CPG Series of Comparative Constitutional Law, Politics and Governance

Edited by the
German-Southeast Asian Center of Excellence for Public Policy and Good Governance

Vol. 5

Dirk Ehlers | Henning Glaser (eds.)

State and Religion

Between Conflict and Cooperation

Nomos

The Deutsche Nationalbibliothek lists this publication in the Deutsche Nationalbibliografie; detailed bibliographic data are available on the Internet at http://dnb.d-nb.de

ISBN 978-3-8487-8000-6 (Print)
978-3-7489-2392-3 (ePDF)

British Library Cataloguing-in-Publication Data
A catalogue record for this book is available from the British Library.

ISBN 978-3-8487-8000-6 (Print)
978-3-7489-2392-3 (ePDF)

Library of Congress Cataloging-in-Publication Data
Ehlers, Dirk / Glaser, Henning
State and Religion
Between Conflict and Cooperation
Dirk Ehlers / Henning Glaser (eds.)
597 pp.
Includes bibliographic references.

ISBN 978-3-8487-8000-6 (Print)
978-3-7489-2392-3 (ePDF)

Onlineversion
Nomos eLibrary

1st Edition 2020

Preface

The relationship between state and religion has been a core problematiqué of societal ordering throughout the history of mankind and subject to continuous philosophical, legal and political reflections and debates across all civilizations from ancient times to today. The present, 5th volume of CPG's Series of Comparative Constitutional Law, Politics, and Governance aims to contribute to the ongoing discussion on this problematiqué. It gathers 20 papers addressing conceptual questions, approaches in international law as well as country-specific problems of state-religion relations. The countries presented in this book allows for a broad comparative perspective and include China, Croatia, Germany, India, Italy, Iran, Japan, Mexico, Poland, Spain, Singapore, Switzerland, and Taiwan.

Particular thanks are, first and foremost, owed to the authors for their time and efforts to make this collection possible. Their analyses and reflections from a broad variety of vantage points are most appreciated.

Furthermore, this publication was only made possible due to the constant support of CPG's work by the German Foreign Ministry, the Federal Foreign Office, the German Academic Exchange Service (DAAD) as well as the CPG-forming universities of Frankfurt am Main, Münster and Passau in Germany and Thammasat University with its Faculty of Law being the host of CPG. To all of them we extend our gratitude.

For support in editing the manuscript we thank Dr. Duc Quang Ly, Jan Lorenzen, Daniel Grünewald, Sandra Blechschmidt, Marie Freitag, Charlotte Wolff and Carla Ingenhorst.

Bangkok, January 2020 *Dirk Ehlers and Henning Glaser*

Table of Contents

Restructuring the Field: Religion, Political Order, Constitution

Henning Glaser

A. Introduction

Since the dawn of human socialization, religion has impacted the realm of politics and law. Religion can evolve as either a serious challenge to, or as a stabilizing factor for, the state and political order. As one of the primordial forces of socialization, religion might thus define, support or disturb a society's political order – or even all of these at once. Every modern constitution has, therefore, to define the place religion is supposed to take. Any legal system will set up a framework to accommodate and regulate the expressions and effects of religious faith and practice where they affect the public order.

The present book deals with these mutual influences and entanglements of the religious and the political from a variety of perspectives, including the philosophical, political, historical, legal and theological. The single chapters are arranged according to two focal points. The first chapters are dealing predominantly with religion as a *source* of impulses affecting social cohesion and the normative fabric and identity of public order in both positive and negative terms. The others focus rather on religion as a *subject* of a given political order's regulatory challenges and responses. These latter articles address the concrete arrangements by which political communities envision and regulate the role of faith and religion according to means of the respective normative and political frameworks.

Given the scope and depth of the collected papers, this introduction merely aims to provide some preliminary and complementary thoughts on this broad and complex field rather than to introduce the individual papers. To this end, I shall begin by attempting a rough outline of the *epistemic field* – how we might perceive the meanings and phenomena that these sparse terms 'religion' and 'politics' address and what patterns dominate their interactions.

This will be followed by some thoughts pertaining to the role of religion as both a source and a subject of the political order.

B. Structuring the Epistemic Field

To reflect on the role of religion as a source or a subject of the political order, it is helpful to briefly set forth the central terms and concepts used, and the basic patterns through which these relations between religion and politics materialize.

The political realm, which is also termed the 'legal-political sphere' in this book, refers simply to that domain of social order that comprises the interrelated and overlapping phenomena of political power and public order, state and constitution, and law in general. However, the question of which phenomena the term 'religion' is supposed to refer to in the present context is much more complicated.

As a starting point, *'religion'* has been defined by Tillich[1] as a worldview that is dealing with a group's "ultimate concern", thereby providing a set of narratives, norms, symbols and practices derived from or related to a supposed reality or truth of sacred, supernatural, otherworldly, or transcendental nature.[2] Behind all attempts to briefly say what religion essentially is, remains, however, a bewildering range of phenomena that might not all fit under this definition whereas they all display a greatly varying impact on the public order. It is therefore instructive to review at least some basic conceptions and dynamics of religious forms and expressions. I shall strive to distinguish between types of religion and faith on the one hand, and different dynamics within a given religion or system of faith on the other.

I. The Complex World of Faith and Religion

To comprehend the broad range of religious thought and practice, its impact on the political, and the ways how the political sphere might respond to this impact, it is helpful to first gain a basic perspective on religions' variety (for the different impact of Catholicism, Protestantism, or Islam on the political realm, see Labuschagne's account on Hegel and Fischer in

1 Tillich, *Dynamics of Faith*, 1957, p. 5.

2 See Labuschagne, "Religion and Order: Philosophical Reflections From Augustine To Hegel On The Spiritual Sources Of Law And Politics," 2009, p. 73; Taylor, *Varieties of Religion Today,* 2002, with a reference to William James' lecture "The Will to Believe".

this volume). It is also important to not essentialize religious experiences, and to take the different possible experiences, expressions and manifestations of religiosity within one and the same religious system or community of faith into account.

At first glance, focusing on the great diversity among and within religious systems might appear banal. However, introducing some structural aspects of this diversity is revealing and helpful for developing viable perspectives on the role of religion as a source and subject of the political order. Different religions, with their patterns of faith, and religious sentiments and practices, can be distinguished by a number of criteria. These include the way they define the sacred, absolute or otherworldly; and the way they envision the nature and content of the respective revelations through their representations, ethical demands or ritual practices. It is suggested here that one criterion among the others stands out: the quality of a religion's ultimate point of ontological reference. This single criterium – the conception of ultimate reality in ontological terms – shall be introduced and developed as a far-reaching epistemic foundation on which large parts of the ensuing discussion will unfold.

There are two qualities of this ultimate ontological reference that have to be distinguished. The first ontological mode a religion refers to is an otherworldly, supernatural or sacred reality that is still conceived as an extension of the mundane or vice versa. Such a perception of ultimate reality often entails a homology – a fundamental unison between apparently distinct ultimate and mundane orders. Corresponding beliefs of a pantheon or an afterlife that brings one close to the divine remain principally comprehensible for the human mind.

Throughout man's socialization, religion has formed according to this model with the otherworldly reality not being ontologically separated from the mundane, being represented for instance by divine forces of nature, homologous deities and spirit beings communicating with the humans. These instances of the supernatural, otherworldly or sacred are perceived as participating in this world, and thus open to human comprehension, communication or even manipulation. Such notions and systems of religiosity can be organized with varying scopes as conceptions of cosmic order, ancestral, animistic and shamanistic cults of smaller groups but also entire states and larger societies or cultural communities.

However, much more significant for the contemporary world are religions of the other type, defined by a totally different conception of reality. These religions have their ultimate point of reference in a transcendent reality. It is incommensurable and incomprehensive from any mundane perspective, and genuinely disconnected from the immanence as the mundane reality of this world. And while the radical schism that ontologically divides the spheres of being might be bridged by prophecy and revelation, radical difference will nevertheless remain in principle according to this worldview.

Belonging to these historically much younger religions based on the ontological discovery of transcendence – the great religions of transcendence – are for instance Hinduism, Buddhism, Judaism, ancient Greek philosophy, Zoroastrian Iran, Christianity, and, finally, Islam.[3] The discourses, norms and institutions that follow in the wake of the respective discoveries of the transcendent have deeply transformed the way the individual, society, power structure, and cosmic order are perceived within the particular religious frameworks.

The distinction within the ontological reference of a given religion is the most important for our discussion. It is thus a distinction according to the basic syntax and semantics of ultimate worldviews, so to say. Within those religions based on their reference to transcendence it has to be further distinguished between the different conceptions of the transcendent reality and its relation to the immanent reality. Comprehending these visions of transcendence and the ensuing differentiations and doctrinal conceptions is indispensable to fully understanding the relation between politics and religion since the religions of transcendence emerged.

In all its different articulation, this transcendent worldview is, first of all, rooted in the historic discovery of transcendence which is as much a watershed moment as it is a relatively late discovery in the course of human civilization. Generally, this discovery of an ontological gap between the mundane and the transcendent reality implies a normative subordination of the former to the latter. This triggered a radical reflection and problematization of all dimensions of the established state of the mundane real-

3 Examined in more detail the picture is much more differentiated. While early Hinduism, Judaism and Greek philosophy had strong immanent characteristics, philosophical Confucianism displays notions of transcendence albeit of much weaker impact than those of the theistic systems. Given that the distinction between the two major types of religion and worldview is an ideal-typical one that is accompanied by flowing transitions in reality, classifications can thus be disputed. For the current perspective, Confucianism is however not counted as fully belonging to the second type of religion or worldview. For Hinduism it might be discussed in how far it gained its 'transcendent' character in response to Buddhism within its tradition.

ity.[4] As a consequence, fundamentally new conceptions of the person emerged, along with reformulations of social, political, and cosmic orders. This civilizational process was accompanied by the birth of new cultures of intellectuality, discourse, and knowledge. Different levels of legal order were introduced, in conjunction with new ethical notions pertaining to human relations and community building that were based on the human condition itself.

Wherever this revolutionary process took shape, the different conceptualization of the fundamental tension between the transcendental and the mundane order resulted in powerful institutionalizations that, driven by new types of intellectual elites, were supported by a strong desire to reshape the mundane reality in light of the respective transcendental vision.[5] Consequently, strong tendencies developed to constitute collectivities distinct from the existing "primordial, ethnic, local, political or religious collectivities". These new collectivities were, ultimately, defined by a universalistic standard on basis of norms that claimed to express a universal truth as derived from the respective transcendental vision. In other words, the various emerging visions of transcendence became the point of origin for entirely new intellectual and societal dynamics so profound, encompassing and strong that they could transform large parts of social life, human agency and the course of history.

This highly transformative civilizational process took place in several civilizations in a time frame that is often dubbed the "axial age" in reference to Karl Jaspers.[6] It manifested for example in the above-mentioned religions and worldviews. Common denominator of the civilizational breakthroughs that occurred along similar patterns in these contexts is, to underline it again, the emergence of a new vision of transcendence. As

---

4 See Eisenstadt, "The Axial Conundrum between Transcendental Visions and Vicissitudes of Their Institutionalizations," 2012, pp. 278 f. Before Eisenstadt initiated a broader academic movement to discuss the axial age Karl Jaspers had noted that during the axial age, "the spiritual foundations of humanity were laid simultaneously and independently in China, India, Persia, Judea, and Greece. And these are the foundations upon which humanity still subsists today." Jaspers, *The Way to Wisdom: An Introduction to Philosophy,* 2003, p. 98; see also Jaspers, *The Origin and Goal of History* [1949], 1953.

5 See Eisenstadt, "The Axial Age Breakthroughs – Their Characteristics and Origins," 1986, pp. 1 ff.

6 See Jaspers, *Vom Ursprung und Ziel der Geschichte*, 1953; Joas, "The Axial Age Debate as Religious Discourse," 2012, pp. 9 ff.

Benjamin Schwartz stated: "[I]f there is nevertheless some common underlying impulse in all these 'axial' movements, it might be called the strain towards transcendence [...] a kind of critical, reflective questioning of the actual and a new vision of what lies beyond."[7]

Starting from their common denominator, the foundational reference to a transcendent reality, the most notable differences among the religions of transcendence derive from their greatly varying visions of transcendence and their conceptualization of the relation between the mundane and the transcendent order.

A central implication of this point of origin is the attitude towards the mundane reality. Long before the axial age theory became rehashed and substantiated under the guidance of Eisenstadt in the course of the 20th century, Max Weber had already suggested an ideal-typical range of these attitudes spanning from an affirmation of the world over notions of 'world adaption' and 'world escape' to total world rejection.[8]

A world-rejecting and world-escaping attitude might be found in a simplifying assessment in particular in the Buddhist vision of transcendence while that of Islam and Judaism remain essentially 'world accepting'. For the latter, the mundane order is created and positively shaped in the light of transcendence and thus ontologically regarded as unequivocally positive as God's creation. The Buddhist vision of transcendence on the other hand, aims lastly at escaping a 'treacherous' mundane order that inescapably suffers from an unresolvable ontological deficit.

The middle-ground between these extremes is occupied by the Christian vision of transcendence. It reconciles in its origin a 'world denying' notion with the mission to transform the mundane reality in both its eschatological deficiency and potential. The Christian vision shares the Buddhist hostility towards the mundane reality in its origin but, instead of aiming to escape it, induces a strong inclination to continuously reshape the mundane reality in a permanent eschatological strive. The Christian vision might therefore be qualified as concomitantly world-sceptic and world-shaping rather than world escaping.

This decisive quality that evolves from central features of the Christian vision of transcendence ensures a maximum of transformative potential whose impact on the Western process of civilization can hardly be overes-

---

7 Schwartz, "The Age of Transcendence," 1975, pp. 3-5.

8 Weber, *Gesammlte Aufsätze zur Religionssoziologie 1*, 1988, p. 554; Schluchter, *Religion und Lebensführung, Bd. 2*, 1988, pp. 62 ff.

timated. Up to date, its transformative spin is still unfolding, even though in largely derived and indirect ways. Conceptually, it has been constituted – among other features of the later dogmatization of the Christian discourse of transcendence – by its pronounced eschatological horizon that is spanning from God's creation of the world over the original sin to God's incarnation and sacrifice at the cross to his resurrection and announced return at the end of times. Moreover, there is the foundational conception of human dignity as a consequence of having been created as an *imago Dei*, the ethics of the Sermon on the Mount and the double commandment of love. These ethics are eschatologically deeply charged and accompanied by the consequent devaluation of the mundane and its traditional social structures[9] combined with a permanent strive towards a utopian replacement by voluntary associations that were defined in terms of their eschatological mission to unfold a certain functional differentiation.[10]

Moving away from the immanent/transcendent dichotomy, a series of tensions exist within the 'transcendental' camp itself. The first lies between theistic and rational forms of transcendent religions. Theistic approaches confine their ideas of ultimate truth to a belief in gods, supernatural beings, revelations, and prophecy. But, the term 'religion' is frequently extended to forms of faith in ultimate truths that are related to purely rational, yet nevertheless eschatologically charged conceptions of a claimed inner-worldly utopian truth of absolute provenance.

Often, these secular, utopian visions of the world display a certainty in their ultimate point of reference that is similar to the transcendental visions of sacral truth, and have similarly advanced claims regarding laws of nature, and humanity's destination within the course of history. Like their sacral counterparts, these secular utopian visions are supposed to transcend any conflicting, man-made norms and practices. Examples of these 'secular religions' include secular humanism, communism, and neoliberalism. Secular humanism, in particular, emerged with the enlightenment and

9 Radical early Christian thought that would emerge as part of especially of the monastic and evangelic thrust within the Christian discourse on transcendence demanded of Jesus' followers for instance to renounce home and family, property and protection (Mt 8:20, Lc 14:26, Mt 6: 25, 5: 38 ff.). See also Kippenberg, "The Role of Christianity in the Depolitization of the Roman Empire," 1986, p. 268.

10 These artificial associations defined themselves by social functions as evidenced most impressively in the various monastic orders. Other examples of such associates are the guilds, municipalities or universities.

forms the conceptional core of Western liberal democracy. All these worldviews provide secular conceptions of an ultimate truth, albeit an inner-worldly one. They encompass visions of a utopian future, a distinct code of universalistic ethics, fundamental norms and governance principles, and a comprehensive set of orthodox interpretations, symbols and narratives of their core vision. The ultimate truths claimed by these systems of believe may be class struggle, universal civil rights and representative democracy, or the market principle, respectively. What they share with religions of transcendence is the assumption of a fundamental gap between the absolute truth and the inner-worldly reality and their inherently discursive, eschatological nature that finds its expression in ongoing attempts to interpret (and reinterpret) the ultimate truth in its doctrinal form. Apropos for this discussion, secular humanism and communism may both be regarded as secular surrogates of important aspects of the Christian discourse on transcendence (apparently different Fischer in this volume), the assumption of additional sources of their emergence and substance notwithstanding.

A second tension arises with the inevitable shifting of discourse. The original core visions of both sacral and secular 'religions' remained prone to constant adaption in response to the shifting socio-political realities and diverging interpretations of competing conceptions. These discourses on ultimate reality could eventually develop new interpretations of the core vision or split up in competing conceptions based on the initial core vision. Ensuing tensions between these competing interpretations could either be captured and integrated within the dominant discursive streams, leading to new institutionalization, or they could eventually transgress the line delimitating the orthodox consensus from heresy. This, then, could lead to the creation of competing orthodoxies or heterodox systems. The latter were either suppressed by the dominant discourse, subjected to extended periods of mutually afflicted violence, or emerged as entirely new denominations that coexisted with the dominant discourse.[11] Often, competing interpretations and accentuations could be contained within the

11 Christian conceptions of transcendence are for example the catholic or evangelical one, the former based on the eschatological centrality of the institutionalized Holy Roman Church, the latter on the common priesthood of all believers. Not any more part of the original vision of transcendence are the various forms of Christian Gnosticism that go beyond the fundaments of the Christian dogma.

frame of orthodoxy, even if at the price of continuing tensions that could have shaping effects on the future course of the overall discourse.

One last differentiation that shall be highlighted pertains to the practical manifestations of transcendental religions among their believers. Regularly, all of the lofty conceptions and doctrinally pure discourses of transcendence coexist with interpretative and practical adaptions that are much more reminiscent of pagan notions of the sacred realities than of the original visions of transcendence they claim to serve.

In daily life, the way a given axial religion's vision of transcendence is actually translated into religious practice will differ greatly from one believer, and even one institution, to the other. If doctrinally 'pure' orientations toward the respective core vision of transcendence would be considered a more original version or 'high form' of that religion, there are regularly also more or less vulgarized notions of belief and religious practice within the respective community of believers that constitute what could be called a 'folk religious' level. The latter focuses more on magic and ritualistic aspects of religious activity than the ethical demands and doctrinal purity and might incorporate different elements of the symbolic and ritual universe of other religions than the more original versions do. Notably, such notions or orientations within axial religions such as Christianity or Buddhism should not be conflated with folk religions even if both share a similar phenomenology. Notably, such folk-religious orientations claim a significant share of actual religious life in most contemporary societies with strong axial religions, and often exert distinct political influence as well. They might appear either as instances of the religious mainstream, or deviant cults, sometimes within the grey zones of orthodoxy, sometimes beyond. Often, they contain some remnants of older religiosity that survived after having seemingly been supplanted by official practice. In many societies officially dominated by axial religions strong influences are actually attributed to the stars, spirits, semi-deities, and to all forms of fortune-telling and magic rituals. In many Buddhist, Christian, Hindu or Islamic societies, these representations of the otherworldly are still considered to represent or invoke powerful forces that can be mobilized to forge alliances or to make political decisions. Occasionally they develop a grave impact on the development of political life.[12]

12 As much as the Romans took it often dead-serious to discover whether the gods would favor a war or a certain time and place for a battle, a journey, or building project as much do elites in Asia and Africa often seek all forms of otherworldly

While most assessments of the politics-religion nexus focus on the respective 'high forms' of religious life, all articulations and shades of a society's religious practice have therefore their significance. Often, the folk dimension appears at least partly intertwined with the high form of a given religious spectrum – sometimes undermining its core assumptions, and sometimes concomitantly contributing to its very relevance. Scholars like Peter Brown or Mary Douglas have pointed out how much folk-religious elements of socio-religious practice are, indeed, not only intertwined with high-religious ones but also respond to essential needs of the given societies, in particular, as Peter Brown shows, with regard to the society's legal-political dimensions.[13]

Things are, however, even more complicated. After all, most contemporary societies experience not only the coexistence of numerous – often shifting and competing – doctrinal and attitudinal notions within the frame of a given orthodoxy. They must countenance also the coexistence of entirely different systems of faith and belief. This coexistence may greatly affect – and even define – the status of legal-political sphere in the respective society. One might think historically of the changing role Christianity played in the Roman Empire, or the religious wars of Early Modern Europe, and their impact on modern state building and the emergence of the international system of states.

Generally, it might be said that tensions between essentially different religious denominations and identities can easily relate to the integrity of societal core values, especially if different axial discourses are competing. In contemporary societies, such tensions often significantly resonate, indeed, with the given political or constitutional process. One might think of the challenges secular Western societies encounter with growing Islamic minorities, especially those adhering to more radical interpretations of Islam (with different notions Pahud de Mortanges, A. Ferrari, S. Ferrari) or, more general, of the tension between adherents of secular and religious

advice in the most auspicious affairs of the state exemplified for instance by military commanders seeking the advice of fortune tellers and astrologers before starting a coup or a revolution. See for example Phongpaichit and Baker, "The Spirits, the Stars and Thai Politics," 2008, at http://pioneer.netserv.chula.ac.th/ ~ppasuk/spiritsstarspolitics.pdf. In fact, the extent to which such folk-religious elements and practices frequently influence politics in a majority of countries seems rather underestimated than accurately conceived by many Western observers.

13 Brown, *Society and the Holy in Late Antiquity*, 1982; Douglas, *Natural Symbols: Explorations in Cosmology*, 1996.

constitutional identities. Examples for challenges of an established public order by newly emerging religious dynamics can be found in Europe in countries such as France, Spain (Torron) and Turkey, in Latin America (Gonzales), or Asia (Laliberté and Thio).

This aspect is related to one last factor, the waning or surging relevance of religion within the given society. Both can be observed today. The waning appeal of some religious identity-offers in many Western societies may be accompanied for instance by a revival or surge of the identity-offers of other religions. In the contemporary world, both trends have been identified, the end of religion or at least a relative decline (Zachhuber) as well as a forceful return of religion that some identify as the dawn of a post-secular age (Alessandro Ferrari). While Fischer stresses the power of secularization in terms of the modern political order in this volume, Ran Hirschl observed that "it is hard to overstate the significance of the religious revival in late twentieth- and early twenty-first-century politics."[14] Both trends do actually not only coexist but coexist most relevantly for the political order often in one and the same society.

II. Religion and the Political

This leads back to the complex *relation* between the religious and the legal-political sphere of society. Basically, this relation shall be contemplated here in line with the suggested perspectives above envisioning religion as a *source* of the political order (which also comprises the state), and or as a *subject* of the state's regulatory challenges and efforts.

The relation between the two realms of politics and religion are manifold and varied. While some ancient cults of state can hardly be separated from the political structure at all, Western modernity's conception of religion and politics as two clearly separated functional societal systems marks the other extreme (see Luhmann[15] and also Fischer). In between these extremes lies a vast and highly dynamic field defined by multiple, mutual influences, and by ways to link politics and religion to each other. Modes of interaction range from intimacy and interdependence, through indifference, to distance and hostility. All these possible modes could,

14 Hirschl, *Constitutional Theocracy*, 2010, p. 1.

15 See for instance Luhmann, *Introduction to Systems Theory*, 2013.

moreover, coincide in the same system. For most societies, it can be said that religion and politics are inextricably intertwined, to a certain degree.[16] After all, politics can shape, or at least influence, the form and substance of the religious discourse, doctrine and institutions, while religious developments and discourses can shape the evolution, performance and impact of politics, law, and state. As Labuschagne points out, there is as much a religious dimension to politics as there is a political dimension to religion.[17]

What has to be stressed here is the fact that the more the respective religious discourses actually refer to a transcendental reality or display an axial potential in their discursive dynamics, the more relations between politics and religion become increasingly complex and dynamic. After all, the axial notion will always claim to supersede the interests and norms of the state in case of conflict. At the same time, it can also exert great leverage on the formation of some of the state's core structures, norms and institutions. The range of possibilities regarding how given axial dynamics relate to the public order differ markedly.

Generally, in Christian, Buddhist or Islamic contexts for example, the political power might simply respect the religious realm's integrity, try to employ its dynamics as a powerful source of social disciplining, or consider it as a fount of adverse influences. Consequently, the state might end up in challenging, containing or repressing these religious dynamics as well as attempting at other occasions to manage, nurture, and employ them.

The Christian discourses and doctrines aiming at implementing the original vision of transcendence have been especially engaged in the endeavor to reconcile the complexities of the relations between the religious and the political sphere that have, for the longest time, been so fraught with irreducible tension and volatility. The Church Authors' discourses of

---

16 See Thomas Mann in his 1,207-page tetralogy "Joseph and His Brothers," claiming that the believe in a fundamental separation of religion and politics would mistake the essential indivisibility of the world whose both spheres [politics and religion] would speak each other's language as complementary parts of the world in its entirety (quoted from Jan Assmann, *Herrschaft und Heil. Politische Theologie in Altägypten, Israel und Europa*, 2000, p. 15). Insofar, Mann reiterates a point already made by Hegel that „it has been the monstrous blunder of our times to try to look upon these inseparables as separable from one another, and even as mutually indifferent." Hegel, Enzyclopedia, § 552, quoted from Labuschagne, "Religion and Order," p. 88.

17 See ibid., p. 71.

the Christian vision of transcendence during the formative decades and centuries of its Catholic version are a case in point. Origenes, for instance, explained to the schismatic Donatists[18] that the state is not in the church but the church in the state which it needs in order to be protected and to enable a Christian life at all.[19] Depenheuer's chapter in this book might well be read along those lines, too. Origenes has, however, also formulated an essentially different, much more radical notion, which in fact, represents his major dogmatic stance on this matter. Here, Origenes describes the nations of the mundane world not as manifestations of an eschatological category but manifestations of an order of a falling away from the divine order. In his radical turn to the eschatological, Origenes ultimately refuses the mundane political order's legitimacy and embraces even the possibility to engage in an outright conspiracy against the state's law for the sake of eternity.[20] – While Depenheuer cannot but understand this point of view from a religious perspective, as a constitutional scholar he takes the side of the state highlighting that the state cannot subscribe to such a stance.

Augustine argues in a similar direction as the radical Origines, albeit with a slightly more moderate stance towards the state. In his *De Civitate Dei*, he reiterates that the temporal and the eternal dimension of society remain separated even if coexisting and interacting *within* the mundane order in which God incarnated in form of his son Jesus, the Christ. Augustine accepts a political reality that strives towards the City of God whose demands, however, eventually supersede those of the city of man which he ultimately also refuses as a category of its own right in case of conflict.[21]

Notably, it is the axiomatic centrality of the incarnation in the Christian vision of transcendence which makes the relation of state and religion so precarious, especially in the Western historical experience. After all, it is hardly possible to claim that the mundane reality has not deeply been

---

18 The Donatists were a rigorist wing of the Christian Church in North Africa who aimed to purge out the 'faulty' Christians who had handed over their holy scriptures to the Roman authorities during the persecutions of the Christians. Eventually, the Donatists were expulsed from the Church for heresy.

19 Origenes, "De schismate Donati," 2,3 in: PL 11, 1000A.

20 Origenes, "Contra Celsum," I 1 GCS Origines 1 (ed. Koetschau), p. 56; see also Ratzinger, *Die Einheit der Nationen. Eine Vision der Kirchenvater*, 2005, pp. 41 ff.

21 Augustine, *De Civitate Dei*, V 16, p. 149; V 19, p. 155. The devaluation of the city of man, the state, is accompanied by the emphasis of the universalistic category of humanity (Augustine, *De Civitate Dei*, V 17, p. 150).

touched by the transformative reality of the incarnation and Christ order to follow his evangelic example. Historically, the enormous impact of the eschatological dynamic and its relevance for all attempts to conceive and shape the mundane political order is reflected throughout the Medieval and Early Modern periods. Some examples are the Gregorian revolution, the Investiture Conflict, and the rise of the Fraticelli. Also, the series of heterodox evangelical movements within the Catholic Church around Europe since the High Middle Ages was consistently centered at the question of how to reestablish a spiritual life within or beyond the reach of the temporal realm of political power, often identified also with the Church itself. All these movements and disputes are witness to the ongoing struggle to delineate the spiritual and the temporal realms within one and the same mundane reality for which both claimed supreme relevance. Echoes of this struggle still resonate in the Christian world wherever the voice of faith is raised against political power, even if with much less impact than before, and without being manifested in doctrinal attempts to redraw the lines of demarcation compared with the Medieval and Early Modern periods.

What seems certain is that the attempt to find a conceptional arrangement of the complex relations between state and religion has been one of the constant themes of political philosophy and practice in Europe over the centuries. Notably, this struggle has left a regular pattern in the history of thought concerning the central question of how to normatively conceive the public order in general. Essentially, these enduring debates always implied the normative opposition between the law and prudence of the 'city' on the one side and a claimed universalistic truth of transcendental providence and its higher law on the other. This fundamental opposition shall be pointed out in more contemporary settings below.

C. Religion as a Source of the Political

The role of religion as a source of the legal-political order is a complex matter that is discussed in various ways, from different perspectives and with different attitudes. Some of the most central issues and perspectives shall be briefly introduced in the following section. Key questions pertain to the *relevance of the religious factor* for the political and to *political theology* as an epistemic concept. Concerning political theology, after some thoughts on political theology in general, the concept is discussed in two regards.

First, the outlines of a general theory of normative order will serve as a broader conceptual frame for different possible configurations of political theology and the religion-politics nexus. This perspective helps to approach analytically the basic tensions between state and religion as an inherent potential of all post-axial political orders but also extends to frequent tensions between the interests of the state and constitutional core values.

Closely related to the general theory of normative order, the second perspective on political theology scrutinizes two opposing points of view of how to conceive the relation between religion and politics practically.

I. On the Relevance of the Religious Factor

The contributions in this volume consider the factor 'religion' with quite different notions. Fischer, for instance, analyzes religion rather as a negative factor where it comes to the shaping of the modern European state and its law. Focusing on the processes of secularization, Fischer highlights the delimitation from the realm of religion, the consequent prioritization of the political over the religious and thus devaluation of the religious factor in the political realm as a major driver that makes the modern state. In this perspective, the Western democratic polity has its roots not in a historical experience that is shaped by the Christian discourse of transcendence and its institutionalization, but in the "Greek discovery of politics" as an autonomous affair of the political community on secular terms.[22] Under the conditions of the Western constitutional state, "politics and religion are [therefore] fatefully tied to one another and each is the other's nemesis".

The opposing notion is represented by Labuschagne who stresses the constructive influence of religion on the political fabric or, in his words, a "more positive, optimistic view on the spiritual infrastructure of society." Labuschagne exemplifies this view through a detailed analysis of Hegel's

22 Among the many scholars who stress the Greek impact on the Western processes of socialization and political formation see only Freeman, *The Greek Achievement: The Foundations of the Western World*, 1999, and Bruce Thornton, *Greek Ways: How the Greeks Created Western Civilization*, 2000. See for a particular significance of a claimed Roman experience in creating a secular system of governance based on the "autonomous principles of judicial reasoning and an explicit statement of the law" Roger Scruton, *The West and the Rest: Globalization and the Terrorist Threat*, 2002, p. 22.

view "on the sources of normative order in society" which appears throughout his philosophical work on state, religion, law, and history. Providing a "Hegelian perspective on religion, law and state today" Labuschagne highlights that it is not only the state which is central for the course of history but also, and even more important, religion.

According to his reading of Hegel, it is in fact religion that is providing the spiritual infrastructure of societal order in which the respective national spirit manifests in form of the state. Interestingly, Hegel differentiates the ways in which this influence manifests depending on the question if a religion mediates a true concept of God, which implies a strong normative bias that should not be a surprise given the historical context of his work. In this sense, Hegel favors the protestant creed as ethically superior to others as a provider of freedom. This point, however, is questioned in Fischer's remarks on the authoritarian side of Protestantism. Similarly, for Hegel, the Catholic or the Islamic creed support a negatively perceived notion of servitude in the people that will also find its way in the respective concretizations of law and state in his account.[23] In any case, for Hegel, religion is a general requisite for the formation of the individual consciousness and a corresponding national spirit that will realize itself in law and state which it enables and shapes.

Alexis de Tocqueville has provided a similarly momentous account on the crucial role of the religious factor for the political order in his 1835 work 'Democracy in America'. He observed that religion, although no official part of America's secular political system, was nothing else than the first of America's political institutions by virtue of its indirect effects upon political life.[24] If we presume that religion does indeed exert a more or less discrete influence on the realities of the legal-political order, in line with authors like Hegel and Labuschagne or Tocqueville respectively, two crucial challenges evolve in the contemporary world.

First, it might be asked whether and to what degree the factor religion is setting a necessary condition concerning the development of those deep

---

23 Although Hegel is more explicit on Catholicism also note Labuschagne's reference to Hegel's remark on Islam in his 'Philosophy of History'. See Labuschagne, "Religion and Order," p. 89; Hegel, *Philosophy of History*, 2004, p. 358. Similar, Ulrich Haltern, a German constitutional scholar, provides a detailed and differentiated account on protestant and catholic emanations of political theology. See Ulrich Haltern, *Was bedeutet Souveränität?*, 2007, especially pp. 24-75.

24 See Tocqueville, *Democracy in America*, 2004, p. 305.

structures of a given society that nurture the normative and institutional fabric of a democratic liberal political order. The practical point in Labuschagne's account is then: "How democratic institutions, rule of law, and protection of human rights should function against a religious and cultural background that did not give birth to these institutions at the first place, is one of the most pertinent and difficult questions societies deal with nowadays, especially in the (Middle) East."[25] The underlying assumption here is that liberal-democracy develops in its certain relation with a Christian influenced historical experience.

In this context it is interesting to have a look at Kuo's text on the Taiwanese democratization project. In his article on "Democratic Prophets and Priests during Taiwan's Democratization," he stresses both the odds for Taiwan's chances for a smooth and successful democratization with regard to the country's countervailing Confucian tradition,[26] as well as what he sees as one of the significant factors that eventually enabled the transition: the country's "democratic prophets and priests."

While the Confucian tradition in Kuo's account is a factor to sustain authoritarian governance, he traces the democratizing impulses for democratic transition in Taiwan to some Buddhist and especially Christian groups that established key conditions for change. In this, he refers especially to the Presbyterians and particular Buddhist organizations as enablers of democracy. Noteworthy in this regard, Kuo distinguishes between the direct shaping impact of the Presbyterians and the merely complementary and indirect supporting role of the Buddhist notion. Concerning the latter, he stresses concepts of human rights, peaceful transition and cooperation. Concerning the Christians Kuo highlights the importance of elections in the Presbyterian framework of participation and governance as well as an inclination to evoke human rights discourses in highly political contexts like the question of Taiwan's sovereignty. Consequently, Kuo suggests we appreciate a positive relationship between religion and democracy in the Taiwanese case. Similar to Labuschagne, he highlights a

---

25 See also Tocqueville, *Democracy in America*, II, p. 23, who, highlighting a nexus between Christianity and democracy, predicts that the introduction of democracy might not fare well in Islamic countries.

26 Francis Fukuyama, "Confucianism and Democracy," 2005, pp. 42-55, who also refers in a similar way, as Kuo does, to the different input provided by Christianity (pp. 51 f.).

significant contribution of the democratic theology of certain Christian organizations to a smooth and sustaining transition to democracy.

The second contemporary challenge concerning the religious factor for political life to mention here is the coexistence of distinct religious denominations which are sending essentially different impulses in terms of their influence on the political order within one and same constitutional framework. Alessandro Ferrari and Pahud de Mortanges are dealing with this question regarding Muslim minorities within the Italian and the Swiss framework respectively.

A. Ferrari, focusing on Islam as one of Italy's two dominant minority religions, describes the difficulties of the state and those of the various Islamic representations to manage Islam's role within the established constitutional framework as a significant 'other' in cultural terms. In Italy, Muslims encounter a state and a society with which it neither shares a colonial heritage – as it is the case in Belgium, France or England – nor a history of state-managed immigration from a single state with a majority Muslim population – as it is the case with Turkish immigrants in Germany. Pahud de Mortanges describes a similar problem for the Swiss constitutional system which finds itself similarly in distress where it has to deal with changing societal realities regarding the impact of certain notions of Islamic religiosity under the precepts of globalization, migration, and an increasing politicization of Islam.

II. Political Theology as an Epistemic Concept and its Discontents

This all leads back to the general question of how to envision the role of religion as a source of the legal-political order more generally, starting with the concurrence of the two basic postures towards the factor religion, the positive and the negative. To repeat, the negative view in context of the secularization thesis stresses the absence of religion in the autonomous realm of politics as a necessary condition of the Western constitutional state. The opposing positive view holds that religion represents a significant constructive factor for the development of the normative-institutional fabric of the political order in general and the political order of the Western constitutional state in particular. Both views are considered here as justified and not mutually exclusive.

The exploration of the complex question of whether religion proved to be a positive or negative factor for the emergence of the modern political order of the West is leading to the central term 'political theology' which has been used by Carl Schmitt to describe a certain form of positive continuity of the religious influence. The idea of political theology has been applied in many ways from Varro in the first century BC, to Spinoza in the 17th century, and then to Carl Schmitt and Eric Voegelin in modern times. The term has been used descriptively as well as prescriptively, often, however, without much reference to a more substantiated concept of how to imagine the interface of religion and the political.

Here, I suggest making use of the term 'political theology' to denote a given prescriptive or analytical approach to conceive a concrete interface of the religious and the political in historical, social, political or legal contexts.

As indicated above, one of the most visible among the numerous modern references to 'political theology' has been made by Carl Schmitt. With the famous dictum that "all significant concepts of the modern theory of the state are secularized theological concepts," Schmitt pointed to the significance of the deep structural influences of the religious on the legal-political sphere.[27] He refrained, however, to give a more differentiated and substantial analysis of the exact trajectories and crystallizations he invoked with the formula.[28]

---

27 Carl Schmitt, *Politische Theologie. Vier Kapitel zur Lehre von der Souveränität*, 2009, p. 43.

28 Schmitt employs his account on "Political Theology" essentially in favor of his central ideological account of decisionism, thus a political concept directly opposed to liberal democracy. This finding is interesting for it exemplifies how different religious impulses can be conceived and have impacted on the political. If Schmitt argues affirmatively in favor of Catholic political theology of decisionism this only reinforces the claim that the Catholic conception of the original Christian vision of transcendence entails very different threads that have coexisted in great tension from the onset. All too often these interpretations have manifested in heterodox notions and violent oppression or longstanding constitutional disputes within the Church, manifested for instances in the conciliar movement. Even after these tensions led to great schism of Western Christianity in the age of the reformation, several interpretations and denominations continued to coexist within the protestant tradition with sometime strongly diverging preferences for notions of hierarchical ecclesiology and evangelical ethics of egalitarian provenance. Schmitt, who often referred to conservative political thinkers of the 19th century such as de Maistre, Bonald or Donoso Cortes who, like him, tried to contain the advancement of the different notions of secular humanism and socialism, thus limits the scope of his political theology to only one aspect and its normatively driven interpretation where he takes recourse on political theology. Under different signs,

Two earlier scholars who laid much of the groundwork of constituting a coherent research paradigm to explore what is denoted here as political theology without using the term, however, were Otto von Gierke and Max Weber. Gierke's monumental work explored the continuity of certain forms of associations in the Western formation of society by which the natural bonds of society were deliberately replaced. These free deliberate associations were strongly influenced by Germanic legal traditions, Roman law, and Christian discourses. In fact, the development of these associations was deeply intertwined with those of Western constitutional thought, including central questions regarding representation, collegiate sovereignty, the distribution of authority, legitimacy, consent, or resistance, to name just a few.[29] Gierke thus provided an immensely valuable contribution to the study of those structures at the interface of religion, law and politics Schmitt denoted with his use of 'political theology'.

Worthy of note, and likely one of the reasons why Gierke is rarely mentioned in deliberations under the label of political theology, is the fact that he does not focus solely on the Christian impact on the development of law and political thought.[30] Instead, by focusing on the normative and institutional infrastructure of artificial associations, he investigated a central phenomenon of Western socialization characterized by the coalescence of several normative, conceptual and institutional developments that interacted, amalgamed, and developed in a likewise complex historical context. Here, the emergence and development of these deliberate, free associations with their tremendous impact on Western constitutional thought was nevertheless heavily influenced by Christian political theology, which

---

Fischer meets the same result as Schmitt when he also stresses a negative relation between liberal democracy and religion while Fischer, contrary to Schmitt, is implicitly arguing in favor of liberal democracy. That Schmitt's account on a political theology of decisionism actually draws on a long discursive line of Catholic theology has been impressively exemplified by Ernst Kantorowicz, "Mysteries of the State: An Absolutist Concept and its Late Medieval Origins," 1965, pp. 381-398.

29 See for instance Tierney, *Religion, Law, and the Growth of Constitutional Thought 1150-1650*, 1982, pp. 103 ff.

30 Carl Schmitt, however, has indeed extensively referred to Gierke. Concerning his study on political theology, see Schmitt, *Politische Theologie*, pp. 31 ff. In another central work, the 'The Concept of the Political', Carl Schmitt also referred to Gierke's work and likeminded scholars in France and England influenced by him such as Léon Duguit and Harold Laski. See Schmitt, *The Concept of the Political*, 2008, pp. 40 ff.

manifested time and again during the long process of the practical reproduction and doctrinal differentiation in the socialization and political organization within the European historical experience.

A similar impression to that of Gierke is offered by Max Weber, who also put great emphasis on the religious factor for the development of civilizational pattern and developments without limiting his focus on the topic. In the introduction to his seminal study on *The Sociology of Religion*, Weber famously identified a distinctly occidental process of civilization that he described as unique in its form and features compared to other civilizational processes. The characteristic pattern of this process that coherently shaped all significant elements of society and human achievement Weber rooted ultimately yet not exclusively in the occidental religious identity whose most fundamental manifestation, he claimed, is a certain form of rationality.

While Weber's approach is sometimes criticized for its claim of a European *Sonderweg* to modernity, it well recognizes the fact that every cultural trajectory based on an axial batter is capable of producing its own remarkable civilizational impact. Weber's political theology of the 'West' should be seen in particular as just one extrapolation of a general paradigm of 'multiple modernities', each of them special due to the respective substance of the different visions and conceptions of transcendence as Eisenstadt and his fellows pointed out.[31]

Despite groundbreaking work of scholars such as Gierke, Weber, Voegelin, Kantorowicz, Löwith, Eisenstadt and many others, political theology remains a challenging concept, as Clifford Geertz claimed, for the modern times under extended conditions of secularity:

> The political theology [...] of the 20th century has not been written, though there have been glancing efforts here and there. But it [the political theology of the 20th century] exists – or, more exactly, various forms of it exist – and until it is understood [...], a great deal of public life of our times is going to remain obscure. The extraordinary has not gone out of modern politics, however much the banal may have entered; power not only still intoxicates, it still exalts.[32]

Geertz, however, focuses on a particular dimension of political theology, one that resonates with Weber's concept of charisma, which seems quite

---

31 See Eisenstadt, "Multiple Modernities," 2000, pp. 1-29.

32 Geertz, "Centers, Kings, and Charisma: Reflections on the Symbolics of Power," 2000, p. 143.

limited given the above-mentioned studies. What might instead be explored through the lens of political theology in historical perspectives are all civilizational threads and influences that have been developed in the interface of politics and religion. Arguably, these continue to nurture vibrant intuitions within the societal fabric that conditions and impacts on the deep structure of state and law. This does not necessarily imply a positive relationship, or exclusively religious roots of such influences at all, as Gierke and Weber have already shown. Actually, political theology denotes deep structural influences in which manifold factors coalesce with a significant input of religion and unfolding on a broad range of evolutionary levels, evolving in several lines of development and developing different dynamics.

III. Political Theology and Normative Order

On that basis, the role of religion as a source of the political order shall be approached from two related perspectives, one descriptive, the other prescriptive.

First, the religious factor will be linked analytically to a general theory of normative order that distinguishes particularly two essentially different, yet co-existing notions of normative order in general. Second, two prescriptive paradigms and their arguments and agendas on the role of religion in the realm of politics will be derived from this ontological distinction.

1. The Conceptual Frame: A Theory of Normative Order

In terms of normative order, the axial discovery of transcendence resulted in the emergence of universalistic normative orders that were characterized by the claim that such an order applies to everyone – to humankind as such. Historically, this was a remarkable novelty of weighty consequences, especially in case of the Christian discourse on transcendence and its secular derivatives, as the corresponding universalistic morality became encoded into law.

The universalistic normative orders whose secular humanist version would eventually spread and sweep around the world with great impact, however, only represent one of the younger notions of normative order in the development of human socialization. As the older forms of normative order were not replaced by the universalistic ones but continued to coexist and interact with the new approaches – as much as the mentioned folk religious and pagan notions do in context of the axial religions – it is instrumental to take a broader view on the syntax of normative order in general.

Overall, three fundamental notions of normative ordering or 'classes' of norms – the *'particularistic'*, the *'central-integrative'* and the *'universalistic'* – are distinguished according to their primary scope. These classes are named for their claimed normative reach. In an evolutionary perspective, these classes of norms represent three emerging levels of normative ordering. As a result, they coexist in varying modes of interaction and balance in every modern legal-political order, all being inhabited by, and exposed to, manifestations of all three of them. The actual locus and relative weight of these representations of order within the normative fabric of a given society will, however, vary significantly in intertemporal as well as comparative perspectives.

Historically, the different classes of norms or notions of normative order respectively emerged in stages over the entire span of human socialization, with the particularistic orders as the first and the universalistic orders as the last ones taking shape. This process of emerging normative orders corresponded with the development of new forms of social formation and the ultimate definition of the political community.

The emergence of the first, the particularistic layer of normative order goes back to the beginnings of the homo sapiens if not beyond, with family and kinship as its nucleus. Based on this nucleus, other forms of socialization and (proto)political formation emerged. They all were derived from the basic model of the family producing an anthropologically ubiquitous set of constructive pattern and normative dispositions. Other forms of social formation that evolved from family and kinship by emulating these structural and normative patterns include clans and tribes, patron-client-relationships, friendship networks and alliances, as well as artificially created ties of kinship based on fiction.

The second evolutionary layer of the development of the present forms of normative order is marked by the emergence of early (proto-)states that politically integrated several particularistic groups that were otherwise not linked by the primordial ties of family and kinship and their mentioned derivates.

Eventually, the third layer of normative order followed after the axial discovery of transcendence. The ensuing idea of collectives governed by universalistic norms were based on radically different conceptions of human agency, as well as a new dynamic of questioning, disrupting, and redefining knowledge and social structures, starting with the nature and role of the self within this order.[33]

The gradual emergence of these three layers of normative order, in correspondence with the related stages of social-political formation, is of special interest here with regard to the second and third layers of normative ordering, namely the central-integrative and the universalistic orders. They shall be described briefly below.

Second-level normative orders are defined by the state, whose essence and rationale it is to serve as the central-integrative unit of the political that remains irreducible to the particularistic layer of ordering and its representations. It is this political order's, thus the state's rationale to constitute, provide, and maintain a common space of peace and safety, symbolized and reinforced by its own laws and cults, beyond those of the particularistic groups. Even if the state develops from the domination of one of these particularistic groups adopting its laws and cults as those of the state, the latter change their meaning and impact in the moment they apply to outsiders not linked to the original group by means of the 'law of the family'.

However, no power of this state or grade of domination by a ruling group, is sufficient to control the inevitable persistence of particularistic groups and norms, to fully subdue their continuous challenge to the state's claim of political and normative supremacy. The ensuing, inherent and inevitable tension between first and second orders follows from both classes of orders' primary rationales.

While the alien who is not pacified by means of an alliance – originally through marriage as Levy-Strauss has pointed out – is an enemy to the particularistic group, the state claims peace within its borders as a prime condition that is applying to everyone within.

While the particularistic group is governed by the 'discriminative preference of the respective own and close' as one of its core principles, the state claims to apply its laws to all subjects on terms basically irrespective of relations on the particularistic level of ordering. The state that grew out of, and comprises, particularistic groups in this sense cannot get rid of

33 Eisenstadt, "The Axial Breakthroughs – Their Characteristics and Origins," pp. 1-4.

them though. Although constantly challenged, the state is also frequently dependent on them and their cooperation.

For the state, this condition is permanent and irrefutable. Irrespective of all its efforts, it will face the centrifugal forces of first order formations continuously permeating the public sphere as long as it consists of human beings organized by the primordial ties of family and kinship. These forces are, after all, constantly evolving from a social condition that the state cannot abandon without undermining its own very substance.

This has two consequences. First, the state finds itself in a position where it is dependent on achieving a certain equilibrium in dealing with the countervailing forces and interests emanating from the particularistic sphere of ordering. This produces an ensuing mode of interaction that is best described as an ever-shifting relation of competition, cooperation and conflict which, as such, forms a constant within the state's order.

On the other hand, this inescapable condition is constantly provoking the state's very raison d'être: the integration of all societal groups and individuals in its unit of peace, security and safety. It thus forces the state to always warily preserve its integrity as one of its primary objectives and supreme duties.

This results in a systemic ambiguity on the side of the state. On the one hand, the majesty of law, if not the provision of equal justice by means of law, proved to be one of the most convincing currencies of the state's symbolic capital. On the other hand, the power and reach of law made, announced and enforced by the state proved also to be too challenged and institutionally too weakly supported to rest on solely. Therefore, the state's ultimate and supreme norm remains its interest to preserve its integrity and to enhance its power and influence in order to increase the chances of its survival by any means necessary. This inherent logic of the central-integrative political unit is nothing less than a depiction of what later became the *reason-of-state*. Together with the closely related concept of *sovereignty*, it is the arguably most significant illustration of the central-integrative notion of normative ordering, which acts as a constant condition and expression of statehood.

Despite the rhetorical prominence of the 'state of exception' in justifying the reason-of-state – be it where it is overtly implemented or where its covert operations are drawn to the light –, the reason-of-state represents an inherent form and regular disposition of political ordering:

> rather than being something exceptional that reaches outside legal orders for their inspiration, reason of state is generally built into the institutional struc-

tures and deeply embedded within the everyday working life of the modern state.[34]

The third layer of normative ordering has already been alluded to briefly above. It has been a relatively recent development, arising with the 'axial breakthroughs' that started to emerge in the 8th century BC. The revolutionary assertion of a fundamental gap between the mundane and the transcendent order spurred the mission to reshape, or at least adjust, the old world in light of the new transcendent order.[35] Based on this imperative, the various religions of transcendence established novel codes of universalistic ethics that did not address particularistic groups or single states but the whole of mankind. At the same time, they all displayed more or less radical and entrenched notions against the 'law of the family', most aggressively in Buddhism and Christianity. Generally, the long axial moment brought about the arguably most transformative "revolution […] in the realm of ideas and their institutional bases which had irreversible effects on several major civilizations and on human history in general."

Its overall effect on the formation of normative order is the lasting emergence of universalistic orders (third-order formations) that competed and strongly interacted with the established first- and second-order formations in their claim to supersede them. At the same time, the societal manifestations of the axial dynamics were shaped and influenced by similar paradoxical entanglements as those that have been described above for the relation between first- and second-order formations (see Depenheuer).

Whereas different manifestations of the normative orders of first and second degree display a largely similar architecture and basic principles, third order figurations develop very different structures and normative concretizations following from their foundation in very different visions and conceptions of transcendence as outlined above.

The different visions of transcendence and the different layers of normative ordering in general produce different forms of political theology. The political theology of a central-integrative unit and its cult – as Varro described it for Rome – is a totally different thing compared to the political theology of any axial religion or derivative worldview given alone the

34 Poole, *Reason of State: Law, Prerogative, and Empire*, 2015, pp. 4 and 6.
35 Eisenstadt, "The Axial Age Breakthroughs – Their Characteristics and Origins," pp. 1 ff.

entirely different dynamic concerning the perception of the individual, the societal discourse and its institutional manifestations.

This difference in terms of political theology explains diverging assessments of the political sphere in ancient times. Taking a perspective on political theology that is informed by the highly dynamic interactions between the spiritual and worldly representations of power in the European Medieval or Early Modern periods, it might indeed appear justified to indicate the existence of a secular realm of politics for ancient Rome or Greece (see Fischer for Greece). This observation might however be questioned as the political realm in ancient times was well permeated with pre-axial notions of religious meaning in both cases, only that the corresponding political theology was one of a very different nature and dynamics than those of the middle ages. These 'pagan' forms of ancient religiousness and political theology were in fact largely state supportive, more controlled by, and conforming with, the interests of the state. The state of the ancient times could carefully nurture, protect and employ the integrity of this political theology as a matter of the reason of state as evidenced by the trial against Socrates. While not autonomy of the political sphere in a modern sense, a different form of political theology is thus the sign of the relations between religion and politics in ancient times in Rome and Greece.

This points to a crucial aspect of the modern discourse. Today, political theology as a normative, prescriptive argument is still shaped through the tension between two camps each favoring another priority in the relations between second-order and third-order norms. On the one side, there are those who favor a principled priority of the state as a second-order formation, somehow resembling the ancient version of political theology in the style of Varro. On the other side stand those who emphasize the autonomy and higher truth of normative formation of the third-order, be they sacral or secular in nature.

Depenheuer, for instance, discusses in this volume the tension between the state as a central-integrative unit of peace and security and the 'axial' morality of the papal encyclical 'Caritas in Veritate'. Doing so, he refers extensively, even though implicitly, to the tension between second- and third-order formations in general. This tension represents one of the most important and recurring problems of constitutional theory and practice, especially in the context of Western constitutionalism which epitomizes secular humanism as the most prevalent third-order formation in contemporary law and politics. Here, the tension is, however, more pressing than between the political mission of the state and the mere morality of a religious community like the Christian Church.

The line between tensions within the political realm and the political and the religious realm are, however, often fluid. This is the case in many Muslim majority countries where the constitutional position of Islam and, thus, the borderline between politics and religion remains blurred. While these states often aim to somehow discipline and control the dynamics related to Islam, they find themselves challenged by movements driven by more autonomous versions of political Islam claiming to refer to a truth that transcends the authority of the state. The fact that these axial dynamics cannot easily be redirected towards the realm of the state and its claim to ultimately control them is one of the central challenges of numerous states in the Middle East, Africa, South Asia and South East Asia that are trying to cope with this unruly potential by means of appeasement, cooptation, control and repression. It seems that these attempts increasingly fail to deliver in countries that were formerly regarded bastions of constitutional supremacy over religious matters such as Turkey or Indonesia. In the new millennium, these states, their institutions and elites, seem to be less and less capable to prevent a creeping Islamic transformation of secular or religiously neutral constitutional core values as they once were adopted in wake of national independence. Ironically though, Turkey's leader Erdogan, who came to power on the ticket of political Islam muting the laic commitment of Turkey's state ideology, increasingly emphasizes policies in line with consequent second-order thought and practice after having dismantled secular constitutional core values.

A similarly increasing impact of political theologies that stress third-order identities over second-order interests can be observed for political Buddhism in Myanmar and, albeit to a lower degree, Sri Lanka. In other countries with a dominant Buddhist population such as Cambodia and Thailand the political potential of Buddhism has – with some notable exceptions – been largely controlled or appropriated by the state.

2. The Prescriptive Reference to Matters of Political Theology: Politicals versus Universalists

The discussion above now brings us to a second and closely related aspect pertaining to the role of religion as a source of the political order, the question of how this relation is perceived and pursued on prescriptive terms. It seems fair to say that pursuing a certain role of religion in the realm of political power in post-axial times has been shaped by a limited set of basic perspectives that can be traced back to the normative theory outlined above. Based on an ideal-typical view, these perspectives can be viewed as two poles bounding a broader spectrum each.

At the one end of this spectrum, one finds those who stress that the public order is shaped by, and ultimately directed toward, a universalistic measure that originates from a transcendent or absolute reality. Where this is put forward as an argument, such a *universalistic* standard would, in case of conflict, even supersede the mere laws and interests of the state. Notably, such a supreme universalistic standard can also represent the secular notions of political theology, especially (liberal) secular humanism and socialism.

At the other end of the spectrum stand those who primarily focus on the interests of the concrete public order – the state they are living in, the 'polis' or the 'city' as, for example, the neocons like to label it often. They place the integrity, stability and security of the state as the central-integrative unit of the political ahead, which they see as the ultimate goal to pursue. For them, the interests of the city trump all others, potentially superseding any countervailing moral or legal norm in case of conflict.

In this volume, the terms 'universalists' and 'politicals'[36] are used to denote the proponents of these two extreme positions in perceiving public order and governance in general and the interface of politics and religion in particular. Universalists align themselves in other words ultimately with third-order, politicals with second-order norms. In terms of political *techne* and the ultimate normative orientation, universalists and politicals will favor entirely different approaches to the same empirical reality. This results in diametrically opposing normative dispositions toward the role of religion, and in fact, any third-order formations including those based on secular universal core values of the constitution, *vis-à-vis* the state.

---

36 The term *politicals* is loosely inspired by the historical designation *politiques* which is used for sixteenth and seventeenth century intellectuals, jurists and power elites in France who put the strength, success and well-being of the state above all else, including especially the ideological demands of the warring religious faiths in the age of the religious wars. This faction of political pragmatists called the *politiques* were in favor of a strong government, predominantly led by national security concerns and a 'prudence' or reason of state that trumped their personal allegiance to a certain faith as most prominently exemplified by Henri IV of France.

Depenheuer's chapter in this book can be read as a forceful argument in favor of the positions of the politicals in regard of both sacral and secular universalism. In fact, Depenheuer prominently represents a notable strand of German constitutional theory that is inclined to put forward the interest of 'state' as argument against the values of 'constitution' if necessary, – much in line with the principled tension between politicals and universalists in general. This tension does not typically result in refuting the respective other's values and principles entirely, but only one's preferences in cases of conflict.

Practically, the two ideal-typical perspectives often coexist and intertwine to a certain degree. Nevertheless, ultimately, one of the two points of view will always be regarded to ultimately dominate the other. Often, the antagonism between the two points of view relates to critical junctures in the development and reproduction of the overarching public order, and represents defining conflicts over foundational decisions and hegemonically adopted, upheld and contested collective identities that are based either on one or the other opposing core values.

a) The Universalists

The universalists' stance concerning the role of religion in the political realm varies according to the kind of universalism in question. Especially in Western contexts, it has to be differentiated between secular and sacral universalists. In the Western context, the most relevant are the secular universalists who orient themselves towards secular humanism regarding liberal democratic constitutions. This type of constitutionalism manifests as a basic structure consisting of mutual reinforcing features like popular sovereignty, representative democracy, civil and human rights, and the rule of law. Secular universalists in Western settings would perceive these constitutional core values as the ultimate measure of how to execute political power in general, and with regard of the role of religion within the public order in particular.

Secular universalists would naturally not condone that the countervailing claims and interests made on behalf of the state as the central-integrative unit of the political would guide or even trump the normative direction set by these core values. The essence of their 'constitutional faith' is that these core values form the supreme and ultimate rallying point of the public order and its reproduction.

For the universalists of secular Buddhist provenance, religion is mostly a matter of individual freedom. Universalists would especially condone various forms of reservations based on their strive to ensure the fundamental right to religious liberty in both a positive and a negative sense, as long as it does not impinge on the freedom of others, or upon secular constitutional core values in general. Universalists would especially condone various forms of reservations based on conscience and faith – much in the tradition of the Augustinian *reservatio mentalis*.

However, where religious values clash with the demands of personal freedom or other constitutional core values, secular universalists might encounter great difficulties to find a consistent stance, which is often the case when faced with more assertive manifestations of Islamic faith. Even if secular universalists are generally inclined to argue in favor of freedom and greater leniency in cases of diverging displays of identity in the public realm, they will have great difficulties to reconcile their faith in secular humanism with an Islamic universalism if the latter is interpreted in ways that clash with precepts of secular constitutional faith, such as the equality of men and women or the fundamental freedoms of those not adhering to Islamic faith. Here, the universalists might partly converge in their policy approach with the politicals who normally argue in favor of a stronger securitization of the constitution and more forceful demands to ensure social cohesion.[37]

But, as a rule, secular universalists will encounter the role of religion in and for the political realm first of all as a problem of constitutional theory, constitutional law and constitutional faith. Compared to the politicals, they

37 A typical example for the opposing discursive preferences of the politicals and secular universalists in general is the question of torture for the sake of state security. While secular universalists tend to emphatically reject any remedy to security threats that contravenes the human dignity, the politicals would be more flexible. For them, torture could, under certain circumstances, be acceptable to safeguard the integrity of public safety and security, even irrespective of existing norms of universalistic morality and law, especially under the conditions of Western constitutionalism as being shaped by secular humanism. The complex entanglements of both ideal-typical positions manifest, however, in the ticking-bomb scenario. Here, the argument is raised that torture is used precisely to safeguard the human dignity of the victim by sacrificing that of the perpetrator who has it still in his hands to end the torture by ending the threat to the victim. Here, a classical position of the politicals is developed by an argument that aims at the core values of the universalists.

would rather accept the dynamic role of any faith as a sort of free societal radical, easier tolerate differences and require less adaption as long as divergence is not directly affecting constitutional core values too greatly.

In states less or not essentially influenced by Western constitutional core values, the universalists are often those in opposition to the hegemonic state of affairs, be it on behalf of a secular or a sacral universalism. In countries with a majority Muslim population, sacral universalists are often in sharp opposition to the hegemonic forces representing the state. In South-East Asia, secular universalists who are calling for a more prominent place for their version of constitutional faith have considerable difficulties overcoming the established power structures dominated either by politicals or sacral universalists or both. This is case for instance in Indonesia, where secular humanists' demands for minority rights of the LGBT community clash with strong representations of the sacral universalists and politicals over the question if human rights should be interpreted in light of Islamic faith and opposing Western human right claims. This last point leads us to a fuller description of the politicals.

b) The Politicals

Generally, the politicals are inclined to represent the more conservative end of the ideological spectrum. Their highest concern is maintaining the integrity of the state as the central-integrative political unit. They care supremely about the state's internal harmony, internal and external security, and oftentimes aim also at sustaining the might and glory of the state.

Politicals are inclined to refer in their decisions and preferences lastly to a 'friend and foe' distinction, per Carl Schmitt. Regarding the religious, the politicals' focus on its effect in terms of the internal cohesion of the central-integrative unit. Ultimately, modern politicals still hold a similar position on religion that Varro took in the Roman Empire: they condone a political theology under the precepts of the state's interest to bind society together and reinforce conservative values. They reject all divisive religious dynamics as much as they deny any universalistic normative order to supersede the interest of the state in principle.

Practically, politicals appear in very different shades ranging from personally religiously committed advocates of the primacy of the state to religiously completely indifferent disciples of an absolute reason-of-state approach that welcome any instrumentalization of the religious for the mere interest of the state. One of the most coherent, consequent and influential representations in the sense of this latter extreme can be found in American neoconservatism.

This comprehensive theory of government which exerts a remarkable influence on the world's most powerful country, where religion is generally referenced significantly stronger in political affairs than in European countries,[38] exhibits a particularly pointed understanding of the role of religion but also for the public order.

In the US, neoconservatism wields enormous influence over the conservative intellectual movement within the Republican Party but also beyond. Its sweep creates in fact a "trickle-down effect on the [entire] political culture" reflected in a significant "influence on both major parties" as claimed by Norman Podhoretz, one of the neocons' foremost intellectual leaders.[39] Be that as it may, the strategic agility, conceptual determination, intellectual engagement, forceful political networking and outreach make their 'neo-' version of conservativism so remarkably influential – somehow similar to the 'neo-version' of liberalism.[40]

The neocon movement took its initial inspiration from Leo Strauss.[41] Based on his philosophy of governance, they developed a view on religion that is deeply embedded in a philosophy of governance which is derived from a distinct ontology. Strauss and the neocons have found their inspiration insofar particularly in and, so to say, merged Plato and Machiavelli.[42]

38 Even a liberal democrat like John F. Kennedy, to put that in a nutshell, famously said in his inaugural address of January 20, 1961 that "the rights of man come not from the generosity of the state but from the hand of God." See Bellah, "Civil Religion in America," 1967, pp. 1-21. For the role of religion in the US see also Bauszus, "The Religious Aspects of the Founding of the American Republic: A Design of Religion and Reason," 2009, pp. 335-362.

39 Norman Podhoretz quoted in Thompson and Brook, *Neoconservatism: An Obituary for an Idea*, 2010, p. 15.

40 Like the neoliberals, neocons know how to work in the backyard of power, know when to either openly play or skillfully conceal their influence.

41 Although Leo Strauss had to leave his home country Germany as a Jew for the US after Hitler's rise to power, he was close to the German Conservative Revolutionaries and in many respects a soulmate of Carl Schmitt whom he attempted to intellectually aid to defeat liberal democracy.

42 See Thompson and Brook, *Neoconservatism*, pp. 128, 138 and 146. Concerning Plato, the neocons' interest is particularly focused on the Plato of the 'Republic'. See for Plato on this matter Bilski, "Plato's Political Ontology: On the Nature of Man and Regime," 2009, pp. 54 ff.

Reminiscent of the Gnostic experience, the neocon's ontology is based on the assumption of an unbridgeable chasm between a perfect transcendental sphere of Platonic ideas and the imperfect, ever-changing reality of this world.[43] The mundane reality is shaped for them by contingency, men's inherently evil nature, and permanent conflict within and between the political communities.[44] Accordingly, the neocons find themselves locked in a world of constant Machiavellian flux of political ascent, descent and decay.[45] In this world, the 'city', the neocon's favored denotation for the state, is the ultimate point of orientation, the pivotal entity within this disappointing reality.

Transcendent ideas are, on the other side, not sought to govern this world's affairs, but rather the inner-worldly realities of expediency, necessity, and force or, to put in a single term: the reason of state.[46]

Neocons base their definition of the public function of religion on this ontologically derived philosophy of governance. Although the ensuing art of statecraft places a high value on religion, the political theology the neocons pursue stands in total opposition to that of the universalists. The epistemic pivot of the neocons' comprehensive concept of ontology, politics and religion again taps into a quasi-gnostic dualism. It manifests in a sharp distinction between two levels of ontological and political knowledge that generates an esoteric elitism as sharply opposed to both the egalitarian nature of the Christian revelation and the normative precepts of liberal secular humanism. Derived from the epistemic distinction between an exoteric level of knowledge accessible for the ordinary man and an esoteric level of knowledge available only for the sages, the neocons endorse two moral and political standards that essentially define their political theology.[47]

---

43 See ibid., p. 123.

44 Notably, the Straussian statesman has to "arbitrate between competing factions in the city" for which he needs the integrative effects of religion and nationalism as an accompanying civic religion. The observation that the statesman has to manage the competing and centrifugal forces within the city describes the very condition of second-order figurations or the central-integrative unit of the political as pointed out above. See Thompson and Brook, *Neoconservatism*, pp. 129 f., see also pp. 144 f.

45 See Kristol, Review of "Persecution and the Art of Writing by Leo Strauss," 1952, p. 394.

46 See Thompson and Brook, *Neoconservatism*, pp. 156 ff.

47 See ibid., pp. 146 ff., 152 f., 154 ff., 159 f.

It is the mission of the neocon leaders – the philosopher and the statesman enlightened by him –, to cope with the world's imperfection and impermanence that only their eyes can penetrate. While regulating the condition of the ordinary people who are trapped in this imperfection, the neocon leaders are supposed to be lastly unconstrained by the rules of inferior men and to hover above ordinary morality and laws.[48] While the masses have to be tightly disciplined and directed, the statesman's success depends on the ability of "looking away from first things, principles, [...]; and looking towards last things, fruits, consequences, facts."[49] – not the elusive realm of the ought, but the hard facts of being, dictate his law of action.

Accordingly, Irving Kristol's 'First Law' of statecraft requires the statesman to be ready to abandon "one's avowed principles" and to act according to what the moment demands.[50] At the same time, to govern the 'city' and regulate the lives of the ordinary men, the statesmen need to create and maintain a public order that meets the requirements of the imperfect and shifting condition of reality.[51] This implies the need to keep the ordinary people in check through social engineering and disciplining for which the neocons regard religion to be one of the most efficient tools.

This art of statecraft and its politics of religion shall be explained in some more detail. Starting point is the practical need to govern ordinary men and women by a morality that suits their condition of ignorance and that aligns the individual's primary identity and self-interest with a love for the 'city'.[52] The recipe for a functional morality that binds together and directs the ordinary people comprises the classical conservative virtues, especially "fidelity, loyalty, piety" for the 'city'.[53] To instill such a morality religion is one of the most powerful tools along with a military valor and a warrior ethos, patriotism, and nationalism.[54] The point of these politics of civic virtue is to make the ordinary man believe in targeted noble

48 See ibid., p. 125.

49 See James, "What Pragmatism Means," 1948, pp. 144 f.

50 Kristol, "When It's Wrong to Be Right," March 24, 1993: "There are occasions where circumstances trump principles. Statesmanship consists not in being loyal to one's avowed principles (that's easy), but in recognizing the occasions one's principles are being trumpeted by circumstances [...].".

51 See Thompson and Brook, *Neoconservatism*, p. 123.

52 See ibid., p. 125.

53 See ibid., p. 123.

54 See ibid., p. 160.

ideas in order to discipline and control his destructive impulses towards society, and to instill a sense for duty and self-sacrifice.[55] The politics of religion are of particular importance in this context as they provide hope and fear as the central tools of governance most effectively.[56] In this view, Strauss' reference to religion in antiquity can be applied timelessly to the present:

> Religion as reverence for gods breeds deference to the ruling class as a group of men especially favored by the gods and reminiscent of the gods. And vice versa, unqualified belief will dispose the people not to believe in what they are told by venerable men. The ruling class will not be able in the long run to elicit this kind of deference if it does not contain man, and especially old men, who are venerable by virtue of their piety.[57]

Instilling public faith and virtue as well as hope and fear, a benevolent deception is the statesmen's duty.[58] To serve the 'city', the statesman must nurture, manage and protect the 'city's' inherited institutions and the conventional system of belief and morality to which the ordinary man must adhere.[59] The leaders must either create the ordering myths that inform this morality or cultivate those that already exist.[60] They themselves, however, do not have to share the faith in these 'public truths'. Overtly, the leaders are thus decisively "pro-religion even though they themselves may not be believers", with some of the most famous neocon thinkers defining themselves as "pro-religion atheists".[61] To them, God might be an illusion

55 See ibid., p. 160; see also Depenheuer, "Das Bürgeropfer im Rechtsstaat," 2007, pp. 75-100.

56 See Thompson and Brook, *Neoconservatism*, pp. 160 ff.

57 Strauss, "Liberalism Ancient and Modern," p. 100, quoted from Thompson and Brook, *Neoconservatism*, p. 127, fn. 34.

58 See ibid., p. 123. In this regard, the neocons draw not only on Machiavelli but also on the Platonic conception of the noble lie and its impact on civil religion in Plato's Republic. See Bilski, "Plato's Philosophical Ontology," pp. 54 ff. The free-floating absence of any traditional moral boundaries concerning the leaders is one of the outstanding characteristics of the neocon version of conservatism and the position of the politicals, besides the particular ontological foundation and gnostic dualism of the neoconservative persuasion.

59 See Thompson and Brook, *Neoconservatism*, p. 127.

60 See ibid., p. 124.

61 Irving Kristol quoted from Thompson and Brook, *Neoconservatism*, p. 160: see also Ledeen, *Machiavelli on Modern Leadership: Why Machiavelli's Iron Rules are as Timely and Important Today as Five Centuries Ago*, 1999, p. 109; Lord, *The Modern Prince*, p. 65; see also Machiavelli, *The Prince*, chapter 18.

but one they understand to be essential for the task to governing the masses. The underlying nexus of epistemic dualism, Gnosticistic esoterism and elitism, philosophy of governance, art of statecraft and politics of religion is perfectly formulated by Irving Kristol:

> If God does not exist, and if religion is an illusion that the majority of men cannot live without [...] let men belief in the lives of religion since they cannot do without them, and let the handful of sages, who know the truth and can live with it, keep it among themselves. Men are then divided into the wise and the foolish, the philosophers and the common men, and atheism becomes a guarded, esoteric doctrine [...]. It would indeed become the duty of the wise publicly to defend and support religion, even to call the police powers to its aid, while reserving the truth for themselves and their chosen disciples.[62]

It is, to underline that again, no transcendent idea or absolute normative standards of third-order provenance but 'city' as the primary unit of social and political reality which forms the ultimate rallying point in the neocons' endeavor to govern. Many of the brightest and most influential minds on the American right buy into this project which, as a corollary, regards the Enlightenment – central to the emergence of secular humanism, and itself arguably a derivative of the Christian discourse of transcendence – to be nothing less than the original sin of modern times.

Religion in this system, to put it from another perspective, is not supposed to be transformative but to preserve and mobilize the 'city' under the inescapable condition of imperfection. For the same end, the leaders enjoy the widest possible latitude in shaping the ever-changing realities by means of the reason of state.[63] The acceptance of what the 'city' essentially is – and the understanding that there is no sense in attempting to impose any normative vision of the good on its deficiency, or even 'a best regime' in order to eschatologically transform it – defines both the prominent place of religion as a tool of governance as well as its strict limitation on merely functional terms.

Finally, it has to be reiterated that the neoconservative point of view represents only the most vocal and radical version of a broad range of different conceptions that seek to subordinate universalistic normative stan-

62 Kristol, *Reflections of a Neoconservative: Looking Back, Looking Ahead*, 1983, p. 300.

63 See Thompson and Brook, *Neoconservatism*, pp. 164 ff. Where moderation does not work however, the leaders have to apply "all manner of nastiness" and might even have "to enter into evil" in order to keep ordinary men and women on track of neocon governance. See Ledeen, *Machiavelli on Modern Leadership*, pp. 89 f.

dards ultimately to those of the 'city', the central-integrative unit of the political. Typically, this view includes a determined preference of the latter's integrity over individualistic liberalism.

Both major ideal-typical stances, those of the universalists and those of the politicals, shape not only the respective political agendas – even if sometimes in discrete and implicit ways – but also the epistemic point of view where an intellectual perspective is directed at the discussion of political theology. In fact, it makes a great difference for the analytical investigation of the problem of political theology, whether one is inclined to take a stance closer to the position of the politicals or the universalists when perceiving the interface of religion and politics. While politicals are inclined to focus more pragmatically on the immediate stabilizing or disruptive effects of the religious factor, universalists tend to pay more attention to the deep structural influences in terms of normative substance and institutional crystallization.[64]

c) Civic religion versus constitutional faith

The conceptual differences between politicals and universalists become especially clear with regards to the concept of 'civil religion', a term coined by Rousseau.[65] For the politicals, civil religion, or civic religion as

64 The single 'structural' factor in the history of religions to which the politicals of neoconservative provenance pay greater attention seems to be the enlightenment-induced secularization. For them, the Enlightenment's call on "unaided reason" that "could accept no authority above itself" and its "promise to strip bare and expose the lies of throne and altar" meant nothing else than a dangerous "assault on the forces […] that had for centuries been the moral and cultural glue holding various societies together." This, and the Enlightenment's underlying equalizing assumption are, in many neoconservatives' view, therefore deceitful if not fatal deconstructions. Much in line with Rousseau's conviction that full knowledge must remain the preserve of a small minority, they believe that "the light of reason destroys the sacred and the transcendental; it undermines the belief of ordinary man in the immortality of souls, of an afterlife, and of divine punishments, all of which are necessary for them to bear […] life in this world. Reason […] shatters everything that gives meaning to the lives of ordinary people; it undercuts their belief in everything that unites and brings order to society." See Thompson and Brook, *Neoconservatism*, pp. 66 and 79.

65 See Rousseau, *Social Contract, Book IV, Chapter VIII.* For an influential earlier assessment, see Bellah, "Civil Religion in America," pp. 1-21. From the perspec-

they often call it, is a crucial complement to the positive inclinations associated with religion as a source of the *polis'* stability. For them, civic religion is neither a substitute for religion on sacral terms, nor is it related to the constitutionally enshrined principles of secular humanism.[66] When Irving Kristol refers to the "holy trinity" of the American civil religion as formed by the '[American] Flag, the Declaration [of Independence], [and] the Constitution […]"[67], the Declaration and the Constitution are arguably rather addressed as symbolic points of reference for the crucial sentiments of patriotism and nationalism than as actual references to discursively shaped and deliberated supreme values of the political or constitutional core values. Similarly, when Samuel Huntington refers to the US civil religion, the "American creed," as a necessary condition to secure a sufficient degree of social and political cohesion,[68] he stresses the effect rather than the principle. This 'creed' does not necessary represent an unquestionable substantial norm to be deliberately reproduced, but merely operates as a functional tool. Finally, for the politicals, civic religion is about merging religion and nationalism,[69] which follows from the essence of governance and statecraft which they see ultimately as a form of "soul-craft".[70]

The universalist stance differs markedly. Here, constitutional core values form the heart of civil religion. They are the exclusive and ultimate point of reference of public faith. This constitutional faith is, thus, the faith in the constitutional order itself as largely defined in Western constitutionalism as a third-order figuration in terms of secular humanism. Constitutional faith in this sense does not complement the constitutional order but reinforces it in another dimension of acknowledgment and effect that is adding up to the technical legal one.

---

tive of the terminology suggested here, Bellah conflates however, political theology and civil religion.

66 From the point of view of the politicals, civic religion is especially important where the cause of religion is weakened, not compelling enough or lost. Moreover, civic religion is supposed to create a unifying rallying point for state-supportive sentiments of those societies which are conditioned by great religious diversity. Here, it is often reinforced by constitutional guarantees that would prevent the establishment of a sufficiently homogenous religious base.

67 Kristol, "The Spirit of '87," 1987, p. 5.

68 Huntington, *America's Politics: The Promise of Disharmony*, 1981, pp. 22 f.

69 Thompson and Brook, *Neoconservatism*, p. 86.

70 Ibid., pp. 167 and 169.

Such a constitutional faith easily clashes with the politicals' understanding of civic religion as evidenced in one of the landmark decisions of the US Supreme Court, the decision West Virginia State Board of Education v. Barnette, a case decided during World War II. Sanford Levinson qualifies this decision as one of "the great testaments" of "constitutional faith" in American constitutionalism, which, at the same time, decisively refuses the politicals' understandings of civic religion. In this case,

> a child who was a member of the Jehova's Witnesses was punished for refusing to enact [....] the pledge to the American flag at the beginning of the public-school day, as requested by state law. The Supreme Court reversed the child's suspension from school, with Justice Jackson writing one of the most quoted sentences in all constitutional law: 'If there is any fixed star in our constitutional constellation, it is that no official, high or petty, can prescribe what shall be orthodox, in politics, nationalism, religion, or other matters of opinion or force citizens to confess by word or deed their faith therein.'[71]

The stance formulated by Justice Jackson (and condoned by Sanford Levinson) is quite the opposite of what the politicals stand for. While the latter strive for homogeneity in terms of social cohesion by means of civic religion, Justice Jackson makes the case for acknowledging the negative freedom of any individual to refuse any demonstration of a public creed. The individual enjoys the natural right to refrain from joining the symbolic ritual of the American civil religion, the "American Creed," on which grounds whatsoever as guaranteed by the secular Constitution. The essence of universalists' constitutional faith is that it credits and respects the autonomous orientation of the individual, that it embraces the emancipating, transcending impetus of the constitutional promises of secular humanism whose negative freedom precludes any order to subscribe to another creed than that chosen by it. These very values protect it from the unifying claims of a cult of the state as many politicals like Strauss or Varro emphatically condoned it.

Other politicals, many European conservatives for instance, would argue in favor of more cohesive and assertive politics of national culture vis-à-vis Islamic civic culture, for example concerning Islamic dress codes for women.

---

71 Levinson, *Constitutional Faith*, 1988, p. 101.

D. Religion as a Subject of the Political

Religion as a subject of the political order, or the *legal*-political order to be more precise, refers to the broad area of concrete frameworks, arrangements and practices by which the political communities regulate their relation with the religious domain. In this sense, 'political community' means not only the state but also other legal-political frameworks such as the European Convention on Human Rights (see Follesdal, Ehlers) or the United Nations' Legal Framework on the protection of the rights of religious minorities[72] (Souza Alves).

On the level of the state, the sister domains of law and politics intersect in the constitution, which is point of reference of most of the contributions dealing either with European, or North American, or Asian states. Additionally, Esser provides an account on the German penal law with regard of the criminal protection against the defamation of religion.

All these legal-political frameworks are ultimately influenced by interests, forces and considerations that can often be broken down to some general perspectives on religion as a source of public order as presented above, especially the particular impact of 'axiality' in the politics-religion interface – the three-layered theory of normative order and the opposition of universalists and the politicals concerning the politics of religion.

On a more concrete level, the different legal-political frameworks can be distinguished and assessed on the basis of some typological considerations as a starting point.

I. Typological Approximation

Despite the inevitable shortcomings and blind spots of all typologies, an overall classification of state-religion relations is helpful to assess the range of possibilities as they are reflected by those chapters of this volume that are dealing with religion as a subject of the legal-political order. To facilitate a comparison of possible approaches to regulating faith and religion, three typologies with strong resemblances by Dirk Ehlers, Pahud de

72 See especially the International Covenant on Civil and Political Rights of 1966, and the Declaration on the Rights of Persons Belonging to National or Ethnic, Religious and Linguistic Minorities of 1992.

Mortanges, and Cécile Laborde provided or mentioned in this volume shall be combined in one model providing three broad categories.

A first category of *separation* is defined in the accounts of Pahud de Mortanges and Ehlers by the absence of any constitutional relation established between the state and the religious communities. Laborde distinguishes, slightly differently, two forms of separation, a militant and a more moderate separation. The category of militant separation features secularist states with outright anti-religious and suppressive tendencies that officially support a skeptical view of religion and provide inadequate protections of religious freedoms. An example would be the People's Republic of China (Laliberté, see also Banic's recourse on Yugoslavia). For a long time, Mexico has also followed this model, but has since developed a more accommodative stance towards religion as presented by Gonzales in this volume. With the constitutional reforms of 1992 and 2013, and the derogation of several anti-clerical provisions from Mexican constitutional and plain law allowing religious communities to obtain eventually legal personality, for example, Mexico has shifted to the separation category featuring states with a more moderated separation that have protections of religious freedoms, but no provision of any administrative, financial or other support by the state. This category accommodates that form of Western constitutionalism that enshrines different laical arrangements such as in France, Turkey, or Mexico but also Japan.

A second category of *subordination* is characterized in Pahud de Mortanges' approach by the subjugation either of the state by a religion, such as in Iran or, *vice versa*, in cases where states authoritatively instrumentalize a state religion. This corresponds with Laborde's model of states which adopt a particular religion or orthodoxy as a state religion and therefore provide only inadequate protection of religious freedoms, discriminating against members of other faiths or those having no religion at all. Similarly, yet slightly more broadly, Ehlers provides the model of an alliance between the state and a particular religion. He does not refer to an alliance on equal terms though, but implies that the state aligns itself with a particular religion that it somehow subdues, imposing a sort of control while controlling or suppressing the other religions on even more rigid terms. Examples would be Turkey after the Islamic transformation of the laically Kemalist state or Malaysia's attitude towards a state sponsored and controlled Islam.

A third category of *cooperation* finally is based in Pahud de Mortanges' account on free and equal relations between independent and autonomous partners with the state recognizing a positive social function of religion. Ehlers speaks here of a *"mediating model"* that combines separation with some sort of cooperation on more liberal and equal terms concerning the different religions. This is very similar to Laborde's category of secular states that complement an adequate protection of religious freedoms with some degree of state support of religious communities, concerning for example religious education and other forms of support with countries such as Germany (Ehlers, Esser) or Switzerland (Laliberté) as examples in case. Especially interesting within this category are those states that feature 'special relations' to a particular, prominent religion without subduing this or other religions while basically fostering cooperative relations with the other religions as well, albeit on a relatively lower level. Examples in this volume are Croatia (Banic), Poland (Brzozowski), Spain (Torron), and Italy (S. Ferrari, Follesdal).

To complement this broader model of the constitutional arrangements regulating the relations between state and religion, I shall define three ideal-typical tendencies of societal development that have historically influenced the modern secular state's relation towards religion especially in Western countries. A first type is characterized by a long tradition of largely *homogeneous historical experience* based on the adherence to a single dominant confession or religion that is reflected by present-day constitutional identity such as in Croatia, Italy, Ireland, Poland, Spain, Russia or the Scandinavian countries.

A second tendency is defined by historical experiences of a *notorious plurality* of Christian denominations in absence of a clearly dominating faith. Here, the notion of a tension-ridden plurality is balanced by the shared experience and reference to basically the same Christian roots. Moreover, these different religious communities share the deep-structure, underlying cultural trajectories and normative-institutional outfit that has developed as part of a larger European civilization. Western societies of this type appear in at least two subtypes though, one represented by the US and another by Germany and Switzerland for instance.

In Germany, the cuius regio, eius religio concept of the 1555 Treaty of Augsburg resulted in a greater compartmentalization of confessional groups and a particular role of state authority as a guarantor of the organization of religious life. Religious freedom is here traditionally very much also the freedom of and state support for organized religiosity.[73] The US experience builds however on the foundational adherence to the individual's religious liberty and freedom of self-organization. As a freedom of a multitude of religious groups from the state it resulted historically in an autonomous and comparatively amorphous religious sphere disconnected from the state.

A third ideal-typical tendency in the formation of Western secular states emerged as result of distinct *ideological splits within a given society between sacral and secular* conceptions of political theology. Here, the development of constitutionalism was historically exposed to deeply entrenched and continuous struggles between groups committed to a homogeneous religious identity, such as Catholics, and those committed to atheism or militant agnosticism on basis of a secular political theology of radical, progressive or socialist provenance.

Sub-types can be distinguished by an eventual constitutional crystallization in terms of a hegemonic establishment in form of a strict separation or a compromise on terms of a special relation between the state and the dominant religion. Both sub-types are often still defined by the presence of the underlying division though, with France and Mexico as example on the one hand and Croatia, Poland, Spain, and Italy on the other.

Today, the historic dividing lines seem to be frequently blurred though, for instance when both, the French secular and sacral political theology are confronted with what they perceive as the impositions of an Islamic political theology. Here, the laical separation seems to be accompanied by notions of a disguised special relation between the state and the predominant religion. This, at least, is the observation of Cécile Laborde who sees "French national republicanism" in danger to culturalize republican values whereby the allegiance to the French "catho-laïque" culture, becomes the guiding particularism that besets French republicanism where laical standards are applied differently in context of Catholic or Islamic expressions of faith respectively.[74] When Laborde argues that the ban on the hijab in schools cannot be defended on grounds of French constitutional core values, that, contrary, the "liberal, difference-blind ideals of equality and im-

73 See for state-religion relations in Germany, besides Ehlers in this volume, also Gerhard Robbers, "Religious Freedom in Germany," 2001, pp. 643-668.

74 Laborde, "Virginity and Burqa: Unreasonable Accommodations? Considerations on the Stasi and Bouchard-Taylor Reports," 2008, at https://booksandideas.net/Virginity-and-Burqa-Unreasonable.html.

partiality" should be applied more consequently instead of emphasizing national identity, she also offers a casebook example of the opposition between universalists and politicals.[75] Starting from these typological reflections some further observations shall be developed.

II. Dealing with the 'Böckenförde Dilemma': 'Special relations' in European Constitutionalism

One of the most influential assessments of the conditions of European secularism comes from Ernst-Wolfgang Böckenförde. The German constitutional court justice and scholar noted the constitutional impossibility of maintaining by duress the empirical conditions for a constitutive influence of a Christian political theology under the normative pretext of secular liberalism. This famous 'Böckenförde Dilemma' reads as follows:

> The liberal secularized state lives by prerequisites which it cannot guarantee itself. [...] As a liberal state it can only endure if the freedom it bestows on its citizens takes some regulation from the interior, both from a moral substance of the individuals and a certain homogeneity of society at large. On the other hand, it cannot by itself procure these interior forces of regulation, that is not with its own means such as legal compulsion and authoritative decree. Doing so, it would surrender its liberal character and fall back [...] into the claim of totality it once led the way out of, back then in the confessional civil wars.[76]

Böckenförde acknowledges first a formative influence of Christianity on Western modernity and its legal-political structure that is in alignment with a broad and settled scholarly discourse going back to intellectual giants like Weber and others. Not so clear is the second assumption by which he explicitly refers to Hegel (see Labuschagne). Two interpretations are possible. Not so different from the politicals, Böckenförde could be understood to focus on a religiously derived morality and social cohesion necessary to sustain the state. Or he could be interpreted as pointing to the need of a sustaining Christian identity to nurture secular constitutional thought and practice on a more subtle basis. This would imply the

75 Laborde, *Critical Republicanism. The Hijab Controversy and Political Philosophy*, 2008, p. 14 at 18 (quotation).

76 Böckenförde, "Die Entstehung des Staates als Vorgang der Säkularisation," 1991, p. 112.

question if a society whose fundamental conceptions are shaped by a particular religion can reproduce a secularized version of this worldview without being somehow in touch with the original religious influence or whether constitutional faith alone can produce enough energy to sustain the deep structure state and law are resting on. This is what Laborde recommends when she rejects both identity politics and affirmative actions to understand constitutional core values as the ultimate answer for the question of how to ensure a good society. Böckenförde on the other hand, is at least as much a universalist too, as he refuses to trade constitutional liberty against the public interest in morality and social cohesion.

Somehow resonating these scholarly thoughts in form of a practical strategy to brace oneself against the elusiveness and inevitability captured in the Böckenförde dilemma are those state constitutions that establish 'special relations' with a particular religion or denomination that is seen to reflect national identity or to ensure social cohesion in a particular way. This leads back to the typology presented above.

As so many constitutional states are going this way, it might be considered to denote a typological category of secular states that are constitutionally built on the explicit or implicit acknowledgment of a particular religion as a decisive source of their social cohesion or constitutional identity without being illiberal concerning the religious freedom in general. Besides the European examples presented in this volume, Thailand and Indonesia are Asian examples.

A general distinction concerning secular states that feature a 'special relation' with a single religion pertains to the mode by which this preference is established. Is it openly acknowledged or disguised by constitutional law, predominantly accepted or significantly contested in legal and societal discourse, for instance? Altogether four European constitutional systems that establish special relations between the state and the Catholic Church are covered in this volume, two Southern European countries, Spain and Italy, as well as two formerly socialist countries, namely Croatia and Poland.

A striking case of these special relations is the Republic of Croatia. Here, special relations between the state and the Catholic Church have been established by four concordats between Croatia and the Holy See. They have emphasized the "irreplaceable role of the Catholic Church in the education of the Croatian people, its historical and present role […] as well as the appreciation that the majority of the Croatian citizens affiliates to the Catholic Church" (Banic). As a consequence, the Catholic Church enjoys a considerable special status concerning its legal status, financial support, and autonomy from the state in comparison to all other religions and denominations albeit religious freedom is generally provided (Banic).

The other Eastern European country with a special relation to the Catholic Church is Poland. This relationship goes even beyond consistently strong support for Catholicism and corresponding special relations on the state-church level, but also embodies the deep entanglements of faith and national identity in context of a struggle for independence, similar to the Irish case. Accordingly, the dominant constitutional discourse acknowledges the commanding position of Catholicism within the religious structure of the country. Brzozowski's rather critical assessment of this special relationship in this volume reflects, however, the fact that the differently accentuated special relations between secular European states and particular religious denominations, while often reflecting a hegemonic mainstream, regularly also have their opponents who prefer a focus on secular constitutional core values in line with Laborde.

Slightly less pronounced than in Croatian and Polish constitutional law, Spain is also establishing its own special relations with the Catholic Church. In Spain, similar to Croatia and Poland, Catholicism still exerts an "enormous" influence on social life (Torron), which is also reflected by the Church's moral authority within the public realm. Like in the other countries, this manifests in direct interventions of the Church in the public discourse on political questions (Torron). In terms of constitutional law, this impact and influence is limited though, given the country's violent history of divisiveness over the role of religion for the political order. Although the Spanish Constitution explicitly denounces the establishment of a state religion in its article 16, it also compels public authorities to take into account the "religious beliefs of the Spanish society" and "to maintain the consequent relationships of cooperation with the Catholic Church and the other denominations." This formulation might be read as reflecting both a sense of special appreciation for Catholicism as well as the consciousness of the highly divisive character of state-religion relations that forbids a too explicit embrace of Catholicism. According to Torron in this volume, the provision should be understood as "a recognition of the fact that Catholicism was part of the 'religious beliefs of the Spanish society'." While the Spanish Concordat with the Holy See confers a superior legal status to the Catholic Church in comparison to that of the other religions, the constitutional court enforced a strong notion of equality when acknowledging the legal status of some other religious communities.

A last example of the European states that exhibit a special relationship with a single religion is Italy. The Italian Lautsi case, which is discussed in the papers of Follesdal and S. Ferrari in this volume, serves as an impressive example for the Italian state's exercise to indeed stand against the elusiveness captured in Böckenförde's dilemma, as it might seem to be reinforced by the European Convention on Human Rights' protection of (negative) religious freedom.

While Follesdal's paper focuses on the decision of the European Court of Human Rights in Lautsi, S. Ferrari analyzes the decision of the Italian Council of State in the same case. In both instances, the case deals essentially with the Italian state's claim that the display of crucifixes in public schools has to be understood as a justified dissemination of Italian societal values (for a similar case in German constitutional law see Ehlers). Follesdal's criticism of the court's recognition of a margin of appreciation in the Lautsi case, is interestingly contrasted by the rather affirmative assessment of the arguments brought forward by Italy in S. Ferrari's assessment. He considers the decision of the Italian Council of State from 2006 as a "lucid attempt to express in legal terms" the affirmation of the actual importance of a particular religion for the society. In this line, he seems to condone the argument of the dissemination of the cross as a "protective umbrella" that extends to other religions as well, with a notable reservation though: "as long they are not in competition with the Catholic" one. For both the Council of State and S. Ferrari, the public dissemination of the cross reflects a positively impacting presence of religiousness in the public sphere that serves as a nurturing ground for the fundamental principles and values on which social cohesion is founded.

The argument that the Christian cross had become one of the *secular* values of the Italian Constitution resonates with the assumption of a structural continuity between the Christian and the secular-humanistic political theology, the claim that the symbolic crystallizations of this structural continuity serve to essentially express and reproduce it and the presumption of an inner relation between sacral and secular political theology on the level of the societal deep structure.

In all four constitutional contexts characterized by a special relationship between state and religion, the respective politics of religion can hardly be reduced to the ideal-typical positions either of the universalists or the politicals, but rather display a strong affirmation of a political theology that is at least aware of what both positions would care of.

III. Confucian/East Asian Constitutionalism: Politicals, Non- and Anti-Universalists

Another interesting issue covered in this volume are the alternative versions of what might be called 'Chinese' secularism for which Laliberté, Kuo, and Thio give fascinating accounts on Singapore, China and Taiwan respectively. In both regional and cultural perspectives, their contributions are complemented by Zhong's piece on Japan. The remarkable difference in how these four systems encounter and manage the factor 'religion' can be read in a coherent way against the background of what has been said above on the role of religion as a source of political order.

Singapore's "secularism with a soul", to start with Thio's contribution, offers the example of a rarely pure constitutional manifestation of the position of the politicals, albeit not that of neoconservative provenance. She derives the baseline structure of her argument from a common observation: "Caesar and God remain in an uneasy relationship, sometimes partners and, at other times, antagonists."[77] What Thio describes, and what might at a first glance appear as a paradox, is however, that in Singapore 'Caesar' always condones the political theology of the politicals and never that of the universalists[78], – especially not under the condition of ethnic and religious plurality in a rather small and densely populated political community.

As much as the state appreciates religion as an instrument to bind society together, to reinforce national values and to reach out to the individuals and groups, it also fears religious contestation among its citizens or directed against itself. Consequently, the city state is generally wary of all 'axial' dynamics; not only in form of Christianity and Islam, but also of secular universalistic systems of belief such as secular humanism or communism. While this brand of secularism does not deny its citizens the right to privately adhere to universalistic religions, it is keen to stay aware of and even participate in the management of these religions' internal affairs.

Markedly different is the militant secularism of the People's Republic of China (PRC). Among all four Asian forms of secularism, the PRC brand is the most assertive. Whereas the current Chinese socialism does

77 Thio, "Constitutionalism and Religious Diversity in Singapore," 2015, p. 233.

78 That does not imply that 'Caesar' is against a universalistic faith but that he does not accept this faith as a public rallying point that supersedes his will within the public realm.

not prohibit every notion of religiosity, the socialist party state exercises a strict hegemony over any, even slight, *institutional* notion of religious faith (Laliberté). All institutionalized religious groups are subjected to a tight regime of state control and state managed religiosity that regulates them increasingly rigidly by law and party discipline. Those groups that are considered to even possibly defy the state's claim of definitional supremacy and control, be they of Buddhist, Muslim, Christian or other provenance, are met with relentless suppression. This is especially true for Uighur Muslims and 'evil cults' like Falun Gong. The predominant reason why a seemingly harmless cult such as Falun Gong moved into the party states' firing line are arguably not merely its exercise techniques and the moral discipline of its disciples but especially its ability to move the masses as a salvationist, partly apocalyptic, movement under charismatic leadership.

In general, the Chinese socialist state's control and repression expresses different strands of the character and development of public order in China. One strand evolves from what can be called the socialist 'political religion', a distinct, encompassing this-worldly view of history, society, and politics that claims absolute superiority and supremacy of its Maoist orthodoxy and is reinforced by a socialist hostility towards the superstitious as it also lies at the cradle of Mexican laicity (Gonzales).

While the first strand is a militantly secular universalist orthodoxy, the second strand of the state's antipathy towards religion is an anti-universalism that reflects the sacralization of the state as a second-order formation that claims to govern the souls of its subjects. Two historical experiences resonate in this anti-universalist notion. One is the more recent memory of devastating upheavals with distinct religious notions. All too often, these at least religiously 'colored' rebellions, uprisings, and civil wars were driven in part by third-order visions that emerged as a dialectical response to the failure of the imperial state (Laliberté).[79] This often-mentioned ex-

79 Examples are the White Lotus Rebellion (1794-1804), the Miao Rebellion (1795–1806), the Eight Trigrams Uprising (1813), the Taiping Rebellion (1850-1864), the Qian Rebellion (1854-1873), and the Boxer uprising (1898-1900), all of them showing signs of millenarianism or notions of salvation. They are accompanied by a series of Muslim rebellions such as the Red Turban Rebellion (1854–1856), the Panthay rebellion (1856–1873) the Tongzhi Hui Revolt (1862–77), or the Dungan Revolt (1895–96). In terms of a secular universalist world-view, one might also count the Cultural Revolution (1966-76) in this list.

perience explains a deep-seated caution towards all uncontrolled universalistic visions that is aligned with a particular appreciation of the state's dignity as the (second-order) central-integrative unit of the political.

Underlying and even more important however, as the second historical experience is the long and pervasive influence of Confucianism. Although philosophical Confucianism has displayed some axial notions it has to be distinguished from Confucianism as a state ideology that developed the greatest influence on the Chinese socio-political universe. The latter elevated essentially a refined version of the ethical and religious notions of the 'law of the family' to become the imperial cult of state and was thus dominated by the amalgamation of first- and second-order structures. With the exception of this Confucianism as a state cult, the imperial state of the third latest dynasties is already characterized by what Laliberté observes for the socialist party state, that its moral basis is radically detached from any established religion.

In comparison, both China and Singapore reject universalistic religious notions; but Singapore pursues the political theology of the politicals while China does not rely on any notion of religiousness beyond the communist party cult and its Maoist orthodoxy.

The third study on Chinese secularism in this volume deals with the Taiwanese case which is totally different from both the Singaporean and that of the Chinese People's Republic. It manifests in a cooperation model that allowed for the development of autonomous religious dynamics of axial provenance that would exert a significant effect on the transformation of the political order in direction of secular Western constitutionalism (Kuo). With a certain unwanted irony, Kuo's account on the Taiwanese secular state[80] seems to confirm that the angst of axial dynamics in China and Singapore is somewhat justified, at least if Kuo is right and a political theology on the basis of third order dynamics was indeed responsible for a liberal-democratic transformation Western-style that leaders in Singapore and China consider to be detrimental to the common good in their countries.

80 See also Kuo, *Religion and Democracy in Taiwan*, 2008. Similar dynamics as those described by Kuo for Taiwan have also been experienced in South Korea. See for example Shik, "The Progressive Christian Church and Democracy in South Korea," 1998, pp. 437-465; Hong, "Evangelicals and the Democratization of South Korea since 1987," 2009, pp. 185-233.

The fourth and last contribution on Asian political theology is Zhong's paper on Japan. He analyses the legal-political dispute over Prime Minister Koizumi's annual visits of the Yasukuni Shrine[81] – a major Shinto holy site supposed to contain the spirits of two million Japanese soldiers, among them a number of convicted war criminals – and the handling of the corresponding complaints by the Supreme Court. The Yasukuni Shrine dispute points to a late reaffirmation of a political theology based on Shinto (State Shinto) that challenged the secular Japanese Constitution's command to implement what could be termed a moderate separation model.[82]

This political theology centered at Shinto is interesting for its non-axial quality. Interestingly, in their search of a firm and comprehensive basis of legitimacy and cohesion for the new state, the architects of the Meiji Restoration reflected initially the possibility to adopt a state ideology linked to Christianity, Buddhism or Confucianism but eventually refused all these options in favor of Shinto. Especially Christianity was refused precisely because its 'axial' nature as pointed out forcefully by Inoue Tetsujirō, for instance, who clearly understood the nature of universalistic axial dynamics and emphatically rejected them as a reference for the design of an imperial political theology. A clear choice against transcendental dynamics that the state would not be able to fully control, the Meiji reformers turned instead to the idea of an organicistic state modelled after the family and based on Shinto. On this fundament, they created a state cult that would serve everything a neocon could wish for including the firm nexus of loyalty towards the government, patriotism, nationalism, military virtues and a sense for self-sacrifice.

Much in opposition to the Taiwanese experience for instance, the Meiji elevation of Shinto as a central element of its state ideology resembles Singapore's preference for a non-axial political theology that represents the ideal-typical position of the politicals on the politics of religion.

---

81 Prime Minister Koizumi's visit was not the only one by a Japanese Prime Minister. Especially, Prime Minister Shinzo Abe, member of the revisionist lobby organization Nippon Kaigi, has also visited the Shrine. All these visits were, however, claimed to be of private nature.

82 While apologists have argued that Shinto is no religion, imperial Meiji scholars who adopted State Shinto as a political theology did so precisely to found the Emperor's lineage from the Sun Goddess and thus the claim to be a divine being, whereas Shinto practice also comprises the belief in spirit beings. Even if no axial religion, Shinto arguably is therefore a form of religion (see also Zhong).

From this perspective, Koizumi's visit of the Yasukuni Shrine represents an interesting notion of a 'non-axial' political theology that reflects a broader stance both in Asia as well as among neo-conservatives.

IV. Constitutional Change and Contestation

A last aspect to ponder pertains to the dynamics of constitutional change and contestation that can easily blur typological lines and, in particular, secular constitutional identities. Especially where the world is "as furiously religious as it ever was" or "in some places [even] more so than ever", as Ronojoy Sen quotes Peter Berger[83] in his account on Indian secularism, a number of secular states experience ongoing attacks on the increasingly brittle walls they had once forcefully erected between the state and religion. The nationalist Hindu challenge to India's secularism (Sen) is, however, only one example of a larger trend.

Ran Hirschl, who is a keen observer of this trend in contemporary constitutionalism, sees even a new kind of legal and political order emerging that he calls 'constitutional theocracy'. Without referring only to theocratic states in the formal sense of the word, countries like Iran, for example, Hirschl describes the amalgamation of "two of the most important phenomena in late twentieth- and early twenty-first-century politics – the triumph of constitutionalism as the prevalent form of governance and the return of religion to the world political stage […]."[84] To a varying degree, this trend seems to affect an increasing number of countries that managed it to uphold their secular constitutions for decades. In the Islamic world, where it gains a particular momentum, this trend becomes especially visible with the transformation of a formerly strictly laical country such as Turkey or the ongoing attempts to reinterpret the Indonesian constitutional basic structure of Pancasila as an affirmation of an Islamic state.[85] The above-mentioned case of the Japanese Yasukuni Shrine case is another, albeit moderate, move in this direction, where the Supreme Court stopped

83 Berger, "Securalism in Retreat," 1996/1997, p. 3.

84 Hirschl, *Constitutional Theocracy*, p. 241.

85 See for Indonesia the contributions in Tim Lindsey and Helen Pausacker (eds.), *Religion, Law and Intolerance in Indonesia*, 2016; Machmudi, "The Development of Political Islam in Indonesia," 2015, pp. 237-248; for Turkey see İnceoğlu, "Constitutional Conflict and the Idea of a New Constitution," 2015, pp. 159-180.

short before declaring the Prime Minister's visit of the shrine unconstitutional despite a clear constitutional ban of any engagement of the state with religious activities (Zhong).

In Europe, the global surge in resorting to a more assertive understanding of religious identity has been particularly critical in dealing with Islamic minorities. As A. Ferrari points out for Italy, the right to religious freedom is increasingly subordinated "to more […] securitarian versions of civic cohesion and public order" while the perception of Islamic challenges to a secular consensus has led "to a crisis of religious freedom as a unified, specific and high standard right."

Similar to Laborde for France, A. Ferrari observes nothing less against this background than a "crisis of religious freedom as a unified, specific and high standard right."

On a global level, one might even see a general crisis of Western constitutional identities that coincide with a rise of more vulgarized forms of the old counter-discourses to Western dominance in terms of values and ultimate norms of governance.

This is not to denounce lock, stock, and barrel all non-secular visions of good governance and the common good. The claim of Pakistan's founder, Muhammad Ali Jinnah, in a 1946 speech, that democracy would be in the very blood of the Muslim who presumed a complete equality of man still resonates as sound reminder to some of the repressive systems in the Islamic world that are lacking any viable legitimacy among their citizens.

Those representations of Islam that are presently particularly vocal in the public sphere seem, however, often to be dominated by rather vulgarized forms of faith and practice. In many countries with a majority Muslim population, the rigidity of the corresponding demands is often inclined to conflict with secular constitutionalism, especially where they aim at rewriting constitutional core values in light of their religious interpretations. An example in case is again Turkey. Here, it is licit nowadays to discuss on state TV slavery and sexual intercourse with minors as religiously condoned practices at prime time. Only few years ago, something like that would have been completely unthinkable under the Kemalist precepts of the Turkish constitution. The social acceptability of such debates underlines how much religious identities are shifting and how strong these shifts can impact on constitutional identities as well.

After this section on religion as a subject of the legal-political order has started with a typological approach to the constitutional frameworks regulating the relations of politics and religion, this introductory chapter is thus closed with a reminder of some of the current dynamics that make the topic of this volume so interesting.

Bibiography

Assmann, *Jan, Herrschaft und Heil. Politische Theologie in Altägypten, Israel und Europa*, München: Carl Hanser, 2000.

Augustine, *De Civitate Dei*: *Book V*, ed. Patrick Gerard Walsh, Oxford: Aris & Phillips, 2009.

Bauszus, Detlev David, "The Religious Aspects of the Founding of the American Republic: A Design of Religion and Reason," in *Religion, Politics and Law: Philosophical Reflections on the Sources of Normative Order in Society*, ed. Bart Labuschagne and Reinhard Sonnenschmidt, Leiden: Brill, 2009, pp. 335-362.

Bellah, Robert, "Civil Religion in America," *Daedalus* ("Religion in America") 96, 1 (1967): 1-21.

Berger, Peter L., "Securalism in Retreat," *The National Interest* 46 (Winter 1996-1997): 3-12.

Bilski, Benjamin, "Plato's Political Ontology: On the Nature of Man and Regime," in *Religion, Politics and Law: Philosophical Reflections on the Sources of Normative Order in Society*, ed. Bart Labuschagne and Reinhard Sonnenschmidt, Leiden: Brill, 2009, pp. 30-69.

Böckenförde, Ernst-Wolfgang, "Die Entstehung des Staates als Vorgang der Saekularisation," in idem, *Recht, Staat, Freiheit. Studien zur Rechtsphilosophie, Staatstheorie und Verfassungsgeschichte*, Frankfurt am Main: Suhrkamp, 1991, pp. 92-114.

Brown, Peter, *Society and the Holy in Late Antiquity*, Berkeley: University of California Press, 1982.

Depenheuer, Otto, "Das Bürgeropfer im Rechtsstaat," in *Staat im Wort, Festschrift für Josef Isensee*, ed. Otto Depenheuer, Heidelberg: C. F. Müller, 2007, pp. 43-60.

Depenheuer, Otto, "Das Bürgeropfer," in *Selbstbehauptung des Rechtsstaates*, ed. Otto Depenheuer, Paderborn: Ferdinand Schöningh, 2007, pp. 75-100.

Douglas, Mary, Natural Symbols: Explorations in Cosmology, London: Routledge, 1996.

Eisenstadt, S. N., "Multiple Modernities," *Daedalus* 129, 1 (2000): 1-29.

Eisenstadt, S. N., "The Axial Conundrum between Transcendental Visions and Vicissitudes of Their Institutionalizations," in T*he Axial Age and its Consequences*, ed. Robert N. Bellah and Hans Joas, Cambridge, MA: Belknap Press, 2012, pp. 277–293.

Eisenstadt, S.N., "The Axial Age Breakthroughs – Their Characteristics and Origins," in *The Origins and Diversity of Axial Age Civilizations*, ed. S. N. Eisenstadt, State University of New York Press, Albany: Suny Press, 1986, pp. 1-28.

Freeman, Charles, The Greek Achievement: The Foundations of the Western World, New York: Penguin, 1999.

Fukuyama, Francis, "Confucianism and Democracy," in *World Religions and Democracy*, ed. Larry Diamond, Marc F. Plattner, and Philip J. Costopoulos, Baltimore, MD: John Hopkins University Press, 2005, pp. 42-55.

Geertz, Clifford, "Centers, Kings, and Charisma: Reflections on the Symbolics of Power," in *Local Knowledge: Further Essays in Interpretative Anthropology*, ed. Clifford Geertz, 3rd ed., New York: Basic Books, 2000, pp. 121–146.

Haltern, Ulrich, *Was bedeutet Souveraenitaet?*, Tübingen: Mohr-Siebeck, 2007.

Hegel, G. W. F, *Philosophy of History*, New York: Dover Publications, 2004.

Hirschl, Ran, *Constitutional Theocracy*, Cambridge, MA: Harvard University Press, 2010.

Hong, Joshua Young-gi, "Evangelicals and the Democraization of South Korea since 1987," in *Evangelical Christianity and Democracy in Asia*, ed. David Halloran Lumsdaine, Oxford: Oxford University Press, 2009, pp. 185-233.

Huntington, Samuel, *America's Politics: The Promise of Disharmony*, Cambridge, MA: Harvard University Press, 1981.

İnceoğlu, Sibel, "Constitutional Conflict and the Idea of a New Constitution," in *Norms, Interests, and Values. Conflict and Consent in the Constitutional Order*, ed. Henning Glaser Baden-Baden, 2015, pp. 159-180.

James, William, "What Pragmatism Means," in *Essays in Pragmatism*, ed. and with an introduction by Alburey Castell, New York: Hafner publishing, 1948, pp. 144 ff.

Jaspers, Karl, *The Origin and Goal of History* [1949], London: Routledge and Kegan Paul, 1953.

Jaspers, Karl, *The Way to Wisdom: An Introduction to Philosophy*, New Haven, CT: Yale University Press 2003.

Joas, Hans, "The Axial Age Debate as Religious Discourse," in *The Axial Age and its Consequences*, ed. Robert N. Bellah and Hans Joas, Cambridge, MA: Harvard University Press, 2012, pp. 9-29.

Kantorowicz, Ernst H., "Mysteries of the State: An Absolutist Concept and its Late Medieval Origins," in idem, *Selected Studies*, J.J. Augustin Publisher, New York: J. J.Augustin, 1965, pp. 381-398.

Kippenberg, Hans G., "The Role of Christianity in the Depolitization of the Roman Empire," in *The Origins and Diversity of Axial Age Civilizations*, ed. S. N. Eisenstadt, State University of New York Press, Albany: Suny Press, 1986, pp. 261-279.

Kristol, Irving, "When It's Wrong to Be Right," *Wall Street Journal*, March 24, 1993.

Kristol, Irving, *Reflections of a Neoconservative: Looking Back, Looking Ahead*, New York: Basic Books, 1983.

Kristol, Irving, Review of "Persecution and the Art of Writing by Leo Strauss," *Commentary* (October 1952): 394.

Kristol, Irving. "The Spirit of '87," *The Public Interest* 86 (1987): 3-9.

Kuo, Cheng-Tian, *Religion and Democracy in Taiwan*, Albany: Suny Press, 2008.

Laborde, Cécile, "Political Liberalism and Religion: On Separation and Establishment," *Journal of Political Philosophy* 21, 1 (2013): 67-86.

Laborde, Cécile, "Virginity and Burqa: Unreasonable Accommodations? Considerations on the Stasi and Bouchard-Taylor Reports," in *La Vie des idées*, 2008, at https://booksandideas.net/Virginity-and-Burqa-Unreasonable.html

Laborde, Cécile, *Critical Republicanism: The Hijab Controversy and Political Philosophy*, Oxford: Oxford University Press, 2008.

Labuschagne, Bart, "Religion and Order: Philosophical Reflections From Augustine To Hegel On The Spiritual Sources Of Law And Politics," in *Religion, Politics and Law: Philosophical Reflections on the Sources of Normative Order in Society*, ed. Bart Labuschagne and Reinhard Sonnenschmidt, Leiden: Brill, 2009, pp. 71-94.

Ledeen, Michaela, *Machiavelli on Modern Leadership: Why Machiavelli's Iron Rules are as Timely and Important Today as Five Centuries Ago*, New York, 1999.

Levinson, Sanford, *Constitutional Faith*, Princeton: Princeton University Press, 1988.

Lindsey, Tim and Helen Pausacker (eds.), *Religion, Law and Intolerance in Indonesia*, London and New York: Routledge, 2016.

Lord, Carnes, *The Modern Prince: What Leaders Need to Know Now*, New Haven, CT: Yale University Press, 2003.

Luhmann, Niklas, *Introduction to Systems Theory*, Cambridge: Polity Press, 2013.

Machiavelli, *The Prince* [1532].

Machmudi, Yon, "The Development of Political; Islam in Indonesia," in pp. 237-248.

Origenes, "Contra Celsum," I 1 GCS Origines 1, ed. Paul Koetschau, Berlin: Julius Hinrichs, 1899.

Origenes, "De schismate Donati," 2,3 in: PL 11, 1000A.

Phongpaichit, Pasuk, and Chris Baker, "The spirits, the stars, and Thai politics," Talk at Siam Society, 2 December 2008, available at http://pioneer.netserv.chula.ac.th/~ppasuk/spiritsstarspolitics.pdf.

Poole, Thomas, *Reason of State: Law, Prerogative, and Empire*, Cambrigde: Cambridge University Press, 2015.

Ratzinger, Joseph, *Die Einheit der Nationen. Eine Vision der Kirchenväter*, Salzburg: Anton Pustet, 2005.

Robbers, Gerhard, "Religious Freedom in Germany," *Brigham Young University Law* 2 (2001): 643-668.

Rousseau, Jean Jacques, *The Social Contract,* ed. Anthony Uyl, transl. G.D.H. Cole, Woodstock: Devoted Publishing, 2016.

Schluchter, *Religion und Lebensführung, Bd. 2*, Frankfurt/M: Suhrkamp, 1988.

Schmitt, Carl, *Politische Theologie. Vier Kapitel zur Lehre von der Souveränität* [1922], 9th ed., Berlin: Duncker & Humblot, 2009.

Schmitt, Carl, *The Concept of the Political* [1932], transl. by George Schwab, Chicago: University of Chicago Press, 2008.

Schwartz, Benjamin, "The Age of Transcendence," in Daedalus (Wisdom, Revelation, and Doubt: Perspectives on the First Millennium B.C.) 104, 2 (1975): 1-7.

Scruton, Roger, *The West and the Rest: Globalization and the Terrorist Threat*, London: Continuum/ISI Books, 2002.

Shik, Chang Zun, "The Progressive Christian Church and Democracy in South Korea," *Journal of Church and State* 40, 2 (1998): 437-465.

Taylor, Charles, *Varieties of Religion Today: William James Revisited*, Cambrideg: Havard University Press, 2002.

Thio, Li-ann, "Constitutionalism and Religious Diversity in Singapore," in *Norms, Interests, and Values*, ed. Henning Glaser, Baden-Baden: Nomos, 2015, pp. 197-237.

Thompson, Bradley, and Yaron Brook, *Neoconservatism: An Obituary for an Idea*, London: Routledge, 2010.

Thornton, Bruce, *Greek Ways: How the Greeks Created Western Civilization*, San Francisco: Encounter Books, 2000.

Tierney, Brian, Religion, Law, and the Growth of Constitutional Thought 1150-1650, New York: Cambridge University Press, 1982.

Tillich, Paul, *Dynamics of Faith*, New York: Harper & Row, 1957.

Toqueville, Alexis de, *Democracy in America*, transl. by Arthur Goldhammer, New York: Penguin, 2004.

Weber, Max, *Gesammelte Aufsätze zur Religionssoziologie*, Tübingen: Mohr Siebeck, 1988.

Religion and State: A Hegelian View on the Sources of Normative Order in Society

Bart Labuschagne

A. Introduction

During the last few years, public debate has been filled with discussions on the role of religion in society in relation to the state. For a long time, the standard-view on this role has been that modernisation and secularisation went hand in hand with each other and that with the gradual advancement of society, religion would wane in the long run, and finally disappear. Freedom, equality, social cohesion and adherence to political institutions would be self-supporting, and would all flourish, independent from any worldview or religion. Democracy, human rights, the rule of law, all these concepts were thought to function properly in any culture, no matter what the religious background of the population was. However, things turned out very different from these liberal dreams. Religion manifested itself as a tough phenomenon, especially since the 'revolt against the West' and the insurgence of Islamism worldwide. Ours is a time of great upheaval, fragmentation, and people seeking for certainty. Religion is on the fore of the agenda and we have to understand and come to terms with it in order to understand the way normative order in society is generated and reproduced.

A very similar period in human history, a period of rapid changes of the social and spiritual infrastructure of society, occurred in the end of the 18th and the early 19th Centuries. The Enlightenment, *Aufklärung* in Germany, at its height, in the aftermath of the French Revolution, when new liberal ideals swept over the European peoples, and traditional forces proved to be more resilient than anticipated. What occurred in Europe back then can still be perceived today on a world scale. For that reason, it can be very inspiring to study and try to understand a great thinker who has tried to grasp the spirit of that age. G.W.F. Hegel, the author who coined the very task of philosophy as the comprehension of its own time in thoughts,[1] is a philosopher who is nowadays increasingly (re)valued for his keen insights and thorough understanding of the nature of man, history and society.[2]

There is almost no other thinker who has had such an extraordinary sharp eye for, and a deep insight in the close and complicated relationship that religion, politics and law have with each other. There is an unmistakable correlation between what people believe in, on the one hand, and what is considered as just and good by them, on the other hand. Religion has, in one way or another, some influence on societal order, law and the state of a country. Hegel pushes his point even so far, as he dares to maintain: "A people that has a bad concept of God has also a bad state, bad government, and bad laws."[3] With this, he suggests that there might also be a positive connection between religion, and law and state: that if a people does have a good concept of God, it will also have a good state, a good government and good laws. But is it really so? The answer to this question shall be the guiding line of this contribution. It is a line along a path with numerous sideways and loose ends that cross over the fields of the sciences of religion, of politics, of law and jurisprudence. However, it is a route that is always philosophical in nature.

Several sub-questions emerge with it. Apparently, Hegel differentiates between religions that mediate a true concept of God, and others that don't. Seemingly, he assumes that there are true and false religions. On what grounds is this distinction based? Where does Hegel derive this from, and is it correct? Furthermore, what is a good state, what are good laws, what is justice? Hegel presupposes also here a qualitative criterion: there are good and bad states. Again, the questions can be asked: on what grounds is this difference based? Where does he derive this from, and is it correct? It will be clear to the reader that Hegel finds the answer to these sub-questions on the truth of religion and of law and state ultimately in philosophy. It is in philosophy, in thought therefore, where we can discover the criteria by which we can discern the true, just and good religion

1 Hegel, *Elements of the Philosophy of Right*, 1991, Preface, p. 21.

2 One of the leading present-day philosophers of religion, society and politics, Taylor (e.g. in his monumental *A Secular Age*, 2007), is deeply immersed in Hegel's philosophy; see his 580 pages counting monograph *Hegel*, Cambridge: Cambridge University Press, 1975. Hegelian themes and approaches can be found throughout his work since then.

3 Hegel, *Lectures on the Philosophy of Religion*, 2007, p. 452.

from the untrue, unjust and bad one; as well as those criteria of the just state. On first sight an unheard-of and exceedingly pretentious enterprise, that sets the bar for modern readers quite too high. Do we really dare to come along with this kind of thinking that demarcates true from false religions, and a good state from a bad one? To what extent indeed is good governance in need of such ultimate justification?

Our present-day intuitions and prevailing ideas are tuned in a much more modest key. Nowadays we are not really inclined to differentiate sharply between true and false religions. Religion is considered primarily as a private matter, protected by all kinds of human rights and the principles of separation of church and state, and of religious neutrality of the state. What for one person is the absolute religious truth, does not have to be so for the other. Should not in a tolerant society several truths co-exist peacefully side by side? And are not law and state – that is: the regulation of external relations between people in society – the result and product of mutual and democratic deliberation according to parliamentary procedures under the rule of law? We tend to measure the quality of good governance by the extent to which actual practice approaches this ideal of free, unhampered deliberation.[4] A good state is a state in which deliberative democracy is enabled to flourish, with a free press and media, and free expression of opinions, and in which the truth is not monopolised. But does this suffice? Is this all that is needed to generate a free society?

What then do religion and state have to do with each other in God's name? The one is after all a matter of private concern, of conscience, in which no one else has anything to say. And have not all religions become a private issue, and are no longer object of attention and concern from the government? The idea that all religions amount to the same thing more or less, and have nothing to do with the way we organise society normatively, is nowadays generally accepted, as well as the notion that religion has nothing to do with the common and fundamental values that enable living peacefully with each other. Law, state and politics are based on rationally acceptable principles, and the outer bond which they provide can function well, on the basis of the enlightened self-interest of each citizen who is primarily interested in the enforcement of the law. But is this all enough? Is society not also a community of shared values?

4 Very much in line of Habermas' *Between Facts and Norms. Contributions to a Discourse Theory of Law and Democracy*, 1996.

These very same questions were heavily debated during Hegel's lifetime, the period of the late Enlightenment and Romanticism, of the French Revolution and the Restoration, from the 1790's unto the 1830's. This is a very important period in which many of our own contemporary ideas and ideals of the organisation of society were settled, also with regard to the place of religion in it. All during his working lifetime, Hegel intensely addressed the questions regarding religion in relation to society and the state. His ideas were not written down in one single monograph, but are laid down in numerous publications, scattered over many years. They reflect a great deal of continuity and coherence, but also discontinuity and changing nuances. It must be noted, however, first of all, that Hegel answers these questions very differently from the way we nowadays would tend to answer them. Where we now would be inclined to diminish and maybe to underestimate the role of religion for people in society, Hegel definitely did not. Religion is inescapable for providing social cohesion and moral infrastructure for society, and the importance of religion here can hardly be overestimated.

In this contribution, the ideas of Hegel, their meaning and their relevance for today will be addressed critically.[5] In section B we will start with an analysis of some of the writings of the young Hegel, comprising the years 1790-1800 when he was in his twenties. These manuscripts were never published by Hegel and became known to us only after publication by Hermann Nohl, under the title *Hegels Theologische Jugendschriften* (Tübingen, 1907).[6] They demonstrate a keen and sensitive understanding of the value of religion for the ethical fabric of society but still lack philosophical argumentation. In the next section C we will focus on the more systematic place of religion in society, according to Hegel's philosophical scheme that has come to maturity in his middle age, where he discusses

---

5 Literature on this subject is recently booming in the English-speaking world: Lewis, *Religion, Modernity, and Politics in Hegel*, 2011; Nuzzo (ed.), *Hegel on Religion and Politics*, 2013, and many others. See also: Labuschagne and Slootweg, *Hegel's Philosophy of the Historical Religions*, 2012, and Labuschagne, "Godsdienst en de grondslagen van recht en staat bij Hegel," 2014, pp. 45-80 (in Dutch). It is this last contribution that provided much material for the present chapter here. Earlier publications on this subject can be found in solid German scholarship, for example in the works of Herbert Scheit, Ernst-Wolfgang Böckenförde, Walter Jaeschke, Andreas Arndt and many others.

6 These texts were (partly) translated in English and published as Hegel, *Early Theological Writings*, 1948, and some others as Hegel, *Three Essays 1793-1795*, 1984.

the foundations of the state in the hearts and minds of the population, their *sittliche Gesinnung* (ethical disposition) towards the commonwealth. The famous text that we will be studying and commenting is the long *Anmerkung* (remark) to § 270 of the *Grundlinien der Philosophie des Rechts* (Berlin, 1821).[7] It is in fact a short treatise on the relationship between religion and state, viewed from his philosophy of law. Hegel stresses the importance of religion for state and society, but doesn't seem to care much about what kind of religion people adhere to, as long as it is any religion. The following paragraph (D.) will deal with the view of the older Hegel, in the final phase of his thinking, which shows remarkable shifts and nuances. The text we will be discussing here is § 552 of the final version of the *Enzyklopädie der Philosophischen Wissenschaften* (Berlin, 1830).[8] In it, Hegel is no longer indifferent as to what kind of religion people should adhere to, but is explicitly positive about Protestant Christianity and negative on Roman Catholicism. We will see how Hegel's view has developed over these years, in particular how these changes should be understood and evaluated for our purposes of coming to terms with the role of religion today. And finally in the conclusion in section E, we will draw some further lines to the present day and ask ourselves what Hegel still has to offer to our understanding of the value of religion in society in relation to the foundations of law and state. Is it really true that a bad concept of God leads automatically to a bad state, a bad government and bad laws? If this would be indeed the case, then we should be very worried about our age in which secularisation and religious pluralism run rampant, which contain all various kinds of concepts of God or the divine, and have serious concerns about the impact that would have on the moral foundations of law and state. Or is a different, more positive conclusion possible?

B. *The young Hegel: In Search of a Contemporary Civil Religion for the Modern State*

Already in the very first (unpublished) writing of Hegel that has come down to us, dated around 1793 and 1794, and that has received the title *Fragmente über Volksreligion und Christentum* – later known as 'The

---

7 Hegel, *Elements of the Philosophy of Right.*

8 Part III of Hegel's *Encyclopaedia*, in which this paragraph is located, is translated as *Hegel's Philosophy of Mind*, 2007.

Tübingen Essay' and 'The Berne Fragments' – he comes to speak about the very problem that occupies us here.[9] Hegel started writing this essay during the final months of his stay as a student in the Tübinger Stift and continued writing after he had been hired as a private tutor to the children of a rich family in Bern, Switzerland. Trained as a theologian and philosopher, he did not write it in this professional capacity but more as a social theorist who explores how a people's religion, in fact a civil religion, could function as a social glue that could provide social cohesion in a disintegrating and fragmenting society. His intended audience was not professionally trained philosophers, but he had a much wider, literary audience in mind. In this period he saw himself as a *Volkserzieher*, an educator of the people, very much in the spirit of Gotthold Ephraim Lessing with his *Nathan der Weise*.

In these fragments, Hegel investigates the extent to which religion enables a people to foster shared intuitions and motivations that can keep a complex but free society together. This would require a civil religion that drives people to act in accordance with practical reason. What Hegel means with practical reason are the requirements of the moral law, formulated by Immanuel Kant as the *Categorical Imperative*: act only according to that maxim whereby you can, at the same time, will that it should become a universal law.[10] A popular translation is the *Golden Rule*: one should treat others as one would like others to treat oneself. We can of course establish with practical reason what people should do and not do, but most people in fact do not act out of sheer sense of duty. That is why auxiliary motives are necessary for these people, and here Hegel sees an important part played by a civil religion, that is: to deliver psychologically effective motives for moral behaviour.[11]

Religion consists according to Hegel not only of arid knowledge of God and his characteristics, our relationship with him and how we should stand in the world (this is what he calls 'objective religion'), but is also something of man's heart and how it pertains to our thought and feelings and to the determination of our will (this is 'subjective religion'). The duties people have and the laws of a nation that need to be complied with can receive a greater emphasis and can impress us more when they are repre-

9 See Hegel, "The Tübingen Essay," 1984, pp. 30-58; "The Berne Fragments," 1984, pp. 59-103.

10 See Kant, *Grounding for the Metaphysics of Morals*, 1993, p. 30.

11 See Hegel, "The Tübingen Essay," pp. 59-103, pp. 31-32.

sented as divine commandments in religion. Religion supplies morality, in particular the motives for ethical behaviour, with a new and elevated *Schwung* (momentum), and stems the tide against the power of sensual passions in a particular and effective manner. A civil religion like that would stimulate our behaviour, by instilling in people from young age onwards, by means of ceremonies, stories and habituation, these collective convictions, thereby intermingling them with the loom of human feelings, and binding them to what effectively propels human behaviour.[12] It is ultimately, in Hegel's words, not about the folding of the hands or the bowing of the knees and the heart for the sacred, but it reveals its presence by the way it suffuses the entire scope of human inclination and makes its presence felt everywhere (without the soul being directly conscious of it). It for a great part moulds our feelings that are necessary for being able to practice virtues like love for one's neighbour, but also for being delivered from feelings of envy for example.[13] In order to be able to fulfil its role of effectively providing social cohesion for society, this civil religion should of course respect the freedom of conscience and essential elements of the freedom of exercise of religion. It should advance the ethos of society, but not impose from above one particular faith, or exclude beforehand that a plurality of (private) religions can exist next to each other. Individual liberty is something definitely to be respected.[14]

Hegel marks out different roles for a civil religion like this on the one hand, and for the actual, historically developed private religions on the other hand. For the latter he has the creation and education of a small elite of very dedicated believers in store. These private religions – and Hegel has in particular the Christian denominations in mind – serve therefore a totally different purpose. The moral excellence that is cultivated in them is something for groups who are voluntarily composed on the basis of free choice of faith. It would lead to moral tyranny to impose these high moral standards on the population as a whole. Therefore it would even be counterproductive to try to do so. A good *Volksreligion* is aimed conversely to the moral cultivation of the population as a whole towards a certain minimum standards, not the formation of ethical adepts or an elite of sages. Trying to mould everyone's character towards these high demands is to

12 See ibid., pp. 59-103, pp. 32-33.
13 See ibid., pp. 59-103, pp. 35-36.
14 See Hegel, "The Berne Fragments," 1984, p. 79. See also extensively Lewis, *Religion, Modernity, and Politics in Hegel*, pp. 25-27.

confuse a civil religion, which is relevant for everybody, with what should be relegated to a private religion.[15]

The big question is of course how such a *Volksreligion* exactly should look like. In the rest of the 'Tübingen Essay' Hegel tries to find an answer, systematically exploring this stubborn field. First of all, its central tenets should be based upon generally acceptable practical reason. A civil religion does not demand from people that they accept unreasonable things. Any religion that asks from people to sacrifice their intellect will not convince people in the long run. What the creed teaches, should at least be accessible for common understanding.[16] Moreover, man's imagination, the heart, and the senses must not go away empty-handed in the process of constituting such a folk, civil religion. Although it can be considered a high ideal (*pace* Kant) that people are morally motivated by respect for duty alone, fact is that for most people non-moral incentives are indispensable as motives for moral behaviour. Love is of course one of the most important, but it can also be tradition, trust, the feeling of being recognised and being part of something greater, etcetera. Ceremonies play an important role here, according to Hegel who dwells in this regard on music, festivals, games and so on. These are forms and practices that are able to touch the heart and move the breast pre-eminently.[17] And finally, civil religion needs to be constituted in such a way, that all of life's needs, including public and official transactions, are bound up with it. It is obvious that Hegel has the classical Greek polis-religion in mind here, where numerous festivals structured public life, ethics and social cohesion in the city-state. They permeated people's entire life and enabled them to feel they were a moral, political, and social unity.[18]

This 'Tübingen Essay' poses the problem in a very clear manner and points in directions where solutions might be found. Nevertheless, Hegel has not very concrete suggestions as to how this all relates to the actual,

15 See Hegel, "The Tübingen Essay," p. 50; Lewis, *Religion, Modernity, and Politics in Hegel*, p. 28.

16 See Hegel, "The Tübingen Essay," pp. 49-52; Lewis, *Religion, Modernity, and Politics in Hegel*, pp. 28-29. Not only does Hegel here join Kant, but also Rousseau in his idea of a civil religion, as proposed in book IV, chapter 8 of his *Du Contrat Social*, 1762.

17 See Hegel, "The Tübingen Essay," pp. 54-55; Lewis, *Religion, Modernity, and Politics in Hegel*, p. 30.

18 See Hegel, "The Tübingen Essay," pp. 55-58; Lewis, *Religion, Modernity, and Politics in Hegel*, pp. 31-32.

existent religions. To what extent can for example Christianity be a supplier for this civil religion? Or do we need to look for and find the sources for it somewhere else? These were the very questions that Hegel addressed in another fragment from this period, one of the 'Berne Fragments' that were written in Bern in 1794, in which he shows himself very critical of the role of Christianity in this respect. Instead, he focusses on a greater appreciation of the role of history and tradition. The state has a great interest in people obeying wholeheartedly the laws of the country, without being forced or pushed to do it. Christianity originated initially as a private religion, as a religion in which the moral perfection of the individual stands at the forefront. Hegel analyses Jesus' advise to sell all one's possessions and give the proceeds to the poor. When we imagine this being put into effect as a rule of conduct for even a small community or a humble village, it yields consequences so absurd that we cannot conceive its extension to a larger populace. For Hegel, this image of perfection that Christ erects carries within itself the proof of how much Christ in his teaching had in mind the cultivation and perfection of the individual human being and how little it can be extended to a society as a whole. Such behaviour cannot be expected from ordinary citizens in order for the state to function properly. When perfectionist ideals are enforced on a whole society, tyranny will be the consequence. The history of Christianity clearly demonstrates this, according to Hegel. Not only in Catholicism with (forced) confession, excommunication and the ban but also in Protestantism the tendency to control man's inner thoughts and feelings was pervasive.[19]

How important is religion for morality? Is moral goodness only attainable through faith (in Jesus Christ e.g.), or is it universally attainable independent from religion? In the 'Berne Fragment' Hegel struggles with these questions, and it is remarkable how he consequently puts the demands for a peaceful and free society first and foremost. And when we focus our attention to this, we discover that Christianity overreaches this aim morally. Hegel tries instead to dwell on the notion that a population should be made accustomed to cordial social ties, with the help of historically grown traditions, with folk tales, legends, stories, music, festivals, and all kinds of institutions etc. in order to strengthen the ethos of a free state and society. Christianity has no role here, according to Hegel, in this phase of his

19 See Hegel, "The Berne Fragments," pp. 69-75, 79-80; Lewis, *Religion, Modernity, and Politics in Hegel*, pp. 33-34.

thought.[20] It is clear that Hegel is still looking for a suitable candidate as a provider for this civil religion. The answers he now is exploring and experimenting with steer him right into the waterways of emerging Romanticism, what would later in the period of the Restoration, after 1815 make furore as romantic nationalism. In this later period, Hegel would distance himself from these tendencies fiercely.

This quest for an appropriate source for this civil religion is further explored by Hegel in several other unpublished texts from this period. During his stay in Frankfurt, also as a private tutor, he wrote several *Entwürfe über Religion und Liebe* (1797/98)[21] in which love is increasingly allotted the role as a source for religion, morality and social cohesion as well. In love, all kinds of opposites can be elevated and solved: between duty and inclination, between 'me' and the 'other', between object and subject etc. It should be noted that Hegel also experimented with other concepts that could fulfil this reconciliatory task, like 'life' and 'spirit'. But he concluded here that 'love' is the philosophical key to open the wells of normative order in society. Especially in a text titled *Der Geist des Christentums und sein Schicksal*, which he wrote in Frankfurt between 1798 and 1800, Hegel elaborated on this idea extensively.[22] Although lack of space here prevents us from discussing this important text at length, we will nevertheless devote some words to it in order to understand how Hegel's thought developed itself towards what was published in his mature works early in the 19th century.[23]

According to Hegel, love constitutes a category beyond morality, even beyond the division between 'is' and 'ought'. Where duty and virtue presupposes a division and a tension between the 'self' (even in the autonomous morality of Kant, there is always a part in ourselves that is in control and a master in command, and a part that is obedient, the servant), love annihilates and elevates this separation, by enabling that which is to

---

20 See Hegel, "The Berne Fragments," pp. 80-92; Lewis, *Religion, Modernity, and Politics in Hegel*, 2011, pp. 36-37, 42-44.

21 Unfortunately, these were not translated into English. I refer to the original source in German: Hegel, "Entwürfe über Religion und Liebe", in *Frühe Schriften, Werke 1*, 1971, pp. 239-254.

22 See Hegel, "The Spirit of Christianity and its Fate," 1948, pp. 182-301.

23 According to Jacques Derrida, *Glas. Que reste-t-il du savoir absolu?*, 1974, p. 78, this work contains the matrix of Hegel's mature philosophical system. Thomas Lewis is more reticent: he notices that Hegel's engagement with love is more like a stepping-stone to his later, systematical work.

be done according to duty or virtue, to be done entirely voluntarily and out of ourselves, namely out of love. Kant would argue that this would amount to acting out of inclination, even though love is a good one. Hegel ignores this point and maintains that with love a category is introduced that moves us beyond these kinds of oppositions and strains that split us and break us up.[24] Love not only unites our inner divided self, but also annihilates the alienation between people, and the rift between man and the world, subject and object. It makes that we see and appreciate the totality and coherence of the world, of man and his place in the larger unity of society.[25]

What then is exactly the role of love in keeping society together? In 'The Spirit of Christianity' Hegel describes how in early Christianity people formed communities tied together by bonds of love. Christians lived in small congregations refrained from private property, and shared their possessions with each other and ate their daily meals together. What we in fact see in these early communities is not the germ of a general and universal people ('mankind'), but on the contrary an intrinsically limited fellowship that stands in contrast and separation to the rest of the world, and therefore is definitely *not* universal. For larger society, private property is indispensable for some kind of order in society, where people are strangers to one another. In the end, Hegel has no other option than to abandon the idea of love in the strong sense that is deeply religiously motivated as a source of social cohesion in larger society. Social coherence does not have to entail that people entertain these strong bonds of love with one another. A different, but not inferior kind of love is sufficient for that. And here comes the role of religion into play again, because religious language, images and stories are indispensable for expressing and communicating a more general human benevolence and consideration. This kind of human, mutual affability is embodied and opened up for the heart and mind in images, representations and inspiring stories, like that of the Good Samaritan (Luke 10: 25-37), in fact a story of simple human solidarity and brotherhood. All this opens up the way for Hegel's greater appreciation of the role of religion for societal order than in his earlier writings.[26]

---

24 See Hegel, "The Spirit of Christianity and its Fate," 1948, pp. 210-217.

25 Hegel, "Entwürfe über Religion und Liebe", p. 246; Lewis, *Religion, Modernity, and Politics in Hegel*, p. 48.

26 See for a thorough discussion Lewis, *Religion, Modernity, and Politics in Hegel*, pp. 33-34, 51-53.

It is in exactly this light that Hegel investigates the 'spirit' of the actual historical religions, more in particular the spirit of Judaism on the one hand and the spirit of Christianity on the other. Studying this spirit of a religion is tantamount to analysing the attitudes of believers, as these are symbolized in religious representations and practices, to the degree that they actually can contribute to this very human, brotherly benevolence. No longer is the concept of love the reference point *par excellence* for social cohesion and moral order in larger society, because true love can only really flourish in small communities. For larger society, we have to rely – besides law of course – on some form of religion. However, religion in some 'light version', as benevolent mutual human solidarity, supported by Biblical stories, images and corresponding moral attitudes. It is this intuition that will prove to have a lasting importance in Hegel's later, mature philosophical thought, to which we will turn our attention right now.

C. *State and Religion in Hegels Grundlinien der Philosophie des Rechts (1821)*

In a long *Remark* of more than thirteen pages to § 270 of the *Elements of the Philosophy of Right*, Hegel explains how the relationship between state and religion should be understood in the light of his philosophy of law.[27] He does this in the final, third section of the third part of this book, where the state is discussed. What is exactly a state? How does Hegel conceive the state? And how does the state relate exactly to religion? In answering these questions, we must first of all keep in mind what Hegel has to say in this book in the first place. In short: law (in the broad sense as 'right') and state serve the purpose of the realization of human freedom. They embody the way by which we humans give freedom an objective existence and by which the consciousness of freedom, which is at the same time human self-consciousness, becomes real. "[T]he system of right is the realm of actualized freedom, the world of spirit produced from within itself as a second nature."[28] The state is the institution of all social institutions that enable this realization on a national level in a concrete way and protects this freedom. For Hegel, the state is more than just the political organiza-

27 Hegel, *Elements of the Philosophy of Right*, Preface, § 270 Remark, pp. 291-304.
28 Ibid., p. 35.

tion of society. It comprises common characteristics of a people, as it is expressed in its culture, civilization, and its spiritual and ethical consciousness. The principle of the modern state, as Hegel saw this emerging in the modern, post-Napoleonic age, has an enormous strength and depth, precisely because it allows individual freedom to flourish, and at the same time bringing it back to substantial unity and so preserving this unity in the principle of subjectivity itself.[29] The individual can completely be himself in the family and in civil society and blossom and develop his talents in all directions while being at the same time assimilated in a larger whole and connected with reasonableness – so that he can be better preserved in the end. In this way, a unity of universality and particularity is realized; individual and society are mediated with each other.

This unity is realized on two specific levels, on the one hand *objectively*, in the actual constitution, the institutions of the state, laws, regulations and the like.[30] On the other hand *subjectively*, that is by the supportive political disposition and the trust that is put in the government by the citizens. This can be indicated as constitutional patriotism, love of one's country, in the most common and simple meaning of the word as political virtue: my confidence that my individual subjectivity is in good hands and safeguarded by the state. This is often a matter of unconscious habit, like the possibility to walk safely on the streets by night. This habit of living in safety has so to speak become a second nature, and we scarcely stop to think that it is solely the effect of specific stately institutions.[31] But it is nevertheless a form of consciousness. In short, the state is a form of conscious universality that enables particularity to participate in it, which is formed (*gebildet*) in a specific way. And this is exactly the point where religion comes into play, because what people believe in, where they have their heart, is of paramount importance to the quality of the foundations of the state.[32] Religion is discussed and scrutinized with regard to this function only. It is not analysed to the extent that it has also a different function or meaning for itself or something else. Hegel has done that in other

29 See ibid., p. 282.

30 See ibid., §§ 265, 266 and 269, pp. 287-288 and 290 Addition, where the constitution is indicated as something organic, an organism.

31 See ibid., § 268, Addition, p. 289.

32 See ibid., § 270 and Remark, pp. 290 ff.

works, for example in the *Phenomenology of Spirit* (1807) and in the *Lectures on the Philosophy of Religion* (1821-1831).[33]

It is typical for Hegel that he does not conceive the relationship between religion and the state in simplistic, contradictory terms. *Neither* that state and religion should have nothing to do with each other (as secularist tendencies nowadays suggest), *nor* that state and religion are essentially one (as reactionary, restorative forces in the 19th century proclaimed under the banner of an alliance between throne and altar). In Hegel's view, state and religion are *both* united *and* separated. This calls for an explanation. The two are *one* with regard to their content. Both share *one and the same foundation*, i.e. the absolute. But each relates in his own peculiar way to the absolute, to the truth. In the state, the truth that it is the realization of freedom comes to the fore. In religion, absolute truth is mediated and experienced not in the way it is done in philosophy, where it is presented in the mode of conceptual understanding, but as intuition, feeling and representational cognition. So is for example the unity of infinitude and finitude, of the human and the divine *believed*, *represented* and *felt* in the symbolism of the divine incarnation in Christ, and *not understood* as such. According to Hegel, Christianity is the truth of religion, because it is the religion of freedom and of the unity of the divine and the human. God appears here as the Father, not as some strange, remote, mere transcendent reality, compared to whom man is only a tiny creature. He also is the Son, in Christ – and the Holy Spirit, who moves and inspires in mysterious ways. We must keep in mind that other religions that have a different concept of God and the divine also have another image and idea of the absolute and how the state is to be conceived.

This all entails that the absolute is present in religion and the state in very different ways. The point in which they converge is where for man his ultimate disposition and deepest loyalty are situated. Faith perceives everything from the view of what God demands from us, and therefore has a binding force that permeates the totality of life. The state and its laws acquire legitimacy and are obeyed wholeheartedly from this perspective only when they are represented and experienced as in accordance with the

33 Hegel, *Lectures on the Philosophy of Religion*, 2007, p. 452, and Lewis, *Religion, Modernity, and Politics in Hegel*; Nuzzo (ed.), *Hegel on Religion and Politics*; Labuschagne and Slootweg, *Hegel's Philosophy of the Historical Religions*, and Labuschagne, "Godsdienst en de grondslagen van recht en staat bij Hegel," pp. 45-80.

divine. True religiosity and a positive attitude towards the state and its laws can go very well together, according to Hegel. Hence, he denounces the position that proclaims that only by turning one's back on the earthly world and politics one can be truly religious. The consequence for human behaviour is such advice as 'To the righteous, no law is given', that can lead to dangerous fanaticism. "Those who 'seek the Lord' and assure themselves, in their uneducated (*ungebildete*) opinion, that they possess everything *immediately* instead of undertaking the work of raising their subjectivity to cognition of the truth and knowledge of objective right and duty, can produce nothing but folly, outrage, and the destruction of all ethical relations."[34] On the contrary: a true believer in the eyes of Hegel recognizes in the state and its laws that which constitutes his substantial freedom, which is the activity of the spirit, of self-consciousness of freedom. There is no dual truth; neither can there be a conflict between thought and faith. Freedom, the infinite dignity of man, and the unity of universality and particularity are in the centre stage of both.

Now that religion in this way comprises the foundation of ethical life and the character of the state (as if they originated from a divine will) it is at the same time *only* their foundation, and from this point onwards they diverge. They need to be separated strictly and consequentially. While spirit provides itself in the state an *external* reality and unfolds itself in the organisation of relations in society, it remains in religion in one's inner self and conscience. Religion and state are distinguished from each other as *internality* from *externality*. From this follows, *on the one hand*, that the state is incompetent in religious matters. The state has no saying in and has nothing to do with this sphere of inwardness and the personal convictions of its citizens, at least when they take no hostile stance towards the legal and ethical order. The latter belongs to the domain of the state. *On the other hand*, it can be inferred that religion has no competence in matters of the state. The system of laws, the rights and duties that citizens have towards one another and towards the state are not subject to religious authority. The state cannot impose one particular religion on its citizens, and religion lacks the rational thinking and organising that is needed to regulate social and political life. From the belief that we are all children of

34 Hegel, *Elements of the Philosophy of Right*, § 270 Remark, p. 294.

one heavenly Father cannot be inferred how society should be rationally ordered in detail. Religious conviction is from a totally different order.[35]

Although the state cannot prescribe the citizens what they should believe or not, Hegel nevertheless requires that citizens be members of some congregation, "since religion is that moment which integrates the state at the deepest level of the disposition [of its citizens]."[36] What community they belong to is of no importance as long as they are members of any community they please, for the state can have no say in the content of religious belief in so far as this relates to the internal dimension of representational thought.[37] A liberal state which is strong because its organisation is fully developed can adopt a more liberal attitude in this respect. It may even completely overlook individual matters which might affect it, "or even tolerate communities whose religion does not recognize even their direct duties towards the state (although this naturally depends on the numbers concerned)."[38] Hegel is thinking about Quakers and Anabaptists who refuse military service. Instead, a compensating duty can be imposed. Anyway, freedom of religion cannot be invoked in order to tolerate practices within religious communities which are contrary to the rights and duties of any citizen in a nation. On the other hand, it is of course also the duty of the state to provide the religious community with every assistance and protection in the pursuit of its religious end.[39]

Finally, Hegel dwells upon the paramount importance of the Reformation and the falling apart of the old Catholic world in a plurality of congregations. Hegel contends that this has in the end, after all been a very favourable situation, both for the state as for religion itself. The modern state, which keeps the banner of freedom high, owes its existence in the first place that it is not connected to a specific church or belief. The modern state can exist only against a backdrop that is religiously plural in character. Not only Catholics and Protestants should have equal rights and freedoms; Jews as well should possess full citizenship with all entailing rights and freedoms, simply because they are human beings in the first

35 Ibid., pp. 292-293.

36 See ibid., p. 295.

37 It is to be noted that precisely on this point the later, older Hegel will differ from view.

38 Hegel, *Elements of the Philosophy of Right*, p. 295.

39 See ibid.

place and not just members of a specific people of religious community.[40] The distinguishing feature of the modern state is that is does not directly identify itself with a specific religion, although Christianity is the carrier of the principle on which the modern state is founded.

Although the state does not comprise of the highest or the absolute, it represents nevertheless the highest instance on the level of 'objective spirit' and has its roots in 'absolute spirit'. In the state, the absolute is present to the extent that the ethical idea of freedom becomes reality. What becomes reality in the state is not something arbitrary or capricious, as if history is only filled with mere chance and luck, but is self-consciousness itself, becoming real as something universal that is known and thought. In a way, the state itself is also a product of religion, also because the state cannot be conceived as something entirely independent of a history of salvation and divine engagement with the world, according to Hegel.[41] Hegel can be very easily misunderstood and misread,[42] as if he divinised the state. The only thing he contends is that the process by which the state realises human freedom gradually more adequately is a means by which God interacts with the world.[43]

To sum up: although state and religion share a deep and common foundation with each other, which in practice pertains mainly to the disposition that citizens have towards political life in the state, each one of them has its specific, demarcated domain in which the other has nothing to say. Hegel posits himself on a moderate pluralistic standpoint and draws the

---

40 See ibid., § 209, p. 240. With this contention, Hegel went directly against the grain of current regulations of the German Federation (Deutscher Bund) that all citizens be members of one of the three officially recognized denominations.

41 See ibid., § 258, Addition, p. 279, where we can read in the English translation: "The state consists in the march of God in the world", which is not an accurate translation of the original German that reads "Es ist der Gang Gottes in der Welt, dass der Staat ist" – therefore we should translate that as "it is the march of God in the world, that there exists a state – something entirely different from what the translation suggests: it suggests that everything a state is and does, is the result of divine providence, but Hegel means to say here that it is God's will that there is a state that realizes the human potential of freedom.

42 For example, due to translational errors mentioned in the previous note.

43 This theme is exposed extensively in Hegel's *Lectures on the Philosophy of History*. See for an excellent commentary Hodgson, *Shapes of Freedo: Hegel's Philosophy of World History in Theological Perspective*, 2012. A very readable introduction, also to Hegel's philosophy as such, is provided by Houlgate, *Freedom, Truth and Histor: An Introduction to Hegel's Philosophy*, 1991.

line of what has to be tolerated along fanaticism with which is frowned upon 'normal' and day-to-day ethical duties that citizens have towards one another and the state. If religion is involved in this fanatic fervor, then Hegel has no mercy. It might be an interesting question what Hegel would have thought of the very opposite of fanaticism: indifference and quietude. Of course, fanaticism of which Hegel speaks forms a direct threat to the foundations of the state, but the (actual) question can be raised whether present tendencies towards indifference or even hostility towards the absolute (maybe caused by still rising secularization, at least in Western Europe) nevertheless poses a danger, although more indirect and less explicitly. Questions like these will be discussed in the final paragraph (E.) of this contribution. But first we have to turn our attention to the views of the older, even more mature and developed Hegel, as we come to the fore in his work of around 1830, only shortly before his sudden death in 1831.

D. Religion and State in the later Hegel: The Encyclopaedia of 1830

As noted in the introduction above, Hegel's ideas on the relationship between religion, law and state have only developed and blossomed fully in the final and most mature phase of his life and work. These ideas are exposed in several works dating from that period, for example his *Lectures on the philosophy of religion*, the *Lectures on the philosophy of history* (both only published after his death) and the third edition of the *Encyclopaedia of the Philosophical Sciences*, published in 1830. Due to lack of space to dwell extensively on all these works, we will concentrate on Hegel's published work, the *Encyclopaedia.* With this, we obtain a good overview of Hegel's final outlook on our subject and we can see where and why nuances have occurred.

Although Hegel's *Encyclopaedia* was published in 1830 as a concise summary of his philosophical system as a whole, and part of it is dedicated to the philosophy of law and state (under the title of 'Objective Spirit'),[44] the treatment of the relationship between religion and state herein

44 Hegel's *Encyclopedia of the Philosophical Sciences* consists of three parts: 1) Logic – metaphysics and epistemology etc. 2) Nature – physics and organics etc. and 3) Spirit – subjective spirit (anthropology, psychology etc.), objective spirit (law, ethics, politics and the state) and absolute spirit (art, religion and philosophy).

differs from that in the *Elements* of 1821. To start with, the systematic place where this analysis is made is very different. Instead of treating it in an introductory text where the general principles of the state are discussed, it is placed at the very end of the entire part of Objective Spirit, after the state, international law and the philosophy of history, in a long Remark to § 552, comprising about 11 pages. Situating the problem right on the border between objective and absolute spirit, between finite existence and infinity, sheds clear light on how we should deal with it. Right on this spot the transition is made philosophically from actual, finite existence (discussed in Objective Spirit) to infinity as it comes to the fore in art, religion and philosophy (Absolute Spirit). It is in this very paragraph where the relationship between the infinity of art, religion and philosophy and the finitude of actual social, political and historical existence is brought to comprehension. How is the sphere of objective spirit anticipated by an absolute spirit? In what way does absolute spirit determine what happens in objective spirit? Right in the focus of these kinds of questions Hegel's considerations of religion in relation to the state take place.

Similar to the *Elements* where religiosity is associated with people's ethical disposition, here also their moral attitude and the way they stand in the world and perceive society and state stand central. "Ethical life is the state drawn back into its substantial interior, while the state is the development and actualization of ethical life, but that the substantiality of ethical life itself and of the state is religion. According to this relationship, the state rests on the ethical disposition, and this rests on the religious disposition."[45] The right religious disposition emerges only from ethical life when it becomes conscious of the free universality of its concrete essence. The ethos of a free society is rooted in a religious disposition towards freedom, an ethos that religiously embraces and endorses freedom. Ethical life is so to speak divine spirit as indwelling in consciousness, in the actual presence of self-consciousness as a people and the individual members of that people as a whole. "[T]his self-consciousness retreating into itself out of its empirical actuality and bringing its truth to consciousness, had in its *faith* and in its *conscience* only what it has in the *certainty* of itself, in its spiritual actuality. The two are inseparable; there cannot be two sorts of conscience, a religious conscience and an ethical conscience, differing

45 Hegel, *Philosophy of Mind*, (1830) 2007, p. 251.

from it in substance and content."[46] According to Hegel, it is up to the religious content to corroborate ethical life in its functioning in empirical reality. For self-consciousness, religion is the basis of ethical life and the state. On this point, Hegel holds pertinently the view that man is a thoroughly religious animal, and that what man believes in is crucial for how he perceives morality, social and political life.

In what follows, Hegel dissociates himself explicitly from his own standpoint in the *Elements* of 1821 that religion is *only* the foundation of the state and that the two of them depart from one another from that point onward and should be considered separated from each other. "It has been the massive error of our times to want to regard these inseparables as separable from one another, in fact even as mutually indifferent. The view taken of the relationship of religion and the state has been that the state already exists for itself in some other way and from some force or power, while religion is the subjective affair of individuals and had to be added, perhaps as something desirable only for strengthening the state, or is even a matter of indifference, since the ethical life of the state, i.e. rational law and constitution, stands firm for itself on its own ground."[47] The idea that law and the state can be something self-supporting, and can be obeyed only on the basis of rational insight of the people, is vehemently rejected by Hegel. Reasonable law and a reasonable constitution cannot stand on their feet alone: a spirit of free consciousness is indispensable for them, and this can only be found in religion, in what people deeply believe in and put their faith, trust and heart in. In the *Lectures on the Philosophy of Religion* (of 1831) Hegel is even more clear about this: "Religion is knowledge of the highest truth, and this truth, defined more precisely, is *free* spirit. In religion, human beings are free before God. Because they make their will conform to the divine will, they are not opposed to the highest will but instead have themselves within it. (…) The state is simply *freedom in the world*, in actuality. What essentially matters here is the concept of freedom that a people bears within its self-consciousness, for the concept of freedom is realized in the state. (…) There is *one* concept of freedom in religion and state. This one concept is the highest concept that humans have,

46 Ibid., p. 251.
47 Ibid.

and it is made real by them."[48] Obviously, Hegel is no longer indifferent towards what religion they adhere to, as long as they confess to any religion of their choice, like he maintained back in 1821. The Hegel of 1830 takes a much more critical stance towards the kind of religion people believe in. When a religion lacks this spirit of freedom and self-consciousness, people can fall prey to a form of spiritual slavery, of a kind that posits itself rigidly in opposition to self-conscious spirit. It is here where Hegel speaks very critical words about Roman Catholicism, and if we listen closely and carefully – and 'read between the lines' that appear as appalling at first sight – we can easily extend this criticism to other kinds of religions and worldviews that keep people in spiritual servitude and understand why that is indeed the case.

The essence of Hegel's criticism on Roman Catholicism is demonstrated by his critical treatment of the consecrated host. In the host, "God is presented to religious worship as an *external thing*. (In the Lutheran church, by contrast, only and solely in the *faith*, i.e. in the annihilation of the externality of the host, and in the faith, i.e. in the spirit that is at the same time free and self-certain, only then is the host first consecrated and exalted to God in his presence.) From that first and supreme relationship of externality flow all the other external, hence unfree, unspiritual and superstitious relationships [among Roman Catholics]."[49] Hegel mentions several examples of these, like the distinction between an estate of the laity which receives knowledge of divine truth (as well as the direction of people's will and conscience) from outside, i.e. from another class, the estate of the clergy. Laity does not itself gain possession of that knowledge in a spiritual way only, but essentially needs an external consecration for it. And there are more examples: for instance the style of praying, "firstly just moving the lips by themselves, then spiritless in that the subject foregoes the direct approach to God and asks others to pray for him; addressing devotion to miracle-working images, even to bones, and expecting miracles from them; in general, *justification* by external works, a merit which is supposed to be gained by actions, even supposed transferable to others, etc. – all this binds the spirit under a self-externality, by which the concept of spirit is misconceived and perverted in its innermost core, and

48 Hegel, *Lectures on the Philosophy of Religion*, p. 452. The next sentence here in the text is the quote cited in footnote 3: "A people that has a bad concept of God has also a bad state, bad government, and bad laws."

49 Hegel, *Philosophy of Mind*, p. 252.

right and justice, ethics and conscience, responsibility and duty are corrupted at their root."[50] Hegel's main objection to Catholicism is that it conflicts with what he regards as a central feature of modern ethical life, namely individual self-consciousness and individual freedom and autonomy.[51]

According to Hegel, corresponding to such a principle and to this development of spiritual unfreedom in the religious sphere there can only be a legislation and constitution of legal and ethical unfreedom, and a condition of lawlessness and ethical depravity in the actual state. He sharply contrasts the sacredness as it is experienced and symbolized in the Catholic world, especially in monasticism where the vows of chastity, poverty and obedience are cast, with Protestant ethics in which sacredness is something entirely inward and a matter of conscience, as it comes to the fore in this (long) quote:

> [T]he divine's spirit self-introduction into actuality, the liberation of actuality to spirit, means that what in the world is supposed to be *holiness* is displaced by *ethical life*. Instead of the vow of chastity, only now does *marriage* rank as the ethical, and, therefore, the *family* as the highest condition in this aspect of humanity. Instead of the vow of poverty (corresponding to which, embroiled in contradiction, is the merit of giving away one's goods to the poor, i.e. enriching them) what counts is the *activity* of acquisition by one's own intellect and industry, and *honesty* in this traffic and use of wealth, ethical life in civil society. Instead of the vow of obedience, what matters is *obedience* to the *law* and the legal arrangements of the state – an obedience that is itself genuine freedom, because the state is one's own reason, self-actualizing reason: *ethical life* in the *state*. Only so can right and morality then obtain.[52]

This (albeit hyperbolic, but rhetorically effective) contrasting between sacredness of the monastic life and civil life is indeed telling. A free legal order is incompatible with a religion of unfreedom. Making laws in a country is useless when people's religion stands in the way of wholeheartedly obeying these laws.

> Principles of lawful freedom can only be abstract and superficial, and political institutions derived from them must be for themselves untenable, if the wisdom of these principles misunderstands religion so grossly that it is unaware that the principles of the reason of actuality have their ultimate and supreme

50 Ibid.

51 See Inwood, "Commentary to Hegel's Philosophy of Mind," 2007, p. 611.

52 Hegel, *Philosophy of Mind*, p. 253. See. Inwood's succinct commentary on pp. 613-614.

> verification in the religious conscience, in subsumption under the consciousness of absolute truth.[53]

It is therefore according to Hegel to be considered a folly of modern times

> to alter a system of corrupt ethical life, its political constitution and legislation without changing the religion, to have made a revolution without a reformation, to suppose that with the old religion and its sanctities a political constitution opposed to it can have internal peace and harmony, and that stability can be procured for the laws by external guarantees, e.g. so-called chambers, and the power given them to determine the budget and the like.[54]

And finally, "it is in fact the most profane, the supreme contradiction to want to bind and subject the religious conscience to a worldly legislation that it regards as a profanity."[55] Hegel concludes that

> only in the principle of the mind that is aware of its essence, is in itself absolutely free, and has its actuality in the activity of its liberation, is the absolute possibility and necessity to be found for state power, religion, and the principles of philosophy to coincide, for the reconciliation of actuality in general with the mind, of the state with the religious conscience as well as with philosophical knowledge, to be accomplished.[56]

And finally,

> [I]n the Protestant conscience the principle of the religious conscience and of the ethical conscience becomes one and the same, – the free mind aware of itself in its rationality and truth. The constitution and legislation, as well as their operation, have as their content the principle and the development of ethical life, which proceeds, and can only proceed, from the truth of religion, when this truth is established as the original principle of ethical life and thereby becomes actual as such. The ethical life of the state and the religious spirituality of the state are thus firm reciprocal guarantees.[57]

In short, Hegel suggests that in order for a free society and a legal order based on liberty to exist and function properly it is necessary that it is protected from within against decline and corruption by letting it root in a spirit of Protestantism. In order to uphold a free state based on the rule of law, one needs honest, incorruptible Protestant citizens, to paraphrase Hegel in summary. Whether this implies that all citizens actually should

---

53 Hegel, *Philosophy of Mind*, p. 253.
54 Ibid., p. 254.
55 Ibid.
56 Ibid., p. 256.
57 Ibid.

be members of Protestant congregations, is not explicitly clear in Hegel's texts. He is more concerned about fostering a *spirit* of Protestantism as an ideal-typical attitude and state of mind that is led by an *inner* understanding and awareness of right and wrong and is not commanded by any external, empirical authority. It is this attitude that moreover leaves room for secularity's and worldliness' own right. Paradoxically, a state founded on such Protestant principles is a state that does not depend on a specific confession, but can leave room for a plurality of religions. In other words: Hegel is more concerned for a *cultural* Protestantism, an attitude that can be embraced across all religions by everyone. Could this cultural Protestantism then be the ultimate candidate that Hegel has elected as the provider for modern societies and states of the so desperately needed civil religion? In the final, concluding paragraph we will elaborate this question further, when we shall try to formulate some observations on the relevance of Hegel's views on the relationship between religion and state for our present age.

E. Conclusion: A Hegelian Perspective on Religion, Law and State Today

In the aftermath of the dramatic developments of the French Revolution and Napoleon's transformation of the European continent, a time that is characterised by the dwindling of old certainties and growing social fragmentation, Hegel tried to conceptualise and develop a contemporary notion of freedom that should benefit not only law and state, but religion itself as well. Not only he wanted to put freedom central in his political and legal thinking, but in theology as well. At the same time however, he had a sharp eye for the conditions under which very diverse and pluralist societies can and should be held together. In Hegel's century, religion was seen as a much more self-evident and taken-for-granted foundation of society and state. Hegel amended this restorative, romantic and nationalistic notion by claiming that the state has indeed a rational foundation, but is in need of religion for its legitimacy and efficacy. What a population believes in, where it puts their trust, their treasure and their heart in, is of influence on how they perceive the authority of law and state. In Hegel's eyes, religion is of decisive influence on man's character formation, especially during our young age, and influences deeply our moral intuitions, dispositions, and how we stand in and look at our individual life itself and our living together in society. The role of religion in the formation, education

(*Bildung*) and cultivation of our consciousness is considered by Hegel of much greater importance than the formal position that religion takes as an institutionalised manifestation as 'church' in society in relation to the state.[58]

Moreover, the state is in Hegel much more than just the external organisation and institution that enables peaceful living together as society, but is also the expression of the common meaning of who we are as society and what is important for us. A vital and vigorous state expresses the import of who we together deeply are: free creatures whose freedom should be reflected, embodied and protected in our legal and political institutions. What is symbolized in religion as representations, feelings, rituals and ceremonies is what is realised in the state in political and legal structures: there is after all only *one* concept of freedom in religion and state, as stated by Hegel. Therefore, we can indeed never be really free in a state when we consider the state as the greatest enemy of our liberty. It is for this reason that religion has such a great significance for our cultivation of a proper civic disposition.[59] This does of course not entail that Hegel demands from citizens a mere blind trust and a servile obedience towards the state. If we understand him properly, we should realise ourselves that our essence is characterised by free spirit, and that we can and may entrust (as we do in faith as well) the realisation and blossoming of it to the instance that embodies this spirit. Faith in God and faith in political institutions run in a certain sense parallel to each other and reinforce one another as well. Not only can our individual liberty flourish better, also the state will function more properly, because it is supported from within and among the citizens. When a discrepancy exists between what law and state require from their citizenry on the one hand, and what their deepest convictions teach them on the other hand, law and state cannot have much meaning. After all: "Religion is the sphere in which a nation gives itself the definition of that which it regards as the true."[60]

This insight of Hegel has far-reaching implications. As discussed above, Hegel strongly inclines towards favouring a moral, civic disposition of mind that is moulded by Protestant Christianity as the spiritual infrastructure of modern, liberal democracies. He is very critical towards the

58 See Lewis, *Religion, Modernity, and Politics in Hegel*, pp. 232-234.
59 See ibid., pp. 234-235.
60 Hegel, *Lectures on the Philosophy of History*, p. 50.

spiritual attitudes of Catholicism, but for example that of Islam as well.[61] In these two religions, individual liberty and a corresponding personal responsibility do not constitute its highest values, nor will states that fit with these religions be likely to uphold these values. Religions characterised by a spiritless servitude and submission[62] can never comprise a fertile ground for free, democratic states, according to Hegel. It is of great importance that we bear this in mind when we investigate what Hegel could offer today for our understanding of the role of religion in society in relation to law and the state. Of course, he could never have expected that the religious landscape in the world, especially in Europe, would change as drastically as it did during the last two centuries. From a thorough Christian world, Europe has secularised drastically and has become a religiously very pluralistic social order, maybe even in some strata of society a hedonist and materialist society. In other parts of the world, in the wake of the decolonisation, and what is called the revolt against the West, we witness a resurgence of religious movements rooted in (Middle) Eastern parts of the world, e.g. (radical) Islam, Hinduism and others. Tensions between (post-)colonial legal and political superstructures, and the underlying religious infrastructure – often fuelled and brought to the fore due to democratisation-processes that unleashed them – are a wide-spread phenomenon. How democratic institutions, rule of law and protection of human rights should function against a religious and cultural background that did not gave birth to these institutions in the first place is one of the most pertinent and difficult questions societies deal with nowadays, especially in the (Middle) East. When we would look at these problems from our Hegelian perspective and apply this way of thinking and looking, I think two very different and even contrary conclusions are possible and philosophically defendable: a pessimistic and an optimistic one. I will start elaborating on a more pessimistic outlook and paint with dark colours ('grey in grey')[63] a world in decline that maybe has nothing to believe or hope in. But finally, I will dwell on a more optimistic position and ex-

---

61 See recent scholarship e.g. Thompson, "Hegel, the Political, and the Theological: The Question of Islam," 2013, pp. 99-118, and Dudley, "The Active Fanaticism of Political and Religious Life: Hegel on Terror and Islam," 2013, pp. 119-132.

62 The literal meaning of 'Islam' is submission.

63 As philosophy does, according to Hegel in the Preface of the *Elements of the Philosophy of Right*, p. 23. "When philosophy paints its grey in grey, a shape of life has grown old, and it cannot be rejuvenated, but only recognized, by the grey in

pound a more hopeful and positive conclusion that will conclude this contribution not in a minor, but in a major key.

Looking with a Hegelian view at our present societies, the conclusion first at hand would of course be that the spiritual infrastructure of liberal democracies is in a very bad situation. Protestant Christianity is already many years on the wane, and only a small percentage of the population consider themselves protestant, with the exception maybe of the Scandinavian countries. Secularisation has raged thoroughly through European countries, and growth of protestant denominations is rare, albeit Pentecostalism is very much alive in Africa. The rest of the world is dominated either by Roman Catholicism, Islam or indigenous religions – and some by other ideologies that have the status of a political religion. The chance that viable liberal democracies will flourish against these religious and cultural backdrops is in the eyes of Hegel very slight of course. Two dangers threat the spiritual infrastructure of these societies: nihilism and materialism on the one hand, which is the result of the fact that people (especially in Europe) have no traditional faith any longer and have come to embrace hedonism and greed for money and wealth instead.[64] And on the other hand there is the danger of fanaticism, in all its various forms, Islamic and non-Islamic; and of course in its most acute form: as terrorism. Faced with these latter dangers, efforts have been made to install and introduce liberal democratic forms in states like Afghanistan, Iraq, and since the so-called Arab Spring, as well in Libya, Egypt and so on. These turned out to be massive failures,[65] in some of these states fuelling civil wars and eventually even leading to the establishing of an Islamic State that calls itself a Caliphate. This recent development would have been no surprise at all for a Hegelian spectator, who would understand that peoples in the Islamic world are best governed by a form of state that suits the Islamic faith best. Despotism is the most adequate form of government for an Islamic society, would his conclusion be, because believers who see God as a remote, uncompromising and harsh being who simply has to be obeyed

grey of philosophy; the owl of Minerva begins its flight only with the onset of dusk." A culture's philosophical understanding reaches its peak only when the culture enters its decline, explains Allan Wood in his "Editorial Commentary," on p. 392.

64 A recent movie of Martin Scorsese, *The Wolf of Wall Street*, exemplified this type of man brilliantly.

65 Except maybe for only one state that seems to do reasonably well, Tunesia.

and with whom no discussion is possible are best ruled by a despot to whom one also merely has to submit and not question his authority. Introducing democracy in the Islamic world only leads to the fatal degeneration of the forms of state, already described by Plato in his *Republic*: a weak and corrupt democracy leads to anarchy, strife and civil war, which ensues finally in a tyranny.[66] Proof of it can be read in every day's newspapers and seen on television each and every day. Do not the only vital, long lasting and stable democracies worldwide have their origin in North-Western Europe, where – not surprisingly – Protestantism has always been the dominant religion? Trying to introduce democratic institutions in other parts of the world is asking for a recipe for disaster, according to this view. And ongoing secularisation in the West will eventually erode democracy there as well in due course.

This utmost critical and even gloomy perception of the present world and the state of affairs regarding religion, society and state leaves no room for hope or any perspective for improvement at all. Soothed by this glumness one could easily lean back comfortably, nostalgically and even lazy – and become a rabid cultural pessimist, complaining that everything was better in the old days, that doom is near and that the world is coming to its end, unless we all convert to the only one and true God. Does this really have to be our conclusion? Is this the cul-de-sac we end up finally? Is this philosophically the only outcome of our Hegelian viewpoint on today's troubles? I think not. There are other possible readings of today's tendencies that have plausible philosophical credentials as well and may on good (even Hegelian) grounds even be preferred. It was Hegel himself who ultimately held an optimistic view on the course and *telos* of world history as "none other than the progress of the consciousness of freedom."[67] Let us by way of an alternative, more optimistic conclusion draw this line a little further in this direction and see where it brings us.

The image of present society might look very different when we are able to see several elements in it that could be interpreted as cultural protestant, be it in a secularised form. Present-day individualism, with its emphasis on personal responsibility for your own life, happiness and the meaning of your life, can undoubtedly be regarded as a heritage of centuries-long leading Protestantism that has imbued North-West European

66 See Plato, *The Republic*, Books 8 and 9, 1987, pp. 311-335.
67 Hegel, *Lectures on the Philosophy of History*, p. 19.

culture. With the spreading and the internationalisation of this personal attitude, going hand in hand with the wish to live in a liberal democratic regime that protects this way of life by means of human rights and the rule of law, especially among younger generations worldwide, we can see a new ethos emerging. Parallel to this development, we see a general rise of the level of education, a decline of illiteracy, the result of steady emancipation and education-programs. With it, new (social) media has led to a forum for many to express and unite themselves, has led to increased political awareness and a willingness to stand up against corrupt and tyrannical regimes. Alongside this, a companying and very personal spirituality is rising, fed by a religious cosmopolitanism that has eye for the fact that the sacred can be found and expressed in many ways, as long as the personal responsibility for each's choice for one's life is respected. The uniqueness of each and every individual is something very deeply believed in, as well as the high value of personal freedom. All this seems to engender a deep commitment to an ethos of freedom, which is not only claimed for oneself, but also mutually granted to others.

All this are but a few tentative and highly impressionist brush-strokes depicting a more positive, optimistic view on the spiritual infrastructure of society. Of course, tendencies in the various parts of the world do not all point in this direction. Younger generations can choose very different and even contrary ideals, as can be seen in the Islamic world where many join the Jihad of IS. But also in the hearts and minds of them, a very personal decision was made to do so, and it is always possible that they choose otherwise (as some do when they grow more mature and have become wiser). Taking personal responsibility seems everywhere the bottom-line. It is the question how everybody can be convinced that it takes a liberal state and society that best embodies this freedom. The task of philosophy here is taken to its limits and should not be overstretched.[68] Which of the two conclusions discussed just above should be preferred, remains of course up to the critical reader. It is nevertheless hoped that Hegel's keen insights will keep our attention focused on the way personal faith interacts with society's ethical regime.

68 See above note 63, on the flight of the Owl of Minerva at dusk. Philosophy can only try to understand its own age, and not predict the future.

Bibliography

Derrida, Jacques, *Glas. Que reste-t-il du savoir absolu?*, Paris: Galilée, 1974.

Dudley, Will, "The Active Fanaticism of Political and Religious Life: Hegel on Terror and Islam," in *Hegel on Religion and Politics*, ed. Angelico Nuzzo, New York: SUNY Press, 2013, pp. 119-132.

Habermas, Jürgen, *Between Facts and Norms: Contributions to a Discourse Theory of Law and Democracy*, Cambridge: Polity Press, 1996.

Hegel, Georg Wilhelm Friedrich, *Early Theological Writings*, tr. T. M. Knox, Chicago: University of Chicago Press, 1948.

Hegel, Georg Wilhelm Friedrich, "The Spirit of Christianity and its Fate," in *Early Theological Writings*, tr. T. M. Knox, Chicago: University of Chicago Press, 1948, pp. 182-301.

Hegel, Georg Wilhelm Friedrich, *Frühe Schriften, Werke 1*, ed. Eva Moldenhauer and Karl Markus Michel, Frankfurt am Main: Suhrkamp, 1971.

Hegel, Georg Wilhelm Friedrich, "Entwürfe über Religion und Liebe," in *Frühe Schriften, Werke 1*, ed. Eva Moldenhauer and Karl Markus Michel, Frankfurt am Main: Suhrkamp 1971, pp. 239-254.

Hegel, Georg Wilhelm Friedrich, *Three Essays, 1793-1795*, tr. Peter Fuss and John Dobbins, Notre Dame: University of Notre Dame Press, 1984.

Hegel, Georg Wilhelm Friedrich, "The Tübingen Essay," in *G. W. F. Hegel, Three Essays, 1793-1795*, tr. Peter Fuss and John Dobbins, Notre Dame: University of Notre Dame Press, 1984, pp. 30-58.

Hegel, Georg Wilhelm Friedrich, "The Berne Fragments," in *G. W. F. Hegel, Three Essays, 1793-1795*, tr. Peter Fuss and John Dobbins, Notre Dame: University of Notre Dame Press, 1984, pp. 59-103.

Hegel, Georg Wilhelm Friedrich, *Elements of the Philosophy of Right*, ed. Allen Wood, Cambridge: Cambridge University Press, 1991.

Hegel, Georg Wilhelm Friedrich, *Lectures on the Philosophy of History*, 1956, tr. John Sibree, Mineola: Dover Publications, 2004.

Hegel, Georg Wilhelm Friedrich, *Hegel's Philosophy of Mind*, tr. William Wallace and Arnold V. Miller, revised by Michael J. Inwood, Oxford: Clarendon Press, 2007.

Hegel, Georg Wilhelm Friedrich, *Lectures on the Philosophy of Religion, Vol. 1, Introduction and The Concept of Religion,* ed. Peter Hodgson, Oxford: Clarendon Press, 2007.

Hodgson, Peter C., *Shapes of Freedom. Hegel's Philosophy of World History in Theological Perspective*, Oxford: Oxford University Press, 2012.

Houlgate, Stephen, *Freedom, Truth and History. An Introduction to Hegel's Philosophy*, London: Routledge, 1991.

Kant, Immanuel, *Grounding for the Metaphysics of Morals*, tr. J. W. Ellington, Indianapolis: Hackett, 1993.

Labuschagne, Bart, and Timo Slootweg, *Hegel's Philosophy of the Historical Religions, Critical Studies in German Idealism, Vol. 6,* Leiden: Brill, 2012.

Labuschagne, Bart, „Godsdienst en de grondslagen van recht en staat bij Hegel,“ in *Hegels godsdienstfilosofie en de monotheïstische religies. Een actuele confrontatie*, ed. Bart Labuschagne, Timo Slootweg and Rico Sneller, Antwerpen: Garant 2014, pp. 45-80.

Lewis, Thomas A., *Religion, Modernity, & Politics in Hegel*, Oxford: Oxford University Press, 2011.

Inwood, Michael J., "Commentary to Hegel's Philosophy of Mind," in Hegel, *Philosophy of Mind*, tr. William Wallace and Arnold V. Miller, revised by Michael J. Inwood, Oxford: Clarendon Press 2007.

Nuzzo, Angelica (ed.), *Hegel on Religion and Politics*, New York: SUNY Press, 2013.

Plato, *The Republic, books 8 and 9,* tr. Desmond Lee, London: Penguin Books, 1987.

Rousseau, Jean-Jacques, *Du Contrat Social*, Amsterdam, 1762.

Taylor, Charles, *Hegel*, Cambridge: Cambridge University Press, 1975.

Taylor, Charles, *A Secular Age,* Cambridge: The Belknap Press, 2007.

Thompson, Kevin, "Hegel, the Political, and the Theological: The Question of Islam," in *Hegel on Religion and Politics*, ed. Angelico Nuzzo, New York: SUNY Press, 2013, pp. 99-118.

Wood, Allan, "Editorial Commentary," in *Georg Wilhelm Friedrich Hegel, Elements of the Philosophy of Right*, ed. Allen Wood, Cambridge: Cambridge University Press, 1991.

Human Rights and Freedom of Religion: Secular Statehood as a Condition for Religious Truth

*Otto Depenheuer**

A. "Caritas in veritate" from a Constitutional Perspective

To commentate on a pontifical social encyclical from a secular perspective and to contrast it in a constitutional and legal way appears to be a daring and multidisciplinary undertaking. For this reason, it seems to be an inappropriate approach relating to the studied object at first glance. But not only the honorable invitation has led me to ignore such concerns. The constitutional perspective on a social-ethical sign-posting also promises a large gain of knowledge: both disciplines – the constitutional law and social ethics – refer to the identical substratum, that is to say they refer both to the people united in the state and have the same function, namely the good order of society.

However, the epistemological starting point and the ordering perspective of social ethics differ fundamentally from those of constitutional law. The modern and necessarily secular constitutional law must not be based on the religious conviction of the individual. Faith is constitutionally legitimate for the individual, religiously essential and theologically necessary: but these beliefs create commitment only for the believers. Anyone pursuing and promoting political concepts of order based on the Christian belief in revelation will, at best, persuade only those members of a not merely religiously fragmented society, who share the same religious premises and contents. In contrast, constitutional law is necessarily secular, equally to the modern state. It acts from the assumption of the – also religious – heterogeneity of humans and claims to be ethically acceptable to all citizens in a similar way, regardless of their religions or other characteristics. Therefore, constitutional concepts of order have to be so convincing, that

---

* Translated from German by Till Karrer.

they don't only persuade the "men of good spirit", but reach a "people of devils" – alluding to a famous dictum of Immanuel Kant.[1]

From the perspective of a modern state and the constitution, social ethic justifications based on religious or ideological truths are legitimate but relative: every human is free to stick to them, to stand up for them and to promote them with convincing arguments.

But they do not legitimate any generally binding claim of validity on their own. Religious convictions and social ethic derivations are only able to prevail in the relativistic and democratic discourse by majority decisions.

The basic principle of modern constitutional law is: auctoritas non veritas facit legem.[2] Apart from that, beliefs of all content are constitutionally legitimate and supportable positions, but without any obligation for those, who do not share them.

B. Statehood as a Condition for Fundamental Rights

Furthermore, the difference between a social-ethical and constitutional approach is that social ethics have to convince people, whereas the public law – which relies on conviction and acceptance of the citizens as well – in borderline cases, could be carried through resistance based on the "state monopoly on the use of force" (Max Weber). This difference is reflected in the terminology of our subject: Human rights are based on an idea, but fundamental rights are guaranteed by the State. This simple sentence demonstrates the difference between the social-ethical and constitutional approach particularly clearly. Opposed are an anthropologically substantiated ethic, which takes the human nature into account, and an institutional

---

1 This formulates exactly the constitutional problem of order, cf. Immanuel Kant, *Zum ewigen Frieden* [1795], VIII, p. 336: "The problem of building a state is, even if it sounds hard, even for a people of devils (as long as they have any sense) solvable and is as follows: 'One have to put a mass of reasonable beings – who all demand general laws for their maintenance – in order and arrange them with their constitution in a way, even though they are all in favor of exempting their selves from the general laws they demand, that they hold back their private and competitive attitudes enough so they succeed with their public conduct, as if they would not have any competitive private attitudes'." (Translation)

2 Thomas Hobbes, *Leviathan*, Kap. 26.

point of view on human rights, which first of all asks for the conditions of their legal reality.

While invoking human rights fulfills especially political-appellative functions, fundamental rights have a concrete guaranteeing institution as well as a locatable recipient: the State, which guarantees the fundamental rights against itself. On the other hand, human rights are not legally enforceable in this way. This relation between legally non-binding human rights and legally binding fundamental rights is reflected in Article 1 of the German Basic Law: in paragraph 2, the people commit to the "inviolable and inalienable human rights". In paragraph 3, the human rights are transformed in fundamental rights and bind the "legislation, executive power and jurisdiction as direct right". The bottom line is: If human rights are guaranteed by the State, this means they transform into legally binding and legally recoverable fundamental rights, and their justification changes: the ideas, which they emerged from, become the philosophical background of a from now on solely secular guarantee by positive constitutional law.

Effectively working statehood becomes a condition for the possibility of legally effective human rights in the shape of fundamental rights. By contrast, the encyclical presupposed a steady state of the community without making it a subject of discussion. For this reason, the encyclical is quasi blind for the institutional conditions of legal freedom. But concept and reality of the modern state are based on the maintenance of peace. Only under this precondition, fundamental rights can "come to life". The peacefulness of the social circumstances is the first and indispensable condition for the possibility to discuss freely and decide democratically about the good order of society. Although the encyclical broaches the issue of peace again and again, it does not frame this aim consistently in an institutional structure. But in framing the human rights constitutionally and thereby guaranteeing their effective validity lies the constitutional challenge. The state function of peacekeeping has structural preconditions and legal consequences, which each social-ethic discussion about the human rights has to presuppose if it wants to be heard in the secular discussion about the good order of society.

Neither can one have human rights without a state, nor can one have the peacekeeping function of the state, unless one accepts the crucial elements of state structure, which includes the constitutionally guaranteed fundamental rights. The history of legally codified and state guaranteed human rights is diversely interwoven with the development of the modern state. Hereinafter, these origins of the modern state shall be outlined.[3]

C. Structural Elements of Modern Statehood

The modern state owes its development to the surmounting of competitive universalistic truth claims, i. e. the neutralization of the religious question of truth in the course of the secularization.[4]

Rise, triumph and success of the idea of fundamental rights and democracy – the freedom of the individual of self-determination and collective co-determination[5] – replace the one clerically managed religious truth, which used to frame politics and law and was broken by the Reformation. Even more explicitly: the idea of freedom required the triumph of the secular state over the religious truths and the disempowerment of their protagonists: the truth was pushed off the throne, so that the freedom of the individual could prevail.

This tremendous process can be seen as a story of state success, but also can be described as a story of religious decline. However, the free, secular and constitutional statehood is the result.

This process of secularization evolved in three steps.

I. The Road to the Secular State

The Holy Roman Empire of the German Nation originally took its unifying strength out of the fact that it was a – in the fashion of Aritstotle – "societas perfecta": a sacred order, which embraced all aspects of life and was religious and secular-political at the same time. Emperor and Pope were not representing the religious order on the one hand and the secular order on the other hand, but holders of different offices of the one "res publica

3 See Depenheuer, "Wahrheit oder Frieden. Die fundamentalistische Herausforderung des modernen Staates," 1999, pp. 5 ff.; also Hillgruber, *Staat und Religion*, 2007, pp. 67 ff.; Ladeur and Augsberg, *Toleranz – Religion – Recht*, 2007, pp. 55 ff., 59 ff.

4 See for the following: Böckenförde, "Die Entstehung des Staates als Vorgang der Säkularisation," 1967, pp. 75 ff.; Schlink, "Zwischen Säkularisation und Multikulturalität," 1997, pp. 306 ff.; Gärditz, "Säkularität und Verfassung," 2010, § 5.

5 See Isensee, "Grundrechte und Demokratie – Die polare Legitimation im grundgesetzlichen Gemeinwesen," 1981, pp. 161ff.

christiana". This concept of unity was dissolved in particular by theology, which was developing into a rational science, and worked out the separation of religious and secular power. The increasing theoretical independence and the separation and competition of the two subsystems state and church also included a real potential of conflict between them. Actually, the hermeneutic disputations and the resulting critical questions led to divergences over the content of the revelation. Even though the pontifical lectureship was able to assert itself for a while against Luther's posting of his theses in 1517 and the postulation "sola scriptura" – that relevant interpreter be the believer himself – the unity of the Catholic faith broke and discharged in the religious and confessional civil wars of the 16th and 17th century.[6]

The secular state first served the religious participants and their claim of truth totally. This self-conception was reflected exemplarily in the vow of Ferdinand II. of Austria when taking power in Styria: "Rather rule over a desert, rather eat bread and water and go begging with wife and child or get one's body cut in pieces, than tolerate injustice against the church or heresy."[7] All participants of the conflict – Catholics, Lutherans and Reformists – agreed on this consequent but bloody and brutal logic of truth. The religious conflict became a political battle and was as merciless and total as it was uncompromising as a religious one. Thereby, large parts of Europe tumbled in decades of massacres and large regions were depopulated. It is this which unintentionally and unconsciously provided the reason for the practical breakthrough of the theoretical idea of a modern, i.e. sovereign and secular state. The outcome of this crisis could only be the deprivation of power of the religious authorities. For this purpose, an absolutely safe point beyond the hermeneutic disputations regarding the veracity of revelation texts had to be found, i.e. a truth, independent of culture and religious denomination that all men can agree with, regardless of their culture, religion, nation or people. This secular truth was about the peace and the absolutistic and the secular state was the administrator of this truth.[8] *Thomas Hobbes*, the great theorist of this emancipation of the

6 See Depenheuer, "Auf dem Weg in die Unfehlbarkeit? Das Verfassungsbewußtsein der Bürger als Schranke der Verfassungsgerichtsbarkeit," 1997, pp. 485 ff.

7 Quote from Burger, "Multikulturalismus im säkularen Rechtsstaat. Eine zivilisationstheoretische Grenzbestimmung," 1997, p. 177. Translated from German.

8 For the de-Christianization of the concept of state: Quaritsch, *Staat und Souveränität*, 1970, pp. 293 ff.

secular authority from the religious one, proceeded thereby from a straightforward, formal and outward term of peace, which did not focus on living in truth, but on the silencing of weapons.[9] Only the state as a sovereignly deciding and ordering force is able to guarantee this peace as the end of the bellum omnium contra omnes. Since then, the modern state is the neutral instance that is above the arguing religious conflict parties. Finally, after the French revolution, the state totally stops being in charge of religion and church. Religion becomes a private matter of the individual and thereby, the development of the secular modern state is structurally finished. Over many decades, the Catholic Church refused the modern world.[10] The Catholic Church did not complete its Aggiornamento on reality of secular statehood until the second Vatican Council declaration on religious freedom ("Dignitatis humanae") in 1965.

II. Peace instead of Truth

The "truth" of the secular state lies in peacekeeping. But the state cannot argue with a transcendent truth anymore, only with a transcendental one, focused on the formal and procedural conditions of a peaceful and free coexistence of the citizens. It consists of the governmentally guaranteed categorical open-endedness of the political process, the results of which have to be accepted by everybody in the interest of peace. The ideologically neutral state contents itself with this penultimate truth of rationality, to be not obliged to take sides at the end. The state renounces last findings in principle: not because of epistemological skepticism, but of commonsense conviction. In the name of its absolute mission of peace, it limits its function on guaranteeing equal freedom to everybody on the same conditions of peace.

The justification of the modern state is its rationality. Therefore, it is independent of culture or confession and for this reason it is superior to other kinds of knowledge – narrative ones as well as hermeneutic ones – inas-

9 See Isensee, "Staat und Verfassung," 2004, § 15, marginal nos. 61 ff.; Böckenförde, "Die Entstehung des Staates als Vorgang der Säkularisation," 1992, pp. 105 f.

10 See Isensee, "Die katholische Kritik an den Menschenrechten – Der liberale Freiheitsentwurf in der Sicht der Päpste des 19. Jahrhunderts," 1987, pp. 138 ff.

much as all men have to be able to realize the rational truth of statehood.[11] As an abstract and formal truth, it unites people by the civilized peace: whereas concrete cultures and religions divide people, the civilized state unites them by providing and guaranteeing the possibility of a peaceful life together. The basis of this state order of peace is the state monopoly on the use of force: it prevents the citizen from the private enforcement of his or her supposed rights. Only the state dispenses "justice" by and in his courts, only the state enforces this justice effectively on the basis of the state monopoly on the use of force and therefore only the state is able to guarantee constitutional freedom in legal practice. Thus, the fundamental rights found their recipient in the state – freedom against the state – as well as their guarantor – fundamental rights accorded by the state.

However, there is no historic necessity reflected in the triumph of the modern state, but its secularism remains vulnerable just as all types of achievements of civilization. The rejection of a truth binding everyone for the benefit of an order of peace for all citizens is neither a logical nor a historical necessity; it developed historically coincidentally in Europe, but it cannot be proved rationally or universally as "true". Solely the historical experience of most bloody wars and the thereby saturated conviction of the value of peace give reasons for the secularity of the modern state as the institutionalized priority of peace within. In shape of Islamic fundamentalism, this conviction is questioned theoretically and politically in principle. Its plea for the absolute applicability of religious truth without any compromise rejects the European answer in the form of the modern state and its order of peace. And indeed, the European debates of the 16th century are now repeated globally in the 21st century and again with military background music. And in fact: there are few logical reasons for a religious truth revealed by God and the transcendental hope of salvation associated therewith to shy away from earthly challenges and threats. That is the root for a latent and at any time refreshable martyrdom, which does not fear death because its belief promises eternal salvation in the hereafter. To understand the stress ratio between state and religion, one has to understand the plausible logics of both systems. But the logic of religious truth and the logic of secular statehood are fundamentally opposite and not transferable into each other. State power still rebounds from religious convictions: precisely because religion deduces its truth "not from this

11 See Depenheuer, "Wahrheit oder Frieden," pp. 19 f.

world", the state cannot defeat it. The state faces an opponent which it does not understand, fights it using all means that are incompatible with the religious sphere and fights against a reality that lies beyond its power: the otherworldly salvation.[12]

In light of the actual challenges of religious fundamentalism, the modern state is called upon to assert itself. Precisely because it should be viewed as an institutionalized rejection of a material foundation of itself in a religious truth, the liberal constitutional state cannot escape the logic of contrary "secular truth". Also the truth of the secular state is not able to compromise. Its function as a guarantor of peace is not under discussion, is non-negotiable and not open to compromise, as long as the modern state wants to maintain its fundamental values – human dignity, freedom, democracy and constitutional state – against hostilities.[13] So, the liberal-democratic basic order as a well-fortified democracy protects the openness of its decision-making procedure, the constitutional freedom to arbitrariness and the relativity of democratic majority decisions. This logic dresses up in a paradox: No freedom for the enemies of peace, respectively no tolerance for intolerance.[14]

D. The Modern State from a Constitutional and Social Ethical Perspective

The social encyclical *caritas in veritate* says nothing explicit about these institutional preconditions of the modern state; it presupposes them. That is not without danger for the logical coherence of the line of argument: the benefits of the modern state – secularism, internal peace, state monopoly on the use of force, freedom and democracy, rule of law – are not available without paying the price for it. One cannot make theoretical and practical peace with the modern state without affirming its structural consequences. So the effective guarantee of fundamental rights presumes a generalized construction of statehood (1.). Moreover, the legal and practical guarantee of freedom against the state are only available for the price of a lack of content of these – defensive – rights. Given positive expression as

12 See Depenheuer, 2008, pp. 940 f.

13 See Depenheuer, *Selbstbehauptung des Rechtsstaats*, 2007.

14 For an overview: Becker, "Die wehrhafte Demokratie des Grundgesetzes," 1992, § 167, marginal nos. 46 ff.

fundamental rights, the human rights as a defensive freedom abstain from giving contents regulation of how to use the freedom, but rather release – for the sake of the freedom of the individual – a relativism of individual freedom and democratic majority decision (2.).

I. Claim of Universality and Bindingness

In democracy, state, constitution and law are carried by all state citizens, legitimate and binding for all. In this respect, the constitutional perspective differs clearly form the social ethical perspective of the encyclical. Under constitutional law, "the problem of state-building […] is solvable even for a people of devils".[15] Neither is the goodwill or participation of "men and women of good will"[16] necessary, nor could contradictions of the modern society be solved only by relegating to "love"[17]. Constitutionally, social conflicts have to be handled within legal procedures and have to be decided in accordance with the solely binding law. Democratically legitimized public officials are constitutionally obliged to perceive their legally given competences dutifully and in accordance with the democratically legitimized law. As a moral solicitation and ethical dictum, the confidence in men's goodwill as well as the appeal to love and ethos may provide helpful orientation to the individual by meeting its obligations. But they provide no license to cover up democratic legitimation and obedience in office as well as legally defined limits of competence.[18] But they become important for the individual bearer of fundamental rights by providing hints, assistance and suggestions for the right use of liberty.

15 Kant, *Zum ewigen Frieden.*

16 *Caritas in Veritate* (CV) 57, at http://w2.vatican.va/content/benedict-xvi/en/encyclicals/documents/hf_ben-xvi_enc_20090629_caritas-in-veritate.html.

17 So the guiding principle and the whole characteristic style of the encyclical, e.g. "Charity is at the heart of the Church's social doctrine." (CV 2.).

18 For the idea and term of the state office, see Depenheuer, "Das öffentliche Amt," 2005, § 36, marginal nos. 26 ff.

II. Constitutionally Legitimized Relativism

But above all, the concept of freedom in the declarations of human rights of the Church differs strikingly from the one of the fundamental rights of the German Basic Law. The secular idea of individual freedom as an attitude towards life and type of thinking became more and more dominant for the political theory since the Italian renaissance and the German reformation.[19] Jakob Burckhardt got to the heart of this radical change of thinking:[20] While the medieval human understood himself "only as a race, people, party, corporation, family or some other general form", now his awareness of his personality – different from all others and to be clearly distinguished from them – awakens. The principle of individuality permeates all ways of life, the moral as well as the social life. Towards limits and laws of all sorts, the modern human has the "sense of own sovereignty". He determines autonomously whether he commits to traditional bonds, assumes them or remodels them rationally ever since. The dictum attributed to Martin Luther from his speech on the imperial diet in 1521 in the city of Worms – "Here I stand. I cannot do otherwise." – is representative for the self-confidence of the individual that sees itself sovereign, that does not accept the institutionalized lectureship of the church and the heterogeneous truth claim any more. The person becomes the last and no longer questionable element of secular life, freed from all social and religious implications. Therefore, human dignity also became sacrosanct in the secular state and the human rights were not at free disposal any more.[21] The sovereign freedom of the individual against every kind of – governmental, clerical or otherwise social – paternalism let the idea of freedom became a defensive and meaningless "freedom from", a freedom to arbitrariness. A society, which is in in a progressive differentiation,[22] accrues from the non-coordinated actions of these sovereign individuals, leading to a predominance of relativism in the complex world in the

19 For the history of individual-mechanistic theory of state, see with further references Depenheuer, *Solidarität im Verfassungsstaat* [2001], 2009, pp. 241 ff.

20 See Burckhardt, *Die Kultur der Renaissance in Italien* [1859], 1976, pp. 123 ff., 128 ff.

21 See Isensee, "Menschenwürde: die säkulare Gesellschaft auf der Suche nach dem Absoluten," 2006, pp. 173 ff.; Depenheuer, "Tabu und Recht – ein Problemaufriß," 2003, pp. 7 ff.; Depenheuer, "Die Kraft des Mythos und die Rationalität des Rechts. Einführung," 2009, pp. 7 ff.

22 Summary analyses: Luhmann, *Die Gesellschaft der Gesellschaft*, 1997.

present tense,[23] sets the individual to growing impositions in dealing with his life.

3. The Impositions of Modern Age: Life in Distinction

But what remains of the concept of meaningful and positive liberty in this modern and extremely differentiated world? Could there still be a comprehensive truth, encompassing all parts of life, which gives orientation to the individual in a world of relativism and which fills the defensive freedom with positive content? Two problems must be treated separately with regard to these obvious questions, which additionally are the basic social problems of western constitutional statehood: firstly, the relation between legally guaranteed defensive freedom against the state and the existential longing for positive realization of this freedom by the individual and thus about the question, what the individual should do with his freedom to live a life in accordance with his human dignity (V.). Secondly, how the various religious groups in their function as signposts handle with their different claims of truth whereas truth conceptually knows no compromise and no plurality of equal truths (VI).

E. Religious Truth under Secular Statehood

I. Truth as a Fundamental Right

The fulfilment of constitutionally guaranteed freedom is not and cannot be objectively predetermined in the modern and liberal constitutional state. In fact, the fulfilment of freedom falls to the individual citizen. Liberal freedom gives the individual the freedom to search, to find and to live his own – subjective – truth of faith, in particular in the "fulfilled truth rooting in

23 See Girard, "Das Christentum ist allen anderen Religionen überlegen," 2005: "The in our days so obvious predominance of relativism has its roots partly in the challenges of our age. A society in that live so many people is inevitably heterogeneous. You have to hold balance between the various religions and do not take sides. Each religion must be seen of the same value. Even if you are no relativist you have to sound like one, or even act like one." (translated from German.).

the transcendental."[24] "This includes the individual's right to orientate his or her whole conduct to the teachings of his or her faith and to act in accordance with his or her inner religious convictions."[25] Although these subjective truths of the individual bearers of fundamental rights are only "possibilities of thinking", they create "the reality of existence" (Viktor E. Frankl). Whoever found his truth in this way knows that "truth will make him free" (Joh. 8, 32). However, this is Moreno longer the state-directed constitutionally liberal "freedom from", but the freedom from the adversities of earthly life with regard to eternity.

Insofar as the individual has not the good fortune to grow into a religious world with its values and meanings through education and socialization in family, school and friends, state guaranteed liberal defensive "freedom from" means a double imposition to each human. On the one hand, he or she could become desperate by reviewing the variety of religious and other offers of meaning and liberal options of emancipation. He or she has to decide, without being empirical and positively sure, whether his or her decision of faith is true. He or she rather has to transform to match his or her decision of truth, bearing in mind that it was him or her who subjectively committed to this truth. His or her concrete faith only roots in its subjectivity and is therefore not objectively predetermined, but could be revised by an actus contrarius at any time. Any faith is and remains a risk for the people – and many shy away from the commitment to truth and therefore submit to the dictatorship of relativism.

II. Risk of Dictatorship of Relativism

In the reality of the western states, the defensive "freedom from" gains a new and quite questionable meaning: to a large extent, freedom is not exercised any more in the way of deciding your options of freedom and questions of meaning on your own responsibility, but instead consists of the conscious and intended non-decision, consists of keeping open to as many answers as possible: you enjoy and perpetuate your freedom to decide freely by not making a decision. In fact you keep your options open to all potential partners as long as you do not marry, but you run the risk of

24 CV 56.
25 BVerfGE 32, 98 (106 f.).

never realizing your freedom practically at the same time, of never filling the abstract freedom with real life.[26] This constant keep-all-options-open, this consicous non-decision-making for the sake of a misunderstood freedom misses not only the practical fulfillment that is laid-out in each option of freedom, but also could degenerate into the "dictatorship of relativism", of which the pope has been warning repeatedly for a long time.[27]

Liberal freedom does not only provide the individual with the freedom to search, to find and to fulfill the freedom. It also expects the decision to faith from the beneficiary of freedom, which fulfills and therefore consumes this freedom, so he or she will be literally "able to move mountains". The fact that there is constitutionally and epistemologically no more objective truth constitutes no title for the individual to handle all truths equally and to remain banal and superficial. In fact, one has to completely devote oneself to something, to stand up for it unconditionally, to totally offer oneself as a person to another person or a cause. The responsibility of human beings towards themselves demands to devote oneself to a position and to bring it fully committed to the very end.[28] Although the subjective truths of the humans are – once again – only "possibilities of thinking", they created "the realities of existence" (Viktor E. Frankl) in the past and the present. And in fact: the most important testimonies of men in the world are regularly "possibilities of thinking that became reality", petrified proofs of religious faiths of prior generations. Beijing's Temple of heaven, the Pyramids of Giza or the Cologne Cathedral are magnificent proofs of lived faith and men's longing for the lost paradise. They give us an example of how much creative power religious truth is able to generate and it also gives us a notion of the truth on the basis of which they were created.

26 A compromise in-between decision and non-decision votes for a temporary and at any time revocable option: so the spouse becomes the temporary life companion.

27 A dictatorship of relativism arises that acknowledges nothing as final and accepts as last measure only the own Ego and its cravings, so Ratzinger, "Pro eligendo Pontifice," 2005, translated from the German edition.

28 So Girard, "Das Christentum ist allen anderen Religionen überlegen".

III. No Freedom against the Truth

Legal, state guaranteed defensive freedom may not remain abstract to itself, but aims at practice. This means to freely choose one option without alternative. The once made decision forms the basis of the subjective truth of the individual and is therefore – at least temporarily – consumed. Logically, there is no more subjective "freedom from" towards this taken decision of truth: freedom comes true in the concrete decision and is the opposite of relativism: those who decide freely are henceforth immunized against the impositions of relativism.

F. The Church and the Plurality of (Un-) Truths

To channel the arbitrariness of constitutional practice of freedom, to give behavior influencing values and perspectives of orientation, that is the noblest task for the social agents family, school, university and last but not least the religious groups. But the diversity of existing and constitutionally legitimized religious groups leads them to a dilemma. Seing themselves as administrators of religious truth, they compete with other agents of truth. This means the biggest challenge imaginable to each religious group. Because truth, especially a truth revealed by God, is logically not prepared to comprise. But how does the own truth get along with the others' simultaneously supported truth, which therefore only could be an untruth? How could an intermediary way be found from "the one truth" that is not open for relativism or compromise to the simultaneous postulate of religious freedom? Doesn't the own claim of truth necessarily get relativized by the state-guaranteed recognition of the "truths of others" or by the own self-conception, at least "darkened"? According to the logic of the modern state, the answer lies in a fundamental differentiation of the question.

From the perspective of the modern state, all religious groups have freedom of action on the one hand. They may live their truth, promote it and missionize, but only within the frame of the constitution, particularly by respecting the law of peace. However, violence is not a justifiable way to proclaim faith in the modern state. But on the other hand, each religious group has the right to argue and to practice their claim of truth and the supremacy deriving therefrom in accordance with their self-conception. Also Caritas in veritate clearly phrases the claim of supremacy of the Catholic truth: "Religious freedom does not mean religious indifference and does not imply that all religions are equal."[29] So in the modern state, there is a kind of distribution of tasks and power between the state and religious groups in the domain of religious truths: the churches may uncompromisingly proclaim and exemplarily act out their belief in their truth in accordance with their religious freedom, but the state expects them all – and forces them if necessary – to mutually exercise tolerance towards other religious and ideological communities and to renounce violence. [30]

Guiding Principles

I. The modern state as guarantor of fundamental rights

1. The modern secular state finds its mission in maintaining peace between the citizens. In the maintenance of peace lies the only and non-negotiable "truth" of the secular state. Apart from that, religious and other truths become pluralized by fundamental rights and democracy in a liberal community.
2. Idea and shape, justification and legal effectiveness of fundamental and human rights are derivations from the development of modern secular statehood. They are the significant expression and the engine of a process of differentiation of the society, unbroken to this day. The fragmented society as well as the "dictatorship of relativism" are unrefusable consequence of a liberal community.
3. Individuals are the only possible and permissible components of a state order of compulsion in a liberal community, fundamental rights and democracy the mode of its effectiveness. The common good is determined formally by majority decision, the fundamental rights release formal freedom of arbitrariness. The state law knows ethical obligations only as – legally, i. e. reinforced, not enforceable – constitutional expectations.

29 CV 55.

30 To the precondition of peace of the human rights and religious missions, see. Depenheuer, "Risiken und Nebenwirkungen menschenrechtlicher Universalität," 2009, pp. 98 ff.

II. Religious freedom and the risk of the truth

4. The concept of truth has split up – parallel to the development of secular statehood – into a scientific-positivistic and a historical-interpretive and humanities concept: the latter is about the reply to needs of meaning ("The truth will set you free" [John 8, 31]), the other about empirical proven knowledge.
5. From a constitutional point of view, religiously based statements of truth are nothing else than – constitutionally legitimate – exercise of freedom of religion and speech. The following applies: "Freedom guaranteed by human rights opens the path to the personally found truth of the individual".
6. Liberal defensive "freedom from" given by the state leaves the crucial human questions of life and truth unanswered. While the state does not want to or is not allowed to answer these questions, the religious groups must answer them – thanks to the religious freedom, of course in competition with other religious and ideological groups.
7. To answer questions of meaning is an imposition for the individual that he or she cannot overcome. He or she has to choose an objective truth subjectively, without being sure about it in an empiric-positivist way. Each decision of faith is not prescribed objectively, but roots in its subjectivity.
8. An alternative strategy of many people in liberal states is the non-decision, i. e. to keep open to as many options as possible. To keep open to the relative answers to the eternal questions – that is exactly what the pope's campaign against the dictatorship of relativism aims at. It is correct: whoever keeps open to everything never receives the following: fulfilment. Freedom means to choose freely and responsibly one option (truth), but at one's own risk.
9. Whoever chooses one truth is not free anymore towards this truth. Fulfilled freedom binds.

III. The person's right and the plurality of truths

10. The state has no problem with the variety of religious truths; it has an indifferent attitude towards them. It supports religious groups if and as far as they are compatible with its structure, accept the state's right for final decision and the relativism of democracy and fundamental rights,

fill the constitutional expectations with content and abstain from any use of violence.

11. From a historic perspective, religions always struggled with the variety of other (un-) truths. In particular missionary truth claims hold conflictual implications. In fact, truth is not open to compromise by itself.
12. To maintain the own clerical truth claim whilst postulating the religious freedom of the individual means a permanent and difficult to endure challenge. Acceptance, tolerance and appreciation of other (un-) truths bears the risk to relativize and "obscure" the own truth claim.
13. In light of this dilemma, the function of the church is – in competition with others – to give the individuals the more convincing guidance in overcoming the "dictatorship of relativism". So on the one hand, the churches are allowed to postulate and live their truths without any compromise. On the other hand, the state expects and, if necessary, enforces mutual tolerance towards other religious groups and the waiving of the use of violence in principle.

Bibliography

Becker, Jürgen, "Die wehrhafte Demokratie des Grundgesetzes," in *Handbuch des Staatsrechts, Bd. VII*, ed. Josef Isensee and Paul Kirchhof, Heidelberg: C. F. Müller, 1992, Article 167.

Böckenförde, Ernst-Wolfgang, "Die Entstehung des Staates als Vorgang der Säkularisation," in *Säkularisation und Utopie. Erbacher Studien, Ernst Forsthoff zum 65.Geburtstag*, Stuttgart et al.: Kohlhammer, 1967, pp. 75–94, re-printed Ernst-Wolfgang Böckenförde, *Recht, Staat, Freiheit*, 2nd ed., Frankfurt am Main: Suhrkamp, 1992, pp. 92-114.

Böckenförde, Ernst-Wolfgang, "Die Entstehung des Staates als Vorgang der Säkularisation," in idem, *Recht, Staat, Freihei. Studien zur Rechtsphilosophie, Staatstheorie und Verfassungsgeschichte*, 2nd ed., Frankfurt am Main, 1991, pp. 92-114.

Burckhardt, Jakob, *Die Kultur der Renaissance in Italien* [1859], Stuttgart: Kröner, 1976.

Burger, Rudolf, "Multikulturalismus im säkularen Rechtsstaat. Eine zivilisationstheoretische Grenzbestimmung," *Leviathan* 25, 2 (1997): 173-185.

BVerfGE 32, 98.

Caritas in Veritate, available at http://w2.vatican.va/content/benedict-xvi/en/encyclicals/documents/hf_ben-xvi_enc_20090629_caritas-in-veritate.html.

Depenheuer, Otto, "Auf dem Weg in die Unfehlbarkeit? Das Verfassungsbewußtsein der Bürger als Schranke der Verfassungsgerichtsbarkeit," in *Staatsphilosophie und Rechtspolitik: Festschrift für Martin Kriele zum 65. Geburtstag*, ed. Burkhardt Ziemske, München: C. H. Beck, 1997, pp. 485-505.

Depenheuer, Otto, "Das öffentliche Amt," in *Handbuch des Staatsrechts, Bd. III*, ed. Josef Isensee/Paul Kirchhof, 3. ed., Heidelberg: C.F. Müller, 2005, § 36, S. 87-130.

Depenheuer, Otto, "Die Kraft des Mythos und die Rationalität des Rechts. Einführung," in *Mythos als Schicksal. Was konstituiert die Verfassung?*, Wiesbaden: Springer, 2009, pp. 7-23.

Depenheuer, Otto, "Risiken und Nebenwirkungen menschenrechtlicher Universalität," in: *Menschenrechte als Weltmission*, ed. Josef Isensee, Berlin: Duncker & Humblot, 2009, pp. 81-100.

Depenheuer, Otto, "Staat – Kirche – Gesellschaft," in *Handbuch der Katholischen Soziallehre*, ed. Anton Rauscher, Berlin: Duncker & Humblot, 2008, pp. 935-956.

Depenheuer, Otto, "Tabu und Recht – ein Problemaufriß," in *Recht und Tabu*, ed. Otto Depenheuer, Wiesbaden: Springer, 2003, pp. 7-23.

Depenheuer, Otto, "Wahrheit oder Frieden. Die fundamentalistische Herausforderung des modernen Staates," in *Essener Gespräche* 33 (1999): 5-35.

Depenheuer, Otto, *Selbstbehauptung des Rechtsstaats*, 2nd ed., Paderborn et al.: Ferdinand Schöningh, 2007.

Depenheuer, Otto, *Solidarität im Verfassungsstaat. Grundlegung einer normativen Theorie der Verteilung* [2001], 2009.

Gärditz, Klaus Ferdinand, "Säkularität und Verfassung," in *Verfassungstheorie*, ed. Otto Depenheuer and Christoph Grabenwarter, Tübingen: Mohr Siebeck, 2010, § 5, pp. 101-146.

Girard, René, "Das Christentum ist allen anderen Religionen überlegen," interview in *Die Welt*, May 14, 2005, at https://www.welt.de/print-welt/article670569/Das-Christentum-ist-allen-anderen-Religionen-ueberlegen.html.

Hillgruber, Christian, *Staat und Religion*, Paderborn: Schöningh, 2007.

Hobbes, Thomas, *Leviathan*: *Or the Matter, Forme and Power of a Commonwealth Ecclesiasticall and Civil* [1651].

Isensee, Josef, "Die katholische Kritik an den Menschenrechten – Der liberale Freiheitsentwurf in der Sicht der Päpste des 19. Jahrhunderts," in *Menschenrechte und Menschenwürde. Historische Voraussetzungen – säkulare Gestalt – christliches Verständnis*, ed. Ernst-Wolfgang Böckenförde and Robert Spaemann, Stuttgart: Klett-Cotta, 1987, pp. 138-174.

Isensee, Josef, "Grundrechte und Demokratie – Die polare Legitimation im grundgesetzlichen Gemeinwesen," *Der Staat* 20 (1981): 161-176.

Isensee, Josef, "Menschenwürde: die säkulare Gesellschaft auf der Suche nach dem Absoluten," *Archiv des öffentlichen Rechts* 131, 2 (2006): 173-218.

Isensee, Josef, "Staat und Verfassung," in *Handbuch des Staatsrechts*, ed. Josef Isensee and Paul Kirchhof, Bd. II, 3rd ed., Heidelberg: C.F. Müller, 2004, § 15, pp. 3-106.

Kant, Immanuel, *Zum ewigen Frieden* [1795].

Ladeur, Karl-Heinz, and Ino Augsberg, *Toleranz – Religion – Recht, Die Herausforderung des »neutralen« Staates durch neue Formen der Religiosität in der postmodernen Gesellschaft*, Tübingen: Mohr Siebeck, 2007.

Luhmann, Niklas, *Die Gesellschaft der Gesellschaft*, Frankfurt am Main: Suhrkamp, 1997.

Quaritsch, Helmut, *Staat und Souveränität*, Frankfurt am Main: Athenäum, 1970.

Ratzinger, Joseph, "Pro eligendo Pontifice," *L'Osservatore Romano*, April 22, 2005 (German edition).

Schlink, Bernhard, "Zwischen Säkularisation und Multikulturalität," in *Recht und Recht: Festschrift für Gerd Roellecke zum 70. Geburtstag*, ed. Rolf Stober, Stuttgart: Kohlhammer, 1997, pp. 301-316.

The Political Problem of Religious Liberality

Karsten Fischer[*]

A. Introduction

The following contribution seeks to shed light on the problematic relationship between politics and religion in its historical, systematic, and normative aspects. To this end, I will reconstruct the process of secularization with regard to its importance for a liberal understanding of politics (B). I will then further specify the political problem of religious liberality as the pre-condition of democratic and constitutional states (C). Finally, from this perspective, I will offer a brief survey of the political ethics of some of the major world religions (D).

B. The Liberal Logic of the Secularization Process

For some time now it has been fashionable to question the rise of the state as a process of secularization[1] and instead to brand the modern secularization process – understood as an increasing autonomy of politics in relation to religion – as a myth that merely reflects the European desire for a *Sonderweg*. But this view, prominently represented in the work of José Casanova,[2] is difficult to reconcile with the historical record. For the peaceful resolution of religious conflicts through legally regulated adversary proceedings is an essential achievement of the state's monopoly of power, and its beginnings are linked directly to the establishment in 1495 of the Imperial Chamber Court by the German King, and later Emperor,

---

* A large portion of the following remarks is based on thoughts expressed in Fischer 2009. I thank Matthias Hansl, Sebastian Huhnholz, Astrid Séville, and Yannick Bassler for their pertinent suggestions.

1 See Böckenförde, "The Rise of the State as a Process of Secularisation," 1991.

2 See Casanova, "The problem of religion and the anxieties of European secular democracy," 2008, pp. 63-74.

Maximilian I.[3] This movement toward juridification was continued in 1555 in the Peace of Augsburg, the first step toward the development of the modern secular institutional territorial state which came into being by detaching the state from the medieval political order based on personal relations (Personenverbandsstaat), a process completed by the Peace of Westphalia.[4]

The process is closely linked to the successive development of religious and ideological neutrality which played an essential role in the later emergence of the liberal-democratic constitutional state. Such neutrality is directly related to the real progress of the religio-political itself, which was therefore no longer a mere exercise in tolerance, as it was in the Edict of Nantes in 1598 and generally in the Age of Reformation. The concept of tolerance implied that the other party was in error and tolerance was exercised in order to diminish the potential for conflict.[5] Neutrality is not tolerance. It suspends a priori the question of truth as one incapable of being solved, and as one that does not need to be solved. It does not merely treat questions of *faith* in this manner but also all questions concerning *truth.* In religio-philosophical terms, neutrality means that in principle one takes an *agnostic* attitude – and it is precisely this stance that constitutes the democratic moment.

The consciousness of this moment has deep roots. From the time of *the Greek discovery of politics*[6] democracy has meant the institutionalization of a benign attitude toward the errors that take place in acts made among the contingencies of the profane world. In fifth century BC Greece, *politics* was understood for the first time to be a matter entirely subject to the decisions of free citizens. From that time on, traditional or transcendental references were dispensed with and considered to be non-political. It now became possible to rigorously examine the problem of domination from the standpoint of the idea of freedom whose only limitation stems from the fact that legal political decisions are made by the *autonomous acts* of citizens themselves. This *discovery of politics* led to a new kind of legal

3 See Voßkuhle, "Religionsfreiheit und Religionskritik – Zur Verrechtlichung religiöser Konflikte," 2010, p. 537.

4 See Mayer, "Die Ausbildung der Grundlagen des modernen deutschen Staates im Hohen Mittelalter," 1974.

5 See Steiger, "Neutralität in Religionssachen," 1978, p. 352; see also: Forst, *Toleration in Conflict: Past and Present*, 2013.

6 Meier, *The Greek Discovery of Politics*, 1990.

thought which emancipated itself from the supposed sensibilities of the gods and from such archaic practices as blood revenge.

This was clearly demonstrated in 458 BC, three years after the overthrow of the Athenian aristocratic council, the Areopagus, when Aeschylus' *Oresteia* was first performed. The tragedy narrates how the Athenian general Agamemnon, who in order to appease the gods sacrificed his daughter Iphigenia, is murdered for the deed by his wife Clytemnestra when he returns in triumph from the Trojan War. In turn, Agamemnon's son Orestes kills his mother; an act for which he is pursued relentlessly by the Erinyes, the goddesses of revenge. With the appearance of the goddess Athena, Aeschylus' *Oresteia* becomes the "*polis* myth"[7] that, for the first time, opposes the traditional moral faith and belief in divinity with a pagan form of the rule of law. "The old law, with its implacable insistence on punishment, is severe and terrible."[8] To the Erinyes' demand to observe the unquestioned validity of the old law, Athena replies that the question to be decided is too difficult for the gods to decide alone and that the case must be brought before a broader assembly, even if this means relativizing the hierarchy of gods and humans. In this democratic process Orestes is finally expiated. The prerequisite for the "clearly more liberal"[9] new law is Aeschylus' awareness of the relativity of legal norms including those of divine provenance. This leads to the empowering of the democratic citizenry to make its own law or – to put it in modern terms: The citizens can claim to be the authors of all valid norms that affect them. Such a change was part of the profoundly disturbing and painful process which eroded faith in convictions that had long been taken for granted and whose ultimate validity had seemed unimpeachable.[10]

The insight into the "awareness that in political decision making a distinction must be made between validity and truth"[11] was related to the process of democratization in 462/461 BC and passed down in *the political art of Greek tragedy*.[12] In this regard, and in order to limit religious claims to truth and validity, we find in *the Greek discovery of politics* not merely a "consciousness of ability" as an historical equivalent of the modern idea

---

7 Ibid., p. 122.
8 Ibid., p. 100.
9 Ibid.
10 See Meier, *Athens: A Portrait of the City in Its Golden Age*, 2000.
11 Meier, *The Greek Discovery of Politics*, 1990, p. 107.
12 Meier, *The Political Art of Greek Tragedy*, 1993.

of progress,[13] but the first secularization *avant la lettre*. Insofar as the *discovery of politics* – understood as the citizens' right to make autonomous decisions on questions of validity – originated at the same time that the first democratization took place, it is easy to see that there is a systematic connection between democracy and secularization.

Of course, it is well known that for a long time this development remained an historical episode since the authoritarianism of Christian political theology that continued into modernity stood in the sharpest possible contrast to ancient Greece's "culture of freedom".[14] Naturally, the medieval annihilation of ancient Greece's proto-liberal understanding of politics was not merely the result of the idea that worldly rulers reign by the grace of God and its orientation to Paul's statement in *Romans* (13:1) that rulers are ordained by God and that therefore when a tyrannical ruler appears it is a sign of the sinfulness of his subjects. For the speculative boldness of the Middle Ages was intended to explore God's possibilities to the fullest, not humankind's.[15] That is why under medieval conditions there was no need to understand *liberal* politics; indeed in the literal sense of the word, there was even no *understanding of politics*. Until the scholastic reception of Aristotle the concept of *politics* did not appear in medieval sources.[16]

However, by the middle of the 11th century, the fragile tension between the worldly *imperium* and the spiritual *sacerdotium* had become a smoldering presence that in 1076 burst into flame in the so-called Investiture Controversy. The solution worked out in the Concordat of Worms in 1122 provided the impulse for long-term changes in the idea of order, which came close to producing an unintended disenchantment of the world.[17] Although on the surface it seemed that the Concordat of Worms confirmed the supremacy of the church and limited the power of kings to worldly matters, at the same time it created the prerequisites for the autonomy of secular statehood.[18] In accord with George Spencer-Brown's (1994) postu-

---

13 See ibid., p. 208.

14 Meier, *A Culture of Freedom: Ancient Greece and the Origins of Europe*, 2011.

15 See Blumenberg, "'Nachahmung der Natur'. Zur Vorgeschichte der Idee des schöpferischen Menschen," 1981, p. 83.

16 See Struve, "Regnum und Sacerdotium," 1993, p. 189.

17 See Weinfurter, *Canossa. Die Entzauberung der Welt*, 2007, p. 187. Böckenförde, "The Rise of the State as a Process of Secularisation," 1991, pp. 28 ff.

18 See Struve, "Regnum und Sacerdotium," 1993, p. 235.

late that in *drawing a distinction*, the creation of preferences within the framework of the distinction is less important than the fact of the distinction itself, the result of the Concordat of Worms had the effect of renewing the consciousness that worldly affairs constitute an independent realm of human action that is endowed with its own logic.

Thus, scholasticism could build on the Aristotelian understanding of politics, something that was radicalized in Marsilius of Padua's 1324 treatise *Defensor pacis* "into a full-scale attack on the hierocratic system".[19] In opposition to the medieval tradition, Marsilius raised the modern question concerning the prerequisites for the establishment of legitimate rule. And he answered with the no less modern view that it is established by means of legislative due process for which responsibility resides in all citizens or in a majority.[20] This further opened scholasticism to historico-political reality and to an understanding of the concerns of the *conditio humana* that had been regained at the time of Thomas Aquinas.[21] In turn, this led to the desacralization of political thought that, in the long term, proved to be the prerequisite for the Protestant doctrine of the two kingdoms.[22]

But the Reformation plunged Europe into schism and, as a result, into bitter civil wars that were not originally religiously motivated. However, denominational differences fanned the flames. This was equally true for the French Wars of Religion, the Eighty Years' War between Spain and the Netherlands, and for the Thirty Years' War which has entered into European collective memory as the worst war up to that time. Its end, brought about by the Peace of Westphalia in 1648, is synonymous with the emergence of the modern institutional territorial state which is characterized by its monopoly in four key areas: It is *sovereign* in the sense of having monopoly powers of coercion, on legislation, on the levying of taxes, and in the power to remain above and neutral toward religious claims to truth and validity. In this way religion was dismissed from its role at the center

19 Wilks, *The Problem of Sovereignty in the Later Middle Ages: The Papal Monarchy with Augustinus Triumphus and the Publicists*, 1963, p. 143.

20 See Marsilius de Padua, *Defensor Pacis*, 1522, Cap. XIII.

21 See Böckenförde, *Geschichte der Rechts- und Staatsphilosophie. Antike und Mittelalter*, 2006, p. 245.

22 Prodi, *Eine Geschichte der Gerechtigkeit. Vom Recht Gottes zum modernen Rechtsstaat*, 2003, p. 49.

of politics and given the status of a private world-view that the state controls to see that it exercises its social role in an acceptable manner.[23]

It is in this sense that *the rise of the state as a process of secularization*[24] is to be understood. However, it can be demonstrated that the concept of secularization was already present in the French canonical disputes of the 16th century. Therefore, it does not originate from the negotiations that led to the Treaty of Westphalia during which the French emissary in Münster, Henri II d'Orléans, Duke of Longueville, used the concept *séculariser* in 1646 to designate – and protest against – the transfer of Church property into worldly hands, nevertheless, the effectiveness of the concept first began in 1648.[25]

The further development toward a world-immanent legitimation of political rule took place in small steps. For it was not liberal constitutionalism and the renewal of democracy during England's Glorious Revolution in 1688/89 that first broke with medieval Christian political theology. Indeed, the political theories of Absolutism had aimed at making any religious legitimation of political order and praxis superfluous; viewing them as seeds that might flower into civil war.

This position is explicitly stated in the works of Thomas Hobbes who believed that the European civil wars, if not religiously or denominationally motivated, were prolonged by religious motives. Nor did he see the wars as historically contingent phenomena that had merely accompanied the Reformation, but as the Reformation's necessary consequence. At the beginning of *Behemoth*, Hobbes therefore sees a problem with translating the Bible into national languages:

> For after the Bible was translated into English, every man, nay, every boy and wench, that could read English, thought they spoke with God Almighty, and understood what he said, when by a certain number of chapters a day they had read the Scriptures once or twice over. And so the reverence and obedience due to the Reformed Church here, and to the bishops and pastors therein, was cast off; and every man became a judge of religion, and an interpreter of the Scriptures to himself.[26]

---

23 See Grimm, "Der Staat in der kontinentaleuropäischen Tradition," 1987. See also Grimm, *Souveränität. Herkunft und Zukunft eines Schlüsselbegriffs*, 2009.

24 Böckenförde, "The Rise of the State as a Process of Secularisation," 1991.

25 See Conze, Strätz, and Zabel, "Säkularisation, Säkularisierung," 1984, pp. 792, 801 ff.

26 Hobbes, *Behemoth or The Long Parliament*, 1990, p. 21.

This destroyed reverence for and obedience to the clergy and gave "colour to the late rebellion".[27] In other words, it contributed to the execution of King Charles I in 1649.

> If it be lawful then for subjects to resist the King, when he commands anything that is against the Scripture, that is, contrary to the command of God, and to be judge of the meaning of the Scripture, it is impossible that the life of any King, or the peace of any Christian kingdom, can be long secure.[28]

However, if political theology that was now seen to encourage civil war was to be replaced by an inner-worldly theory of government and civil order, one cannot say that the latter first came into being with Thomas Hobbes' contractually legitimized justification of the absolutist *Leviathan*. Jean Bodin's equally absolutist theory of sovereignty had already rested on the foundation of the post-Westphalian order that had inaugurated the modern era. And if one shares Luhmann's view on the unfolding (*Entfaltung*) of paradoxes in the history of ideas as the motor of the progress of ideas,[29] Bodin's theory is of the greatest interest in the attempt to understand what subsequently took place.

In *Les Six livres de la République* Bodin formulated his famous definition of sovereignty as

> une puissance perpétuelle et absolue, sans restriction de temps ou de condition: Elle consiste à pouvoir donner loy à tous en général, et à chacun en particulier, sans le consentement d'autruy, n'en recevoir de personne.[30]

The elements of this definition that legitimize political rule establish that the sovereign ruler, in contrast to the ruler in the Middle Ages' state based on an association of persons (*Personenverbandsstaat*), is no longer tied to a metaphysical corrective like the *lex divina* or to any other elements of traditional political legitimacy. To express Bodin's concept of sovereignty in Max Weber's categories, it is rational-legal authority. In relationship to the tradition the sovereign is free: He is entirely exempt from the laws of his predecessor, but absolutely bound by his own. Otherwise, with this freedom, he would be a tyrant. But fostering tyranny was no part of Bodin's intention – tyranny has no need of theory. Bodin's concept of

---

27 Ibid., p. 49.

28 Ibid., p. 50.

29 See Luhmann, "Tautologie und Paradoxie in den Selbstbeschreibungen der modernen Gesellschaft," 1997.

30 Bodin, *Les six livres de la République*, 1583, p. 142.

sovereignty aims to establish the rule of law. He equates sovereignty with legislation. In other words, sovereignty finds its concretization in legislative monopoly. And here, for the first time, we find this form of the concept of state authority. The essence of sovereignty is legislative sovereignty. Thus, Bodin would have found the concept of the *Rechts-Staat* tautological, since for him sovereign statehood, or state sovereignty, is constituted in the function of creating law (*Rechtsetzungsfunktion*). In this regard, Bodin's absolutist concept of sovereignty marks an early step toward the rule of law. It attempts to prevent religiously motivated civil wars by relying exclusively on the binding nature of formal laws as the ultimate measure, and no longer relies on a faith in legitimate resistance in the name of God. In modern terms: For Bodin, there is no legitimacy beyond legality; a fact that shows that Schmitt's attempt to claim Bodin and Hobbes as his predecessors was a blatant attempt to try to disguise his own totalitarianism.[31] We see that, in its genesis, the concept of sovereignty is implicitly anti-clerical. To this extent, it constitutes the, at first glance, seemingly counterintuitive alliance between absolutism and liberalism that was further developed in the "pre-liberal" aspect of Hobbes' religio-political approach in the distinction made between private *fides* and public *confessio*.[32] This alliance declares religion to be a private matter and thus defuses its explosive power. Just as Hobbes's later concept of sovereignty, Bodin's concept aimed to strengthen state power absolutely in order to dominate the conflicting sects.

The fact that Bodin had no intention of legitimizing tyranny but rather intended to bind the sovereign by his own laws, is also rooted in the paradox of his idea of sovereignty, namely, that limited power is more potent than limitless power.[33] This paradox can be resolved if one looks at Bodin's concept of sovereignty neither from the perspective of the sovereign himself, nor from the perspective that looks toward the sovereign. Nor should one think of the sovereign in terms of persons – as was done in 20th century totalitarianism and is still done in today's neo-authoritarianism. Rather, one must look at sovereignty as an institution that is an attribute of the state in its entirety. Viewed in this way, sovereignty is intended to eliminate the arbitrary acts of individuals – i.e. of ruling persons

31 See Fischer, "Hobbes, Schmitt, and the Paradox of Religious Liberality," 2010.

32 See Holmes, *Passions and Constraints: On the Theory of Liberal Democracy*, 1995, p. 131.

33 See ibid., pp. 108 ff.

– for the modern territorial state is no longer an association of persons as the state of the Middle Ages was. If sovereignty were an attribute of the ruler as a person, instead of the office, it would be subject to the person's arbitrariness. But according to Bodin, the sovereignty of the state as a political institution is above individual arbitrariness and in no way subordinate to the individual ruler. The ruler has an obligation to legality, even when this obligation cannot be externally enforced – a problem first solved by modern liberalism. According to Bodin, sovereignty is an unlimited power but, paradoxically, one that also governs the individual who exercises it. Of course decisions can be reversed, but then they are new decisions. And in this respect they are anything but arbitrary since they are made according to a methodological procedure.

Thus, sovereignty means the unity of state authority in a limited territory in which the traditional rival sources of law such as customs and mores are excluded. Only these conditions make it possible for such a sovereign state to arbitrate denominational controversies in which the disputing parties call upon other sources of legitimacy than that of the state's institutional law.

The unfolding of the paradoxical structure of the absolutist conception of sovereignty became the driving force in the concept's historical development. For, if Bodin's concept of sovereignty had been the legitimation of tyranny, what would tyranny be? Like anything else, arbitrariness can only be conceived when it is differentiated from something else, and its opposite is obligation. What then is the unity in the distinction between arbitrariness and obligation in which the unity of the political system must lie? This question leads directly to the concept of the rule of law. But the demand on the sovereign that he subjects himself to the law was not conceivable before the end of the 17th century. To bind oneself was viewed as a *contradictio in adiecto*; only contracts could bind. But if the sovereign were to bind himself by contract he would bring an end to his sovereignty. This point can also be seen in Hobbes' theory of the social contract to which the sovereign is not a partner but the one who benefits from the contract; he is the third party that cannot be held to account for any alleged breach of contract. But in order to insure that his laws will be obeyed, the sovereign must limit his own authority, and to this extent it may be said that limited sovereignty is more potent than unlimited:

> Bodin overcomes his own injunction against self-binding by claiming that constitutional precommitments, institutional constraints that cannot be waived on an ad hoc basis, are vehicles of royal freedom – strategies by which

> sovereigns may most effectively assert their authority. Applied imaginatively to a democratic sovereign, this important argument eventually became the basis of the modern theory of liberal constitutionalism.[34]

This solution opened the gate to liberal constitutionalism which, by reformulating the contractual argument, overcame its early absolutist form. And it demonstrates the correctness of Habermas's statement "that there is a conceptual or internal relation, and not simply a historically contingent association, between the rule of law and democracy".[35] In this way, Bodin's paradox of sovereignty, that the sovereign cannot be subject to anyone else, yet is still bound, is overcome, and it is this idea that constitutes the rule of law. It is related to a new idea of differentiation that distinguishes between legal obligation and the control necessary to insure that the obligation is fulfilled. In this way, the theory of sovereignty is extended to the democratic idea of the sovereignty of the *people*. For now those who rule – and under the conditions of democratic rule we must use the plural – constitute such a large majority (whose members are always replacing one another), that it can be internally differentiated in order to make possible the division of state power. This is Locke's argument, and especially, Montesquieu's, whereby the latter – with his great example always before him, England's constitutional monarchy – takes the decisive step beyond Locke toward the *rule of law*. If the differentiation of state authority into legislative and executive branches would have been unthinkable for Bodin and Hobbes, the theorists of sovereignty in the early modern period, Montesquieu now introduces a third element, the independent judiciary whose power extends to the control of political decisions. From now on political decisions can be appealed, i.e. they are subject to judicial review. In this way, in modern society, politics and law can be differentiated as functional systems of the same rank and the principle of *princeps legibus solutus* ceases to exist. Legislation is now, and remains hereafter, what it was in the classical concept of sovereignty, an act of the supreme political authority, but now the reverse is also true: politics is bound by law.

34 Ibid., p. 152.

35 Habermas, *Between Facts and Norms: Contributions to a Discourse Theory of Law and Democracy*, 1998, p. 449.

Here we find both the real and the historical core of secularization theory[36] long before and independent of Napoleon's 1803 decree and the adoption of the concept in the same year in the legal language of the Final Recess of the *Reichsdeputation*. At the center of secularization we find the explosiveness that religious claims to truth and validity have for a democracy; for were they to be pursued consequently they would not only rule out the possibility of democratic control but would cancel each other. In so far it was terrible, but logical, that the break-up of the long standing unity of faith in Europe brought bitter religious wars in its wake and that the emergence of the institutional territorial state drew the fire of religious conflict to itself. For then, the politically organized state asserted that religious claims to validity must be placed under the caveat that they present no danger to public order. In this way, the liberal state of Occidental modernity took charge of religious conflicts and transformed them into the legal question of the legitimate exercise of freedom – itself limited where it clashed with the legitimate exercise of the freedom of those of other faiths. Previously, these conflicts had affected politics "*only*" indirectly, but in the form of religiously fueled civil wars all the more violently. Then, the liberal state – the long-term product of these conditions – became a party to the conflict by asserting its claim to ideological neutrality and by trying to establish its authority. Thus, the liberal-democratic constitutional state is not merely a result of secularization[37] but also a *heritage* of Europe's religious civil wars. For this reason it is still in danger today of being targeted as the enemy by groups with comprehensive religious demands based on claims to truth and validity who oppose the state with the same fervor with which they opposed each other in the pre-modern era. Under the conditions of modernity such groups are termed 'fundamentalists', a concept that also reveals the current issue's deep historical dimension: The charge brought by fundamentalists of every kind, that the liberal state is blasphemy, is itself an index of the reality of secularization; otherwise the anger of the fundamentalists would be pointless.

Therefore, the conditio sine qua non for the fruitful coexistence of religious groups within, and with, the liberal state is the development of *reli-*

---

36 See Gorski, "Historicizing the Secularization Debate: Church, State, and Society in Late Medieval and Early Modern Europe, ca. 1300 to 1700," 2000. See also Schlögl, *Alter Glaube und moderne Welt. Europäisches Christentum im Umbruch (1750-1850)*, 2013.

37 See Böckenförde, "The Rise of the State as a Process of Secularisation," 1991.

gious liberality in the sense of a *voluntary willingness on the part of communities of faith to accept the primacy of democratic political decisions over the truth and validity claims of world-views, and thus to tolerate the convictions of rival religious communities*. Especially the monotheistic religions of revelation, based on their comprehensive claims to truth, find it difficult in principle to accept the primacy and autonomous logic of democratic politics, and their acceptance came about only under particular historical conditions. For democratic politics have their roots elsewhere; in the *Greek discovery of politics* based on the political autonomy of the human being, the person who understands herself as a free citizen and whose sovereignty alone decides on the allocation of legitimate political power.

> Whether God or Satan will rule is not what is at stake, and that makes politics less 'interesting', less dangerous, hence less exciting than it might otherwise be. Denying God's authority in political life is a shorthand phrase for making politics safe for human beings doomed to unending disagreement and conflict.[38]

In this respect, it is not just true in ancient Greek history but also in accord with a trans-historical logic that every act of democratic politics is an act of secularization. Their binding nature for all is the product of a procedure that takes place under the auspices of equality and transparency; it is these that insure that responsibility can be accorded to the makers of decisions and that the decisions can be enforced. Thus, democratic rule is legitimate to the extent that those subject to it can hold the rulers accountable, and based on the reversibility of power relations, can also change decisions.

Under the democratic conditions of liberal modernity, politics and religion are fatefully tied to one another and each is the other's nemesis. For it is a characteristic of functional social differentiation that each functional sub-system takes itself for the whole, and in this sociological megalomania religion and politics are closely related. But the function of politics is "*to maintain the capacity for making binding decisions for the collective*" through the medium of *power*.[39] However, through its medium of *faith*, religion guarantees the "determinability of all meaning in the face of life's experience which points to the indeterminable."[40] If, against the logic of functional differentiation, these functions are short-circuited we are con-

38 Walzer, "Drawing the Line: Religion and Politics," 1998, p. 305.
39 Luhmann, *Die Politik der Gesellschaft*, 2000, p. 84.
40 Luhmann, *Die Religion der Gesellschaft*, 2000, p. 127.

fronted with religio-political pathologies, the dangerous anti-modernism of which has been observed now for the last one hundred years: At one extreme end, totalitarian *political religions* lay claim to quasi-religious meaning in decisions that bind the collective. But the democratic will of the people has no need of 'meaning', it is not a means but an end – therein lies its freedom. At the other extreme end, we find the various forms of fundamentalism, each with its claim that politics should make binding decisions for the collective under the auspices of a religious meaning. The need to reach a balance between these extremes was concisely formulated by Michael Walzer:

> Politics separated from religion in this extended and qualified sense – that all the crusaders, religious or secular alike, are denied the sword (but allowed to fly their banners) – is an open-ended conflict over interests and values among people who understand that they have to co-exist with one another. [...] We have to set ourselves against the closure that God's name, again and again, has licensed – but also against every other kind of closure, licensed by any of the secular substitutes for God's name. Only someone who has never experienced, or who can't imagine experiencing, the dangers of politics gone bad, could possibly complain about that.[41]

It would therefore be wrong to consider the process of secularization as one in which religious meaning was completely lost. In this erroneous assessment, radical enemies of religion and critics of secularization theory, which misunderstand its nature, or deliberately attribute religious enmity to its representatives, meet – *les extrêmes se touchent*! Finally, not only does the modern liberal state threaten to use its monopoly on coercion but, beyond that, it is also true that "the autonomy of politics increases simultaneously with the autonomy of religion."[42] To put it pointedly, religious convictions are to be treated as individual private views and therefore restricted, but precisely for that reason they are also to be protected against any form of political influence. In this constructive result of secularization for both parties – for the official state relationship toward religion and the corresponding dimension of religiousness that follows from it – we find one of the main differences of liberalism to previous regimes.

In this perspective, modern secularization can be understood as the process of establishing a status of equality among functions within a functionally differentiated modern society. In modern society, politics, law, econo-

---

41 Walzer, "Drawing the Line: Religion and Politics," p. 305.

42 Holmes, *Passions and Constraints: On the Theory of Liberal Democracy*, p. 207.

my, science, religion, art and other social subsystems are at work, each according to its own binary coded functional logic. In the pre-modern world, "religion and society were indistinguishable."[43] In modern society, both religion and politics are only two social function systems among others. There is no longer total social inclusion such as there was in pre-modern society – a society which, at least nominally, represented the entire population in a *community of the faithful*. This, of course, is the condition that fundamentalist and totalitarian political movements want to re-establish. Under modern conditions it is valid to say:

> Today, religion does not protect one against inflation, nor against an undesired regime change, nor against a love relationship growing stale, nor against the scientific refutation of one's theories. Religion cannot jump in and do the work of other functional systems.[44]

Thus, on the one hand, the liberal and democratic constitutional state opposes religious encroachments that violate the *individual pursuit of happiness* in the sense intended by the American Declaration of Independence. On the other hand and in order to protect against tyranny, the state emphasizes its own functional artificiality of being an entity created by contract the role of which is in no way to be inflated ideologically or morally. The guarantee of liberality lies in limiting the state to proper procedures and institutional protections. Thus, pluralism is guaranteed wherever the ideologically neutral state is defended against religious claims to exclusion and closure. It is also defended by the fact that every goal set by the state is made under the reservation that it not violate an individual's right to freely choose his or her own convictions or the right to religious freedom. At an early date, these points were established by the United States Supreme Court which underlined their importance:

> [I]f there is any fixed star in our constitutional constellation, it is that no official, high or petty, can prescribe what shall be orthodox in politics, nationalism, religion, or other matters of opinion or force citizens to confess by word or act their faith therein.[45]

The model to separate politics and religion which was developed in modern liberal constitutionalism and made in the interest of religious freedom,

43 Luhmann, "Die Ausdifferenzierung der Religion," 1993, p. 259.

44 Ibid.

45 US-Supreme Court, West Virginia State Board of Education v. Barnette, 319 U.S. 624 (1943).

limits the power of both religion and politics. It views political tyranny and the hardening of religion in the pursuit of domination as two sides of the same coin. Likewise, religious freedom and political freedom are inseparable; both culminate in the concept of civil liberty.

With the unfolding (*Entfaltung*) of Bodin's paradox of sovereignty, the successively emerging liberal self-limitation is again linked to a paradox. For, in the interest of liberality, the secular state that confines itself to its functional political institutions, must refrain from trying to influence the social morals of its sovereign, the people. Indeed, it must refrain from even trying to find out the state of their moral views, for this would come close to trying to control them. At the most, the liberal state can try to administer homeopathic doses of its social and moral resources. The paradox of the liberal state is that it apparently needs the binding powers of the traditional world-views that were guaranteed by religion, but at the same time it had to pacify and limit religion to private conviction in order to establish itself.[46]

Here, with this so-called Böckenförde paradox, the early modern period's paradox of sovereignty which led to the transformation of Bodin's theory returns in a changed form. This is not as much an irony of history as a demonstration of the importance of the role that the unfolding of paradoxes play in the history of political ideas. Like the power of the early modern period's absolutist sovereign, the power of a democracy's sovereign people requires a limit placed on its power to act; and this in the interest of insuring its ability to engage in practical politics. This limitation is the constitution: "Citizens need a constitution, just as Ulysses needed to be bound to his mast."[47] Just as Ulysses was able to enjoy the song of the sirens without having to suffer the sorrows of a deadly shipwreck only by having himself tied to the mast, the experiment of democratic freedom also needs to take security measures. These consist in making sure that, by means of constitutional statutes, the democratic society's core moral norms are taken out of the hands of the democratic majority's power to act upon them.[48] Thus, one paradox is answered in the unfolding of the next: "Democracy means that the people rule. Over whom? Over the people, of course."[49] Constitutionalism responds with a form of the act of

---

46 See Böckenförde, "The Rise of the State as a Process of Secularisation," 1991.
47 Holmes, *Passions and Constraints: On the Theory of Liberal Democracy*, p. 135.
48 See ibid., p. 163.
49 Luhmann, *Die Politik der Gesellschaft*, p. 353.

Ulysses that one might call the 'paradox of intangibility' (*Unverfügbarkeitsparadox*): The liberal constitutional state opposes any transcendental legitimation of social order and political domination. It does not view them as being subordinate to divine determination but rather as emerging from the will of those subject to political domination, and therefore as objects of practical action. This state of affairs is mirrored in the fact that all laws, up to and including the constitution, are made by the sovereign people's democratically elected representatives. But then, this procedure and its principle institutional expression are made absolute and removed from the people's power to act upon; and precisely in order to prevent any possible return of the religious postulate that such elements are reserved for the divine sphere. Thus, out of the political will creating a constitution in which the right to fashion all elements of the world-immanent factual and symbolical order is proclaimed, emerges the second order paradox that not all matters are within the people's power to act upon. This solution is also intended to solve the problem of cohesion that is alleged to plague the liberal order: "The rule of law [...] is the great mucilage that holds society together."[50]

As the result of the paradox regarding the things that are not within the power of the people to determine, one might indeed call the concept of *constitutional democracy* an "oxymoron"[51] because the basic norms are beyond the power of the people's will to act upon. The logical and normative advantage of the "'auto-paternalism'"[52] that is found in the constitutional paradox of aspects that cannot be changed by the people is that no one can voluntarily agree to surrender his right to voluntariness, and that therefore, "to preserve voluntariness, voluntariness itself must be restricted".[53]

The result for the relationship between politics and religion is that the ideologically neutral and liberal-democratic constitutional state profits from the fact that the scarce resource of 'meaning' is not within the power of the state to determine. It is constituted and re-produced outside the state and codified in the sphere of transcendence. And, for its part, religion profits from the fact that the question of power is treated in the political

50 US-Supreme Court, Papachristou v. City of Jacksonville, 405 U.S. 156, 171 (1972).

51 Holmes, *Passions and Constraints. On the Theory of Liberal Democracy*, p. 136.

52 Ibid., p. 174.

53 Ibid., p. 176.

system and its limits set by law. In this way, religion enjoys the state's legal protection against political persecution and the pretensions of totalitarian political religions and avoids the dysfunctional temptation of trying to substitute – or of mistaking – its own sphere of faith for that of politics. Let us take a closer look at this *win-win-situation*[54] in systematic perspective.

C. Demands of Liberal Constitutionalism

Even if the religio-political *win-win-situation* is theoretically convincing, proven historically and consequently without alternative, it is still impertinent to the truth and absolutist claims of monotheistic revealed religions. For being compelled to differentiate between politics and religion presents a permanent challenge to religious conviction. From the standpoint of a neutral position, both realms are viewed as two different forms of social action. In this way, religion is denied its traditional priority that once included social meaning, metaphysical mission, scientific truth, and political praxis.

All the more, the liberal-democratic constitutional state is in need of "*complementary* life forms",[55] especially on the part of those whose earlier conflicts with each other, and with the collective order, contributed decisively to *the rise of the state as a process of secularization.*[56] Such a complementary approach can be found in the prerequisites that led to the development of *religious liberality* in the just described sense of the term: the voluntary willingness of communities of faith to accept the primacy of democratic political decisions over their world-views' claims to validity and to tolerate rival religious faiths. It is therefore necessary for the pious to interpret God's law religiously and morally and, precisely in the discursive arguments about the truth of various religions, recognize that, in the long run, only an autonomous state of the rule of law can guarantee the arguing groups' free, legal, and peaceful life of coexistence.[57] For the suspicion that, in the last instance, the secularized western state derives its

---

54 Stepan, "Religion, Democracy, and the 'Twin Tolerations'," 2000.

55 Habermas, *Erläuterungen zur Diskursethik*, 1991, p. 25.

56 Böckenförde, "The Rise of the State as a Process of Secularisation,".

57 See Graf, *Moses Vermächtnis. Über göttliche und menschliche Gesetze*, 2006, p. 87.

strength from the inner forces and binding powers that religious faith communicates to the state's citizens, means that religious citizens of every provenance must acknowledge that the liberal secular state provides the opportunity for freedom and that it is their responsibility to maintain it.[58]

This places a far reaching demand on the development of systems of interpreting religion: within the medium of religious language itself, the difference between the mundane order and the religious ethos must be established, and thus the constructive notion of the legitimate and freedom-serving secularity of the state must be affirmed.[59] The members of religious communities must therefore learn to limit themselves to their own articles of faith, i.e., they must learn to distinguish between what in a liberal democratic, and therefore ideologically neutral, state can be considered valid for everyone, and what can be considered valid only for a specific community.[60] This paradoxical requirement of an internally self-imposed limitation on religious claims and symbol systems, in the form of the genuine religious insight that the state must not be allowed to be religiously determined, sensitizes against any possible essentialist and a-historical notion of a supposed principle compatibility – or incompatibility – in the relationship of democracy and liberality to religion.[61]

However, one can hardly suppose that the conditions of religious liberality depend exclusively on internal religious developments.[62] Rather, in view of the historical record, what is called for is that attention be paid to the process of exchange between politics and religion whose positive – or negative – experiences have an influence on both sides' potential for liberality.

On the political side of this question we find the religio-political governance structure of the free and democratic constitutional state which we may characterize – with reference to Abraham Lincoln's famous praise in his Gettysburg Address of 19 November 1863 of "government of the people, by the people, for the people" – as *governance of religions*, *governance by religions* and *governance for religions*. The vanishing point of this threefold constellation is found in the voluntary religious liberality described above. In view of the necessary regulatory components of a *gover-*

58 See Böckenförde, "The Rise of the State as a Process of Secularisation," pp. 45 ff.
59 See Graf, "Einleitung," 2013, p. 39.
60 See ibid., pp. 39 ff.
61 See ibid.
62 See ibid., p. 43.

nance of *religions*, as we find, for example, in the prohibition of unconstitutional fundamentalist activities, the acceptance of the democratic caveat is a necessary condition for a *governance for religions* being able to be extended to a *governance* by *religions*, such as we find in the German constitutional rights of religion. These rights have now been extended to the Islamic communities of faith and allow them to make their own program of instruction in schools and to establish Islamic theological faculties at state universities. In such a way, on the one hand, religio-political governance practices induce complex reciprocal processes and thus positive, resp. negative, political incentives for religious liberality; on the other hand, religious communities acquire experience ranging from the repressive *governance of religions* to the autonomy-supporting *governance by religions*, all the way up to the liberal *governance for religions*.

This demonstrates that it is precisely the functional separation of politics and religion that allows church and state to work together to accomplish common tasks.[63] The specific pre-condition for this achievement is the ideological neutrality of the liberal democratic constitutional state.[64] Naturally, such a state has a minimal tendency toward hegemony, insofar as the liberal democratic rule of law must, at the very least, require that the framework it creates, and thus the fundamental order of values it upholds, be accepted.[65] In this regard it places faith in a force of transformation.[66] "Thus, by definition, the democratic and liberal state's neutrality cannot be absolute"; instead "the state [...] takes the side of equality and autonomy, allowing citizens to choose their life plan and mode of life."[67]

The liberal constitutional state must watch over the return of religiosity, administer it in a secular way, and remain neutral.[68] From this perspective, the widespread notion that liberalism turned religion into a private matter and intended to marginalize it in the public realm is a misunderstanding.

63 See Graf, *Götter global. Wie die Welt zum Supermarkt der Religionen wird*, 2014, p. 102.

64 See Patten, "Liberal Neutrality: A Reinterpretation and Defense," 2012.

65 See Galston, *Liberal Purposes: Goods, Virtues, and Diversity in the Liberal State*, 1991, p. 3.

66 See Macedo, "Transformative Constitutionalism and the Case of Religion: Defending the Moderate Hegemony of Liberalism," 1998. See also Woodberry, "The Missionary Roots of Liberal Democracy," 2012.

67 Maclure and Taylor, *Secularism and Freedom of Conscience*, 2011, pp. 16 ff.

68 See Dreier, *Säkularisierung und Sakralität. Zum Selbstverständnis des modernen Verfassungsstaates*, 2013, p. 112.

Quite the opposite is true; in a pluralistic and democratic society, it is entirely legitimate and desirable that religious communities attempt to exercise political influence. What is essential is that they remain open toward the results of such an attempt, and that no claim be made that the right to take such influence is based on being in possession of divine truth.[69]

Cécile Laborde has therefore distinguished aptly between "four ideal-typical models of the public place of religion":[70]

> (A) Militant Separation: Inadequate protection of religious freedoms; official support and promotion of scepticism or atheism by the state; secularist anti-religious state.
>
> (B) Modest Separation: Adequate protection of religious freedoms; no official support of religion(s) by the state; no public funding of religious education and no state aid to religious groups.
>
> (C) Modest Establishment: Adequate protection of religious freedoms; official support of religion(s) by the state; public funding of religious education and state aid to religious groups.
>
> (D) Full Establishment: Inadequate protection of religious freedoms; official support and promotion of religious orthodoxy by the state; theocratic anti-secular state.

Models (A) and (D) are unacceptable to political liberalism, but liberalism is "potentially compatible" with both models (B) and (C) "(or any intermediary model)".[71]

Not only in view of the highly desirable and manifold civil society activities preformed by religious communities, for example the caritative ones, but also with regard to their political engagement, the distinction between public and private functions is sometimes misunderstood because these functions are confused with the distinction between the state and socicty:[72] religious communities are as free as any other social group to engage in political activity in the public and social sphere; but such activity must be distinguished from a collective political activity that claims to be

69 See Böckenförde, "Der säkularisierte, religionsneutrale Staat als sittliche Idee – Die Reinigung des Glaubens durch die Vernunft," 2011, p. 86.

70 Laborde, "Political Liberalism and Religion: On Separation and Establishment," 2013, p. 68.

71 Ibid., p. 69. See now in more detail Laborde, *Liberalism's Religion*, 2017.

72 For this idea I am indebted to Professor Rainer Schmalz-Bruns (University of Hannover).

binding for everyone and which, in the liberal democratic constitutional state, is reserved for elected institutions.

Whily pre-conditionally accepting this caveat, a fortiori, further research is urgently necessary in order to examine and to more closely determine the reciprocal relationship between political structures of incentives and religious dispositions. This calls for comparative studies of the political conditions of religious liberality. Following, I will outline some initial thoughts on such a project.

D. The Political Ethics of World Religions

The starting point for such an investigation can be found in the work of the Protestant theologian Ernst Troeltsch. In a manner analogous to Max Weber's famous question, why did capitalism develop originally only in the Occident, Troeltsch asked why liberalism has remained a Western discovery. Like Weber, who sought and found the answer to his question in the economic ethics of the major world religions, Troeltsch addressed their political ethics.

Support for this perspective can be found in the religio-philosophical reflections of Jürgen Habermas who, after initial skepticism, now thinks that he "can lend an unproblematic meaning to Böckenförde's theorem":[73] "For, as a constitutional democracy, it depends on a mode of legitimation founded on convictions."[74]

In view of this requirement, Habermas calls on citizens of secular conviction to join with their fellow citizens who hold religious convictions in order to translate the language of religious meaning into a language accessible to all.[75] With this reasonable postulate, Habermas hopes to make it possible for religious experience, with its potential for solidarity, to become a part of the process of societal self-interpretation. To this end, he has offered a memorable description of the process of secularization: "Secularization functions less as a filter separating the contents of traditions than as a transformer which redirects the flow of tradition."[76] In keeping with the liberal tradition, Habermas writes:

73 Habermas, *Between Naturalism and Religion: Philosophical Essays*, 2008, p. 110.
74 Habermas, "An Awareness of What is Missing," 2010, p. 20.
75 See Habermas, *Between Naturalism and Religion. Philosophical Essays*, p. 132.
76 Habermas, "An Awareness of What is Missing," p. 18.

> The truth contents of religious contributions can enter into the institutionalized practice of deliberation and decision-making only when the necessary translation already occurs in the pre-parliamentarian domain, i.e. in the political public sphere itself.[77]

The concept of translation is at the heart of Habermas's religio-theoretical extension of discourse ethics. It replaces the liberal concept of conflict-shy *gag rules* which were meant to "preclude [the] cooperation-shattering debate of emotionally charged issues."[78] For his part, Habermas defends "Hegel's thesis that the major world religions belong to the history of reason itself."[79] In this way, Habermas departs from the liberal position, at least insofar as it fails to impute a rationality postulate to religions, but rather treats religions – for their own protection – as private matters that are to be spared the test of any criteria of reason.

Habermas's partial correction of the liberal model may well be justified and have a future. Still, it is not immediately clear why liberalism that was a rival of the *major world religions* for hundreds of years should trust its former enemies, or indeed grant them credit for rationality. Thus Habermas's religio-philosophical reflections also culminate in the question concerning the conditions of religious liberality, and Habermas indicates his intuitive feeling for this problem when, with regard to "religious consciousness", he places his hope in a "modernization from within".[80]

Encouraged in this way by Habermas, when looking at the comparative examination of the major world religions' political ethics by Troeltsch, one sees that there is reciprocity between, on the one hand, political incentive structures resp. modes of conduct and, on the other hand, genuine religious dispositions resp. forms of reaction.

Thus, until the Second Vatican Council, Catholicism held the ideologically neutral liberal state for apostasy, the fall from faith, because the Catholic idea of the unity of morals and law was incompatible with Kant's principle distinction between morality and legality and the idea of an individual's right to self-defense against the state. Reflections on the liberal potential of natural rights under Pope Leo XIII did not arise from that fact that "there is no obstacle in principle to an autonomous foundation of

---

77 Habermas, *Between Naturalism and Religion. Philosophical Essays*, p. 131.

78 Holmes, *Passions and Constraints: On the Theory of Liberal Democracy*, 1995, pp. 10, 202 ff.

79 Habermas, *Between Naturalism and Religion. Philosophical Essays*, p. 6.

80 Ibid., p. 311.

morality and law [...] from the Catholic side, which is congenial to the lumen natural."[81] Rather, this development came directly from the insight that communism was a far more dangerous enemy than liberalism.[82] But when the Second Vatican Council's Pastoral Constitution *Gaudium et spes* expressly recognized human rights, including religious freedom and the constitution, as constituting the foundation of modern statehood, it did so on the basis of the so-called differentiation thesis in number 76 of the Pastoral Constitution according to which the political community and the church are "autonomous in their respective spheres of activity."[83] This new position was undoubtedly indebted to the positive experience that the Catholic Church had made in the United States with liberal religious policy and governance – an experience John Courtney Murray S.J. communicated to the Second Vatican Council.[84]

But Protestantism has its problems with liberal democratic constitutionalism either. For Calvinism "is related not with modernity but with modernization, that is, with the process far more significantly than with its outcome."[85] For this reason, Calvinism tends to overemphasize the political, indeed to the point of institutionalizing a theocratic or Christocratic commonwealth[86] which is the very opposite of the liberal model. Complementary to this ambivalence, Lutheranism stands for the peerless nadir of a religiously connotated authoritarianism as well as, in its two-kingdom-doctrine, for a liberal moment that amounts to an "anarchy of the inner man".[87] With this position, worldly affairs can be relativized and acknowledged to be an independent realm with its own dignity. Thus, with regard to Protestantism, the findings concerning liberality are ambivalent.

---

81 Ibid., p. 102.

82 See Uertz, *Vom Gottesrecht zum Menschenrecht. Das katholische Staatsdenken von der Französischen Revolution bis zum II. Vatikanischen Konzil (1789-1965)*, 2005.

83 Tanner, *The Church and the World: Gaudium et spes, Inter mirifica*, 2005, p. 58.

84 See Hooper, *Bridging the Sacred and the Secular: Selected Writings of John Courtney Murray, SJ*, 1994. See Murray, *We hold these Truths: Catholic Reflections on the American Proposition*, 2005. See also Weigel, "Catholicism and Democracy, The Other Twentieth-Century Revolution," 1990.

85 Walzer, *The Revolution of the Saints: A Study in the Origins of Radical Politics*, 1965, pp. 18 ff.

86 See Graf, *Der Protestantismus. Geschichte und Gegenwart*, 2006, p. 44.

87 Graf, "Der Protestantismus," 2007, p. 116.

If one enlarges this cursory and comparative overview beyond the Western Christian denominations one finds an anti-liberal position in Orthodox Christianity;[88] a problem that, fatally, was one of the most underestimated in the eastward expansion of the European Union.[89] Characterized by its ethnic orientation and organization and endowed with a strong apocalyptic strain, Orthodox Christianity, due to its so called principle of sympathy with the state, continues to have difficulty distinguishing between the realms of the sacred and the profane, and thus between religion and politics. This rules out the possibility of constitutionally limiting political and ecclesiastical power. In his revealing book, *Politische Theologie in der griechisch-orthodoxen Kirche*, Dimitrios Kisoudis renews this anti-liberal tradition with reference to Carl Schmitt and finds that the current enemy of the Greek Orthodox Church is constitutional law the insistence of which that state and church observe human rights is an outgrowth of Western theology.[90]

Konstantin Kostjuk finds the root of this attitude of Orthodox Christianity in the fact that it is far more oriented to authoritarian Platonism than to more liberal Aristotelianism.[91] This is of particular interest because here we find agreement between Orthodox Christianity and Islam, for the political dimension of Islam's reception of ancient Greek thought was strictly Platonic. In the first instance, this can be attributed to the simple fact that no Arabic translation of Aristotle's *Politics* existed while there were translations of both Plato's *Politeia* and *Nomoi*. For this reason, "few were aware of the difference" between Platonic and Aristotelian political philosophy.[92] Thus, Ibn Rušd wrote a commentary on all of Aristotle's works except *Politics*; in the political sphere we find instead a commentary on Plato's *Politeia*.[93] And Ibn Sīnā noted in his discussion of the three practical sciences, ethics, economics and politics – a division based on Aristo-

---

88 See Anderson, "Sovereignty vs. liberalism: some Russian Orthodox responses to democracy and pluralism," 2013.

89 See Olteanu and de Nève, *Eastern Orthodoxy and the Processes of European Integration*, 2014.

90 See Kisoudis, *Politische Theologie in der griechisch-orthodoxen Kirche*, 2007, p. 114.

91 See Kostjuk, *Der Begriff des Politischen in der russisch-orthodoxen Tradition. Zum Verhältnis von Kirche, Staat und Gesellschaft in Rußland*, 2005, pp. 28 ff.

92 See de Bour, *The History of Philosophy in Islam*, 1903, p. 27. See also Walzer, *Greek into Arabic. Essays on Islamic Philosophy*, 1962, p. 243.

93 See ibid., p. 19.

tle's *Nicomachean Ethics* – that the last of these was treated by Plato and Aristotle in their teachings on government but that *both philosophers* treated questions of prophecy and (divine) right in their works on law.[94] This erroneous reference of Iban Sīnā to a non-existent work of Aristotle on law seems to go back to a false entry in a list of Aristotle's writings[95] and with this puzzling reference, and the suspicion that Aristotle's *Politics* was completely unknown in the Orient during the Middle Ages, we can let the matter rest.[96] But even if Ibn Sīnā had known Aristotle's *Politics*, that would change nothing; quite the contrary, in that case the lack of a reception of Aristotle's political writings would be all the more significant.[97]

That Platonic politics were particularly suited to the then prevailing circumstances and corresponding philosophical needs can already be seen at the beginning of the 10th century in the writings of al-Fârâbî who, in the turmoil of civil war and in view of the impotence of the caliphate, turned to the concept of the ideal state in Plato's *Politeia* "as a guide to practical action to renew the theocratic state."[98]

In contrast to the unintended disenchantment of the world-view that followed from the Investiture Controversy and the successive re-discovery of politics as an autonomous sphere by scholastic Neo-Aristotelians, the Islamic reception of the ancient Greek world developed far less favorable conditions for the later adoption of a liberal attitude and democratic structures – and for contingent reasons.

This is especially true for Sunni Islam. In contrast, the Shiite tradition which was influenced by neo-Platonism and in which political Aristotelianism was also unknown recognized in the beginning the separation of religion and politics. (It is still an erroneous commonplace in the public discussion in the West that the principle of the separation of religion and politics is universally absent in Islam.) The Shiite doctrine of 'occultation' and the return of the twelfth Imam at the end of time have existed since

---

94 See Avicenna, "On the Divisions of the Rational Sciences," 1984, p. 97.

95 See ibid., p. 2.

96 See Morris, "The Philosopher-Prophet in Avicenna's Political Philosophy," 1992, p. 169.

97 See Peters, *Aristotle and the Arabs: The Aristotelian Tradition in Islam*, 1968, pp. 168 ff.

98 Endreß, "'Der Erste Lehrer.' Der arabische Aristoteles und das Konzept der Philosophie im Islam," 1991, pp. 163 ff. See Corbin, *History of Islamic Philosophy*, 1993, p. 162. See also Walzer, *Greek into Arabic. Essays on Islamic Philosophy*, pp. 19, 243 ff.

934. This mystical interpretation of the Koran goes back to the sixth Shiite Imam who died in 765 and was developed in compensation for the humiliating experience of having to live under foreign rule. Still, it amounted to a theocratic perversion of a centuries old secular Shiite tradition rooted in mysticism, when, in the course of the Islamic Revolution, the Ayatollah Khomeini succeeded in establishing his doctrine of the 'guardianship of the scholar of the law' (Velâyat-e Faqîh). In doing so, he destroyed the attempt that had been made in the 1904/1905 Iranian constitutional revolution to connect with modern political thought in the West.[99]

Remarkably, there must be historically marginalized independent, rationalist, and liberal developments in Islam, the recovery of which might open some promising possibilities. For the Sunni tradition in particular, Reinhard Schulze has reconstructed an original enlightenment stream, whose further development was tragically interrupted – and now we would say ironically prevented by Western colonialism.[100]

Even this brief tour de force through a desideratum of scholarly research brings into focus the necessity of undertaking a comparative study of the political ethics of the major world religions from the perspective of whether conditions may be found in them that favor religious liberality. This suggests the working hypothesis that radicalism does not take place due to the experience of the loss of meaning under the conditions of the secular liberal state. Indeed, quite the opposite seems to be true, there is a *paradox of transcendence in religious liberality.* While prima facie one might think that a religion is more liberal the more it is open to the world and the more it is politically engaged, as a matter of fact, the existence of a pronounced orientation toward transcendence seems to be a theological and religio-psychological condition for religious liberality, for it leaves a sphere free for the autonomous laws of worldly existence. This is especially true if, at the same time, such a religion has positive experiences with the liberal political institutions that guarantee religious freedom.

In conclusion, and with regard to the hypothesis that I have developed here with the help of Christian and Islamic examples, let us take a brief

99 See Armstrong, *The Battle for God*, 2000, p. 156.

100 See Schulze, "Das islamische 18. Jahrhundert. Versuch einer historiographischen Kritik," 1990; see Schulze, "Was ist die islamische Aufklärung?," 1996; see Schulze, *A Modern History of the Islamic World*, 2002; see Browers and Kurzman, *An Islamic Reformation?*, 2004. See also Kurzman, *Liberal Islam: A Sourcebook*, 1998.

look at Buddhism which is not a monotheistic religion of revelation and the fundamental position of which is well known to be compatible with freedom.

First, we must correct the caricature of Buddhism that depicts it as passive and wanting to flee from the world; a view that hardly pays attention to social and political issues, and which was unfortunately encouraged by Max Weber's highly influential sociology of religion. Weber asserted that Buddhism is determined by "quietism"[101] and is a "specifically apolitical and anti-political status religion"[102] which "has established no 'social-political' goal".[103]

But these judgments "are based on an arbitrary interpretation of the evidence and the drawing of equally arbitrary conclusions", for Gautama Buddha and his disciples turned toward the world "in order to provide a model of how, at one and the same time, one can distance oneself and yet remain in symbiotic relationship with the world."[104] Finally, the Buddha himself experienced politics as the decisive factor in existence, and not just because his father was the elected ruler of the Śâkya-Republic that had lost its autonomy, but also because he took the larger historical context into account. During Gautama Buddha's life, profound social changes took place in north India, brought about by the introduction of a money economy, the use of iron, and the rise of crafts, commerce, and small business, which in turn led to the emergence of larger cities with their social differentiations. As far as political organization is concerned, smaller territorial principalities developed where previously republican forms of government had been widespread. All these far reaching changes were reflected in the transformation of values and in new world-views to which the Buddhist questioning of the caste system must be reckoned.[105] In addition,

---

101 Weber, "Religion of India: The Sociology of Hinduism and Buddhism," 2000, pp. 206, 215.

102 Ibid., p. 204.

103 Ibid., p. 224.

104 Tambiah, "Max Webers Untersuchung des frühen Buddhismus. Eine Kritik," 1984, p. 208.

105 See Gokhale, "Dhamma as a Political Concept in Early Buddhism," 1968, p. 251. Gombrich, *Theravada Buddhism: A Social History from Ancient Benares to Modern Colombo*, pp. 5 ff. Ilaiah, *God as Political Philosopher: Buddhism's Challenge to Brahmanism*, 2001, pp. 33 ff. Schumann, *Der historische Buddha. Leben und Lehre des Gotama*, 1995, pp. 13 ff. Zotz, *Buddha. Mit Selbstzeugnissen und Bilddokumenten*, 1998, pp. 16 ff., 27 ff.

the princes sought Gautama Buddha's counsel, and at the height of his fame he was also approached for an activity that today we would call political consultation.[106]

Consequently, the sutras of Gautama Buddha reveal a modernizing tendency of thought that replaces the ritual collectivism of the Vedic tradition with a socially accented ethical individualism the object of which is to lead "to the formation of a viable economy, a strong and solid social structure and a healthy and durable state."[107] Here we find a parallel between Buddhism and Protestantism since both, the one directed against Hinduism and the other against Catholicism, place a higher value on individual achievement than on inherited social status. And it was this affirmation of social mobility that made both of these reform religions attractive to the aspiring middle classes and especially to merchants.[108]

Seen in this perspective, the question of Buddhism's religio-political potential for liberality must be understood as "religious individualism".[109] At first glance, this view would seem to contradict the rejection of the notion of an individual soul; but the idea of an egoless spirit supports the teaching of limited genesis in mutual dependency, and precisely because acts, according to this Buddhist conception, are subject to thoroughly observed causality – since they determine a variety of conditions – the intentional ethical act (*kamma*) is all the more important.

This leads to an understanding of politics as an autonomous realm and to a benign attitude toward republicanism and human rights:

> In short, each person should share in the responsibility of making decisions, and […] the community should present a united front. Here, obviously, the moral character of the individual must be a factor of primary importance.[110]

106 See Gokhale, "The Early Buddhist View of the State," 1969, pp. 731 ff.

107 Upreti, *Early Buddhist World Outlook in Historical Perspective*, 1997, p. 168. See also Harris, „Buddhism and Politics in Asia: The Textual and Historical Roots," 2001.

108 See Bailey and Mabbett, *The Sociology of Early Buddhism*, 2003, pp. 17 ff., 26. See also Gombrich, *Theravada Buddhism: A Social History from Ancient Benares to Modern Colombo,* 2006, pp. 171 ff.

109 Gombrich, *Theravada Buddhism: A Social History from Ancient Benares to Modern Colombo,* 2006, pp. 73 ff.

110 Saddhatissa, *Buddhist Ethics*, 1997, p. 125.

That Gautama Buddha was a believer in tribal republicanism[111] is also evident in his skillful policy advice on the occasion when a king sent his counselor to him to seek advice on a pending military campaign. Gautama Buddha responded by asking whether the king's enemies often held assemblies, were peaceful and law-abiding, honored and followed the counsel of their oldest members, did not commit acts of rape, and whether they granted religious freedom. And because the king's enemies did in fact live according to these principles, or in other words had a republican political order, the Buddha concluded that they were almost invincible. Confronted with this answer, the king dropped the notion of using force against them.[112]

In other sutras, Gautama Buddha explained how rulers should deal with civil unrest, lawlessness, and plundering. They should not reply with harsh penalties but rather with loans, alimentations, and investments that would lead to prosperity, peace, and harmony.[113]

As a consequence, the notion that systems of political rule are either natural or divine was called into question – and in this "'demystification' of the world" we find another parallel between Buddhism and Protestantism[114] which is all the more surprising since Max Weber, of all people, overlooked it.

In any case Gautama Buddha emphasizes "that societal status depends on man-made conventions";[115] a statement that situates religion in its principle duality to politics and thus underscores the fact that the liberal political order is endowed with a logic of its own.[116] This view which is open to differentiation rules out the kind of paternal rule by philosophers that we

---

111 See Ilaiah, *God as Political Philosopher. Buddhism's Challenge to Brahmanism*, p. 217.

112 See "Mahāparinibbāna Sutta: The Great Passing. The Buddha's Last Days," in *The Long Discourses of the Buddha*, 1996, pp. 231-277, 231 ff.

113 See "Kūṭadanta Sutta: About Kutadanta. A Bloodless Sacrifice," in *The Long Discourses of the Buddha*, pp. 133-141. See "Cakkavatti-Sīhanāda Sutta: The Lion's Roar on the Turning of the Wheel," *The Long Discourses of the Buddha*, pp. 395-405.

114 See Gombrich, *Theravada Buddhism: A Social History from Ancient Benares to Modern Colombo,* p. 88.

115 "Aggañña Sutta: On Knowledge of Beginnings," in *The Long Discourses of the Buddha*, pp. 407-415. See also Ilaiah, *God as Political Philosopher. Buddhism's Challenge to Brahmanism*, pp. 82 ff.

116 See Gokhale, "The Early Buddhist View of the State," p. 732.

find in Plato.[117] Instead a "balance of forces" between politics and religion shall prevail,[118] which, at one and the same time, limits political domination *with the help of* religion and also limits the domination *of religion*. It can function in this way because the transcendent *dhamma* can only develop its corrective power in the differentiation of political concerns.

Thus, for Buddhism too, it would seem that the paradox of transcendence, which we have detected in religious liberality, retains its plausibility. This question deserves further research. Pursuing it might allow substantial insights that facilitate dealing with the political problem of religious liberality.

Bibliography

Anderson, John, "Sovereignty vs. liberalism: some Russian Orthodox responses to democracy and pluralism," in *Risky Liaisons? Democracy and Religion: Reflections and Case Studies*, ed. G.J. Buijs, J.T. Sunier and P.G.A. Versteeg, Amsterdam: VU University Press, 2013, pp. 161-177.

Armstrong, Karen, *The Battle for God*, New York: Knopf, 2000.

Avicenna, "On the Divisions of the Rational Sciences," in *Medieval Political Philosophy: A Sourcebook*, ed. Ralph Lerner and Muhsin Mahdi, Ithaca and New York: Cornell University Press, 1984, pp. 95-97.

Bailey, Greg, and Ian W. Mabbett, *The Sociology of Early Buddhism*, Cambridge: Cambridge University Press, 2003.

Blumenberg, Hans, "Nachahmung der Natur. Zur Vorgeschichte der Idee des schöpferischen Menschen," in idem, *Wirklichkeiten in denen wir leben. Aufsätze und eine Rede*, Stuttgart: Reclam, 1981, pp. 55-103.

Bodin, Jean, *Les six livres de la République*, Paris: Jacques du Puis, 1583.

Böckenförde, Ernst-Wolfgang, "The Rise of the State as a Process of Secularisation," in idem, *State, Society and Liberty. Studies in Political Theory and Constitutional Law*, New York: Berg, 1991, pp. 26-46.

Böckenförde, Ernst-Wolfgang, *Geschichte der Rechts- und Staatsphilosophie. Antike und Mittelalter*, Tübingen: Mohr Siebeck, 2006.

117 See "Aggañña Sutta: On Knowledge of Beginnings," 1996, pp. 408 ff; Gokhale, "The Early Buddhist View of the State," p. 735; Ilaiah, *God as Political Philosopher. Buddhism's Challenge to Brahmanism*, pp. 94 ff.; Saddhatissa, *Buddhist Ethics*, 1997, pp. 115 ff.

118 See Gokhale, "The Early Buddhist View of the State," p. 738.

Böckenförde, Ernst-Wolfgang, "Der säkularisierte, religionsneutrale Staat als sittliche Idee – Die Reinigung des Glaubens durch die Vernunft: Biographisches Interview von Dieter Gosewinkel," in *Wissenschaft, Politik, Verfassungsgericht. Aufsätze von Ernst-Wolfgang Böckenförde*, ed. Ernst-Wolfgang Böckenförde and Dieter Gosewinkel, Berlin: Suhrkamp, 2011, pp. 84-93.

Browers, Michaelle, and Charles Kurzman (eds.), *An Islamic Reformation?*, Lanham: Lexington Books, 2004.

Buddha, Gautama, *The Long Discourses of the Buddha. A Translation of the Dīgha-Nikāya by Maurice Walshe*, Somerville MA: Wisdom Publications, 1996.

Casanova, José, "The problem of religion and the anxieties of European secular democracy," in *Religion and democracy in contemporary Europe*, ed. Gabriel Motzkin and Yochi Fischer, London: Alliance Publ. Trust, 2008, pp. 63-74.

Conze, Werner, Hans-Wolfgang Strätz, and Hermann Zabel, "Säkularisation, Säkularisierung," in *Geschichtliche Grundbegriffe. Historisches Lexikon zur politisch-sozialen Sprache in Deutschland*, Vol. 5, ed. Otto Brunner, Werner Conze, and Reinhart Koselleck, Stuttgart: Klett-Cotta, 1984, pp. 789-829.

Corbin, Henri, *History of Islamic Philosophy*, London and New York: Keagan Paul, 1993.

De Bour, T.J., *The History of Philosophy in Islam*, London: Luzac, 1903.

Dreier, Horst, *Säkularisierung und Sakralität. Zum Selbstverständnis des modernen Verfassungsstaates*, Tübingen: Mohr Siebeck, 2013.

Endreß, Gerhard, "'Der Erste Lehrer'. Der arabische Aristoteles und das Konzept der Philosophie im Islam," in *Gottes ist der Orient, Gottes ist der Okzident. Festschrift für Abdoldjavad Falaturi zum 65. Geburtstag*, ed. Udo Tworuschka, Köln and Wien: Böhlau, 1991 pp. 151-181.

Fischer, Karsten, *Die Zukunft einer Provokation. Religion im liberalen Staat*, Berlin: Berlin University Press, 2009.

Fischer, Karsten, "Hobbes, Schmitt, and the Paradox of Religious Liberality," *Critical Review of International Social and Political Philosophy* 13 (2010): 399-416.

Forst, Rainer, *Toleration in Conflict. Past and Present*, Cambridge: Cambridge University Press, 2013.

Galston, William A., *Liberal Purposes: Goods, Virtues, and Diversity in the Liberal State*, Cambridge: Cambridge University Press, 1991.

Gokhale, Balkrishna G., "Dhamma as a Political Concept in Early Buddhism," *Journal of Indian History* 46 (1968): 249-261.

Gokhale, Balkrishna G., "The Early Buddhist View of the State," *Journal of the American Oriental Society* 89 (1969): 731-738.

Gombrich, Richard F., *Theravada Buddhism: A Social History from Ancient Benares to Modern Colombo*, New York: Routledge, 2006.

Gorski, Philip S., "Historicizing the Secularization Debate. Church, State, and Society in Late Medieval and Early Modern Europe, ca. 1300 to 1700," *American Sociological Review* 65 (2000): 138-167.

Graf, Friedrich Wilhelm, *Moses Vermächtnis. Über göttliche und menschliche Gesetze*, München: Beck, 2006.

Graf, Friedrich Wilhelm, *Der Protestantismus. Geschichte und Gegenwart*, München: Beck, 2006.

Graf, Friedrich Wilhelm, "Der Protestantismus," in *Säkularisierung und die Weltreligionen*, ed. Hans Joas and Klaus Wiegandt, Frankfurt/M.: Fischer, 2007 pp. 78-124.

Graf, Friedrich Wilhelm, "Einleitung," in *Politik und Religion. Zur Diagnose der Gegenwart*, ed. Friedrich Wilhelm Graf and Heinrich Meier, München: Beck, 2013 pp.7-45.

Graf, Friedrich Wilhelm, *Götter global. Wie die Welt zum Supermarkt der Religionen wird*, München: Beck, 2014.

Grimm, Dieter, "Der Staat in der kontinentaleuropäischen Tradition," in *Recht und Staat in der bürgerlichen Gesellschaft*, Frankfurt/M., 1987 pp. 53-83.

Grimm, Dieter, Souveränität. Herkunft und Zukunft eines Schlüsselbegriffs, Berlin: Berlin University Press, 2009.

Habermas, Jürgen, *Erläuterungen zur Diskursethik*, Frankfurt/M.: Suhrkamp, 1991.

Habermas, Jürgen, *Between Facts and Norms: Contributions to a Discourse Theory of Law and Democracy*, Cambridge MA: Polity Press, 1998.

Habermas, Jürgen, *Between Naturalism and Religion. Philosophical Essays*, Cambridge and Malden MA: Polity Press, 2008.

Habermas, Jürgen, "An Awareness of What is Missing," in *An Awareness of What is Missing. Faith and Religion in a Post-Secular Age*, ed. Jürgen Habermas et al., Cambridge and Malden MA: Polity Press, 2010, pp. 15-23.

Harris, Ian, "Buddhism and Politics in Asia: The Textual and Historical Roots," in *Buddhism and Politics in Twentieth-Century Asia,* London: Pinter, 2001, pp. 1-25.

Hobbes, Thomas, *Behemoth or The Long Parliament*, ed. Ferdinand Tönnies, with an Introduction by Stephen Holmes, Chicago: Chicago University Press, 1990.

Holmes, Stephen, *Passions and Constraints. On the Theory of Liberal Democracy*, Chicago: University of Chicago Press, 1995.

Ilaiah, Kancha, *God as Political Philosopher: Buddhism's Challenge to Brahmanism*, Kolkata: Popular Prakashan, 2001.

Kisoudis, Dimitrios, *Politische Theologie in der griechisch-orthodoxen Kirche*, Marburg: Diagonal, 2007.

Kostjuk, Konstantin, *Der Begriff des Politischen in der russisch-orthodoxen Tradition. Zum Verhältnis von Kirche, Staat und Gesellschaft in Rußland*, Paderborn: Schöningh, 2005.

Kurzman, Charles (ed.), *Liberal Islam. A Sourcebook*, Oxford: Oxford University Press, 1998.

Laborde, Cécile, *Liberalism's Religion*, Cambridge, MA: Harvard University, Press, 2017

Laborde, Cécile, "Political Liberalism and Religion: On Separation and Establishment," *Journal of Political Philosophy* 21 (2013): 67-86.

Luhmann, Niklas, "Die Ausdifferenzierung der Religion," in *Gesellschaftsstruktur und Semantik. Studien zur Wissenssoziologie der modernen Gesellschaft*, Vol. 3, Frankfurt/M.: Suhrkamp, 1993, pp. 259-357.

Luhmann, Niklas, "Tautologie und Paradoxie in den Selbstbeschreibungen der modernen Gesellschaft," in *Protest. Systemtheorie und soziale Bewegungen*, ed. Kai-Uwe Hellmann, Frankfurt/M.: Suhrkamp, 1997 pp. 79-106.

Luhmann, Niklas, *Die Politik der Gesellschaft,* Frankfurt/M: Suhrkamp, 2000.

Luhmann, Niklas, *Die Religion der Gesellschaft*, Frankfurt/M.: Suhrkamp, 2000.

Macedo, Stephen, "Transformative Constitutionalism and the Case of Religion. Defending the Moderate Hegemony of Liberalism," *Political Theory* 26 (1998): 56-80.

Maclure, Jocelyn and Charles Taylor, *Secularism and Freedom of Conscience*, Cambridge MA: Harvard University Press, 2011.

Marsilius de Padua, *Defensor Pacis*, ed. Matthäus J. de Tiege and Winand Paffen, Basel, 1522.

Mayer, Theodor, "Die Ausbildung der Grundlagen des modernen deutschen Staates im Hohen Mittelalter," in *Herrschaft und Staat im Mittelalter*, ed. Hellmut Kämpf, Darmstadt: Wiss. Buchgesellschaft, 1974 pp. 284-331.

Meier, Christian, *The Greek Discovery of Politics*, Cambridge (MA): Harvard University Press, 1990.

Meier, Christian, *The Political Art of Greek Tragedy*, Baltimore: Johns Hopkins University Press, 1993.

Meier, Christian, *Athens. A Portrait of the City in Its Golden Age*, New York: Metropolitan Books, 2000.

Meier, Christian, *A Culture of Freedom: Ancient Greece and the Origins of Europe*, Oxford: Oxford University Press, 2011.

Morris, James W., "The Philosopher-Prophet in Avicenna's Political Philosophy," in *The Political Aspects of Islamic Philosophy. Essays in Honor of Muhsin S. Mahdi*, ed. Charles E. Butterworth, Cambridge MA: Harvard University Press, 1992 pp. 152-198.

Murray, John Courtney, SJ, *Bridging the Sacred and the Secular. Selected Writings of John Courtney Murray, SJ*, ed. J. Leon Hooper, SJ, Washington DC: Georgetown University Press, 1994.

Murray, John Courtney, SJ, *We hold these Truths. Catholic Reflections on the American Proposition*, Lanham MD: Rowman & Littlefield, 2005.

Olteanu, Tina and Dorothée de Nève, "Eastern Orthodoxy and the Processes of European Integration," in *Eastern Orthodox Encounters of Identity and Otherness. Values, Self-Reflection, Dialogue*, ed. Andrii Krawchuk and Thomas Bremer, New York: Palgrave Macmillan, 2014 pp.179-206.

Patten, Alan, "Liberal Neutrality: A Reinterpretation and Defense," *Journal of Political Philosophy* 20 (2012): 249-272.

Peters, Francis E., *Aristotle and the Arabs: The Aristotelian Tradition in Islam*, New York and London: New York University Press, 1968.

Prodi, Paolo, *Eine Geschichte der Gerechtigkeit. Vom Recht Gottes zum modernen Rechtsstaat*, München: Beck 2003.

Saddhatissa, Hammalawa, *Buddhist Ethics*, Boston: Wisdom Publications, 1997.

Schlögl, Rudolf, *Alter Glaube und moderne Welt. Europäisches Christentum im Umbruch (1750-1850)*, Frankfurt/M.: Fischer, 2013.

Schulze, Reinhard, "Das islamische 18. Jahrhundert. Versuch einer historiographischen Kritik," *Die Welt des Islams* 30 (1990): 140-159.

Schulze, Reinhard, "Was ist die islamische Aufklärung?," *Die Welt des Islams* 36 (1996): 276-325.

Schulze, Reinhard, *A Modern History of the Islamic World*, New York: New York University Press, 2002.

Schumann, Hans Wolfgang, *Der historische Buddha. Leben und Lehre des Gotama*, München: Diederichs, 1995.

Spencer-Brown, G., *Laws of Form*, Portland OR: Cognizer, 1994.

Steiger, Heinhard, "Neutralität in Religionssachen," in *Geschichtliche Grundbegriffe. Historisches Lexikon zur politisch-sozialen Sprache in Deutschland*, Vol. 4, ed. Otto Brunner, Werner Conze, and Reinhart Koselleck, Stuttgart: Klett-Cotta, 1978 pp. 337-365.

Stepan, Alfred, "Religion, Democracy, and the 'Twin Tolerations'," *Journal of Democracy* 11 (2000): 37-57.

Struve, Tilman, "Regnum und Sacerdotium," in *Pipers Handbuch der politischen Ideen*, Vol. 2, ed. Iring Fetscher and Herfried Münkler, München: Piper, 2000, pp. 189-242.

Tambiah, Stanley J., "Max Webers Untersuchung des frühen Buddhismus. Eine Kritik," in *Max Webers Studie über Hinduismus und Buddhismus. Interpretation und Kritik*, ed. Wolfgang Schluchter, Frankfurt/M.: Suhrkamp (1984): 202-246.

Tanner, Norman P., *The Church and the World: Gaudium et spes, Inter mirifica*, New York: Paulist Press, 2005.

The Long Discourses of the Buddha, A Translation of the Dīgha-Nikāya by Maurice Walshe, Somerville MA: Wisdom Publications, 1996.

Uertz, Rudolf, *Vom Gottesrecht zum Menschenrecht. Das katholische Staatsdenken von der Französischen Revolution bis zum II. Vatikanischen Konzil (1789-1965)*, Paderborn: Schöningh, 2005.

Upreti, G. B., *Early Buddhist World Outlook in Historical Perspective*, New Delhi: Manohar, 1997.

Voßkuhle, Andreas, "Religionsfreiheit und Religionskritik – Zur Verrechtlichung religiöser Konflikte," *Europäische Grundrechte-Zeitschrift* 37 (2010): 537-543.

Walzer, Richard, *Greek into Arabic. Essays on Islamic Philosophy*, Cambridge MA: Harvard University Press, 1962.

Walzer, Michael, The *Revolution of the Saints: A Study in the Origins of Radical Politics*, Cambridge MA: Harvard University Press, 1965.

Walzer, Michael, "Drawing the Line. Religion and Politics," *Soziale Welt* 49 (1998): 295-307.

Weber, Max, *Religion of India: The Sociology of Hinduism and Buddhism*, New Delhi: Manohar, 2000.

Weigel, George, "Catholicism and Democracy, The Other Twentieth-Century Revolution," in *The New Democracies. Global Change and U.S. Policy*, ed. Brad Roberts, Cambridge MA: Harvard University Press, 1990, pp. 17-37.

Weinfurter, Stefan, *Canossa. Die Entzauberung der Welt*, München: Beck, 2007.

Wilks, Michael, *The Problem of Sovereignty in the Later Middle Ages. The Papal Monarchy with Augustinus Triumphus and the Publicists*, Cambridge: Cambridge University Press, 1963.

Woodberry, Robert D., "The Missionary Roots of Liberal Democracy," *American Political Science Review* 106 (2012): 244-274.

Zotz, Volker, *Buddha. Mit Selbstzeugnissen und Bilddokumenten*, Reinbek: Rowohlt, 1998.

US-Supreme Court, West Virginia State Board of Education v. Barnette, 319 U.S. 624 (1943).

US-Supreme Court, Papachristou v. City of Jacksonville, 405 U.S. 156, 171 (1972).

Religion and National Identity in Modern Western Societies: Theological Reflections on a Political Problem

Johannes Zachhuber

A. Introduction

Connecting religion with collective identity formation in the West today is counter-intuitive. The privatisation of religion, which in the nineteenth century was the political programme of radicals and progressives, has become the rather unspectacular reality of early twenty-first century liberal societies. Secularisation has not brought the end of religion, and most observers by now accept that this is not going to happen in the foreseeable future either, but it has transformed religion in various ways.[1] One aspect of this transformation is that religion is no longer considered a public good, but is viewed as part of people's private existence, an expression of their personal freedom.

Consequently, the traditional alignment of religion with national identity must appear a thing of the past. Like other, similar traditions it may continue to linger, for example in institutions such as the Church of England, but these would be what the anthropologist E.B. Tylor has called 'survivals': leftovers from history that have lost their erstwhile function. The real battles about religion today are waged about individual world views, their practical consequences, and their integration into a secular and pluralistic society.

And yet, there are indications that this perception may not capture the whole of reality. Quite generally, we may observe that wherever and whenever national identity becomes elusive, religion tends to get invoked

1 Recent literature on secularisation includes: Asad, *Formations of the Secular*, 2003; Bruce, *God is Dead: Secularization in the West*, 2002; Casanova, *Public Religions in the Modern World*, 1994; Connolly, *Why I am not a Secularist*, 1999; Jakobsen and Pellegrini, *Secularisms*, 2008; Cady and Fessenden, *Religion, the Secular, and the Politics of Sexual Difference*, 2013; Taylor, *A Secular Age*, 2007; Ward, "The Myth of Secularism," 2014, pp. 162-179; Zachhuber, "Die Diskussion über Säkularisierung am Beginn des 21. Jahrhunderts," 2007, pp. 11-42.

by those seeking to instil a sense of belonging and thus a measure of stability into those groups of people. In recent decades, this has most obviously been the case in the newly emerging nation states of Eastern Europe, such as Ukraine, or in transition states, such as Russia, but the same mechanism is applied almost intuitively by Western politicians in countries such as the United Kingdom or Germany.[2]

In this situation, my paper has two purposes. On the one hand, it will attempt to elucidate the current situation by tracing its genealogy back to pivotal movements in the nineteenth century. On the other hand, I shall offer a theological assessment or rather a theological critique of the use of religion to facilitate collective, national identity. Overall, it is my intention to highlight the continuing power of religion as a source of collective identity while sounding a warning with regard to its theological and ultimately political implications which often go unnoticed when the virtues of such an arrangement are extolled. Religion, I shall argue, works best when it transforms the individual towards an existence with and for other people. Where, on the other hand, it is predicated on a collective body as an expression of, for example, national unity, it shows many of its most deeply problematical sides which have understandably led many to turn away from the faith.

B. Public Religion in a Secularised World

The most influential recent argument for the perseverance or even return of a public dimension of religion in our own time has been presented in José Casanova's book *Public Religions in the Modern World*.[3] Casanova countered the narrative of religious privatisation with a detailed analysis of five very different cases in which religion more recently regained a public role – for better or worse. The instances he looked at were Poland with its Catholic Church famously contributing to the overthrow of the Communist regime in the 1980s; Spain where by contrast the Catholic

---

2 See for a recent example the discussion about a discussion paper in the German CSU emphasising the German 'order of values on a Christian basis' in the context of limiting the influx of refugees. Online source: https://www. bayernkurier.de/wp-content/uploads/2016/09/Klarer-Kurs-bei-der-Zuwanderung-Vorlage.pdf, accessed on 21 November 2016.

3 See Casanova, *Public Religions in the Modern World.*

Church keeps struggling from the aftereffects of its close alliance with Franco's dictatorship; Brazil where the Church has for the first time managed to emancipate itself from the shackles of its long-time close association with the state. Casanova chose his final two examples from the USA in order to illustrate the public role of churches within civil society: the rise of the so-called 'religious right' as a transformation of American Protestantism, and the development of the American Catholic Church from a ghettoised subculture into a self-confident public voice.

Casanova's analysis led him to a twofold conclusion: first, the salient trend in religious life since the late 1970s has been "deprivatisation."[4] Secondly, contrary to common assumptions, a long-term close association between church and state does not enhance the church's public relevance, but hampers it. The church becomes little more than a department of the state, and its public engagement, including its contribution to social and political controversies, is inevitably tainted by this association. Often, these churches find it difficult to distinguish their specific, religious message from the essentially political context in which they are embedded.[5] Characteristically thus, the churches with longstanding ties to their respective governments, in Casanova's analysis these were the Catholic churches in Spain and Brazil, were far less successful as public agents than their counterparts in the US and Poland – two countries which, in spite of obvious differences, shared the radical separation between church and state (at least until 1989). Ultimately, Casanova concludes that "only public religions at the level of civil society are consistent with modern universalistic principles and with modern differentiated structures."[6]

C. Religion as a Source of Identity

My own approach here will be different not least because, unlike Casanova, I am not a social scientist but a theologian with historical interests. But my results will in many ways echo those yielded by his research: I too shall seek to show that it is far from evident that in today's world religion has ceased to perform a public or social role. This function may recede in-

4 Ibid., p. 10.

5 See ibid., chs. 3 and 5.

6 Ibid., p. 219.

to the background in times of social and political stability, but it is ready to come to the fore as soon as the latter becomes more elusive.

In arguing this case, however, my ultimate interest is different or at least more specific than Casanova's was. I am not going to consider any form of social or political activity in which religious communities may engage, but shall enquire into their potential or actual role for social integration and collective identity. This, it seems to me, is a much more serious, problematic, and contentious issue than the more general assumption that religious communities have their part to play in the social and political realm. The latter may pose a problem for an extreme interpretation of religion as 'private' as it was understood, for example, in the former communist countries in Eastern Europe, but, as Casanova has convincingly shown, it can be integrated into a pluralistic framework as long as churches understand themselves as agents within civil society and agree to play by its rules.[7]

If religion underwrites collective identity, however, a religious community (and probably only one or only a few) will occupy a unique and privileged position in society and state by virtue of its ability to stem the centrifugal forces that threaten to compartmentalise and even atomise societies.[8] This evidently is a rather major claim with considerable political, legal and even financial implications. Not surprisingly therefore it has been, and continues to be, controversial: it is easy to see that it exists in tension, to say the least, with the principle of the separation of church and state which, albeit to various degrees and in different forms, underlies most modern democratic systems. It also has serious implications for religious pluralism which it endangers on account of the privileges extended to one religion over against all others.

In fact, one may take this consideration one step further and suspect that a strong link between collective religious and political identities unmasks religious pluralism as an illusion. For if religion is aligned to col-

---

7 This is not to deny the serious tensions that can emerge (and have emerged more recently) when religious groups struggle to accept social and political developments on topics such as gay rights and the end of life.

8 The need to preserve social cohesion in the face of impending 'anomy' has been a central concern in modern political thought at least since Thomas Hobbes declared the 'natural state' of human society to be bellum omnium contra omnes. Emile Durkheim famously saw religion essentially as society's cohesive force. See Durkheim, *The Elementary Forms of Religious Life*, 1995, p. 429.

lective identity, might one not conclude that it can only be either conducive or detrimental to the flourishing of a particular society? In other words, will not perhaps the existence of a minority religion pose an actual threat to the cohesion of the society? This certainly was right into the nineteenth century the suspicion towards Roman Catholics in countries such as England or Prussia (we shall see more of this later on). Along the same lines, however, a French conservative could equally lash out against the Protestants and their subversive influence on his country:

> Louis XIV trampled Protestantism, and he died in his bed shining with glory and laden with years. Louis XVI caressed it, and he died on the scaffold.[9]

For the author of these lines, who of course was no other than the notorious Joseph de Maistre,[10] the mere existence of a sizeable minority unwilling to join in with majority rituals and accept their values was sufficient to challenge and undermine social and political stability. Was this merely a problem of early modern Europe with absolutist monarchies built on religious establishment? Without denying that acceptance of religious pluralism is deeply built into the self-definition of twenty-first century Western democracies, it is difficult not to recognise in the distinctive mix of apprehension and suspicion characteristic of many instinctive responses to Islam today an attitude remarkably similar to that expressed by de Maistre two centuries ago.

The question about the relationship between religion and collective identity thus takes us right to the heart of two central problems of modern Western nation states: how can they have stable existence in a state of internal peace, and, secondly, how can and should religion be integrated into such a commonwealth? I have neither the space nor the competence to sketch these two issues even in their broadest possible outlines; for my present topic it is, however, crucial to see that they have framed the debate about Christianity and national identity in Europe and North America at least since the nineteenth century. I shall now illustrate this with three examples from the nineteenth century which, I hope, will show how diverse the responses were while also demonstrating some crucial similarities.

---

9 See de Maistre, "Réflexions sur le protestantisme," 1874, pp. 8, 82; quoted from Armenteros, "Preparing the Russian Revolution: Maistre and Uvarov on the history of knowledge," 2011, p. 224.

10 See on de Maistre: Berlin, *Freedom and its Betrayal: Six Enemies of Human Liberty*, 2003, pp. 131-154.

D. Historical Interlude: Three Narratives from the Nineteenth Century

I. John Keble: Disestablishment as National Apostasy

My first example takes us back to Britain in the early 1830s. This was a time of considerable change in the relationship between church and state. The so-called Corporation and Tests Act from 1673, which made an affiliation with the Church of England practically the precondition for any public office, had been repealed in 1828.[11] In the following year, the Roman Catholic Relief Act was a decisive step towards Catholic emancipation. Even so, the predominantly Catholic population in Ireland, which since 1800 had been united to Britain in the Act of Union, continued to pay tithes to the established Anglican Church of Ireland. This unsurprisingly led to considerable tensions culminating in the so-called Tithe War of the 1830s. To remedy this intolerable situation, a bill was introduced into Parliament in 1833 seeking to reduce the number of Irish Anglican bishoprics with a view to using the income generated by these sees for the purposes that had previously been levied on Irish Catholic taxpayers.

In this situation, a number of academics and churchmen (most of them were both) in Oxford joined up to organise resistance against this development. They were angered in particular by the role played by Robert Peel, Home Secretary under the Duke of Wellington and Member of Parliament for Oxford University. Peel had been elected by Oxford not least on account of his staunch opposition to Catholic emancipation (in recognition of his "services to Protestantism"[12]), but had under mounting pressure changed his position and voted for the repeal of the Corporation and Tests Act as well as the subsequent Roman Catholic Relief Act. Consequently, the first action by the defenders of the Anglican status quo at Oxford was a campaign aimed to oust him from his parliamentary seat. In this they succeeded, but this did nothing to prevent continuing changes to the fabric of Britain's religious establishment; in fact, Peel himself stayed in government for the time being, as he was returned for the 'rotten borough' of Westbury.

---

11 See here and in what follows Gelpi, "14 July 1833: John Keble's Assize Sermon, National Apostasy," at http://www.branchcollective.org/?ps_articles=barbara-charlesworth-gelpi-14-july-1833-john-kebles-assize-sermon-national-apostasy, accessed on 30 July 2014.

12 Ibid.

One of the main campaigners against Peel was John Keble (1792-1866), an immensely talented young theologian and writer whose *The Christian Year*, published in 1827, became one of the most enduringly popular collections of religious poems throughout the nineteenth century and secured its author the election to Oxford's Professorship of Poetry in 1831.

Keble's most influential intervention in the political and religious developments of his time was a sermon preached on 14 July 1833.[13] For this he chose the topic of 'national apostasy' – the apostasy of the nation was, of all things, the disestablishment of the Church of Ireland which Keble saw emerging on the horizon.[14] For the preacher, such a prospect amounted to the nation's renunciation of its age-old pact with God himself. Keble based his argument on an Old Testament text, Samuel's critique of the popular wish in Israel for a monarchy (1 Samuel 12,23) which, according to him, offered the analogy not that a Christian people should not have a king, but that its special relationship with God must not be affected by contemporary popular opinion.

He speaks of

> [...] a nation, having for centuries acknowledged, as an essential part of its theory of government, that, as a Christian nation, she is also a part of Christ's Church, and bound, in all her legislation and policy, by the fundamental rules of that Church – the case is, I say, conceivable, of a government and people, so constituted, deliberately throwing off the restraint, which in many respects such a principle would impose on them, nay, disavowing the principle itself; and that, on the plea, that other states, as flourishing or more so in regard of wealth and dominion, do well enough without it.[15]

Keble is very careful in this text to avoid too explicitly political overtones. Throughout the sermon he does not mention words such as 'establishment' and does not commend any one model of the relationship between throne and altar as normative.[16] Instead, he insists that the Church of England and the Church of Ireland are the 'apostolical churches' of these countries and for this reason deserve special recognition by the govern-

---

13 John Henry Newman famously made this sermon the beginning of the Oxford Movement: *Apologia Pro Vita Sua*, 1994, p. 50.

14 It finally happened in 1869 through the Irish Church Act.

15 Keble, "National Apostasy Considered in a Sermon Preached in St Mary's Oxford, before His Majesty's judges of Assize, on Sunday, July 14, 1833," 1833, p. 12.

16 See Turner, *John Henry Newman: The Challenge to Evangelical Religion*, 2002, p. 70.

ment as well as the people. Changes to the role of religion in British society, as envisaged by the government of the time, are therefore illegitimate attempts to interfere in the relationship between God and his people.

One of the dangers about which Keble specifically warns his audience is the growing acceptance of religious diversity; at the time this was mainly confined to Protestant dissenters and Roman Catholics:

> One of the most alarming, as a symptom, is the growing indifference, in which men indulge themselves, to other men's religious sentiments. Under the guise of charity and toleration we are come almost to this pass; *that no difference, in matters of faith, is to disqualify for our approbation and confidence, whether in public or domestic life.* Can we conceal it from ourselves, that every year the practice is becoming more common, of trusting men unreservedly in the most delicate and important matters, without one serious inquiry, whether they do not hold principles which make it impossible for them to be loyal to their Creator, Redeemer, and Sanctifier? Are not offices conferred, partnerships formed, intimacies courted, – nay, (what is almost too painful to think of,) do not parents commit their children to be educated, do they not encourage them to intermarry, in houses, on which Apostolical Authority would rather teach them to set a mark, as unfit to be entered by a faithful servant of Christ?[17]

Keble's sharp rejection of religious plurality is important as an indicator of his concern for religion as a source of national identity. His dire warning that liberal toleration for deviant religious views poses a grave risk to the wellbeing of the nation is analogous to de Maistre's invectives against Protestantism. Yet while de Maistre couched his critique of religious deviancy in political language, Keble shies away from the latter and prefers to express his concern as one of religious truth alone.

The main line of argument is, nevertheless, unmistakeable. As far as the purposes of this paper are concerned, Keble represents a first and, in a way, the most expected response from a religious leader to a tendency to loosen the bonds between church and state: the attempt is denounced as an illegitimate attack on God's own prerogative. The special bond between God and nation is presented as sacred and the source of unequivocal benefits to everyone. Neither the people nor the government are permitted to change it.

Thus far, Keble's position can legitimately be characterised as conservative. Yet it would be facile to reduce him and his allies to reactionaries going against the grain of modern developments. In spite of his defence of

17 Keble, "National Apostasy Considered," p. 15 (italics in original).

the close bond establishment had created between Christianity and the British people, Keble perceived clearly the ambiguous nature of its political aspect, as it allowed politicians, parliamentarians and members of the government to make decisions in the religious realm on the basis of political expediency.

So it may be no coincidence that throughout the sermon Keble refers to the English people and to the English nation rather than the monarch as the counterpart of God in this particular relationship. Keble's analogy is carefully chosen: the people of Israel were in a special relationship with God. For this reason, their attempt to anoint a king is a violation of the terms of that covenant and, consequently, undermines their specific identity as a people. The allusion to identity is evident from the emphasis both in the biblical text and in Keble's sermon on the contrast with other nations. Keble gives no particular reason why the Anglican Churches of England and Ireland are apostolical churches more than, for example, the Roman Catholic Church, but he is clear that looking beyond the nation's borders for guidance in this question is as wrong today as it was wrong for the Ancient Israelites to emulate the example of the Near Eastern monarchies of their time. Preserving their particular, even idiosyncratic form of religious establishment therefore was imperative if the British nation wanted to stay faithful to its own character and preserve its vitality in Keble's own time.

For all its conservative overtones, then, Keble's sermon contains a whiff of the recognition that any defence of the ecclesiastical *status quo* could only work if religious identity became anchored in the populace as a whole. It is for this reason that the Oxford movement reformed the Church of England especially with regard to its roots in the general population: many of its proponents worked with the industrial working classes and devoted themselves to the care for those suffering in the horrendous conditions of the country's slums.

Keble's response to the threat to religious establishment in his own time, then, is less straightforward than might appear at first sight. In some ways one may even say that he inverts its traditional logic: the royal privilege extended to a single faith *produced* religious homogeneity by marginalising and ultimately excluding those unwilling to abide by its terms. It was therefore in the first instance a political tool chosen by monarchical rulers to enhance the nation's coherence and stability. Its modern variant, by contrast, *presupposes* the existence of religious homogeneity and argues from there for its political and social benefits. This modern argument, characteristically, is often presented by representatives of the churches themselves in opposition of political tendencies to loosen the bonds between church and nation.

In this inversion, however, lies the weakness of this position. There are many reasons to believe that religions if left to themselves tend towards plurality; charismatic religious leaders may be able to rouse popular opinion on behalf of their group for a while, but most historical evidence would suggest that the withdrawal of political privilege for a particular faith leads to increased religious diversity including abstention from religion.[18] Keble therefore, quite understandably, warned against the dangers of what he called "the growing indifference, in which men indulge themselves, to other men's religious sentiments." If for all intents and purposes it does not matter which faith a person holds; if there is complete civic equality between people of all religions: what does it even mean to speak of a Christian nation any longer?

II. Nikolai Grundtvig and the Cause of National Religion

Keble, while a religious rebel of sorts and at odds with the Anglican establishment in the Oxford of his time, hoped to regain for his nation a Christian identity in the traditional sense of the word. Yet not everyone in the nineteenth century was orthodox. On the contrary, part of the fascination of this period in religious history derives from the emergence of various novel forms of religion within the Christian churches and beyond. My second example, while in some ways staying close to Keble, illustrates this trend.

The Danish intellectual Nikolai Grundtvig (1783–1872)[19] had a complex religious biography; his period of significance for religion in Denmark began with what he himself called his 'matchless discovery' (mageløse opdagelse) in the 1820s: "his insistence that the true Church is defined by and founded on the oral transmission of the Apostles' creed, and not on scripture."[20] The essence of this discovery was the devaluation of the 'dead letter' of the Bible over against the 'living faith' of a Chris-

18 Cf. Bruce, *God is Dead: Secularization in the West*, p. 36.

19 For what follows I rely heavily on Backhouse, *Kierkegaard's Critique of Christian Nationalism*, 2011.

20 Ibid., p. 67.

tian community. Grundtvig then combined this religious insight with a theory of historical development and on this basis assigned to the Nordic peoples in his own time the task to "demonstrate to the world authentic Christianity".[21] That this understanding of Christianity was rather different from the official Lutheranism preached by the Danish state church only increased its attractiveness to Grundtvig who, as a political thinker, was deeply concerned about growing German and in particular Prussian influence and hoped to kindle the spirit of Danish nationalism as an antidote against this tendency.

Like his quasi-contemporary Keble, Grundtvig sought to re-establish Christianity at the centre of Danish society. Also comparable is his clear perception that the subject of such a national church now has to be the people. This line of thought is more extenuated in the Danish thinker, however, who is much closer than the English priest to the new European nationalism, rooted in Romanticism, which he seeks to integrate into his own idiosyncratic version of Christianity.

These similarities notwithstanding, we find in Grundtvig a second and very different type of religious response to the debate about religion and national identity in the nineteenth century: an unashamed alignment of the cause of Christianity with that of nascent nationalism. In the words of a recent scholar,

> It is not an exaggeration to call Grundtvig's theology 'nationalistic'. Nationalism is not an afterthought or an addendum to Grundtvig's theology, it is integral to it, and Grundtvig's concern to foster national identity has rightly been described as "the crimson thread" that runs throughout the span of his writings.[22]

For Keble, as we have seen, the emphasis on national identity is carefully and subtly woven into a narrative informed by traditional Christianity. Grundtvig, by contrast, brings modern ideals of national cohesion and national identity much more to the centre of his own thinking and makes no apology for demanding fundamental alterations to the orthodox fabric of the Christian religion in order to make it fit for the modern world.

Grundtvig and his followers always remained firmly within the tradition of the Danish Lutheran church, but it is easy to see that his approach

---

21 Ibid., pp. 68-69.

22 Ibid., p. 68. The reference in Backhouse is to Thanning, *N. F. S. Grundtvig. Aus dem Leben eines kritischen dänischen Theologen*, 1972, p. 15.

made the transition between Christian nationalism and national Christianity an easy one. Motivations for further moves along this trajectory are not difficult to identify: with its universalistic character, Christianity has often been pronounced ultimately incompatible with the necessities of political identity formation. For this reason, Jean-Jacques Rousseau already opined that the Christian tradition could not provide for the civil religion his perfect state needed. Add to that the nineteenth-century pressure on Christianity to adapt its traditional character to the insights produced by modern science and historiography, and the allure of modernised national Christianities becomes as obvious as their regular, albeit short-lived, appearance throughout the nineteenth and early twentieth centuries.

III. German Unification and the Quest for Protestant Identity

My third example is different in kind from the first two in that I focus not on an individual person but a country. Germany was newly unified in 1871. It was the largest of the many new nation states created in Europe during the nineteenth and early twentieth century, desperately trying to find their own sense of national identity. One important aspect of the German quest for national identity was the attempt to define itself as Protestant. The choice of this particular label was neither historically nor theologically innocent: after all, there had been century-long divisions within the Protestant tradition. In the German territories, the most enduring and significant of them was the one separating Lutheran and Calvinist churches. Administrative attempts to overcome this division, such as the Prussian Union of 1817,[23] encountered fierce resistance, especially from the Lutherans.[24]

What exactly a Protestant identity was, was therefore far from obvious. In fact, it is arguable that such an identity was in many ways only the result of nineteenth-century developments; and these developments were at least partly inspired by political concerns for national identity. The intentional character of this construction of identity is evident, for example, in buildings such as the huge Berlin Cathedral, inaugurated in 1905, as a 'Protestant' counterpart to Rome's St Peter, or the multi-denominational

23 See Landry, *Ecumenism, Memory, and German Nationalism, 1817-1917*, 2013, pp. 9-17.

24 See Nipperdey, *Germany from Napoleon to Bismarck: 1800-1866*, 2014, p. 382.

Memorial Church of the Protestation of Speyer erected in remembrance of the Diet of Speyer of 1529, from which the term Protestant originated.

Another central element for the construction of national, Protestant identity in nineteenth-century Germany was the person of Martin Luther. The Reformer was presented as standing at the twin-origin of Protestant Christianity and the modern German nation, its language, literature, and music. Like no other historical figure he could therefore be appealed to as vouchsafing the formative role of 'Protestantism' for German identity.[25]

The German case shows a new facet of our topic: since the nineteenth century, new nations or at least nations without a clearly defined historical narrative or genealogy of their identity actively sought out the ideological support of religious communities.[26] The latter willingly agreed – after all they were previously often facing the same issues John Keble had protested against, the increasing erosion of their traditional position of privilege and political, social, and educational influence. The advantage could therefore appear mutual: a church that had lost its sway over much of the educated public at that time or was in the process of losing it came out in support of a political entity desperately in need of identity. It is for this reason that, in the words of one leading scholar, "the success of nationalism [i.e. in the Wilhelmian era] could also be read as the success of 're-christianisation'."[27] The newly constructed 'Protestant' Christianity of Prussian-dominated Germany provided the newly created German nation state of the late nineteenth and the early twentieth century with a much-needed source of collective identity and gained in turn a reinvigoration of its public acceptance as the guardian of a concept which at that time was cherished by large parts of the population.

Yet the German case also reveals the Janus face of this kind of attempt. For Germany at the time was, of course, far from being a Protestant nation. While a majority of the inhabitants of the Reich belonged to Lutheran and Reformed churches, Catholics still made up more than one third of the total population. And so what may have helped many Germans develop

25 See Dewhurst, *The Legacy of Luther: National Identity and State-Building in Early-Nineteenth Century Germany*, 2013, p. 64, at http://scholarworks.gsu.edu/cgi/viewcontent.cgi?article=1065&context=history_theses, accessed on 23 December 2016.

26 See Wood, *Christianity and National Identity in Twentieth-Century Europe*, 2016.

27 Graf, "Dechristianisierung. Zur Problemgeschichte eines kultur-politischen Topos," 1997, p. 64.

their feelings of national identity in the Wilhelmian era produced considerable difficulties for those who were effectively excluded by the decidedly Protestant brand of this political religion. Catholics, consequently, felt consistently the strain between their religious and their national identities, a conflict that came to a head in the so-called *Kulturkampf* (1871-87). Most notorious, and rightly so, became the pressure on the Jewish population which faced an increasing confrontation with an aggressive nationalism constructed in a way that would by definition exclude them from its notion of community.[28]

IV. Summary

The list of examples could easily be extended. Yet the three I have chosen illustrate, arguably, the major scenarios that have arisen as a result of the historical transformations in Europe over the past two hundred years. I have ignored attempts to replace the Christian religion with an alternative source of collective identity, such as the so-called political religions of National Socialism and Communism. The reason for this omission is not that I consider those experiments insignificant but that the purview of my paper is more narrowly concerned with the role of Christianity. For the same reason I have also excluded the fascinating case of American civil religion.

Within these limitations, I hope that my account so far demonstrates that and how the argument for a relation between religion and collective identity has been made in very different guises and yet displays some common features. By way of a brief summary, the following may perhaps be said:

1. Increasing religious pluralism, or at least the need to recognise this more than previously, casts into doubt traditional forms of religious establishment.
2. In response to this development, ecclesiastical and, more broadly, religious figures have found their sphere of influence under threat and searched actively for new inroads that would allow for their voice to be heard in crucial political and cultural matters.

---

28 See Pickus, "Native Born Strangers: Jews, Catholics and the German Nation," 2004, pp. 141-156.

3. There is general recognition that the 'people' must be the new point of reference if the identity of church and nation is to be upheld. This provides for a link with emergent forms of nationalism and could lead to the development of novel forms of national Christianity.
4. Newly emerging or transforming nations clamoured for ideological support and often gratefully accepted the moral and historical narratives that religious communities can provide.

E. Religion and Collective Identity Today: Where do we stand?

Considering these nineteenth century developments, I would now suggest, can shed light on the relationship of religion and collective identity today if we take note of both similarities and dissimilarities. In many ways we are still – to use Charles Taylor's phrase – the Victorians' 'contemporaries'. Few if any of the problems troubling our ancestors during that period have entirely gone away though all of them have changed, some arguably beyond recognition. The public role of religion and its significance for identity formation are hardly an exception to this rule.

The first interesting observation is that of the three models the second, which at first sight might seem the most modern option, is the most obviously outdated one. After a promising career throughout the nineteenth and way into the twentieth century, the idea that a modernised form of national Christianity could supplant the more traditional versions of the faith today appears a remote possibility if that. Its erstwhile success, of course, is at least partly to be blamed for its more recent fall from grace. Any attempt to revitalise this kind of project would be tarnished from its associations with totalitarian regimes in the earlier twentieth century.[29] Yet I do not think that this historical link is the only or even the main reason why an idea such as Grundtvig's seems so far-fetched and unattractive today. Rather, none of the modernised forms of traditional religion have managed to shed the air of artificiality and technicality; their purpose was too obvious to make them convincing and successful *as* religions. None of them, in a word, has lived up to Durkheim's prophetic vision:

29 See Heschel, *The Aryan Jesus: Christian Theologians and the Bible in Nazi Germany*, 2008.

> A day will come when our societies once again will know hours of creative effervescence during which new ideals will again spring forth and new formulas emerge to guide humanity for a time.[30]

It is true, some commentators speak of 'consumerism' as the official religion of Western, secular countries, but whatever truth such an observation may contain, it is insignificant for the larger question under investigation in the present paper as there is no evidence that an obsession with material goods provides for the communal structures that made traditional religions and some of their modern successors attractive from the point of view of identity formation.

It may surprise that the first option, by contrast, has proved more resilient. Religious establishment continues to exist in parts of the United Kingdom as well as some other European countries. In fact, the number of countries that recognise the special significance of one or a small number of churches for the nation's identity is considerably larger and includes countries such as Poland and Ireland. Thus far, Keble's worst fears have not materialised. The theologian's stern warnings could not, however, stem the tide of religious diversification, and today the United Kingdom is one of the most religiously diverse countries in Europe. Consequently, today's defenders of religious establishment do not any longer rail against religious plurality but, on the contrary, argue that the co-existence of people of various faiths is compatible with the established status of the Church of England. Thus Nigel Biggar, in his brilliant *Between Kin and Cosmopolis: An Ethic of the Nation*,[31] points to this fact as an argument against the critics of the *status quo*: apparently, so his argument, the remaining ties between the Anglican Church and the British monarchy do not make this country inhospitable to people of different faiths. In fact, apart from the remaining ban on a Roman Catholic monarch, there is no single law discriminating on the basis of religion; on the contrary, such discrimination is forbidden by strict equality legislation.

Yet while this argument weakens the claims of those who reject religious establishment as incompatible with religious pluralism, it is equally hard to see what in the circumstances the specific advantages of such a settlement are? Biggar sets out his case by suggesting that nations are in need of a moral foundation; liberalism, he charges, is in danger of creating

30 See Durkheim, *The Elementary Forms of Religious Life*, p. 429.

31 Biggar, *Between Kin and Cosmopolis: An Ethic of the Nation*, 2014.

a moral vacuum that can be filled by the enemies of freedom. This is an important point to which I shall return, but whatever the legitimacy of this observation, it remains unclear – and I suspect Keble would have agreed – how a church can provide for such a foundation if its role has become so largely ceremonial as it was bound to happen once the state had assumed religious neutrality for all practical purposes? Biggar points to the implicit admission by liberal theorists that political freedom must have limits, but fails to mention that in the United Kingdom these limits are in no obvious way defined with regard to the teachings of the Church of England. Instead, for all practical purposes, British legislators adjudicate between individual rights and their restrictions in the public interest on the basis of the same liberal and utilitarian principles that are applied in other secular Western countries as well.

In spite of its perseverance, therefore, the traditional model of religious establishment or even quasi-establishment has in practice run its course. The reason was precisely identified by Keble and before him de Maistre when they pointed to the incompatibility of this model with religious pluralism – they were right even though the purpose of their argument was the rejection of pluralism. For this reason, defenders of the special relationship between a particular faith and a nation today find themselves between a rock and a hard place: they either insist on the necessity to maintain the specific identity mandated by that religion and face challenges of religious discrimination; or they emphasise the compatibility of religious establishment with religious pluralism but then struggle to explain the tangible benefits of the settlement they defend.

In their current coexistence with religious pluralism on the one hand and political and legal secularism on the other, contemporary forms of this model pose little danger to any political or religious agenda. It is therefore quite possible that they will continue to exist for some time if only by virtue of the law of inertia. Yet they offer little room for development as the force that brought them about, the political support for religious homogeneity, has long ceased to exist, and the promise of religious leaders that the factual existence of a predominant religious culture could lend support of collective identity, sounds increasingly hollow in the face of radical religious pluralism.

This leaves the third model, and I would indeed argue that it offers the most powerful template for the interplay of religion and national identity today. The German case from the late nineteenth century maps almost perfectly on to the much more recent situation of many Eastern and South-

Eastern European, so-called transition states. Countries across the region have, since the fall of communism very consciously referred to their specific religious roots as part of their search for a new national identity.[32] This became perhaps most evident to a wider public at the time of the Yugoslav Wars, when the various parties aligned their identities to their Orthodox, Catholic, and Muslim traditions respectively.[33] It is difficult not to be struck by the irony of the fact that this happened in places in which organised religion had been suppressed for the better part of the twentieth century. The same, of course, is supremely the case in Russia where Vladimir Putin has skilfully played up Russian Orthodoxy as an important element of the country's historical identity.[34] In all these cases, the churches have willingly played along, and it is easy to see why. Whether in the long run this strategy is successful (even in the merely institutional sense of the term), is, of course, very much an open question. Still, if we seek to understand the enduring allure of an alignment of religious and national identities, this is the type most worthy of consideration as it is most likely to be replicated wherever new political entities clamour for a sense of identity in the interest of internal stability on the basis of affective civic attachment to the nation. It is this model, therefore, that I will have primarily in mind in my subsequent theological assessment and critique of the use of religion in support of collective identity.

F. Religion and Collective Identity: A Theological Critique

My aim so far has been to describe and analyse the predominant forms in which the idea of religion as a prop of collective identity has been introduced since the nineteenth century and into our own time. What I have not yet asked is whether or how this idea can be justified. The latter question can be approached in several ways. One might, for example, consider how evident it is that particular religions have this effect. One would then have to look comparatively at nations with very different religious settlements and see how they fare in terms of stability as well as, broadly speaking,

32 Leustean, *Eastern Christianity and Politics in the Twenty-First Century*, 2014. I am grateful to Mr Andrey Levitskiy for pointing me to this publication as well as that mentioned in note 30.

33 Perica, *Balkan Idols: Religion and Nationalism in Yugoslav States*, 2002.

34 See Fagan, *Believing in Russia: Religious Policy after Communism*, 2012.

success. Another interesting question might be how realistic it is that this kind of settlement can be reintroduced or renewed in societies that have become religiously more diverse.

I shall, however, leave these legitimate questions to others better qualified than myself to assess them. My own aim in the remainder of this chapter will be to look at this problem from the point of view of the religious communities themselves, specifically the Christian churches. On the basis of their self-understanding, which it is the task of the theologian to elucidate, is it a legitimate expectation that they should provide this kind of ideological support for nations and similar communities? Should they understand themselves as providers for the values that hold society together?[35]

The need for this question is evident, I believe, even for the non-theologian. An agreement to make use of a religion in support of collective national identity is not without its risks for both sides that enter into it. Casanova, whose study I mentioned earlier in my paper, pointed out the utterly negative consequences for the churches in Spain and Brazil from their close association with a succession of political regimes.[36] The Church of England has at some point been called "the Tory party at prayer" – and this surely was not meant as a compliment.[37] In Germany it is also arguable that the least religious areas today, especially the traditionally Lutheran territories in the East, are the ones that historically saw the closest alliance between 'throne and altar'.[38] Generally, one could say that churches (or for that matter, religious communities) tying themselves to certain political settlements share in both their success and their failure.

But my concern goes beyond the pragmatic disadvantages potentially resulting from a close alliance with a nation state. How persuasive is specifically the Christian justification of collective identities? How easily is it compatible with the fundamental ideas of that religion? It is in this

35 I have addressed this question elsewhere. See Zachhuber, "Churches as 'Value Mediators'? Religion and Collective Identity in Germany," 2007, pp. 187-200.

36 See Casanova, *Public Religions in the Modern World.*

37 The phrase goes back to the preacher and suffragist Agnes Maude Royden as reported by *The Times of London* on 17 July 1917.

38 Detailed references in Hölscher, *Datenatlas zur religiösen Geographie im protestantischen Deutschland. Von der Mitte des 19. Jahrhunderts bis zum Zweiten Weltkrieg*, 4 vols., 2001.

sense that my paper in its title promised a theological assessment of a political problem.

To facilitate this assessment I start from the observation that any definition of identity works with both inclusion and exclusion.[39] At one level this may seem trivial and innocent enough: to be British means, for example, not to be French or German. To be Polish means to be neither Russian nor Czech. And yet it is evident that in most cases this formation of one's own identity by defining it over against others, is by no means innocent: In different ways both English and German national identities have crucially involved the notion of the French as 'the other'; and this idea contains a considerable degree of hostility which could, and was, used to justify competition, enmity, and even warfare.

Today we are aware of the constructed character of these identities: the other who needs to be excluded from our understanding of the self changes depending on the situation. This is particularly evident in the case of religious identities: a notion now extremely popular all over the Western world is that of a 'Judaeo-Christian tradition' which is usually brought up in order to emphasise the need to keep Islam at bay in Europe. Yet it is perhaps not too cynical to point out that one hundred years ago a considerable part of European Christians felt that the religious and cultural 'other' who had to be excluded was precisely Judaism. The idea of a Judaeo-Christian tradition would have made no sense to these people (or indeed, I suspect) to anyone prior to the 1950s. If we go another fifty or hundred years back, we find that 'Christian' as a generic marker of identity meant little given that collective identities were formed along confessional lines. 'Christendom' usually mattered in confrontation with the (Muslim) Turks.

My point is this: the truly worrying aspect of Christian contributions to political and social identity formation comes into view if we zoom in on those whose exclusion is the precondition for the consolidation of collective identity: the Protestant identity in late nineteenth century Germany, as I have pointed out before, came at the cost of the marginalised Catholic population and even more dramatically the Jewish minority. Contemporary attempts to found national (or even European) identity on its 'Judaeo-Christian' heritage is similar in that the implicit connotation of this

39 For a more detailed treatment of the problems resulting from the use of exclusion in Christian constructions of identity see my "The Rhetoric of Evil and the Definition of Christian Identity," 2013, pp. 193-217.

rhetoric is the exclusion of immigrant religions that have grown and increased in importance over the last decades.

This mechanism may at some level be inevitable: social entities are apparently in need of an identity and, as I argued above, exclusion seems to be part of how this operates. Be this, however, as it may, it seems more than doubtful that this practice is even remotely compatible with the fundamental tenet of the Christian faith. It would take more than the space of a single chapter to develop this insight in more detail, but in a nutshell I would say that this fundamental tenet can be precisely identified as the turn towards those who are otherwise excluded. The reader of the gospel is directed to notice and regard those who are cast aside; those who become invisible on the margins of society (cf. Mt 25, 31-46): the paradox of the crucified God, which turns the object of capital punishment into an object of worship, was certainly not lost on the contemporaries of the early Christians.[40]

This is not to deny that the Christian Church has itself over the centuries contributed to the exclusion of others – nonbelievers, heretics, Muslims, Jews etc.[41] It has, and it has also, in fact, contributed to political identity formation not least in European nation states for the better part of the last millennium. While all this is evident to all, the case can and should still be made that the decisions that led to these policies were at the least deeply problematic, inspired by the kind of logic Fyodor Dostoevsky has masterfully illustrated in his parable of the Grand Inquisitor.[42]

Where does this, however, leave the problem of religion and collective identity? If there is need for it to be provided, and if (for the sake of the argument) we assume that 'religion' can serve this purpose, does not the refusal of one religious community to offer this service simply mean that another one will do the job instead? Is there not, in other words, a burden of responsibility placed on certain churches whose rejection would be a sign of irresponsibility? A full answer to these questions cannot be given in the present place, but I would propose that the best answer to this conundrum today is that collective identity is specifically to be found in the

---

40 As the infamous Alexamenos graffiti shows; cf. http://penelope.uchicago.edu/~grout/encyclopaedia_romana/gladiators/graffito.html, accessed on 23 December 2016.

41 See Zachhuber, "The Rhetoric of Evil and the Definition of Christian Identity," 2013, pp. 195-200.

42 See Dostoevsky, *The Brothers Karamasov*, 2005, part II, ch. 5.

acceptance of plurality and openness to what Britain's former Chief Rabbi Jonathan Sacks has called the "dignity of difference."[43] If this is so, then perhaps this kind of identity formation could indeed be a contribution religious communities in the Judeo-Christian tradition can make to contemporary Western societies.

Bibliography

Armenteros, Carolina, "Preparing the Russian Revolution: Maistre and Uvarov on the history of knowledge," in *Joseph de Maistre and his European Readers: From Friedrich von Getz to Isaiah Berlin*, ed. Carolina Armenteros and Richard A. Lebrun, Brill: Leiden, 2011, pp. 213-248.

Asad, Talal, *Formations of the Secular*, Stanford: Stanford University Press, 2003.

Backhouse, Stephen, *Kierkegaard's Critique of Christian Nationalism*, Oxford: Oxford University Press, 2011.

Berlin, Isaiah, *Freedom and its Betrayal: Six Enemies of Human Liberty*, ed. Henry Hardy, Missoula: Pimlico, 2003.

Biggar, Nigel, *Between Kin and Cosmopolis: An Ethic of the Nation*, Cambridge: James Clark, 2014.

Bruce, Steve, *God is Dead: Secularization in the West*, Oxford: Wiley-Blackwell, 2002.

Cady, Linell E., and Tracy Fessenden, *Religion, the Secular, and the Politics of Sexual Difference*, New York: Columbia University Press, 2013.

Casanova, José, *Public Religions in the Modern World*, Chicago: University of Chicago Press, 1994.

Connolly, William E., *Why I am not a Secularist*, Minneapolis: University of Minnesota Press, 1999.

de Maistre, Joseph, "Réflexions sur le protestantisme," in *Oeuvres complètes*, 14 vols., Lyons: Vitte and Perrussel, 1874.

Dewhurst, Ruth L., *The Legacy of Luther: National Identity and State-Building in Early-Nineteenth Century Germany*, Georgia: Thesis Georgia State University, 2013.

Dostoevsky, Fyodor, *The Brothers Karamasov*, tr. C. Garnett, Mineola, New York: Dover, 2005.

Durkheim, Emile, *The Elementary Forms of Religious Life*, tr. Karen E. Fields, Karen E., New York: The Free Press, 1995.

Fagan, Geraldine, *Believing in Russia: Religious Policy after Communism*, London: Routledge, 2012.

43 Sacks, *The Dignity of Difference: How to Avoid the Clash of Civilisations*, 2004.

Gelpi, Barbara Charlesworth, "14 July 1833: John Keble's Assize Sermon, National Apostasy," in *BRANCH: Britain, Representation and Nineteenth-Century History*, ed. Dino Franco Felluga, at http://www.branchcollective.org/?ps_articles=barbara-charlesworth-gelpi-14-july-1833-john-kebles-assize-sermon-national-apostasy.

Graf, Friedrich Wilhelm, "Dechristianisierung. Zur Problemgeschichte eines kulturpolitischen Topos," in *Säkularisierung, Dechristianisierung, Re-christianisierung im neuzeitlichen Europa. Bilanzen und Perspektiven der Forschung*, ed. Hartmut Lehmann, Göttingen: Vandenhoeck & Ruprecht, 1997, pp. 32-66.

Heschel, Susannah, *The Aryan Jesus: Christian Theologians and the Bible in Nazi Germany*, Princeton/Oxford: Princeton University Press, 2008.

Hölscher, Lucian, *Datenatlas zur religiösen Geographie im protestantischen Deutschland. Von der Mitte des 19. Jahrhunderts bis zum Zweiten Weltkrieg*, Berlin: De Gruyter, 2001.

Jakobsen, Janet A., and Anne Pellegrini, *Secularisms*, Durham, NC: Duke University Press, 2008.

Keble, John, "National Apostasy Considered in a Sermon Preached in St Mary's Oxford, before His Majesty's judges of Assize, on Sunday, July 14, 1833," Oxford: J.H. Parker, 1833.

Landry, Stan M., *Ecumenism, Memory, and German Nationalism, 1817-1917*, New York: Syracuse University Press, 2013.

Leustean, Lucian N., *Eastern Christianity and Politics in the Twenty-First Century*, London: Routledge, 2014.

Newman, John Henry, *Apologia Pro Vita Sua*, London: Penguin, 1994.

Nipperdey, Thomas, *Germany from Napoleon to Bismarck: 1800-1866,* Princeton: Princeton University Press, 2014.

Perica, Vjekoslav, *Balkan Idols: Religion and Nationalism in Yugoslav States*, Oxford: Oxford University Press, 2002.

Pickus, Keith H., "Native Born Strangers: Jews, Catholics and the German Nation," in *Religion und Nation, Nation und Religion: Beiträge zu einer ungbewältigten Geschichte*, ed. Michael Geyer and Hartmut Lehmann, Göttingen: Wallstein, 2004, pp. 141-156.

Sacks, Jonathan, *The Dignity of Difference: How to Avoid the Clash of Civilisations*, London: Continuum, 2004.

Taylor, Charles, *A Secular Age*, Cambridge MA: Harvard University Press, 2007.

Thanning, Kaj, *N. F. S. Grundtvig. Aus dem Leben eines kritischen dänischen Theologen*, tr. David Hohnen, Copenhagen: Det Dankse Selskab, 1972.

Turner, Frank M., *John Henry Newman: The Challenge to Evangelical Religion*, New Haven: Yale University Press, 2002.

Ward, Grahameorge, "The Myth of Secularism," *Telos* 167 (2014): 162-179.

Wood, John Carter, *Christianity and National Identity in Twentieth-Century Europe*, Göttingen: Vandenhoeck & Ruprecht, 2016.

Zachhuber, Johannes, "Churches as 'Value Mediators'? Religion and Collective Identity in Germany," in *Religion and Politics in the United States and Germany: Old Divisions and New Frontiers*, ed. Dagmar Pruin, Rolf Schieder, Johannes Zachhuber, Münster: LIT, 2007, pp. 187-200.

Zachhuber, Johannes, "Die Diskussion über Säkularisierung am Beginn des 21. Jahrhunderts," in *Säkularisierung: Bilanz und Perspektiven einer umstrittenen These*, ed. Christina von Braunn, Wilhelm Gräb, and Johannes Zachhuber, Münster: LIT, 2007, pp. 11-42.

Zachhuber, Johannes, "The Rhetoric of Evil and the Definition of Christian Identity," in *Vom Bösen reden/Rhetoric of Evil*, ed. Paul Fiddes, and Jochen Schmidt, Würzbung: Ergon, 2013, pp. 193-217.

Analysis of the Amendments to Articles 24 and 40 of the Political Constitution of the United Mexican States: Implications for Public Policies of Religious Diversity Management

María Concepción Medina González

A. Introduction

The basis for the legal relationship between State and Church is to be found in the Mexican Constitution of 1917. Since that date, there have been amendments to Articles 24 and 130 on few but important occasions. Before constitutional reform of 28 January 1992, Articles 24 (at the time freedom of belief) and 130 (at the time Supremacy State on Church) contained anti-clerical provisions, religious associations could not obtain legal personality and the principle of Supremacy State on Church predominated.

With the constitutional reform of 28 January 1992 to Articles 3 (right of education), 24 (at the time freedom of belief), 27 (right of property) and 130 (at the time Supremacy of State on Church), several anti-clerical provisions were derogated, religious communities and churches could obtain legal personality as "religious associations" (asociaciones religiosas) by the Ministry of Interior.

This constitutional reform showed several processes, such as: construction of laicity on the recognition of religious diversity, the visibility of the "religious minorities" at the possibility of being registered as religious associations and obtain legal personality, and recognition of religious diversity within a framework of inclusion and tolerance.

In particular, Article 130 (today Principle of Separation of State and churches) allowed the Churches and religious communities acquire legal personality once they obtain their registration as religious associations by the Ministry of Interior.

Now, the last constitutional reform to Article 24 on 19 July 2013 implied the substitution of the expression "every man" for "every person", the introduction of the right to freedom of ethical convictions, right to freedom of conscience and right to freedom of religion. It makes clear that this freedom includes the right to participate individually or collectively, both in public and in private, in ceremonies, devotions or acts of worship, provided they do not constitute an offense punishable by law. Although a prohibition is incorporated: "No one can use the public acts of expression of this freedom for political purposes, proselytism or propaganda."

Before this reform several civil and non-catholic religious associations demonstrated in about 20 states in the Mexican Republic to warn that would not allow the reform of article 24 of the Constitution, because it threatens the secular nature of the Mexican State and it considers privileges for Catholics. They expressed three arguments:

1. The intention of the reform is the dismantling of the secular state. It is intended to use it to demand clerical privileges: mainly replacement of secular education for religious instruction in public schools and control of mass media.
2. The handling of the reform in the concept of "freedom of religion". The redefinition of "freedom of religion" that the Catholic hierarchy seeks to establish, offers a tendentious and biased concept of that freedom to provide religious education in public schools as a religious privilege.
3. The consequences of reform are an affectation of the freedoms of religious minorities. For example, religious education in public schools will cause that children and adolescents who profess a different faith to Catholic are victims of acts of intolerance and discrimination. Religion is also represented as a factor of division among students professing different faiths and as an element of social polarization that will damage seriously the living together.

On the other side, the constitutional reform to Article 40 on 30 November 2012 to include the "lay character" of the State was not really necessary to know that "Laicity" is the scenario and presuppose for the effective exercise of fundamental freedoms. Laicity and religious freedom are not opposed and are not mutually excluding. Reference to an "open Laicity", "positive Laicity" or even "healthy Laicity" is made. For example, religious freedom includes the teaching of religion too, and the state has to guarantee it. The current dimension of Laicity is particularly in the field of cultural identities and protection of minorities. The issue of Laicity is not only an issue of "political" but also one of "minorities" who defend their "vulnerability". The concept of the lay state is dynamic, and is linked to social processes. In the debate on Laicity new actors are present, and not only the traditional State-Church or churches, but women, academics, homosexuals, indigenous people. Certainly "pathology" of Laicity would be to reduce religion to the private sphere alone. The formula "for greater religious freedom" less "lay state" is a fallacy. However, the exercise of religious freedom recognizes limits.

There is no doubt that the recent constitutional reforms involve two key elements of the rule of law (*Estado de derecho*): Popular sovereignty, under Article 40 of the Constitution (linked to Article 39) and human rights, including the right to religious freedom established in Article 24 of the Constitution.

For the following analysis I will focus my remarks on three fundamental aspects:

- Binomial "Law and Religion" (B.);
- Analysis of the amendments to Articles 24 and 40 of the Constitution (C.); and
- Approaches to public policy management of religious diversity (D.)

B. Law and Religion

This conceptual binomial gives me the opportunity to analyze the amendments to Articles 24 and 40 and their constitutional implications, from the perspective of the *Mexican Law of Religion*,[1] whose core is religious freedom, and its ground the dignity of the human person, so that I will not focus only on the so-called "Churches- State relations", which at least in its formal name apparently may be restrictive and not open to religious communities that are not churches.[2]

---

1 It is worth noting that the concept of "Mexican ecclesiastical law" is formally limited, because it refers to the ecclesiastical, to the institutional, to the churches, but not all religious communities are erected in this way, as churches; for example, the case of Jewish, Buddhist, Hindu communities. For that reason, among others, I prefer to refer to the "Mexican Law of Religion" as the set of rules of the State concerning the religious factor that attends to the religious needs and interests at the individual level (individual juridical person), corporate level (religious communities and religious associations) and collective level (indigenous peoples, with respect to their religious practices and customs), under the principles of religious freedom, laicity (laicidad) and separation of state and churches (or religious communities).

2 I mean Jewish, Buddhist and Islamic religious communities.

Here I want to refer to the important intervention of *François Houtart* in the Assembly of the United Nations in 2008,[3] which noted that the world needs alternatives and not merely regulations, since it is not sufficient to rehabilitate or maintain a system but to transform it

It is a question of permitting all forms of knowledge, including traditional forms of all philosophies and cultures, to participate in the construction of alternatives[4] "in breaking the monopoly of Westernization". This author considers various aspects among religions:

> [T]he wisdom of Hinduism in relationship to nature, the compassion of Buddhism in human relations, the permanent quest for utopia in Judaism, the thirst for justice which defines the prophetic current in Islam, the emancipatory power of the theology of liberation in Christianity, the respect for the sources of life in the concept of the land itself among the indigenous peoples of the Americas, the sense of solidarity expressed in the religions of Africa, can all make important contributions in the context of mutual tolerance guaranteed by the impartiality of political society.

This consideration has its own specific weight to the topic at hand, since to democratize society within a framework of laicity (*laicidad*) is to allow multiculturalism be expressed through religious freedom. A lay (*laico*) state which renounces religious freedom, renounces the claim of this human right in all its dimensions; it loses its right to exist as such, i.e. as a lay (*laico*) state.

C. Analysis of the amendments to Articles 24 and 40 of the Mexican Constitution

This second aspect focuses primarily on distinguishing between the justification for the existence of the constitutional reform to Article 24 of

---

3 Cf. General Assembly of the United Nations, Panel on the financial crisis, October 30, 2008.

4 Here I want to refer to an indigenous representative Chamula, expert in Tzotzil indigenous language of the National Commission for the Development of Indigenous Peoples, who – in December 2010 – questioned the application of human rights in indigenous communities, since in these – he says – "there is no freedom but complementarity, there is no equality but reciprocity, there is no fraternity but relatedness." How to translate the Universal Declaration of Human Rights into the indigenous context? It is a challenge for the indigenous peoples themselves.

28 January 1992 and the reason for the existence of the recent amendments to Articles 24 and 40 of the Constitution.[5]

Regardless of the political nature attributed to the constitutional reforms of January 28, 1992 about a "search for legitimacy of the Federal Executive", it was rather to combat obvious anachronism and open simulation with:

- the adequacy of the rules in religious matters to social reality, to prevent thereby any simulation;
- the updating of the regulations on religious freedom. It demands that the Mexican government complies with international treaties signed by the Mexican state to ensure that fundamental right; and
- the need to promote, in the awareness of Mexican society, respect for the legal system and proper implementation of the law on religious matters.

With this constitutional reform and the subsequent issuance of the *Law on Religious Associations and Public Worship* (July 15, 1992) several processes took place:

- The construction of laicity (*laicidad*) on the recognition of religious diversity.
- The visibility of religious minorities, which may be registered as religious associations before the *Ministry of Interior* to obtain juridical personality.[6]
- The recognition of religious diversity that creates conditions for inclusion and tolerance that are essential for peaceful coexistence

5 Amendments to Articles 24 and 40 of the Mexican Constitution were approved by the Senate on March 28, 2012. The amendment to the first paragraph of Article 24 received 72 votes in favor and 35 votes against; while the amendment to Article 40 was approved by 97 votes in favor, 3 against, and one abstention. The amendment to the first paragraph of Article 24 of the Mexican Constitution was published on July 19, 2013 in the Diario Oficial de la Federación. The amendment to Article 40 of the Mexican Constitution was published on November 30, 2012 in the Diario Oficial de la Federación.

6 In the year 1992 were registered as religious association only three communities of Catholic orientation (the Catholic, Apostolic, and Roman Church in Mexico, the Mexican Episcopal Conference, and the Primatial Archdiocese of Mexico); in 1993 and 1994 were registered diverse religious associations, mostly, different than Catholic.

among different believers, religious communities and religious associations.

I. Amendment to Article 40 of the Constitution

Article 40, in close connection with Article 39 of the Mexican Constitution,[7] establishes the fundamental characteristics adopted by the political organization of the Mexican people.

One reason, apparently, "to raise the lay (laica) nature of the state to constitutional rank"[8] was the reaction to assumed acts that "violated" this lay nature (for example: to allow religious services at public hospitals;[9] to deny minority rights; to impose the beliefs of the majority;[10] and to dictate public policies based on religious criteria for 110 or 120 million Mexicans as if they were Catholics).[11]

Generally, in the case of the amendment to Article 40 of the Constitution, it was argued that this reform was made to ratify, to reaffirm the lay (*laica*) nature of the Mexican state, even to defend and strengthen it against the *backward and obscurantist temptation*,[12] and against attacks on laicity (*laicidad*), and that "*postponing the fullness of secularity of the State*" means the "*risk of a successful [attack] from the rhetoric of intransigence.*"[13]

---

7 "Article 39. National sovereignty is vested essentially and originally in the people. All public power derives from the people and is instituted for their benefit. The people have at all time the inalienable right to alter or amend their form of government.".

8 "Deplora el Senado que el carácter laico del Estado haya sido vulnerado," *La Jornada*, February 18, 2010, p. 10. And here I want to ask: was the Mexican state not lay (laico) already? And if this is so, then the article 3 of the Law of Religious Associations and Public Worship, which establishes „The Mexican state is lay (laico)", was unconstitutional.

9 "Intelectuales piden a senadores ratificar el carácter laico del Estado mexicano," *La Jornada*, February 19, 2010, p. 10.

10 "Censuran a Rivera por su postura sobre el Estado laico," *Rumbo de México*, February 19, 2010.

11 See ibid.

12 See "Navarrete confía en que el Senado apruebe reforma para Estado laico," *La Crónica*, February 19, 2010, p. 9.

13 The Mexican state is lay (laico), a-confessional, and does not subscribe to any religion or religious denomination as its own. The conception of a lay (laico) state is

In sum, this constitutional reform was rather "confirmatory", "declarative" and not "foundational" or "constitutive" in character. Therefore, even if there had not been any constitutional reform to Article 40, the laicity (*laicidad*) of the Mexican state would have remained intact.[14]

Here I would refer comparatively, while maintaining a proper sense of proportion, the case of the German law of religion, where, although there is no principle of laicity (*laicidad*), there is the principle of neutrality. The *Fundamental Law* of the Federal Republic of Germany does not explicitly contain the word "neutral", this nature of the German state has been recognized and developed by the jurisprudence of the Federal Constitutional Court.[15]

---

dynamic, also linked to social processes. Precisely, one of the dimensions of laicity (laicidad) is in the field of cultural identities and the defense of minorities, of course in attention to the following guiding principles:

- religious freedom;
- separation of state and churches (or rather, religious communities);
- no intervention by the authorities in the internal affairs of religious associations (linked to respect for the right of self-determination of religious communities);
- authorities may not attend in an official character any religious act of public worship;
- churches and other religious communities should not interfere in the functions of the state;
- state laicity (laicidad).

On November 6, 2012, the Senate declared approved the amendment of Article 40 of the Constitution, establishing formally the lay (laica) nature of the Mexican State, as follows: "Article 40. It is the will of the Mexican people to constitute a representative, democratic, lay (laica), and federal Republic composed by States, free and sovereign in all matters concerning their internal affairs; but united in a federation established according to principles of this fundamental law." (The underlined is mine). This can be assumed to be a platform to strengthen the management of religious diversity.

14 From the freedom of belief – Article 4, paragraph 1 of the Fundamental Law – derives the principle of neutrality towards different religions and confessions. The ideological-religious neutrality is a binding mandate for the state. The state's obligation to neutrality implies that the state must conduct itself equally before various religious orientations; the state cannot generate religious indifferentism. The state is prohibited from favoring certain denominations, also from making distinctions between religious communities and valuing the belief or non-belief of its citizens, and noting their convictions as correct or false. See BverfGE 24, 236 (246), BVerfGE 32, 98 (106), BVerfGE 33, 23 (28), BVerfGE 93, 1 (16).

15 "Pathology" of the laicity (laicidad) is to reduce religion to the private sphere.

In my opinion, the "laicity" is a scenario, which may be presupposed, where the effective exercise of fundamental freedoms – including the freedom of religion – takes place.[16] Therefore "*laicity*" and "religious freedom" are not opposed and are not mutually exclusive, since a lay (*laico*) state must ensure full enjoyment of religious freedom.

Certain documents such as the Universal Declaration of Laicity (laicidad) of 21st Century[17] and the Lay (laica) Charter[18] do not address in its true size, at least explicitly, religious freedom; rather, they include it only by reference, for example, that it is related to "freedom of religion" and to the "right to profess or not to profess religious beliefs". The "*Alphabet of the lay (laica) Republic*"[19] simply refers to "freedom of worship" or "to exercise any religious option or not practice any one."But it is evident that religious freedom in its complexity implies this and much more.

---

16 See Libertades laicas. Red Iberoamericana por las Libertades Laicas. Programa Interdisciplinario de Estudios sobre las Religiones. El Colegio Mexiquense, A.C.

17 See Extraordinary Chair "Benito Juárez" of UNAM, January 14, 2013.

18 José Woldenberg, ex-counselor of the Federal Electoral Institute introduced this alphabet during the Forum "Laicidad y democracia: 150 aniversario de la libertad de pensamiento".

19 A large majority were evangelical groups, as shown by the various demonstrations that occurred in more than 20 states of the Mexican Republic.

II. Amendment to Article 24 of the Constitution

1. An Approach to the Three Argued Reasons for Rejecting the Amendment to Article 24 of the Constitution

There were several groups,[20] which expressed different reasons for rejecting the amendment to Article 24 of the Constitution. These were linked to:[21]

- The intent of reform. It was argued that this was *"the dismantling of the lay (laico) state"*.
- The manipulation of reform. It was argued that redefining "freedom of religion" was offering a tendentious and biased concept of that freedom.
- The consequences of reform. There was reference, in this respect, to the effect on the freedoms of religious minorities.

It was noted that reference to the supposed "danger" of religious teaching in public schools was common in these three reasons.

The reference to religious freedom only as *"teaching religion in public schools"* represented, rather than a serious approach to the dimensions or areas of religious freedom, a manipulation of the discourse on religious freedom that prevented a serious analysis of its real scope.

---

20 Approximately 50 organizations and associations publicly opposed the amendment to Article 24, among which are Pentecostal churches, the Light of the World, Apostolic Church of Mexico, Presbyterian churches and Masonic Grand Lodge. Moreover, it was expressed that some small religious groups are in opposition to this reform, because they considered that the reform would benefit the Catholic associations. Historic churches – such as the latter – and Jewish, Orthodox, Anglican or traditional evangelical churches supported the amendment to Article 24.

21 The text of Article 24 of the Constitutional Reform from January 28, 1992 establishes: "Every man is free to embrace the religion of his choice and to practice the ceremonies, devotions and acts of worship, provided they do not constitute a crime or an offense punishable by the Law" (first paragraph). "The Congress of the Union may not enact laws establishing or prohibiting any religion" (second paragraph). "Religious acts of public worship must regularly be performed inside the temples. Those extraordinarily performed outside of them shall be subject to the Law" (third paragraph).

2. *Analysis of Article 24 of the Constitution*

The Article 24 in force provides that:

> Every person has the right to freedom of ethical convictions, conscience and religion. This freedom includes the right to participate individually or collectively, in public or private, in the ceremonies, devotions and acts of worship, provided they do not constitute a crime or an offense punishable by law. No one may use the public acts of expression of this freedom for political purposes, proselytism or propaganda.[22]

Although the new version of this Article uses an inadequate legislative technique, the substance of the constitutional reform of Article 24 focuses on:

- Replacement of "every man" by "every person" in accordance with the terminology adopted by all international instruments on human rights.
- The formal introduction of the right to freedom of ethical convictions:

Freedom of ethical convictions. Its inclusion – it seems to me – was linked *mutatis mutandis* to a formulation used in Article 4 of the *Fundamental Law* of the Federal Republic of Germany, which refers to the profession of religious and ideological beliefs (or non-religious worldview) called *Weltanschauung*,[23] whose translation into Spanish is complex, but in the case of Article 24 was adopted simply as "ethical convictions", which creates some confusion especially when this is disassociated from the "freedom of religion".

---

22 "Art und Weise, wie jemand die Welt und ihren Sinn sowie sein Dasein betrachtet und beurteilt" (Mode and form how someone observes and judges the world, its reason and its existence), Wahrig, *Deutsches Wörterbuch*, 1997. Gerhard Anschütz considers Weltanschauung as the doctrine comprising the total and universal world that seeks to recognize and to value the position of man in the world.

23 While it is true that the Constitution of the United Mexican States did not establish expressly the freedom of conscience, this was considered by the Constituent Assembly of 1856-1857 in the sense that freedom of conscience, based on the most intimate convictions of the person, could not be subject to regulation by the state legal order. Meanwhile, the Constituent of 1916-1917 considered freedom of conscience as presupposed and included in Article 24 of the Constitution, since, in the opinion of the liberals of the period, Article 24 expressed, on the one hand, a large freedom of conscience and on the other hand, limitation only for religious acts which constitute a crime or an offense punishable by law.

Freedom of conscience.[24] Various international instruments establish, unanimously, freedom of conscience as a fundamental right, where "consciousness" is precisely its subject.

Note that within the elements of freedom of conscience are:

- "Freedom of formation of consciousness" as the right guaranteed to every person to follow his own representations in the formation of concepts of religious-moral value or disvalue without any influence of state coercion or social pressure, and perform this purpose under the constitutional legal order.[25]
- "Freedom of realization of consciousness"implies "to omit" the legal prescribed behavior and "to not observe" the legally established rules of "not to do". It is here that the "right of conscientious objection" is linked with the fundamental right to "freedom of conscience".

The *International Covenant on Civil and Political Rights* does not explicitly refer to a right of conscientious objection, however, in *General Comment No. 22* to Article 18 of the *Covenant* it considers that such right can be derived precisely from Article 18, paragraph 1, and there shall be no differentiation among conscientious objectors on the basis of the nature of their particular beliefs.

At the bottom of the issue about conscientious objection[26] there is a relationship of tension between constitutional freedom and equality.[27]

---

24 See Listl and Pirson (eds.), *Handbuch des Staatskirchenrechts der Bundesrepublik Deutschland*, 1994, p. 468.

25 "Conscientious objection" comes to be defined as "the attitude of a person who refuses to comply with a rule of law under a binding mandate from his consciousness, which is in radical opposition to the implicit ethical content of the legal norm." See Lima Torrado, *Desobediencia civil y objeción de conciencia*, 2000, p. 25.

26 See Bleckmann et al., *Die Rechtsstellung des Wehrdienstverweigerers aus Gewissensgründen in den Mitgliedsstaaten des Europarats, Ein vergleichender Überblick*, 1967, p. 231.

27 For example, this is the case of Article 10 of the Military Service Law (Ley del Servicio Militar) and Article 38, paragraph III of its Regulation (Reglamento) concerning the ministers of worship, who may be exempted from compulsory military service; also this is the hypothesis in the case of Article 59, Health Law for the Federal District, where it is provided that doctors, for reasons of a religious nature, may refuse to perform an abortion.

Of course, freedom of conscience does not exclude or exempt, without further ado, the objector, of having to fulfill civic obligations, because a person who is recognized as a conscientious objector must perform, in principle, an alternative service (*servicio sustitutorio*), in order to reconcile precisely the right to freedom of conscience with the observance of common duties for all within the rule of law.

The Mexican Law of Religion provides what one might describe as "*conscientious objection secundum legem*", for example, that the legislation itself establishes a certain "right to object" to justify the breach of a legal mandate.[28]

In addition it is essential to examine carefully the second paragraph of Article 1 of the Law of Religious Associations and Public Worship,[29] in order to align its content with the current Article 24 of the Constitution, which expressly guarantees freedom of conscience.

- Freedom of religion. Notwithstanding the constitutional reform on human rights from June 10, 2011 (the rules on human rights shall be interpreted in accordance with the Constitution and international treaties on this matter, favoring to the people all the time the more extensive protection), and in addition to the requirements of the New Law of Amparo,[30] (the sphere of protection of rights is extended, the human rights established within international treaties are subject of direct protection) still, the reform of Article 24 reinforces full religious freedom, from the interpretation of this in international instruments and from the contributions of comparative law.

Religious freedom consists of an *internum forum* and an *externum forum*.

The *internum forum* relates to the freedom of belief. "Positive freedom of belief", i.e., to have or to adopt[31] a belief of one's choice "or preference" (International Covenant on Civil and Political Rights) as well

---

28 This establishes: "Religious convictions do not exempt in any case from complying with laws of the country. No one may invoke religious motives to evade the responsibilities and obligations established in the laws.".

29 Published on April 2, 2013 in the Diario Oficial de la Federación.

30 The "freedom to adopt a belief" consists usually in search of a community of believers, learn about it, and take its doctrine.

31 The "freedom to change one's religion" implies in the background "the right to abandon or to resign from being a member from a community of believers and to enter another." This formulation has been considered in many cases instead of "to change one´s religion" because it has usually been objected by Islamic countries,

as to maintain or to "change his belief"[32] (American Convention on Human Rights); this *internum forum* includes the "negative freedom of belief", which is summarized in not having any belief.

The *forum externum* relates to the "freedom to profess a belief". "Positive freedom of profession" involves the right to say what one believes, which includes the freedom to propagate one's belief, and also the freedom of dispreading other beliefs (what is known as a missionary activity) and to say that one doesn´t believe at all.

"The negative freedom of profession" guarantees the right to keep what one believes secret, or the right to silence (*Schweigerecht* in German law of religion).

Moreover, the freedom of exercise of religion in any form involves exercising it alone, in a community, in private (for example, the called *devotio domestica simplex* – private devotion without the intervention of a minister of worship of one's religious confession – and *devotio domestica qualificata* – private devotion involving a minister of worship of one's religious confession), and in public (the called *exercitium religionis publicum*).[33]

Moreover, the manifestations of the exercise of religion include, for example:[34]

- Religious service: as the typical form of religious adoration or proclamation, for example, worship.
- Religious uses: among which are processions, wearing/carrying of religious clothing or (a certain style of) beard, circumcision, prayers, tolling of bells, flying of church banners; in short, rites and rituals of different religions.

---

such as Saudi Arabia. See Nowak, *UNO-Pakt über bürgerliche und politische Rechte und Fakultativprotokoll. CCPR-Kommentar*, 1989, "Artikel 18 des Paktes", p. 333.

32 See Listl and Pirson, *Handbuch des Staatskirchenrecht des Bundesrepublik Deutschland*, p. 458.

33 See ibid, pp. 461-462.

34 Article 18 of the Covenant: 1. "Everyone shall have the right to freedom of thought, conscience and religion. This right shall include freedom to have or to adopt a religion or belief of his choice, and freedom, either individually or in community with others and in public or private, to manifest his religion or belief in worship, observance, practice and teaching.".

- Praxis (practice): conducting religious assemblies, foundation and support of charities and humanitarian institutions; manufacture or acquisition of ritual objects; collecting donations; training of religious leaders; observance of days of rest and specific holidays; missionary activity; sustaining religious hospitals; implementation of development projects; distribution of flyers; pacifists, motivated by a pacifist spirit.
- Teaching: transmission of content from one religion or worldview in religious schools, in public schools, in various forms of non-formal education and in missionary work.

Also freedom of religious association is part of the fundamental right of religious freedom in its positive and negative aspect.

In this regard, religious freedom in Mexico should not be a taboo subject. Hence the importance of serious and open debate on issues such as:

- The right to self-determination of religious communities as well as freedom of expression of their ministers of worship.
- Mass media in the ownership or possession of religious associations.
- The right of parents to ensure the religious and moral education of their children in conformity with their own convictions, even in public schools.
- The protection of cultural property of a religious character.
- Attention to the problems of displaced indigenous people because of "religious intolerance".

It clarifies that this freedom includes the right to participate individually or collectively, in public or private, in ceremonies, devotions, or acts of respective worship, provided they do not constitute a crime or an offense punishable by law.

In this respect, it is not that "this freedom includes the right...", but rather "this right includes freedom..." (in accordance with Article 18 of the International Covenant on Civil and Political Rights,[35] and Article 12 of the American Convention on Human Rights[36]). In addition to the ob-

35 Article 12 of the Convention: "Everyone has the right to freedom of conscience and of religion. This right includes freedom to maintain or to change one's religion or beliefs, and freedom to profess or disseminate one's religion or beliefs, either individually or together with others, in public or in private.".

36 Papal Mass held on March 23, 2012 at Bicentennial Park in Silao, Guanajuato.

servation about the inadequate legislative technique used, it is considered that such provision falls far short in scope, at least formally, when it refers only to ceremonies, devotions and acts of respective worship.

Finally, a prohibition is incorporated: no one can use the public acts of expression of this freedom for political purposes, proselytism or propaganda. The questions are: who is the addressee of this? Any person? What specifically does "using public acts of expression of this freedom" mean? What does "this freedom" mean? The "freedom of ethical convictions, conscience and religion"or the "freedom to participate individually or collectively, in public or private, in ceremonies, devotions, or acts of respective worship"? Is this prohibition applicable during an electoral campaign and also in non-election times? What would be the sanction for contravening this provision?

By reading this provision, suddenly the image of the presidential candidates came to my mind who gathered at the Mass celebrated by Pope Benedict XVI in Silao Guanajuato in 2012,[37] where some of them even took communion publicly. If at the time a prohibitive provision like this had been in force, would this prohibition have been applicable to them?

Moreover, it appears that prohibitions against ministers of worship engaging in political matters existed before, for example:

- to hold public offices and not be elected for public offices.[38] Those who have ceased being ministers of worship with anticipation and in the manner established by law, may be elected (Article 130 of the Constitution d) and Article 14, first paragraph, LARCP);
- to associate for political purposes, to proselytize in favor of or against any political candidate, party or association (Article 130 of the Constitution, and Articles 12 and 29 LARCP);
- to celebrate political meetings in temples (Article 130 of the Constitution and Article 21 LARCP);

---

37 In the doctrine it is discussed on the legal nature of this constitutional impediment of the ministers of worship to exercise a passive vote, placing it within three possible explanations: 1. An incompatibility on the basis of the principle of State-churches separation. 2. A mutilation of human rights of ministers of worship, or 3. A discriminatory treatment.

38 It is recommended to carry out this derogation also in local regulations (electoral codes and civil codes), where the word "sect" is present.

- in developing public acts of their own ministry, to induce the electorate to vote or not vote for a particular candidate or political party (Article 404 Cófigo Penal Federal (CPF)).

To these, it has been added: "no one can use the public acts of expression of this freedom for political purposes, proselytism or propaganda" as a "burden" additional to the bans for ministers of worship, especially if this prohibitive requirement seems an "open letter" to the exercise of discretional activity of governmental authorities in its application.

D. Public Policies for Managing Religious Diversity

The *laicity* (*laicidad*) of the state, as a scenario and presupposed, where the effective exercise of religious freedom and other fundamental freedoms occurs, also involves the generation of appropriate public policies for the management of religious diversity.

At the legislative level, it is necessary to legislate without discrimination, as happened with the derogation of the word "sect" in federal regulations. This word was removed from the Federal Code of Electoral Institutions and Procedures (COFIPE) but this has not been done in case of the Federal Civil Code, because Article 1330 still includes the word "sect".[39]

Moreover, the *National Council to Prevent Discrimination* (CONAPRED) published a *Handbook for lawmaking without discrimination*, which will undoubtedly contribute to that purpose.

39 "Libertad religiosa. Sus diferentes facetas", in Semanario Judicial de la Federación, Ninth Epoch, First Chamber, Thesis 1a LX/2007, Subject: Constitutional, isolated thesis, February 2007. "Freedom of worship" means "freedom to practice the ceremonies, rites and meetings associated with the cultivation of certain religious beliefs.".

At the jurisdictional level, the interpretation of "religious freedom and their different facets"[40] and "differences of religious freedom and freedom of worship"[41] is developed.

At the federal executive level, it is necessary to comply with the generation of an appropriate public policy of management of religious diversity.

Among the public policies for management of religious diversity are the following:

- Political-administrative attention for the transformation

Regardless of the circumstances that involved a significant shift of the administrative body of the federal executive in charge of religious affairs before 1992, it was called "*Underdirectorate of Religious Worship, Firearms and Explosives*"; and with the reform from January 28, 1992 the situation changed toward the formation of a *General Directorate of Religious Associations*, within an "*Undersecretariat for Population, Migration and Religious Affairs*". Here it is expedient to review the vision, mission and objectives of this Undersecretariat.

40 "Libertad religiosa y libertad de culto. Sus diferencias", in Semanario Judicial de la Federación y su Gaceta, Ninth Epoch, First Chamber, Thesis 1a LXI/2007, Subject: Constitutional, isolated thesis, February 2007. "Acts of public worship" as "the acts specifically oriented to develop collectively rites, ceremonies and practices of different religions recognized as institutionalized or formalized expressions of religious faith, defined and governed by pre-established rules by them.".

41 The management of the Federal Executive relations with religious associations (churches and religious communities), with full respect for the lay (laico) spirit of public institutions, formally has had as guidelines: a) Improving the relationship with religious communities, religious associations and religious traditions existing in the country; b) Greater openness and fairness for different religions; c) Assumption of a positioning of "non-control" by the authority on religious associations; d) Respect of the internal life of religious associations and religious pluralism; e) Strengthening of interfaith dialogue and coexistence; e) Permanent dialogue with religious organizations and ministers of worship; f) Transparency and access to information on religious matters; g) Improving the administrative service to attend the religious associations; h) Application of modern technology for recording and processing information in religious matters.

While the services offered by the General Directorate of Religious Associations formally involve administrative attention to religious diversity, this is only part of public management policy. [42]

Since the new administration took office on 1 December 2012, a rethinking of public policy for the management of religious diversity under the National Development Plan 2013-2018 is expected, and depending mainly on the implementation of the constitutional reform of Article 24.

- Extraordinary acts of public worship are not "public spectacles"

It must be insisted that in the case of holding acts of extraordinary public worship of religious associations provisions should not be applied which strictly correspond to "public performances",[43] since it is not possible to fulfill the same requirements for implementation and because "extraordinary acts of public worship" are not "public spectacles".

- Spiritual assistance

It is required further to facilitate spiritual support in health, social care and rehabilitation institutions, making this effectively one of the dimensions of the right to religious freedom of internal people and users.[44]

- Prohibition of discrimination on religious grounds

The constitutional and legal normativity on religious matters assumes the principle of non-discrimination in favor of religious diversity.

Article 1 of the Constitution explicitly prohibits discrimination based on religion and establishes that the authorities have the obligation to promote, protect and ensure the human rights of all people.

Article 2 of the Law of Religious Associations and Public Worship recognizes the right of individuals to be free from discrimination, coercion

---

42 See Law for Holding Public Events in the Federal District (Ley para la celebración de espectáculos públicos en el Distrito Federal), article 4, V. Public spectacle; article 25, VII, Requirements of permissions to hold public spectacles.

43 Based on article 6 of the Regulation of the Law on Religious Associations and Public Worship, published on November 6, 2003, in the Diario Oficial de la Federación.

44 Agreements – that were ready to be signed – are those corresponding to the states of Coahuila, Jalisco, Puebla and Veracruz. Agreements in process of elaboration, in case of the states: Campeche, Guerrero, Queretaro, San Luis Potosi, Sonora, Tamaulipas, Tlaxcala.

or hostility because of their religious beliefs and the prohibition to restrict the exercise of any work or activity for religious reasons.

Article 4 of the Federal Law to Prevent and Eliminate Discrimination prohibits all discriminatory practice. This law establishes the following in Article 9 as discriminatory behaviors: to hinder freedom of religion, religious practices or customs, provided they do not violate public order (paragraph XVI), and to deny religious assistance to persons deprived of liberty, serving in the armed forces or interns in assistance or health care institutions (paragraph XVII).

- Conscientious objection

Education authorities have refrained from punishing students – Jehovah's Witnesses – because of their religious beliefs, who refuse to salute the flag and sing the national anthem at civic ceremonies that take place in schools, according to the *General Recommendation Nr. 5*, issued by the *National Commission of Human Rights* (May 14, 2003).

However, in the case of basic education teachers – for example, Jehovah's Witnesses – are required, in respect of their right to conscientious objection to honoring national symbols, to complying instead of this with an alternative service, so that they should not be separated from their charges – as this happens at the present – because they "*do not inculcate love for the country in their students*".

- Coordination agreements in religious matters[45]

It is necessary to review the status of coordination agreements on religious matters signed by the Ministry of Interior with the governments of the states of Zacatecas,[46] Chiapas,[47] Chihuahua,[48] Michoacan,[49] Nuevo Leon[50] and Quintana Roo,[51] to update them, and to promote the signing of agreements with the remaining states.

- Translation of the Law of Religious Associations and Public Worship and its regulation into indigenous languages

45 Published on January 28, 2005, in the Diario Oficial de la Federación.
46 Published on January 28, 2005, in the Diario Oficial de la Federación.
47 Published on March 9, 2005, in the Diario Oficial de la Federación.
48 Published on April 25, 2005, in the Diario Oficial de la Federación.
49 Federación.
50 Published on April 28, 2005, in the Diario Oficial de la Federación.
51 Published on May 3, 2005, in the Diario Oficial de la Federación.

The Ministry of Interior has promoted the translation of the *Law on Religious Associations and Public Worship* into various indigenous languages in at least five states. These languages are: *Tzotzil*, *Tzeltal*, *Tojolabal*, *Zoque* (in Chiapas); *Mazahua* (in State of Mexico); *Nawatl* (in Puebla); *Nahuatl*, *Tenek* (in San Luis Potosí); *Nahuatl*, *Totonaca* (in Veracruz).[52] However, translation of the law by itself is not enough, but there should also be informed knowledge about its content, so this topic must be addressed, too.

- Interreligious dialogue

The state must encourage the development of the work of interreligious dialogue at different levels, for example: 1. At national level: the Interfaith Council of Mexico. 2 At state level: the Interreligious Councils of Chiapas and Guerrero; and 3. At municipal level: the Municipal Evangelical Interfaith Council in Larrainzar. Also with respect to those who, exercising their right of self-determination, have decided not belong to any Interfaith Council, as has been the case of the *Christian Congregation of Jehovah's Witnesses*.

On April 14, 2016, the first encounter between Deputies and Interfaith Councils took place.[53] While the deputies pronounced to elaborate a political agenda and initiatives to advance in a regulation of the Article 24 constitutional, representatives of interreligious councils manifested the necessity to legislate in the matter of freedom of conscience and to improve the Law of Religious Associations and Public Worship, as well as its regulations, in order to defend and promote religious freedom. Finally, it was assumed that Mexico has much to learn about religious freedom, since the

---

52 The translation of the law into indigenous languages took place in states that have concluded a coordination agreement with the Ministry of Interior in religious matters: Chiapas, State of Mexico, Puebla, San Luis Potosi and Veracruz.

53 Proposals: A) Develop a political agenda with these issues and advance in the constitution of a better society. B) In no public schools should be imposed or teached any religious line of thought. C) Legislate on conscientious objection; improve both Law of Religious Associates and Public Worship, and its regulations to defend and promote religious freedom. D) That religious associations may own and operate radio and television stations. E) That a fiscal legislation be elaborated according to the aims and objectives of the religious associations and churches, because they are not economic companies with the objektive of trading.

1992 reforms, although they recognized that guarantee, said reforms "are still far from what Mexico has signed on human rights issues."[54]

- Migration

It should support religious associations that make use of their right to bring into the country ministers of worship and associated religious persons to participate in pastoral interchanges, as well as for international events held in Mexico, so it is necessary to reduce administrative obstacles on matters of inviting foreign ministers of worship into the country.

A positive aspect of the Mexican lay (*laico*) state has been to allow special diets in migration centers for people who for religious reasons so request (*Immigration Law*,[55] Article 107, II, second paragraph). This shows more openness to guaranteeing religious freedom.

It requires greater collaboration between government and religious associations for the defense and the protection of the rights of migrants, especially of unaccompanied migrant children.

Finally, members of the Tohono otham indigenous people, as it is written on the other side of the Rio Grande; tojono o'tam, as pronounced on the Mexican side, are part of the 82,000 indigenous people, of whom some 42,000 reside in Mexico and around 40,000 live in the United States, in the desert territory of Sonora and Arizona, divided by 120 kilometers of border that was imposed upon them without having been consulted. To that is added the construction of the "wall" as proposed by Donald Trump, which represents a double offense fot this indigenous population.[56]

- Official recognition of studies in religious institutions

Since 1995 there has been a policy of openness by the *Ministry of Education* to recognize studies in religious matters, such as theology or religious sciences, provided they comply with the established legal requirements.

For example, official validity was recognized by the *Ministry of Education* for the curriculum in Judaic at the upper level (October 2012), which is unprecedented in the history of the Jewish Community of Mexico.

---

54 Promote secondary legislation on religious freedom and worship, which strengthens social value. See Bulletin No. 1341.

55 Published on May 25, 2011, in Diario Oficial de la Federación.

56 See http://www.proseco.com.mx/488808/pueblo-indigena-separado-la-frontera-va-contra-muro-trump

- Tax matters

The tax treatment of religious associations is regulated through a "general resolution" for all of them. However, the religious associations are not yet considered "non-profit legal entities" (*personas morales sin fines de lucro*);[57] they are not authorized to receive donations deductible from income tax;[58] so this situation should be changed.

- Donations in kind from abroad

Various religious denominations in Mexico – especially evangelical churches[59] – have close relationship with churches from the United States of America who are willing to support them with donations in kind, especially: food, used clothing in good condition, medicines, toys, medical equipment, among others.

The current problems, in this case, are customs procedures that carry a high cost, which often turns out to be more expensive than the amount donated, and churches or religious communities do not have sufficient financial resources to cover such costs.

It seeks to guide religious associations to find the most appropriate way to receive donations from abroad. At present, they do this through civil associations for welfare; however, it insists that religious associations as "non-profit legal entities" also should come to be considered authorized donees.

- Labor matters

In this item it is necessary to determine that ministers of worship are not employees or workers of religious associations, because there is a general assumption that considers religious associations as their employers, who therefore have to pay patronal contributions to the *Mexican Social Security Institute* (IMSS)

57 Although the Law of Income Tax (Ley del Impuesto sobre la Renta) does not expressly refer to religious associations, it establishes that: "For the purposes of this Law, are considered non-profit legal persons (...) the following: XVI. Civil associations or societies with political, sporting or religious purposes."

58 See Tax Administration System (SAT). Rules for Religious Associations for the Fiscal Year 2012, of February 16, 2012.

59 For example, in the state of Tamaulipas.

- Security

State authorities have recognized that religious associations, churches and religious communities have much to contribute to Mexican society, to rebuild the social net (*tejido social*), especially in prevention matters, so their specific involvement in the new National Security Plan of the federal government must be known.[60] For now, they work on voluntary disarmament programs[61] which are usually carried out in the atrium of Catholic churches.

- Reservations to international treaties

It is necessary to review and to update the interpretative declarations and reservations made at the time by the Mexican state in concluding international treaties relating to religious freedom and ministers of worship.

- Religious tourism

At the federal level, the Ministry of Tourism (SECTUR) has conducted coordinated actions with state governments and non-governmental agencies to strengthen religious tourism in Mexico.

At the local level, on June 14, 2014 the "religious tourism program" was presented by the Federal District Government. The program involves three routes for visitors: 1) The Guadeloupian way (*El camino guadalupano*), 2) Bastions of Catholicism (*Baluartes del catolicismo*), and 3) Ways of faith (*Caminos de la fe*). This program considers not only Catholic, but also Buddhist, Jewish, Methodist, Mormon and Orthodox temples.

- Environmental education for sustainability

The Ministry of Environment and Natural Resources (SEMARNAT), in coordination with the Ministry of Public Education (SEP), has developed since 2008 a program to encourage the called "green schools", which perform actions and environmental management strategies to combat climate change.

---

60 See Speech of Enrique Peña Nieto, Second Special Session of the National Public Security Council, December 17, 2012.

61 For example, since 2007 are developed voluntary disarmament programs in the Federal District under different names: "Entrega voluntaria de armas de fuego" (voluntary handing over of firearms) and "Por tu familia, desarme voluntario" (For your family, voluntary disarmament).

In 2012, for example, the Tarbut Hebrew College was recognized as "Green school. Environmental leader" and the Israeli College of Mexico as "Green school", implying that in the field of environmental sustainability, institutions representing a diversity of religions are taken into consideration for such programs.

- Resolution of religious conflicts

The General Directorate of Religious Associations must address in a more timely and prudent manner the conflicts on religious intolerance matters that are characterized by the combination of several factors, including political, partisan, economic and agrarian, also caciquism (*cacicazgo*). These have even instrumentalized religion to cover up political actions or justify violence, so it makes it difficult to identify intolerance as purely religious and to achieve an immediate peaceful solution to the conflicts.

E. Conclusion

With the amendments to Articles 24 and 40 of the Mexican Constitution it is clear that a truly lay (*laico*) state has to facilitate the effective exercise of religious freedom. The state has to generate a public policy that engages a significant change in the way in which it manages the religious diversity, which makes it comprehensible to decision makers that this field is not in the sphere of persuasion or negotiation but in the necessary observance of rules that ensures religious freedom effectively.

This management is expressed in developing actions and strategies for the implementation of in force legal instrumentarium, consistent with Mexico's international obligations in this regard; plus informed dialogue between state authorities and religious actors in the meaning of full religious freedom and the responsibility that implies its exercise in the context of a lay (*laico*) state respectful of religious diversity.

Bibliography

Bleckmann, Albert, Konrad Buschbeck, Volker Haak, Meinhard Hilf, Josef Jurina, Alfred Maler, Werner Morvay, Hartmut Schiedermair, Dimitris Tsatsos, Hannfried Walter, and Axel Werbke, *Die Rechtsstellung des Wehrdienstverweigerers aus Gewissensgründen in den Mitgliedsstaaten des Europarats, Ein vergleichender Überblick*, Heidelberg: Max-Planck-Institut für ausländisches Recht und Völkerrecht, 1967.

Constitution of the United Mexican States.

Federal Constitutional Court of Germany, BverfGE 24, 236 (246).

Federal Constitutional Court of Germany, BVerfGE 32, 98 (106).

Federal Constitutional Court of Germany, BVerfGE 33, 23 (28).

Federal Constitutional Court of Germany, BVerfGE 93, 1 (16).

La Jornada, "Deplora el Senado que el carácter laico del Estado haya sido vulnerado," February 18, 2010.

La Jornada, "Intelectuales piden a senadores ratificar el carácter laico del Estado mexicano," February 19, 2010.

Lima Torrado, Jesús, *Desobediencia civil y objeción de conciencia*, Mexico: National Commission for Human Rights, 2000.

Listl, Josef, and Dietrich Pirson (eds.), *Handbuch des Staatskirchenrechts der Bundesrepublik Deutschland, Vol. 1*, 2nd ed., Berlin: Duncker & Humblot, 1994.

Nowak, Manfred, *UNO-Pakt über bürgerliche und politische Rechte und Fakultativprotokoll. CCPR-Kommentar*, Strassburg: Engel, 1989.

Rumbo de México, "Censuran a Rivera por su postura sobre el Estado laico," February 19, 2010.

Wahrig, Gerhard, *Deutsches Wörterbuch*, Gütersloh: Bertelsmann Lexikon, 1997.

The State and Religious Communities: Their Relationship and its Development in Germany

Dirk Ehlers

A. Introduction

Today's national law controls the behavior of people and their co-existence in a community. At the same time, religions and religious communities address the person holistically and claim – in reference to transcendental deduction – to harmonize human action with religious rules. Significant conflicts can arise if the requirements diverge. The constitutional order of a state determines to a high degree how national law deals with religion and religious communities. In order to evaluate the constitutional order it is of significant importance whether religious freedom – and religious equality as its sister – is ensured. From an historical point of view the guarantee of religious freedom is one of the oldest guarantees of fundamental rights. There is no general freedom without freedom of religion. This is why freedom of religion today is considered as a human right. It is not only guaranteed by national constitutions, but also by International Human Rights Covenants such as the Universal Declaration of Human Rights (Article 18), the International Covenant on Civil and Political Rights (Article 18) and the European Convention for the Protection of Human Rights and Fundamental Freedoms (Article 9).

To assume that this freedom is fully secured would not only be hasty, but wrong. Firstly, there are still states which do not recognize freedom of religion. Secondly, one has to differentiate between the law in the books and the law in action. According to matching and reliable reports, violations of religious freedom around the world increase.[1] Some reports even claim that 75% of the world's population lives in countries which do not

1 See (UN-Special Correspondent) Bielefeldt, *Streit um Religionsfreiheit. Aktuelle Facetten der internationalen Debatte*, 2012; Hainbach-Steinz, *Religionsfreiheit. Ein Menschenrecht unter Druck*, 2012.

fully guarantee free exercise of religion.[2] For instance, it is not uncommon that there are persecutions of Christians[3], violent (to some extent also militant international or non-international) clashes between various Islamic persuasions and hostile activities between Buddhists and Muslims. These interferences are initiated only to a certain extent by the state. Often they are a result of social forces. However, this does not relieve the State from its duty to protect: the right of freedom of religion is not only a right of defense against the public authority, but also asks for state protection against unlawful interference by individuals.[4]

Then again, the state's duty to guarantee religious freedom is not fulfilled by admitting uncontrolled freedom of religion or by allying with a particular religion. Freedom can also be suppressed by religion. A theocratic reign is as dangerous as any state-run tyranny. Based on a dictum of a 20th century German revolutionary one can say that freedom is always also the freedom to dissent.[5] All this indicates that conflicting interests must be fairly balanced since there is no freedom without any commitment: in this case this means the recognition of certain rules in the community.

States react differently to the challenges they currently face. It is possible to differentiate (not only in theory, but also in reality) between three ways of how states deal with religion: an alliance of the state with a religious community, the strict separation of the two units or a mediating model on the basis of a separation between the state and religious communities, which does not exclude a cooperation.

---

2 See the report "Rising Tide of Restrictions on Religion," by Pew Research Centers on Religions & Public Life, available at http://www.pewforum.org/2012/09/20/rising-tide-of-restrictions-on-religion-findings/, 2012 (Index, pp. 52 ff.).

3 For more information see EKD, "Bedrohung der Religionsfreiheit, Erfahrungen von Christen in verschiedenen Ländern," 2003, available at http://www.ekd.de/EKD-Texte/44616.html. In some Islamic states the conversion to Christianity will be punished with the death penalty.

4 For general information about the duty to protect against infringements of basic rights (through private third parties) in the German law see Calliess, "Schutzpflichten," 2006, § 44; concerning the duties to protect laid down in the European Convention on Human Rights see Grabenwarter and Pabel, *Europäische Menschenrechtskonvention*, 2012, § 19 par. 3 ff.; for freedom of religion in particular see Unruh, *Religionsverfassungsrecht*, 2011, § 4, mn. 104 f.; von Ungern-Sternberg, "Art. 9," 2012, par. 52.

5 Luxemburg, *Die Russische Revolution. Eine kritische Würdigung*, 1920, p. 109.

An alliance may be created by the incorporation (control) of a religious community into the state along with the simultaneous suppression or control of any other religious communities (as it tended to be in the past in Turkey[6], where after the proclamation of Islam as the state religion, the caliphate was abolished and religion had been nationalized). Contrarily, the religious community can subdue the state (as it tends to be in the Islamic Republic of Iran with the religious leader's right of final decision[7]) or the connection may more or less only have historical significance (as it is the case in the United Kingdom, in which the respective monarch is the head of the Church of England without having spiritual functions[8]). A separation of state and religious communities aims to keep secular and sacred matters apart. Strict is the separation if its main aim is to banish religious communities from the public to the private sector. As a European example the French "Laïcité" can be named. It was mainly introduced by the separation law of 1905[9] and focused on this particular issue. The mediating model which merges fundamental separation and simultaneous cooperation has received its specific expression in Germany.[10] In the following chapter, the development of the mediating model in Germany shall be briefly described because its development is characteristic for the European region in many ways and it may and should inspire to legal comparison.

6 For "state secularism" in Turkey see the preamble and Art. 2, 136 and 174 of the Turkish Constitution of 1982. For more information about this – and about Diynaet İşleri Başknliği – see VerfGE 1970/53, 1989/1; Uslubaş, *Das Präsidium für Diyanet-Angelegenheiten der Republik Türkei*, 2014, pp. 188 ff.

7 Art. 107 ff. of the Iranian Constitution.

8 See Mückl, *Europäisierung des Staatskirchenrechts*, 2005, pp. 78 ff., 99 ff.

9 See Art. 2 I of the Constitution of the Fifth Republic of 4.10.1958 and especially the law of seperation of 9.12.1905. For more information see von Campenhausen, *Staat und Kirche in Frankreich*, 1962; Mückl, *Europäisierung des Staatskirchenrechts*, pp. 143 ff.

10 See von Campenhausen and de Wall, *Staatskirchenrecht*, 2006, §§ 24 ff.; Heckel, "Zur Zukunftsfähigkeit des deutschen 'Staatskirchenrechts' oder 'Religionsverfassungsrechts'?," 2009, pp. 309 ff.; Ehlers, "Staatskirchenrecht," 2013, § 130, mn. 3 ff.

B. Early Period and Middle Ages: State Church under a more Religious or more Secular Impact

In ancient Europe political commonwealth and religion were usually inseparably linked together.[11] In the Roman Empire many subjected peoples had been permitted to retain their religions as long as they surrendered unconditionally to the roman emperor cult. This relation changed to a significant extent with the appearance of Christianity. There are different statements in the Bible about this relationship. On the one hand, the Bible says that one has to obey God more than humans (Acts. 5, 29), on the other hand everybody shall be subject to a human authority (Romans 13,1). The different ways of defining this relationship were not relevant as long as Christians were persecuted. However, they became relevant when Christianity was elevated as state religion in 380. In the Eastern Roman Empire a Caesaropapism developed.[12] The Emperor was the head of the Church, which was dependent on him, insofar political and religious power remained combined. Conversely, in the Western Roman Empire the papacy (the Roman Catholic Church) claimed the sovereignty over religious and even secular law. Eventually, conflicts with secular rulers occurred and became more intense in the Middle Ages. According to the so-called two-swords theory[13], God ruled the world by a religious and a secular sword. Both had been given to the Pope with the order to hand the secular one to the Emperor, the Kings or Princes who had to comply with his (the Pope's) instructions.[14] One explanation for this theory was the gift that the Roman Emperor Constantine had given to the Church.[15] However, this Donation of Constantine actually never happened, as it has been proven hundreds of years later.[16] It will not surprise that secular powers, including communes, often did not accept their subsidiarity even in profane matters. Sometimes, they even claimed the right to appoint a bishop for their

---

11 See Classen, *Religionsrecht*, 2015, par. 5 f.

12 De Wall and Muckel, *Kirchenrecht*, 2014, § 2, par. 10.

13 Based on Lukas (22,38) by Gelesius I, Epistula 12 (494), and further developed by Bonifatius VIII, *Unam Sanctam* (1302); similarly Augustinus, who differentiates civites terrena and civites dei in *De Civitate Dei*, 413-426, German translation by Thimme, 1978, pp. 216 ff.

14 See Bonifatius VIII, *Unam Sanctam* of 1302, see also Link, *Kirchliche Rechtsgeschichte*, 2010, § 7, par 1.

15 See Fuhrmann, *Das Constitutum Constantini*, 1968, pp. 187 ff.

16 See Link, *Kirchliche Rechtsgeschichte,* § 5, par. 10.

own.[17] The whole Middle Ages were affected by conflicts between religious and secular powers. An exception existed where the creation of prince-bishoprics succeeded, in which religion and politics merged. Regarding the relations with other religions, there were multiple military conflicts, particularly the crusades in Muslim ruled areas. But the Roman Catholic Church also had inner conflicts, for example the election of rivaling popes, leading to its temporary separation and intensive prosecution of heretics by the roman inquisition, which was established as the supreme clerical tribunal in 1542.

C. From the Reformation to the End of the First World War: Approaches to Ensure Religious Freedom and Religious Equality

The legal situation in Germany changed radically with the Reformation because, besides the Roman Catholic Church, the Protestant Church established itself as a second confession. If one includes not only the followers of Luther, but also of the reformers Zwingli and Calvin one could even speak of three confessions. The new situation led to cruel religious wars which were not even ended by the Augsburg Religious Peace of 1555. However, this agreement framed the legal situation from that time on. The peace accord included a dual solution: Within a given territory, the local sovereign determined the religion. The principle was *cuius region, eius religio*. This means that the local sovereign had the power to dictate the religion of all the people within the given territory. People with a different belief were allowed to emigrate if they left their belongings behind. On the level of the Holy Roman Empire (which was an association of different countries) the coexistence and equality of different religions (Roman Catholic and Protestant Church) was granted for the first time in the occident's history. About 100 years later, with the end of the Thirty Years' War (1648), this solution was appeased: From then on, confessional issues were governed by the territory's status of confession of the year 1624.[18] If the territorial sovereign changed his belief, the subjects did not have to follow him. Subjects with a different confession were tolerated and not hindered from divine services or private religious practices. This was a

---

17 For the Investiture Controvery cf. de Wall and Muckel, *Kirchenrecht*, § 3 par. 3.
18 Art. V § 3 ff., Instrumentum Pacis Osnabrugense.

first step towards individual protection of basic rights, long before the Bill of Rights of Virginia and the French Revolution. Furthermore, the powers of the territorial sovereign in religious matters were limited in the Protestant territories compared to the Roman Catholic territories. This can be traced back to the beginning of the Age of Enlightenment. The words of the Prussian King Frederick II (Frederick the Great) that everyone should find his personal luck according to his own inclinations became a guiding principle. Persons from religious minorities, such as Jews or Huguenots, also benefited from these changes. Many Roman Catholic princedoms became secularized in the Napoleon area, especially by the Principal Decree of the Imperial Deputation (*Reichsdeputationshauptschluss)* of the 25th of February 1803. The attempt of 1849 to create a uniform constitution (*Paulskirchenverfassung*) with freedom of faith and conscience for the German Federation (*Deutscher Bund*), which was influenced by the American Constitution and the French Declaration of Civil Rights, failed due to conservative forces aiming at preserving and restoring the monarchies on German soil. Nevertheless, several state constitutions contained important provisions regarding individual freedoms (particularly in the Constitution of Prussia from 1850[19]). Until 1914 civil rights and liberties such as freedom of religion had been increasingly enlarged. This is why the period from the Reformation to the end of the First World War can be characterized as the long way to a state under the rule of law.

D. Current Law

The current German law on state-church-relations is primarily governed by constitutional law.

I. Constitutional Basis

A distinction has to be made between the Weimar Constitution of the German Empire of 1919 and the Basic Law of the Federal Republic of Germany of 1949.

19 See in particular Art. 12 (freedom of religious belief, to unite as a religious community and freedom of private and public practice of religion) and Art. 15 (clerical right to self-determination).

1. Weimar Constitution

The breakthrough and final recognition of basic rights – including the freedom of religion and religious equality – took place when the monarchy was replaced by the so-called Weimar Republic. The Weimar Constitution (*Weimarer Reichsverfassung*, WRV) of 1919 guaranteed "full freedom of faith and conscience" to all inhabitants of the empire (Art. 135 WRV) and introduced the separation of state and church (Art. 137 I WRV) along with the prohibition of a state church and the provision of a right to self-determination of the religious community (Art. 137 III WRV). It protected both the positive and negative freedom of religion (negative freedom of religion meaning the right not to have or express a religious or philosophical creed and the right to conceal the creed). Traditional religious communities are recognized as public bodies with the right to collect church taxes (Art. 127 V, VI WRV). This also applied to other religious communities, otherwise regarded as organized under private law, if they existed on a permanent basis. In addition to public inter-denominational schools, public denominational schools (denominationally directed state schools) were permitted if the parents of a child (or other legal guardians) insisted (Art. 149 II WRV). Moreover, public schools had to offer denominationally bound religious education. However, participation was voluntary (Art. 149 I WRV). Previous (meaning Christian) theological faculties of the universities remained. Sundays (Art. 139 WRV) as well as the property of religious communities got special state protection and the communities were supposed to be compensated for former secularization during Reformation or in the Napoleonic Era. Finally, religious communities were granted the right to exercise pastoral care in state institutions (e.g. hospitals and prisons).

2. Basic Law

Generally speaking, the German Basic Law (*Grundgesetz*) incorporates most of the Weimar Constitution's provisions on the relationship between the state and religious communities. However, it puts a stronger emphasis on the Basic Rights which form the core of the constitution. Thus, the right of religious freedom (Art. 4 I, II Basic Law) has a larger impact than during the Weimar Republic. Undoubtedly, basic rights are enforceable subjective rights. After the exhaustion of all domestic legal remedies one can file a constitutional complaint to the Federal Constitutional Court (Art. 94 I Nr. 4a Basic Law). Both freedom of religion and equality of religion form the basis of the law on state-church-relations and play a significant role in the arrangement of this law and the still persistent institutional regulations of the Weimar Constitution by giving directions and striking the balance. However, religious freedom is not guaranteed without limits. The individual religious freedom needs to be balanced whenever it interferes with colliding constitutional law, especially Basic Rights of others (as for example freedom of expression)[20]. Additionally, religious communities are bound by the law like any other (natural or juristic) person (Art. 137 III 1 WRV in conjunction with Art. 140 Basic Law).[21] Any kind of interference with freedom of religion needs to be proportional. Proportional means suitable, necessary and adequate to achieve a legitimate purpose derived from the Constitution. The standard of proportionality developed in the German law is applied in a very strict way in comparison to other constitutions. However, in extreme situations even religious communities may be banned[22] – for example if they violate human dignity or cause acts of violence.

3. Essential Characteristics of the German Religious Law

If one tries to point out the essential characteristics of the German law on state-church-relations, one can firstly point out that it is state law and not law enacted by both the state and religious communities. This also applies to state-church agreements which are widespread in Germany, because they are concluded according to state law and have to be measured against the respective national legal requirements. State-church agreements are Concordats (traditional name with regard to the RomanCatholic Church) and other contractual agreements between the State and religious communities, which need the approval of the legislature or the parliament.[23] With

20 See BVerfGE 28, 243 (260 ff.); 108, 282 (297). Regarding the dispute of the Mohammed caricatures see (from an international perspective) Nathwani, "Freedom of expression and religious feelings," 2009, pp. 507 ff.; Langer, "The Rise (and Fall?) of Defamation of Religions," 2010, pp. 257 ff.

21 BVerfGE 67, 157 (173); 70, 278 (286); 104, 337 (347 ff.).

22 BVerfG (K), NJW 2004, 47 (48); BVerwG, DBVl 2003, 873 f.; EGMR, EuGRZ 2007, 543.

23 See Ehlers, "Staatskirchenverträge," 2011, § 130, pp. 75 ff.

respect to the Catholic Church the treaties are international treaties, because the Holy See is regarded as sovereign entity under international law, with respect to everybody else they are of constitutional nature. The interpretation, specification and application of state law are done by state authorities; in case of a dispute it is handled by the state courts. This is one reason why it cannot be left to the understanding of each individual subject of fundamental rights to decide what the constitution's understanding of the terms religion, freedom of religion and religious communities is.[24] What the state cannot define, it cannot protect either. The statement of US-Chief Justice Hughes "The constitution is, what the judges say it is"[25] does not only apply to the United States. The jurisdiction of the federal courts in Germany defines religion or belief as a person's certainty about certain statements concerning the world as a whole, as well as the cause, nature and purpose of human life. This certainty is connected to the character of the individual. According to this understanding, religion is based on a transcendent reality which exceeds and encompasses the human being whereas belief is limited to secular references.[26] When defining the area of protection of freedom of religion, the self-conception of the believers and the religious communities play a significant role and has to be respected, as long as it is plausible. For example, an economic activity is primarily neutral with respect to religion. However, if the activity serves a religious aim a different evaluation, namely a protection of the activity by the freedom of religion, might be necessary. All this indicates that freedom of religion is a very broad concept. Of course, in the end it is the decision of the subject which is protected by this freedom if, how much and how it wants to make use of this generously offered constitutional freedom.

Furthermore, state-related and religious issues are separated concerning organization and content. On the one hand, there shall be no state church (Art. 137 WRV in conjunction with Art. 140 Basic Law), on the other hand, the state is obliged to ensure its denominational neutrality.[27] This

---

24 BVerfGE 83, 341 (353 ff.); cf. Morlok, *Selbstverständnis als Rechtskriterium*, 1993, pp. 431 ff.

25 See "Speech before the Chamber of Commerce, Elmira, New York (3 May 1907)," published in *Addresses and Papers of Charles Evans Hughes, Governor of New York, 1906-1908*, 1908, p. 139.

26 BVerwGE 90, 112 (115).

27 BVerfGE 19, 206 (216); 24, 236 (246); 33, 23 (28); 93, 1 (16); 102, 370 (383); 108, 282 (299 ff.); 123, 148 (178 f.).

means that the state is not allowed to identify itself with religious or irreligious beliefs or institutions. However, this does not exclude certain cooperation between the state and the religious communities. The German law may claim for itself that it shaped this cooperation in a special way. According to the German understand, the separation of state and religious communities is considered favorable, not adversarial.[28] According to this notion, the state shall support and realize the freedoms granted by the Basic Law. As indicated earlier, the basic rights do not only include rights of defense against the state, but also obligations of protection and guarantees in an objective sense both authorizing and binding the state to provide the conditions necessary for the realization of the freedom rights. Today, freedom does not only mean freedom of the state, but also freedom in the state and by the state.[29] This notion refers to all freedom rights and thus also to religious freedom. How should religion otherwise develop itself facing the great amount of state-dominated parts of public life, if it was not allowed to be brought up in for example public kindergarten, schools, universities, hospitals, military and penal institutions, retirement homes or within the scope of funeral on municipal cemeteries? The Basic Law does not demand that religious practice be confined to private life. The state may even fund religious communities. In the past, only Christian communities benefited from this. Nowadays, all religious communities can refer to the freedom of religion and the principal of equal treatment. As the state is prohibited to judge religious communities, the state may not rank them in a certain way or make the promotion dependent on manifestations of loyalty[30] or considerations of usefulness.[31] Any kind of funding needs to be done without any special purpose. By its openness towards plurality of ideological and religious beliefs the liberal state of the Basic Law preserves religious and ideological neutrality.[32]

28 See Ehlers, "Art. 140 GG," 2014, par. 9 with further references.
29 See Heckel, "Zur Zukunftsfähigkeit des deutschen 'Staatskirchenrechts' oder 'Religionsverfassungsrechts'?," 2009, pp. 309 ff.
30 BVerfGE 102, 370 (392 ff.).
31 Ehlers, "Staatskirchenrecht," § 130 par. 7.
32 BVerfGE 41, 29 (50).

II. European Convention for the Protection of Human Rights and Fundamental Freedoms

The authority of the state is not only bound by the national constitutional law, but also by the European Convention for the Protection of Human Rights and Fundamental Freedoms and thus on common European requirements, which include the guarantee of the freedom of conscience, thought and religion (Art. 9 ECHR). The European Court of Human Rights (the "Court") supervises the compliance with the European Convention for the Protection of Human Rights and Fundamental Freedoms. The Court's jurisprudence may deviate from the jurisprudence of the Federal Constitutional Court. The Federal Republic of Germany is obliged by international law to abide by the judgments of the European Court of Human Rights. From a domestic perspective the European Convention on Human Rights ranks only as an ordinary law below the constitution. However, the Federal Constitutional Court interprets the Constitution in a way to accommodate international law[33], as long as the standard of protection of fundamental rights is not reduced or limited. Therefore, the decisions of the European Court of Human Rights are used as an auxiliary of interpretation and determination of the content and range of the German basic rights and fundamental principles of the Basic law.

In fact, more and more appeals are addressed to the European Court of Human Rights in order to clarify essential questions related to religious law. Its administration of justice in this regard is however characterized by reluctance.[34] Due to the different cultural and moral concepts regarding the role of religion in the European society the Court generally concedes every member state a wide margin of appreciation in religious issues in order to balance the conflicting freedoms (as the positive and negative freedom of religion or freedom of religion and freedom of expression). In these cases, the Court does not apply a strict test of proportionality (be-

---

33 BVerfGE 74, 358 (370); 111, 307 (317 ff.).

34 For a typical example, see the decision of the ECHR concerning the presence of a crucifix in Italian school classes (footnote 43). For the question whether the Burka ban in public places is a breach of the Convention, see ECHR (Grand Chamber), Judgment of 1.7.2014 (Application no. 43835/11).

cause otherwise there would be no margin of appreciation[35]). There might be exceptions in specific cases: In Germany, employees of the Church are subject to a particular clerical obligation of loyalty. This, for example, led to the case that an organist and choir director employed by the Catholic Church was dismissed because he had separated from his wife and moved to his new partner who was expecting a child from him. This is against catholic moral concepts. The German courts including the Federal Constitutional Court all considered the dismissal legal[36], whereas the European Court of Human Rights[37] claimed a violation of the right to privacy (Art. 8 ECHR). This shows that the German religious law sometimes needs to accept selective corrections by European law. However, huge corrections should not be expected.

III. Current Problems

The challenges religious law is currently facing and will face in the near future especially refer to the constant trend of secularization and pluralization in Germany. Approximately 33% of the German population does not belong to any religious community. Only 48% are members of one of the Christian Churches.[38] Moreover, according to surveys, approximately four million Muslims are living in Germany with a rising tendency. Besides these religions, there are numerous religious communities with a smaller number of members: for example Jewish, Buddhist and Hindu communities or so called “Youth religions” (questionable term referring mostly to religious-ideological communities propagating syncretic beliefs and attracting primarily young people[39]). The problems resulting from this diversification shall be illustrated by the following two examples.

---

35 Dissenting Follesdal, “Religion and the State – the European Court of Human Rights and the ‘Lautsi’ Case” about Kruxifixes in Italien Class Rooms (in this Volume).

36 Judgement of the Federal Labour Court, NJW 2000, 1286; BVerfG (K), file no. 2 BvR 1160/00.

37 ECHR, EuGRZ 2010, 560.

38 Figures of the Federal Agency for Public Education (Bundeszentrale für politische Bildung) for the year 2010.

39 For example transcendental meditation societies like Rayneesh Chandra Mohan (Osho-Movement).

1. Secularization

Secularization in this context shall not only mean alienation from religion, but also atheism (the belief that there is no God or that there are not any gods). The atheistic beliefs and ways of behavior are also protected by the basic right of religious freedom. Within public institutions, such as schools, one might ask the question how positive and negative freedom of religion may be brought into a balance. In the past, crucifixes were affixed to class room walls in public schools in many areas in Germany. This corresponded with the will of the Christian majority. However, during the eighties and nineties of the last century parents took legal action against this because they conceived the crucifix as a Christian symbol and did not want their children to be educated "under the crucifix" on the basis of their atheistic conviction. Although neither a commandment nor a ban was imposed on those pupils, the Federal Constitutional Court decided in a highly controversial judgment that the daily confrontation with a Christian symbol violates the negative religious freedom of the dissenting pupils and rather that of their parents and that this violation cannot be justified in as the crucifix has a missionary significance.[40] Nevertheless, the German state of Bavaria left all crucifixes in classrooms referring to its history and culture while conceding the right to object against a crucifix in a classroom to all pupils and parents on the basis of severe and respectable reasons of belief or ideology. The school director needs to find a compromise whenever there is a dispute between those welcoming the crucifix and those objecting it.[41] The Federal Administrative Court thus decided that the school needs to accept the objections of parents if they are atheist or regard it as unacceptable that their child is exposed to religious influences in its upbringing because of irreligious beliefs. Mere ideological indifference does not constitute a basis for objection.[42] With regard to this matter there is no matching decision of the European Court of Human Rights concerning Germany. However, in a case concerning Italy, the European Court of Human Rights decided that it falls into the appreciation of the contracting state to determine the legality of displaying a Christian cross in a class room of a public school.[43]

---

40 BVerfGE 93, 1 ff.

41 Art. 7 III BayEUG, in the version dated 23.12.1995.

42 BVerwG, NJW 1999, 3063 ff.

43 ECHR (Grand Chamber), NVwZ 2011, 737.

2. Pluralism

Religious Pluralism means a rising diversification of religions and religious communities, thus evoking questions of equal treatment. In Germany, for example, there is a discussion on the question whether a female Muslim teacher employed as a civil servant and working in a public school may wear a headscarf for religious reasons. Pupils are allowed to do so. As public servants represent the state, a different situation might apply to them. At the same time, one needs to take into account the religious freedom of public servants which must not be completely suppressed by their status as public servants. The Federal Constitutional Court had initially hesitated to decide how to solve this conflict. It had restricted itself to demand a legal provision.[44] The German states thus enacted different and not always clear laws. Some of them can be interpreted as a general ban on religiously motivated clothing, whereas the depiction of Christian-Western cultural symbols is allowed. But, this is not in accordance with the denominational neutrality of the state and the principal of equality: If religious avowals in the outer appearance of educators are strictly banned to protect neutrality and peace of the school, this principle has to apply to all religions indiscriminately.[45]

It is not acceptable to argue that religious freedom is not guaranteed in all Islamic-orientated states and thus to conclude that the religious freedom of Muslims in Germany does not need to be taken seriously. Religious freedom and the principle of equality are human rights which apply to all people living in Germany, independent from the situation in other countries.

E. Conclusion

Before the background of this volume's title "Political and religious communities – partners, competitors and aliens" it shall be noted that the times in which the state and the religious communities competed for the power within a community belong to the past. The separation of state and religion ensures both the liberality of the political community and the free development of religion. Therefore, one can hardly speak of "competitors"

---

44 BVerfGE 108, 282 ff.
45 BVerfG, NJW 2015, 1359 ff.

or "enemies". In some ways these communities remain aliens or become aliens because they both primarily fulfill different tasks and have different opinions. Abolition for example is under certain conditions legally permitted, although fundamentally repudiated by several religious communities. However, also religious communities claim to influence the actions of their members living in the real world. Especially in state-run institutions such as schools, universities, cemeteries and other institutions, the state and religious communities normally face each other in a cooperative way. However, the fewer people make use of their positive religious freedom, the more often citizens will claim their negative religious freedom in public institutions and the more often the state will be confronted with difficult questions of equal treatment and it will be more probable that the state will limit cooperation with and promotion of the churches as these are not legally obligatory.

In conclusion, the degree of cooperation between the state and the religious communities is on a stable level even though it is likely to decrease in the future.

Bibliography

Augustinus Aurelius, *De Civitate Dei*, translated by Thimme, Münster: dtv, 1978.

Bielefeldt, Heiner, *Streit um Religionsfreiheit. Aktuelle Facetten der internationalen Debatte,* Erlangen: Friedrich-Alexander-Universität Erlangen-Nürnberg, 2012.

Callies, Christian, "Schutzpflichten," in *Handbuch der Grundrechte*, *Vol. 2*, ed. Detlef Merten and Hans-Jürgen Papier, Heidelberg: C.F. Müller, 2006, § 44.

Campenhausen, Axel Freiherr von, *Staat und Kirche in Frankreich*, Göttingen: Otto Schwarz, 1962.

Campenhausen, Axel Freiherr von, and Heinrich de Wall, *Staatskirchenrecht*, 4th ed., Munich: C.H. Beck, 2006.

Classen, Claus Dieter, *Religionsrecht*, 2n ed., Tübingen: Mohr-Siebeck, 2015.

De Wall, Heinrich, and Stefan Muckel, *Kirchenrecht*, 4th ed., Munich: C.H. Beck, 2014.

Ehlers, Dirk, "Staatskirchenrecht," in *Leitgedanken des Rechts, Paul Kirchhof zum 70. Geburtstag*, ed. Hanno Kube, Rudolf Mellinghoff, Gerd Morgenthaler, Ulrich Palm, Christian Seiler, and Thomas Puhl, Heidelberg et al.: C.F. Müller, 2013, pp. 1417-1426.

Ehlers, Dirk, "Staatskirchenverträge," in *Die Privilegien der Kirchen und das Grundgesetz, 4. Berliner Gespräche über das Verhältnis von Staat, Religion und Weltanschauung*, ed. Rosemarie Will, Norderstedt: Books on Demand, 2011, § 130.

Ehlers, Dirk, "Art. 140 GG," in *Grundgesetz*, ed. Michael Sachs, 7th ed., Munich: C.H. Beck, 2014.

Evangelische Kirche Deutschlands, "Bedrohung der Religionsfreiheit, Erfahrungen von Christen in verschiedenen Ländern," 2003, available at http://www.ekd.de/EKD-Texte/44616.html.

Follesdal, Andreas, "Religion and the State – the European Court of Human Rights and the 'Lautsi' Case" (in this Volume).

Fuhrmann, Horst, *Das Constitutum Constantini, Monumenta Germaniae Historica – Fontes Iuris Germanici antiqui 18*, Hannover: Hahn, 1968.

Grabenwarter, Christoph, and Katharina Pabel, *Europäische Menschenrechtskonvention*, 5th ed., Munich: Beck, 2012.

Hainbach-Steins, Marianne, *Religionsfreiheit. Ein Menschenrecht unter Druck*, Paderborn: Ferdinand Schönigh, 2012.

Heckel, Martin, "Zur Zukunftsfähigkeit des deutschen 'Staatskirchenrechts' oder 'Religionsverfassungsrechts'?," Archiv des öffentlichen Rechts 134 (2009): 309-390.

Hughes, Charles Evans, *Addresses and Papers of Charles Evans Hughes: Governor of New York*, ed. Jacob Gould Schurman, New York, 1908.

Karpenstein, Ulrich, and Franz C. Mayer, *EMRK. Konvention zum Schutz der Menschenrechte und Grundfreiheiten. Kommentar*, Munich: C.H. Beck, 2012.

Langer, Lorenz, "The Rise (and Fall?) of Defamation of Religions," *Yale Journal of International Law* 35 (2010): 257-263.

Link, Christoph, *Kirchliche Rechtsgeschichte*, 2nd ed., Munich: C.H. Beck, 2010.

Luxemburg, Rosa, *Die Russische Revolution. Eine kritische Würdigung*, Berlin: Verlag Gesellschaft und Erziehung, 1922.

Morlok, Martin, *Selbstverständnis als Rechtskriterium*, Tübingen: Mohr Siebeck, 1993.

Mückl, Stefan, *Europäisierung des Staatskirchenrechts*, Baden Baden: Nomos 2005.

Nathwani, Niray, "Freedom of Expression and Religious Feelings," in *Yearbook of Muslims in Europe, Vol. 1*, ed. Jørgen S. Nielsen, Samim Akgönül, Ahmet Alibašić, Brigitte Maréchal, and Christian Moe, Leiden: Brill, 2009, pp. 507-532.

Pew Research Centers on Religions & Public Life, "Rising Tide of Restrictions on Religion," 2012, available at http://www.pewforum.org/2012/09/20/rising-tide-of-restrictions-on-religion-findings/.

Schilling, Heinz, and Heribert Smolinsky, *Der Augsburger Religionsfrieden 1555*, Gütersloh: Gütersloher Verlagshaus, 2007.

Ungern-Sternberg, Antje von, "Art. 9," in *EMRK. Konvention zum Schutz der Menschenrechte und Grundfreiheiten. Kommentar*, ed. Ulrich Karpenstein and Franz C. Mayer, Munich: C.H. Beck, 2012.

Unruh, Peter, *Religionsverfassungsrecht*, 2nd ed., Baden-Baden: Nomos, 2011.

Uslubaş, Ramazon, *Das Präsidium für Diyanet-Angelegenheiten der Republik Türkei*, Frankfurt a.M.: Peter Lang, 2014.

Should Criminal Law Protect Against Religious Defamation? Some Reflections on the Applicability of Sec. 166 of the German Criminal Code and the Current Situation in Germany

Robert Esser[*]

A. Protection of Religious Belief by Means of Criminal Law?

To punish a specific behaviour with a criminal sentence is considered the *ultima ratio* of the legislator's reaction to certain grievances in society. In German law, the legal basis for the criminalization of religious defamation would be Art. 4 of the Basic Law (*Grundgesetz* – GG), the Constitution of the Federal Republic of Germany:

> [Freedom of faith and conscience]
>
> (1) Freedom of faith and of conscience, and freedom to profess a religious or philosophical creed, shall be inviolable.
> (2) The undisturbed practice of religion shall be guaranteed.
> (3) No person shall be compelled against his conscience to render military service involving the use of arms. Details shall be regulated by a federal law.

What may seem unusual at first becomes clearer when taking a look at the nature of fundamental rights in the German legal system. Nearly all fundamental rights are above all defensive rights which protect the individual from infringement by the state. However, to be capable of actively making use of their fundamental rights, citizens have to be provided with effective legal protection by the state. In the present context that means: while the believer certainly enjoys his freedom to practice his religious beliefs and has to be protected to be able to do so, the non-believer and even the "blasphemer", too, may claim to have their rights protected by the Constitution.

---

* The chapter was completed in October 2015.

The Basic Law of 1949 is guided and inspired by a liberal spirit. The Federal Constitutional Court (*Bundesverfassungsgericht* – BVerfG) expressed in one of its leading verdicts that neither the protection of a "general feeling of peace" nor the protection from "poisoning the spiritual climate" could justify an infringement of fundamental rights.[1]

Other courts in Germany emphasize the liberal spirit of the freedom to profess a religious belief, too. The Administrative Tribunal (*Verwaltungsgericht* – VG) in Hamburg once proclaimed:

"Art. 4 § 1 GG protects believers against incursion by the state in their religious beliefs and activities and obliges the state to ensure an environment in which one's personality can unfold in the field of religious beliefs; it especially obliges the state to protect believers from attacks or other ways of infringement by believers of other religious groups. Art. 4 § 1 GG does not, however, give a right to state support in order to express one's religious beliefs."[2]

I. Arguments in Favour of Criminalization of Religious Defamation

Nonetheless, there are of course arguments speaking in favour of criminalizing religious defamation:

1. The protection of religious freedom may only be effective by means of specific statutory criminal norms. Every other form of legal protection might not be as effective in preventing religious defamation.
2. German criminal law already knows the criminal offences of "Incitement to hatred" (*Volksverhetzung*), Sec. 130 of the German Criminal Code (*Strafgesetzbuch* – StGB), and "Insult" in Sec. 185 ff. StGB. The StGB also contains Sec. 166 entitled "Defamation of religions, religious and ideological associations" (*Beschimpfung von Bekenntnissen, Religionsgesellschaften und Weltanschauungsvereinigungen*). Those criminal offences have, to some extent, proven ineffective for protecting religious beliefs because of their narrow approach and due to some forms of "overlapping": the offence of "Incitement to hatred" interferes with Sec. 166 StGB if verbal harassment is not only directed against the religious belief in respect of the institution, but also against an indi-

---

1 BVerfGE 124, p. 334.

2 VG Hamburg, 2012, p. 2536 (translated).

vidual personally, amounting to an attack against that person's human dignity. In that case, Sec. 166 StGB steps back behind Sec. 130 StGB. Sec. 166 StGB has an autonomous meaning and scope if verbal abuse is not directed against a person and that person's human dignity is thus not under attack. The scope of Sec. 185 ff. StGB does not comprise verbal abuse of the contents of religious beliefs if the attack is not directed at a person or a community at the same time.
3. Other arguments that militate in favour of criminalizing religious defamation are: the danger of compromising public morality if religious defamation is not considered a criminal offence; the protection of public peace; the protection of believers; the social value of religion which justifies special protection; and the right to recognition of religious beliefs and the predetermination set by the Basic Law in its Art. 4, guaranteeing the freedom of religion, and in its preamble ("Conscious of their responsibility before God and man…").

II. Arguments Against Criminalization of Religious Defamation

Despite the multitude of arguments that would speak in favour of criminalizing religious defamation, there are quite a few arguments against it.

1. One of these is plain and simple: criminalization of religious defamation is superfluous because there simply is no necessity to punish. In Germany, there are around a dozen condemnations for religious defamation (Sec. 166 StGB) per year.[3] This low number of cases simply does not justify widening the scope of the offence.
2. In addition, there are grave constitutional concerns regarding Sec. 166 § 1 StGB and the principle of legal certainty (*nulla poena sine lege certa*) enshrined in Art. 103 § 2 of the Basic Law.
3. Criminal law has to restrain itself from governing every aspect of life. It is no moral codex but seeks to protect society from *grave* breaches

3 See for instance BT-Drucks. 16/3579 of 27 November 2006, pp. 2-4; Landtag-NRW Drucks. 16/4408 of 21 November 2013, pp.2-3; *Hörnle*, "Bekenntnisbeschimpfung (§ 166): Aufheben oder Ausweiten," 2015, p. 293; Statistisches Bundesamt, Fachserie 10, Reihe 3, Tab. 2.1, at https:// www.destatis.de/DE/Publikationen/Thematisch/Rechtspflege/StrafverfolgungVollzug/Strafverfolgung2100300137004.pdf?__blob=publicationFile, accessed 18 September 2015.

of fundamental norms – like the right to life, the right to physical integrity or the right to property.

4. A return to the blasphemy statute of olden times is unwanted by a majority of the German population because society has evolved and become more liberal.
5. The protection of religious beliefs considered to be "right" or "acceptable" versus the non-protection of those considered "wrong" or "unacceptable" could prove to infringe upon the right to equality guaranteed in Art. 3 of the Basic Law.
6. Most certainly, the criminalization of religious defamation would collide with the freedom of expression and art guaranteed in Art. 5 of the Basic Law and Art. 10 of the European Convention on Human Rights (ECHR).[4] It is possible that criminalizing religious defamation would effectively prohibit an open and critical discussing of topics with religious content.
7. Another imminent danger in the discussion concerning the criminalization of religious defamation is that big religious communities have a far greater lobby than smaller ones. They could foster their special interests much more effectively than smaller ones which in the end might lead to an imbalance among the religious communities themselves.
8. Last but not least it has to be considered that public peace is not an autonomous legal interest as such that can be protected by criminal law. It is thus inconceivable to criminalize religious defamation for the sake of public peace alone.

B. Structure of Sec. 166 StGB

In order to decide if a deficiency of protection of religious beliefs by means of criminal law exists in Germany it is important to visualize the structure of Sec. 166 of the German Criminal Court which reads as follows:

Sec. 166

4 See for a detailed analysis: Arslan, *Meinungs- und Kunstfreiheit gegen die Religionsfreiheit – Wie viel Schutz für religiöse Empfindlichkeiten*, 2015.

Defamation of religions, religious and ideological associations

(1) Whosoever publicly or through dissemination of written materials (Sec. 11 § 3) defames the content of the religious or ideological conviction of others in a manner that is capable of disturbing the public peace, shall be liable to imprisonment not exceeding three years or a fine.
(2) Whosoever publicly or through dissemination of written materials (Sec. 11 § 3) defames a church or other religious or ideological association within Germany, or their institutions or customs in a manner that is capable of disturbing the public peace, shall incur the same penalty.

I. The Legal Interest Protected by Sec. 166 StGB

Sec. 166 StGB is conceived as a strict liability tort (*abstraktes Gefährdungsdelikt*). Its protected legal interest (*Rechtsgut*) is the public peace only. This view is disputed but still prevails in the German legal community.[5] It is thus clear that neither God nor religions or ideologies nor religious feelings of believers nor individual convictions are protected.[6]

II. The Object of the Offence

The object of the offence is split in § 1 and § 2:

1. In § 1 the object is the content of a religious or an ideological conviction of another individual. An individual is convinced of something if she is "manifestly convinced of higher beliefs beyond mere persuasion". "Conviction" within the meaning of Sec. 166 StGB does not require that an individual relies on a complex set of convictions as a whole; relying upon essential parts of a conviction is sufficient.[7] It is thus not necessary that a believer include each and every teaching of a certain belief into her personal conviction to be actually convinced of the said belief.

5 See Lackner, Kühl, and Heger, *StGB*, 2014, § 166, marginal no. 1.

6 See OLG Karlsruhe, 1986, p. 364; OLG Nürnberg, 1999, p. 239; Lackner, Kühl, and Heger, *StGB*, § 166, marginal no. 1; Schönke, Schröder, Lenckner, and Bosch, *StGB*, 2014, Vor § 166, marginal no. 2; Muckel, "Kein Anspruch eines Privaten auf Untersagung eines blasphemischen Bühnenstücks – 'Gólgota Picnic'," 2013, p. 73.

7 See Schönke, Schröder, Lenckner, and Bosch, *StGB*, § 166, marginal no. 4.

2. In § 2, churches and other religious groupings and ideological groups as well as their facilities and customs have to be targeted. Outside the scope of Sec. 166 § 2 StGB are attacks against individuals, objects of religious worship or other religious objects.[8] Sec. 166 StGB is an offence against the institution as such.

III. "Defamation" Within the Meaning of Sec. 166 StGB

1. Defamation in the sense of Sec. 166 reads as an expression of disrespect that is especially damaging through its form or content. Not every disrespectful comment amounts to defamation.[9] Even provoking, disapproving or harsh critique is permitted.[10] Defamation cannot be defined as mere touting with the aim of ridiculing or the mere negation of holiness. Neither can defamation be committed by stating true facts.[11] Every statement has to be evaluated objectively and impartially.[12]
2. Defamation can be committed orally, in written form and by means of symbolic acts and pictures. However, questions and problems may arise when the meaning of symbols and pictures is in doubt.
3. Defamation has to be interpreted in a restrictive manner because of the inherent conflict with the freedom of expression enshrined in Art. 5 § 1 of the Basic Law and Art. 10 § 1 sentence 1 of the European Convention on Human Rights (ECHR):

   Article 5 Basic Law/German Constitution [Freedom of expression, arts and sciences]

   (1) Every person shall have the right freely to express and disseminate his opinions in speech, writing and pictures, and to inform himself without hindrance from generally accessible sources. Freedom of the press and

---

8 See Maurach, Schröder, and Maiwald, *Strafrecht Besonderer Teil*, 2012, § 61 II, marginal no. 11.

9 See Hörnle, in *Münchener Kommentar zum StGB*, 2012, § 166, marginal no. 15.

10 See for instance VG Sigmaringen, Judgment of 19 January 2011 – 1 K 1561/10 –, juris § 35; VGH München, 2011, p. 795; ECtHR, *NVwZ* 2007, p. 316; Fahl, "Zur Strafbarkeit des Auftritts der Punk-Rock-Band 'Pussy Riot' nach deutschem Strafrecht," 2013, p. 2.

11 See Hörnle, in *Münchener Kommentar zum StGB*, § 166, marginal no. 17.

12 See Satzger, Schluckebier, Widmaier, and Hilgendorf, *Strafgesetzbuch*, 2014, § 166, marginal no. 16.

freedom of reporting by means of broadcasts and films shall be guaranteed. There shall be no censorship.

(2) These rights shall find their limits in the provisions of general laws, in provisions for the protection of young persons, and in the right to personal honour.

(3) Arts and sciences, research and teaching shall be free. The freedom of teaching shall not release any person from allegiance to the constitution.

Article 10 ECHR [Freedom of expression]

(1) Everyone has the right to freedom of expression. This right shall include freedom to hold opinions and to receive and impart information and ideas without interference by public authority and regardless of frontiers. This article shall not prevent States from requiring the licensing of broadcasting, television or cinema enterprises.

(2) The exercise of these freedoms, since it carries with it duties and responsibilities, may be subject to such formalities, conditions, restrictions or penalties as are prescribed by law and are necessary in a democratic society, in the interests of national security, territorial integrity or public safety, for the prevention of disorder or crime, for the protection of health or morals, for the protection of the reputation or rights of others, for preventing the disclosure of information received in confidence, or for maintaining the authority and impartiality of the judiciary.

The task of criminal courts is to balance the freedom of expression and the respect for freedom of religion, of thought and of conscience in every individual case.[13] According to the German Federal Constitutional Court (BVerfG) even exaggerated criticism falls in principle within the scope of freedom of expression unless it can be regarded as "mere abusive" criticism ("Schmähkritik"). Even excessive and polemical criticism, in itself, does not make a statement defamatory provided that the statement is connected to a dispute in the matter, so that contempt of a person does not come to the foreground.[14]

The problems criminal courts face when they have to decide on defamation cases in connotation with religious matters can be illustrated by two leading judgments of the European Court of Human Rights (ECtHR) in Strasbourg which has been set up in order to ensure the observance of the engagements undertaken by the High Contracting Parties in the Convention and the Protocols thereto (Art. 19 ECHR).

---

13 See for example Isensee, "Meinungsfreiheit im Streit mit der Religion – 'Gotteslästerung' heute," 2013, pp. 190 ff.

14 BVerfG, Decision of 28 July 2014 – 1 BvR 482/13, *ZUM* 2014, p. 965; see also: LG Düsseldorf, *NStZ* 1982, p. 291.

4. In Tatlav vs. Turkey the European Court of Human Rights (ECtHR) in Strasbourg ruled in 2006 that the freedom of expression (Art. 10 ECHR) is not only guaranteed "for 'information' or 'ideas' that are well perceived or being considered as inoffensive or irrelevant, but also for those that hurt, shock or disturb."[15] This judgment of the ECtHR was preceded by a conviction of the Turkish journalist Erdogan Aydin Tatlav (born 1957 and living in Istanbul). The District Court of Ankara sentenced *Tatlav* in 1998 for a "publication which aims at the defamation of a religion".[16] The occasion for the sentence of *Tatlav*, who worked as a journalist, was the publication of the five books comprising work entitled "Islamiyet Gerçegi" ("The reality of Islam") in 1992. The work criticized the Islam as a religion legitimizing social injustice by portraying the injustice as "God's will"; 16,500 copies were sold within only a few years.[17] Only after the fifth edition was published in 1996, Tatlav was charged with blasphemy against "God, the Religion, the Prophet and the Holy Book" according to Art. 175 of the Turkish Criminal Code. He was sentenced to one year imprisonment, which was later reduced to a fine. After the Turkish Court of Cassation had confirmed the sentence of the previous instance, Tatlav complained before the European Court of Human Rights (ECtHR) that this judgment was a violation of the right to freedom of expression (Art. 10 ECHR).
Finally, the ECtHR held unanimously that there had been a violation of Art. 10 of the Convention. The Court continued saying that "[w]ith regard to religious beliefs there can exist an obligation to refrain from insulting or profaning statements".[18] However, in the view of the Court, "[t]hose exercising their right to religion […] cannot […] expect to be protected from any form of critique. […] [They] have to tolerate others disapproving of their religious beliefs and even teachings defying their faith".[19]
The Court concluded that certain parts of the book indeed contained criticism of the religion in a socio-political context, but that these passages did not offend Muslims or their sacred symbols to an extent that

15 Translated from the binding French version of the judgment: ECtHR, Tatlav v. Turkey, Judgment of 2 May 2006, no. 50692/99, § 22, *NVwZ* 2007, p. 314.
16 Ibid., §§ 8-17.
17 See ibid., §§ 9-10.
18 Ibid., § 23.
19 Ibid., § 28.

would justify a criminal charge. The court also considered the fact that the alleged offence was prosecuted for the first time in 1996 and concluded from the "delay" in prosecution that the insult was not very intense. Furthermore, the Court also included into its reasoning the danger that other journalists and editors would feel discouraged to publish their opinions on religion, which the Court sees as an essential part of a democracy.

5. In I.A. vs. Turkey (2005) the ECtHR had already ruled on a condemnation of a journalist for defamation of Islam.[20] In 1996 a Turkish Court had sentenced a journalist and editor for publishing the novel "Yasak Tümceler" ("The Forbidden Phrases") according to Art. 175 §§ 3 and 4 of the Turkish Criminal Code. The work was accused of containing theological concepts critical to Islam[21] and insults relating to "God, the Religion, the Prophet and the Holy Book". For example it mentioned that "Mohammed did not forbid sexual intercourse with a dead person or a living animal".
   The European Court of Human Rights held that Art. 175 of the Turkish Criminal Code (TCC) restricted the author's freedom of expression. However, the court found that the reason behind Art. 175 TCC was primarily the prevention of disorder and the protection of morals and the rights of others thereby justifying a restriction of the right to freedom of expression. Therefore, the Court held that it was necessary to assess every individual case as to whether there had been a violation of the freedom of expression included in Article 10 of the Convention.[22]
   The Court considered the claimant's right to publish and distribute views on religious theory on the one side; on the other side, the Court found that every individual's right to freedom of opinion, conscience and religion has to be respected. It has to be tolerated that not everyone has the same religion or even adopts a particular religious orientation at all. However, intentional attacks on a religious group do not have to be accepted or tolerated. In the Turkish case, the Court held that parts of the book actually contained insulting attacks on the Prophet Mohammed and some of his statements. According to this it found that be-

20 ECtHR, I. A. v. Turkey, Judgment of 13 September 2005, no. 42571/98, *ECtHR 2005-VIII*, §§ 25-32.

21 See ibid., §§ 5-6, 13.

22 See ibid., §§ 30-32.

lievers could rightfully feel violated in their religious feelings. Hence, they found no violation of Article 10 of the Convention.

IV. Public

In order for public peace to be endangered and to give rise to the protection by Sec. 166 StGB, the defamation has to be made publicly. 'Public' can be defined as a sufficiently large group of people not bound by personal relations.[23] Defamation in public could be committed by divulging scripts, sound and image carriers, hard disks, pictures and any depiction accessible by a large group of people. Of course, defamation in public can also be done by means of the Internet.

V. Limited Scope of Application of Sec. 166 StGB due to Freedom of Art

As mentioned above, Sec. 166 StGB conflicts not only with the freedom of expression of others but also with the freedom of art guaranteed by Art. 5 § 3 of the Basic Law.[24] That is why some works of art, especially those bearing an ironic and critical character, cannot be considered defamatory. The Higher Administrative Court (*Oberverwaltungsgericht*) of Berlin-Brandenburg ruled that publishing caricatures of Islamic Prophet Mohammed during a demonstration cannot usually be seen as defamation.[25] That decision points out that Art. 4 of the German Constitution does not protect the freedom of belief in any case against the hurting of religious feelings by private persons, at least if the defendant can also can claim a fundamental right for their activities (such as the freedom of art)

---

23 See Satzger, Schluckebier, Widmaier, and Hilgendorf, *Strafgesetzbuch*, § 166, marginal no. 18.

24 See BVerfG, *NJW* 1971, pp. 1645 f.; Isensee, "Meinungsfreiheit im Streit mit der Religion – 'Gotteslästerung' heute," p. 192.

25 OVG Berlin-Brandenburg, *NJW* 2012, p. 3116 (preliminary review); Cornils, "Gefühlsschutz, negative Informationsfreiheit oder Staatliche Toleranzpflege: Blasphemieverbote in rechtlicher Begründungsnot," 2013, p. 200.

that prevails over the the freedom of belief by way of so-called "practical concordance" of the basic rights concerned by the conflict.[26]

VI. Ability to Disturb Public Peace

1. In Germany religious defamation is only subject to criminal prosecution if it is able to disturb public peace. Defamation that "only" disturbs religious feelings does not fall within the scope of Sec. 166 StGB.[27]
   However, in a judgment delivered in 1999 the Court of Appeal (Oberlandesgericht – OLG) of Nuremberg decided that public peace is disturbed "either by shattering justifiable confidence of those affected in the respect and tolerance of their beliefs protected by the legal order or by encouraging intolerance against the defamed belief with regard to third parties".[28]
   In contrast to the aforementioned, the German Constitutional Court (BVerfG) has in one of its fundamental verdicts opted for a rather narrow approach and presumed that in order for the assumption of the capability of a special behaviour to qualify as disturbance of public peace, the threatening of the legally-protected interest needs to already have transitioned into aggression or breach of law.[29]
   The definition used by the Court of Appeal (Oberlandesgericht) of Nuremberg is also criticized by Tatjana Hörnle[30] who points out that "defaming" includes, in most cases anyway, an impairment of faith on behalf of the victims. Thus, the characteristic "capability of disturbing public peace" does not constitute a "filter effect". However, if one

---

26 Kau, "Polizeiliches Filmverbot im Spannungsverhältnis von Kunst- und Meinungsfreiheit – der sog. 'Mohammed-Film' im Lichte von Art. 5 GG," 2015, pp. 72, 78.

27 See Schönke, Schröder, Lenckner, and Bosch, *StGB*, § 166, marginal no. 12; Maurach, Schröder, and Maiwald, *Strafrecht Besonderer Teil*, Teilband 2, § 61 II, marginal no. 14.

28 OLG Nürnberg, *NStZ-RR* 1999, p. 240.

29 BVerfG, Decision of 4 November 2009 – 1 BvR 2150/08, § 77, *NJW* 2010, p. 51 – concerning § 130 para. 4 StGB; VGH München, *NJW* 2011, p. 795; Hörnle, "Bekenntnisbeschimpfung (§ 166): Aufheben oder Ausweiten," p. 294.

30 See Hörnle, "Strafbarkeit anti-islamischer Propaganda als Bekenntnis-beschimpfung," 2012, p. 3417.

based the "capability of disturbance of public peace" solely on the reaction of the believers, it would, in the light of the significant differences concerning the reactions of Muslims and Christians, lead to "false emphasis" on the subtext of Sec. § 166 StGB. In fact, it is much more decisive whether the defamation of the confession/religious belief reveals "that the intentionally pursued objective is the emotional incitement of third parties against the religious confession/belief".

2. Some critique is voiced in the German legal community that the requirement of the disturbance of public peace has developed into an instrument to restrain the application of the offence.[31] Whenever big religious communities are concerned, no defamation is able to cause perturbation because of its irrelevance. Whenever small religious communities are concerned, the number of believers offended is just too small to disturb public peace.[32] Whenever those offended retain their composure, no perturbation is perceived. On the other hand, whenever those offended lose their composure, their reaction is considered inadequate and thus irrelevant for public peace.

VII. Examples Constituted by Jurisdiction or Examples of Different Courts' Decisions

A recent example of developments in the interpretation of the term "ability to disturb public peace" was provided by a Local Court (Amtsgericht – AG) located in Berlin which ruled that naming the Catholic Church a "sect of paedophiles" on the Internet (i.e. publicly) was *defamation*, but was unable to disturb public peace.[33]

Similarly, the Regional Court (Landgericht – LG) of Bochum decided with reference to a caricature in which a crucifix (the main Christian symbol) is depicted as a mousetrap and where the person lying on the crucifix beats a mouse to death when see-sawing forward. Indeed, the court af-

---

31 See Maurach, Schröder, and Maiwald, *Strafrecht Besonderer Teil*, § 61 II, marginal no. 15; OLG Karlsruhe, *NStZ* 1986, p. 365.

32 See for instance Isensee, "Meinungsfreiheit im Streit mit der Religion – 'Gotteslästerung' heute," p. 190.

33 AG Berlin-Tiergarten, Judgment of 6 February 2012 – (263b Ds) 224 Js 3745/11 (228/11), 263b Ds 228/11, *StraFo* 2012, 110.

firmed in this case *defamation* in the sense of Sec. 166 StGB, but did not conclude that a disturbance of public peace had occurred.[34]

In addition, in the case of criticism of the church-designed float on the occasion of Christopher Street Day, the Higher Administrative Court (Verwaltungsgerichtshof – VGH) of Munich concluded that a disturbance of public peace had not occured. The float represented a "popemobile"[35] and contained illustrations of the Pope, inter alia with a HIV ribbon and condoms. Yet the court did not see, on account of a lack of transition to a threatening of the protected legal interest, an impairment of the peaceful coexistence in the expressed criticism of the Church.[36]

Finally, in the case of the satirical television series "Popetown"[37], a disturbance of public peace was also not assumed by the Regional Court (Landgericht) of Munich.[38]

C. *Sec. 166 StGB as Subject in the World of Politics*

The widening of the scope of Sec. 166 StGB in the area of criminal law through a removal of the passage "Capability to disturb public peace" has already been the subject of parliamentary initiatives on multiple occasions. It is noteworthy that those were, most of the time, initiatives from federal states via the Bundesrat and did not originate from the center of the German Bundestag. This emphasises that the widening of the criminal protection of religious convictions and feelings is rather a regional concern, more specifically a concern of the German South, which is also in religious questions rather conservatively orientated.

The removal of the passage "Capability to disturb public peace" in the norm of Sec. 166 StGB, and by this a criminal widening of the provision,

34 See LG Bochum, *NJW* 1989, pp. 727 f.

35 The "Popemobile" is a specially designed motor vehicle used by the Catholic Pope when travelling abroad during outdoor public appearances for transport and for communication with believers on the street.

36 VGH München, *NJW* 2011, pp. 793, 795.

37 "Popetown" is about the everyday life of padre *Nicholas* living in Popetown – a satirical imitation of the Vatican. The series portrays the Pope as childish and mad. The cardinals are greedy for money and corrupt.

38 LG München I, Decision of 3 May 2006 – 9 O 8051/06, §§ 5 f.; Liesching, "Anmerkung zu LG München, Beschluss vom 3. Mai 2006 – 9 O 8051/06," 2006, pp. 578 ff.

was already demanded by means of a "Länder-initiative" in the years 1986 and 1998.[39] A majority for this initiative could not even be found in the Bundesrat, the representation of the Länder (federal states) in the German Parliament.[40] In its reasoning the Bavarian Federal Government quoted, inter alia, that the scope of the norm was restricted too much by the interpretation of the characteristic *"Capability to disturb public peace"* in literature and jurisdiction whereby the protection of religious and ideological beliefs could not be sufficiently guaranteed anymore. First and foremost, the victims could not be expected to turn to peace-disturbing means in order to realise the offence.[41]

Besides that, the Länder-initiative referred to the increased sharpness and intensity of attacks on Christian belief which is proved by the rising amount of complaints submitted to public bodies and politicians by citizens. It is therefore regarded necessary that the State guarantees within the scope of its duty, the validity of constitutional fundamental values; the punishment of inappropriate disturbances (exceeding the previous extent) of the exercise of religion of fellow citizens and stipulates a standard of tolerance.

Even the reform proposal of the Free State of Bavaria dating back to 2007 which aimed, without a removal of this passage, at a widening of the sope of Sec. 166 StGB, failed.[42] The concrete proposal was as follows: in the norm of Sec. 166 StGB the word *"defames"* should have been replaced by *"degrades and ridicules."* Furthermore it was proposed to add a third paragraph which should incorporate a broad definition of *"Capability to disturb public peace."*[43] The background of this reform proposal was

39 See BR-Drucks. 460/98 of 14 May 1998; BR-Drucks. 367/86 of 11 August 1986.

40 The Parliament of the Federal Republic of Germany comprises the German Bundestag, consisting of directly elected representatives (Art. 38 GG – Basic Law), and the Bundesrat (Federal Council of Germany), consisting of members of the governments of the federal states (Art. 51 GG). An initiative for an amendment of the Criminal Code can be proposed, as with every other federal law, by the German government, by the center of the Bundestag or by the Bundesrat (Art. 76 § 1 GG).

41 See BR-Drucks. 460/98 of 14 May 1998; BR-Drucks. 367/86 of 11 August 1986.

42 See BR-Drucks. 683/07 of 1 October 2007.

43 See ibid.

the ongoing debate in 2006 on the caricatures of the Prophet Mohammed and satirical television series like "Popetown".[44]

In the end it must therefore be concluded that, in the last more then 60 years, a parliamentary majority for the widening of Sec. 166 StGB could not be built.[45]

D. Sec. 166 StGB as Subject of Academic Writing

Concerning academic writing, there are two totally opposing views regarding the future of criminalization of religious defamation.

One view proposes to eliminate the clause "capable of disturbing the public peace" to widen the scope of Sec. 166 StGB. It also proposes to define the "respect for religious and ideological tolerance" as the protected legal interest of Sec. 166 StGB. That would include a protection of believers' feelings and wishes to be appreciated.

Martin Mosebach[46] thinks it would "serv[e] art and social climate in general if blasphemy is punishable again." In particular, restrictions on the freedom of art by rules and prohibitions inspire artists to create sophisticated, creative and audacious works. The same applies, according to Mosebach, to satire in the religious sphere. The artist, conscious of the prohibition of blasphemy, would then utilise blasphemous elements more deliberately and aesthetically. Moreover, a society in which God and religious convictions are (more) present again, is to be welcomed.

Robert Spaemann[47] also militates in favour of criminalizing religious defamation. He argues that "German law and even more so the German Courts allow for public defamation and ridiculing of the holiest goods of religious citizens." The disturbance of public peace would only apply to the defamation of Islam as Christians would just not react as violently as Muslims to defamation. *Spaemann* continues saying that

---

44 See Steinke, "'Gotteslästerung' im säkularen Staat, Ein Plädoyer für die Streichung des § 166 StGB," 2008, p. 456.

45 See also Cornils, "Gefühlsschutz, negative Informationsfreiheit oder staatliche Toleranzpflege: Blasphemieverbote in rechtlicher Begründungsnot," p. 202.

46 Mosebach, "Kunst und Religion – Vom Wert des Verbietens," *Berliner Zeitung*, 18 June 2012.

47 See Spaemann, "Beleidigung Gottes oder der Gläubigen," *Frankfurter Allgemeine Zeitung (FAZ)*, 25 July 2012.

> [p]eople that are concerned with God, that do believe in God have to be protected. They are the ones insulted by religious defamation and more deeply so than by insulting themselves as individuals. [...] A state not protecting the holiest goods of its citizens cannot expect those people to feel like a part of society.

In addition, according to Müller-Neuhof, [48] Sec. 166 StGB should not be abolished for now. The norm is rather an important signal for victims who suffer from defamation of their belief, and shows behavioural limits as a message for potential offenders. However, Müller-Neuhof adds that the norm should only be applied rarely or, in case of doubt, not at all.

The contrasting view proposes the elimination of Sec. 166 StGB. That would strengthen the freedom of expression. Recently published opinions on this subject have sparked the debate once more:

Barbara Rox[49] argues that the right to practise one's religion is not impaired by defamation. Neither is the believer's internal religious freedom nor the freedom of decision to believe impaired. The denial of respect of religious believers is directed against an individual and thus falls under the scope of Sec. 185 ff. StGB (Insult). Rox consequently finds that the state has no duty to protect the believer based on fundamental rights. In her opinion, the "State has to protect the foundations of human coexistence – if necessary with means of criminal law. When the freedom of expression is affected, caution is required. [...] Not only blasphemers are expected to behave respectfully towards people of other beliefs." This effectively means that those affected have the same rights within the limits of the freedom of expression. *Rox* argues that a standstill of any public discussion concerning religious content would follow from criminalizing blasphemy whereas the public sphere should serve as a room for intellectual controversy in a democratic society.

Tatjana Hörnle[50], too, speaks up for the abolition of Sec. 166 StGB. This would be due to the norm's "lack of purpose". In particular, Hörnle sees in the legally-protected interest "public peace" no substantial reasoning for the maintenance of the norm, since the violence could often not be ascribed to the defamer, but rather to those who thereupon act violently or incite others as agitators to act in this way. Furthermore, she argues that it

48 Müller-Neuhof, "Der Bart des Propheten, " 2012, p. 907.

49 Rox, "Vom Wert der freien Rede – Zur Strafwürdigkeit der Blasphemie," 2013, p. 30 ff.

50 Hörnle, "Bekenntnisbeschimpfung (§ 166): Aufheben oder Ausweiten," p. 295.

should not be encouraged to let people define themselves solely via a single essential key group membership.

E. Current Discussion in Germany in the Light of the Terrorist Attacks in Paris in January 2015

On the occasion of the terrorist attack on the offices of the French satirical magazine Charlie Hebdo on Wednesday 7 January 2015, a discussion on the reform of Sec. 166 StGB (Defamation of religions, religious and ideological associations) unfolded in Germany. The current debate provides a good example of how the development of criminal law is not only subject to the formal international framework conditions (compulsory penalisation in public international and European law), but also to the influence of international political trends and social incidents in foreign countries.

The current reform proposals cover the whole conceivable spectrum of thoughts, i.e. they range from the abolition of the criminal provision on the one hand[51], to its notable tightening (of offence and legal consequence)[52] on the other.

A tightening of Sec. 166 StGB is in the present discussion primarily demanded by members of conservative parties. Thus the CSU-politician Stephan Mayer supports, in view of the events in France, a tightening of the penalty range of Sec. 166 StGB.[53] Wolfgang Bosbach (CDU) also stresses that a widening of the offence's range by the cancellation of the formulation "that is capable of disturbing the public peace" is right, although there is no majority prevailing for this in the Bundestag at the moment.[54]

In the context of the current debate regarding the terrorist attack on the offices of the satirical magazine Charlie Hebdo in January 2015, it is frequently postulated that Sec. 166 StGB should be abolished as a whole. This was particularly expressed in an online petition (started in January

51 See Hörnle, "Abschaffung des Blasphemie-Paragrafen?," 2015, p. 62; Steinke, "'Gotteslästerung' im säkularen Staat, Ein Plädoyer für die Streichung des § 166 StGB," p. 451.

52 See Hillgruber, "Abschaffung des Blasphemie-Paragrafen?," 2015, p. 62.

53 See Berliner Zeitung, www.bz-berlin.de/deutschland/csu-fordert-haertere-strafen-fuer-blasphemie, accessed 18 September 2015.

54 See ibid.; for this argumentation see also Hillgruber, "Abschaffung des Blasphemie-Paragrafen?," p. 62.

2015 and released on the website of the Bundestag) on the abolition of Sec. 166 StGB, which ended on 17 February 2015.[55] The petition, attracting far-reaching attention, is now in the parliamentary screening process.[56] In its rationale, the petition particularly aims at the protection of the freedom of expression, art and press.[57] Thus, it shall be underlined that intolerance and the inability of fundamentalistic-minded human beings to take criticism cannot restrict the freedom of art.[58] Other advocates for the abolition rely primarily on the conviction that no one who reacts to religious provocations with peace-disturbing acts should be protected.[59] Steinke, who pleads likewise on that score for the abolition, also criticises the vagueness of Sec. 166 StGB, since the characteristic "disturbance of the public peace" is not measureable in an objective, but only in a subjective-judgmental manner.[60]

In addition, leading politicians of the party Freie Demokraten (Free Democrats – FDP) advocate the criminal provision's abolition and argue inter alia that the defamation offences' scope already guarantees enough protection.[61] In principle, the party Bündnis 90/Die Grünen (The Greens) approves of this but nonetheless argues in favour of the retention of the norm at this time, and so do the Social Democratic Party (SPD) and the majority of the Christian Democratic/Social Union (CDU/CSU).[62]

---

55 See Deutscher Bundestag, "Petition 56759," at https://epetitionen.bundestag.de/petitionen/_2015/_01/_08/Petition_56759.html, accessed 18 September 2015.

56 See Giordano Bruno Stiftung, "Petitionsausschuss prüft Petition zur Abschaffung des 'Gotteslästerungsparagraphen'," at http://www.giordano-bruno-stiftung.de/ meldung/petition166-pruefverfahren, accessed 18 September 2015.

57 See Deutscher Bundestag, "Petition 56759," at https://epetitionen.bundestag.de/petitionen/_2015/_01/_08/Petition_56759.html, accessed 18 September 2015.

58 See. Giordano Bruno Stiftung, "Petitionsausschuss prüft Petition zur Abschaffung des 'Gotteslästerungsparagraphen'," at http://www.giordano-bruno-stiftung.de/meldung/charlie-hebdo-paragraph166-abschaffen, accessed 18 September 2015.

59 Vgl. Norouzi, "Kultur, Religion, Strafrecht – auch ein Thema für die Anwaltschaft, Herausforderungen für das Strafrecht in einer pluralistischen Gesellschaft," 2014, p. 596; Steinke, "'Gotteslästerung' im säkularen Staat, Ein Plädoyer für die Streichung des § 166 StGB," p. 456; Hörnle, *ZRP* 2015, p. 62.

60 Vgl. Steinke, "'Gotteslästerung' im säkularen Staat, Ein Plädoyer für die Streichung des § 166 StGB," pp. 453-456.

61 See Lindner and Buschmann, "Signal für mehr Meinungsfreiheit," 2015, p. 123; Zeit Online, "Grüne gegen Diskussion um Blasphemie-Paragrafen," at http://www.zeit.de/politik/deutschland/2015-01/blasphemie-charlie-hebdo-bosbach, accessed 18 September 2015.

62 See ibid., accessed 18 September 2015.

It is predominantly emphasised that the abolition of the criminal provision of the Sec. 166 StGB at this time, would by no means be a sign of solidarity vis-à-vis a country (in this case France) that was afflicted by a religiously motivated assault.[63]

In the light of the increase of religiously motivated infringements, Nils Muižnieks (Commissioner for Human Rights of the Council of Europe) stresses especially for France the need for political measures in the field of criminal law and through ratification of the Protocol No. 12[64] to the ECHR.[65]

F. Final Views

In Germany an expansion of criminal law provisions concerning blasphemous behaviour is not advisable, not to say unnecessary, even after the terrorist attack on the offices of the satirical magazine *Charlie Hebdo* in January 2015. In a democratic society pertinent criticism on deficiencies within a religious community is not only tolerable but requires a positive protection by the criminal law – by means of a narrow interpretation of existing criminal law provisions covering blasphemous behaviour.

Due to its strong basic rights protection (freedom of expression) and in conformity with human rights standards Germany has opted for a quite reluctant criminal approach concerning blasphemous behaviour and favours an open discourse on different religious topics including sharp and direct criticism on religious institutions and representatives of religious communities. Against meaningless, nasty or even abusive criticism of religious communities and their members in public, Sec. 130, 166 and 185 ff. of the Criminal Code (StGB) already offer sufficient protection.

---

63 See Osnabrücker Zeitung, "Bosbach weist FDP-Vorschlag zurück," at http://www.noz.de/deutschland-welt/politik/artikel/536986/bosbach-weist-fdp-vorschlag-zuruck, accessed 18 September 2015.

64 Protocol No. 12 to the Convention for the Protection of Human Rights and Fundamental Freedoms, 4 November 2000, entry into force on 1 April 2005 (CETS No. 177).

65 See Council of Europe, "Nils Muižnieks: Racism, discrimination and hate speech 'are on the rise' in France," at http://www.humanrightseurope.org/2015/02/nils-muiznieks-racism-discrimination-and-hate-speech-are-on-the-rise-in-france/, accessed 18 September 2015.

As in many other areas of life, the call for an extension of criminal law does not solve the core problems of society but merely leads to an atmosphere of unreasonable fear and democratic self-restraint in the end. Those who want to live in an openminded, pluralistic community have to tolerate criticism on religious topics even if it hurts their personal feelings.

Even in case of an attack on religious feelings criminal law can and should only – according to its very nature and basic concept of "ultima ratio" – protect the "unbearable" instead of the "moral".

Bibliography

AG Berlin-Tiergarten, Judgment of 6 February 2012 – (263b Ds) 224 Js 3745/11 (228/11), 263b Ds 228/11, *StraFo* 2012: 110.

Arslan, Canadar, *Meinungs- und Kunstfreiheit gegen die Religionsfreiheit – Wie viel Schutz für religiöse Empfindlichkeiten*, Hamburg: Verlag Dr. Kovač, 2015.

Berliner Zeitung (B.Z.), "CDU fordert härtere Strafen für Blasphemie," at www.bz-berlin.de/deutschland/csu-fordert-haertere-strafen-fuer-blasphemie.

BR-Drucks. 367/86 of 11 August 1986.

BR-Drucks. 460/98 of 14 May 1998.

BR-Drucks. 683/07 of 1 October 2007.

BT-Drucks. 16/3579, 27 November 2006.

BVerfGE 124, 300.

BVerfG, *Neue Juristische Wochenschrift (NJW)* 1971: 1645.

BVerfG, Decision of 4 November 2009 – 1 BvR 2150/08, § 77, *Neue Juristische Wochenschrift (NJW)* 2010: 47.

BVerfG, Decision of 28 July 2014 – 1 BvR 482/13, *Zeitschrift für Urheber- und Medienrecht* (*ZUM*) 2014: 965.

Cornils, Matthias, "Gefühlsschutz, negative Informationsfreiheit oder staatliche Toleranzpflege: Blasphemieverbote in rechtlicher Begründungsnot," *AfP – Zeitschrift für Medien- und Kommunikationsrecht* 44, 3 (2013): 199-211.

Council of Europe, "Nils Muižnieks: Racism, discrimination and hate speech 'are on the rise' in France," at http://www.humanrightseurope.org/2015/02/nils-muiznieks-racism-discrimination-and-hate-speech-are-on-the-rise-in-france/.

Deutscher Bundestag, "Petition 56759," at https://epetitionen.bundestag.de/content/_2015/_01/_08/Petition_56759.html.

European Court of Human Rights, I. A. v. Turkey, Judgment of 13 September 2005, no. 42571/98, *ECtHR*, 2005-VIII.

European Court of Human Rights, Tatlav v. Turkey, Judgment of 2 May 2006, no. 50692/99, § 22, *Neue Zeitschrift für Verwaltungsrecht (NVwZ)* 2007: 314.

Fahl, Christian, "Zur Strafbarkeit des Auftritts der Punk-Rock-Band 'Pussy Riot' nach deutschem Strafrecht," *StraFO – Strafverteidiger Forum* 1 (2013): 1-6.

Giordano Bruno Stiftung, "Petitionsausschuss prüft Petition zur Abschaffung des 'Gotteslästerungsparagraphen'," at http://www.giordano-bruno-stiftung.de/meldung /petition166-pruefverfahren.

Hillgruber, Christian, "Abschaffung des Blasphemie-Paragrafen?," *ZRP – Zeitschrift für Rechtspolitik* (2015): 62.

Hörnle, Tatjana, in *Münchener Kommentar zum StGB*, ed. Olaf Hohmann et al., 2nd ed., Munich: C. H: Beck, 2012, §§ 166–168.

Hörnle, Tatjana, "Abschaffung des Blasphemie-Paragrafen?," *ZRP – Zeitschrift für Rechtspolitik* 48, 2 (2015): 62.

Hörnle, Tajana, "Bekenntnisbeschimpfung (§ 166): Aufheben oder Ausweiten," *JZ – Juristenzeitung* 70, 6 (2015): 293-297.

Hörnle, Tatjana, "Strafbarkeit anti-islamischer Propaganda als Bekenntnisbeschimpfung," *NJW – Neue Juristische Wochenschrift* 47 (2012): 3415-3418.

Human Rights Europe, "Nils Muižnieks: Racism, discrimination and hate speech 'are on the rise' in France," at http://www.humanrightseurope.org/2015/02/nils-muiznieks-racism-discrimination-and-hate-speech-are-on-the-rise-in-france/.

Isensee, Josef, "Meinungsfreiheit im Streit mit der Religion – 'Gotteslästerung' heute," *AfP – Zeitschrift für Medien- und Kommunikationsrecht* 44, 3 (2013): 189-199.

Joecks, Wolfgang, and Klaus Miebach (eds.), *Münchener Kommentar zum Strafgesetzgesetzbuch, Vol. 4, §§ 185-262*, 2nd ed., München: C.H. Beck, 2014.

Kau, Marcel, "Polizeiliches Filmverbot im Spannungsverhältnis von Kunst- und Meinungsfreiheit – der sog. 'Mohammed-Film' im Lichte von Art. 5 GG," *AöR – Archiv des öffentlichen Rechts* 1 (2015): 31-88.

Lackner, Karl, and Kristian Kühl, *Strafgesetzbuch, Kommentar*, ed. Kristian Kühl and Martin Heger, 28th ed., München: C.H. Beck, 2014.

Landtag NRW Drucks. 16/4408, 21 November 2013.

LG Bochum, *Neue Juristische Wochenschrift (NJW)* 1989: 727.

LG Düsseldorf, *Neue Zeitschrift für Strafrecht (NStZ)* 1982: 290.

LG München I, Decision of 3 May 2006 – 9 O 8051/06.

Liesching, Marc, "Anmerkung zu LG München, Beschluss vom 3. Mai 2006 – 9 O 8051/06," *ZUM – Zeitschrift für Urheber- und Medienrecht* (2006): 578-580.

Lindner, Christian, and Marco Buschmann, "Signal für mehr Meinungsfreiheit," *DRiZ – Deutsche Richterzeitung* 4 (2015): 122-124.

Maurach, Reinhart, Friedrich-Christian Schröder, and Manfred Maiwald, *Strafrecht Besonderer Teilband 2, Straftaten gegen Gemeinschaftswerte*, 10th ed., Heidelberg: C.F.Müller, 2012.

Mosebach, Martin, "Vom Wert des Verbietens," *Berliner Zeitung*, 18 June 2012.

Muckel, Stefan, "Kein Anspruch eines Privaten auf Untersagung eines blasphemischen Bühnenstücks – ‚Gólgota Picnic'," *JA – Juristische Arbeitsblätter* (2013): 72-74.

Müller-Neuhof, Jost, "Der Bart des Propheten, " *AnwBl – Anwaltsblatt* (2012): 907.

Norouzi, Ali B., "Kultur, Religion, Strafrecht – auch ein Thema für die Anwaltschaft, Herausforderungen für das Strafrecht in einer pluralistischen Gesellschaft," *AnwBl – Anwaltsblatt* (2014): 595-597.

OLG Karlsruhe, *Neue Zeitschrift für Strafrecht* (*NStZ*) 1986: 363.

OLG Nürnberg, *Neue Zeitschrift für Strafrecht – Rechtsprechungsreport* (*NStZ-RR*) 1999: 238.

Osnabrücker Zeitung, "Bosbach weist FDP-Vorschlag zurück," at http://www.noz.de/deutschland-welt/politik/artikel/536986/bosbach-weist-fdp-vorschlag-zuruck.

OVG Berlin-Brandenburg, *Neue Juristische Wochenschrift* (*NJW*) 2012: 3116 (preliminary review).

Rox, Barbara, "Vom Wert der freien Rede – Zur Strafwürdigkeit der Blasphemie," *JZ – Juristenzeitung* (2013): 30-34.

Satzger, Helmut, Wilhelm Schluckebier, and Gunter Widmaier, *Strafgesetzbuch, Kommentar*, 2nd ed., Köln: Carl Heymanns, 2014.

Schönke, Adolf, and Horst Schröder, *Strafgesetzbuch, Kommentar*, ed. Bosch, Nikolaus et al., 29th ed., München: C.H. Beck, 2014.

Spaemann, Robert, "Beleidigung Gottes oder der Gläubigen," *FAZ – Frankfurter Allgemeine* Zeitung, 25 July 2012.

Statistisches Bundesamt, "Fachserie 10 Reihe 3, Tab. 2.1," at https:// www.destatis.de/DE/Publikationen/Thematisch/Rechtspflege/StrafverfolgungVollzug/Strafverfolgung2100300137004.pdf?__blob=publicationFile.

Steinke, Ron, "'Gotteslästerung' im säkularen Staat, Ein Plädoyer für die Streichung des § 166 StGB," *KJ – Kritische Justiz* 41 (2008): 451-457.

VG Hamburg, *Neue Juristische Wochenschrift* (*NJW*) 2012: 2536 (translated).

VG Sigmaringen, Judgment of 19 January 2011 – 1 K 1561/10 –, juris § 35.

VGH München, *Neue Juristische Wochenschrift (NJW)* 2011: 793.

Zeit online, "Grüne gegen Diskussion um Blasphemie-Paragrafen," at http:// www.zeit.de/politik/deutschland/2015-01/blasphemie-charlie-hebdo-bosbach.

How Law Incorporates Religious Communities: A New Look on State-Religion Relationships Explained by Using the Example of Switzerland

René Pahud de Mortanges

A. Introduction

Until the 1970s Switzerland was a religiously very homogenous country. Most citizens were either member of the Roman-catholic church or the Protestant church. Both churches were granted on the cantonal level a form of recognition under Public law, which gave them many privileges as well as some duties. The states' policy and governmental practice focussed entirely on the demands and needs of these two Churches. Discussion or even conflicts were rather seldom. The needs or even the presence of other, minority religious groups were hardly taken into consideration.

With this policy Switzerland was indeed perfect in line with other countries in Western Europe, which, apart from France, all had some form of establishment of the large Christian churches.

The situation however has dramatically changed since then. Switzerland has experienced a large-scale immigration from many South European and North African countries in the last four decades. With a growth of Muslim population from nearly zero in 1970 to 4.5 percent in 2010, Islam in Switzerland has become a topic of general interest and, especially after 9-11, also of many heated debates – unfortunately often with a rather islamophobic prefix.

During the past fifteen years, the discussion on state and religion in Switzerland was dominated by the question: What effect does the presence of Islam and other non-Christian religions have on the Swiss legal system?[1] New religious practices, religious clothing and cultural conceptions

---

1 This essay is a shortened, translated and updated version of my original essay "Das rechtliche Inkorporationsregime für Religionsgemeinschaften," in *Integration durch Religion? Geschichtliche Befunde*, gesellschaftliche Analysen, rechtliche Perspektiven, ed. Edmund Arens, Martin Baumann, Antonius Liedhegener, Wolfgang W.

seem to challenge the majority of the society and the state government. How to handle a request for a dispensation of certain school activities for religious reasons? When to allow the construction of a building for a new religion or cult? Is it legal to arrange a special sector in a cemetery for the deceased of a certain religion? In Switzerland such specific questions often led to pragmatic and casuistic solutions. By this, the traditional state-law system experiences some sort of a patchwork-style development.

So far so good, but as it seems to me, this raises a more fundamental question: Is the Swiss legal system still capable of providing an *adequate legal frame* for the activities of the different religious communities, both the older and the newer ones, and the practice of their members? Does the fact that nowadays the discussion on state and religion at least in Switzerland is closely related to the topic of migration demand a new state policy?

This paper shall analyse these questions in the following order: The first chapter introduces the notion of incorporation of religious communities. Furthermore, it will be explained what basic options a state may choose regarding this notion. In the second chapter, I will present the concrete legal incorporation system in Switzerland, including the fundamental rights of the Swiss constitution, the specific legal levels of the Confederation, the constitutional system of the cantons as well as some case law of the Swiss Supreme Court. A final conclusion shall be drawn in the third chapter.

B. Conditions of Incorporation

I. Notion

How do states regulate religious communities and religious practice – and do they act adequately in times of growing religious diversity nowadays? Differently asked: What are the state-given conditions for the development of the activity of religious communities and their adherents? What are the rules for established religious communities and what for the novel ones?

First, it is evident that there is more to this topic than just religious freedom. This is, of course, a very important but by far not the sole element of the state policy. There are other fundamental rights and constitutional pa-

Müller, and Markus Ries, Zürich: Pano-Verlag 2014, pp. 179-211. Many thanks to the editor for the permission to re-utilise the essay.

rameters in addition, as well as rules in other legal sectors, such as, for instance, in family law, construction law or criminal law. Furthermore, there is school law, naturalisation law, international private law, or – in Switzerland – the cantonal law of recognition of religious communities – and much more.

Thus, there is a conglomerate of legal norms and governmental practices that provides the state-given condition for religious communities and religious individuals. Could we call this a state's regime of *integration*? This seems not appropriate. What is integration at all? The general understanding of this notion equates it with assimilation to the "intake"-society. The pattern of thinking behind this may be the following: A group of immigrated persons that is perceived as a foreign body to the society evolves to a group that lives within the surrounding society "as everybody else does". There are indeed clear normative conceptions behind this notion. The majority, thus the "intake"-society provides the normative scale. However, I wonder if such a majority still exist in Western countries nowadays or if societies today are much more a mix of different groups with a wide spectrum of values and goals?

The question therefore is: What political and legal frame conditions must the state establish in order that religious communities and its members can evolve freely, be and become a part of the society and, as the case may be, integrate?

According to a concept proposed by Yasemin Soysal[2] and in Switzerland amongst others by Martin Sökefeld and Virginia Suter Reich, we should be talking about *incorporation* instead of integration. This means a multidimensional and interactive process of integration which includes not only the efforts of the particular groups but also those of the "intake"-society and its institutional equipment.[3] The scope of groups and individuals are of course dependent on their own cultural, social and demographic characteristics. However, the existing institutional, legal and political frame conditions have a significant influence. Those conditions can either have a supportive or repressive effect or then be indifferent. As the case may be, they can work including or excluding. There is thus a correlation between the frame conditions and the process of integration. How an (religious) individual integrates into society and how he organises his life de-

2 See Soysal, *Limits of Citizenship, Migrants and Postnational Membership in Europe*, 1994, pp. 31.

3 See Allenbach and Sökefeld, *Muslime in der Schweiz*, 2010, p. 19.

pends partly on the frame conditions. They urge him to make choices regarding his strategy: his path of incorporation is influenced by them.[4]

The state policy on religion can have social effect of inclusion or exclusion, depending on how it is designed and for whom it applies. If, for instance a religious community can offer religious education in public schools and spiritual care in public institutions, and if this is even financially supported by the state the social effect will be an including one. If, on the other hand, apparent and significant legal restrictions for religious practice exist, these restrictions will work out in an excluding manner for the religious groups affected. The incorporation system can be either way.

Apart from the conditions of incorporation for religious groups as a whole there are additional ones for their members, for religious individuals. For example, to what extent do they have access to the employment and residential market? Do they have a fair chance in the political process? Are they allowed to practise their religion without problems or just with restrictions? All these questions have to be answered when it comes to immigrants and their religious practice – but also for members of established Christian communities, in this case often with a reverse prefix.

II. Types of Conditions

Conditions of incorporation are therefore conditions which government and society set up for groups and individuals to be socially accepted. They may be of different nature, such as a result of a conscious action and active decision or just by unreflecting and unconscious acting. Regarding the religious communities and its members, we can also distinguish, besides the legal conditions of incorporation, some *social*, *economic* and *political* conditions. Of importance, for instance, is also the economic situation of the religious community and its members as well as their education and social and professional position, the possibilities of participating in the political process, the appearance in the media and therewith related also the perception in the public.

Often, there is a correlation between the different categories of these conditions of incorporation. For example, the possibilities of participating

4 Suter Reich, *Zwischen Differenz, Solidarität und Ausgrenzung. Inkorporationspfade der alevitischen Bewegung in der Schweiz und im transnationalen Raum*, 2011, p. 207.

in the political process is sometimes limited for members of migrating religions because they have not obtained citizenship yet – the pre-condition for voting rights – or because they dispose only of limited financial resources which do not allow efficient lobbying. Prohibition or limitations to their religious practice can be the consequences.

III. Basic Options

A state's legal system of incorporation constitutes of a plurality of legal norms and governmental practices. It is founded on certain basic options that a state defines explicitly or tacitly. With these basic options, first significant positions are set for the particular system of incorporation.

1. First and foremost, every state has its own method of assignment of the religious communities, may this be explicitly, for instance based on the constitution, or simply as a result of the existing policy and practice. In simple terms, this relation can consist in a relation of subordination of religion to the state (or vice versa) or in a cooperation of both institutions:
   In the case of a *separation* of state and religion, the state does not establish a constitutional relation to the religious communities. This may be in a positive sense, as for instance in the U.S. (non-establishment clause) or in France, or may it be in an adversarial sense, as for example in the former Soviet states, where religion was seen as something to be fought against. Separation can thus be the expression of very different political concepts. Such a program, however, does have consequences for the incorporation of the religious communities and its members in the particular state, because such a state does not provide any administrative, financial or other support.
   Subordination means that the religious community is subordinate to the state authority (or reverse). The state claims a more or less strict sovereignty over the religious communities. This brings to mind the concept of a state church that was dominating many European States. Contrariwise, there are nowadays still examples of governing religious authorities over state authority, such as the Vatican or Iran.[5] In such a relation between the state and the religion, other religious communities

5 See ibid, p. 72.

and their members have only limited freedom, if any at all. Religious compulsion is the normal case and religious minorities are forbidden or (strongly) restricted in their practice.
A relation of *cooperation* between the state and the religious communities means that the parties are equal, independent and autonomous.[6] The state does no longer identify with a particular religion, but recognises the positive social function of religious communities in general. Nowadays, this is the case in most of the Western-European states. The state's position is religiously neutral and the freedom of religion is granted. The state may offer a legal frame (e.g. establishment, recognition under public law) for historical reasons or because the cultural and social function of the religious communities seem socially valuable to the state. This concept is favourable for the incorporation of religious communities.

2. Of importance is also the *organisation of a state*: Is it a unitary or a federally organised state? And in the latter: How big is the autonomy of the member state when it comes to own policies dealing with religious groups? The unitary state has only *one* system of incorporation. The federal state, on the other hand, has maybe as many as the number of its states. Due to the different levels of a federal state, there is the possibility of having different incorporation systems in the different states. There are many examples such as the U.S., India and Germany – and of course also Switzerland with its cantonal diversity. But even in a unitary state as France things are more complicated than one may think: even though there is a strict separation in the laic republic since 1905, the two departments Elsass and Mosel have a different, cooperative relation with the churches.[7]
3. The system of incorporation is furthermore influenced by the *democracy type* a state has adopted. In a representative democracy, the state policy on religion is – next to the executive and the judiciary – dictated only by parliament. In a (semi-)direct democracy, citizens have the possibility to participate in this process by the instruments of the initiative and the referendum. A popular vote means that the majority decides over the minority – and mostly not in favour of the latter.

6 See ibid, p.74.
7 "Art. France," *Dictionnaire Droit des religions*, 2010, pp. 358 f.

4. Of great significance, lastly, is the standard of constitutional rights: To what extent are fundamental rights granted and protected? At this point, we shall not only think of religious freedom, but also of other fundamental rights, such as the right of assembly for religious communities and their members, the right of property with regard to their material goods. To what extent can these rights be enforced by law? Do they exist only on paper when it namely comes to members of ethnic-religious minorities and is the political reality in fact a different one? A Western European point of view, coined by the ECHR, may lead to an over-optimistic contemplation of the situation. According to a report of the Pew Research Centre (in Washington) 70 percent of the world population lives in countries which restrict religious freedom massively or in which a large social discrimination exists for religious reasons.[8] These restrictions and discriminations have increased over the last years in many countries – and this particularly in those countries where the situation was already tense.

C. The Legal System of Incorporation in Switzerland

I. General Policy

How is the legal system of incorporation for religious groups and individuals shaped in Switzerland?

The Swiss Confederacy is a federal state that consists of the Confederacy and the Cantons. The Cantons are sovereign as far as their sovereignty is not limited by the constitution (art. 3 Swiss Constitution, Cst.).[9] The Cantons' sovereignty plays an essential role regarding the religious constitutional law (see below chap. 2.4.). All Cantons have an autonomous policy regarding their relation with religious communities, which leads to a multitude of different systems of incorporation. For historical reasons – the church authority was always a Cantonal competence – the Confederacy abstains from imposing a nationwide policy. In fact, this leads to a sep-

---

8 Pew Forum on Religion and Public Life, "Rising Restrictions on Religion, one-third of the world's population experiences an increase," at http://pewforum.org/Government/Rising-Restrictions-on-Religion.aspx, last visited 9 November 2017.

9 A translation of the Federal Constitution of the Swiss Confederation (Cst.), can be found at http://www.admin.ch/ch/e/rs/1/101.en.pdf, last visited 17 July 2014.

aration of state and religion on the level of the Confederacy. On this level exists thus implicitly a non-establisment policy, meanwhile, as we will see in chap. 2.4., on the level of the member states (the Cantons) there are many (mild) forms of establishment. But even on the federal level the separation is not to strict. At a closer glance one can see that between the Confederacy and the religious communities there are many points of contact and fields of cooperation.

In the Swiss federal state, there are three levels of state-activities: on the level of the Confederacy, the Cantonal level and at last, the level of the municipalities. This leads to three levels of state activity with partly different conditions for incorporation. The municipalities of the big cities often set up own policies dealing with religions, this often to create better conditions for migrant regions. For instance, they establish own agencies or special projects to facilitate integration, or they install on public cemeteries burial places for particular religions in order to meet their special burial requirements.

Important to note is that the democratic civil rights of citizens in Switzerland are large. They cannot only elect the governmental authorities but also, via initiative and referendum, vote on concrete factual questions (art. 138 Cst.). The Swiss Confederacy is by this a semi-direct democracy.[10] Questions regarding the policy on foreigners, integration or religion are often the subject of heated public debates and lead to initiatives and referendums. Decisions of citizens thus become part of the different incorporation regimes, which by this not seldom contain some *contradictory elements*, some religion-friendly, some limiting or even discriminating religions. As the official governmental policy will often try to integrate migrants, popular initiatives aiming at restriction of immigration or religious symbols (2009: ban of minarets on federal level; 2014: ban of Burka in Canton of Ticino) will send totally opposite signals.

10 See Biaggini, Gächter and Kiener, *Staatsrecht*, 2011, pp. 44.

II. The Legal Situation on the Level of the Confederacy

1. The Swiss Constitution

a) Fundamental Rights

The three levels of the Confederacy are legally bound by the Constitution that builds the framework which does not only organise the state activity but also defines the fundamental rights of the citizens. The protection through fundamental rights has strongly developed in Switzerland since the 1970s.

The fundamental rights can only be restricted under concrete conditions defined in the constitution: A restriction may be allowed if there is a legal basis, there is further the necessity of a public interest or the need for protection of a third party's fundamental rights, and at last, this restriction has to be proportional. The core value cannot be touched (art. 36 Cst.).

In this context, the most significant fundamental right is certainly the freedom of religion and conscience (art. 15 Cst.). This right includes, on the one hand, the inner freedom to believe or not to believe and, on the other hand, also the external freedom of being allowed to express religious beliefs or (other) convictions, to practise and to spread them. This right protects the religious beliefs or convictions of every individual and that in a positive and negative sense: The latter also in terms of protection from governmental compulsion in religious matters. This protection manifests itself, inter alia, in the obligation of the state to *religious neutrality*. Whenever public institutions deal with religious topics, as for example in public schools, this shall not happen in a single-sided or partial manner. Religion, religious traditions and symbols may also have a rightful place in public institutions, however only in a way that non-believers are not hurt in their opinion.[11]

The freedom of belief and conscience is of great significance in this context because it (partly) leads to a freedom of culture – which is not explicitly anchored in the constitution.[12] Religious and cultural practices – as for instance wearing a certain piece of clothing or following a specific diet

---

11 See Tappenbeck and Pahud de Mortanges, "Religionsfreiheit und religiöse Neutralität in der Schule," 2008, pp. 105.

12 See Kälin, *Grundrechte im Kulturkonflikt. Freiheit und Gleichheit in der Einwanderungsgesellschaft*, 2000, p. 30.

– are often closely related, which leads to the fact that cultural practices, exercised in the name of religious freedom, are also protected by the state.

Within the fundamental rights, the *right to equality* (art. 8 Cst.) is of further importance as well as the *prohibition of discrimination* – besides others for religious reasons – and the therewith connected claim of *equal treatment* of women and men. The latter is perceived as an essential accomplishment of the Western society of the 20th century which, however, seems to oppose the understanding of gender roles of some religions.[13] The prohibition of discrimination is furthermore important regarding the naturalisation law or the law of construction. Since 2009, Switzerland has after a successful popular initiative incorporated a prohibition of constructing minarets into its Constitution (art. 72 section 3 Cst.). Such a unilateral restriction on religious freedom can be seen as a discrimination of Muslims but cannot be successfully claimed to the Swiss Supreme Court, since these two constitutional norms (prohibition of constructing minarets and the prohibition of discrimination) have the same level in hierarchy.

The *right of marriage and family* is anchored in art. 14 of the Constitution. As a consequence of the secularisation in the 19th century, Switzerland has adopted a state-based marriage and family law. In the beginning, it was strongly coloured by Christian values and forms. Due to the social development in the second half of the 20th century it has oriented itself to an own and more secular direction. The patriarchal concept disappeared and equal rights of the spouse as well as the best interests of the child became the primary values of society.[14] A marriage according to religious law can still take place, but only after the civil marriage and on a purely optional level. This is the same for members of religious minorities as for members of traditional religious communities. A religious marriage or divorce has no legal value for the state. This leads – differently from other states – to a compulsory civil marriage.

---

13 See Wyttenbach, "Partnerwahl, Familienplanung und sexuelle Gesundheit zwischen verfassungsrechtlich geschützter Selbstbestimmung und religiösen Vorschriften," 2010, p. 126.

14 Pahud de Mortanges, *Schweizerische Rechtsgeschichte. Ein Grundriss*, 2007, pp. 237.

b) Further Constitutional Elements of the Incorporation Regime

A further constitutional aim and value expressed in the Swiss Constitution is the *integration* of everybody in society (art. 2 Cst.). Integration is percieved not only a political objective, but also a state task. Equality of treatment and equal participation are in this context of special importance. Art. 41 Cst. states the social objectives of the Constitution, which includes the support of children and young adults in their social, political and cultural integration. Some Cantonal constitutions oblige governmental authorities as well to undertake efforts of integration.[15]

A last governmental task in this context finally is the duty to preserve religious peace. Art. 72 section 2 Cst. empowers the Federation and the Cantons to take necessary measures to preserve the *public peace* between the members of the different religious communities. Nowadays, this should probably be complemented with "between religious and non-religious persons".

III. Further Elements of the Legal System of Incorporation

As an example for a specific sector of Swiss law, criminal law shall be explained hereafter. Likewise relevant would be e.g. family law, naturalisation law, construction law or international private law.

The states' task of preserving religious peace is anchored in several norms of criminal law, namely, amongst others, art. 261 of the Swiss Criminal Code (SCC)[16] and art. 261bis SCC. Both norms part of the 12th chapter of the SCC, which contains a rather heterogeneous group of offences called "offences against the public peace".

15 See Caroni, "Religion und Integration – Gedanken zum Umgang mit religiösen Minderheiten," 2010, p. 16.

16 An officially translated version of the Swiss Criminal Code can be found at http://www.admin.ch/ch/e/rs/311_0/, last visited 17 July 2014.

Art. 261 (*attack on the freedom of faith and the freedom to worship*) is a conglomerate of four alternative elements:[17]

- Any attack on the freedom of faith and the freedom to worship by any person who publicly and maliciously insults or mocks the religious convictions of others,
- any malicious desecration of objects of religious adoration,
- any person who maliciously prevents, disrupts or publicly mocks an act of worship guaranteed by the Constitution (this refers to Art. 15 Cst.),
- any person who maliciously desecrates a place or object that is intended for a religious ceremony or an act of worship guaranteed by the Constitution.

This norm contains a rather mild punishment.[18] It does not intend the protection of God (in a biblical sense), nor of a certain *religion.* Objective of this norm is solely the protection of all religious opinions.[19] Even atheism is seen as being protected.[20] Neither does the norm protect specific religious *communities*.

Art. 261 must be interpreted in connection with art. 15 Cst. (freedom of belief and conscience). The Constitution protects all forms of religious and non-religious understanding of the world.[21] The object protected by art. 261 SCC is "the freedom of belief, more precisely the esteem of the fellow human being and their conviction in religious matters and therewith at the same time also the religious freedom".[22] Therefore, the object of protection is primarily the *religious feelings of individuals*,[23] the protection of

---

17 Stratenwerth and Bommer, *Schweizerisches Strafrecht, Besonderer Teil II*, 2008, pp. 202.

18 A monetary penalty not exceeding 180 daily penalty units.

19 Schwander, *Von den Religionsdelikten*, 1955, p. 105.

20 Ibid., p. 107; Fiolka and Niggli, "Strafrechtlicher Schutz von Religionsgemeinschaften im realen und virtuellen Raum," 2005, p. 710; Stratenwerth and Bommer, *Schweizerisches Strafrecht, Besonderer Teil II*, p. 203; Fiolka, "Kommentar zu Art. 261 StGB," 2007, N. 12 regarding art. 261.

21 See Winzeler, *Einführung in das Religionsverfassungsrecht*, 2009, pp. 63.

22 Translation of "die Glaubensfreiheit, genauer die Achtung vor dem Mitmenschen und seiner Überzeugung in religiösen Dingen und damit gleichzeitig auch der religiöse Friede," decision of the Swiss Supreme Court (BGE 86 IV 19, 23).

23 Fiolka, "Kommentar zu Art. 261 StGB," N. 7 regarding art. 261.

the "person who relinquishes him-/herself in the irrational."[24] Secondarily, the norm aims also at the preservation of the *public peace*.

Art. 261bis SCC (*racial discrimination*) was introduced to the SCC in 1993.[25] It targets a person or a group of persons who are victims of discrimination because of their race or ethnicity, but also because of their religion. Religion has here to be understood both in a large sense, i.e. including all traditional, but also any smaller or novel religion; the jurisprudence regarding freedom of religion can be helpful in interpretating.[26] As art. 261bis SCC shows, minoritarian religious communities with a migration background (which are probably more often target of discriminatory pronouncement or actions than the established churches) are seriously protected by the criminal law. Swiss criminal law makes special efforts to create favourable conditions of incorporation.

IV. The Cantonal System of Incorporation

1. An Element of Great Importance: The Recognition under Public Law

In concretization of the general norms of competence in art. 3 Cst., art. 72 section 1 Cst. states the competence of the cantons to regulate the relationship between "State and Church". In Switzerland, there are 26 different cantons. Therefore 26 different autonomous relationships exist between "State and Church". Apart from the two Geneva and Neuchatel, who have adopted the French "Laicié-model", the cantons have all adopted a similar system nevertheless.[27] This system grants the two main religious denominations, the Roman-Catholic and the Protestant Church, as well as the small Christian-Catholic Church a status under Public law. This gives them a favourable position with several rights and advantages, as well as some duties.

The recognised churches, firstly, have the right to raise church taxes from their members. In those cantons in which corporations are obliged to

24 Translation of "im Irrationalen preisgebenden Menschen," Krauss, "Der strafrechtliche Konflikt zwischen Glaubensfreiheit und Kunstfreiheit," 1984, p. 220.

25 Trechsel, *Schweizerisches Strafgesetzbuch. Praxiskommentar*, 2008, Rz. 3 regarding art. 261bis SCC, 1123.

26 See ibid, N.13 to Art. 261bis SCC, 1127.

27 See Winzeler, *Einführung in das Religionsverfassungsrecht*, pp. 77.

pay church taxes as well, they participate in the profit thereof. Furthermore, some cantons provide for historical reasons unconditional financial support. In many cantons, the recognised communities also have the possibility to offer pastoral care in state institutions such as hospitals, schools and prisons; the state is then financing this work as well. Moreover recognized religious communities have at public primary and secondary schools the right to use the schools' infrastructure for their confessional education.

In return for all these privileges, the state claims a limited right to supervise the activities of the Churches and their financing.

Also, several cantons claim democratic decision structures for the election member of the local Church government. For the Protestant Church this is nothing new, as its members elect its government in a democratic way. But in the case of the Roman-Catholic Church, this led to the creation of an additional governmental structure besides the (hierarchical) diocesan structures.[28]

The recognition under Public law leads to significant advantages for the recognized religious communities. As they can work in many state institutions, they are thereby able to reach not only their members, but also other people. Furthermore, they receive financial support from the state for their activities. Equally important: the official recognition of a religious community gives them a kind of "governmental approval", a "certificate of non-objection". Those which are recognised by the state are declared as *socially integrated* at the same time. The recognition under Public law by this also has an important *symbolic value*. As a result many minoritarian religious communities aim for this recognition in order to overcome the social disadvantages.

This growing interest of the minor religious communities is interstingly in coincidence with the opening up of the cantonal law of recognition, as seen in the last decades. After the revision of the Swiss Constitution in 1999, many cantons followed the path and revised their Constitutions as well.[29] In certain cantons, this led to a cautious and pragmatic reform of the legal system of recognition.

In a first step, the local Jewish communities were recognised. After their recognition in Basel City, St. Gallen, Fribourg and Bern, the cantons Waadt and Zurich followed.

---

28 See ibid., pp. 55.

29 Pahud de Mortanges, "Im Laufe der Zeit. Vom Stand des kantonalen Religionsverfassungsrechts," 2010, pp. 14.

Furthermore, some cantons created a legal basis for the recognition of "other" religious communities. Some cantons introduced a form of a *small public recognition*: In this case, the recognised community maintains its legal status under Private law, but receives some of the above named privileges (in particular, this small recognition does not include the right to raise church taxes). This is some sort of intermediate stage on the way to a full recognition under Public law. By this a significant step was made towards fairer conditions for the incorporation of minor religious communities. The Canton of Basel City has in the last years recognized three minority communities, amongst others the local Alevit community.

A clear disadvantage is that there is no enforceable right to obtain the recognition in any canton. Due to the fact that the Swiss Supreme Court has no right to constitutional review, a religious community cannot claim recognition grounded on the right to equality (art. 8 Cst.). A cantonal parliament can refuse a request for recognition; sometimes government authorities advice religious communities not to hand in a request. This tool of incorporation is thus not set up in a totally fair way. Even though in theory the norms may look decent and fair, in practice they are not when the decision is left more or less entirely to the discretion of government officials. For historical reasons the cantons speeded up recognizing their local Jewish communities, for actual political reasons they repeatedly avoid to recognize local Muslim communities. The result is rather discriminatory – but there is no constitutional way to claim that.

V. The Jurisprudence

The incorporation system of the state is not only influenced by the lawmaking process of the legislative and the practices of the executive authorities but also by the case law of the courts. The court is the last deciding instance when there is a collision of private interests of religious practise with public ones and individuals do not accept decisions of governmental autorities.

Particularly, the Swiss Supreme Court has not seldomly to give guidance in state-religion matters.[30] In the last years its jurisdiction repeatedly

30 See Winzeler, "Die öffentliche Schule als Werkstatt der Integration," 2010, pp. 149 ff.; Kley, "Kutten, Kopftücher, Kreuze und Minarette – religiöse Symbole in öffentlichen Räumen," 2010, pp. 229.

dealt with the religious practice of Muslims in public institutions. The fast augmentation of the Muslim population in Switzerland led to several legal questions for which legislation did not have any answer. Therefore, it was ultimately the court that had to solve these conflicts. Some of the Supreme Court jurisprudence was afterwards included into cantonal law.

How does the Supreme Court deal with the religious freedom of Muslims in Switzerland? Comparing older and newer decisions one can see that some years ago the Supreme Court was quite easy with waiving limitations of religious freedom: (BGE 123 I 296 ff.: ban on headscarves for teachers in primary schools in the canton of Geneva; BGE 125 I 300 ff.: no right to Islamic burial rites; BGE 135 I 79 ff.: no right to dispensation of mixed-gender swimming instructions at school). But this seems to have changed: more recent decisions do not support half-cooked limitations of local authorities any more (e.g. BGE 1 C_35/2015: no ban on veil for female students in public primary school; 2 C_121/2015: no interdiction for an event of a wahabid muslim organisation on public ground; BGE 134 I 56: no refusal of naturalisation because the applicant wears a headscarf).

It seems to me that the Supreme Court has changed to a more open interpretation of freedom of religion especially for Muslims. The Court takes religious neutrality more serious. It cannot give in to the pressures of those groups in Swiss society, who do not want to see Muslim religious practice at all.

Court decisions regarding matters of state and religion are often a topic of wide and controversial discussions in Switzerland. However, such decisions are the rare case because in general, a consensual solution can be found. Nevertheless, these decisions show the change from a homogeneous, Christian coined society towards a religious pluralistic one. Governmental authorities have to find their position in this new situation. Thereby, freedom of religion and religious neutrality become very important. And like the legal instrument of recognition under Public law, the principle of the religious neutrality – as blurry as it may seem – is a 'incorporation tool' of essential significance.

D. Conclusion

This overview of some aspects of the incorporation system in Switzerland leads to the assumption that the state and religion system is currently directed towards more acceptance of religious plurality. Rights which were in earlier times only granted to the two majoritarian Christian churches are nowadays also given to non-Christian religions. The initial point and motor of this development is – besides the principle of neutrality – primarily the constitutional principle of equal treatment, respectively the prohibition of discrimination. This principle requests a state policy of *acceptance* of religious and cultural diversity in society. In the last years, the Federal state as well as the cantons tried to enforce these constitutional aims and values e.g. by opening-up of the cantonal recognition under Public law and by several important decisions of the Supreme Court. Direct democracy on the other hand, has rather a braking effect in this process: initiatives on the federal and cantonal level were and are still used in order to keep mainly Muslim religious practice invisible. But this seems to me a rather transient phenomenon. What used to lead to protest some years ago, e.g. the opening of special burial sites for specific religious groups, is widely accepted these days. And the opening of a "Center for Islam and Society" at Fribourg University in summer 2016 had an overwhelming positive echo.

Bibliography

Allenbach, Brigit, and Martin Sökefeld (eds.), *Muslime in der Schweiz*, Zürich: Seismo, 2010.

Biaggini, Giovanni, Thomas Gächter, and Regina Kiener (eds.), *Staatsrecht*, Zürich and St. Gallen: Dike, 2011.

Caroni, Martina, "Religion und Integration – Gedanken zum Umgang mit religiösen Minderheiten," in *Religion und Integration aus der Sicht des Rechts. Grundlagen-Problemfelder-Perspektiven*, ed. René Pahud de Mortanges, Zürich: Schulthess, 2010, pp. 11-37.

Dictionnaire Droit des Religions, sous la direction de Francis Messner, CNRS Edtitions, Paris, 2010.

Fiolka, Gerhard, and Marcel Alexander Niggli, "Strafrechtlicher Schutz von Religionsgemeinschaften im realen und virtuellen Raum," in *Kooperation zwischen Staat und Religionsgemeinschaften nach schweizerischem Recht*, ed. René Pahud de Mortanges and Erwin Tanner, Zürich: Schulthess, 2005, pp. 705-734.

Fiolka, Gerhard, "Kommentar zu Art. 261 StGB," in *Strafrecht II, Basler Kommentar*, ed. Marcel Alexander Niggli, Marcel Alexander and Hans Wiprächtiger, 2nd ed., Basel: Helbing Lichtenhahn, 2007.

Kälin, Walter, *Grundrechte im Kulturkonflikt. Freiheit und Gleichheit in der Einwanderungsgesellschaft*, Zürich: NZZ libro, 2000.

Kley, Andreas, "Kutten, Kopftücher, Kreuze und Minarette – religiöse Symbole in öffentlichen Räumen," in *Religion und Integration aus der Sicht des Rechts. Grundlagen-Problemfelder-Perspektiven*, ed. René Pahud de Mortanges, Zürich: Schulthess, 2010, pp. 229-257.

Krauss, Detlev, "Der strafrechtliche Konflikt zwischen Glaubensfreiheit und Kunstfreiheit," in *Gedächtnisschrift für Peter Noll*, ed. Robert Hauser, Jörg Rehberg and Günter Stratenwerth, Zürich: Schulthess, 1984, pp. 209-230.

Pahud de Mortanges, René, *Schweizerische Rechtsgeschichte. Ein Grundriss*, Zürich: Dike, 2007.

Pahud de Mortanges, René, "Im Laufe der Zeit. Vom Stand des kantonalen Religionsverfassungsrechts," in *Wo Gottes Wort ist. Die gesellschaftliche Relevanz von Kirche in der pluralen Welt. Festgabe für Thomas Wipf*, ed. Thomas Flügge, Martin Ernst Hirzel, Frank Mathwig and Peter Schmid, Zürich: Theologischer Verlag, 2010, pp. 141-155.

Pew Forum on Religion and Public Life, "Rising Restrictions on Religion, one-third of the world's population experiences an increase," at http://pewforum.org/ Government/Rising-Restrictions-on-Religion.aspx.

Schwander, Vital, *Von den Religionsdelikten*, Freiburg: Universitätsverlag, 1955.

Soysal, Yasemin Nuhoglu, *Limits of Citizenship, Migrants and Postnational Membership in Europe*, Chicago: Chicago University Press, 1994.

Stolz, Jörg, "Religion und Integration aus der Perspektive der erklärenden Soziologie," in *Religion und Integration aus der Sicht des Rechts. Grundlagen-Problemfelder-Perspektiven*, ed. René Pahud de Mortanges, Zürich: Schulthess, 2010, pp. 41-80.

Stolz, Jörg, and Martin Baumann, "Religiöse Vielfalt: Kulturelle, soziale und individuelle Formen," in *Eine Schweiz – viele Religionen*, ed. Martin Baumann, and Jörg Stolz, Bielefeld: Transcript, 2007, pp. 21-38.

Stratenwerth, Günter, and Felix Bommer (eds.), *Schweizerisches Strafrecht, Besonderer Teil II*, 6th ed., Bern: Stämpfli 2008.

Suter Reich, Virginia, *Zwischen Differenz, Solidarität und Ausgrenzung. Inkorporationspfade der alevitischen Bewegung in der Schweiz und im transnationalen Raum*, Dissertation Universität Bern, 2011.

Swiss Supreme Court, BGE 86 IV 19, 23.

Tappenbeck, Christian, and René Pahud de Mortanges, "Religionsfreiheit und religiöse Neutralität in der Schule," in *Religiöse Neutralität. Ein Rechtsprinzip in der multireligiösen Gesellschaft*, ed. René Pahud de Mortanges, Zürich: Schulthess 2008, pp. 105-136.

Trechsel, Stefan, *Schweizerisches Strafgesetzbuch. Praxiskommentar*, Zürich andSt.Gallen: Dike 2008.

Winzeler, Christoph, *Einführung in das Religionsverfassungsrecht*, 2nd ed., Zürich: Schulthess, 2009.

Winzeler, Christoph, "Die öffentliche Schule als Werkstatt der Integration," in *Religion und Integration aus der Sicht des Rechts. Grundlagen-Problemfelder-Perspektiven*, ed. René Pahud de Mortanges, Zürich: Schulthess, 2010, pp. 149-171.

Wyttenbach, Judith, "Partnerwahl, Familienplanung und sexuelle Gesundheit zwischen verfassungsrechtlich geschützter Selbstbestimmung und religiösen Vorschriften," in *Religion und Integration aus der Sicht des Rechts. Grundlagen-Problemfelder-Perspektiven*, ed. René Pahud de Mortanges, Zürich: Schulthess, 2010, pp. 123-147.

Islam in Italy: A Religion Under Construction

Alessandro Ferrari

A. Introduction

For some years now, Islam has been, with Eastern Orthodox Christianity, the second largest religion in Italy after Roman Catholicism. In fact, although precise data are not available, the number of Muslims in Italy is approximately 1.9 million.[1] Nevertheless, Islam is still perceived in Italy as a foreign religion, and its integration into the Italian civic and institutional landscape has been, until a very recent time, mainly left to the "goodwill" of local practices, often promoted by civil society actors. As a consequence, Islam in Italy, although it represents one of the most powerful symbols of the "post-secular" age and the "return of religion" in the public arena, is not still officially recognized as a "religion" within the law but as a more generic and fluid cultural or ethnic experience. In very few cases, in fact, are Muslims able to take advantage of the special dispositions on religious freedom available under Italian law. Islam, then, exists mainly as a "non-religion" in a "religious country," relying on organizational forms that disguise its religious dimensions.

This situation reflects the traditional character of the Italian nation-state, which bases civic cohesion more on proximity or private relationships than on the voluntary engagement of public institutions.[2] However,

---

1 As in most European countries, the national census does not consider religious affiliation, and the data for the foreigners are most often inferred from the surveys published in the annual reports on immigration by the Italian Caritas, the Roman Catholic relief, development, and social service organization. See for example, regarding the 2016 Report http://www.integrazionemigranti. gov.it/Documenti-e-ricerche/Sintesi_OK%20(1).pdf, and http://www.cesnur.com/lislam-e-i-movimenti-di -matrice-islamica-in-italia/lislam-sunnita-unintro duzione/: both accessed 30 June 2017. See, for a first overview, Razzali and Equizi, "*I musumani e i loro luoghi di culto*," 2013, pp. 47-72, and Coglievina, *Annotated Legal Documents on Islam in Europe: Italy*, 2016.

2 I have analyzed this ideal-typical condition in "Laïcité et multiculturalisme à l'italienne," 2008, pp. 133-154, and in "Civil Religion in Italy: 'A Mission Impossi-

the legal status of Italian Islam also reflects a broader, deeper contemporary change in the perception of religions and the right to religious freedom.

In fact, the difficulty in reconciling globalized and 'post-modern' religious experience with the traditional paradigm of 'religious belonging' based on clear 'religious constellations'; the advent of a "third age" of secularism[3] and the subordination of the right to religious freedom to more ideological and securitarian versions of civic cohesion and public order have provoked contradictory dynamics within the European right to religious freedom. On one side, these changes have brought to a crisis of religious freedom as a unified, specific and high standard right. On the other, they have exacerbated the efforts to transform Islam in a "religious denomination", although its all-encompassing, multifaceted and transnational nature complicates references to the traditional Church-oriented European right to religious freedom.

Consequently, if Islam is too broad to be encapsulated by the only right to religious freedom, the Italian experience witnesses the ongoing political role of this latter as state's protector through its function of watershed between "sacred alterities" and "secular" institutions.

B. *Sociological Frameworks*

Setting aside the far memory of Muslim Sicily, Islam only arrived and became established in Italy in the 1970s, coming from Tunisia, and later from Morocco, Syria, Jordan, and Senegal. From the 1990s on, migration to Italy grew, including from new countries such as the Balkans and Southeast Asia. Consequently, unlike other European Islams, Italian Islam is neither a colonial Islam, as in France, nor is it an Islam based on ar-

---

ble'?," 2010, pp. 839-859. This nation-state character avoids simple recourse to the often hypocritical principle of neutrality, but it certainly does not avoid evident tensions between a "Kelsenian" and a "Böckenfördian" approach, making it difficult for a (Kelsenian) law to limit the (Böckenfördian) weight of majority and, above all, of history.

3 With "secularity 3" Taylor, *A Secular Age*, 2007, p. 3 intends "a move from a society where belief in God is unchallenged and indeed, unproblematic, to one in which it is understood to be one option among others (...). Secularity in this sense is a matter of the whole context of understanding in which our moral, spiritual or religious experience and search takes place."

rangements between Italian companies and a specific country rich in manpower, as is true, for example, in the case of Turkish Islam in Germany. Italian Islam is rather, a group of very different people who arrived in random order largely for economic reasons (except in these very recent years) and who have formed, over time, a real plural community.[4]

Among the approximately 1.9 million Muslims in Italy, Moroccans comprise about 500,000; the largely secularized Albanians about the same, followed by 118,000 Bangladeshis, 110,000 Egyptians, about 100,000 Tunisians, the same number of Pakistanis and Senegalese and about 20,000 Turkish.[5] Although the different faces of Sunni Islam are clearly the majority, groups of Shiites are also represented.[6] The distribution of this diversified community within Italy reflects the economic geography of the country, the possibility to find a job, such that there is a stronger Muslim presence in the Northern regions. Recently, there has been an exchange between unskilled workers who returned to their countries of origin or moved to other European countries due to the Italian economic crisis, and younger graduates who have arrived in Italy after the events following the 'Arab Spring'.

Despite the forty years since Muslims' stable settlement in Italy and its overcoming of the symbolic "second generation" threshold, Muslim ethno-national groups have not only not been merged into a single religious entity, but, above all, Islam still remains a foreign religion in Italy. This is due, first of all, to the fact that the majority of "Italian Muslims" are still foreign citizens and Italian citizenship is deeply rooted in a very strong conception of *ius sanguinis* and its acquisition depends on a complicated process full of bureaucratic obstacles. As a result of these challenges, there are only about 100,000 naturalized "Italian Muslims," or, in any case, less

4 See Allievi, *Islam italiano: Viaggio nella seconda religione del paese*, 2003, passim.

5 See Bombardieri, "Islam in Italia: Numeri, protagonisti e dinamiche sociali," 2013, pp. 7-24, and for more recent data: http://www.tuttitalia.it/ statistiche/ cittadini-stranieri-2016/, accessed 30 June 2017.

6 There are, in fact, six Shi'a associations and one small Ismaili group. About the non-Arabic Muslim groups, Senegalese murids associations are spread all over the national territory, while various Turkish associations (Süleymanci, Fetullah Gülen or Milli Görüsh) are especially prevalent in the North. In 2009 the Union of Muslim Albanese in Italy was also founded, see Bombardieri, "Mappatura dell'associazionismo islamico in Italia," 2014, pp. 11-34.

than 10 percent of the total Muslim population.[7] This formal and ascribed "foreign" character, which prevents Muslims from having an influential political voice,[8] directs public discourse about Islam mainly on immigration, ethnicity, and security, a discourse that rarely addresses Muslims' right to religious freedom.[9] At the same time, this foreign character also leads public institutions to focus more on the role of foreign "Muslim" states and private international law than on investigating the role of autochthonous leaderships and Italian sharī'a.[10]

---

7 The Law 91/1992 defines an Italian as one who is born of an Italian mother or father. Young people do not automatically acquire Italian citizenship simply by being born on Italian soil. The acquisition of citizenship is possible through marriage to an Italian citizen or after ten years of legal residence. Moreover, Article 4, para 2 of the same law allows people born in Italy of foreign parents to apply for citizenship after reaching legal age (eighteen years) if they have legally resided in the country "without interruption". Nevertheless, each year 37 percent of these young "foreigners" – but not immigrant – who are resident in Italy at their majority cannot become Italian citizens because of some interruption of their residence, and they have to remain in the strange condition of "Italian with foreign citizenship": See Milena Santerini, "Le seconde generazioni e il nodo della cittadinanza," 2014, pp. 137-148. In October 2015 the Chamber of Deputies had approved a new law on citizenship which introduced a soft form of *ius soli* but the Senate didn't approve it.

8 In the present legislature there is only one Muslim MP, native Moroccan journalist Khalid Chaouki, of the Democrat Party. In the XV legislature (2006-2008), the sociologist Khaled Fouad Allam, native to Algeria, was elected in the same party and in the XVI legislature (2008-2013) the journalist Souad Sbai, native to Morocco, was MP for the right-wing coalition. No political Muslim movement to date has participated in any Italian election, and the civic electoral list "Milano Nuova" that ran at Milan's 2011 municipal election in Milan and proposed the president of an Islamic center as a candidate for mayor, presented itself as "secular, pluralist and open", see https://it-it.facebook.com/Milano Nuova, accessed 25 August 2014.

9 See *I musulmani e la società italiana. Percezioni reciproche, conflitti culturali, trasformazioni sociali*, ed. Stefano Allievi, 2009; Bruno, *L'islam immaginato. Rappresentazioni e stereotipi nei media italiani*, 2009, and the Report of the National Institute of Statistics (ISTAT), "Il contesto italiano nei dati Istat," at http://www.camera.it/leg17/1264, accessed on the 30 June 2017.

10 See Conetti, "Il matrimonio: conflitti di leggi o di culture?," 2008, pp. 111-120, and Domianello, "Il pluralismo in materia religiosa nel settore matrimoniale," 2012, pp. 120 ff. For a wider picture see Anello, "Passato e futuro della minoranza musulmana in Italia, tra islamofobia e pluralismo pragmatico-giuridico," 2016.

Nevertheless, the hundred thousand Italians who have converted to Islam[11] and, most importantly, the youth, the so-called second generation, already Italian or still not, could change this perspective.

On one hand, because of their mastery of the Italian language and of the Italian 'way of life', converts are natural mediators between their new religious community and Italian institutions and civil society. Mario Scialoja, the former Italian ambassador in the Saudi Arabia, who worked in support of the 'Great Mosque' of Rome and the Shaykh' Abd al-Wahid Felice Pallavicini, founder of COREIS, an influential Muslim association which mainly gathers Italian converts, were pioneers in this role.[12] On the other hand, a bridging role is played today by the young of the 'second generation', men and women born in Italy who, interpreting their multiple identities as a strength rather than a limitation, are moving away from a purely symbolic or "decorative" role to assume leadership positions in the building of an Italian Islam more autonomous from foreign states.[13]

C. *Muslim Actors: The Main Actors*

The "foreign" character of Islam in Italy clearly has a strong impact on Muslim organizations born to transplant Islam in the country and, in particular, to open places of worship, promote religious education and other

---

11 In 1999 Allievi, *I nuovi musulmani. I convertiti all'islam*, quoted at ten thousand the number of converts. Today, after fifteen years, that number has increased tenfold: Bombardieri, "Mappatura dell'associazionismo islamico in Italia," p. 12.

12 See infra in the paper.

13 See Abis Analisi e strategie, "G2: una generazione orgogliosa. Una ricerca sui musulmani in Italia," at http://www.italianieuropei.it/it/le-iniziative/convegni/ item /2308-g2-una-generazione-orgogliosa-unaricerca-sui-musulmani-in-italia.html, accessed on 25 August 2014, and Frisina, *Giovani musulmani d'Italia*, 2007. See also, Branca, *Yalla Italia! Le vere sfide dell'integrazione di arabi e musulmani nel nostro paese*, 2007, and, written by two young "2G" leaders: Chaouki, *Salaam, Italia! La voce di un giovane musulmano italiano*, 2005, and Qader, *Porto il velo, adoro i Queen. Nuove italiane crescono*, 2008. It is worth noting that today Khalid Chaouki is the only Italian Muslim MP and Sumaya Abdel Qader the only sitting in the Council of the city of Milan where another young Italian Muslim, Davide Piccardo, plays an important role as coordinator of the CAIM (Coordination of Islamic Associations of Milan), which gathers more than twenty Muslim associations: see https://www.facebook.com/pg/ilcaim/ about/?ref=page_internal, accessed 10 November 2016).

community activities. In fact, the internal life of the main Italian Islamic organizations is still strongly influenced by the financial and ideological links with foreign governments, with homelands.

Three main Sunni associations traditionally contend for the representation of Italian Muslims: the Union of Islamic Communities and Organizations in Italy (UCOII); the Islamic Cultural Center of Italy, called the 'Great Mosque' of Rome; and the Islamic Religious Communities in Italy (COREIS).

I. The Union of Islamic Communities and Organizations in Italy

UCOII, ideologically related to the Tunisian An-Nahada and the Egyptian Muslim Brotherhood[14] and associated with the Federation of Islamic Organizations in Europe (FIOE), aspires to represent the 'people of mosques', a 'bottom-up Islam', and aims to promote an Islamic identity fully integrated within Italian society as a public moral force. The Union was founded in 1990 by former students of the University for Foreigners of Perugia who came to Italy in the 1970s and by the first Italian converts coming from leftist ranks.[15] Present throughout the country the Union brings together about two hundred places of worship, and in recent years has managed to build two mosques with dome and minaret, in Ravenna and Colle Val d'Elsa,[16] near Siena, and to inaugurate a third in a redeveloped building in Catania. With time, the Union has been able to develop a visible presence within civil society and is today considered a central in-

---

14 These are, in any case, rather flexible and sensitive references. For Ahmed Abdel Aziz, former spokesman of the Italian Muslim Youth and now responsible for the Committee for the Freedom and Democracy for Egypt, «the Muslim Brotherhood does not exist in Italy and there are not even brothers Muslims». For Aziz, in fact, "the Brotherhood is an important political and social movement in Egypt, but (in Italy) we do not have a corresponding, and it does not intend to have it. This is why it does not make sense to replicate in Italy the model of another country that is based on a different reality," at http://www.popoli.info/Easy Ne2/Primo_piano/Fratelli_(musulmani)_d_Italia.aspx, accessed 20 August 2014.

15 See Bombardieri, "Mappatura dell'associazionismo islamico in Italia," pp. 15-18.

16 This mosque has a very long history: see the 2005 study by Fiorita and Tarchiani, "L'Islam a Colle Val d'Elsa: pregi e difetti di un protocollo d'intesa," at http://www.olir.it/areetematiche/85/documents/Fiorita_Tarchiani_Islam_Colle.pdf, accessed 25 August 2014, and Bombardieri, *Moschee d'Italia. Il diritto al luogo di culto. Il dibattito sociale e politico*, 2011, pp. 147-153.

terlocutor by the state.[17] But the path for joining this position has been long and marked by vicissitudes.

In 1992, the Union presented a proposal of agreement (*intesa*) to the state with the aim to be placed on the same level as the Roman Catholic Church and other "established religions."[18] The fact that this proposal came from only one of the Muslim groups not already recognized as a "religious institution" according to Italian law[19] gave the impression of a propagandistic initiative addressed more to the internal Muslim audience than to the Italian government. As such, the proposal remained unilateral, ephemeral, and inconsequential. In any case, UCOII's lack of clear organization as a recognized religious association has not been the only source of tension between it and the state; the perception of UCOII as a representative of a political and fundamentalist Islam also has weighed heavily.[20]

The lowest point of these relations occurred in 2007 at the signing of the Charter of Values of Citizenship and Integration, promoted by the Home Ministry.[21] The official aim of the Charter was the promotion of a model of integration able to settle new religious and cultural pluralism and Italian constitutional principles thanks to the recognition of the role played

17 Apart from 'Muslim activities', UCOII is especially attentive to relationships with non-Muslims and to interreligious dialogue. UCOII also provides scholarships for the master's in European Islam at the inter-university Centre FIDR, based at the University of the "Piemonte Orientale", also sponsored by Morocco.

18 The third paragraph of art. 8 of the Italian Constitution foresees that relationships between the state and religious denominations (*confessioni religiose*) "shall be regulated by law on the basis of agreements with their respective representatives." See Ventura, *Religion and Law in Italy*, 2013, pp. 58-59 and 101-104.

19 UCOII does not have any recognition as a "religious legal entity" on the basis of the 1929-1930 legislation (see below). Recognition has always been considered by the administrative praxis the condition *sine qua non* for asking the state to open talks for the signature of an agreement.

20 This perception was also encouraged by some organization leaders themselves, who have slipped up on ambiguous anti-Zionist demonstrations or on ingeniously conservative and misogynistic theological statements, thus provoking a barrage of criticism by anti-Muslim right-wing opinion makers. See Bombardieri, *Moschee d'Italia*, pp. 30-33.

21 See http://www.interno.gov.it/mininterno/export/sites/default/it/sezioni/sala_stampa/speciali/accordo_integrazione/carta_dei_valori.html, accessed 24 August 2014, and see also below in the text.

by the Catholic character of the nation as a bedrock of the societal system.[22] Nevertheless, at the same time, the Charter aimed also at encouraging unity among moderate (i.e. state-centered) Islamic organizations and marginalizing the Union, which was perceived as an expression of a transnationalism without state and too politically radical.[23] Consequently, although UCOII formally signed the Charter, the Home Ministry, citing controversial statements by some Union leaders, declared the signature meaningless.[24] In 2011, this resulted in the Union being excluded from the new Committee for Italian Islam established by the Home Ministry. This also caused difficulties at the local level, where having signed the Charter was considered an indispensable requirement for opening places of worship, especially by right-wing local administrations.

It was the Arab Spring to restore the political – and religious – centrality of the Union which, in the interim, had chosen a renewed leadership, more able to cope with Italian landscape. In fact, in 2012 UCOII was among the religious groups represented at the Permanent National Consultation for Religions, Culture and Integration, and since then, regardless of the fall of the Egyptian President Morsi and the recent 'Qatar crisis', it always officially appears in all important institutional events. Above all, in February 2017, UCOII has been the main actor of the signature of the "Pact for an Italian Islam" promoted by the Home Ministry.[25]

It is worth to note that, until the signature of this last document, the Union has not used its institutional role for structuring itself as a religious entity, but rather for continuing its expansion from the bottom as a simple private association within the more flexible and generic framework provided for the civil code and charity legislation.[26] Given the government instability and the state's awkwardness towards the Islamic question, it appears that the Union leadership was convinced that, *rebus sic stantibus*, it

22 This character was particularly evident, for example, in n. 25 for which "(O)n the basis of its religious and cultural tradition, Italy respects the symbols and the signs of all religions."

23 See the following para 5.

24 See Bombardieri, *Moschee d'Italia*, pp. 107 ff. and para. 7.3.

25 See, infra, at para. 5.

26 Things didn't change after the gift, between 2013-2016, of more than 20 millions of dollars by the Qatar Charity Foundation for the places of worship of this organization. See http://www.repubblica.it/esteri/2016/08/04/news/chi_ finanzia_le_moschee_dal_qatar_alla_turchia_fondazioni_e_tanti_soldi_per_l_islam_italiano-145334232/, accessed 20 September 2016.

was better not to get involved in the complex and highly discretionary procedures necessary of being recognized as a religious entity. Rather UCOII, indulging the growing search by the state for safe and loyal imams has heavily invested in creating an "Italian imamate" as a premise for a subsequent greater and structural recognition.

Consequently, on one hand, in 2013, it has signed an agreement with the Tunisian Ministry of Religious Affairs for the arrival of imams who will be retrained by UCOII with respect to the linguistic, sociological, and juridical skills necessary for their work in the Italian context.[27] On the other, UCOII has cultivated strong links with the Italian Islamic Association of Imams and Religious Guides, which is connected with the European Council for Fatwas and Research and that aspires to become the referent for an "Italian fiqh."[28] On the 5th November 2015, the UCOII's attention to the "imam question"[29] has been rewarded an agreement with the Department of Prisons of the Ministry of Justice for the access of cultural mediators and imam of this organization in Italian prisons.[30]The signature of the "Pact for an Italian Islam", which is accompanied by the explicit commitment of the government to engage itself in the process of institutional recognition of Islamic religious associations, has opened a new phase where UCOII is destined to play a leading role.

27 See http://www.dirittodicritica.com/2013/01/03/islam-ucoii-imam-italia/, accessed 25 September 2015.

28 See Bombardieri, "Mappatura dell'associazionismo islamico in Italia," pp. 16-17, and https://www.facebook.com/Associazione.ImamItalia/?ref=page_ internal, accessed 5 November 2016.

29 See also the circular of the 18 January 2015 to the associations linked with UCOII for a khutba in Italian, as the common language of Italian Muslims: http://www.ucoii.org/category/comunicati-stampa/page/2/, accessed 5 November 2016.

30 The convention indicates that there are only 9 imam and 14 cultural mediators for more than 10,000 Muslim prisoners. See https://www.giustizia.it/giustizia/it/mg_1_7_1.page;jsessionid=94smZhGhJwx9+tbWYfBn4lKi?facetNode_1=0_2&facetNode_2=1_1(2015)&facetNode_3=1_1(201511)&facetNode_4=1_1(20151105)&contentId=SCA1196726&previsiousPage=mg_1_7, accessed 25 November 2015, and Cuciniello, "L'Islam nelle carceri italiane," 2016, at http://www.ismu.org/wp-content/uploads/2016/10/Cuciniello_Islam-e-carcere_paper_ottobre2016.pdf, accessed 10 July 2017.

II. The Islamic Cultural Center of Italy

The Islamic Cultural Center of Italy (ICCI) is the other main Muslim institution in Italy. ICCI is the traditional antagonist of the Union and represents a 'top-down Islam', strictly controlled by foreign state authorities. Based in Rome, it is the only Islamic organization in Italy recognized as a religious entity according to the 1929-1930 legislation.[31] Nevertheless, the date of the recognition, 1974, and the name assigned to this institution, which emphasize its cultural before the religious character are the mark of a very peculiar reality. In 1974, Italy was in the midst of the oil crisis, and the Italian government, in cooperation with the Vatican, determined it would be a good political investment to recognize an institution directed by the ambassadors of Muslim countries appointed to the Italian government and the Holy See. The nature of this foreign-state leadership and the fact that Islam was still perceived as a far reality, determined the choice to define the center with a less engaging cultural reference rather than with a more demanding religious denomination. In any cases, in 1995 ICCI officially inaugurated the Great Mosque, designed by Paolo Portoghesi and funded mainly by Saudi Arabia and Morocco, which have since competed for ICCI leadership. The mosque is directed by a council of administration, in which fifteen of the twenty-eight Muslim country ambassadors based in Rome sit in rotation, and by an assembly of the general membership that also includes Italian Muslims, among whom is the vice-president of the Islamic Religious Community in Italy (COREIS), the third most influential Muslim institution in Italy. Currently, Saudi Arabia appoints the president of the council of administration and Morocco appoints the general secretary, who is in charge of the effective administration of the Mosque and ICCI. The imam, in turn, is appointed by Egypt.

Due to its seniority, its location in Rome and official legal status, ICCI presents itself as the primary "natural" representative of Islam in Italy. However, it faces a challenge among the general Muslim population because of its evident foreign character and top-down nature, both of which distance it from the "people of mosques" courted by UCOII.

Conscious of these limits – and within the context of its competition with Saudi Arabia – Morocco has used its influence through the position of the general secretary of the Great Mosque to regroup Moroccan Mus-

31 Decree of the President of the Republic no. 212 of 21 December 1974.

lims living in Italy into regional associations since 2008. After March 2012, these associations were merged into the Islamic Italian Confederation (IIC), which aspires to become the more qualified representative of Italian Islam by combining top-down diplomacy and bottom-up dissemination Consequently, the Confederation aims at two interconnected goals: first, to influence and control the Moroccan diaspora and avoid anti-royalist influences on it; and second, to strengthen the Maliki school in Italy and sign an agreement with the state as the more reliable Muslim representative. Nevertheless, governance of the Confederation has not proved easy. In fact, already at its inaugural meeting, five out of fifteen regional federations refused to join the national confederation complaining a lack of transparence and democracy in the decisional process. Then along came criticisms of Moroccans eager to integrate in the new Italian context and break free from too obliging ties with their native country. Regardless, actually the deed of incorporation speaks about thirteen regional federations as being part of the Confederation with a total of 269 associations[32] and which counts about the same number of places of worship as UCOII. The Confederation also tries to organize its own imamate in relationship with the European Council of the Moroccan Ulema.[33]

Its undeniable spreading together with its Moroccan governmental supervision, give Confederation important advantages over its competitors also because the debate about radicalization among European Muslim youth has strongly re-legitimated the role of Morocco as guarantor of 'moderate Islam'. Nevertheless, the foreign supervision, although it could reassure Italian authorities, slows down the consideration of the ICCI Islam as an "Italian religion" limiting the possibility for the Center to become, just as it is, without formal statutory changes, a partner of the state for the signature of an agreement.[34]

---

32 See Bombardieri, "Mappatura dell'associazionismo islamico in Italia," pp. 20-21, and idem, "Una federazione prevalente," 2012, p. 314, and http://www.conf-islamica.it/confederazione-islamica-italiana/struttura/#, and http://www.conf-islamica.it/confederazione-islamica-italiana/atto-costitu tivo/, accessed 30 June 2017.

33 See http://www.conf-islamica.it/confederazione-islamica-italiana/corso-di-fiqh-in-lingua-italiana/, accessed 5 November 2016.

34 In fact, due to their too overt foreign character, it is very unlikely a signature of an agreement only between the Italian state and the Great Mosque or the Confederation. See Casuscelli, "Le proposte d'intesa e l'ordinamento giuridico italiano. Emigrare per Allah/emigrare con Allah," 2009, pp. 83-105. See also, idem, "La libertà religiosa alla prova dell'Islām: la peste dell'intolleranza," 2008, pp. 53-70. See

III. The Islamic Religious Community in Italy

The third relevant Italian Muslim organization is the Islamic Religious Community in Italy (COREIS) founded in the 1990s by the Shaykh' Abd al-Wahid Felice Pallavicini, an Italian convert to Islam, who led the association until passing the leadership to his son, Yahya, in the spring of 2016.[35] Despite only having about one hundred official members, COREIS is the only Muslim association clearly established and organized as a religious association. It is led by Italian converts and mainly composed of Italian citizens. Founded in the gnostic esoteric line of the French thinker René Guenon, it represents an independent branch of the *tarīqa* Ahmadiyya Idrīsiyya Shādhiliyya and cultivates the reputation of embodying a 'moderate Islam', open to interreligious and intercultural dialogue.[36] COREIS's Italian character, 'moderation', theological focus, and intensive dialogue with the Catholic Church and its institutions are presented as the best credentials for good relationships with state authorities. This activism also differentiates this association from the ICCI and ICC, where COREIS has been 'junior partner', sharing a similar top-down approach and close ties with foreign institutions unsympathetic towards any 'Muslim brothers style'. This also explains why relationships between COREIS and UCOII have often been quite strained. Especially in the past, UCOII has overtly accused COREIS of 'esotericism', which has led the latter to tout its own moderate stance in opposition to the perceived fundamentalism of the Union. This was particularly evident by the signing of the Charter of Values of Citizenship and Integration, which was endorsed and strongly promoted by COREIS acting in opposition to UCOII.

---

also, for a complete and updated overview, *Comunità islamiche in Italia. Identità e forme giuridiche*, ed. Carlo Cardia and Giuseppe Dalla Torre, 2015. At the same time, it is also very unlikely that the Italian state sign an agreement without considering the role played by Morocco within the Italian and Mediterranean scenarios.

35 Moreover, the daughter-in-law of the founder, the wife of the present President, IlhamAllah Chiara Ferrero, is the General Secretary of the association.

36 See Bombardieri, "Mappatura dell'associazionismo islamico in Italia," pp. 18-19. The present President, Yahya Pallavicini, is the only Italian among the 138 Islamic scholar signatories of the letter "A Common Word between US and YOU" written to Pope Benedict XVI in 2007.

COREIS's website proudly references the public recognitions enjoyed by the association over the years.[37] Aside from the participation at many thematic seminars organized by local and central institutions, these recognitions include, in particular, a 2013 agreement with the Italian Ministry of Education aimed at starting educational projects in schools and universities for the development of studies on religious diversity, and the 2009 interministerial agreement in support of "Halal Italy," a trademark of halal certification recorded by COREIS.[38] Nevertheless, these qualifications struggle to make effective and, above all, have been insufficient not only to obtain a signature of agreement with the state but also, to achieve the status of religious entity, as the "foreign" ICCI. In fact, not only did COREIS's 1996 proposal of an agreement with the state remain unanswered, but more surprisingly, two requests proposed by this association to the Home Ministry for obtaining the recognition of the legal status as religious entity have been unsuccessful as well. The first request, at the beginning of 2000, was frozen by political reasons despite the favorable opinion of the Council of State, probably because of the state's indecision about the broadening of the number of Islamic recognized institutions without a clear global "Muslim policy."[39] The second request, has been stopped in 2015 by the refusal of the Council of State to recognize the religious character of the association,[40] a decision which has completely overturned the position taken by the same institution fifteen years before but which seems have also convinced the Government that the time was ripe for getting out from a simply dilatory attitude and for deciding a more direct involvement in the process of institutionalization of Italian Islam.

37 See http://www.coreis.it/13/riconoscimenti.php, accessed 20 August 2014.

38 See http://www.halalitalia.org/, accessed 24 August 2014.

39 See Pallavicini, "Un itinerario nell'Islam italiano: dalla Costituzione verso l'Intesa?," 2010, p. 21.

40 To be recognized as cult institution the religious goals and activities of the associations have to be "prevalent" in relation to those qualified as merely cultural. In 2015 the Council of State as qualified as cultural – and not religious – the COREIS's activities directed to the diffusion of their creed and the interreligious dialogue. This refusal of the Council of State has had the form of a negative advice to the Home Ministry. See https://www.giustizia-amministrativa.it/cdsintra/cdsintra/AmministrazionePortale/DocumentViewer/index.html?ddocname=UAQ4E2ATUZRXLVJMGS2OMS2XFM&q, accessed 30 June 2017. Therefore, COREIS has decided not to publicize this refusal for not compromising its potential revision and the relationships with the state administrations.

D. Muslims Before the State: In Search for a Law

Faced with this new and plural religious presence, for many years the Italian state ignored Islam or choose paralysis regarding to it. This has been the result of two interrelated factors. At the beginning, was the loss of importance of the "religious question" in political discussion together with the lack of perception of the deep transformations of Italian society. From the Seventies the idea that "religious issue" had ended and that changes were only in the direction of more individualistic and privatized approaches favored the underestimation of the growth of a "Muslim question". In a second time, when to ignore globalization and the settlement of Muslim communities became impossible, the state appeared to be reluctant and without clear categories to address a topic suddenly as sensitive as Islam.

This situation not just confirms the fact that the "Muslim question" as a "religious question" is inseparable from multiple and very complex political factors but also points out a specific trait of the relationship between Islam and the Italian right to religious freedom. This is a widespread tolerance for some forms of public exhibition of Muslim religiosity and, at the same time, the extreme difficulty for Muslim associations to be formally recognized as religious entities or, much more, to sign an agreement with the state because of the weight of the political discretion of state authorities.

Clearly, this state of affairs not only highlights the special place reserved for religion within the Italian scenario, but also the rigidity and the distinctive political character of the right to religious freedom, which forces 'religious' groups into legal patterns that reflect very specific histories and interpretations of 'religiosity' and 'religious freedom'.

This framework fosters a system of coexistence that has been (generously) praised by the judges of Strasbourg on the occasion of the Great Chamber "Lautsi" decision.[41] In fact, unlike some other European coun-

41 See, for example, the § 74 of the Application no. 30814/06 of 18 March 2011. The generosity of the Strasbourg Court is especially referred to its benevolent acceptance of the Italian government's statement (see § 39) following which the beginning and end of Ramadan were "often celebrated" in schools; and optional religious education could be organized in schools for "all recognized religious creeds". In reality, not only are these "celebrations" really exceptional, but the optional religious education is unlikely to be organized by Muslims due to the fact that only the "foreign" Cultural Islamic Centre has obtained the legal status of

tries, Italy does not consider some practices – e.g. wearing the hijab in public and institutional spaces and, unless a few exceptions, even the burqa, asking food compatible with religious prescriptions (although not always formally certified as halal food) in hospitals, school and prisons – as ideological and dangerous communitarian displays, and they are pragmatically accommodated.[42] Still, this pragmatism does not follow from a conscious application of the constitutional rights. It is rather a form of toleration resulting both from Italy being a Roman Catholic country long accustomed to the public visibility of its religion, and also, paradoxically, a reflection of the lack of real reception of the cultural and religious changes of the Italian society. In fact, problems immediately arise as soon as from this more fluid level we move on to institutional one, concerning the legal status of Muslim associations. In fact, in this matter, Italy suffers both the limits connected to a legislation that dates back to 1929-1930, at the times of the Fascist regime and the consequent lack of an updated legislation.

This situation can be explained by two main reasons. The first is that, despite the great consideration given by the Constitution to religion(s),[43] in nearly seventy years since its approval, the major political energy has been spent addressing the long and difficult reform of the Lateran Pacts (1929) between the state and the Catholic Church, and the extension of this same bilateral model to other religions, according to a system of dis-

---

"recognized religious creed", namely "religious entity", indispensable for using the possibility offered by art. 23 of the Royal decree no. 289 of 28 February 1930.

42 See, for example, the resolution of the Consiglio Superiore della Magistratura (the self-governing body of Italian judges) of 22 February 2012, which declared that once a person has been identified, he/she can attend court hearings with the head and also the face covered, at http://www.olir.it/documenti/index.php? argomento=127&documento=5782, accessed 25 August 2014. It is worth to note that recent discussions about wearing the burka in France and Germany have not changed this perception at all. Nevertheless, this data has to be combined with the 2015 Pew Forum's survey from which Italy appears to be one the most "islamophobic" European country. See http://www.pewglobal.org/2015/06/02/ chapter-3-anti-minority-sentiment-not-rising/#jews-seen-favorably, accessed 13 September 2016.

43 Religion is the most quoted social factor in the Italian Constitution, which refers to it in at least six articles (2, 3, 7, 8, 19 and 20), representing for some authors a sign of a real *favor religionis*: See Torre, *Il fattore religioso nella Costituzione. Analisi e interpretazioni*, 1995, pp. 28-29.

cretionary selection by public authorities.[44] Accordingly, if the Parliament approved a new concordat with the Catholic Church in 1985 and twelve general agreements with as many religious denominations between 1984 and 2016,[45] no bill has been approved that grants a general basic standard of religious freedom enjoyable by religions that remain outside of the contractual relationships with the state.[46] The second, more general reasons, is that a new legislation would have meant the formal recognition of an open

44 Nevertheless, a new comprehensive legislation, designed to provide a right to religious freedom for all, was already presented by Bettino Craxi, the President of the Council of Ministries responsible for the new Concordat with the Catholic Church of 1984, as the natural framework for the new bilateral relationships between the state, the Catholic Church, and the other religious denominations: See Francesco Margiotta Broglio, "La politica religiosa della Repubblica italiana. Elementi e riflessioni," 2014, pp. 29-30.

45 Agreements have been approved with the Tavola Valdese (Valdensians), the Seventh-day Adventists, the Assemblee di Dio (Assemblies of God, a Pentecostal church), the Union of Jewish Communities, the Christian Evangelical-Baptist Union, the Lutheran Church, the Italian Buddhist Union, the Italian Hindu Union, the Apostolic Church in Italy, the Church of Jesus Christ of Latter-day Saints, the Greek Orthodox Archdiocese of Italy and Exarchate of Southern Europe and the Soka Gakkai. The Jehovah's Witnesses signed an agreement in 2000 and later in 2007, but parliament has never approved these agreements. All the agreements, except that of the Church of Jesus Christ of Latter-day Saints, foresee the participation of the religious denomination signatory to the "0,8% system." See http://www.governo.it/Presidenza/USRI/confessioni/intese_indice.html#2, accessed on 5 November 2016.

46 This is the so-called legislation on the "admitted cults" formed by the law no. 1159 of the 1929 and its executive royal decree no. 289 of the 1930 clarified by the Home Ministry circular no. 111 of 20 April 1998. See Ferrari, *La libertà religiosa in Italia. Un percorso incompiuto*, 2012, passim. This legislation allows religious associations to enjoy the legal status of "religious entity" after a procedure that, starting from the Home Ministry and passing through an (formally not compulsory but always requested) advocate of the Council of State and a (political) vote of the Council of Ministers, ends with a decree of the President of the Republic. Religious associations recognized as a "religious legal entity" enjoy fiscal advantages because their finalities of religion and cult are assimilated to that of instruction and beneficence. Getting this recognition requires presenting for the approval of the public administration a clear organizational statute, a detailed balance sheet, and a report on the religious principles followed by the organization. Once recognition is granted, the religious entity is subject to the supervision of the Home Ministry, which is in charge of monitoring adherence to the approved organizational statutes and the other conditions of the law: See Finocchiaro, *Diritto ecclesiastico*, 2012, pp. 315-317.

and fluid religious pluralism[47] and, necessarily the erosion of the present highly institutional right to religious freedom modeled on the Catholic paradigm. It is true that a formal appreciation of pluralism occurred in 1989, when the Constitutional Court recognized a principle of *laicità* implying "the protection of the freedom of religion in a context of confessional and cultural pluralism."[48] But the fulfilment of this "supreme constitutional principle" is yet to be completed.

The result of this situation is that in the absence of a fair suit specifically tailored for the exercise of religious freedom and in an effort to avoid the unpredictable scrutiny of the public administration connected with the application of the 1929-1930 legislation, Muslim groups prefer to camouflage their religious identity and act as no-profit associations, within the more beneficial frames of the private law.[49] In this way, they enjoy simplified procedures for gaining recognition of private legal status, as well as advantageous and flexible organizational forms and fiscal advantages formally only foreseen for the exercise of non-profit charity activities. Although this choice entails the abandonment to openly display a religious identity, this is also the only available alternative to the poor status of non-recognized religious association, which would be the only available in the impossibility to benefit from the 1929-1930 legislation, but which also does not provide for any benefit.[50]

---

47 In the national census of 1931 non-Catholics were 130,000; see Broglio, "La politica religiosa della Repubblica italiana," pp. 30-31. Today they have reached five million, not to count the non believers. See Pace, *Le religioni nell'Italia che cambia,* and idem,, "Achilles and the tortoise. A society monopolized by Catholicism faced with an unexpected religious pluralism," 2013, pp. 315-331. .

48 See decision no. 203 of 12 April 1989, at http://www.giurcost.org/decisioni/ 1989/ 0203s-89.html, accessed on 24 August 2014.

49 This Muslim consciousness has been confirmed by the negative outcome of COREIS's attempt to obtain legal recognition as a "religious entity" (2015) and confirms the exceptional case of the Islamic Cultural Centre, recognized more for its diplomatic character than for its contribution to the "religious freedom", as also demonstrated by the tolerance shown by the ministerial authorities toward some opacity in the administration of the Institute. See the previous paragraph.

50 The Council of State is firm in pretending that the only possibility for becoming a recognized religious association, and obtaining a religious legal status, is the process prescribed by the special legislation of 1929-1930. Consequently, no religious association can achieve legal status according to private, general law. See decision no. 2331 of 17 April 2009, at http://www.olir.it/documenti/? documento=4988, accessed 20 August 2014.

The unavailability of the special religious associative typology foreseen by the 1929-1930 legislation and the impossibility of religious groups achieving legal status on the basis of the civil code are really problematic. The Constitution, in fact, prohibits discrimination based on the religious character of the activities carried out by an association[51] and aims at overcoming the eighteenth-century royalist idea that associates religion with unjustified privileges and a highly discretionary public scrutiny.

As a result, most influential Muslim associations still do not have a clear religious physiognomy (UCOII); or if they have it, it is without any recognition by the state (COREIS), or only through a peculiar "extraterritorial" organization recognized by the state as a "cultural" Muslim entity (ICCI). But the camouflage of the religious character is even more evident at the bottom, where the hundreds of Muslim associations that comprise the three main national organizations are mainly structured as cultural associations, associations of social promotion, charities, non-profit associations, and so on.[52] On the one hand, this mimicry forces important dimensions of social capital underground, first of all not allowing the full recognition of the important public role played by Muslim religious organizations in the integration of their members in the Italian society. On the other hand, the use of forms of association intended for goals other than religious activities is against the law and turns out to be counterproductive for religious groups.[53] In fact, some non-profit associational schemes absolutely prevent any profit, whereas a religious group may be able to pursue profit secondarily. In other cases, the law prohibits any form of discrimination in the choice of members or imposes a democratic organization, two points that could be hardly acceptable for a religious group. Moreover, some organizational forms used by Muslim groups are for specific activities only, among which religious activity is not included. Even

51 See, for example, the Art. 20 of the Constitution, for which: "(N)o special legislative limitation or tax burden may be imposed on the establishment, legal capacity or activities of any association or institution on the ground of its ecclesiastical nature or its religious or worship purposes," and Angelucci, "L'associazionismo religioso nel quadro delle garanzie costituzionali del diritto di libertà religiosa," 2014, pp. 35-52.

52 See Ferrari, "Libertà religiosa e nuove presenze confessionali (ortodossi e islamici): tra cieca deregulation e super-specialità, ovvero del difficile spazio per la differenza religiosa," 4 July 2011, www.statoechiese.it.

53 See Angelucci, "L'associazionismo religioso musulmano tra diritto speciale e diritto comune: la centralità dello statuto," 2014, pp. 71-93.

more limiting, if a religious group chooses to act as a 'generic' cultural or no-profit organization, it cannot formally provide religious assistance in prisons, in the army, or in hospitals because of the lack of a religious physiognomy. For the same reason, public authorities will also refuse both the recognition of such association as a religious entity on the basis of the 1929-1930 legislation and, obviously, the signature of an *intesa*, which requires that the organization is a 'religious denomination' (*confessione religiosa*).

Moreover, without a clear religious character, an association may exercise worship only privately, within the premises of the organization, and without the possibility of opening an 'official' public space of worship, open to anyone who wishes to participate. In fact, Muslim places of worship are quite numerous but they are not legally considered as such. Between 2008 and 2009, a survey counted 769 'places of worship': one for every 1,723 Muslims, which is more or less in line with the European average.[54] Today, the numbers have not changed significantly, and only six

---

54 Cfr. Bombardieri, *Moschee d'Italia*, passim. Some years later, another study identified 655 of them: Rhazzali and Equizi, "I musumani e i loro luoghi di culto," pp. 47-72. See also, for the European framework, Allievi, *Conflicts over Mosques in Europe. Policy issues and trends*, 2009, pp. 22 ff., at http://www.nef-europe.org/wp-content/uploads/2013/03/Conflicts-over-mosques_NEF-RelDem-RELIGION-MOSQUES-Final-1.pdf, accessed on 26 August 2014. In 1992 these places numbered about one hundred (Allievi and Dassetto, *Il ritorno dell'Islam. I musulmani in Italia*, 1993). Self-financed and often supported with financial assistance from abroad (see the note 26), Italian mosques are often open to all Muslims, without ethnic or national distinctions. There exist, however, some ethnic places of worship, mostly attended by Pakistani, Bangladeshi, Senegalese and Turkish Muslims looking for a less Arabic-speaking environment, although an Italian summary of the *khutba* is common today (see note 29). Apart from the ethnic-national divide, the other distinguishing factor depends on the leadership of the places of worship. Thus, these places may be more or less open to a new and younger leadership, while other places are more or less "fundamentalist". Some years ago, in the notorious case of Jenner Street in Milan, the imam who was involved in an unlawful operation of kidnapping organized by the CIA and Italian security services was sentenced in December 2013 to six years in prison for conspiracy with the aim of international terrorism. See http://www.ilgiornale.it/news/cronache/lex-imam-abu-omar-condannato-sei-anni-carcere-973783.html, accessed 5 October 2014; Hendricks, *A Kidnapping in Milan: The CIA on Trial*, 2010, and Vidino, *Il jihdaismo autoctono in Italia: nascita, sviluppo e dinamiche di radicalizzazione*, 2014, at http://www. ispionline.it/it/EBook/Il_jihadismo_autoctono_in_Italia.pdf, accessed on 26 August 2014.

of them (Segrate, near Milan; Brescia; Ravenna; Colle di Val d'Elsa, near Siena; Roma and Catania) have architectural features which make them recognizably Muslim. Anyway, only very few of them have followed the special dispositions foreseen by regional laws for places of worship, which means they are open not as headquarters of a private cultural associations but as places open to anyone who wishes to practice Muslim worship. On the contrary, the great majority are simply garages, sheds, and places where worship can only legally be a secondary 'lawful activity', confined to the members of the particular association. The situation is also exacerbated because some Northern regions starting with the Lombardia, use their powers regarding urban planning to impose draconian conditions for the opening of places of worship, and make changing the use of a building from 'civil' to 'religious' particularly difficult. These regions are able to use their powers regarding urban planning because there is a lack of fundamental principles dictated by the central state, forcing religious groups to hard and uncertain recourses to regional administrative courts.[55]

Finally, this context does not help Muslims associations in seeking greater transparency and rather helps to continue to practice their worship in a "private" way, in a vicious circle that hinders their integration, feeds local suspicions, and, obviously, deprives them of eligibility for government grants for the construction of places of worship.

The result is that Islam in Italy is moving into a 'no-law area'.

E. Looking for (a Policy of) Religious Freedom

The legal condition of Islam that has been summarily described highlights the weakness – or even the absence – of coherent 'ecclesiastical politics'[56]

---

55 On the current legislation in the matter See Marchei, "Il diritto alla disponibilità degli edifici di culto,"2012, pp. 171 ff., and idem, "Le nuove leggi regionali 'anti-moschee'," 10 July 2017, www.statoechiese.it. See also Ferrari, "È possibile costruire una moschea in Italia?," 2008, pp. 35-52, and for the case of the Lombardia region Marchei, "La legge della Regione Lombardia sull'edilizia di culto alla prova della giurisprudenza amministrativa," 31 March 2014, at www.statoechiese.i t.

56 See the editorial and the papers of Francesco Margiotta Broglio, Luciano Musselli, Pasquale Annicchino, Marco Ventura, Pierluigi Consorti, Fabiano Di Prima, and Antonio Angelucci in the first part of the journal *Quaderni di diritto e politica ecclesiastica* 1 (2014), pp. 5-158, about "Politica e rapporti fra Stato e confessioni

in contemporary Italy: a "construction without a project."[57] More precisely, this situation is suggestive of the extreme difficulty in the transition from an 'ecclesiastical policy' based on the relationships between the state and Roman Catholic-like structured religious groups (*confessioni religiose*), to a policy of religious pluralism aimed at offering individuals and (all different) groups access to a fair right to freedom of religion and conscience. In fact, the 'Muslim policy' of the Italian authorities on one side, replicates the patterns of the traditional ecclesiastical policy, which favors diplomatic, political, and institutional contacts; on the other, it tends to emphasize the 'exceptionality' of the "Islamic question."[58] This policy, even more than the political colour of the Government, depends very much on the personality and the political strength of the single Home ministers and has often risked to lead to further divisions and discrimination.[59]

Apart from the Italian Parliament, the Government is the main institution responsible for the religious policy trough both the Presidency of the Council of the Ministries and the Central Directorate for the Cult's Affairs of the Home Ministry, two institutions that not always act in full coordination between them.

The Presidency of the Council is directly responsible for negotiating the signing of agreements (*intese*) between the state and religious denominations (*confessioni religiose*), agreements that enter into force in the Italian legal order after the approval of the Parliament. As I have already mentioned, the agreements represent the top level of protection of religious freedom, which certifies the full political and institutional recognition of the religious group and can open the doors of important public funding for the group.[60] The Home Ministry, in turn, is responsible for recognition of 'religious entities', which are finally chosen by the Council of Ministries and are the only eligible to request the start of the negotiation with the state for the signing of the *intesa*. Finally, according to the article 117, 1c of the Constitution, local authorities do not have general competences in

---

religiose. Il sistema italiano (Politics and relationships between the state and religious denominations: The Italian system)".

57 See Naso and Salvarani (eds.), *Un cantiere senza progetto. L'Italia delle religioni. Rapporto 2012*, 2012.

58 See Ferrari, "'Deislamizziamo' la questione islamica," 2007, at http://www. cipmo .org/analisi/2007/silvio-ferrari-newsletter-cipmo.html, accessed 25 August 2014.

59 See Angelucci, "Una politica per l'islam?," 2014, pp. 141-158.

60 See note 47.

the matter: nevertheless, their role is far from insignificant and they meet – and manage – religious needs by exercising their powers in the fields of health, integration, and urban planning.

As explained earlier, no Muslim group has been granted an agreement with the state; only one of the groups, the ICCI, is recognized as a religious entity, and all of them struggle to receive even minimal attention from local governments. Although the lack of a unitary representation should not constitute an obstacle to the conclusion of an agreement *per se*,[61] the question of representation has for long time prevented not only access to this highest level of recognition, but also recognition of more than one Muslim association as a religious entity,[62] with a 'slippery slope' effect that also influences the local level by slowing down the process for constructing places of worship.[63] Nevertheless, the institution, in January 2016, of the Council for Relationships with Italian Islam at the Home Ministry seems to have injected a new dynamic, as we will see later on.

A part from the recognition, in 1974, of the ICCI, the Italy's contemporary 'Muslim policy' basically begins after September 2001. It is true that in the 1990s the unilateral proposal of agreements from some Muslim associations were made public, and in the first half of 2000, thanks to the intervention of the secretary-general of the League of the Islamic World, the ICCI promoted the creation of the Islamic Council of Italy with the

61 See, for example, the treatment foreseen for the Orthodox churches: not only have associations with different affiliations been recognized as religious entities, but the state has also signed an agreement with an only partial representative of the Orthodox world that directly depended on the Ecumenical Patriarchate. Even more evident is the situation of Buddhists. In fact the state has already signed two different agreements with two different entities: the Italian Buddhist Union and the Italian Buddhist Institute Soka Gakkai.

62 See the already mentioned case of the COREIS: in fact, so far, to have recognized the Cultural Islamic Center of Rome as a "religious entity" seems to be interpreted as precluding other (Muslim) recognitions.

63 Against the regional law that forbids religions without an agreement with the central state to open places of worship, the Constitutional Court has strongly clarified that the right to build places of worship, as an essential part of the right of religious freedom, belongs to all religious groups. So Muslims also can benefit from the regional laws that assign special areas and public funding for this purpose in each municipality: see, e.g., the decisions no. 195 of 19 April 1993, http://www.governo.it/Presidenza/USRI/confessioni/norme/sentenza_195_1993.pdf, against the Abruzzo Region, and no. 346 of 16 July 2002, http://www.giurcost.org/decisioni/2002/0346s-02.html, against the Lombardia Region.

aim of including all main Muslim associations.[64] But these attempts were quickly replaced by the post-2001 phase where securitarian approach was central and the 'moderate' role of the Great Mosque of Rome greatly evaluated. In this period, Italian state administration tried to encourage a unitary Islamic representation able to cope with the values of a Western democratic country.[65] The apex of this attempt was reached on 10 September 2005, with the creation, by the Home Minister, of a consultative institution: the Council for Italian Islam.[66] The tasks of this Council were far from homogeneous. They concerned not only matters specifically linked with specific Muslim religious needs, but also matters generically connected to immigration and integration. This multiplicity of purposes was reflected in the members of the Council, who were chosen by the minister from among representatives of religious associations (UCOII to COREIS), journalists, ostensibly secular intellectuals, social workers, and so on. It was always difficult to conceive of this body as actually being in a position to influence the debate and encourage concrete initiatives.[67] A change in this rather unproductive routine occurred a year later, with the arrival of a new Home Minister who decided to approve a 'manifesto' on citizenship and Islam. This project represented a strong politicization of the works of the Council and highlighted the overlaps between the debate on rights, duties, and citizenship and the search for a moderate Muslim representation. Consequently, the exclusion of UCOII from the consultative table after the approval of the Charter of Values of Citizenship and Integration,[68] and, one year later, the 13 February 2008 the signature of a Declaration of Intent for the Federation of Italian Islam by the "constitu-

64 See Mancuso, "La presenza islamica in Italia: forme di organizzazione, profili problematici e rapporti con le istituzioni," 22 February 2010, pp. 17-18, at www.statoechiese.it, and Pacini, "I musulmani in Italia. Dinamiche organizzative e processi di interazione con la società e le istituzioni italiani," 2000, pp. 50-51.

65 See the influential Sartori, *Pluralismo, multiculturalismo e estranei. Saggio sulla società multietnica*, 2000, that was the ideal forerunner of those who denied this possibility.

66 See Alessandro Ferrari, "L'intesa con l'islam e la Consulta: osservazioni minime su qualche questione preliminare," 2006, pp. 29-53.

67 See Angelucci, "Una politica per l'islam?," pp. 150-151.

68 See the decree of the Home Minister of 23 April 2007. The Charter was conceived as a programming guide for the administrative action of the Ministry: for a critical comment see Colaianni, "Una 'carta' post-costituzionale?," 11 June 2007, at www.statoechiese.it.

tional Muslims" (ICCI and COREIS), did not come as a surprise.[69] Nevertheless, these initiatives didn't reach their expected results.

From 2008 to 2011, at the time of the last right-wing Berlusconi government, Italy experienced a tide of vociferous public expression that portrayed Islam as being in irreconcilable opposition to 'Western civilization'. This time, among the parties to this debate were Muslims who were individually involved in politics and who made the fight against Islamic fundamentalism the core business of their public engagement. The future convert to Catholicism, Magdi Allam and slightly more nuanced the rightist MP, Souad Sbai, founded their political legitimation in alliances with "devout atheists"[70] and other ardent defenders of so-called Western values accusing the Italian Muslim leadership to be too weak in the defense of human and – especially – women rights.[71]

In such a heated political context, a comprehensive, efficient and constitutionally fair Muslim policy was clearly not feasible. Instead, the Council for Italian Islam was replaced by a more modest Committee for Italian Islam, which worked within the Home Ministry from 2010 to the end of 2011, when the Berlusconi government fell. Established after the affair of UCOII's "missing signature" on the Charter of Values of Citizenship and Integration,[72] the Committee was composed of experts in Islamic studies and religious freedom, right-wing pundits, and "constitutional Muslims", with ICCI and COREIS in the front line and the obvious exclusion of UCOII.

Backing 'moderate Islam' remained on the agenda, but in the mind of the new Home Minister the goal of the Committee was simply to support

69 The Federation was actively promoted by the state administration that "posted" it on the website of the Home Ministry. See Angelucci, "Una politica per l'islam?," pp. 151-154; for the text of the Declaration http://www.interno.gov.it/ mininterno/export/sites/default/it/assets/files/15/0679_DICHIARAZIONE_DI_INTENTI.pdf, accessed 26 August 2014, and Fantelli, "La 'Dichiarazione di intenti per la federazione dell'Islam italiano': un primo commento," 21 July 2008, at www.statoechiese.it.

70 The sociologist Renzo Guolo had already highlighted this phenomenon in *Xenofobi e xenofili. Gli italiani e l'Islam*, 2003, pp. 44-80 and 100-124. See also idem, *Chi impugna la croce. Lega e Chiesa*, 2011, on the "identity Catholicism" of this political movement.

71 See, among others, Allam, *Europa cristiana libera. La mia vita tra verità e libertà, fede e ragione, valori e regole*, 2009, and Sbai, *L'inganno. Vittime del multiculturalismo*, 2010.

72 See, above, in the text.

parliamentary initiatives about Islam with 'neutral' and 'technical' expertise. The first case facing the Committee was the proposal of a law to ban the burqa from public space, with MP Sbai in the forefront.[73] The endorsement of this ban was unsurprisingly the first act of the Committee which was approved by all the Muslim members with only two votes against from two non-Muslims experts. The Committee continued its work by producing other soft law documents, sometimes pressed by the minister (e.g., opinions on *kafala* and on the Mediterranean Arab Spring), and other times acting mostly on its own initiative, as in the case of the opinions on mosques and imams. It is worth noting that except for the first opinion on the burqa, which responded to an imperative political need, the Committee's later opinions tried to draft general answers to the most delicate issues using the limited spaces of the 1929-1930 legislation, given the impossibility of counting on Parliament for a (constitutionally oriented) renewal of the latter.[74] Regardless, no proposal of the Committee was realized and this entity ended its work in uncertainty and awaiting policy directives.

The simultaneous end of the Committee and of the Berlusconi government in November 2011 closed a first time of the Italian Muslim policy.

The Conference of Religions, Culture, and Integration, which replaced the previous Committee between March 2012 and February 2014, can be seen as the beginning of a new phase. The Conference, established at the Ministry on Integration and International Cooperation, was the first outside the Home Ministry and so, the first that acted without clear competences over the right to religious freedom. Nevertheless, thanks to the personal skills of the Minister, Andrea Riccardi, founder of the Community of Sant'Egidio, the Conference had been able both to officially renew the dialogue between the state and UCOII, bypassing the fracture between moderate and fundamentalist Islam and also to try to surmount Muslim exceptionalism through a global approach to the public role of religions and religious freedom, far from "islamophobic" feelings.[75]

---

73 See Ferrari, "A Besieged Right: Religious Freedom and the Italian War on the Burqa and the Niqab," 2013, pp. 37-58.

74 The opinions are published in *Il Regno* 3 (2012), pp. 115-128 (with a comment of Maria Bombardieri, "Sul burqa, le moschee e la formazione degli imam,") and have also been commented on by Macrì, "Brevi riflessioni sui pareri espresso dal Comitato per l'Islam italiano," 2012, pp. 407-423.

75 See Ferrari, *La libertà religiosa in Italia*, pp. 107-108.

Nevertheless, the weak jurisdictions of the new Ministry of Integration, which operated without an effective coordination with the Home Ministry and the weakness of the government as a whole prevented the inauguration of a constructive phase able to concretely address the needs of Italian Muslims.[76] In the same period, even at the local level, promising initiatives that have shown formal goodwill on the part of some municipalities were also left at the stage of good intentions, without concrete developments.

The most notorious case was that of Milan, chosen as the site of the 'Exposition 2015' and still devoid of suitable Muslim places of worship. In 2012, thinking at the forthcoming EXPO and with the aim of becoming a real European multicultural metropolis, the municipality pressed Muslim groups to explicitly organize themselves as religious associations, with coherent and appropriate statutes, in order to benefit from the regional dispositions regarding places of worship.[77] Nevertheless, this encouragement didn't achieve its target, especially because of the intervention of the Region, which changed the urban development law in order to make the construction of Muslim places of worship almost impossible[78] and turning the initiative of the city of Milan in another frustrated opportunity for Mus-

76 As a partial exception of this picture it is possible to quote the experience of cooperation of some universities of Northern Italy with Muslim associations in order to address two crucial issues: the civic training of imams and the statute for religious associations. See Bombardieri, "Un percorso d'integrazione. Fra università, associazioni islamiche e Ministero," 2010, pp. 732-733; idem, "Il dialogo continua... Università, Associazioni islamiche e Ministero," 2012, p. 4, and Angelucci, "L'associazionismo religioso musulmano tra diritto speciale e diritto comune." See also the website www.fidr.it/index_eng.asp.

77 See (at the time much too optimistic) Ferrari, *La libertà religiosa in Italia*, pp. 108-112; Angelucci, "L'Albo delle associazioni e organizzazioni religiose del Comune di Milano," 2013, pp. 461-478, and Bombardieri, "Un albo per il culto," 2012, p. 597.

78 Moreover, the action of the municipality of Milan was strongly opposed by the Lombardia Region, ruled by the right-wing. In fact, on 27 January 2015 the Region, to impede the legitimation of Muslim places of worship, passed the law n. 2/2015 which imposed severe burdens to religious groups without agreement with the state. The law, challenged by the central government and only partially declared against Constitution by the Constitutional Court (decision no. 63 of 23 February 2016) is still in force, posing serious questions to Lombard municipalities. See, for a wise indication of the limits of local policies not backed by a coherent general regulatory framework, Floris, "La tutela delle esigenze religiose in ambito locale tra regole giuridiche e buone pratiche. Il contesto italiano," 2013, pp.

lims, convinced once more of the empty rhetoric of public statements regarding their status.

Two years after the Conference of Religions, Culture, and Integration, the state management of the 'Muslim question' returned to the Home Ministry, which established, in the January 2016, the Council for the Relationships with the Italian Islam. The Council, still in charge, is composed by two different commissions: one composed by experts and one composed by members of Islamic associations.[79] The Council, although benefiting from the 'ecumenical' action of the Minister Riccardi's Conference, started its work in a climate of international uncertainty and fear, marked from the 'caliphate' terrorism. This situation also explains the fact that the Council began its activities since the start, in a sort of never-ending task, analysing the usual topics – imam and places of worship – already examined by the previous analogous commissions. So, in July 2016, the Council approved an advice about imams, very similar to that already adopted in 2011 by the Committee for Italian Islam, and again focused on the need to make the 1929-1930 legislation effective also for Muslim clergy by implementing an action of 'civic training' carried out by Universities in partnership with the Ministry itself.[80] However, no special financial resources have been devoted by the Italian state to this task. Funding rests only upon European funds for integration, whose use complies more with formal and bureaucratic logics than with strategic considerations connected with a state policy on the matter. Another document about places of worship, containing the usual pleas for a coordinated action between central and local state administrations in order to implement the basic constitutional right to religious freedom, was approved some months later.

These documents, which aim at assuring Muslim communities in Italy in that difficult time, have soon appeared as a premise of a much more ambitious project. This latter has been revealed on 1st of February 2017 with the approval of the "National Pact for an Italian Islam, expression of an

---

175-206 (and especially pp. 200-202), and, about the Regional law and the Court decision: Oliosi, "La Corte costituzionale e la legge regionale lombarda: cronaca di una morte annunciata o di una opportunità mancata?," 24 October 2016, at www.statoechiese.it. See also note 57.

79 See http://www.interno.gov.it/it/notizie/rapporti-stato-islam-alfano-passo-impor ta nte-nella-pace-e-sicurezza-attraverso-dialogo, accessed 5 September 2016.

80 See an unofficial version of the document in http://www.olir.it/documenti/ index.p hp?argomento=26&documento=6710, accessed 13 August 2016.

open and integrated community, recognizing the values and principles of the state legal order."[81]

The contents of this document, divided into three sections, are not, *per se*, a total novelty. They are aimed at fighting Islamic radicalism through a common engagement between Muslim associations and the Italian state. The former commit themselves in order of ensuring both a selection of well-trained imam able to preach in Italian according with the national context and the transparence of their organization, with special regards to the financial matters. The latter shall ensure to overcome any further delay in making operational the legislation about the recognition of Muslim religious entities also in the light of the signature of one (or more) general agreement(s) between Muslim representation(s) and the state. If these engagements can seem quite usual, their formulation is not. In fact, in a concordatarian country such Italy, it must not pass unnoticed the contractual-bilateral character of the "pact" where, for the first time, the Home Ministry and Muslim associations appear on an equal footing in front of the need to comply with Constitutional directives. Moreover, for the first time, this bilateral structure, which emphasizes the role of religious autonomy, another pillar of the Italian way to cope with religious groups, openly preludes to a conclusion of one or more agreement(s) with one or more Muslim representation(s).

The signature of the 'Pact' could have opened a new phase characterised by a process of institutionalization, more precisely of 'ecclesiasticization', of Muslim communities. Of the consequences of this Pact, on one hand single religious Muslim associations, counting now on the government's commitment, are working for recognition as legal entities, following the 1929-1930 legislations. On the other, they try again to build a confederal representation, again with the endorsement of the government which would unsurprisingly prefer to interact with a single umbrella Muslim federation.

81 See http://www.interno.gov.it/sites/default/files/patto_nazionale_per_un_islam _it aliano.pdf, accessed 10 July 2017.

F. Towards an Italian "Muslim Church"?

The description of the legal condition of Islam in Italy seem to confirm the argument of those who have suggested that a 'right to religious freedom' is inevitably politically oriented, discriminatory and even impossible.[82] Nevertheless, this description, reveals also the inexorable path toward the building of a 'Muslim Church' Westphalian style.[83] The Pact for the Italian Islam goes in this direction. Nevertheless, faced with economic priorities, as well as with the political instabilities of both Mediterranean shores and the connected migratory flows, Italy as a whole must decide what to do regarding religious and cultural pluralism, religious freedom, and Islam: the recent debates about the new law on citizenship, so harshly discussed but not approved, are part of the same picture. The decision about the (degree and the ways of the) metabolism of globalization will also determine not only internal social cohesion but also Italy's international status and possibilities for reaching its potential in Europe and especially in the Mediterranean area.[84] The so far peaceful coexistence with Islam, which has also avoided Italy to completely fall into the traps of the securitization of the 'Islamic question', together with the needs of the cooperation of Italian Muslims in the management of the significant migratory flow and, more widely, as a new social capital, could be seen by the political establishment as crucial opportunities for experiencing and metabolizing an Italian style of "living together" where the establishment of a 'Muslim Church' could play a fundamental role.

Bibliography

Abis Analisi e strategie, "G2: una generazione orgogliosa. Una ricerca sui musulmani in Italia," at http://www.italianieuropei.it/it/le-iniziative/convegni/item/2308-g2-una-generazione-orgogliosa-unaricerca-sui-musulmani-in-italia.html.

Allam, Magdi, Europa *cristiana libera. La mia vita tra verità e libertà, fede e ragione, valori e regole*, Milano: Mondadori, 2009.

---

82 See Sullivan, *The Impossibility of Religious Freedom*, 2007, and Hurd, *Beyond Religious Freedom: The New Global Politics of Religion,* 2015.

83 See Ferrari, "Le droit européen de liberté religieuse au temps de l'islam," May 2017, at www.statoechiese.it.

84 See in this regard Annicchino, "La tutela e la promozione del diritto di libertà religiosa nelle recenti iniziative di politica estera italiana," 2014, pp. 51-65.

Allievi, Stefano, and Felice Dassetto, *Il ritorno dell'Islam. I musulmani in Italia*, Roma: Edizioni Lavoro, 1993.

Allievi, Stefan, *I nuovi musulmani. I convertiti all'islam*, Roma: Edizioni Lavoro, 1999.

Allievi, Stefano, *Islam italiano: Viaggio nella seconda religione del paese*, Torino: Einaudi, 2003.

Allievi, Stefano (ed.), *I musulmani e la società italiana. Percezioni reciproche, conflitti culturali, trasformazioni sociali*, Milano: Franco Angeli, 2009.

Allievi, Stefano, *Conflicts over Mosques in Europe. Policy issues and trends*, Alliance Publishing Trust, London 2009, at http://www.nef-europe.org/wp-content/uploads/2013/03/Conflicts-over-mosques_NEF-RelDem-RELIGION-MOSQUES-Final-1.pdf.

Anello, Giancarlo, "Passato e futuro della minoranza musulmana in Italia, tra islamofobia e pluralismo pragmatico-giuridico," *Stato e Chiese e pluralismo confessionale, Rivista telematica*, www.statoechiese.it, 17 October 2016.

Angelucci, Antonio, "L'Albo delle associazioni e organizzazioni religiose del Comune di Milano," Quaderni di diritto e politica ecclesiastica 2 (2013): 461-478.

Angelucci, Antonio, "L'associazionismo religioso nel quadro delle garanzie costituzionali del diritto di libertà religiosa," in *Islam e integrazione in Italia*, ed. Antonio Angelucci, Maria Bombardieri, and Davide Tacchini, Venezia: Marsilio, 2014, pp. 35-52.

Angelucci, Antonio, "L'associazionismo religioso musulmano tra diritto speciale e diritto comune: la centralità dello statuto," in *Islam e integrazione in Italia*, ed. Antonio Angelucci, Maria Bombardieri, and Davide Tacchini, Venezia: Marsilio, 2014, pp. 71-93.

Angelucci, Antonio, "Una politica per l'islam?," *Quaderni di diritto e politica ecclesiastica* 1 (2014): 141-158.

Annicchino, Pasquale, "La tutela e la promozione del diritto di libertà religiosa nelle recenti iniziative di politica estera italiana," Quaderni di diritto e politica ecclesiastica 1 (2014): 51-65.

Bombardieri, Maria, "Un percorso d'integrazione. Fra università, associazioni islamiche e Ministero," in *Il Regno* 22 (2010): 732-733.

Bombardieri, Maria, *Moschee d'Italia. Il diritto al luogo di culto. Il dibattito sociale e politico*, Bologna: EMI, 2011.

Bombardieri, Maria, "Il dialogo continua... Università, Associazioni islamiche e Ministero," *Il Regno* 2 (2012): 4-5.

Bombardieri, Maria, "Una federazione prevalente," *Il Regno* 10 (2012): 313-314.

Bombardieri, Maria, "Un albo per il culto," *Il Regno* 18 (2012): 597.

Bombardieri, Maria, "Islam in Italia: Numeri, protagonisti e dinamiche sociali," Ad Gentes – Rivista di teologia e antropologia della missione, 1, 33 (2013): 7-24.

Bombardieri, Maria, "Sul burqa, le moschee e la formazione degli imam," Il Regno, 3 (2012): 115-128.

Bombardieri, Maria, "Mappatura dell'associazionismo islamico in Italia," in *Islam e integrazione in Italia*, ed. Antonio Angelucci, Maria Bombardieri, and Davide Tacchini, Venezia: Marsilio, 2014, pp. 11-34.

Branca, Paolo, *Yalla Italia! Le vere sfide dell'integrazione di arabi e musulmani nel nostro paese*, Roma: Edizioni Lavoro, 2007.

Broglio, Francesco Margiotta, "La politica religiosa della Repubblica italiana. Elementi e riflessioni," *Quaderni di diritto e politica ecclesiastica* 1 (2014): 29-30.

Broglio, Francesco Margiotta, Luciano Musselli, Pasquale Annicchino, Marco Ventura, Pierluigi Consorti, Fabiano Di Prima, and Antonio Angelucci, "Politica e rapporti fra Stato e confessioni religiose. Il sistema italiano (Politics and relationships between the state and religious denominations. The Italian system)," *Quaderni di diritto e politica ecclesiastica* 1 (2014): 5-158.

Bruno, Marco, *L'islam immaginato. Rappresentazioni e stereotipi nei media italiani*, Milano: Guerini e Associati, 2009.

Cardia, Carlo, and Giuseppe Dalla Torre, *Comunità islamiche in Italia. Identità e forme giuridiche*, Torino: Giappichelli, 2015.

Casuscelli, Giuseppe, "Le proposte d'intesa e l'ordinamento giuridico italiano. Emigrare per Allah/emigrare con Allah," in *I musulmani e la società italiana. Percezioni reciproche, conflitti culturali, trasformazioni sociali*, ed. Stefano Allievi, Milano: Franco Angeli, 2009, pp. 83-105.

Casuscelli, Giuseppe, "La libertà religiosa alla prova dell'Islām: la peste dell'intolleranza," in *Identità religiosa e integrazione dei musulmani in Italia e in Europa. Omaggio alla memoria di Francesco Castro*, ed. Roberta Aluffi Beck-Peccoz, Torino: Giappichelli, 2008, pp. 53-70.

Chaouki, Khalid, *Salaam, Italia! La voce di un giovane musulmano italiano*, Reggio Emilia: Alberti editore, 2005.

Coglievina, Stella, *Annotated Legal Documents on Islam in* Europe: Italy, Leiden/ Boston: Brill, 2016.

Colaianni, Nicola, "Una 'carta' post-costituzionale?," *Stato e Chiese e pluralismo confessionale, Rivista telematica*, 11 June 2007, at www.statoechiese.it.

Conetti, Giorgio, "Il matrimonio: conflitti di leggi o di culture?," in *Islam in Europa/ Islam in Italia tra dritto e società*, ed. Alessandro Ferrari, Bologna: Il Mulino, pp. 111-120.

Constitution, Art. 8 (IT).

Constitution, Art. 20 (IT).

Constitutional Court, Decision No. 203, 1989 (IT).

Constitutional Court, Decision No. 195, 1993 (IT).

Constitutional Court, Decision No. 346, 2002 (IT).

Constitutional Court, Decision No. 63, 2016 (IT).

Council of State, Decision No. 2331, 2009 (IT).

Cuciniello, Antonio, "L'Islam nelle carceri italiane," Report of the ISMU Foundation, October 2016, at http://www.ismu.org/wp-content/uploads/2016/10/Cuciniello_Islam-e-carcere_paper_ottobre2016.pdf.

Domianello, Sara, "Il pluralismo in materia religiosa nel settore matrimoniale," in *Diritto e religione in Italia. Rapporto nazionale sulla salvaguardia della libertà religiosa in regime di pluralismo confessionale e culturale*, ed. Sara Domianello, Bologna: Il Mulino, 2012, pp. 120 ff.

Fantelli, Paola, "La 'Dichiarazione di intenti per la federazione dell'Islam italiano': un primo commento," *Stato e Chiese e pluralismo confessionale, Rivista telematica*, 21 July 2008, at www.statoechiese.it.

Ferrari, Alessandro, "L'intesa con l'islam e la Consulta: osservazioni minime su qualche questione preliminare," in *Il dialogo delle leggi. Ordinamento giuridico italiano e tradizione giuridica is*lamica, ed. Ida Zilio-Grandi, Venezia: Marsilio, 2006, pp. 29-53.

Ferrari, Alessandro, "Laïcité et multiculturalisme à l'italienne," *Archives des Sciences Sociales des Religions* 53, 141 (2008): 133-154.

Ferrari, Alessandro, "Civil Religion in Italy: 'A Mission Impossible'?," *The George Washington International Law Review* 41, 4 (2010): 839-859.

Ferrari, Alessandro, "Libertà religiosa e nuove presenze confessionali (ortodossi e islamici): tra cieca deregulation e super-specialità, ovvero del difficile spazio per la differenza religiosa," in *Stato e Chiese e pluralismo confessionale, Rivista telematica*, 4 July 2011, at www.statoechiese.it.

Ferrari, Alessandro, *La libertà religiosa in Italia. Un percorso incompiuto*, Roma: Carocci, 2012.

Ferrari, Alessandro, "A Besieged Right: Religious Freedom and the Italian War on the Burqa and the Niqab," in *The Burqa Affair Across Europe. Between Public and Private Space*, ed. Alessandro Ferrari and Sabrina Pastorelli, Farnham: Ashgate, 2013, pp. 37-58.

Ferrari, Alessandro, "Le droit européen de liberté religieuse au temps de l'islam," *Rivista telematica*, May 2017, at www.statoechiese.it.

Ferrari, Silvio, "'Deislamizziamo' la questione islamica," 2007, at http://www.cipmo.org/analisi/2007/silvio-ferrari-newsletter-cipmo.html.

Ferrari, Silvio, "È possibile costruire una moschea in Italia?," in *Identità religiosa e integrazione dei musulmani in Italia e in Europa. Omaggio alla memoria di Francesco Castro*, ed. Roberta Aluffi Beck-Peccoz, Torino: Giappichelli, 2008, pp. 35-52.

Finocchiaro, Francesco, *Diritto ecclesiastico*, Bologna: Zanichelli, 2012.

Fiorita, Nicola, and Francesca Tarchiani, "L'Islam a Colle Val d'Elsa: pregi e difetti di un protocollo d'intesa," at http://www.olir.it/areetematiche/85/documents/Fiorita_Tarchiani_Islam_Colle.pdf.

Floris, Pierangela, "La tutela delle esigenze religiose in ambito locale tra regole giuridiche e buone pratiche. Il contesto italiano," in *Diversidad religiosa y gobierno local. Marco jurídico y modelos de intervención en España y en Italia*, ed. Adoración Castro Jover, Cizur Menor (Navarra): Thomson Reuters Aranzadi, 2013, pp. 175-206.

Frisina, Annalisa, *Giovani musulmani d'Italia*, Roma: Carocci, 2007.

Guolo, Renzo, *Xenofobi e xenofili. Gli italiani e l'Islam*, Roma-Bari: Laterza, 2003.

Guolo, Renzo, *Chi impugna la croce. Lega e Chiesa*, Roma-Bari: Laterza, 2011.

Hendricks, Steven, *A Kidnapping in Milan: The CIA on Trial*, New York: W.W. Norton & Company 2010.

Hurd, Elizabeth Shakman, *Beyond Religious Freedom: The New Global Politics of Religion*, Princeton-Oxford: Princeton University Press, 2015.

Law No. 91/1992 (IT).

Law No. 1159/1929 (IT).

Macrì, Gianfranco, "Brevi riflessioni sui pareri espresso dal Comitato per l'Islam italiano," *Quaderni di diritto e politica ecclesiastica* 2 (2012): 407-423.

Mancuso, Anna Sveva, "La presenza islamica in Italia: forme di organizzazione, profili problematici e rapporti con le istituzioni," *Stato e Chiese e pluralismo confessionale, Rivista telematica*, 22 February 2010, pp. 17-18, at www.stato echiese.it.

Marchei, Natascia, "Il diritto alla disponibilità degli edifici di culto," in *Diritto e religione in Italia. Rapporto nazionale sulla salvaguardia della libertà religiosa in regime di pluralismo confessionale e culturale*, ed. Sara Domianello, Bologna: Il Mulino, 2012, pp. 171 ff.

Marchei, Natascia, "La legge della Regione Lombardia sull'edilizia di culto alla prova della giurisprudenza amministrativa," *Stato e Chiese e pluralismo confessionale, Rivista telematica*, 31 March 2014, at www.statoechiese.it.

Marchei, Natascia, "Le nuove leggi regionali 'antimoschee'," *Stato e Chiese e pluralismo confessionale, Rivista telematica*, 10 July 2017, at www.statoechiese.it.

Marzo, Luzio di, "Abu Omar, ex imam di viale Jenner, condannato a sei anni di carcere," *Il Giornale*, 6 December 2013, at http://www.ilgiornale.it/news/cronache/leximam-abu-omar-condannato-sei-anni-carcere-973783.html.

Naso, Paolo, and Salvarani, Brunetto (eds), Un cantiere senza progetto. L'Italia delle religioni. Rapporto 2012, Bologna: EMI, 2012.

National Institute of Statistics (ISTAT), "Il contesto italiano nei dati Istat", in *Report of the Commission "Jo Cox" on intolerance, xenophobia, racism and hate phenomena presided by the President of the Chamber of Deputies, Laura Boldrini*, at http://www.camera.it/leg17/1264.

Oliosi, Francesca, "La Corte costituzionale e la legge regionale lombarda: cronaca di una morte annunciata o di una opportunità mancata?," *Stato e Chiese e pluralismo confessionale, Rivista telematica*, 24 October 2016, at www.statoechiese.it.

Pace, Enzo, "Achilles and the tortoise: A society monopolized by Catholicism faced with an unexpected religious pluralism," *Social Compass*, 9, 60 (3) (2013): 315-331.

Pace, Enzo (ed.), *Le religioni nell'Italia che cambia. Mappe e bussole*, Roma: Carocci, 2013.

Pacini, Andrea, "I musulmani in Italia. Dinamiche organizzative e processi di interazione con la società e le istituzioni italiani," in *Musulmani in Italia. La condizione giuridica delle comunità islamiche*, ed. Silvio Ferrari, Bologna: Il Mulino, 2000, pp. 21-52.

Pallavicini, Yahya S. Y., "Un itinerario nell'Islam italiano: dalla Costituzione verso l'Intesa?," in *La costituzione italiana in lingua araba nell'ambito del dialogo interculturale e delle relazioni tra ordinamenti giuridici*, ed. Gaetano Zilio Grandi, Rubano (Padova): ANCI, 2010, p. 21.

President of the Republic, Decree No. 212, 1974 9 (IT).

Qader, Sumaya Abdel, *Porto il velo, adoro i Queen. Nuove italiane crescono*, Milano: Sonzogno editore, 2008.

Razzali, Khalid, and Massimiliana Equizi, "I musumani e i loro luoghi di culto," in *Le religioni nell'Italia che cambia. Mappe e bussole*, ed. Enzo Pace, Roma: Carocci, 2013, pp. 47-72.

Royal Decree No. 289, 1930 (IT).

Santerini, Milena, "Le seconde generazioni e il nodo della cittadinanza," in *Islam e integrazione in Italia*, ed. Antonio Angelucci, Maria Bombardieri, and Davide Tacchini, Venezia: Marsilio, 2014, pp. 137-148.

Sartori, Giovanni, *Pluralismo, multiculturalismo e estranei. Saggio sulla società multietnica*, Milano: Rizzoli, 2000.

Sbai, Souad, *L'inganno. Vittime del multiculturalismo*, Siena: Cantagalli, 2010.

Sullivan, Winnifred Fallers, *The Impossibility of Religious Freedom*, Princeton-Oxford: Princeton University Press, 2007.

Taylor, Charles, *A Secular Age*, Cambridge, MA, and London: The Belknap Press of Harvard University Press, 2007.

Torre, Giuseppe Dalla, *Il fattore religioso nella Costituzione. Analisi e interpretazioni*, Torino: Giappichelli, 1995.

Ventura, Marco, *Religion and Law in Italy*, Alphen aan den Rijn: Wolters Kluwer, 2013.

Vidino, Lorenzo, *Il jihdaismo autoctono in Italia: nascita, sviluppo e dinamiche di radicalizzazione*, Milano: Istituto per gli Studi di Politica Internazionale, European Foundation for Democracy, 2014, at http://www.ispionline.it/it/EBook/Il_jihadismo_autoctono_in_Italia.pdf.

Law and Religion in Italy: A new Model of Civil Religion?

Silvio Ferrari

A. Introduction

Italy is a Member State of the European Union and, at the same time, a country whose history and culture has been strongly influenced by Catholicism. On the one hand, the questions underlying the relations between law and religion are shared by Italy with many other countries of the Old Continent; on the other hand, the answers given to these questions often reflect the Italian specificity. To understand the Italian pattern of law and religion relations and its current transformations it is therefore necessary to take into consideration both the European and the national dimensions: in some cases the first will prevail, in some others the specific characteristics of Italian history will gain the upper hand.

In this paper I shall not provide a description of the Italian system of State-religion relations. I shall focus on its most interesting feature, the attempt to govern religious plurality by transforming Catholicism into the Italian civil religion. Once the European context has been outlined (B), the Italian pattern will be described focusing the attention on the attempt to transform Catholicism into the Italian civil religion (C): the debate about the crucifix in the classrooms will provide a good example of this transformation (D). A short description of the French model of civil religion will highlight the peculiarities of the Italian model (E) and will open the way to an assessment of its strong and weak points (F).

B. The European Context

Europe is in the middle of a process of transformation which can be defined as the passage from religious pluralism to cultural and ethical pluralism, often characterized by a strong religious foundation. Due to this transformation, the traditional systems of relations between States and religions do not work smoothly anymore and, after a period of relative stability, they have entered a phase of transition. The direction of this change is sufficiently clear but it is hard to pinpoint its point of arrival with similar precision.

Religious pluralism is a well-known fact in Europe. For centuries, Europe had been split up into Catholic, Protestant, and Orthodox communities, with dividing lines which frequently crossed the same town or the same region. But this pluralism was contained within a shared horizon, defined by the reference to the same sacred books (Old and New Testament) and the same interpretative corpus (Patristic). Of course, Jewish and Muslim communities have been living in Europe for a long time: but the Jews were faced quite early on with the alternative between assimilation or persecution (and they chose the first, without avoiding the second), and the Muslims were confined to a peripheral region of Europe after the Catholic "reconquista" of Spain in the fifteenth century. As a consequence, religious pluralism in Europe has predominantly been intra-Christian pluralism and the religious conflicts which divided Europe after the Great Schism and above all the Protestant Reformation did not create insuperable cultural divisions. It is true that the relations between man and woman, citizen and State, State and religion were and partly still are conceived in a different way in the Catholic, Orthodox, and Protestant countries, but this difference did not become so huge as to generate incompatibility and to prevent mutual understanding. The unification process of Europe, with all its shortcomings, is the proof that a shared notion of citizenship exists.

This common horizon has become progressively weaker. Two factors – the first internal and the second external to Europe – have played an important role in this weakening process and have paved the way to the birth of a culturally and ethically pluralistic society.

The first factor is immigration, which brought an increasing number of people into Europe who do not know and do not share some central features of the European cultural heritage. The way political or family relations are conceived or, at a more day-to-day level, the way people dress or what they eat mark a difference between a part of these immigrant groups and the majority of Europeans. It is not only a difference of religion, but something larger which concerns lifestyles, beliefs, values, behaviour: in a nutshell, a cultural difference.

Second, there is individualism, which questions assumptions that used to be taken for granted.[1] Secularisation had already weakened the control historical Churches exercised on the central passages of human life, birth, marriage, death, and so on: now the way these experiences are conceived and lived is in the process of changing. The range of possibilities has become far larger and the individual is in a position to make choices which were unconceivable only a few years ago. Europe is moving towards the coexistence of different ways of procreating, marrying and dying which correspond to the different ethical views of individuals and which enjoy the same legal legitimacy. The debate on bioethics all over Europe and the recent reform of family law in a number of European countries show that the historic Churches have largely lost their capacity to lead the public debate on central ethical issues and to influence the corresponding political decisions (although there are exceptions, and I am thinking of Italy, which should not be overlooked).

What I have said confirms that today we are faced with something more than simple religious pluralism: we have to deal with a veritable cultural and ethical pluralism. But to understand this new challenge properly, we need to take into consideration its most interesting feature. This cultural and ethical pluralism is by no means a result of the dissolution of the religious dimension in contemporary society: on the contrary, it is frequently characterized by a strong religious connotation or, at least, takes place in a context still dominated by the "revanche de Dieu".[2] On the one hand, the decline of the historical Churches' power to speak on behalf of the whole European society has been balanced by the development, within these same Churches, of new groups and movements, like the Pentecostals and the "Born Again Christians" in the Protestant field and movements like "Communion and Liberation" and the Opus Dei in the Catholic one. They all are motivated by the aim to manifest their strong religious identity in all fields of human life and, consequently, they want to affirm the religious

1 "The changing nature of churchgoing in modern Europe" is underlined by Grace Davie, who highlights the passage "from a culture of obligation or duty to a culture of consumption or choice. What until somewhat recently was simply imposed (with all the negative connotations of this word), or inherited (a rather more positive spin), becomes instead a matter of personal choice" (Davie, "Is Europe an exceptional case?," 2006, p. 26, in Turkish).

2 See Kepel, *La revanche de Dieu. Chrétiens, juifs et musulmans à la reconquête du monde,* 1991. See also Casanova, *Public Religions in the Modern World*, 1994.

foundation of ethical, cultural and political choices. On the other hand, the distinction between religion, ethics, culture and politics which had been accepted – willingly or unwillingly – by most Christian Churches is not part and parcel of the heritage of many religious communities which have arrived in Europe in the last forty years, starting with Islam and some of the "new religious movements". Consequently, cultural and ethical choices are frequently justified through a direct reference to religion. The affair of the Islamic headscarf is a good example: what had been regarded, until a few years ago, as an ethnic custom is now perceived primarily as a religious expression.

The final outcome of this mix between religion, culture, ethics and politics has been that negotiation and compromise are much more difficult today than in the past: when ethical and cultural choices are directly connected to the will of God, they tend to become non-negotiable.

What are the legal consequences of this transformation of the European religious landscape? What is its impact on the systems of relations between States and religions? Today the traditional legal mechanisms which regulated the different areas where human activity takes place do not seem to work properly: confronted with a pluralism which is at the same time cultural, ethical and religious such mechanisms have difficulty in granting the freedom of social communities without falling into the anarchy of particularisms. It is necessary to find new legal mechanisms which take into account the public role of religions. But how is it possible to do so without falling into "communautairisme" which erodes the hard core of shared principles and values and risks endangering social cohesion?

C. The Italian Case or Catholicism as the Civil Religion of Italy

Many and different meanings can be given to the expression "civil religion". Jean Jacques Rousseau employed it in a very broad sense, to indicate a set of universal religious beliefs that every human being is bound to accept;[3] Robert Bellah's most famous essay is entitled "Civil religion in America" and it links civil religion to the specific history, culture and mission of a given country.[4] Sometimes civil religion is viewed as a specific,

---

3 See Ball, "Rousseau's Civil Religion Reconsidered," 1995, pp. 108-118.

4 See Bellah, "Civil Religion in America," *1967, pp. 1-21.*

sectarian religion competing with other religions;[5] sometimes it is conceived as a set of principles and values that the members of all religions can accept without giving up their beliefs.

It seems to me that the current debate on civil religion has to do with the identification of a core nucleus of values that bind individuals together and make a people out of them. This linkage is revealed by the debate timeline: it started in the United States in the '60s, during a time of trial when the national covenant had been broken (to quote Bellah again), and resurfaced in Europe a couple of decades ago, when immigration from Asia and Africa raised the question of the identity of Europe and of its Member States. In a religiously plural society civil religion provides a set of values, symbols and rituals upon which the spiritual unity and social cohesion of a nation (or a group of nations, as in the case of Europe) can be re-built.[6] These remarks help to explain why the debate on civil religion concerns all the European countries: but each of them has its own way of dealing with this issue.

In the European context, is there an Italian way of shaping its own civil religion, which is to tackle the challenges deriving from religious plurality? The answer is affirmative: the central core of the Italian experience is the attempt to govern ethical, cultural and religious plurality through the Catholic religion, raised to the rank of civil religion of the country. More precisely, Catholicism supplies the cultural and ethical principles on which citizenship is based: provided they are ready to accept this horizon, non-Catholic religions can fully enjoy religious rights. Governing diversity by stressing (Catholic) identity is the narrow path Italy is trying to follow.

Is this attempt bound to fail, just an impossible dream to revive a long-faded past, or can it be seen as a way to introduce diversity (albeit a "domesticated" diversity) into a largely homogeneous country? If so, can this model be applied in other countries where the Catholic (or another) religion plays a dominant role? In a broader perspective, does it have the capacity to assuage the fears raised by the growth of religious, cultural and ethical diversity, framing it in a traditional, familiar and reassuring context?

---

5 See Bellah, *The Final Word: Can Christianity Contribute to a Global Civil Religion*, 2010, pp. 351-366.

6 See Bellah, *The Broken Covenant: American Civil Religion in Time of Trial*, 1975, p. 3.

If we answer in the affirmative, then a second set of questions needs to be addressed. Assuming that the Italian model is viable, what are the conditions it requires to be successful? What are its strong and weak points? In other words, what is the price to pay, regarding both the dominant and the minority religions, when a particular faith is elevated to the level of civil religion of a country?

D. The Crucifix as Symbol of the Italian Civil Religion

The question of religious symbols provides a good research field for studying the Italian pattern of civil religion. While in France and in other European countries, the debate focused on the symbols of non-Christian religions (first of all the Islamic headscarf), in Italy the same debate concentrated on the symbols of the Catholic religion.[7] The Islamic headscarf was never a real issue in Italy: but when some requests were made to remove the crucifix from schools, hospitals, and tribunals a chorus of disapproval could be heard. This different approach to the religious symbols issue needs to be carefully taken into consideration, as it enlightens both the elevation of Catholicism to the rank of civil religion of Italy and the implications this process has on the legal status of other religions.

To date the Islamic headscarf has not raised significant problems in Italy. There is no law that forbids wearing a headscarf in public places: in particular, there is no provision that prevents students from wearing a scarf at school. It is possible to wear a headscarf when taking a photograph for an official document (driving licences, identity cards, etc.), provided that the face and the ears are visible. Wearing a headscarf in the workplace can be limited only for health or safety reasons and in cases where a uniform has to be worn.

How is it possible to explain this apparent lack of importance of the headscarf issue in Italy? Two elements can be of help in finding an answer. First, this issue is likely to emerge when the Muslim community has reached a certain level of development in a country and it has acquired the strength to affirm its religious and cultural identity. In Italy the number of

7 On the issues connected to religious symbols in Italy see Dieni, Ferrari, and Pacillo (eds.), *Symbolon/Diabolon. Simboli, religioni, diritti nell'Europa multiculturale*, 2005; Dieni, Ferrari, and Pacillo (eds.), *I simboli religiosi tra diritto e culture,* Milano, Giuffrè, 2006.

Muslim women who have a regular job in the public administration is still small and, when they work, they do not have very high and visible positions: female Muslim teachers, medical doctors, judges etc. are very few. The same can be said of female Muslim students wearing the headscarf at school. It is possible that, by some kind of imitative process, the headscarf issue will be imported into Italy and become an element of conflict: but the endogenous motivations for such a conflict are not yet in place.

The second and more interesting element is connected to the position of the Catholic Church. Even when the conflict between Church and State in Italy was at its peak in the nineteenth century, no prohibition to wear religious symbols in public was enacted: clothing regulations for priests and nuns – like the ones that were in force in Mexico – have always been unknown. Moreover, until recently Catholic religion was taught in State schools by priests dressed in clerical attire (now most of the teachers are laymen): differently from France, no official or unofficial prohibition to enter a school with garments that clearly reveal a religious membership or faith has ever been in force. Finally, television broadcasts daily show the Pope, bishops and priests dressed as Popes, bishops and priests: clerical clothes are so common and visible in Italy that people do not understand why other religiously qualified ways of dressing should be prohibited. In this way the dominance of Catholic religious symbols created some kind of protective umbrella extended to all religious symbols: as long as they are not in competition with the Catholic ones, non-Catholic religious symbols can benefit from the presence of religion in the public life that is a consequence of the social importance of the Catholic Church. But when a Muslim requested to remove the crucifix from the classroom attended by his sons and a judge accepted his petition, a wave of indignation crossed the country: the President of the Republic criticized the decision, the Minister of Justice threatened to take disciplinary measures against the judge, political leaders on both sides of the Parliament reaffirmed in the strongest terms that the crucifix had to remain on the classroom walls[8].

A few years later the issue of the crucifix was brought again to the attention of the courts and the media. This time the request to remove the crucifix from the classroom came from a lady of Finnish origin who lived in Veneto. The court rejected the request, stating that the crucifix is not on-

8 On the debate about the crucifix in the classrooms see Temperman (ed.), *The Lautsi Papers: Multidisciplinary Reflections on Religious Symbols in the Public School Classroom*, 2012, in particular the chapter written by Carlo Panara, pp. 301-325.

ly a religious symbol but also the symbol of Italian identity: according to the court, it manifests the historical and cultural tradition of Italy and is a sign of a system of values based on freedom, equality, human dignity, and religious tolerance. As citizenship is founded on these same values, that are to be respected by everybody, the presence of the crucifix in the classroom cannot be made dependent on the religious convictions of the students.[9]

So far, nothing really new: similar remarks can be found in the case law of other European countries. But the Council of State, which judged the appeal against this decision, opened a new perspective by stating that the crucifix is the symbol of the Italian model of *laïcité*. According to the Council of State, in Italy the principles that are at the base of the idea of *laïcité* cannot but have a religious origin: therefore the best way to manifest the secular character of the Italian school is the crucifix in the classroom. This conclusion does not mean that the crucifix is deprived of its religious significance. But it has a different meaning depending on the place where it is situated: when the crucifix is placed in a church or another place of worship, it is only a religious symbol; when it is placed in a school, it becomes a tool for educating students, independently from their religious beliefs, to the values of tolerance, mutual respect, dignity of the human being, human solidarity, non discrimination, etc., that is to the values that are at the core of the notion of *laïcité*.[10]

It would be a mistake to dismiss the Council of State decision as a bundle of paradoxical and incoherent statements. On the contrary, it is a lucid attempt to express in legal terms the idea – supported by large part of the Catholic hierarchy, the governing political coalition and the public opinion – that only Catholicism can perform the role of civil religion of Italy and provide the set of fundamental principles and values on which social cohesion is founded. This conviction does not imply that non-Catholic religions have no standing in this country: as it has been shown by the issues

9 The court went even further: the fact that Italian schools are attended by a growing number of non-Christian students underlines the need of the crucifix, because it contributes towards propagating the principles of respect of diversity and rejection of radicalism (both religious and secular) that are at the foundation of the Italian legal system and that may not be familiar to students of other cultures and religions. See Administrative Court of Veneto, decision of March 17, 2005, n. 1110, at http://www.olir.it/ricerca/index.php?Form_Document =2075).

10 Council of State, decision of February 13, 2006, n. 556, at http://www.olir.it/ricerca/index.php?Form_Document=3517.

of the headscarf and the Muslim places of worship,[11] they can benefit from the dominant position of Catholicism in Italian society. But the integration of non-Catholic religious communities passes through the acceptance of Catholicism as the civil religion of the country. This point was clearly stated in an article published in a newsletter that is inspired by Cardinal Angelo Scola, then Patriarch of Venice and now Archbishop of Milan and one of the most influential personalities among the Italian bishops. Commenting the Archbishop of Canterbury's speech on the opportunity of giving *shari'a* some place in the English legal system[12], the newsletter affirmed that "rather than trying to defend religion through the guise of secular multiculturalism, the Archbishop of Canterbury should have been defending religious pluralism through Christianity" as

> only Christianity can integrate other religions into a shared European project by acknowledging what secular ideologies cannot: a transcendent objective truth that exceeds human assertion but is open to rational discernment and debate. […] Paradoxically, what other faiths require for their proper recognition is the recovery of the indigenous European religious tradition – Christianity.[13]

In this perspective State support of Catholicism and integration of non-Catholic communities into Italian society are linked together. One could wonder why secular symbols and values cannot perform the same job of integrating religions in the Italian society. The answer is provided by history. Different from what happened in France and other European countries, Italian history did not provide a set of secular symbols and values that are strong enough to replace Catholic symbols and values as the civil religion of the country.

11 In many cases the right of Muslims to have their own places of worship has been defended by the representatives of the Catholic Church, who underlined that having a place where to pray is part of religious freedom. See Ferrari, "Le moschee in Italia tra ordine pubblico e libertà religiosa," 2009, pp. 219-236.

12 The speech, given on February 7 2008, can be read in *Ecclesiastical Law Journal*, v. 10, n. 3, September 2008, pp. 262-275.

13 Blond and Pabst, "A new kind of "laïcité" to integrate Islam in the West," 2008, at http://www.oasiscenter.eu/index.php?page=36&lang=en&table=contributi&directory=contributi&name=contributi_doc&news=429&group=contributi&subgroup=doc_2008.

E. Italy v. France: Two Models of Civil Religion

Taking briefly in consideration the French conception of civil religion will help in understanding the peculiarities of the Italian model.

As already said, civil religion has many facets. One of them is the sacralization of secular concepts and symbols that become the axis around which civil society is organized. This is the case, in France, of *laïcité,* conceived as the general principle that can include and reconcile the particular values of the religious, racial, ethnic, cultural, and political communities living in the country. In this perspective *laïcité* is seen as a cluster of universal and abstract values – liberty, equality, tolerance, etc. –that every citizen and group must embrace independently from his origins, preferences, belongings. Citizenship is built around these values that are, as was stated by the past French President Jacques Chirac, "at the heart of our republican identity".[14] Coherently with this approach, the contract of "accueil et integration" that each immigrant has to sign when entering France[15] lists *laïcité*, together with democracy and equality, among the non-negotiable values on which the French Republic is founded.

This secular conception of civil religion is not without consequences as to the way the relations between State and religions are shaped. I shall give three examples. In the field of education, the French schools curricula (with the exception of Alsace and Moselle) include neither a teaching of religions nor a teaching about religions: this is a very exceptional case, as all the EU States and almost all the European countries comprise this teaching in the school curricula, as a compulsory or optional subject[16]. At the European level, France is spearheading the fight against the so called new religious movements: a law has been enacted and a governmental body has been created to combat the sects and the "derive sectaires"[17]. Also in the field of religious symbols, France has taken a very clear-cut

14 This passage of a speech given by Chirac in 2003 is quoted by Chelini Pont and Gunn, *Dieu en France et aux Etats-Unis. Quand les mythes font la loi*, 2005, p. 15.

15 The text of the contract can be read at http://www.anaem.fr/IMG/pdf/ Contrat_200 8.pdf.

16 On the teaching of religion in the French schools see Willaime, "Teaching Religious Issues in French Public Schools: From Abstentionist Laïcité to a Return of Religion to Public Education," 2007, pp. 87-102; Kuyk, Jensen, Lankshear, Manna, and Schreiner (eds.), *Religious Education in Europe,* 2007, pp. 71-75.

17 See Beckford, "'Laïcité', 'Dystopia', and the Reaction to New Religious Movements in France," 2004, pp. 27-40; Duvert, "Anti-Cultism in the French Parlia-

position, by passing a law that prohibits the wearing at school of religious symbols that are too visible[18] and, a few years later, another law that prevents women from wearing a full-face veil in the public spaces[19]. Once more, we are confronted with a case of French exceptionalism: almost no other EU country has followed this path.

In my opinion there is a link between the secular conception of civil religion prevailing in France and these legal and political choices. If national identity has to be built around the notion of *laïcité,* "it is the role of the state to create laïque citizens"[20] by educating them to the values of *laïcité* and shielding them from the competing values upheld by religions. This attitude explains the exclusion of the teaching of religion from schools curricula, the prohibition of religious symbols in public institutions and the need to protect citizens from the threat to freedom posed by the new religious movements. This conclusion is confirmed by an exam of how the same issues have been dealt with in Italy, starting from a completely different conception of civil religion. In the Italian public schools, the teaching of the Catholic religion is compulsory, in the sense that the State has the obligation to provide it and the students or their parents can decide whether to attend or not Catholic religion classes; other religions can be taught but only at the request of the students and the teachers are not paid by the State (as the teachers of the Catholic religion are). In Italy there is no specific law concerning new religious movements nor an official institution charged with controlling or combating them: but these movements are far from enjoying the same legal status other religious communities have. Finally, the symbols of the minority religions – like the Islamic headscarf, the Jewish kippa, or the Sikh turban – are not a matter of concern in Italy, while the debate focused on the symbols of the majority religion: when the Catholic symbols were threatened almost everybody – from the President of the Republic to the Prime Minister – felt compelled to heed the public outcry in their defense. The different impact of the two

---

ment: Desperate Last Stand or an Opportune Leap Forward? A Critical Analysis of the 12 June 2001 Act," 2004, pp. 41-53.

18 On this issue see Bowen, *Why the French Don't Like Headscarves: Islam, the State, and Public Space,* 2006.

19 On this second law see Ferrari and Pastorelli (eds.), *The Burqa Affair Across Europe*, 2013, in particular the chapter written by Anne Fornerod, pp. 59-76.

20 Berger, Davie and Fokas, *Religious America, Secular Europe? A Theme and Variations,* 2008, p. 76.

conceptions of civil religion on the Church-State system could not be more evident.

How much the French conception of civil religion can cope with the two driving forces that are changing the European religious landscape – the increasing plurality of religions and their growing public character – is open to discussion. The weakest point of the French pattern is the assumption that not only the State and its institutions but also society and politics have to be independent from particular traditions and conceptions of life.[21] To attain such a goal these traditions are to be pushed to the margins of public life: but privatization of religion is increasingly rejected by a consistent part of the European historical religions and of the immigrant communities, which come from countries where law and politics are intermingled with religion and by a part of the autochthonous Europeans.

F. What Future for the Italian Civil Religion?

Italy is a country with a strong Church and a weak State. Italy does not have a "state-nation identity, such as France, which aims to achieve social cohesion through a common bond of citizenship based on public institutions"; instead it has a "nation-state identity […] in which social cohesion is principally entrusted to a natural, cultural-religious homogeneity"[22]. This historical weakness of the State has been accentuated by the radical transformation of the political landscape that took place in the '90s, when the Socialist and the Christian Democrat parties disappeared under the blows of the judges who jailed most of their leaders under accusation of corruption. Their place was taken by new parties that had no real ideology beyond the idea of running Italy as an economic enterprise (in the case of Berlusconi's Forza Italia) and of reviving an implausible Celtic tradition to distance the Italian Northern regions from the South and connect them to Central and North Europe (in the case of Bossi's Lega Nord). This ideological void gave the Catholic Church the opportunity to expand its influence.

---

21 This assumption emerges clearly in the "Déclaration sur la laïcité" prepared by Jean Bauberot, Roberto Blancarte and Micheline Milot and published on December 9, 2005 (see art. 4 and 9). The text is published in Bauberot, *L'intégrisme républicain contre la laïcité,* 2006, pp. 247-265.

22 Ferrari, "Religious Education in a Globalized Europe," 2008, p. 113.

Italy has a long Catholic past and also a relatively strong Catholic present[23], if compared with other traditionally Catholic countries like France, Belgium and Spain where secularisation has had a far stronger impact. Moreover the Pope and the Holy See, that are the central governing bodies of the Catholic Church, are in Rome – not in Paris or Madrid – and this fact has a significant influence on the political, cultural and social life of Italy. Just to give one example, when John Paul II died, the whole country virtually stopped: football matches were cancelled, political activity was suspended, schools and universities closed. The Catholic Church is not only a powerful institution: it is also a deeply rooted presence in Italian society. On Sundays churches are reasonably full, there is an impressive network of Catholic voluntary associations that are active in the fields of assistance to immigrants, poor and sick people, Catholic oriented schools are quite strong at the level of pre-primary and primary education, and every parish has an "oratorio", that is a place where young people meet, play and socialize under the vigilant eye of the parish priest. For these reasons the Catholic Church in Italy is something more than the "vicarious Church" described by Grace Davie[24]; it is a "popular" Church, that is something that still has an impact on civil society.[25]

In this context Catholicism was the natural candidate to provide the values and principles on which social cohesion is built, that is to become the civil religion of Italy.

It would be a mistake to conclude hastily that the religious rights of non-Catholic individuals and communities cannot be safeguarded in this context: as some scholars have underlined, "the cross in Italy's state schools is the main defender of the headscarves of Muslim pupils".[26] But

23 Until not long ago over 90% of the pupils at state schools took part in Catholic religious education classes, 70% of all marriages were concluded according to Catholic rites and about 30% of the population regularly attended Sunday mass. See Garelli, Guizzardi, and Pace (eds.), *Un singolare pluralismo. Indagine sul pluralismo morale e religioso degli italiani*, 2003.

24 Davie, *Religion in Modern Europe: A Memory Mutates,* 2000.

25 See Garelli, *La Chiesa in Italia*, 2008; see also Sciolla, *La sfida dei valori. Rispetto delle regole e rispetto dei diritti in Italia*, 2004.

26 Ferrari, "Religious Education in a Globalized Europe," p. 119. The same remark can be extended to other situations: a number of non-Catholic communities has benefitted from the right to conclude a Catholic marriage with civil validity, to have the Catholic religion taught in State schools, to devolve a part of the State income tax to the Catholic Church, as these rights have been extended to them.

non-Catholic religions have to accept "the Catholic Church's role of gate-keeper" of the Italian identity: those groups that are not ready to accept this condition "are not recognized as part of the national heritage."[27] In other words, religious plurality can develop in Italy as long as it is confined within a cultural and ethical horizon defined by the Catholic tradition. When the 'civil' Catholic values are in conflict with the values of other religions – as it happened in the field of family law for example – tensions emerge and the Italian model shows its shortcomings.

Governing religious plurality through Catholic cultural and ethical tradition can provide a short-term solution. The public reaffirmation of the Catholic identity of Italy contributes towards reassuring its citizens and helps them to come to terms with changes that are of unusual speed and magnitude: it makes the whole process of integration more sustainable. But, in the long run, this project is not viable as religious plurality inevitably implies cultural and ethical plurality. It is understandable that Muslim immigrants in Italy are not yet in a position to affirm their cultural identity and concentrate their efforts on gaining full enjoyment of their religious rights. But sooner or later Italy will have a substantial number of socially well-integrated Muslim citizens and they will demand their say in defining the cultural profile of Italy, that is of their own country.

Two other profiles of the Italian experience deserve attention. First of all, Catholicism itself can undergo a transformation in the process of becoming Italy's civil religion. On the one hand this process links a universal religion (Catholicism) to a specific nation (Italy), by emphasizing the role of the Catholic Church as the custodian of the Italian memory and tradition; on the other hand the cultural and ethical dimension of Catholicism come into the forefront, while its religious meaning risks being left in the background. Second, the claim of Catholicism to be Italy's civil religion has an impact on the Church-State system, as it gives a new justification for the State's support of the Catholic Church. Until recently this support was defended through "democratic" arguments, based on the fact that the majority of Italian citizens were members of the Catholic Church. In the 'civil religion' perspective, the Catholic Church can claim public support because it constitutes a fundamental component of the Italian tradition. Its privileged position is disconnected from popular will: the number of the faithful could decrease but, once the Church has repositioned itself on the

27 Ibid.

terrain of the Italian cultural heritage, it is entitled to claim State support as the custodian of Italian identity. This would be a step backwards in the direction of the old-fashioned confessional models.

Bibliography

Administrative Court of Veneto, Decision no. 1110, 17 March 2005.

Ball, Terence, "Rousseau's Civil Religion Reconsidered," in idem, *Reappraising Political Theory: Revisionist Studies in the History of Political Thought*, Oxford: Clarendon Press, 1995, pp. 108-118.

Bauberot, Jean, *L'intégrisme républicain contre la laïcité,* Paris: Aube, 2006.

Bauberot, Jean, Roberto Blancarte, and Micheline Milot, "Déclaration sur la laïcité," (December 9, 2005), in *L'intégrisme républicain contre la laïcité*, ed. Jean Bauberot, Paris: Aube, 2006, pp. 247-265.

Beckford, James A., "'Laïcité', 'Dystopia', and the Reaction to New Religious Movements in France," in *Regulating Religion: Case Studies from Around the Globe*, ed. James T. Richardson, New York: Kluwer, 2004, pp. 27-40.

Bellah, Robert, "The Final Word: Can Christianity contribute to a global civil religion?," in *Christianity and Human Rights: An Introduction*, ed. John Witte Jr. and Frank. S. Alexander, Cambridge: Cambridge Univ. Press, 2010, pp. 351-366.

Bellah, Robert, *The Broken Covenant: American Civil Religion in Time of Trial*, New York: Seabury Press, 1975.

Bellah, Robert, "Civil Religion in America," *Daedalus: Journal of the American Academy of Arts and Sciences* 96, 1 (1967): 1-21.

Berger, Peter, Grace Davie, and Effie Fokas, *Religious America, Secular Europe? A Theme and Variations,* Farnham: Ashgate, 2008.

Blond, Phillip, and Adrian Pabst, "A new kind of "laïcité" to integrate Islam in the West," *Oasis*, 2008, at http://www.oasiscenter.eu/index.php?page=36&lang=en&table=contributi&directory=contributi&name=contributi_doc&news=429&group=contributi&subgroup=doc_2008.

Bowen, John R., *Why the French Don't Like Headscarves: Islam, the State, and Public Space,* Princeton: Princeton University Press, 2006.

Casanova, José, *Public Religions in the Modern World*, Chicago: University of Chicago Press, 1994.

Chélini Pont, Blandine, and Jeremy Gunn, *Dieu en France et aux Etats-Unis. Quand les mythes font la loi*, Paris: Berg, 2005.

Council of State, Decision no. 556, 13 February 2006.

Davie, Grace, "Is Europe an exceptional case?," in *State and Religion in Europe*, Istanbul: Center for Islamic Studies, 2006, pp. 23-33.

Davie, Grace, *Religion in Modern Europe: A Memory Mutates*, Oxford: Oxford University Press, 2000.

Dieni, Edoardo, Alessandro Ferrari, and Vinzenzo Pacillo (eds.), *Symbolon/Diabolon. Simboli, religioni, diritti nell'Europa multiculturale*, Bologna: Mulino, 2005.

Dieni, Edoardo, Alessandro Ferrari, and Vinzenzo Pacillo (eds.), *I simboli religiosi tra diritto e culture,* Milano: Giuffrè, 2006.

Duvert, Cyrille, "Anti-Cultism in the French Parliament: Desperate Last Stand or an Opportune Leap Forward? A Critical Analysis of the 12 June 2001 Act," in *Regulating Religion: Case Studies from Around the Globe*, ed. James T. Richardson, New York: Kluwer, 2004, pp. 41-53.

Ferrari, Alessandro, "Religious Education in a Globalized Europe," in, *Religion and Democracy in Contemporary Europe*, ed. Gabriel Motzkin and Yochi Fisher London: Alliance Publ. Trust, 2008, pp. 113-124.

Ferrari, Alessandro, and Sabrina Pastorelli (eds.), *The Burqa Affair Across Europe*, Farnham, Ashgate, 2013.

Ferrari, Silvio, "Le moschee in Italia tra ordine pubblico e libertà religiosa," in *Quattordicesimo rapporto sulle migrazioni 2008*, ed. Fondazione ISMU, Milano: Franco Angeli, 2009, pp. 219-236.

Fornerod, Anne, "The burqa affair in France," in *The Burqa Affair Across Europe*, ed. Alessandro Ferrari and Sabrina Pastorelli, Farnham, Ashgate, 2013, pp. 59-76.

Garelli, Franco, Gustavo Guizzardi, and Enzo Pace, (eds.), *Un singolare pluralismo. Indagine sul pluralismo morale e religioso degli italiani*, Bologna: il Mulino, 2003.

Garelli, Franco, *La Chiesa in Italia*, Bologna: Mulino, 2008.

Gau, Justin, Ruth Arlow, and Will Adam, "Trustees of the Roman Catholic Church v Ellis," *Ecclesiastical Law Journal* 10, 3 (2008): 262-275.

Kepel, Gilles, *La revanche de Dieu. Chrétiens, juifs et musulmans à la reconquête du monde,* Paris: Seuil, 1991.

Kuyk, Elza, Roger Jensen, David Lankshear, Elizabeth Löh Manna, and Peter Schreiner (eds.), *Religious Education in Europe,* Oslo: Iko-ICCS, 2007.

Panara, Carlo, "Back to the Basics of Fundamental Rights: An Appraisal of the Grand Chamber's Judgment in Lautsi in Light of the ECHR and Italian Constitutional Law," in *The Lautsi Papers: Multidisciplinary Reflections on Religious Symbols in the Public School Classroom*, ed. Jeroen Temperman, Leiden: Brill, 2012, pp. 301-325.

Sciolla, Loredana, *La sfida dei valori. Rispetto delle regole e rispetto dei diritti in Italia*, Bologna: Mulino, 2004.

Willaime, Jean-Paul, "Teaching Religious Issues in French Public Schools: From Abstentionist Laïcité to a Return of Religion to Public Education," in *Religion and Education in Europe: Developments, Contexts and Debates,* ed. Robert Jackson, Siebren Miedema, Wolfgang Weisse, Jean-Paull Willaime, Münster: Waxmann, 2007, pp. 87-102.

Temperman, Jeroen (ed.), *The Lautsi Papers: Multidisciplinary Reflections on Religious Symbols in the Public School Classroom*, Leiden: Brill, 2012.

Religion and the State: The 'Lautsi' Case of the European Court of Human Rights About Crucifixes in Italian Class Rooms

Andreas Follesdal

A. Introduction[1]

The relationship between political authorities and religious communities is complex and controversial. One area where the tensions are evident is in public education. A central task of public authorities is to ensure the education and socialisation of children to become well informed and responsible citizens with a sense of justice. The children must on the one hand appreciate the history and past culture of their society, and at the same time be prepared for their present and future multi-cultural society. Tensions between these objectives are visible when the state seeks to include or exclude contested religious symbols and teachings within the public educational system. The European Court of Human Rights (ECtHR, 'the Court') has been brought in to address and resolve some of these issues, insofar as they fall under relevant paragraphs of the European Convention for the Protection of Human Rights and Fundamental Freedoms (ECHR).

---

1 This article was written under the auspices of the European Research Council under the European Union's Seventh Framework Programme (FP7/2007-2013)/ERC Grant agreement no 269841 – "MultiRights: On the Legitimacy of the Multi-Level Human Rights Judiciary"; and partly supported by the Research Council of Norway through its Centres of Excellence Funding Scheme, project number 223274 – "www.PluriCourts.net: The Legitimacy of the International Judiciary". It was first presented November 24, 2013 at the German – Southeast Asian Center of Excellence for Public Policy and Good Governance (CPG) Conference on "Political and Religious Communities – Partners, Competitors, or Aliens," on the panel on "How Neutral is the State? – State Power and Religious Practice." It was then discussed at the programme on "Justice in Conflict" at the University of Tromsø. I am grateful to the organizers for these opportunities, and for very constructive suggestions by participants.

The ECtHR track record may seem inconsistent. It has restricted religious teaching in textbooks[2] allowed Turkey to prohibit students from wearing religious headscarves at university,[3] allowed Switzerland to prohibit primary school teachers from wearing headscarves,[4] and allows Italy to require crucifixes on school walls – after first denying Italy that authority.[5]

There are several ways to try to make some sense of this cluster of decisions. The explanation which will be addressed here is the ECtHR's practice to grant states a 'Margin of Appreciation' (MA). Other approaches merit mention, only to leave them aside here: One is to look closely at the various rights and vulnerabilities at stake: the rights of the school authorities vs those of parents, or the teacher's right to freedom of expression vs parents' rights, etc. Alternatively, one could elaborate on the distinctions and relations between the public sphere, universities and compulsory public schools. Yet another approach may be to explore the presumed different impacts of statements in schoolbooks intended to influence beliefs explicitly, versus 'passive' crucifixes on school room walls in societies where such symbols are not perceived as salient, versus teachers wearing head scarves in communities where this is experienced as unusual.[6]

The Court's practice of a 'Margin of Appreciation' occurs when the Court gives states some but not full discretion to decide whether they are in compliance with their treaty obligations. This typically concerns questions whether states are justified in violating some individuals' rights because the violations are 'proportionate' to acceptable social objectives – or other human rights.

Many may argue that international or regional courts and treaty bodies should be particularly hesitant in reviewing the legislation of well functioning democracies, out of respect for the citizens' autonomy.[7] Indeed, the rampant value pluralism and variations in natural and social conditions

---

2 See Folgero v. Norway, 2007.

3 See Leyla Sahin v. Turkey, 2004.

4 See Dahlab v. Switzerland, 2001.

5 See Lautsi v. Italy I, 2009, and Lautsi v Italy II, 2011.

6 I owe these points to Jan Harald Alnes, Annamari Vitikainen and Claudio Corradetti.

7 Note that criticism of the ECtHR that it interferes in 'political' issues is misplaced: the objective of the treaty and its court has clearly been to limit legislation and other state decisions that violate the Convention. Thus, the Italian government's argument in this regard concerning the Lautsi case seems mistaken when it held that "1. The

across states counsels a certain leeway concerning how states should best respect and promote various objectives – including human rights. Thus, one explanation of the pattern of decisions by the Court with regard to religion in the class room is that it has declined to overturn several of the national laws or regulations in the cases mentioned.

Critics often challenge the Court's application of a MA as being inconsistent.[8]

To explore these worries, this article seeks to bring a more precise MA doctrine to bear on the Lautsi case concerning crucifixes on school walls, to assess whether the ECtHR decision and doctrine withstands criticism that it is too vague, or that it is poorly applied in this particular case. The case is one where privacy and family life is at stake, thus an area where scholars claim that the Court usually applies a heightened standard of scrutiny.[9] Was this the case in the Lautsi case, and if not, what should the Court have done?

The focus of this article is not to deny that there are other criticisms of the first Lautsi decision – which required crucifixes to be taken down – and the second Lautsi decision which permits them. Such criticisms merit attention – some of which has been presented by others.[10]

Government did not contend that it was necessary, advisable or desirable to keep crucifixes in classrooms, but that the decision whether to keep them there was a political one and therefore one to be taken on the basis of what was expedient, rather than according to legal considerations." (Lautsi I [2009]) Thus Lautsi II (2011): 68. The Court takes the view that the decision whether or not to perpetuate a tradition falls in principle within the margin of appreciation of the respondent State. The Court must moreover take into account the fact that Europe is marked by a great diversity between the States of which it is composed, particularly in the sphere of cultural and historical development. It emphasises, however, that the reference to a tradition cannot relieve a Contracting State of its obligation to respect the rights and freedoms enshrined in the Convention and its Protocols."

8 See Benvenisti, "Margin of Appreciation, Consensus, and Universal Standards," 1999, pp. 843-844; Brauch, "The Margin of Appreciation and the Jurisprudence of the European Court of Human Rights: Threat to the Rule of Law," 2005; Del Moral 2006, "The Increasingly Marginal Appreciation of the Margin-of-Appreciation Doctrine," p. 621; Yourow, *The Margin of Appreciation Doctrine in the Dynamics of European Human Rrights Jurisprudence*, 1996.

9 See Arai-Takahashi, *The Margin of Appreciation Doctrine and the Principle of Proportionality in the Jurisprudence of the ECHR*, 2001.

10 See Zucca, "Lautsi: A Commentary on a Decision by the ECtHR Grand Chamber," 2013, doi:10.1093/icon/mos008; Smet, "Lautsi v. Italy: The Argument from

The first section presents the Lautsi case, the following sections attend to various elements of the MA doctrine of the court. We return at the end to consider whether critics of the MA doctrine are right.

B. Lautsi

The Lautsi case concerns complaints by a parent (Mrs Soile Lautsi) who challenged Italy's administrative law requiring display of the crucifix in every State school classroom. She held that this violated the right of parents to "to ensure [their children's education] in conformity with their own religious and philosophical convictions" (Article 2 of Protocol 1 to the ECHR). Mrs Lautsi pointed out that crucifixes in rooms used as polling stations for voting in political elections had already been found in violation of the principle of a secular state.[11]

Italy argued to the contrary that "the cross had become one of the secular values of the Italian Constitution and represented the values of civilian life". "The democratic values of today are rooted in [...] the Gospel message. The message of the cross would be a humanist message, which could be read independently of its religious dimension, consisting of a set of principles and values that form the basis of our democracies." Therefore, "the display of the cross does not undermine the secular state", and since "there is no European consensus on how in practice to interpret the concept of secularism [...] states should have a wider discretion in the matter."

C. The Margin of Appreciation

Skeptics object that the MA doctrine is too vague: it is hardly a "doctrine" in the sense of a principle or position that forms part of a legal system.[12]

Neutrality," 2011, at https://strasbourgobservers.com/2011/ 03/22/lautsi-v-italy-the-argument-from-neutrality/.

11 See Ronchi "Crucifixes, Margin of Appreciation and Consensus: the Grand Chamber ruling in Lautsi v Italy," 2011, at https://www.cambridge.org/ core/journals/ecclesiastical-law-journal/article/crucifixes-margin-of-appreciation-and-consensus-the-grand-chamber-ruling-in-lautsi-v-italy/0C8445F5BD6C88BA 4A4B6BC0EA9A9E42.

12 One reason that is put forward for an MA is the respect for democratically accountable decisions. However, we should note that this is not obvious in this case.

One concern is that the vague MA doctrine leaves too much discretion to the judges who may be tempted to treat states differently. In particular, the procedure to determine an "emerging common practice" – or "some abstract sense of common standards" is exceedingly opaque – sometimes also contested by the participating judges.[13]

A more precise MA doctrine could specify how to determine whether there is a 'common practice', in particular whether to only include legislation and stated policies, or also include practices of permitting a practice which is technically not legal, and a minimum threshold, for instance 60% of states, to maintain that there is a consensus. Still, such improvements do not avoid other objections: that such discretion entails a failure of the ECtHR to protect human rights in the short and long run. The Court thereby "side-step[s] its responsibility as the ultimate interpretative authority in the Convention system."[14] Indeed, "[t]he essence of the international control mechanism may evaporate if there is in fact no effective check upon national power."[15]

Of central concern here is that when the ECtHR discusses the MA, the general issue is whether there is 'proportionality' or 'fair balance' between the means a state chooses and the aim sought.[16] Discretion might be granted with regard to at least five different elements of the 'proportionality test' as developed in later cases and by various authors.[17] As part of this decision the Court assesses

1. The legitimacy of the social objective pursued.
2. How important the restricted/derogated right is, e.g., as a foundation of a democratic society.
3. How invasive the proposed interference will be.

Judge Malinverni, in a dissenting opinion to Lautsi II, noted that. "With regard to the regulations governing this question, I would point out in passing that the presence of crucifixes in Italian State schools has an extremely weak basis in law: a very old royal decree dating back to 1860, then a fascist circular of 1922, and then royal decrees of 1924 and 1928.

13 See Rasmussen v. Denmark 1984, para 40; X v. United Kingdom 1997, 13; cf. Brems, "The Margin of Appreciation Doctrine in the Case-law of the European Court of Human Rights," 1996, p. 248.

14 Yourow, *The Margin of Appreciation Doctrine in the Dynamics of European Human RightsJurisprudence* 1996, p. 181.

15 Yourow, *The Margin of Appreciation Doctrine*, p. 181; cf Z v. Finland 1998.

16 *James and others v. the United Kingdom* 1986, 50.

17 See Follesdal, "Appreciating the Margin of Appreciation," 2018, pp. 264-294.

4. Whether the restriction of the right is necessary.
5. Whether the reasons offered by the national authorities are relevant and sufficient.

For each of these, the Court may grant the state a narrow or broad MA. Note that some of these factors may well change over time in light of experiences about what rights are necessary for a 'democratic society'[18], or concerning realistic alternative policies. The following sections address each of these factors.

D. The Legitimacy of the Social Objective Pursued

The issue at stake is the interest of the state to pursue its educational objectives through the curriculum and teaching environment of the public schools.

Public education contributes in important ways to a sustainable and legitimate society: it surely prepares students to be full and equal citizens – but what is required, and what is permitted regarding the teaching of religions and values? Clearly, in order to navigate within several European societies, all citizens must know a bit about Christian culture as it has shaped institutions, discourse, and everyday phrases – 'to be a good Samaritan', 'to turn the other cheek'. But Christianity is also a set of religions, with beliefs about the supernatural and norms about human morality that are worthy of respect, but not shared by every reflective and honourable citizen.

Three important elements are worth noting:

1. Issue: Not 'Public Sphere' but Public Schools

The social interest at stake in the Lautsi case – and the policy that is challenged – is not the presentation of religious symbols in the 'public square' or in the 'public sphere' or in 'public life' more generally. Rather, the concern is about crucifixes in public schools, attendance to which is obliga-

18 Arts. 8-19; Moral, "The Increasingly Marginal Appreciation of the Margin-of-Appreciation Doctrine," 2006, p. 613.

tory, and whose role is to educate citizens. This distinction has been overlooked in some of the discussions.[19]

2. Public education about religion is not prohibited, but should be objective, critical, and pluralistic.

The Court allows religious teaching in schools, but insists that it must be objective and pluralistic.[20]

The Government[21] seems to justify the obligation to display the crucifix by referring to the positive moral message of Christian faith. This message is said to transcend secular constitutional values, concerning the role of religion in Italian history and to the deep roots of religion in the country's tradition.

The Court did not accept this argument as sufficient grounds to grant the Italian state a Margin of Appreciation on this issue, and thus apparently did not accept that the crucifix is part of an objective, critical and pluralistic religios education. In particular, the Court disputed the government's claims about the 'secular' symbolism of the crucifix:

The Government[22] justified the obligation to display (or the fact of displaying) the crucifix by referring to the positive moral message of Christian faith, which transcended secular constitutional values, to the role of religion in Italian history and to the deep roots of religion in the country's tradition. They attributed to the crucifix a neutral and secular meaning with reference to Italian history and tradition, which were closely bound up with Christianity. They submitted that the crucifix was a religious symbol but one which could equally represent other values.[23]

In the Court's opinion, the symbol of the crucifix has a number of meanings among which the religious meaning is predominant.[24]

The Grand Chamber joined other parties in dismissing claims by the government that the crucifix in this setting should not be regarded as a re-

19 See Weiler, "Lautsi: Crucifix in the Classroom Redux," 2010.
20 See e.g. Folgero v. Norway, 2008.
21 See Lautsi I, paras. 34-44.
22 See ibid.
23 See citing "The Veneto Regional Administrative Court's judgment," 2005, § 16 and § 13.
24 See Lautsi II, p. 51.

ligious symbol: "The Court further considers that the crucifix is above all a religious symbol."[25]

3. What are State's objectives when requiring crucifixes on the school walls?

It remains very difficult to understand the state's objectives in requiring crucifixes as not including a concern to favour the Catholic religion. A variety of appropriate objectives concerning the dissemination of national culture and history can be secured by several other means. Note that this point is also granted by some who have criticized the Lautsi I judgment: Weiler remarks that:

> By this reasoning, Ms. Lautsi is perhaps entitled to her damages because the Italian government failed to demonstrate that the use of religious symbology in its classroom was part of a credible programme of education for tolerance and mutual respect. It is that which should be the guideline and constitutional imperative of contemporary Europe.[26]

E. How Important is the Restricted/Derogated Right

The right to education is protected by Article 2 of Protocol 1:

> No person shall be denied the right to education. In the exercise of any functions which it assumes in relation to education and to teaching, the State shall respect the right of the parents to ensure such education and teaching in conformity with their own religious and philosophical convictions.

It is difficult to determine how important this right is, but both this and the right to family life appear to be threatened or violated in the Lautsi case. What is at stake is precisely thatthe state's education efforts are at odds with the parents' religious and philosophical convictions concerning how the school dispalys the crucifix. Several authors note that the ECtHR should not grant a broad MA of appreciation to rights of minorities that are at risk by majoritarian decision-making.[27] The *latter* does seem to be at stake here.

---

25 Lautsi II, p. 66.

26 Weiler, "Lautsi: Crucifix in the Classroom Redux."

27 E.g., Benvenisti, "Margin of Appreciation, Consensus, and Universal Standards," 1999, p. 853.

Note that the right to education does not prohibit all teaching of religion, but that this education must be 'objective.'

F. How InvasiveWill the Proposed Interference be

This particular issue is controversial. The Italian government appears to have held that the Crucifix was not primarily a religious symbol at all, so did not raise an issue. The Grand Chamber rejected this argument, – as did various Catholic and Christian organizations.[28]

The Court held that the display was religious in nature, yet rejected unsubstantiated claims by Mrs Lautsi that it had a noticable impact on children:

There is no evidence before the Court that the display of a religious symbol on classroom walls may have an influence on pupils and so it cannot reasonably be asserted that it does or does not have an effect on young persons whose convictions are still in the process of being formed. However, it is understandable that the first applicant might see in the display of crucifixes in the classrooms of the State school formerly attended by her children a lack of respect on the State's part for her right to ensure their education and teaching in conformity with her own philosophical convictions. Be that as it may, the applicant's subjective perception is not in itself sufficient to establish a breach of Article 2 of Protocol No. 1.

The Court here seems on the verge of an inconsistency with its rejection of the Dahlab case. The Swiss ban on Muslim teachers wearing headscarves while teaching was justified in order to 'protect the religious beliefs of the pupils and their parents and to apply the principle of denominational neutrality in schools enshrined in domestic law'.[29] In this case the Court regarded headscarves as 'a sign that is immediately visible to others and provides a clear indication that the person concerned belongs to a particular religion'.[30] It went on to claim that

> [t]he Court accepts that it is very difficult to assess the impact that a powerful external symbol such as the wearing of a headscarf may have on the freedom of conscience and religion of very young children. The applicant's pupils were aged between four and eight, an age at which children wonder about

28 See Lautsi II, p. 9.
29 See Lautsi II, para 73.
30 Dahlab v. Switzerland, 2-3.

> many things and are also more easily influenced than older pupils. In those circumstances, it cannot be denied outright that the wearing of a headscarf might have some kind of proselytising effect.[31]

It is not easy to understand how a headscarf can be a more powerful symbol, nor why the burden of proof shifts according to the government's preferred position between Dahlab and Lautsi. One possible – but problematic – explanation may be that in the former case the religion of concern was one of a minority, while in the latter case it was one of the majority. Another possibility is that under such circumstances of uncertainty the Court grants the state a broader MA – though the right at stake concerns minorities.

G. Whether the Restriction of the Right is Necessary

A central issue here concerns what alternative policies are available to the state that might avoid all rights violations of a similar weight. There are at least three central issues worth considering related to the Lautsi case.

I. Are Crucifixes Necessary?

Firstly, it is not clear from the state's arguments that crucifixes on the school room walls are at all necessary to achieve the legitimate objectives of public education. To the contrary, according to the Court:

> The Government did not contend that it was necessary, advisable or desirable to keep crucifixes in classrooms, but that the decision whether to keep them there was a political one and therefore one to be taken on the basis of what was expedient, rather than according to legal considerations.[32]

It would be a mistake to assume that the fact that the decision was a political one does not reduce the conflict between the ECHR rights and the particular policy. Other symbols of 'secularism' would seem less objectionable; as might other symbols of the historical impact of the Catholic Church on Italian life.

---

31 Ibid.
32 See Lautsi II, p. 42.

II. Did the State Consider Less Rights-Infringing Alternatives?

Secondly, even if crucifixes were regarded as a required component of public education, there is little evidence that the state considered other less burdensome alternatives. For instance, it appears that Bavaria maintains similar practices but allows parents to challenge the practice in particular school rooms – this opportunity for parents was introduced after the Federal Constitutional Court struck down a previous Bavarian school law.[33]

III. Will all Alternatives Violate Some Citizens' Human Rights?

Thirdly, a more complex issue, is whether all alternatives will violate other citizens' similar rights with regard to their world view.

Will any Crucifix policy violate objectivity? The state – and Joseph Weiler, and at least some of the judges of the ECtHR[34] – seems to assume that 'secularism' is on a par with Christianity. The Lautsi I Court held that: The State's duty of neutrality and impartiality is incompatible with any kind of power on its part to assess the legitimacy of religious convictions or the ways of expressing those convictions.[35]

Weiler claimed that: The position adopted by the Chamber is not an expression of the pluralism manifest by the Convention system, but an expression of the values of the laique State. To extend it to the entire Convention system would represent, with great respect, the Americanization of Europe. Americanization in two respects: First a single and unique rule for everyone, and second, a rigid, American style, separation of Church and State, as if the people of those Members whose State identity is not laique, cannot be trusted to live by the principles of tolerance and pluralism. That again, is not Europe.[36]

---

33 See Zucca, "Lautsi: A Commentary on a Decision by the ECtHR Grand Chamber." I am grateful to an anonymous referee for the information about why the Bavarian legislation was changed.

34 See Bonello, 2.10, and Power, pp. 44-45.

35 See Lautsi I, p. 47.

36 See Weiler, "Oral Intervention by Professor Weiler on Behalf of Armenia, Bulgaria, Cyprus, Greece, Lithuania, Malta, Russia, and San Marino – States Who Intervene as Third Parties in the Lautsi Case Before the Grand Chamber of the European Court of Human Rights," 2010, p.17.

The Grand Chamber noted that: In the Government's view, neutrality meant that States should refrain from promoting not only a particular religion but also atheism, "secularism" on the State's part being no less problematic than proselytising by the State. The Chamber's judgment was thus based on a misunderstanding and amounted to favouring an irreligious or antireligious approach of which the applicant, as a member of the Union of atheists and rationalist agnostics, was asserted to be a militant supporter.[37]

Some hold that "secularism (which was the applicant's preferred belief or world view) was, in itself, one ideology among others."[38] On this view, to require the removal of crucifixes amounts to the same sort of endorsement of a particular conception of the good life, a competitor to religious world views.

I submit that this is a mistake.[39] There are certainly secular comprehensive conceptions of the good life that deny the existence of transcendent beings, just as there are comprehensive liberal views that cherish individual autonomy.[40]

But there are political theories that seek to elaborate standards for justifiabe policies precisely where citizens have different such comprehensive views. Some such contributions are known as 'political liberalism',[41] others use the term 'constitutional secularism'[42] about standards appropriate for the constitutional essentials' of a state committed to treat all on a footing of equality, respecting all citizens' status as free and equally participant in a society regarded as a fair scheme of social cooperation. That perspective on the constitution and the central institutions of a state may be better characterized as agnostic than atheistic:

There is, or need be, no war between religion and democracy. In this respect political liberalism is sharply different from and rejects Enlightenment Liberalism, which historically attacked orthodox Christianity.[43]

---

37 See Lautsi II, p. 35.

38 Judges Bonello 2.10, Power 44-45.

39 See Kyritsis and Tsakyrakis, "Neutrality in the classrom," 2013.

40 See Mill, *On Liberty*, 1978, and Kant, *Grounding for the Metaphysics of Morals* 1980.

41 Rawls, *Political Liberalism,* 1993.

42 Zucca, "Lautsi: A Commentary on a Decision by the ECtHR Grand Chamber."

43 See Rawls, *Political Liberalism*, p. 176.

Note that this 'constitutional neutrality' – at least the version argued by Rawls – is limited in scope – and hence is not a full 'alternative' to a world view. It only concerns the basic structure of society – its constitution and central institutions – such as schools. The institutions of the basic structure must be "framed to leave individuals and associations free to act effectively in pursuit of their ends and without excessive constraints."[44] This account will entail that it is impermissible to display crucifixes in courtrooms, polling stations – and presumably public primary schools.[45] Other aspects – such as symbols of national identity – flags etc – or other appearances of religion in the public sphere would not obviously be part of this, so Weiler's objection would not hold against this account:

In the cultural, social and political circumstance of Europe today one does not want to win on such ground – because it implies that if a symbol still maintains its religious significance, it has no place in the public square. That cannot be a correct reflection of the European constitutional sensibility.[46]

A second point is that the required 'neutrality' does not need be one of *effects*, but of *aims*. Neutrality of aim rules out legislation that is "intended to favor any particular comprehensive view"[47] – and instead insists that such rules must be justified based on premises that are acceptable to all, regardless of their reasonable comprehensive conception of the good.

I submit that this version of neutrality may be a suitable reinterpretation of the ECtHR's claim in Lautsi I, that: The State's duty of neutrality and impartiality is incompatible with any kind of power on its part to assess the legitimacy of religious convictions or the ways of expressing those convictions.[48]

So the government's interpretation is mistaken and unfortunate, and the Court's ruling is unfortunate.

---

44 Rawls, *Political Liberalism*, p. 55.

45 See Kyritsis and Tsakyrakis, "Neutrality in the classrom," p. 210.

46 See Weiler, "Lautsi: A reply (to Kyritsis and Tsakyrakis)," 2013.

47 Rawls, *Political Liberalism*, p. 197.

48 See Lautsi I, p. 47.

H. Whether the Reasons Offered by the National Authorities are Relevant and Sufficient

The possibility of 'constitutional neutrality' suggests that the Italian government did not consider plausible alternatives. Furthermore, I submit that the state did not offer convincing arguments why hanging crucifixes was necessary for disseminating Italy's history and values. It did not discuss any alternatives as required by the proportionality test. Moreover, the government's claim that crucifixes are a non-religious symbol of the secular state seems implausible. Of course, if the crucifix did not convey uniquely Catholic values, there would be no problem. This argument appears specious, and was not accepted by the Grand Chamber.

The Administrative Court held that inter alia. Moreover, with the benefit of hindsight, it is easy to identify in the constant central core of Christian faith, despite the inquisition, despite anti-Semitism and despite the crusades, the principles of human dignity, tolerance and freedom, including religious freedom, and therefore, in the last analysis, the foundations of the secular State.[49]

In Lautsi II, Catholic groups conceded this point: The non-governmental organisations Zentralkomitee der deutschen Katholiken, Semaines sociales de France, and Associazioni cristiane lavoratori italiani stated that they agreed with the Chamber that, whilst the crucifix had a plural meaning, it was primarily the central symbol of Christianity. They added, however, that they disagreed with its conclusion, and found it difficult to understand how the presence of crucifixes in classrooms could be "emotionally disturbing" for some pupils or hinder the development of their critical thinking. In their submission, that presence alone could not be equated with a religious or philosophical message; it should rather be interpreted as a passive way of conveying basic moral values.[50]

I. Concluding Assessment

Leaving aside the substantive issue – whether crucifixes on public school walls aviolate the ECHR – let us briefly return to consider whether this decision should be taken by ECtHR or by the Italian authorities. On the basis

49 See Lautsi II, 11.6.
50 See ibid., p. 9.

of the discussion above, I conclude that the ECtHR should not have granted Italy a margin of appreciation in this case, on the basis of the policy the Court itself has laid out. Italy's arguments fail on several points of the proportionality test. This case seems to confirm the criticism that the Court's granting of a MA is inconsistent.[51] Some might argue that this supports a general conclusion that the MA practice should be abolished. I submit that we should instead use this and other cases to explore how the practice may be developed even further, to ensure that the Court contributes to strengthen domestic protections of human rights in Europe.

Bibliography

Arai-Takahashi, Yutaka, *The Margin of Appreciation Doctrine and the Principle of Proportionality in the Jurisprudence of the ECHR*, Antwerpen: Intersentia, 2001.

Benvenisti, Eyal, "Margin of Appreciation, Consensus, and Universal Standards," *International Law and Politics* 3 (1999): 843-854.

Brauch, Jeffrey A., "The Margin of Appreciation and the Jurisprudence of the European Court of Human Rights: Threat to the Rule of Law," *Columbia Journal of European Law* 11 (2005): 113-150.

Brems, Eva. "The Margin of Appreciation Doctrine in the Case-law of the European Court of Human Rights," *Heidelberg Journal of International Law* 56 (1996): 240-314.

European Court of Human Rights, 1984, Rasmussen v Denmark, 7 EHRR 371 Application no 8777/79 (ECtHR) European Court of Human Rights, 1986, James and others v. the United Kingdom, 8 EHRR 123, Application no 8793/79.

European Court of Human Rights, 1997, X v United Kingdom, IHRL 32 Application no 7215/75.

European Court of Human Rights, 1998, Z v. Finland. 25 EHRR at 371, Application no 22009/93.

European Court of Human Rights, 2001, Dahlab v Switzerland, Application no 42393/98

European Court of Human Rights, 2004, Leyla Sahin v. Turkey. Application no 44774/98.

European Court of Human Rights, 2007, Folgero and others v. Norway, Application no 15472/02.

---

51 See Benvenisti, "Margin of Appreciation, Consensus, and Universal Standards," pp. 843-844; Brauch, "The Margin of Appreciation and the Jurisprudence of the European Court of Human Rights,"; Moral, "The Increasingly Marginal Appreciation," 2006, p. 621; Yourow, *The Margin of Appreciation Doctrine*.

European Court of Human Rights, 2009, Lautsi v Italy I, Application no 30814/06.

European Court of Human Rights, Grand Chamber, 2011, Lautsi v. Italy II. Application no 30814/06.

Follesdal, Andreas, "Appreciating the Margin of Appreciation," in *Human Rights: Moral or Political?*, ed. Adam Etinson, Oxford: Oxford University Press, 2018, pp. 269-294.

Kant, Immanuel, *Grounding for the Metaphysics of Morals*, Indianapolis: Hackett Publishing Company, 1980.

Kyritsis, Dimitrios, and Stavros Tsakyrakis, "Neutrality in the classrom," *International Journal of Constitutional Law* 11, 1 (2013): 200-217, at https://academic.oup.com/ i con/article/11/1/200/776146.

Mill, John Stuart, *On Liberty*, Indianapolis: Hackett, 1978.

Moral, Ignacio de la Rasilla del, "The Increasingly Marginal Appreciation of the Margin-of-Appreciation Doctrine," *German Law Journal* 7, 6 (2006): 611-624.

Rawls, John, *Political Liberalism*, New York: Columbia University Press, 1993.

Ronchi, Paolo, "Crucifixes, Margin of Appreciation and Consensus: the Grand Chamber ruling in Lautsi v Italy," 2011, at https://www.cambridge.org/core/journals/eccle siastical-law-journal/article/crucifixes-margin-of-appreciation-and-consensus-the-gr and-chamber-ruling-in-lautsi-v-italy/0C8445F5BD6C88BA 4A4B6BC0EA9A9E4 2.

Smet, Stijl, "Lautsi v. Italy: The Argument from Neutrality," Strasbourg Observers, 2011, at https://strasbourgobservers.com/2011/03/22/lautsi-v-italy-the-argument-fro m-neutrality/.

Weiler, Joseph, "Lautsi: Crucifix in the Classroom Redux," *European Journal of International Law* 21, 1 (2010): 1-6.

Weiler, Joseph, "Oral Intervention by Professor Weiler on Behalf of Armenia, Bulgaria, Cyprus, Greece, Lithuania, Malta, Russia, and San Marino – States Who Intervene as Third Parties in the Lautsi Case Before the Grand Chamber of the European Court of Human Rights," Ilsussidiario.net, 2010.

Weiler, Joseph, "Lautsi: A reply (to Kyritsis and Tsakyrakis)," *International Journal of Constitutional Law* 11, 1 (2013): 230-233.

Yourow, Howard Charles, *The Margin of Appreciation Doctrine in the Dynamics of European Human Rights Jurisprudence*, Leiden: Brill, 1996.

Zucca, Lorenzo, "Lautsi: A Commentary on a Decision by the ECtHR Grand Chamber," *International Journal of Constitutional Law* 11, 1 (2013): 218-229, at https://a cademic.oup.com/icon/article/11/1/218/776139.

Political Community and Religion in Croatia: Thorny Path Towards Partnership

Slavica Banić

A. Justice of the Constitutional Court of the Republic of Croatia

I. Historical Overview from the 19th Century to 1945

Croatia has traditionally been a country with a major population being Catholic. Throughout the history it has been accepted how Catholicism in Croatia shaped the value set of the Croatian people. In that regard the privileged position of the Catholic Church in Croatia during the history was never brought in question. The Kingdom of Croatia, Slavonia and Dalmatia which existed within the Austro-Hungarian Monarchy accepted the Concordat between the Monarchy and the Holy See from 1855 and did not refrain to show its loyalty to the Church. The Catholic Church was considered as the "state" religious community.[1] However, the reforms that were undertaken within the Monarchy by time extended to Croatia as well. Already in 1873 the Croatian Parliament enacted a law which equalized Jews with other legally recognized religious communities.[2] This law was the basis for the subsequent legal recognition of the Orthodox Church, the Greek Catholic Church, the Evangelical Church etc. In the following year, in 1874, reform was carried out in the school system by which the Catholic Church lost its leadership in education and was obliged to fulfil the legal preconditions in the case of the establishment of public confessional schools.

The position of religious communities during the time of the Kingdom of Serbs, Croats and Slovenians, later on known as Kingdom of Yugoslavia, to which Croatia belonged from 1918 to 1941 was variable. In general, it was conditioned by their legal recognition. This implied a sig-

1 Frane Staničić, for the purposes of the paper taken from "The Legal Status of the Religious Communities in Croatian Law," 2014, pp. 225-254.

2 Law from 1873, Art. 61 which establishes the equality of Isrealis with followers of the rest in the Kingdom of Croatia and Slavonia by the Law of recognized religions.

nificant influence of the state in their matters and in no way meant the separation of the state and Church. There were also strong tendencies of favouring the Serbian Orthodox Church[3] and undermining at the same time the Catholic Church whose legal position remained ambiguous during the whole period of its existence.[4] Although the Kingdom of Yugoslavia signed the Concordat with the Holy See in 1935, the ratification procedure which started in 1937 was never finished due to, among other reasons, resistance and disagreement of the Serbian Orthodox Church. Still, the Catholic Church enjoyed trust and recognition within the Croatian society and its role remained stable.

World War Two and the following world events were the turning point in the change of the position of religion, religious communities and accordingly of the exercise of the freedom of religion in Croatia. The Croatian history during the Second World War marks the existence of the Independent State of Croatia which supported fascism. The religious communities accordingly shared the destiny of the fascistic policy of the "proper" and "improper".[5] The Catholic Church was, however, misused for the political purposes of the fascists in spite of the clear rejection of the Croatian Archbishop to be a part of such policy. Additionally, some clerics supported fascism against the Church's will. This image of the Church during the War caused an open contempt of the Communist Party which conducted the partisan movement during the war and led it subsequently to clash with the Church after the war.

II. Position of the Religious Communities in the Socialist Time (1945-1990)

The communists who carried out the victory over fascism on the territory of the former Yugoslavia embraced the socialist political order proclaim-

---

3 For example, the Day of Saint Sava, the saint of the Orthodox Church and the protector of Serbia was a national holiday in the the whole territory of the Kingdom of Yugoslavia.

4 See Staničić, "The Legal Status of the Religious Communities in Croatian Law."

5 The regime recognized catholicism, protenstantism and islam. The Serbian Orthodox Church was considered as dangerous enemy. Already in 1941 it did not function since more than half of the orthodox priesthood was deported or killed.

ing communism as the highest expression of equality among the people. Croatia became one of the republics within the federal state of Yugoslavia.

The socialist regime that lasted from 1945 up to 1991 was marked by the gradual, but steady secularization of the Croatian society. Communists followed the Marx's statement that "religion is the opium for the people" and deemed that "the religious communities may not interfere in the political life of believers."[6]

The earliest socialist Yugoslav Constitution from 1946 guaranteed the freedom of religion and conscience but at the same time it clearly separated the Church from the state. The religious communities were free in the exercise of their religious activities and the state could financially support the religious communities. The early years of the new state were especially marked by the open oppression of the Catholic Church. The reasons were twofold. One of them lies in the fact that the Catholic Church openly deemed communism as a world danger and something that was against Christianity. Another one lies in the communists' conviction that the Catholic Church was an ally of the fascists.[7] The president of post-war Yugoslavia, Josip Broz Tito, openly advocated the separation of the "domestic" Catholic Church from the Holy See.[8] Legal measures against the religious communities were aimed at depriving them of property, denying their clerics different rights, abolishing the social involvement and excluding them from the public life at all. These measures especially hit the Catholic Church and the Serbian Orthodox Church in Croatia, which was the second largest religious community. The Serbian Orthodox Church though was partly saved from the communist oppression because it was deemed as patriotic during the Second World War and therefore considered as less dangerous than the Catholic Church. The Act on Agrarian Reform and Colonization was the first in the line of later legislation which deprived religious communities of the property. Under the moto "the land to peasants" it prescribed deprivation of the land that exceeded the provided legal limits. This Act reasonably affected the material position of the

6 Jandrić, "Položaj Katoličke crkve u Hrvatskoj u poslijeratnim godinama (1945-1953)," p. 49, at http://hrcak.srce.hr/file/161026.

7 See Matijević, "Religious communities in Croatia from 1945 to 1991: Social causality of the dissent between Communist Authorities and Religous Communities Leadership," p. 1, at http://hrcak.srce.hr/15850.

8 See Jandrić, "Položaj Katoličke crkve u Hrvatskoj u poslijeratnim godinama (1945-1953)," p. 50.

Catholic Church which was considered as one of the largest land owners in Croatia. The land which, in turn, remained in the ownership was subsequently severely taxed forcing thus the Church to give away from it often. The imposition of the obligatory primary schools as the precondition for further priesthood education was aimed at diminishing the religious education and abolishment of the religious schools. The parents whose children went to religious schools and did not attend the state primary schools were punished. A large number of the priests and monks was arrested, accused and killed for the national betrayals or cooperation with fascists.

In spite of the harsh relation of communists toward the religious communities, mainly toward the Catholic Church, the position of Croatian Catholic clerics stayed firm while the orthodox priesthood reduced reasonably. The clash between the Church and communists came to its peak with the arrest of the Croatian Archbishop Alojzije Stepinac and trial against him. This led to a breakup of the diplomatic relationships between Yugoslavia and the Vatican in the beginning of the 1950s. Tensions decreased during the 1960s by their reestablishment. The constitutional provision from 1963 which recognized a right to religious communities to own real estate within the limits provided by the federal law in a way opened the door to loosening the rigid approach toward the religious communities in socialism.

Generally said, the socialist political order advocated atheism and over time, by the coordinated legal and quite often illegal actions, pushed the exercise of the freedom of religion completely to the private domain of life. Religious communities in general were excluded from any participation in the social development and, in the socio-political context of that time, were considered as potential danger for the socialist political order. The religious affiliation or any kind of religious behaviour was an obstacle for the public functions the consequence of which was the exclusion from the active involvement in political life.

III. Revitalization of Religion after 1990

After the fall of communism, the newly established political order maintained the general principle of the secular state. The Croatian Constitution of 1990 provided that all religious communities shall be equal before the law and separate from the state. Yet, the practical denial of the freedom of religion in the past 45 years due to the institutionalized contempt for religion and all religious people was suddenly converted to its national "embrace". Being unreligious was related to communism while religiousness was related to capitalism and Croatianhood. The process of religious revitalization was largely supported by politics. The politics unilaterally did not hesitate to develop a relationship which would procure support of religious communities in maintaining the political power. Religion became a powerful political force in the way that the leading party of that time was performing its religiousness in order to obtain a larger degree of legitimacy.[9] The distinguished Croatian scholar in this field, Vrcan, claimed that the 1990s were the witness of the political mobilization of a significant part of present religious traditions as well as the witness of the political mobilization of religious symbolism of all three religions which were present in the former Yugoslavia.[10]

In the case of Croatia, its relation toward religion started with the political mobilization of Catholicism aimed at redefining the Croatian national identity. The Croatian national identity was built up on the politicization of the cultural differences[11] among which the most recognizable was exactly the affiliation to the Catholic Church. The process of mutual affirmation was happening on the Croatian scene: the Catholic Church became an important resource for politics, but at the same time politics became an important factor for the affirmation of the Catholic Church.

How the things went on could be best illustrated by an event which happened in 1992 by the first Croatian president's oath. By the oath before the Constitutional Court on the loyalty to the Constitution, the elected president of the Republic arbitrarily changed the text of the oath and added the words "*So help me God*" although those words were not part of

---

9 The leading party of that time was the Croatian Democratic Union (CDU) (Hrvatska demokratska zajednica (HDZ)) which was firstly considered as national-democratic movement and which actively worked on the establishment of Croatia as independent state and its secession from Socialist Federative Republic of Yugoslavia. After 1992, it was formed as political demochristian party. CDU was the prevailing political power in Croatia until 2000 when a coalition led by the Social Democratic Party (SDP) (Socijaldemokratska partija (SDP)) won the elections.

10 See Vrcan, "Religija i politika – simptomatičan primjer bivše Jugoslavije devedesetih godina dvadesetog stoljeća," 2003, at http://postjugo.filg.uj.edu.pl/baza/files/373/Religija%20i%20politika20Simptomati%C4%8Dni%20primjer%20biv%C5%A1e%20Jugoslavije%20devedesetih%20godina%2020.%20stolje%C4%87a.pdf.

11 See ibid.

the legal text of the oath. The President's discretionary change of the oath text was legalized by the respective law in 1997 and ever since is a part of the presidential oath regardless of the constitutional principle of the secular state.

IV. The Croatian Constitutional Framework Regarding Religion

The starting point of the constitutional framework regarding religion is the constitutional principle in Article 14 which prohibits any kind of discrimination including the discrimination on the basis of religion.[12] Article 17 further on, provides that even in the cases of clear and present danger to the existence of the state, no restrictions may be imposed upon the provisions of the Constitution stipulating, inter alia, the freedom of thought, conscience and religion. However, regarding freedom of religion under the Constitution of 1990 (hereinafter: the Constitution), the Articles 40 and 41 are of particular importance.[13] Article 40 guarantees the freedom of conscience and religion and the freedom to demonstrate religious or other convictions, while Article 41 guarantees that all religious communities are equal before the law and separate from the state. The Constitution manifested the awareness of the importance of the freedom of religion. Therefore, the same article states that religious communities shall be free, in compliance with law, to publicly conduct religious services, open schools, academies or other institutions, as well as welfare and charitable organizations and to manage them. They shall enjoy the protection and assistance of the state in their activities.

---

12 Article 14 of the Constitution: "All persons in the Republic of Croatia shall enjoy rights and freedoms, regardless of race, colour, gender, language, religion, political or other conviction, national or social origin, property, birth, education, social status or other characteristics."

13 Article 40 of the Constitution: "Freedom of conscience and religion and the freedom to demonstrate religious or other convictions shall be guaranteed." and Article 41 of the Constitution: "All religious communities shall be equal before the law and clearly separate from the state. Religious communities shall be free, in compliance with law, to publicly conduct religious services, open schools, academies or other institutions, and welfare and charitable organizations and to manage them, and they shall enjoy the protection and assistance of the state in their activities."

The latter provision gave a slight guess that the Croatian state will exercise the so-called cooperative model of separation of the religious communities from the state.

V. The Legal Framework for the Religious Communities from 1990 to 2002

The blossom of religion in practice and the constitutional determination on the free exercise of the freedom of religion did not mean, at the same time, its institutionalization. For a long time, the state did not provide the proper legal frame on the status of the religious communities which would be the realization of the previously mentioned constitutional principle. The socialist Act on the Legal Status of the Religious Communities from 1978 (hereinafter: ALSRC 1978)[14] continued its legal life within the new political order until 2002 when Croatia enacted the new Act on the Legal Status of the Religious Communities (hereinafter: ALSRC 2002).[15]

The ALSRC 1978 completely reflected the socialist approach towards religion. As such, it was inappropriate for the new political order and the established constitutional framework. According to it, religious communities had the status of civil legal entities without providing any criteria for their foundation; there were no provisions on registration or evidence on them; the functioning of the religious communities was completely in the private sphere; there were restrictions on organizing or conducting of any kind of social activity which would fall out of the religious domain, and material help was just a legal possibility which could have been conditioned by the prescribed purpose.

The whole Act was, actually, "overwhelmed" by the interdictions for religious communities' possible public engagement. Such determination directly contravened the new constitutional guarantee of free foundation of schools, social and charity institutions or public conduct of religious services. In such circumstances, this Act was actually a dead letter except in the aspect of the legal status of the religious communities as civil legal entities. It was the only link of the law with the real life, and not because it

14 The Act on the Legal Status of the Religious Communities (The Official Gazette no. 14/78, 52/88).

15 The Act on the Legal Status of the Religious Communities (The Official Gazette, no. 83/02).

was a suitable solution for the new political order, but because it was necessary for their normal legal functioning. Yet, the only way to confirm the status of religious community was the evidence by the State Bureau of Statistics which was the only valid proof of their existence as legal entities.

The neglect of the newly established state to install the legal framework according to the Constitution had far-reaching consequences on the development of the religious communities and multicultural society in Croatia. Although there were laws that partly overcame this situation by regulations which reaffirmed the freedom of religion and free conduct and foundation of religious schools or institutions, they could not substitute all issues related to the religious communities. In some aspects, it could be said that this factual situation later contributed to the uncertain legal status of some religious communities under the ALSRC 2002. The reasons for such a long non-regulation of this field are not well-known. In general, it was thought that the constitutional framework was quite enough for the time being as it secured the freedom of religion without any major obstacles for its exercise.

VI. The Legal Status of the Catholic Church in Croatia – the Concordats between the Holy See and Croatia and Their Impact on the Croatian Legal Order

The Catholic Church, as the dominant religious community in Croatia[16], in the first decade of independence did not share the same destiny with other religious communities. The perennial recognition of the special position of the Catholic Church in Croatia and its political ascent resulted in the establishment of a special relationship between Croatia and the Holy See. From 1996 to 1998, Croatia signed and subsequently ratified four International Treaties, i.e. Concordats, with the Holy See: on legal issues, on

16 See Padjen, "Vjera u narod bez vlasti i vlasništva: Crkvena šutnja 1961-1971. i glasnost 1990-," 2012, pp. 175-211, at http://hrcak.srce.hr/index.php?show= clanak&id_clanak_jezik=144139. The statistic on the population of the Republic of Croatia from 1991, between the period of the first multiparty elections and independence of the state according to the international law show that Croatia had 4,784,265 inhabitants from which 3,678,787, i.e. 76,6% are Catholics (12.003 of Greek-Catholics), see ibid., p 192.

chaplaincy of the Catholic believers, soldiers and police officers of the Republic Croatia, on cooperation in the field of education and culture, as well as on economic issues.[17] According to Article 141 of the Constitution,[18] these Concordats have become part of the internal legal order and by their legal force are above the law. It means that the legal position of the Catholic Church established by the Concordats may not be altered by the law.

Generally speaking, the pillar of all four Concordats is the one on legal issues. Its Preamble, inter alia, emphasizes the irreplaceable role of the Catholic Church in the education of the Croatian people, its historical and present role in the social, cultural and educational field as well as the appreciation that majority of Croatian citizens affiliate to the Catholic Church.

Croatia granted the Catholic Church the status of a public legal entity. Moreover, all Church institutions which have legal entity status according to the canon law were recognized as such in Croatia. Further on, the Concordat on legal issues provided freedom of Catholic Church to establish its church organization, to found, change or abolish church regions, archdioceses, dioceses, etc. This enabled the Catholic Church the complete independence within the Croatian territory. Croatia accepted Sundays and Catholic solemnities to be non-working days within the territory of Croatia, as well as the Church's right to establish foundations, to build churches and church buildings (where the diocese decides on the building need and location), to have free access to public media owned by the state as well as to found its own radio and television activities in accordance with the Croatian legislation. The Concordat introduced the canon marriage which

---

17 Ugovor o dušobrižništvu katoličkih vjernika, pripadnika oružanih snaga i redarstvenih službi Republike Hrvatske (The Official Gazette, Addition – International Agreements, no. 2/97); Ugovor o suradnji u području odgoja i kulture, (The Official Gazette, Addition – International Agreements, no. 2/97); Ugovor o pravnim pitanjima (The Official Gazette, Addition – International Agreements, no. 3/97) Ugovor o gospodarskim pitanjima, (The Official Gazette, Addition – International Agreements, no. 18/98).

18 Article 141 of the Constitution: "International treaties which have been concluded and ratified in accordance with the Constitution, published and which have entered into force shall be a component of the domestic legal order of the Republic of Croatia and shall have primacy over domestic law. Their provisions may be altered or repealed only under the conditions and in the manner specified therein or in accordance with the general rules of international law."

produces civil effects provided there are no civil barriers according to the Croatian legislation. A very interesting provision is related to the position of the clerics in the case of criminal investigations which obliges Croatian authorities firstly to inform the respective church authorities on such investigation.

With regard to the other three Concordats, several rights of the Church are worth mentioning due to their far-reaching impacts on the Croatian legal order as a whole. One of the major commitments of the Croatian State was the introduction of Catholic religious education at schools as the equal subject when and if the parents decide to have it as a school subject for their child. The content of the program of religious education is authorized by the Church but expenses related to it are on the side of the state. Religious teachers may teach only upon the canon mandate given by the Church. The Holy See took the obligation to establish the Military Ordinary in Croatia equated with the diocese and led by the Bishop, while Croatia took the obligation to secure all material conditions necessary for its functioning, to establish the proper seat of the Ordinary as well as to finance all the Ordinary's staff. Croatia exempted the Catholic Church from the Croatian tax system and obliged itself to return to the Church all nationalized property during the communist time, exchange it with other property or pay a certain amount of compensation for it. Furthermore, Croatia obliged itself to pay a certain amount of money on a monthly basis for the proper functioning of the Church. The amount was agreed according to the percentage of the Croatian citizens who considered themselves as Catholic. Although Concordats allege donations and different kind of contributions as vital source of Church's functioning, it is evident that the state has become a powerful and significant source of Church's funding.

The Catholic scholar Eterović defined Croatia's ratification of the Concordats as a historical happening with important ecclesiastical, social and political characteristics. He is of the opinion that these Concordats were the expression of Croatia's recognition of the Catholic Church as an equal interlocutor. Furthermore, he claims that by them Croatia wants to be an open state which accepts the principle of subsidiarity enabling the Church to contribute to the betterment of man and the social community.[19] On the other side, there are scholars who do not share this view. Uzelac, for ex-

19 See Eterović, "Ugovori između Svete Stolice i Republike Hrvatske," 1997, p. 181, at hrcak.srce.hr/file/78759.

ample, challenges the constitutionality of the Concordats due to the privileged status of the Catholic Church in relation to other religious communities claiming, inter alia, that any form of contractual arrangements with religious community is not permitted because of the constitutional principle which demands a regulation by law and for all religious communities.[20] Padjen submits that Concordats are not necessary because every religious community without Concordat ought to enjoy the complete internal autonomy and right to communicate with its centre abroad. Besides that, he deems that the Concordat would be contrary to the constitutional equality of all religious communities.[21] Staničić, on the contrary, thinks that the international subjectivity of the Holy See would be discriminated if disabled to enter into a treaty as an international subject. Furthermore, he deems that the Concordats are constitutional because the Constitution does not prescribe that the status of the religious communities can be regulated only by law.[22] Jelčić criticises burdensome financial obligations on the side of the Croatian state and pledges for the revision of the Concordats.[23]

It is evident that all the Concordats produce a substantial financial impact on the state budget for the fulfilment of the commitments undertaken. According to some published data, the Catholic Church in Croatia receives around 85 million Euros per year on the basis of the implementation of the Concordats.[24] The financial obligations which mainly fall on the side of the Croatian state are the subject of many public disputes with regard to the lack of transparent financing of the Catholic Church, the questions of the need to amend the Concordats or even to withdraw from them.

---

20 See Uzelac, "Od liberalizma do katolicizma: neki aspekti pravnih odnosa između crkve i države u Republici Hrvatskoj – novo pravno uređenje braka," 1999, pp. 367-368, at http://alanuzelac.from.hr/pubs/A27Od%20liberalizma%20do%20 kato licizma_Zbornik.pdf.

21 See Padjen, "Veliko bezglavo ništa," 1995, at http://www.aimpress.ch/dyn /pubs/archive/data/199512/51201-001-pubs-zag.htm.

22 See Staničić, "The Legal Status of the Religious Communities in Croatian Law."

23 See Jelčić, "Koliko košta Hrvate Crkva: prava istina o novcima koji se slijeva u crkvenu blagajnu," 2013, at http://www.jutarnji.hr/koliko-hrvate-kosta-crkva/1140001/.

24 In the research made by Ana Benačić and presented in the article „Financiranje Katoličke u Hrvatskoj" („Financing of the Catholic Church in Croatia"), at htt p://www.fcjp.ba/templates/ja_avian_ii_d/images/green/Ana_Benacic.pdf, there is a thorough overview of the financial obligations on the basis of Concordats. The article also claims how Croatian authorities are not keen in monitoring the expenditure of those means and tolerate the absence of the necessary reports.

Leaving aside the financial issue, it is apparent, as it has been previously said, that the Concordats "affected" the Croatian legal order in different aspects. The most significant impacts are within the family law by the introduction of the canon marriage as being equal to the civil one and, within the education system, by the introduction of the Catholic religious education in public schooling. However, the aspects of the exemption of the Catholic Church from taxation, the position of the Military Ordinary in relation to the public administration system as well as the different position of the Catholic Church with regard to the Act on the compensation for seized property during the communist regime[25] are also issues which raise a legitimate question on the position of the Catholic Church in relation to the constitutional principle of the separation between the state and religious communities as well as the equality of all religious communities before the law. The issue of the seized property seems to be especially interesting because Croatia obliged itself to return to the Catholic Church, within reasonable time, in kind all the property that is possible to return according to legal provisions. In case of the impossibility of return, the adequate exchange of goods will be made. For the property that cannot be returned though, Croatia is obliged to annually pay out appropriate compensation in four rates as of 2000. Total amount of that compensation will be made upon the evaluation of the goods. On the other side, according to the Act on Compensation for Seized Property, all individuals and legal entities (including other religious communities) are entitled to compensation firstly and exceptionally to return of the property in kind. Although the Concordat obliges both sides to adhere to the legal provisions in case of compensation, the Church refuses to be compensated according to the Act's provisions (which provide measures for evaluation) but insists on the evaluation of the market value of the property that is not possible to return.[26]

VII. Relationship between the State and the Catholic Church

It was evident that politics was one of the main drivers of the Church's revitalization in Croatia. The Concordats clearly reflect the opportunity of

25 The Act on the Compensation for the Seized Property during the Communist Regime, (The Official Gazette, no. 92/96, 92/99, 80/02, 81/02).

26 See Benačić, "Financiranje Katoličke crkve u Hrvatskoj," p. 6.

the Catholic Church to take part in the desecularization[27] of society. By simple application of the basic desecularization features on the Concordats, it can be concluded that they deeply affect the state by reshaping their secular institutions, return the Catholic Church to the public sphere, and enable the resurgence of religious belief and practices and allow the Catholic Church to reassert its social influence.

They were more than sufficient a legal basis for building a partnership. However, in spite of its privileged legal and social status, the Catholic Church has been on a thorny path toward partnership with the state.

Distinguished Croatian scholar Banac deems that in spite of many dilemmas, the Catholic Church has remained the main moral arbiter of the Croatian society, regardless of the fact that Croats themselves as well as the Church were on both sides of modern divisions many times.[28] This view supports the fact that researches show high percentage of the trust in the Catholic Church. The Church is on the second place after the military. The lowest trust is in the Government and the political parties.[29] If it is

---

27 See Karpov, "Desecularization: A Conceptual Framework," 2010, at http://jcs.oxfordjournals.org/content/52/2/232.full. "*Desecularization* is a process of counter-secularization, through which religion reasserts its societal influence in reaction to previous and/or co-occurring secularizing processes. The process manifests itself as a combination of some or all of the following tendencies: (a) a rapprochement between formerly secularized institutions and religious norms, both formal and informal; (b) a resurgence of religious beliefs and practices; (c) a return of religion to the public sphere ("de-privatization"); (d) a revival of religious content in a variety of culture's subsystems, including the arts, philosophy, and literature, and in a decline of the standing of science relative to a resurgent role of religion in world-construction and world-maintenance; (e) religion-related changes in society's substratum (including religiously inspired demographic changes, redefinition of territories and their populations along religious lines, reappearance of faith-related material structures, growing shares of religion-related goods in the overall economic market, and so on)."

28 Taken from Tanjić, "Uloga i značenje Katoličke crkve u Hrvatskoj," 2013, at http://www.unicath.hr/wp-unicath/wp-content/uploads/2013/10/OST-WEST-Uloga-i-znacenje-Katolicke-Crkve-u-Hrvatskoj.pdf.

29 See Ponoš, "Research: Croatians trust the most in the Church and military, the least in the Government and the political parties," 2015, at http://www.novilist.hr/Vijesti/Hrvatska/Istrazivanje-Hrvati-vjeruju-Crkvi-i-vojsci -ne-vjeruju-Vladi-i-strankama?meta_refresh=true. In the article it is noted that research made in 2015 shows how the first place of trust (out of 10 it is rated with 5,62) is given to the military and the Church is on the second place (out of 10 it is rated 5,23). Further are the president of the Republic (4,89). The Government is rated with 2,4 and the political parties with 2,05.

added that around 86 percent[30] of Croatian population are considered to be catholic, the potential of the Catholic Church for reassertion is very high. So why is this path a thorny one?

In order to return to the public scene, the Catholic Church allowed the then leading party, Croatian Democratic Union (CDU), to use it for political aims. This alliance was at a certain point of time seen as a symbiosis of the state and church. The Church participated in events like the construction of highways, schools and pre-school buildings and blessed these projects. Politicians of the highest rank were present at all major Christian events or messes. Many distinguished sociologists and theologians deem that the Church at that time developed a certain client-relationship with the leading political party which contributed to the loss of the Church's institutional reputation and supra-party status. As much as the Church tried to be critical, the shadow of 'flirting' with the CDU became a constant burden with regard to the Church's objectivity. The Catholic scholar Tanjić admitted that the Church, after perennial isolation did not manage to adequately interpret the roles of the state and of society in the 1990s.[31]

It seems that the Church has not used the religious revitalization in order to go for a new evangelism but it got lost in the whirls of politics which, in the case of Croatia, is still in a transitional process. Tanjić criticizes that the Church failed in recognizing those Marxist elites who continued to influence the social life in Croatia under the veil of cosmopolitism disabling the development of the Croatian society. However, he states that the Church in the socialist time was in a forced exile while today it is in a voluntary exile within the Croatian society. He sees the reason for this in the lack of the cultural, social and political elite who, inspired by Christian values, could contribute to the development of the Croatian society. Further on, he is critical toward the Church since it has fared not particularly well in the field of culture, and with regard to general participation in the democratic society.[32]

Padjen states that the Church from the independence of Croatia was more an observer of the social and economic circumstances than an initiator of deliberations. Furthermore, he thinks that the Church, in spite of being critical toward CDU which was in power at the end of the 1990s, was

30 Census from 2011.

31 See Tanjević, "Uloga i značenje Katoličke crkve u Hrvatskoj."

32 See ibid.

not entirely objective because of the fact that the same political power brought some good to the Church – the Concordats.[33]

The barrier to the reassertion of its societal influence might be exactly the Concordats with the Holy See. In the general public, they are seen as the cause for the Church's alienation from society since it was more concerned with the return of its property rather than the resurgence of beliefs. The amount of money that is given to the Church without any justification from its side is becoming a leading question of the advocates on secularism. Very burdening financial clauses in Concordats raise scepticism. Despite the fact that all four Concordats contain a provision which allows both sides to start the negotiations on changes if any of them deems that the circumstances under which the Concordat has been concluded are essentially changed, there has been no impetus for that until now. In the time of the overall economic crisis which has become deeper and deeper in Croatia, more and more voices claim that the Church does not share the destiny of all within the state. Although politicians are voicing that the Concordats should be reconsidered, no power so far has approached to it in a structured manner. On the other side, Cardinal Bozanic claims that Concordats do not determine the privileged position of the Catholic Church. They are concluded in the atmosphere of general recognition of the religious freedoms. The Concordats promote transparent relationship between the state and the Church, their norms protect the Church against possible dependence and blackmails from any of the actual powers.[34] As much as this statement can be supported in a wider political context, it can also be a starting point in turning the Church to the civil society through which it can reaffirm its social, cultural and spiritual function. This view stems from the opinion of the Franciscan theologist Šago who stated that the

> Church will show its authentic face the best if demonstrates that it does not care for the former external glow and material power, but that it prefers to be poor and free in free society which respects every individual, that it is sensitive for social moral, social justice and solidarity with all who suffer any kind

---

33 See Padjen, "Vjera u narod bez vlasti i vlasništva: Crkvena šutnja 1961-1971. i glasnost 1990," p. 197.

34 Cardinal Bozanić presenting the book on twenty years of diplomatic relations between the Republic of Croatia and the Holy See; see http://www.glas-koncila.hr/index.php?option=com_php&Itemid=41&news_ID=2563130, November 2014.

of justice and that it is above all on the side of poor people and those who are humiliated by the present transition.[35]

VIII. The Legal Framework for Religious Communities from 2002

Considering the fact that the Catholic Church in Croatia achieved a high degree of independence within the Croatian legal order, the question is: What was the position of other traditionally present, known or newly founded religious communities in Croatia? How did politics behave toward other religions and was it fully in line with the constitutional principle that all religious communities are equal before the law?

After many years of 'legal passivity' on the issue of the legal status of religious communities in general, the Croatian Parliament enacted the ALSRC in 2002.

At first sight, the ALSRC 2002 contains many 'freedom-like' provisions. It is not necessary to look into the Explanatory Memo of the Act to realize how it followed the patterns of the Concordats. Nevertheless, the part of the explanation which refers to the position of the Catholic Church should be greeted as it showed the striving of the State to bridge possible problems with regard to the status of the Catholic Church vis-a-vis other religious communities. The Explanatory Memo of the Act further on gives an overview of the number of laws which affected the functioning of the religious communities and underlined those which have already taken into account the constitutional framework for religious communities. The Explanatory Memo explicitly defined the religious communities as the social formations sui generis. In the Act, they are non-profit legal entities defined as communities of physical persons which realize the freedom of religion by equal public exercise of religious services and by other expressions of their faith and that they are recorded in the Register of the religious communities of Croatia.

It is noted that the Act accepted the legal personality of religious communities obtained by the ALSRC 1978 in the way that it asked only for their registration in the Register of religious communities. However, all the religious communities which did not have this quality up to enforcement of the Act or which would be founded in the future had to exist first-

35 Taken from Badjun, "Financiranje Crkve u Hrvatskoj: Trebaju li nam crkveni porezi?," at http://zaklada-hanzekovic.ijf.hr/2000/badjun.htm.

ly like religious associations with legal entity status for five years. It means that they ought to be subject to the Act on Associations firstly and after expiration of five years could be registered as religious communities.

In the basic provisions of the ALSRC 2002 it is expressively prescribed that the *issues of the common interest* for the Republic of Croatia and one or more religious communities may be regulated by the agreement between the Government and the religious community. In the part which is defined as specific provisions, the legislator prescribed the rights of religious communities. So, they are entitled to religious education in public schools, the right to spiritual care in health institutions and social care institutions, the right to spiritual care in penitentiaries and prisons, and the right to spiritual care of members of the Armed Forces and the police. However, realization of these rights depends on the agreement concluded between the religious community and the Croatian Government. It means that only upon the concluded agreement the prescribed legal rights may be exercised. It further means that the ALSRC 2002 is ineffective for those communities which do not conclude the agreement. In that regard, the practice went one step forward: the Croatian Government interpreted the Act in a way that the agreement on issues of common interests is actually the agreement on the implementation of legal rights. It signed several agreements at the beginning, but obviously being overwhelmed by different religious communities' requests to conclude the respective agreements with all of them, in due time it imposed conditions which had to be primarily fulfilled for it. They were given within a governmental act, the so called Conclusion, whose legal basis was not the ALSRC 2002 but the Act of the Government of the Republic of Croatia.[36] The Government asked from religious communities to fulfil at least one of two conditions for the agreement: either that they acted within the territory of the Republic of Croatia on April 6, 1941 and continued to act and existed legally including that the membership of believers exceeded the number of six thousand, or that the historical religious community is one of the European cultural circle (Catholic Church, Orthodox Church, Evangelical Church in the Repub-

36 The Act on the Government of the Republic of Croatia (The Official Gazette, no. 101/98, 15/00, 117/01, 199/03), Article 30 par. 3: "By Conclusion, the Government determines the views on its implementation of politics and establishes the tasks to the state administration bodies." By its legal nature, the Conclusion does not fall into the field of regulations.

lic of Croatia, Reformed Christian Church in Croatia, Islamic community in Croatia, Jewish community in Croatia).

Shortly said, the legal obligation to conclude the agreement on the realization of the rights was discretionally converted to the Government's right. Therefore, only those religious communities which fulfilled one of the two conditions set up by the executive discretion could realize their legal rights and obtain the agreement on common interests.

With regard to financing, religious communities are free to obtain the means from different resources. The state obliges itself to grant them financial means depending on the kind and importance of the religious objects and on their activities in educational, social, health and cultural fields as well as depending on their contribution to the national culture and humanitarian activities. Moreover, a religious community could be granted state aid especially for the construction or renovation of its objects. For the latter, the religious community has to submit the elaborated request. They are also exempted from taxation like the Catholic Church including the donations from abroad. From this overview, it can be concluded that legal position of other religious communities differs to a large extent from the position of the Catholic Church. While Concordats foresee secure and regular state's financial aid for the Catholic Church, other religious communities depend on the state's free evaluation on the importance of the religious communities and in that connection their contribution for Croatian society. The Catholic Church is free to decide where and when to build their institutions while other religious communities fall under regular legal regime which is additionally conditioned by the Government's decisions.

IX. The Relationship of the State and Other Religious Communities

The legal status of other religious communities shows that they are in the shadow of the state's relationship with the Catholic Church. In spite of the state's will to follow the patterns from the Concordats, it did not succeed to equalize the positions of religious communities in general. Firstly, the alliance of politics and the Catholic Church already in the beginning of the Croatian independence contributed to the stagnation in the development of a multicultural society which evidently had a negative impact on the smaller religious communities. Secondly, while the Concordats between the state and the Holy See enabled total independence and freedom of the Catholic Church in its functioning, the rights of other religious communities depend very much on the different approvals or decisions of the state. The Catholic Church is defined as a public legal entity whereas religious communities hold the status of non-profit legal entities. Moreover, the programs for religious education of all other religions are approved by the respective ministry which is not the case vis-a-vis the Catholic Church. The financial aid for other religious communities depends on the kind and importance of the respective religious objects and activities of the religious community in the society while the Catholic Church independently decides on its activities. In practice, this means that the state aid depends very much on the state's discretionary evaluation of the degree of their contribution to society. The previously mentioned imposition of severe conditions by the *(ultra vires)* governmental act complicated the realization of legally granted rights of religious communities thereby also violating Convention rights. The judgement of the European Court softened the state's approach toward the status of religious communities, and opened the space for a more liberal approach of the state toward the religious communities. So far, the state has signed eight agreements on the issues of common interests by which it regulated the status of nineteen religious communities. These agreements show that the ALSRC 2002 seems to be just a formal legal base for the conclusion of agreements by which the executive power and respective religious community arrange the rights and obligations of both sides. A glance at the agreements shows that they follow the pattern of the Concordat in many ways, but with evident difference in the legal force. Therefore, the ALSRC 2002 is only an instrument for the Government to proceed with the agreements which become a legal source for legal functioning of the religious community.

X. The Case-Law of the Constitutional Court with Regard to the Religious Communities

The Constitutional Court of the Republic of Croatia met with the issue of religion, religious communities and the right to freedom of religion several times. Already in 1992, the Constitutional Court of the Republic of Croatia has made a breakthrough regarding freedom of religion by instituting the constitutional procedure on the provision of the Act on Marriage and

Family Relations[37] which prohibited the conclusion of a marriage by religious conduct before the legal conclusion of the marriage. The provision was quashed two years later, in 1994. The Court was of the opinion that the marriage by religious conduct falls in the field of free exercise of religion and therefore could not, as such, jeopardize constitutional values. It was quite clear that this provision, enacted during the socialist time, did not go along with the proclaimed values with regard to the free conduct of religious service. At the same time, it was evident that it did not correspond to the actual social reality and that, as such, it was ineffective within the new political circumstances. The zeal of the Constitutional Court for this issue is challenged here by the question on the silence of the Court on the constitutionality of the whole ALSRC 1978. Namely, the Constitutional Court is entitled to institute the constitutional proceedings ex officio. It is hard to believe that this ALSRC 1978 stayed aside of the Court's interest in spite of its obvious inconsistence with the Constitution. Therefore, this approach of the Constitutional Court, nevertheless welcome, seemed yet more like distraction of the attention from much more serious problems in that field. In addition, it seems like it went along with the trend of that time which was reflected in public reaffirmation of the religion. The interest for the constitutionality of the Concordats has been previously mentioned. The expressed views dealt more with formal issues of the constitutionality than with the substantial ones. The Constitutional Court was, nevertheless, challenged to review their constitutionality but it rejected its competence on the review[38] simply alleging that the Article 129 of the Constitution, which establishes the competences of the Constitutional Court, did not contain the competence for the review of international agreements. Such approach has been justified in the literature by invoking Article 141 of the Constitution which provides that the concluded and ratified international agreements may be altered or repealed only under the conditions and in the manner specified therein or in accordance with the general rules of international law.[39] In spite of the clear constitutional provisions on the way of possible interventions in the content of the ratified

---

37 The Act on Marriage and Family Relations (The Official Gazette, No. 51/89, 59/90, 25/94) was a republic law enacted during the socialist time which continued to be in force until the Family Law, enacted in 1998.

38 Decision of the Constitutional Court, no. U-I-825/2001 from 14 January 2004 (The Official Gazette, 16/04).

39 See Smerdel, "Ustavno uređenje europske Hrvatske," 2013, p. 432.

international agreements, the Constitutional Court's approach is disputed here. First of all, the international agreements are above the law, but below the Constitution. Secondly, the international treaty which is ratified becomes a part of the internal legal order through the act of ratification. Although this act by its procedural aspects and content differs from the ordinary laws, it is still a law which is enacted by Parliament through the legislative procedure. In that regard, neither the Constitution nor the Rules of Procedure of the Croatian Parliament prescribe a different legislative procedure with regard to the acts on ratification in relation to other laws. Therefore, there are no obstacles for the constitutional interpretation that the act on ratification falls under the constitutional competence of reviewing whether the laws comply with the Constitution. Even if the Court is not authorized to "touch" the content of the international agreement in any way, it could review its constitutionality and in case of unconstitutionality just declare the violation of the Constitution. This declaration could be further considered like a justified reason for the Croatian side to start procedure on alternation of the Concordat because of changes in circumstances.

With regard to the position of the religious communities which fall under the reach of the ALSRC 2002, the Constitutional Court had the opportunity to review the Government's Conclusion from 2004 (previously mentioned) which regulated the conditions under which a certain religious community could conclude an agreement on the issues of the common interest with the Government. The Court rejected the proposal on the constitutional review limiting itself to the formal aspects. Its reasoning was that the Conclusion did not contain the characteristics which are essential for "other regulations" in order to be examined by the Constitutional Court.[40] The religious communities in question tried to obtain a decision from the ordinary court as well and subsequently from the Constitutional Court via constitutional complaint. After no success before domestic bodies they ended up before the European Court of Human Rights which established a violation of Article 14 in connection to Article 9 of the ECHR[41]. In the merits of the case, the European Court started from its for-

---

40 Decision of the Constitutional Court, U-II-3961/2005 from June 5th, 2007, at http://sljeme.usud.hr/usud/praksaw.nsf/Ustav/C12570D30061CE53C12572F2002843B9?OpenDocument.

41 The case Savez Crkava "Riječ života" and Others v. Croatia (App. no.7798/08), Judgement of the ECtHR from 9 March 2011.

tification that State had a duty to remain neutral and impartial in exercising its regulatory power in the sphere of religious freedom and in its relations with different religions, denominations and beliefs. The European Court found then that Government's treatment of the religious communities in question did not have any "objective and reasonable justification."

The formalistic approach of the Constitutional Court was severely criticised by Staničić and Ofak who deemed that the Constitutional Court made a huge mistake when it considered itself incompetent to review the Conclusion. According to their opinion, the disputed Conclusion was the Government's decree on the execution of the ALSRC 2002 and as such it was suitable for review.[42] It is not the purpose of this paper to discuss the legal nature of the disputed Conclusion.[43] It will be enough to state that the Conclusion represented a typical *ultra vires* act and the Court could have quashed it easily because neither does the ALSRC 2002 in general prescribe any conditions regarding the status of religious communities, nor does it contain any provision which would authorize the Government to set up the conditions at all. Additional reason for substantive approach of the Court would be whether the content of the Conclusion complies with its definition in the Act of the Government as an act without regulative features.

An interesting test for the position of religious communities arose in the face of the Act on Trade which in 2004, after very strong public pressure by the Catholic Church, prohibited work on Sundays for shops and trade centres. The aim of this Act was to improve "the protection of labour rights and families" of those who worked in the shops, and to introduce legal mechanisms for "combating the exploitation of the workers" employed in the shops with a special emphasis on the protection of women and believers.[44] The initiatives for the constitutional review came from the side of entrepreneurs who claimed violation of entrepreneurial rights but also from two citizens, members of the Christian Adventist Church, who

42 See Staničić and Ofak, "Registracija vjerskih udruga i vjerskih zajednica u svjetlu Europske Konvencije za zaštitu ljudskih prava i temeljnih sloboda," 2011, p. 236.

43 The writer of this article disagrees with the opinion on legal nature of the Conclusion. Even a decree on execution of an act should be within its legal boundaries which was not the case in the current Conclusion. The Conclusion introduced completely new legal premisses in the implementation of the ALSRC 2002 and went beyond legal ratio of the ALSRC 2002.

44 Decision of the Constitutional Court, no. U-I-3824/03, from 28 April 2004 (The Official Gazette, no. 55/04).

claimed violation of the right to freedom of religion. They claimed that the Agreement which their Church signed with the Government on the issues of the common interest provided for the members of the respective religious community a right not to work on Saturdays. Their right to freedom of religion is confirmed in the Labour Act which forbids any kind of discrimination including the one on the basis of religion. The Act on Trade by their opinion contravened to the concluded Agreement and the Labour Act. In its review, the Constitutional Court referred to the Act on Holidays and Work-Free Days of the Republic of Croatia, on the Concordat on the legal issues with the Holy See, but also on the aforementioned Agreement between the Government and three religious communities on the issues of the common interest. However, the reasoning of the decision on abolishment of the Act on Trade did not take into account the issue of religious freedoms at all. It was directed on the aspects of the rule of law and the equal rights of all entrepreneurs on the Croatian market. The question is, why did then the Constitutional Court refer at all to the respective Concordat and Agreement if did not take into account these issues? Moreover, the initiative of two members of Advent Church claimed violation of their religious rights in connection to discrimination. Although there is no answer to it, this case showed how the issue of legal status of the religious communities and in that relation of the religious rights of their members is not yet clearly defined in the Croatian legal order. It also showed how even an act from the market field may have an impact on the position of the religious communities. This decision of the Constitutional Court did not prevent the legislator to enact the new Act on Trade four years later prohibiting working on Sundays again, however, slightly different than the previous one. The new constitutional review was established again by entrepreneurs who claimed, among other reasons, that the constitutional principle on equality of all religious communities and principle of separation of the Church from state are violated because one of the aims of the disputed Act was to promote certain world views which reflected only the views of the Catholic Church. The Court noted that in Croatian tradition and its customs Sunday is the day in the week which is recognized as the day for rest. It is also confirmed by the national legislator. In relation to the disputed aim of the Act, the Court defended itself by stating how such an aim could not be recognized. The Court abolished the respective provisions,[45] again taking into account entrepreneurs' constitutional rights and did not touch the issue of status of the religious communities.

The problem for the Constitutional Court in both cases was in the fact that none of the allegations on privileging the Catholic Church could be recognized directly in the disputed Acts exactly because Sunday is traditionally non-working day in Croatia. The claims mainly referred to the Church's public opinion on the respective issue and its firm publicly presented determination to promote its values and defend them legally. In that regard, it could be said that Church's aim to prohibit Sunday as working day showed high degree of Church's socio-political strength in the Croatian society.

With regard to the individual cases, recent case law of the Constitutional Court shows its rather restrictive approach towards 'religious issues'. One case dealt with a teacher for Catholic religious education who lost his job due to a civil divorce and another one dealt with the termination of a religious servant's labour contract. The Catholic religious education teacher entered the high school with the Church's canon mandate, possession of which is the main prerequisite for teaching Catholic religious education according to the Concordat on cooperation in the field of education and culture. The mandate may be withdrawn by the respective Church's authority in which case the person in question loses the right to teach Catholic religious education. The teacher in question became a public servant and acquired all respective rights like any other public servant. Meanwhile, the teacher divorced. When the Church found out about the divorce, it withdrew the mandate and the school terminated his labour contract since he did not possess the mandate anymore. He sued the school for the illegal notice and lost the case up to the Supreme Court. He submitted a constitutional complaint alleging the violation of his right to private and family life since he lost his work because of the divorce. During the constitutional procedure, the Court came to the conclusion that there are no precise regulations on the position, rights and obligations of religious teachers and that the state did not make a proper regulation on the conduct of religious education. The Court referred directly to the respective Concordat as the legal basis for possession of the mandate and concluded that it was not competent to review the Concordat's provision on receiving and

45 The Decision of the Constitutional Court, no. U-I-642/09 et al., from 19 June 2009 (The Official Gazette, no. 76/09).

loosing that mandate. Then, the Court confirmed the statement of the lower courts that teacher did not lose his job exclusively because of withdrawal of the mandate, but also because a school where he taught had no possibility to offer him another similar job. At the end, the Court was firm in the view that withdrawal of the mandate did not constitute a violation of his constitutional rights.[46] However, a more accurate and profound approach was given in the dissenting opinion of the president of the Constitutional Court who claimed the violation of the applicant's right to respect private and family life because of the omission of the positive obligations of the state to form the normative frame which will accord the position of religious teachers with the international obligations and Croatian legal order. This case did not only reveal a grey zone in the field of implementation of the Concordat and its compliance with the Constitution but also touched the issue of exercise of rights by individuals who enter the school system under privileged conditions which stem from the Concordat and continue to enjoy rights as other teachers who entered the school system under sever legal regime.

The other case dealt with the issue of the religious servant who concluded the labour contract with his parish. After some disputes, the parish terminated the contract. The ordinary courts, including the Supreme Court of the Republic of Croatia denied its competence on ruling on this issue. They considered that such a situation did not fall into the jurisdiction of the courts because the competence of the respective religious community for its religious appointments, elections and assignment of the religious services comprised the competence for terminating the labour contract with the religious servant. The Constitutional Court accepted such interpretation of the Supreme Court and refused the constitutional complaint.[47] However, the Court did not take into consideration the provision of the ALSRC 2002 which provides that for the execution of the religious services, the religious community may enter into legal relationships and conclude the labour contracts with religious servants and other workers. Religious servants exercise their rights according to the labour contract and on the basis of the provided work like all other (non-religious) workers.

The restrictive attitude of the Constitutional Court could be explained by assuming that the Court was not yet ready to interpret the constitutional

46 The Decision of the Constitutional Court, no. U-III-702/2009 from 22 May 2013 (The Official Gazette no. 69/13).

47 Decision of the Constitutional Court, no. U-III-461/2009 from 30 January 2014.

provision on separation between the state and religious communities which would demand a thorough analysis of the border line between the cooperation of the state and the religious communities and undue interference of the latter in the secular postulates of the state.

XI. Croatian Society Between the State and Religion

The Croatian society has been in the process of re-examining values. Is it closer to Christian values, ethics and moral, or is it changing in accordance with the views of a liberal society? Like in many European countries, issues like health (sexual) education, homosexual marriages, artificial insemination or the ban on abortion occupy the Croatian social and political scene. Already in 1991, the Constitutional Court received the initiative on the constitutional review of the Act on the Health Measures for Realization of the Right to Decide Freely on Birth of Children which was enacted in the socialist time, i.e. in 1978, and is still valid. In the public it is known as the Act on Abortion. The Court is still silent about it. From time to time conservative parts raise the issue of abortion and provoke the liberal parts which defend the right of women on a free choice.

The health education at schools became a matter of interest when the Minister of Science, Education and Sports enacted the Decision on the health education curriculum with the content which disturbed a huge part of parents due to infringements of their ethical and moral stands. Behind the critics was the view of the incompatibility of the health education issues with the religious education. It was also stated that certain parts directly disturbed the religious beliefs of parents and children. The Catholic Church stood beside the views of parents since they overlapped with its views if not even driven by it. The decision of the Minister failed at the Constitutional Court because of the lack of democratic, pluralist procedure in issuing it.[48]

The Government was in the procedure of the rearrangement of religious education at schools by replacing the hours of religious education on the beginning or at the end of school day in order to facilitate the position of the pupils and students who do not attend the religious education. The

48 Decision of the Constitutional Court, no. U-II-1118/2013 et al. from 22 May 2013 (The Official Gazette, no. 63/2013).

Church considered it an attack on it and stated how the government's approach is not in the interest of the children and the schools. The Catholic Church, supported by other religious communities clearly announced the disagreement about the possibility to extend the institution of marriage for homosexual couples. Although the Government did not clearly refer to marriage as such but to broadening of the rights of homosexual couples, the Church used its social and religious influence and supported the civil initiative for national referendum on the definition of marriage as the union of a man and a woman. The referendum succeeded proving that the Government underestimated and ignored the influence of the Church in the Croatian society.

Although Croatian society has features of conservative and Christian oriented one, it cannot be said that it is not aware of the position of the largest religious community in Croatia, i.e. Catholic Church. The consideration of Croatian citizens being catholic did not deprive them of critical approach toward its legal position. This puts a task before the Catholic Church to reconsider the possible ways to reassert its position.

B. Conclusion

This paper tried to reveal the relationship between the Croatian state and the religion as well as religious communities in general. Throughout history, the Catholic Church has been an important factor in the construction of the Croatian identity. Its revitalization after the forced exile during the period of socialism was largely supported by politics which did not hesitate to use it for its legitimization. The Church did not succeed to resist such attitude and it developed a relationship with the state which, from that point onwards, threw a shadow on its position of a moral arbiter within the Croatian society. Even Catholic scholars pointed to this aspect and sadly admitted that the Croatian people perceive the Catholic Church as a part of the political power or as an ally of authorities.[49]

The burden of the Catholic Church for its sympathy toward the right-oriented party resulted in a lack of dialogue and mutual understanding, respect and appreciation with all political factors in the state. The Church

---

49 See Padjen, "Vjera u narod bez vlasti i vlasništva: Crkvena šutnja 1961-1971. i glasnost 1990-," p. 179.

expects the state to respect traditional family values and the opinion of the majority which expresses itself as religious, while in the state are forces (like the left-oriented party) which promote neoliberal values and resist to social role of the Church. As much as the Church is stuck in its own vision of how Croatian society should look like, as much the left-oriented Government undermines the pure fact that the Catholic Church in Croatia enjoys a high percentage of trust among the citizens. This shows that both sides need to reset their own views and reached positions about issues that shape the Croatian values.

The implementation of the Concordats poses too many questions on the position of the Catholic Church in the Croatian society, the relationship between the state and the Church as well as the position of other religious communities as a whole. A number of burdening financial provisions, unclear limits of the independence of the Catholic Church within the Croatian territory, the impact on the legal order and public administration, the significance of the constitutional principle of the equality of all religious communities before the law and the separation between the state and religious communities are the issues that soon will ask for their answers. On the other hand, the focus of the state on the Catholic Church slowed down the development of other religious communities and their rights. The ASLRC 2002 has basically implemented the freedom of religion but also provided many obstacles for an easy realisation of the granted rights. The Act itself showed that the state is much more involved in the activities of the other religious communities than it is with the Catholic Church. In spite of the fact that the state followed the rights granted to the Catholic Church by Concordat, it showed at the same time resistance to the full follow-up on it. All of this shows how both the Catholic Church as the dominant religious community and all other religious communities are striving to achieve a partnership with the state. While the Catholic Church was in more comfortable situation because of its historical influence on the essence of the Croatian identity and because of the international agreements which facilitated its legal status, the other religious communities needed to struggle for recognition and acceptance by the state as a social factor which contributes to the multiculture and diversity of the Croatian society. However, both of them want to be an equal interlocutor with the state in shaping the Croatian society as a society based on each religious community's values.

Bibliography

Akmadža, Miroslav, Katolička crkva u komunističkoj Hrvatskoj, 1945-1980. Despot Infinitus d.o.o., Zagreb-Slavonski Brod, 2013.

Badjun, Marijana, "Financiranje Crkve u Hrvatskoj: Trebaju li nam crkveni porezi?," at http://zaklada-hanzekovic.ijf.hr/2000/badjun.htm.

Benačić, Ana, "Financiranje Katoličke Crkve u Hrvatskoj," paper presented at the Foundation Centre for Public Law Conference, Secularism and Religion: Bosnia and Herzegovina and the Region, pp. 1-11, at http://www.fcjp.ba/templates/ja_avia n_ii_d/images/green/Ana_Benacic.pdf.

Constitutional Court of the Republic of Croatia, Decision no. U-I-825/2001, 14 January 2004.

Constitutional Court of the Republic of Croatia, Decision no. U-I-3824/03, 28 April 2004.

Constitutional Court of the Republic of Croatia, Decision no. U-II-3961/2005, 5 June 2007.

Constitutional Court of the Republic of Croatia, Decision no. U-III-702/2009, 22 May 2013.

Constitutional Court of the Republic of Croatia, Decision no. U-III-461/2009, 30 January, 2014.

Eterović, Nikola, "Ugovori između Svete Stolice i Republike Hrvatske," 1997, pp. 181-186, at http://hrcak.srce.hr/file/78759.

European Court of Human Rights, Savez Crkava "Riječ života" and Others v. Croatia (App. no.7798/08), Judgement, 9 March 2011.

Jandrić, Berislav, "Položaj Katoličke crkve u Hrvatskoj u poslijeratnim godinama (1945-1953)," 1998, pp. 49-62, at http://hrcak.srce.hr/file/161026.

Jelčić, Božidar, "Koliko košta Hrvate Crkva: prava istina o novcima koji se slijeva u crkvenu blagajnu," 2013, at http://www.jutarnji.hr/koliko-hrvate-kosta-crkva/ 1140 001/.

Jerolimov Marinović, Dinka, "Društvene i religijske promjene u Hrvatskoj: teorijsko-hipotetski okvire istraživanja," 2005, pp. 289-302, at http://hrcak.srce.hr/index.php?show=clanak&id_clanak_jezik=52668.

Karpov, Vyachesla, "Desecularization: A Conceptual Framework," Journal of State and Church 52, 2 (2010): 232-270, at http://jcs.oxfordjournals.org/content/52/2/232.full.

Matijević, Margareta, "Religious communities in Croatia from 1945 to 1991: Social Causality of the Dissent Between Communist Authorities and Religous Communities Leadership," 2007, pp. 117-140, at http://hrcak.srce.hr/15850.

Padjen Ivan, "Vjera u narod bez vlasti i vlasništva: Crkvena šutnja 1961-1971. i glasnost 1990-," *Politička misao* 49, 4 (2012): 175-211.

Padjen, Ivan, "Veliko bezglavo ništa," 1995, at http://www.aimpress.ch/dyn/pubs / archive/data/199512/51201-001-pubs-zag.htm

Ponoš, Tihomir, "Research: Croatians trust the most in the Church and military, the least in the Government and the political parties," Novilist, July 2015, at http://www.novilist.hr/Vijesti/Hrvatska/Istrazivanje-Hrvati-vjeruju-Crkvi-i-vojsci-ne-vjeruju-Vladi-i-strankama?meta_refresh=true.

Smerdel, Branko, Ustavno uređenje europske Hrvatske, Zagreb: Narodne novine, 2013.

Staničić, Frane, "The Legal Status of the Religious Communities in Croatian Law,". *Zbornik PFZ* 64, 2 (2014): 225-254.

Staničić, Frane, and Lana Ofak, "Registracija vjerskih udruga i vjerskih zajednica u svjetlu Europske Konvencije za zaštitu ljudskih prava i temeljnih sloboda," in Vjernici, društva, pokreti, ed. Josip Šalković, Zagreb: Glas Koncila, 2011, pp. 217-242.

Tanjić, Željko, "Uloga i značenje Katoličke crkve u Hrvatskoj," OST-WEST Europäische Perspektiven 3 (2013), at http://www.unicath.hr/wp-unicath/wp-content/uploads/2013/10/OST-WEST-Uloga-i-znacenje-Katolicke-Crkve-u-Hrvats koj.pdf.

Uzelac, Alan, "Od liberalizma do katolicizma: neki aspekti pravnih odnosa između crkve i države u Republici Hrvatskoj – novo pravno uređenje braka," Zbornik PFZ 49, 3-4 (1999): 341-374, at http://alanuzelac.from.hr/pubs/A27Od%20liberalizma%20do%20katolicizma_Zbornik.pdf.

Vrcan, Srđan, "Religija i politika – simptomatičan primjer bivše Jugoslavije devedesetih godina dvadesetog stoljeća," Republica 15 (2003): 1-30, at http://postjugo.filg.uj.edu.pl/baza/files/373/Religija%20i%20politika20Simptomati%C4%8Dni%20primjer%20biv%C5%A1e%20Jugoslavije%20devedesetih%20godina%2020.%20stolje%C4%87a.pdf.

State and Religion in Spain

Javier Martínez-Torrón

A. Some Historical Remarks

Spain has been traditionally – and even more in the last five centuries – a nation in which the vast majority of the population is Catholic.[1] In the late 15th century, after almost eight hundred years of wars between Christian and Islamic kingdoms (the so-called *Reconquista*), Spain forged its national unity together with its religious unity. The unity of the new nation was shortly joined by a much more ambitious enterprise: the building of an enormous overseas empire, in which the binomial political unity/religious unity would also exercise a decisive influence.[2] To be a Spaniard and to be a Catholic were understood as equivalent, as two sides of a single national identity. As a consequence, the faithful of other religions – Jews and Muslims – who refused to convert were expelled from the kingdom. And, following the same political logic, pseudo-converts, and those who abandoned Catholicism to profess a heresy – particularly the doctrines of

1 The following paragraphs contain a brief description of well-known facts. Therefore, a few and general bibliographical references will suffice here (although I will cite some more specific studies in due course). For an attractive summary of the same topic in the last centuries – in Spanish language – see Lombardía, "Precedentes del derecho eclesiástico español," 1980, pp. 151-174. As a larger reference book on the history of the Catholic Church in Spain, see the seven volumes of *Historia de la Iglesia en España*, ed. Ricardo García Villoslada, 1979-1982. For a foreign historian's perspective, see Payne, *Spanish Catholicism: An Historical Overview*, 1984. For a Spanish historian's perspective, written in English, on the last decades of Spain's history, see Tusell, *Spain: From Dictatorship to Democracy*, 2007.

2 I am not suggesting that the Spanish kings were determined to guarantee the kingdom's religious unity under Catholicism for merely political reasons. The Spanish monarchy – perhaps more than other monarchies of that period – was committed to defend the nation's religion largely for strictly religious reasons, at least throughout the 16th century and probably also into the 17th century. Proof of this intent is found in the policy the monarchs followed for the incorporation of the American Continent into the Kingdom of Spain.

Luther or Calvin – were persecuted and, if they did not repent, publicly condemned (this function was in the hands of the Spanish Inquisition[3]). This fact explains why, in Spain, until recently, Protestantism was virtually inexistent and only a few residual, and concealed, groups of Jews and Muslims remained.

We should note that, during the same historical period, national states were constituted all over Europe following analogous interpretations of the principle *cuius regio eius et religio* (the religion of the prince is the religion of the nation). It is thus natural that the Catholic Church exercised a tremendous influence in Spain over the last five hundred years, in spite of the numerous sways of our internal politics – which witnessed some intense episodes of anti-clericalism – and in spite also of the repercussions that events occurred beyond the peninsula's borders had in Spain – from the dismantling of the American empire to the influx of French-Style liberalism and its subsequent withdrawal after Napoleon Bonaparte's Spanish adventure.

From this perspective, the situation was not essentially different in the 20th century, which began marked by the disappearance of overseas Spain and by the social convulsions provoked by socialist and anarchist movements, fuelled by circumstances of severe economic shortage. A significant part of 20th century Spain's politics revolved around church-state relations, which oscillated between two extremes: on the one hand, a confessional state (i.e., a state officially Catholic) that protected, and somehow also controlled, the Catholic Church at the cost of the freedom of other religions or ideologies; and, on the other hand, an anti-religious, and more precisely anti-Catholic, hostility.

We can find a clear and relevant example of the latter approach in the Spanish Second Republic (1931-1936), Spain's last democratic experiment prior to the political transition of the 1970s.[4] It is well known that the 1931 Republican Constitution, as well as subsequent legislation on re-

3 The Spanish Inquisition – which was controlled by the Spanish monarchy through the Dominican Order rather than by the Pope – had jurisdiction only over Christian heretics, i.e. over people who had been baptized. Therefore, they prosecuted Protestants and pseudo-converts from Judaism, but they could not prosecute Jews or Muslims that had never received baptism.

4 For a more detailed description with further bibliographical references, see Martínez-Torrón, "Derecho de Asociación y Confesiones Religiosas en la Constitución de 1931," 2000, pp. 91-120.

ligious issues, adopted a markedly hostile regulation of religious institutions, which severely restricted the Catholic Church's freedom without actually creating an environment of freedom for other religious denominations.[5] Republican legislatures and governments, especially at the beginning and at the end of the Republic, were determined to reduce the Catholic Church's social influence, which they considered excessive and incompatible with a democratic and secular state. They failed to accept the incontrovertible fact that the Church had an enormous weight in Spain's social structure. Consequently, they refused to enact moderate legislation that could reconcile the ecclesiastical influence with a democratic system and, at the same time, attract the ecclesiastical hierarchy towards the Republican cause.[6] It seems that Second Republic politicians – especially those aligned with left-wing parties – were more interested in freeing the country from religion than in establishing the basis for freedom of religion, resembling the attitude of the French government of the Third Republic, especially from 1880 to 1905.[7]

That excessive anti-ecclesiastical reaction led to opposite reactions on the other side. Spanish society became divided in two halves from the religious perspective. This fact seriously disturbed social peace and was one of the main causes that triggered the Civil War (1936-1939), which in turn ended with the dictatorship of General Franco, who ruled the country for the next thirty-six years. During that period, Spain remained largely disconnected from the democratic nations of Europe that, after World War II, rebuilt their economies, their political life, and their cultural strength in a

5 For a complete and interesting study on the making of the Republican Constitution's provisions on religious issues, see Meer, *La cuestión religiosa en las Cortes constituyentes de la Segunda República Española*, 1975.

6 Although it is certainly difficult to judge the protagonists of history from a contemporary perspective, it is very significant that neither the Republican Constitution's provisions on religious issues nor the legislation later enacted to implement them would be permitted today in light of international documents for the protection of human rights. In any event, the attitude of the diverse Second Republic governments was not always uniform with regard to religion in general and to the Catholic Church in particular. For some time, there were attempts to conclude some sort of agreement with the Holy See; see García-Peñuela, *El intento concordatario de la Segunda República (1933-1935)*, 1999.

7 See in this regard, in the context of an interesting comparison between the constitutional principles on religion in France and in the United States, Chélini-Pont and Gunn, *Dieu en France et aux États-Unis: Quand les mythes font la loi*, : 2005, pp. 25-33.

gradual process that developed alongside a series of increasingly significant supranational institutions. Only after Franco's death in 1975 could Spain revive its connection with Europe.

The religious policy of General Franco's dictatorship produced, as a pendulum reaction against Republican extremism, an unmistakable return to the notion of a Catholic confessional state.[8] It is likely true that the acceptance and support of the anti-republican forces winning the civil war by large parts of the ecclesiastical establishment was more the outcome than the cause of the violence exercised against the Church during the Republic,[9] but the fact is that the Catholic Church and Franco's dictatorship held each other for long years. The state declared itself officially Catholic (*Estado confesional*), and its protection of the Catholic Church permeated legislation and administrative praxis at all levels, at the cost of other religions' freedom. The mutual concession of privileges acquired an international dimension, as well as reinforcement in domestic law, with the 1953 Concordat between the Holy See and the Spanish state. This reciprocal support, however, did not prevent that a tension between the ecclesiastical hierarchy and Franco's regime arose with the passage of time. This began especially in the 1960's, as a consequence – among other reasons – of the change of perspective provided by the Second Vatican Council on the relations between religious and civil society.[10]

---

8 See generally the studies by Hera, "Actitud del Franquismo ante la Iglesia," and Lombardía, "Actitud de la Iglesia ante el franquismo," 1987, pp. 43-70 and pp. 81-102.

9 See Rafael Navarro-Valls, "Cómo actuó la Iglesia frente a la Guerra?," 2005, pp. 203 ff.

10 Significantly, the first Spanish law on religious freedom – which legalized non-Catholic religions' public worship – was enacted in 1967, against Franco's own reluctance, as a consequence of the political pressure exercised by Spanish bishops. See Blanco, *La primera ley española de libertad religiosa*, 1999; Tusell, "El impacto del Concilio Vaticano II en la política y en la sociedad española," 1988, pp. 377-390; and the study, written in moments close to the enactment of the law, by Corral, "Valoración comparada de la legislación española de libertad religiosa," 1968, pp. 315 ff.

B. The Constitutional Framework of Religion

I. The new Approach of the 1978 Constitution on Church-State Relations

The current legal and political framework of religion in Spain was designed by the Constitution promulgated on 27 December 1978,[11] which transformed the precedent regime into a democratic state that meets entirely the standards of freedom characteristic of Western democracies and international law. In the years that followed, the Spanish state signed the most relevant international documents regarding human rights, including the European Convention on Human Rights (in force in Spain since 1979) and the International Covenant on Civil and Political Rights (in force in Spain since 1977). Spanish society, in its largest part, accepted rapidly and enthusiastically the new model of political life. The increasing religious and ideological pluralism of society was soon no longer seen by Spaniards as a negative reality, or as contrary to the Spanish traditional identity, but rather as a normal effect of freedom.

Inspired by the experience of other European countries, the system of relations between state and religion designed by the 1978 Constitution contrasted sharply with the record of religious and anti-religious extremism described above. In this, as in other aspects of Spain's political development, the Constitution was aimed at three fundamental objectives, which were absent in Spain's previous constitutional experience: a high degree of freedom, a broad consensus among the Spanish population and political parties, and a reasonable chance of stability.[12]

The 1978 Constitution is the first Spanish constitution that has provided an adequate solution to the social and political conflicts that religious ideas have traditionally caused in Spain. With the constitutional change operated in 1978, religion ceased to be, for the first time in centuries, a major divisive factor in Spanish society. The reason for this success was the transformation of the confessional state into a regime based on religious freedom, but without breaking abruptly with the nation's historical tradition. The Constitution abandoned the customary Catholic confessionality of the state – there is no more an official religion in Spain – but

---

11 The Constitution was officially published and entered into force on 29 December 1978.

12 See López Alarcón, "La superación de la 'cuestión religiosa' como tema clave de la transición: su expresión jurídica," 2005, pp. 303-314.

looked at religion as a positive social phenomenon and adopted a system of state cooperation with religion instead of a separationist model. This secured the support of the Catholic Church, of vital importance in those times of political transition to democracy, which were still full of uncertainties after thirty-six years of dictatorship.[13]

II. Constitutional Provisions Relevant to Religion

Two articles of the 1978 Constitution deal directly with religion. Article 14 guarantees that no one can be subject to discrimination on the ground of religion (among others), and Article 16 recognizes the right to religious freedom and establishes the main principles that define the constitutional status of religion in Spain.

> *Article 14:*
> The Spanish are equal before the law and shall not be subjected to any discrimination on the ground of birth, race, sex, religion, opinion or any other condition or circumstance, personal or social.[14]
>
> *Article 16:*
>
> 1. Freedom of ideology, religion and worship of individuals and communities is guaranteed with no other limitations, in their manifestations, than those necessary for the maintenance of the public order protected by law.
> 2. Nobody shall be obliged to declare about his ideology, religion or beliefs.
> 3. There shall be no state religion. Public authorities shall take into account the religious beliefs of Spanish society and shall maintain the consequent relationships of cooperation with the Catholic Church and the other denominations.

The terminology employed by both articles – especially Article 16 – is explained in the light of the Spanish historical tensions with regard to religion. Thus, in Article 16.1, 'worship' is explicitly mentioned because the past repression of this specific manifestation of religion in moments of anti-religious hostility. 'Ideology' was the word chosen to indicate that all beliefs are protected by the Constitution, and not only religious beliefs. Article 16.2 reflects the deeply felt need to prevent that any religious test

---

13 See Martínez-Torrón, "Religious Freedom and Democratic Change in Spain," 2006, pp. 777-809.

14 Author's translation from the Spanish original into English. Unless otherwise indicated, the author is responsible for all translations included in this paper.

could be used, once again, to discriminate people in public and social life. Article 16.3, whereas it abolished the traditional Catholic confessionality of the state, made clear that public authorities, at any level, cannot ignore religion as a social phenomenon – on the contrary, when organizing public life within the limits of their respective competences, they are obliged to take into account the religious choices of citizens.

Other articles of the Constitution are also relevant to religion. Article 10.2 provides that the constitutional rules on fundamental rights and freedoms shall be interpreted in the light of international treaties ratified by Spain.[15] Article 27, when recognizing the right to education, enshrines the rights of parents to guarantee that their children will receive moral and religious teaching in accordance with their own convictions; and recognizes all natural and legal persons the freedom to create educational centres – this is of the utmost importance for a number of churches and religious organizations. Article 30.2 recognized the right to conscientious objection to military service. Article 32.2 recognized the right of men and women to marry 'with full legal equality', and was interpreted since the beginning as implicitly accepting a plurality of religious marriages with civil effects in Spain (such interpretation was later confirmed, by a modification of the Civil Code in 1981,[16] and by state cooperation agreements with the Catholic Church in 1979, and with the Protestant, Jewish and Islamic communities in 1992).[17]

We should also take into account that the religious choices of individuals, as well as religious communities, enjoy the general constitutional protection of freedom of expression (Article 20), freedom of assembly (Article 21) and freedom of association (Article 22).

15 As the Spanish state ratified the European Convention on Human Rights in 1979, Articles 16 and 14 must be interpreted in the light of Article 9 and 14 of the European Convention on Human Rights, respectively, and also in the light of the relevant case law of the European Court of Human Rights. Those articles of the Constitution must be interpreted also in accordance with Articles 18 and 26 of the International Covenant on Civil and Political Rights, which was ratified by Spain in 1977.

16 See Arts. 59 and 60 of the Spanish Civil Code.

17 See below, subsection C.III. of this paper.

III. Four Fundamental Principles

Four principles constitute the basic structure of the constitutional framework of religion in Spain. Scholars often call them 'fundamental' or 'informing' principles (*principios informadores*).[18] No strict hierarchical order governs the relationship between these principles, and they altogether establish a system of coordinates that define the plane of constitutional legitimacy to which legislator and government must limit their activity.[19]

1. Religious freedom

The first principle is *religious freedom*. According to it, all state laws on religious issues must be aimed at protecting this fundamental right, which many international documents call 'freedom of thought, conscience and religion',[20] and which Art. 16 of our Constitution names 'freedom of ideology, religion and worship' (*libertad ideológica, religiosa y de culto*).[21] The exercise of religious freedom may be limited only when it is necessary for the protection of public order and of the rights and freedoms of others, according to international standards and to the doctrine of our Constitutional Court.[22]

---

18 The bibliography on the constitutional principles of the Spanish law on religious issues is abundant. For a more detailed exposition of the ideas mentioned in the following paragraphs, and for further bibliographical references, see Martínez-Torrón, *Religión, derecho y sociedad. Antiguos y nuevos planteamientos en el derecho eclesiástico del Estado*, 1999, pp. 172-204.

19 See Ortiz, "Los principios constitucionales del derecho eclesiástico como sistema," 1989, pp. 309-322.

20 See, for instance, the 1948 Universal Declaration of Human Rights (Art. 18), the 1950 European Convention on Human Rights (Art. 9), or the 1966 International Covenant on Civil and Political Rights (Art. 18).

21 We could also add the expression 'freedom of religion or belief', which has been gaining ground since the 1981 UN Declaration on the Elimination of All Forms of Intolerance and of Discrimination Based on Religion or Belief, especially within the OSCE environment. With regard to the conceptual questions implied in the use of that diverse terminology, see Martínez-Torrón, *Religión, derecho y sociedad*, pp. 126-139.

22 See Combalía, "Los límites del derecho de libertad religiosa," 1994, pp. 471-510; Martínez-Torrón, "Limitations on Religious Freedom in the Case Law of the European Court of Human Rights," 2005, pp. 587-636.

Although this principle is not, strictly speaking, in a position of hierarchical pre-eminence with respect to the other principles, religious freedom certainly constitutes the primary objective that should define the state policies in this realm. It is conceived as a sort of lodestar that gives sense to and delineates the true dimension of the other constitutional principles. Protection of religious freedom is not only a limit to the legislative or governmental activity – in the sense that unjustified restrictions on freedom of religion or belief are unconstitutional – but it serves also a positive teleological function with regard to public policies. In other words, the higher the degree of guarantee of religious liberty provided by public policies the better they comply with the constitutional mandate.

The other three principles, however, cannot be regarded simply as mere developments of the principle of religious freedom. On the contrary, those other principles define and cement the functional efficiency of religious liberty in Spanish legal order. And, at the same time, the right to freedom of religion or belief acquires a particular meaning when understood in the light of neutrality, equality and cooperation.

2. *Equality*

The second principle is *equality* and entails that all citizens and groups are equal before the law with respect to the exercise of the right to freedom of religion or belief. Equality's immediate consequence is that the same degree of freedom must be recognized for all, and that religion or non-religion cannot be factors of discrimination in Spain.[23] In addition, the principle of equality influences the rules governing more generally the legal position of churches in Spain.

Thus, differences between the legal statuses of various religious denominations are legitimate only if they are not discriminatory. Such differences are allowed when a specific legal treatment is deemed necessary to provide adequate guarantee of the freedom of a certain group or individual in accordance with their particular circumstances. In other words, according to the case law of the European Court of Human Rights and of the Spanish Constitutional Court, differences in legal treatment are legitimate when

23 Public officials or employers who refuse to grant a service to certain people because of their religion or belief commit an offence punished by the Spanish Criminal Code (cf. Arts. 511-512).

they are grounded on a reasonable and objective justification, when they pursue a legitimate aim, and when there is an adequate relationship of proportionality between the aim pursued and the means employed.[24]

3. *Neutrality*

The third principle is state *neutrality* on religious matters,[25] which appears to be the main instrument chosen by the Constitution to protect the religious liberty of all citizens and groups in equal conditions. The deep meaning of neutrality goes beyond mere formal impartiality. Neutrality implies that Spain has no official religion and requires that the state, and its legal system, conceive themselves as *incompetent* with regard to purely religious questions and therefore unable to make value judgments on them.

According to the Constitutional Court, neutrality prohibits all confusion between state and religious functions in society.[26] The state must respect

---

24 The first decision of the European Court of Human Rights establishing its doctrine on equality was the so-called 'linguistic Belgian case': *Case "relating to certain aspects on the laws on the use of languages in education in Belgium"*, 23 July 1968 (see especially 'The Law' n. 1.B.10). The European Court has subsequently reiterated this doctrine in numerous decisions, including some relating to religious freedom. The case law of the Spanish Constitutional Court on the equality principle is directly inspired by the case law of the Court of Strasbourg. See, for instance, STC 49/1982, FJ 2; STC 144/1988, FJ 1; STC 45/1989, FJ 4, among many others. For further references, see Martínez-Torrón, "La protección internacional de la libertad religiosa", 1994, pp. 229-237. With regard to the principle of equality in the case law of the Constitutional Court of Spain, see Calvo Álvarez, *Los principios del derecho eclesiástico español en las sentencias del Tribunal Constitucional,* 1999, pp. 129-164; and Rodríguez Chacón, *El factor religioso ante el Tribunal Constitucional*, 1992, pp. 33-38.

25 Some authors, as well as some decisions of the Constitutional Court and other Spanish courts, often call this principle *aconfesionalidad* (aconfessionality) or *laicidad* (i.e., secularity, which is not exactly equivalent to the French understanding of *laïcité*). The use of one or other term implies certain differences with regard to how the meaning of this principle is understood. I prefer the expression 'neutrality', which I deem more appropriate to avoid misunderstandings with respect to its content (Martínez-Torrón, *Religión, derecho y sociedad*, pp. 177-189). On the complexities inherent to the notion of state neutrality, see Palomino, "Religion and Neutrality: Myth, Principle and Meaning," 2011, pp. 657-689.

26 See STC 24/1982, *fundamento jurídico* 1.

religious pluralism in society, and therefore may not favour the development of some religions while hindering the progress of others. Such notion of neutrality does not imply that public authorities must be indifferent towards the results produced by the exercise of freedom of religion or belief, or that they ignore completely the content of personal choices in this particular area of human rationality. Neutrality means that public authorities cannot judge the truth or falsity of the dogmas or tenets of the diverse religions. However, state action with respect to religion may be based on other judgments. In particular, it may take into account the social effects of the religious activity, or the predictable effects of religious moral doctrines, including the cases in which those effects conflict with the law or with values that the legal system considers essential.

Two important consequences derive from the foregoing. First, state action with regard to religion must be, for the most part, a legal action – i.e., an action defined by law, with a narrow margin for public authorities' discretion that could lead in practice to value judgments on religious doctrines or customs. Second, neutrality implies recognition of the reciprocal autonomy of state and religion and, therefore, state's interference with religious autonomy must be reduced to a minimum and its necessity must be clearly justified.[27] We must keep in mind that, as indicated above, neutrality – or *laicidad* – is conceived not as an aim in itself but as a means to guarantee and facilitate the exercise of freedom of religion or belief by all individuals and groups on equal grounds.

4. Cooperation

Finally, the principle of state *cooperation* with churches or religious communities provides a specific profile to neutrality. The reciprocal autonomy of state and churches is not understood in terms of strict separation but rather in terms of friendly relations and mutual cooperation – at least, co-

27 The European Court of Strasbourg has often emphasized this idea since the late 1990s. See, for instance, *Serif v. Greece*, 14 December 1999; *Hasan and Chaush v. Bulgaria*, 26 October 2000; *Metropolitan Church of Bessarabia v. Moldavia*, 13 December 2001; or *Agga v. Greece*, 17 October 2002. However, some recent cases concerning the labour relations between churches and their employees demonstrate that defining the limits of religious autonomy is far from easy. See, for example, *Obst v. Germany* and *Schüth v. Germany*, both of 23 September 2010.

operation of the state with religious denominations. In the words of Article 16.3 of the Constitution, "public authorities shall take into account the religious beliefs of Spanish society and shall maintain the consequent relationships of cooperation with the Catholic Church and the other denominations". This is consistent with Article 9.2 of the Constitution, which requires public authorities to create the conditions to make "real and effective" the freedom and equality of individuals and groups.

In the years after the Constitution was enacted, Spanish scholars widely discussed the potential legal effects of the specific mention of the Catholic Church by Article 16.3. The passage of time has demonstrated that the specific mention of the Catholic Church should not be interpreted as a sign of *sociological confessionality* of the state, but rather as recognition of the fact that Catholicism was part of "the religious beliefs of the Spanish society". The *mens legislatoris* in that article seems to be explained by the need to achieve what could be described as a 'tranquilizing' effect. In brief, as the new regime of relations between state and religion implied a deep change in Spanish tradition and opening the doors to religious freedom and state neutrality, the drafters of the Constitution wanted to avoid any suspicion on the part of the Catholic Church that the democratic change in Spain could degenerate into the anti-religious direction that characterized the 1931 Republican Constitution.[28] Including the name of the Catholic Church in Article 16.3 was a way to prevent the risk of a negative reaction on the part of the most conservative religious circles in Spain.[29]

The principle of cooperation poses some interesting questions with respect to which are, or should be, the criteria that determine state cooperation with churches. Two questions are particularly important: a) how, when, and in which areas, is the state obliged to cooperate with religions denominations? and b) which factors could, or should, be taken into account to justify differences in state cooperation with diverse religious denominations?

Scholars have endeavoured to answer the second question indicating that state cooperation should differ depending on three main elements.[30] First, the particular characteristics of each religious denomination (e.g.,

28 See above "Introduction" of this paper.

29 See Amorós, *La libertad religiosa en la Constitución española de 1978*, 1984, pp. 128 ff.

30 See Martinez-Torrón, *Religión, derecho y sociedad,* pp. 191-193.

some religions keep a strict observance of sabbatical rest and some others are more flexible; some religions have precise inhumation requirements and while others do not, etc.). Second, the social utility of religious denominations, including their specific contributions to educational, humanitarian or charitable initiatives (this factor tends to me more and more used to define the state economic cooperation with religion, on equal grounds with other non-profit institutions without specific religious nature). And third, the social roots of each religious denomination, which, as indicated below,[31] is one of the criteria used by the law to determine which religious communities can reach a formal cooperation agreement with the state.

With regard to the first question, it is commonly understood that Article 16.3 of the Constitution imposes on the state a general duty to cooperate with religion but does not specify when, in which areas or through which channels state cooperation must materialize. There is an implicit agreement that public authorities have a wide discretion to decide how to concretize state cooperation, limited only by the principles of neutrality and equality. For instance, the alleged aim of cooperation would not allow the government to invade the realm of religious autonomy; all differences in cooperation with religious denominations must have an objective and reasonable justification, etc.

5. *Case Law of the Constitutional Court*

The Spanish Constitutional Court, since its establishment, substantially accepted the prior description of the constitutional principles that govern church-state relations, although, naturally, the Court's application of these four fundamental principles to actual cases has been sometimes problematic. Some of these problems involve the compatibility of the principles of equality and cooperation with the legal position of the Catholic Church, and some others relate to the Court's interpretation of the neutrality principle. For instance: religious symbols or religious ceremonies in public places, civil effects of religious marriages, religious assistance to members of the armed forces, religious education in public schools, state's financial

31 See below, subsection C.III.2. of this paper.

support of religion, or the state's attitude towards new religious movements.[32]

C. The Legal Framework of Religion

The legal framework of religion in Spain is designed by two different types of norms. On the one hand, unilateral state laws (and regulations); on the other hand, bilateral norms negotiated between the state and some religious communities.

I. The Organic Law on Religious Freedom

Among state laws, the most important statute on freedom of religion, and more generally on the relations between state and religion, is the Organic Law on Religious Freedom (*Ley Orgánica de Libertad Religiosa*, hereinafter 'LOLR'), enacted in 1980 with the aim of providing the framework for all future laws and regulations dealing with religious issues.[33]

This was the first organic law enacted to develop some of the fundamental rights recognized by the 1978 Constitution,[34] which reveals that there was a sense of urgency to pass a new law that settled the legal status of religion and replaced the law promulgated by Franco in 1967. Interestingly, the LOLR kept the spirit of consensus that prevailed in the political forces during the elaboration of the Constitution and was approved by an

32 For an analysis of these problems, in English, see Martínez-Torrón, "Freedom of Religion in the Case-Law of the Spanish Constitutional Court," 2001, pp. 711-754. See also Martínez-Torrón, *Religion and Law in Spain*, 2013, pp. 92-100. For a more comprehensive study, in Spanish, see the books by Calvo Álvarez, *Los principios del derecho eclesiástico español en las sentencias del Tribunal Constitucional*, and Chacón, *El factor religioso ante el Tribunal Constitucional*, passim.

33 *Ley Orgánica* 7/1980, 5 July 1980, *de Libertad Religiosa*. The text of the LOLR, and other legislation or regulations on religion, can be found in the Internet pages of the Ministry of Justice, at http://www.mjusticia.gob.es/cs/Satellite/Portal/es/areas-tematicas/libertad-religiosa/normativa-materia-libertad/legislacion-estatal, accessed 6 January 2018.

34 The so-called 'organic laws' require an absolute majority in Congress to be approved, modified or abrogated. The laws governing fundamental rights and public freedoms must be organic. Cf. Art. 81 of the Constitution.

overwhelming majority of the Congress, indeed almost unanimously.[35] This fact was indicative of the acceptance of the new constitutional system of church-state relations. Considering that, at the time, Spain hardly had any experience in the protection of religious freedom and that religious pluralism in the country was very limited, the LOLR was a great step forward and contributed immensely to the normalization of religious freedom in Spain and to secure the constitutional design of relations between state and religion.

The 1980 LOLR is a short law, with only eight articles. Roughly speaking, it is possible to distinguish two parts in the text. The first half (Articles 1-4) refers strictly to freedom of religion or belief, especially on its individual aspects, while the second half (Articles 5-8) deals with the basic legal status of religious denominations in Spain and on the main coordinates and instruments of the relations between state and religion.

Article 2 LOLR is particularly important, for it specifies the content of the right to religious freedom, which corresponds to the provisions of the most well-known international documents. It includes the following aspects: freedom to profess any religion or to profess none; freedom to change religion or to abandon one's own church; freedom to worship; freedom to express and disseminate one's own beliefs (including proselytism effected by lawful means); parents' right to choose the religious and moral orientation of their children's education; freedom to meet publicly for religious purposes; right to receive religious assistance in the army, in hospitals or in prisons (which the state is obliged to facilitate). It also recognizes the churches' right to establish places for worship and meeting, to appoint and instruct their own ministers or religious leaders, to spread their doctrines and to maintain relationships with their own organizations or with other churches, inside or outside Spanish territory. This article also emphasizes (para. 3) that the state's role in the protection of religious freedom is not purely passive or negative but active and positive – the state must adopt appropriate measures to ensure that the right to religious freedom can actually be exercised by everybody, which is consistent with Article 9.2 of the Constitution, where the same role is assigned to the state with respect to fundamental rights in general.

35 More precisely by 294 votes in favour, with only 5 abstentions and no votes against it. See, for a detailed description of the parliamentary itinerary of the LOLR, Ciáurriz, *La libertad religiosa en el derecho español. La Ley Orgánica de Libertad Religiosa*, 1984, pp. 31 ff.

The 1980 LOLR, in line with the principle of cooperation between state and religion, is specifically intended for the protection of religious groups, which receive a special protection in respect to their autonomy.[36] Indeed, article 3 specifically provides that the law is not applicable to non-religious groups.

Other articles of this law create some state offices with competence on religious issues and introduce a new legal figure in the Spanish legal system, the cooperation agreements between state and religious denominations, which are explained in the following subsections II. and III.

II. State Offices with Competence on Religious Issues

1. The Registry of Religious Entities

To control the religious character of groups or communities in Spain, Article 5 LOLR created a specific instrument: the Registry of Religious Entities (*Registro de Entidades Religiosas*). The Registry of Religious Entities (RER) is a public registry in the Ministry of Justice, currently depending from the department of the government with competence to deal with religious juridical persons and, in general, with competence on religious freedom issues: the Vice-Directorate General of Relations with Religious Communities, which is part of the Directorate General of Foreign Juridical Cooperation and Relations with Religious Communities. The provisions of Article 5 LOLR on the RER were developed by a specific royal decree of 1981, which has been replaced by another royal decree of 2015.[37]

---

36 See article 6 of the Law; for an analysis of this article, see Jorge Otaduy, "Las cláusulas de salvaguarda de la identidad de las instituciones religiosas. Doctrina y jurisprudencia", 1989, pp. 363 ff.

37 *Real Decreto* 594/2015, 3 July 2015, *por el que se regula el Registro de Entidades Religiosas*. For an analysis of the problems caused by the former configuration of the RER, see Olmos, "Personalidad jurídica civil de las entidades religiosas y Registro de Entidades Religiosas," 2009, pp. 577-620, and López-Sidro, "La cuestión de la reforma del Registro de Entidades Religiosas: examen de as propuestas reglamentarias de 2003 y 2004," 2009, pp. 621-643. See also the more comprehensive and systematic study by Herrera Ceballos, *El Registro de Entidades Religiosas. Estudio global y sistemático*, 2012. It is still too soon to say if the 2015 regulation has had an actual positive impact on the resolution of those problems. For a comment on the changes introduced by the 2015 royal decree, see Herrera Cebal-

Registration in the RER is necessary to be officially recognized and to acquire legal personality as a religious entity in Spain. Registration is *an option and not a legal obligation.* All religious groups or communities enjoy the freedom of ideology, religion and worship recognized by Article 16 of the Constitution, irrespective of the fact that they have or have not obtained legal personality as religious entities. In practice, however, most churches or religious communities are interested in obtaining legal personality specifically as groups of religious nature.

Normally, registration in the RER is relatively simple and easy. Only limited evidence is required, and no minimum number of members or adherents is necessary. The process commences with a written application of the relevant religious entity, accompanied by authenticated document attesting its creation or establishment in Spain, as well as other formal data, such as the name of the applicant entity, domicile, regulations, structure and legal representatives. Explanation of he entity's religious nature and aims must be also provided.

The fact that only entities with religious purposes can be registered in the RER has posed in the past some important questions about *the notion of religion* that pervades the Spanish law.[38] Article 3.2 LOLR is of no much help in this respect. Apart from indicating that it is not applicable to non-religious entities and activities, this provision only mentions a few examples of activities that must not be considered religious, such as the study of psychic and parapsychological phenomena or the dissemination of spiritualistic or humanistic values. Apparently, the LOLR departed from the assumption that it was *easy* to know what was religious and what was not. In this context, for many years the praxis of the RER, confirmed by the Spanish courts, was to perform a moderate filtering of applicant groups, based upon an explicit notion of religion elaborated for legal purposes and inspired in the Judaeo-Christian religious tradition of the West. More precisely, to be considered a religious community, the RER required

los, "Hacia la construcción de un registro fiel reflejo de la realidad. La reforma del Registro de Entidades Religiosas," 2015, pp. 1-35.

38 For a detailed analysis of the theoretical and practical challenges that a legal notion of religion implies for the protection of religious freedom in Spain, and generally in Western societies, see Palomino, *Religión y derecho comparado*, 2007. By the same author, with specific reference to the notion of religious community in Spanish law, see Palomino, "Iglesias, confesiones y comunidades religiosas: el concepto legal de confesión religiosa en la LOLR y la doctrina," 2009, pp. 556-575.

three main elements: a) it had to be composed by a group of people that professed and shared a common and relatively homogeneous system of doctrines – dogmas and morals – derived from the belief in a supreme being; b) they should have a collective worship expressed in external rites or practices; and c) they must be structured around an organization relatively clear and stable.[39]

On this conceptual basis, the Spanish courts confirmed the denial of registration of, for example, the Church of Scientology,[40] the Monist Order of the Perfect Reflection[41] and the Unification Church,[42] holding that they did not meet the legal requirements to be deemed a religion in Spanish law. Nevertheless, in 2001 a judgment of the Constitutional Court changed completely this situation.[43]

This decision of the Constitutional Court addressed the issue of the refusal of registration of the Unification Church in the RER, on the ground, among others, that it was not properly a religious group. The Court decided in favour of the plaintiff and ruled that the Unification Church was entitled to register as a religious entity. The Court's judgment, however, was not very illuminating. Instead of shedding light on the questions raised by the legal concept of religion in Spain, the Court opted for rendering this concept inoperative. According to the judgment, the authorities in charge of the RER do not have any discretion, or margin of appreciation, to examine the religious nature of any group that has applied to register; they must limit themselves to confirm that this group is not excluded from registration by Article 3.2 LOLR.[44] The problem is that this legal provision specifically excludes not only entities focused on "the study of and experimentation with psychic and parapsychological phenomena, to the dissemination of humanistic or spiritualistic values", but also entities with "similar non-religious aims". Consequently, administrative authorities do of necessity have to make, implicitly or explicitly, a judgment about the religious nature and purposes of the applicant entity.

In spite of the contradictions inherent in the holding of the Constitutional Court, the judgment was sufficiently clear to be understood as prohibit-

39 See Javier Martínez-Torrón, *Religión, derecho y sociedad,* pp. 199-202.

40 See SAN of 23 June 1988, confirmed by STS of 25 June 1990 (RJ 5700/1990).

41 See SAN of 8 November 1985.

42 See SAN of 30 September 1993, confirmed by STS of 14 July 1996.

43 STC 46/2001.

44 See STC 46/2001, *fundamento jurídico* 10.

ing public authorities in charge of the RER from evaluating the religious nature of applicant entities. The consequence is that the Registry must accept, without further inquiries, all applications from entities that claim to be religious, except in the unlikely hypothesis that the applicant group explicitly presents itself as an organization for the study of psychic or parapsychological phenomena, or for the dissemination of humanistic or spiritualistic values. In application of these judicial doctrine and criteria, in 2007 the National Court held that the Church of Scientology in Spain was entitled to register in the RER.[45]

2. *The Advisory Commission on Religious Freedom*

Article 8 LOLR created another public office with competence on religious issues: the Advisory Commission on Religious Freedom (*Comisión Asesora de Libertad Religiosa*, CALR), which, like the Registry, depends from the Directorate General of Foreign Juridical Cooperation and Relations with Religious Communities. The Advisory Commission's structure and activity is governed by a royal decree of 2013.[46]

The CALR is a consultative body composed by three types of members, in conditions of parity. First, representatives of governmental departments or agencies that may have an interest in issues related to religion (presidency, foreign affairs, interior, education, employment and social security, social affairs, and finance), designated by the relevant ministries and appointed by the Minister of Justice. Second, representatives of the most influential religious denominations, those with 'well-known roots' (*notorio arraigo*) in Spain,[47] appointed by the Minister of Justice following the proposals made by the relevant religious denominations. And third, renowned experts on religious issues (usually University professors specialized in law and religion issues), appointed by the Council of Ministers

---

45 SAN 4394/2007, 11 October 2007. This church, under a new name, had applied again for registration in 2004, unsuccessfully.

46 *Real Decreto* 932/2013, 29 November 2013, *por el que se regula la Comisión Asesora de Libertad Religiosa.*

47 With regard to the concept of 'well-known roots' see below, subsection C.III.2. of this paper. The Catholic Church never registered or requested recognition of 'well-known roots'. It was commonly considered unnecessary, in view of the specific constitutional mention of the Catholic Church (Art. 16.3) and the 1979 Concordat.

upon proposal of the Minister of Justice.[48] Their term of office is four years, and can be extended without limitation. At present, the second third is composed by representatives of the Catholic Church (proposed by the Bishops Conference), Protestantism (proposed by the Evangelical Federation, FEREDE), Judaism (proposed by the Jewish Federation, FCJE), Islam (proposed by the Islamic Federation, CIE), the Mormon Church, the Church of Jehovah's Witnesses,[49] Buddhism (proposed by the Buddhist Federation, FCBE) and Christian Orthodoxy (proposed by the Assembly of Orthodox Bishops in Spain and Portugal).

According to the law, the Advisory Commission must study and give an opinion on all legislative and governmental initiatives with respect to all issues relating to the application of the LOLR, i.e. regarding religious freedom. The CALR is also competent to make proposals to the government. It is, therefore, a qualified forum in which churches can propose initiatives, discuss law drafts, and in general have their voice heard by the government. In practice, however, looking at the experience of the CALR in the past years, it is possible to find lights and shadows.

On the positive side, we can mention that the CALR has been a useful forum for dialogue, in which representatives of the main religions existing in Spain have been able to explain their position and interact with the government in relation to a variety of issues. It has effectively intervened in some new regulations, especially in the area of religious assistance in public institutions. The Commission has also asserted its undisputed competence with regard to the applications for recognition of 'well-known roots' (*notorio arraigo*); its opinions, affirmative or negative, on these applications have always been followed by the government. In addition, the CALR has elaborated interesting and detailed studies, published by the Ministry of Justice, with proposals for legal reforms in the area of religious freedom.

48 As the number of members is different in each of the thirds of the CALR, parity is preserved by given a different number of votes to each category of members. For instance, the vote of the experts counts twice the vote of representatives of religious denominations, for in the CALR there are six experts and twelve representatives of religious communities.

49 In practice, the representative of Jehovah's Witnesses never attended the meetings of the CALR and this church has renounced its right to have a seat in the Commission.

On the negative side, we can mention that the CALR has been often ignored in practice. The conclusions of its studies of legal reforms have been often disregarded for one or another reason. Many important laws and regulations susceptible of having an impact on the lives of religious communities and their members – for instance, in the areas of education, abortion, marriage, or economic cooperation – have been enacted without requesting the previous opinion of the CALR, with patent infringement of the LORL. Moreover, the Commission has been too dependent from the director general competent on religious affairs in the Ministry of Justice, with two consequences. On the one hand, as the CALR is not functionally autonomous, the personality – and interests – of the relevant director general have determined the actual extent of its work and contributions. Some directors have worked in close collaboration with the CALR and others simply have let it languish for months or years without convoking the plenary. On the other hand, being the directorate general competent on religious affairs a low-level directorate in the context of the ministerial structure, the CALR has inherited its lack of political leverage. Indeed, this has been one of the main causes of the scarce intervention of the Commission in legal initiatives promoted by other ministries with a potential impact on religious freedom. Often, the praxis has led to a sort of schizophrenic system in which the 'big issues' – typically those affecting the Catholic Church – are negotiated at high political level between the government and the Bishops' Conference, while the Advisory Commission, as well as the General Directorate, remain for 'residual issues' concerning minority religions.

III. Cooperation Agreements between State and Religious Denominations

1. The Concordat with the Catholic Church

In Spain, concordats with the Catholic Church have an old history that dates back to the 18th century.[50] Conceived initially as an instrument for

---

50 The main milestones were the Concordats of 1753, 1851 and 1953. For many years they were, in the context of a Catholic monarchy of regalist orientation, a formal channel for the reciprocal concession of privileges between church and state, with a particular emphasis on the right of patronage (*ius patronatus*) and on the regulation of ecclesiastical offices and benefices. With regard to Spanish his-

reciprocal concession of privileges, concordats were evolving, with the passage of time, towards a bilateral norm – always with the rank of an international treaty – aimed at determining more comprehensively the legal status of the Catholic Church in Spain.[51]

When Spain's political transition to democracy began, in 1976, it did not seem desirable – or even feasible – to eliminate the bilateral relationships between the Catholic Church and the Spanish state. As the Concordat signed by Franco in 1953 was not appropriate for the model of state towards which Spain's political transition was moving, both the ecclesiastical and the civil authorities soon felt the need for a new concordat.

The negotiations commenced in 1976[52] and, on 3 January 1979, a few days after the Constitution was enacted, the Spanish state signed four agreements with the Holy See, which together form a concordat and are assimilated to international treaties in Spanish law.[53] Those four agreements deal, respectively, with juridical affairs, economic affairs, education and cultural affairs, and religious assistance to the army and military ser-

---

toric Concordats, see Martín Martínez, "En el segundo centenario del Concordato español de 1753," 1953, pp. 745 ff.; Suárez, "Génesis del Concordato de 1851," 1963, pp. 65 ff.; del Torco, "Los primeros años de vigencia del Concordato de 1953," 1957, pp. 7 ff.; and the collective volumes *El Concordato de 1953 entre España y la Santa Sede*, 1956, and *La institución concordataria en la actualidad. Trabajos de la XIII Semana de Derecho Canónico*, 1971.

51 This is clearly visible in the Concordat of 1953 – under Franco's regime –, although we can still observe in it the protectionist attitude of the state and the Church's disposition to grant concessions in ecclesiastical matters.

52 The starting point of the negotiations was the signature of an agreement, on 28 July 1976, by which the Spanish state and the Holy See renounced the main reciprocal privileges that characterized their relationship in the past: clergymen's right to be exempted from ordinary criminal jurisdiction (benefit of clergy) and the state's right to intervene in the appointment of bishops.

53 The four agreements of 1979 are: Agreement on Juridical Issues (*Acuerdo sobre Asuntos Jurídicos*), Agreement on Education and Cultural Issues (*Acuerdo sobre Enseñanza y Asuntos Culturales*), Agreement on Economic Issues (*Acuerdo sobre Asuntos Económicos*) and Agreement on Religious Assistance to the Armed Forces and on the Military Service of Clergymen and Members of Religious Orders (*Acuerdo sobre Asistencia Religiosa a las Fuerzas Armadas y Servicio Militar de Clérigos y Religiosos*). Many other agreements of inferior relevance have been subsequently signed between the Catholic Church and the central state or autonomous communities. Among the abundant bibliography on this subject, see Fornés, *El nuevo sistema concordatario español: Los Acuerdos de 1976 y 1979*, 1980; Tirapu, "Acuerdos Iglesia-Estado en España," 1991, pp. 185 ff.

vice of the clergy and members of religious orders. The purpose of the new Concordat was to preserve, according to the constitutional principle of cooperation, those traditional privileges of the Catholic Church that were deemed compatible with the new constitutional principles – e.g., civil effects of canonical marriage, religious education in public schools, financial support, religious assistance in the Army or in other public centres, etc.

The Concordat confers to the Catholic Church in Spain a legal status superior to the status of other religions in aspects relating to state cooperation with religion. However, not every provision of the Concordat contains a privilege granted to the Catholic Church. Sometimes, Concordat provisions merely make explicit some consequences of the autonomy of religious communities, which is part of their collective right to religious freedom, and apply them to the specific circumstances of the Catholic Church. This is the case, for example, of those articles of the 1979 Agreement on Juridical Affairs that recognize the Church's right "to exercise its apostolic mission"; to publicly engage in worship and teaching activities; to provide spiritual assistance to persons staying in military establishments, hospitals, penitentiaries, orphanages or alike centres; to carry out charitable activities; to freely design and modify its internal administrative organization around dioceses or parishes; and the Holy See's and bishops' right to enact and publish provisions related to the Church's government, and to freely communicate between them as well as with the clergy and the faithful.[54]

Since 1979, the Concordat has been modified in one occasion, through an atypical channel. On 22 December 2006, through an exchange of letters between the Spanish Ministry of Foreign Affairs and the Apostolic Nunciature in Spain, the Catholic Church renounced the exemption from paying VAT granted by the 1979 Agreement on Economic Affairs. This renouncement was done to accommodate the Spanish law to European Union law and in exchange for a raise in the percentage of income tax that citizens could voluntarily donate every year to the Catholic Church.[55]

54 See Agreement on Juridical Affairs, Arts. I, II, IV and V.

55 *Intercambio de Notas entre la Nunciatura Apostólica en España y el Ministerio de Asuntos Exteriores y Cooperación, referidas a los acuerdos sobre asignación tributaria a favor de la Iglesia Católica*, 22 December 2006. The text of this exchange of letters has not been officially published, but its text is available in Internet, for example at http://www.unav.es/ima/legislacion_prueba/eclesiastica/2006/6.html, accessed 6 January 2018.

Some of the Concordat provisions have been developed by other domestic agreements, either at a national level, normally between the government and the Bishops Conference, without the need of a parliamentary ratification; or at a regional level, between a regional government and the relevant diocesan bishops. These agreements are usually known as 'minor' agreements. At a national level, for instance, there have been agreements on the Catholic religious assistance in hospitals[56] and penitentiaries;[57] and on the salaries of religion teachers in public schools.[58] Some other Concordat provisions have been developed by unilateral state regulations that had been previously negotiated with the Bishops Conference, as, for instance, the royal decrees on the social security of the clergy and members of religious orders.[59]

2. *Cooperation Agreements with Other Religious Communities*

The system of cooperation agreements in Spain constitutes an innovation without precedents in Spanish law and has its origin in the maintenance of the Spanish tradition of concordats with the Catholic Church after the 1978 Constitution. If the Concordat of 1979 with the Holy See constituted the first juridical materialization of the constitutional principle of state cooperation with religion, the principles of equality and neutrality moved the legislator, one year and a half later, to introduce in the 1980 Organic Law

56 See *Acuerdo* of 24 July 1985, *sobre asistencia religiosa católica en centros hospitalarios públicos*; and *Convenio* of 23 April 1996, *sobre asistencia religiosa católica en los Centros hospitalarios del Instituto Nacional de Salud.*

57 See *Orden* of 24 November 1993, *por la que se dispone la publicación del Acuerdo sobre la asistencia religiosa católica en los Establecimientos penitenciarios.*

58 See *Orden* of 9 April 1999 decreeing the publication of the *Convenio* of 26 February 1999 *sobre el régimen económico-laboral de las personas que, no perteneciendo a los Cuerpos de Funcionarios Docentes, están encargadas de la enseñanza de la religión católica en los centros públicos de Educación Infantil, de Educación Primaria y de Educación Secundaria.*

59 See *Real Decreto* 2398/1977, of 27 August 1977, *por el que se regula la seguridad social del clero*; and *Real Decreto* 3325/1981, of 29 December 1981, *por el que se incorpora al Régimen Especial de la Seguridad Social de los Trabajadores por Cuenta propia o Autónomos a los religiosos y religiosas de la Iglesia Católica.*

on Religious Freedom a sort of adapted version of the concordats and make it available for other religious denominations.[60]

The LOLR took as a main point of reference the analogous pre-existing institutions in Italian law (the *intese*, created by the 1948 Republican Constitution), and added some nuances. Among them, the most important is perhaps the element of 'well-known roots' as the key criterion utilized to determine the religious denominations that can be entitled to a formal cooperation agreement with the state because of their social rooting. According to Article 7 LOLR, the state may conclude, when appropriate, cooperation agreements with those churches or religious communities that meet two requirements: first, to be registered in the Registry of Religious Entities; and second, to have acquired "well-known roots" (*notorio arraigo*) in Spain. Naturally, the latter is the most significant requirement.

Article 7 LOLR is not very precise in providing criteria for determining if a religious community has well-known roots in Spain.[61] It only refers to the territorial extension and the number of believers of a community. Historical rooting, expansion in other countries, transparent organization and a substantial minimum – but imprecise – number of adherents in Spain are some of the criteria used in practice to decide on particular cases, but they have been utilized with vagueness in order not to limit the government's discretion. The only clear rule was a practical one, namely that recognition of well-known roots requires an affirmative opinion of the Advisory Commission on Religious Freedom. In 2015, the government introduced a new regulation aimed at avoiding imprecisions and arbitrariness in the future recognition of well-known roots.[62] According to Article 3 of this regulation, a religious community must meet five requirements to be recognized well-known roots. Three of those requirements are clear and relatively easy to prove. First, they must be registered in the RER for at least 30 years (or 15 years, in the case of religious communities at least 60 years old that can provide evidence of recognition in foreign countries).

60 For further details and bibliography, see Martínez-Torrón, *Separatismo y cooperación en los acuerdos del Estado con las minorías religiosas*, 1994, pp. 20-36.

61 On the possible meanings of this new and peculiar concept of Spanish law, see Martínez-Torrón, *Separatismo y cooperación*, pp. 88-95. See also, from a perspective closer in time to the Organic Law on Religious Freedom, Villa Robledo, "Reflexiones en torno al concepto de 'notorio arraigo' en el art. 7 de la Ley Orgánica de libertad religiosa," 1985, pp. 143 ff.

62 *Real Decreto 593/2015*, 3 July 2015, *por el que se regula la declaración de notorio arraigo de las confesiones religiosas en España*.

Second, they must be present in at least 10 Spanish regions (Spain has 17 regions and 2 autonomous cities, Ceuta and Melilla). And third, they must have at least 100 places of worship or internal communities registered in the RER. Two other requisites, however, are less precise and leave much room for discretionary assessment: they must have "an adequate structure and representation" and they must show "evidence of their presence and active participation in Spanish life".

In any event, recognition of well-known roots is not sufficient, by itself, to reach a cooperation agreement with the state. The procedure normally begins when a religious denomination communicates to the government – in particular to the general directorate competent on religious affairs – its desire to conclude an agreement. The government is free to provide an affirmative or negative answer – or no answer at all – for the law does not stipulate any objective legal criteria that limit or compel the government's decisions on the acceptance or refusal of churches' requests. The decision to initiate the proceedings eventually leading to a cooperation agreement relies entirely on the political will of the government.

If we look at the years passed since the enactment of the LOLR, it is logical to think that cooperation agreements have been an under-applied institution thus far. Only three agreements have been concluded, respectively, with three federations of religious communities: Evangelical, Jewish and Islamic. All of them have a very similar content and were approved by statute the same day: 10 November 1992.[63] The issues addressed by the 1992 Agreements are inspired by the Concordat experience. Moreover, the content of the three Agreements is very similar, for the government was determined to establish the same level and essentially the same expressions of cooperation for the three religions. There are only minor differences between them.

In the last two decades, the three federations signatories of the 1992 Agreements have addressed the government asking for a development of

---

63 *Ley* 24/1992 (*Federación de Entidades Religiosas Evangélicas de España*, FEREDE), *Ley* 25/1992 (*Federación de Comunidades Israelitas de España*, FCI) and *Ley* 26/1992 (*Comisión Islámica de España*, o CIE), all of them of 10 November 1992. Among the abundant bibliography published on the agreements regulated by the Organic Law on Religious Freedom, see Martínez-Torrón, *Separatismo y cooperación*, pp. 20-36; Mantecón, *Los acuerdos del Estado con las confesiones acatólicas*, 1995; and *Acuerdos del Estado español con confesiones religiosas minoritarias*, ed. Victor Reina and M Ángeles Félix, 1996.

diverse aspects of their respective agreements, with varying degrees of success. Their claims refer above all to religious assistance in public institutions, state economic cooperation, and religious instruction in public schools. So far, there are two main aspects of the 1992 Agreements that have been developed by other 'minor' agreements, or by unilateral state regulations previously negotiated with the respective religious federation: religious assistance in penitentiaries,[64] and the conditions for the appointment and salaries of religion teachers in public schools (with the Evangelical and Islamic Federations).[65]

Since 1992, no government – socialist or conservative – has expressed a minimum interest in starting the negotiation of a cooperation agreement with any other religious community, despite the fact that, since 2003, four other religious denominations have been recognized well-known roots: the Church of Jesus Christ of Latter-Day Saints (Mormons), Jehovah's Witnesses, the Spanish Buddhist Federation and a consortium of Christian Orthodox Churches. These religious groups have repeatedly expressed to the government their wish to have a cooperation agreement, or at least to enjoy some of the legal benefits granted by the 1992 Agreements, but none of them has a reasonable perspective to commence a negotiation process in the next future.

IV. Current Challenges

The Spanish system of relations between state and religion, though reasonable overall, is certainly perfectible. Equality is perhaps the principle most

---

64 *Real Decreto* 710/2006, 9 June 2006, *de desarrollo de los Acuerdos de Cooperación firmados por el Estado con la Federación de Entidades Religiosas Evangélicas de España, la Federación de Comunidades Judías de España y la Comisión Islámica de España, en el ámbito de la asistencia religiosa penitenciaria*; and *Convenio de colaboración del estado con la comisión islámica de España para la financiación de los gastos que ocasione el desarrollo de la asistencia religiosa en los establecimientos penitenciarios de competencia estatal*, of 24 October 2007.

65 *Convenio sobre designación y régimen económico de las personas encargadas de la enseñanza religiosa evangélica, en los centros docentes públicos de educación primaria y secundaria*, published by *Resolución* of 23 April 1996; and *Convenio sobre designación y régimen económico de las personas encargadas de la enseñanza religiosa islámica, en los centros docentes públicos de educación primaria y secundaria*, published by *Resolución* of 23 April 1996.

difficult to apply in practice, in this as in other areas of constitutional law, for there is not always a clear dividing line marking the end of what is open to the discretion of public authorities and the beginning of what is obliged by the Constitution. Indeed, probably the biggest challenges of the current Spanish system of relation between state and religion refer to the implementation of the equality principle.

The 1980 Organic Law on Religious Freedom, together with the 1978 Constitution, created a common legal framework applicable to all individuals and religious groups, and guaranteeing a comparable protection of religious freedom for all of them. However, the LOLR left a door open to inequalities in the application of the constitutional principle of state cooperation with religion. As a consequence of the subsequent implementation of the LOLR by various governments, such inequalities are today a reality and not a mere possibility. These inequalities refer to a variety of issues, in areas such as state's economic cooperation with religion, recognition of religious marriages, or religious teaching in public schools, among others.[66]

The inequalities in state cooperation with religion have their main cause in two characteristics of the Spanish system of relations between state and religion, connected both with its legal design and its practical application. First, registration in the Registry of Religious Entities, as such, does not confer any privileged or specific legal position to religious denominations (apart from some protection by criminal law, more theoretical than real). No particular legal benefit is attached to registration. Second, according to Article 7 LOLR, well-known roots in Spain are an indispensable requisite to sign a cooperation agreement with the state but, on the one hand, the decision about concluding a cooperation agreement is entirely in the hands of the government and, on the other hand, recognition of well-known roots does not produce, per se, any other specific legal effects (apart from the right to have a member in the CALR).

The combination of those two factors have produced the result that, in practice, the specific state cooperation with religion foreseen by the Constitution is reserved exclusively to those religious communities that have signed a formal agreement or covenant with the state[67] – only three, so far, dating back to 1992, as indicated above. There is almost no state coopera-

66 For an explanation and analysis of these issues, see Martínez-Torrón, *Religion and Law in Spain.*

67 Religious groups can also obtain legal benefits or advantages through the legislation generally applicable to foundations or to non-profit activities – provided, nat-

tion with other minority religious denominations registered in the RER or even with the five religious communities that have been recognized 'well-known roots' (even though some of them count more members than the Jewish Federation). This has led to a multi-tier system of church-state relations in Spain that, in its actual configuration, is certainly questionable from the perspective of the constitutional principle of equality. To make things worse, the Constitutional Court has not taken a clear stance against those apparent – and unjustified – inequalities in the Spanish law on religious denominations.[68]

In the last two decades, there have been numerous claims on the part of religious minorities alleging that they are subject to discriminatory treatment in comparison with the Catholic Church or with the Evangelical, Jewish and Muslim federations. Those minorities request a fair and equal treatment in issues such as tax benefits and other means of state economic cooperation, recognition of the civil effects of religious marriages, or the possibility of imparting religious instruction in public schools. Many scholars have the clear perception that religious equality is still under-achieved in the Spanish law, especially with regard to minority religions without cooperation agreement with the state. However, neither the governments nor the courts have been receptive, thus far, to the situation of minority religions without cooperation agreement.

Part of the problem resides in the fact that, although there are many of these minority religions, they represent only a residual percentage of the country's population – but still several hundred thousand people. Since 1992 (the year in which the cooperation agreements with the Evangelical, Jewish and Islamic communities were signed), no government, either socialist or conservative, has taken seriously the need to put an end to these 'residual' inequalities of the Spanish law on religion. This fact could be expressive of a certain degree of satisfaction with the status quo. Or perhaps it is just an expression of conformism, and of lack of clear political will, in view of the difficulties to effect legislative amendments in this area.

---

urally, that they meet the relevant legal requirements. This is applicable, in particular, to the area of tax benefits. But this is no specific state cooperation with religion, as mandated by Art. 16.3 of the Constitution.

68 See, in more detail, Martínez-Torrón, *Religious Freedom and Democratic Change*, pp. 802-809.

D. Religion and Politics

I. Influence of Religion in Politics

As Spain is a country of ancient Catholic tradition, the influence of the Catholic Church and institutions in social life is enormous – from the many religious symbols that can be seen everywhere to the presence and activity of Catholic organizations in public life. However, there are no specific positions reserved for Catholic bishops or other religious leaders either in parliament or in regional legislatures. Apart from their representatives in the Advisory Commission on Religious Freedom, formal representation of churches or religious communities in the realm of politics is reduced to mixed consultative commissions constituted for specific purposes (including the commissions established for the application of the cooperation agreements with the state or the temporary commissions for the negotiation of difficult issues of common interest). There is no other churches' representation in governmental, administrative or legislative bodies. That would be considered incompatible with the principle of state neutrality as established by the Constitution and interpreted by the Constitutional Court, which has clearly affirmed that neutrality "bans any sort of confusion between state and religious functions".[69]

Catholic bishops do not endeavour to intervene directly in strictly political issues of secular nature, but they often address the general public to express publicly and clearly what they consider to be the right doctrine with regard to questions of moral consequence. To a large extent, their public discourse places great emphasis on the preservation of Spanish Catholic identity, both formally and substantially. Spanish bishops often speak out – individually or collectively, as the Bishops Conference – against governmental or legislative actions deemed to be detrimental for public morals. In the recent past, the most important cases have been some measures adopted by a socialist government, in particular the legal reforms on family law in 2005 (above all, the legalization of same-sex marriages, and the simplification and facilitation of divorce proceedings[70]),

69 STC 24/1982, *fundamento jurídico* 1.

70 Operated, respectively, by the *Ley* 13/2005, 1 July 2005, *por la que se modifica el Código Civil en materia de derecho a contraer matrimonio*, and by the *Ley* 15/2005, 8 July 2005, *por la que se modifican el Código Civil y la Ley de Enjuiciamiento Civil en materia de separación y divorcio.*

the liberalization of the right to abortion in 2010,[71] and the introduction of a compulsory school subject called 'education for citizenship', which touched upon sensitive moral issues and was deemed to pave the way for moral indoctrination in public schools.[72] In all those cases, Spanish bishops have expressed plainly their views in formal pronouncements and have spread them widely through the media and the web pages of the Bishops Conference. In addition, they also try to stimulate Catholic citizens to move them to take an active part in changing those laws. In the last years, the economic crisis has been another recurrent theme in the bishops' public discourse, urging Catholics to act in solidarity with people in need.

With the same aim of reminding Catholic moral doctrines vis-à-vis specific issues, the Bishops Conference normally makes some pronouncements before general elections. They never make any explicit reference, positive or negative, to political parties but they mention moral questions that Catholics must take into account when deciding their vote; these questions can easily be linked to the programmes of the relevant political parties. The main topics mentioned in those public statements are: the protection of the right to life, family policies, social and distributive justice, the guarantee of parents' rights over the moral education of their children, violence and terrorism. The Bishops Conference has made similar pronouncements before other political consultations of significance – for instance, the 2005 referendum on the European Constitution – and with the occasion of other events with political impact, including relevant decisions adopted by the Constitutional Court or by the European Court of Human Rights.[73] In recent years, the political crisis generated by pro-independence movements in Catalonia has divided Spanish bishops. Although most bishops are against the separation of Catalonia, the Bishops Conference has taken no official stance on this issue and has just insisted that it is

---

71 Operated by the *Ley Orgánica* 2/2010, 3 March 2010, *de salud sexual y reproductiva y de la interrupción voluntaria del embarazo.*

72 Operated by the *Ley Orgánica* 2/2006, of 3 May 2006, *de Educación.* For a detailed (and critical) analysis of the law, see Ruano Espina, "Objeción de conciencia a la Educación para la Ciudadanía," 2008, pp. 1-61.

73 For example, the Constitutional Court's judgment on the constitutionality of same-sex marriages (STC 198/2012), or the ECtHR's chamber judgment *Sindicatul Păstorul Cel Bun v. Rumania,* 31 January 2012. The documents of the Spanish Bishops Conference can be found in its data base at http://www.conferenciaepiscopal.es/base-documental/, accessed 6 January 2018.

necessary to respect democratic rules and institutions as well as to engage in a dialogue between opposite political positions.[74]

Minority religions' leaders tend to intervene much less in public debate. They normally avoid making public pronouncements similar to those of the Catholic bishops, even if they share the same moral views, and tend to intervene only apropos of issues that concern them directly. This has been the case, for example, of some questions of interest for Muslims, as the use of hijab in public schools or the prohibition of full veil in municipal facilities, which have led representatives of Islamic communities to publicly defend the Muslim women's right to wear the garments of their choice. In 2005, in the first anniversary of the jihadist terrorist bombing of 11 March 2004 in Madrid, the Secretary General of the Islamic Commission of Spain published a fatwa against Bin Laden and Al Qaeda, in very strong terms, declaring out of Islam all those who misuse the sharia to commit and justify terrorist attacks.[75] Among minority religions, Islam tends to play a more active role in public debate through the Internet.[76] In recent years, with the occasion of various terrorist attacks by self-proclaimed Islamist organizations, it has been frequent that Islamic communities and leaders make public statements condemning such attacks and claiming that Islam is a religion of peace.[77] The Jewish Federation is very active in denouncing and disseminating information about anti-Semitism.[78]

In Spain there are no religious political parties. Most people of Christian-Democrat ideas are now militant in the Popular Party, one of the two most powerful parties in Spain, which does not have religious affiliation but claims to be based on – among other values – 'the Christian humanism of Western tradition'. More clear and explicit used to be the Christian-Democrat inspiration of a regional Catalan party (*Unió Democràtica de Catalunya*), which, in coalition with other Catalan Party (*Convergència Democràtica de Catalunya*), had representation both in the regional and

74 See http://www.conferenciaepiscopal.es/declaracion-la-comision-permanente-ante-la-situacion-cataluna/, accessed 6 January 2018.

75 See the text of the fatwa at http://www.webislam.com/noticias/43520-la_comision_islamica_de_espana_emite_una_fatua_condenando_el_terrorismo_y_al_gru.html, accessed 6 January 2018.

76 See, for instance, http://www.webislam.com, accessed 24 October 2016.

77 See, for instance, http://comisionislamicadeespana.org and https://www.webislam.com, both accessed 6 January 2018.

78 See http://observatorioantisemitismo.fcje.org, accessed 6 January 2018.

national legislatures; the coalition broke in 2015, and two years later, as a consequence of electoral setbacks, the party decided to dissolve. No other religion has inspired a political party in Spain. At a national level, it is commonly assumed that the relationships of Catholic bishops are normally better with the Popular Party than with the Socialist Party.

Although Spain is no longer a Catholic state, the Spanish monarchy and the royal family do not conceal or dissimulate their traditional links with the Catholic Church. All married members of the royal family have celebrated a Catholic canonical marriage. Religious Christian symbols are frequently visible in the royal palaces and offices. In the King's formal Christmas address, which is broadcast by TV and radio to the entire country in the evening of every 24 December, a traditional Christmas crèche can be clearly seen in the King's office. These facts are commonly accepted and have been only occasionally criticized by left-wing politicians of republican orientation.

II. Political Influence in Religion

In Spain, the government does not control the life of religious communities or, more generally, the religious lives of citizens. In the Ministry of Justice, there is a department with specific competence to deal with religious juridical persons and, in general, with competence on religious freedom issues: the Vice-Directorate General of Relations with Religious Communities, which is part of the Directorate General of International Legal Cooperation and Relations with Religious Communities.[79] Its function, however, is not to control religion in Spain but to facilitate and organize the relationships of cooperation between the government and religious communities, in application of Article 16.3 of the Constitution, as well to take the appropriate measures for a better protection of religious freedom of individuals and groups.

Article 6 LOLR specifically guarantees the autonomy of religious communities with respect to their internal affairs. This includes their self-organization and the appointment of their leaders and ministers. There are some partial exceptions in the case of the Catholic Church. For example,

79 See the Directorate General's site in: http://www.mjusticia.gob.es/cs/Satellite/es/1215197982464/Estructura_P/1215198297241/Detalle.html, accessed 6 January 2018.

according to the 1976 Agreement between Spain and the Holy See, the Catholic Church is obliged to notify the government the name of a newly elected bishop prior to his appointment, in case the government wants to express some political objection (which the Holy See is not bound to accept). Moreover, the appointment of the Vicar General for the Army (*Vicario General Castrense*) continues to be appointed according to a system similar to the one stipulated in 1941 and 1953 – the Spanish government and the Vatican nuncio, by common agreement, propose a tern of names, authorized by the Holy See, out of which the King will choose one and propose him to the Pope for appointment. These rules tend to be justified by historical reasons, as well as by the special social and legal position of the Catholic Church in Spain. In practice, the selection of the Vicar General is done by the Catholic Church with full independence.

No similar state intervention exists with respect to other religious communities. The government, however, has indirectly intervened once in the organization of religious minorities in Spain. After the promulgation of the LOLR in 1980, when the main minority religious communities took the initiative to begin the negotiations of cooperation agreements with the state – in particular Protestants, Jews and, later, Muslims – the government made very clear to them that it would only negotiate with one interlocutor of the respective religion, i.e., one Protestant interlocutor, one Jewish interlocutor and one Islamic interlocutor. This forced the relevant communities to organize themselves in three respective federations. These three federations were formed for the exclusive purpose of the dialogue with the government, before and after the Agreements. Nevertheless, their representatives have acknowledged that, in the long run, the existence and functioning of the federations has had an influence on the internal life of those religious communities – a positive influence, in their opinion, for it has contributed to create stronger links of collaboration between independent religious communities.

III. Interaction between Religion and State

The Advisory Commission on Religious Freedom (CALR), created by the 1980 LOLR, is the main body in which interaction between government and religious communities is supposed to occur. As explained above,[80] this commission is competent to study and give opinions on all legislative and governmental initiatives relating to religious freedom, and one-third of its members are representatives of the main religions existing in the country – those with recognized 'well-known roots' or *notorio arraigo*. Nevertheless, the negotiation of the most important measures affecting the interests of the Catholic Church has often taken place out of the CALR. For religious minorities, instead, the CALR is a useful forum to manifest their needs and proposals to the government, without prejudice to their respective efforts for parallel bilateral negotiations.

In accordance with the international legal personality of the Holy See, the Spanish state and the Vatican have diplomatic relationships. There is a papal nuncio in Madrid, as well as a Spanish ambassador to the Holy See, in Rome. In the numerous times that, since the election of John Paul II, the Pope has visited Spain, he has been received not only as a spiritual leader but also with the honours befitting a head of state.

There are diverse expressions of the interaction between Catholic religion and state in public life. The following are just some examples. When public official takes office, he is given the choice between pledging allegiance to the Constitution by oath on the Bible and the crucifix or by promise 'on his conscience and honour'.[81] Many Catholic religious holidays are considered also civil labour holidays – at a national, a regional or a local level – e.g., Christmas, Epiphany, Good Friday, Saint James (patron saint of Spain), the Assumption of the Virgin, and Saint Joseph. It is considered normal, in some places, the tradition of a protocolary presence of public authorities, as well as army or police units, in public solemn manifestations of Catholic worship, such as religious processions in Corpus Christi day or during the Holy Week. The Constitutional Court has found nothing unconstitutional in these customary practices, as far that no public official is obliged to take part in religious ceremonies against his will.[82]

Although more reduced, there is also some interaction between state and other religions. For instance, the public foundation *Pluralismo y Convivencia* has been disseminating, in the last years, a calendar with indica-

80 See above, subsection C.II.2. of this paper.

81 See *Real Decreto* 707/1979, 8 April 1979, *por el que se establece la fórmula de juramento en cargos y funciones públicas*.

82 See STC 177/1996 and STC 101/2004.

tion of the festivities of the most important religious communities existing in Spain, including not only Christian (Catholic, Protestant and Orthodox), Jewish and Islamic holidays, but also Mormon, Jehovah's Witnesses and Buddhist holidays; and the same foundation has cooperated with the Evangelical and Islamic federations in the production of textbook for religious instruction in public schools.[83] Since 2004, Spain commemorates the Holocaust Remembrance Day in January; on that date, there are various public commemorations in Spanish cities, in national and regional legislatures – with particular solemnity in Madrid – with the presence of representatives of the Jewish communities together with high public officials.

Religious leaders or ministers are not subject to any disqualification to stand for elections or to become public officials. No religious leader is appointed as such for a position in state bodies, with the exception, for obvious reasons, of the Advisory Commission on Religious Freedom.

E. Religion and Culture

I. Religion and Art

The Constitution (Article 46) provides that "public authorities shall guarantee the preservation and shall foster the enrichment of the historical, cultural and artistic heritage of the peoples of Spain […] irrespective of its legal regime and ownership". This obligation of the state, therefore, extends to heritage of religious origin and ownership, which in Spain is almost entirely Catholic. Articles 148 and 149 of the Constitution distribute this public responsibility between central and regional authorities.

Protection of religious freedom requires that, in the preservation of religious cultural heritage, which is often destined to worship, evangelization or other religious purposes, the state harmonizes its *cultural* value with its *religious* value for the Catholic Church. This may sometimes raise difficult questions, for instance when the remodelling or renovation of a historical temple for purposes of worship enters into conflict with the preservation of the original shape of the building.[84]

---

83 See http://www.pluralismoyconvivencia.es/publicaciones/, accessed 3 January 2018. This foundation is under the protectorate of the Ministry of Justice.

84 This was, for instance, the situation in a case decided by the Supreme Court in 2009, in relation to some works done in the cathedral of the city of Avila (STS

The Concordat with the Catholic Church refers to ecclesiastical heritage, in terms of mutual collaboration between Church and state, in the 1979 Agreement on Education and Cultural Affairs. After emphasizing in the preamble that ecclesiastical heritage constitutes an essential part of the national legacy, Article XV, first paragraph, of the Agreement embodies the compromise of mutual cooperation that must dominate the activity of church and state in this area. This paragraph has been sometimes criticized for its too general approach, as well as for the fact that it mentions specifically only the cultural side of ecclesiastical heritage but not its religious value, purposes and inspiration. In any event, the second paragraph of the same article envisaged the constitution, within a year, of a mixed church-state commission. That commission was created in 1980 and elaborated a legal framework for the joint activity of church and state in this area. The guidelines that defined such framework were, in summary, the following: the preferential religious use of ecclesiastical heritage must be respected; the religious use of ecclesiastical heritage must be harmonized with activities of scientific and artistic study; ecclesiastical heritage must be widely available for public visits but without detriment to its religious use and scientific study; and ecclesiastical heritage, as far as possible, shall be exhibited in their original location. These guidelines are supposed to be applied to all types of ecclesiastical heritage or historical, cultural and artis-

528/2009, 10 February 2009). The diocese, after obtaining the appropriate administrative licenses, carried out some remodeling works in the main chapel, with the aim of adapting its old structure to the norms of the Second Vatican Council and facilitating that the largest possible number of faithful could duly attend liturgical ceremonies and keep the altar in sight. Upon request of the Royal Academy of History, which argued that the remodeling could endanger the conservation of some old gravestones, the superior regional court ordered that the chapel be returned to its original condition. The Supreme Court confirmed the judgment with a reasoning that tried to reach a balance between the cultural and the religious values present in the cathedral. After examination of the expert evidence, the Court reached the conclusion that there were technical choices that permitted to make compatible the conservation of the endangered gravestones with the adaptation of the main chapel to the religious purposes legitimately pursued by the diocese; and in such situation, the regional court was right in ordering the removal of the remodelling works already realized. Had there been a situation of incompatibility of interests, the Supreme Court added, the liturgical use of a religious building would have prevailed over its secular use (understood as the citizens' right to contemplate the original funerary monuments). See, for a comment on this decision, Meseguer, "Hacia una nueva comprensión de la regulación estatal del patrimonio cultural eclesiástico," 2012, pp. 8-10.

tic value, including movable and immovable property, archives and documents, libraries and archaeological sites.

A large part of the church-state cooperation in the area of ecclesiastical heritage has taken place at a regional level (Spain is divided into regions or *comunidades autónomas*). Regional legislation and regulations are many and diverse but some common features are identifiable. First, the reference to future specific agreements; second, the constitution of mixed commissions with members that represent regional authorities and the Catholic Church; these commissions are conceived as consultative bodies with limited decision-making power; third, the interest in harmonizing the religious and the cultural aspects of ecclesiastical heritage; and fourth, the interest in fostering the collaboration with local authorities.[85]

Article 13 of the 1992 Agreements with the Jewish and Islamic communities also refer to the collaboration between the state and the relevant federation in order to preserve, catalogue and make available to society Jewish and Islamic heritage, respectively, of historical, artistic and cultural value. This reference must be understood broadly to heritage of Jewish and Islamic origin and nature, not necessarily ownership, for the largest part of the heritage that was originally Jewish or Islamic has become secularized or has passed to the Catholic Church in the course of time. As in the Concordat, it seems surprising that Article 13 of the Agreements only mentions the cultural value of Jewish and Islamic heritage but not its religious signification. The 1992 Agreements did not envisage the creation of ad hoc mixed commissions. The Evangelical Federation renounced having this article in its agreement, considering that there was not sufficient Protestant historical heritage in Spain to justify it. In contrast to the Spanish experience on Catholic ecclesiastical heritage, Article 13 of the 1992 Agreements has had virtually no further development.

Historical, artistic or cultural heritage of religious origin and ownership attracts many visitors all over Spain and is – directly and indirectly – a large source of income for the country within the tourism sector. This in-

---

85 See, for instance, *Ley* 10/1998, 9 July 1998, *de Patrimonio Histórico de la Comunidad de Madrid*; *Ley* 3/1999, 10 March 1999, *del Patrimonio Cultural Aragonés*; *Ley* 4/1999, 15 March 1999, *de Patrimonio Histórico de Canarias*; *Ley* 27/1999, 29 March 1999, *de Patrimonio Histórico y Cultural de Extremadura*; *Ley* 7/2004, 18 October 2004, *de Patrimonio Cultural, Histórico y Artístico de La Rioja*. For a complete guide of the laws and agreements on ecclesiastical heritage, see Aldanondo and Corral, *Nuevo código del patrimonio cultural de la Iglesia,* 2013.

cludes not only religious buildings but also many other artistic expressions, such as paintings, sculptures, codices, liturgical ornaments, music and religious celebrations (e.g., the Catholic processions during the Holy Week, above all in southern Spain and Castile). Festivals of religious music are more and more popular in Spanish cities. Christian music is naturally the main focus, but the music of traditional religious minorities is gradually gaining attention from the public. There is, for instance, an annual festival of Sephardic music held in Cordoba since 2001.

II. Religion and Media

The Spanish Criminal Code imposes some limitations on freedom of expression for the protection of religious feelings as well as with the intention to eradicate hate speech.[86] Those limitations are conceived as means to protect religious and ideological pluralism by fostering religious tolerance and respect.

In line with those provisions, the Concordat, in particular Article XIV of the 1979 Agreement on Education and Cultural Affairs between Spain and the Holy See, provides that "safeguarding the principles of religious freedom and freedom of expression, the state shall ensure that the feelings of Catholics are respected in state-owned media, and shall establish the appropriate agreements with the Bishops Conference on this issue." No subsequent agreement has been actually signed with the Bishops Conference in application of this provision of the Concordat. The 1992 Agreements with the Evangelical, Jewish and Islamic Federations contain no equivalent article.

In any event, both the provisions of the Criminal Code and the Concordat are very rarely applied. Religion and religious communities are often in the media and not necessarily depicted in objective or merely informative terms. Frequently, information about religion is biased and based on an emotional view rather than on factual data. Strong criticism of religion or religions is not an exception, especially in privately owned media. When referred to Christianity, such critic language not rarely becomes blasphemous. Islam is often implicitly or subliminally associated with ter-

86 See Arts. 510, 515 and 525 of the Spanish Criminal Code. For further details about the protection of religious freedom by means of criminal law, see Martínez-Torrón, *Religion and Law in Spain*, pp. 477-485.

rorism, violence or women's discrimination. Now and then, there are sensationalist campaigns or prejudiced information about atypical minority religions, usually qualified, indiscriminately, as 'sects'.

From a different perspective, the media provide some occasions for state cooperation with religion, in line with Article 16.3 of the Constitution. Spanish law and praxis grants religious communities the right to access state-owned media – radio and television, for there are not state-owned journals in Spain. Article 20.3 of the Constitution recognizes such right to access, in very general terms, for all "significant social and political groups", and not only for religious communities.

Those constitutional guidelines have been applied to the particular case of state radio and television (RTVE) by Article 28 of the Law 17/2006,[87] also in very general terms. Such provision emphasizes the need to guarantee, in RTVE programmes, "the expression of the social, ideological, political and cultural plurality of Spanish society", and envisages the possibility that social and political groups are granted specific programmes in radio and television. The development of this article has been very precise with respect to political parties, but has remained very vague with reference to religious groups. For instance, there is no specific definition of the concept 'significant group' as applied to religious communities. This term is often understood as applicable, at least, to all those communities that have been recognized 'well-known roots' (*notorio arraigo*) in the light of Article 7.1 LOLR.[88]

In practice, however, religious programmes have been mostly granted in RTVE to the Catholic Church and, with less time and programmes assigned, to the three religious federations signatory of the 1992 Agreements.[89] Thus, the practical recognition of Spanish religious pluralism from the perspective of state cooperation is restricted, once again, to those religious communities that have concluded a formal cooperation agreement with the state. The situation is rather similar in the norms that regulate the media owned and managed by the regions or *comunidades autóno-*

87 *Ley* 17/2006, 5 June 2006, *de la radio y la televisión de titularidad estatal.*

88 See above, subsection C.III.2. of this paper.

89 The religious programs in RTVE can be found in the relevant Internet pages: http://www.rtve.es/alacarta/programas/tve/religiosos/1/, accessed 6 January 2018, and http://www.rtve.es/alacarta/programas/rne/religiosos/1/, accessed 6 January 2018.

mas, whose respective laws are also comparable to the law on RTVE in this aspect.[90]

While the Protestant, Jewish and Islamic Federations each have a weekly programme in RTVE (television and radio), the Catholic Church has several weekly programmes. They include the broadcast of the holy mass on Sundays. In addition, the big Catholic festivities on Christmas and the Holy Week have traditionally received a special treatment, which includes the broadcast of pontifical masses and other religious services from the Vatican.

The Catholic Bishops Conference has its own news agency[91] and controls several media, in the areas of radio, television and written press.[92] Of particular influence is one of its two radio stations (COPE), which ranks third in radio audience share in Spain. The Evangelical and Jewish Federations control one radio station each, with low audience share. In Spain, there is no prohibition or restriction of religious programming in radio and television. The only limitations on religious broadcasting are indirect, derived from the administrative general regulations of media using radio and television waves, which is a state-regulated and not a free market.

Bibliography

Aldanondo, Isabel, and Carlos Corral, *Nuevo código del patrimonio cultural de la Iglesia*, 2nd ed., Madrid: Edice, 2013.

Amorós, Jose Javier, *La libertad religiosa en la Constitución española de 1978*, Madrid: Tecnos, 1984.

Blanco, María, *La primera ley española de libertad religiosa*, Pamplona: Eunsa, 1999.

Calvo Álvarez, Joaquín, *Los principios del derecho eclesiástico español en las sentencias del Tribunal Constitucional*, Pamplona: Navarra Gráfica, 1999.

Chélini-Pont, Blandine, and Jeremy Gunn, *Dieu en France et aux États-Unis: Quand les mythes font la loi*, Paris: Berg, 2005.

Ciáurriz, María J, *La libertad religiosa en el derecho español. La Ley Orgánica de Libertad Religiosa*, Madrid: Tecnos, 1984.

90 See for further details and references Rossell, "El derecho de acceso de las minorías religiosas a los medios públicos de comunicación," 2010, pp. 127-150.

91 See http://www.agenciasic.es, accessed 6 January 2018.

92 See http://www.conferenciaepiscopal.es/medios-comunicacion-participa-la-cee/, accessed 6 January 2018.

Combalía, Zoila, "Los límites del derecho de libertad religiosa," in VV.AA., *Tratado de Derecho eclesiástico*, Pamplona: Eunsa, 1994, pp. 471-510.

Corral, Carlos, "Valoración comparada de la legislación española de libertad religiosa," *Revista Española de Derecho Canónico* 24, 68 (1968): 315-338.

del Torco, José Maldonado y Fernández, "Los primeros años de vigencia del Concordato de 1953," *Revista Española de Derecho Canónico* 12 (1957): 7-28.

El Concordato de 1953 entre España y la Santa Sede, Madrid: Universidad Complutense, 1956.

European Court of Human Rights, *Case "relating to certain aspects on the laws on the use of languages in education in Belgium"*, 23 July 1968.

European Court of Human Rights, *Serif v. Greece*, no. 38178/97, 14 December 1999.

European Court of Human Rights, *Hasan and Chaush v. Bulgaria*, no. 30985/96, 26 October 2000.

European Court of Human Rights, *Metropolitan Church of Bessarabia v. Moldavia*, no. 45701/99, 13 December 2001.

European Court of Human Rights, *Agga v. Greece*, nos. 50776/99 and 52912/99, 17 October 2002.

European Court of Human Rights, *Obst v. Germany*, no. 425/03, 23 September 2010.

European Court of Human Rights, *Schüth v. Germany*, no. 1620/03, 23 September 2010.

Ferrer Ortiz, Javier, "Los principios constitucionales del derecho eclesiástico como sistema," in VV.AA., *Las relaciones entre la Iglesia y el Estado: estudios en memoria del Profesor Pedro Lombardía,* Madrid: Edersa, 1989, pp. 309-322.

Fornés, Juan, *El nuevo sistema concordatario español: Los Acuerdos de 1976 y 1979*, Pamplona: Eunsa, 1980.

García-Peñuela, José M. Vázquez, *El intento concordatario de la Segunda República* (1933-1935), Madrid: Ministerio de Asuntos Exteriores, 1999.

García Villoslada, Ricardo (ed.), *Historia de la Iglesia en España*, Madrid: BAC, 1979-1982.

Hera, Alberto de la, "Actitud del Franquismo ante la Iglesia," in V V.AA., *Iglesia Católica y regímenes autoritarios y democráticos*, Madrid: Edersa, 1987, pp. 43-70.

Herrera Ceballos, Enrique, *El Registro de Entidades Religiosas. Estudio global y sistemático*, Pamplona: Eunsa, 2012.

Herrera Ceballos, Enrique, "Hacia la construcción de un registro fiel reflejo de la realidad. La reforma del Registro de Entidades Religiosas," *Revista General de Derecho Canónico y Derecho Eclesiástico del Estado* 39 (2015): 1-35.

La institución concordataria en la actualidad. Trabajos de la XIII Semana de Derecho Canónico, Salamanca: CSIC, 1971.

Lombardía, Pedro, "Precedentes del derecho eclesiástico español," in VV.AA, *Derecho Eclesiástico del Estado español*, Pamplona: Eunsa, 1980, pp. 151-174.

Lombardía, Pedro, "Actitud de la Iglesia ante el franquismo," in VV.AA., *Iglesia Católica y regímenes autoritarios y democráticos*, Madrid: Edersa, 1987, pp. 81-102.

López Alarcón, Mariano, "La superación de la 'cuestión religiosa' como tema clave de la transición: su expresión jurídica," *Anales de Derecho* 23 (2005): 303-314.

López-Sidro, Ángel, "La cuestión de la reforma del Registro de Entidades Religiosas: examen de as propuestas reglamentarias de 2003 y 2004", in *La libertad religiosa y su regulación legal,* ed. Rafael Navarro-Valls, Joaquín Mantecón and Javier Martínez-Torrón, Madrid: Iustel, 2009, pp. 621-643.

Mantecón, Joaquín, *Los acuerdos del Estado con las confesiones acatólicas*, Jaén: Universidad de Jaén, 1995.

Martín Martínez, Isidoro, "En el segundo centenario del Concordato español de 1753," *Revista Española de Derecho Canónico* 8 (1953): 745-759.

Martínez-Torrón, Javier, *Separatismo y cooperación en los acuerdos del Estado con las minorías religiosas*, Granada: Comares, 1994.

Martínez-Torrón, Javier, "La protección internacional de la libertad religiosa," in " in VV.AA., *Tratado de Derecho eclesiástico*, Pamplona: Eunsa, 1994, pp. 229-237.

Martínez-Torrón, Javier, *Religión, derecho y sociedad. Antiguos y nuevos planteamientos en el derecho eclesiástico del Estado*, Granada: Comares, 1999.

Martínez-Torrón, Javier, "Derecho de Asociación y Confesiones Religiosas en la Constitución de 1931," *Cuestiones Constitucionales* 3 (2000): 91-120.

Martínez-Torrón, Javier, "Freedom of Religion in the Case-Law of the Spanish Constitutional Court", *Brigham Young University Law Review* 2 (2001): 711-754

Martínez-Torrón, Javier, "Limitations on Religious Freedom in the Case Law of the European Court of Human Rights," *Emory International Law Review* 19 (2005): 587-636.

Martínez-Torrón, Javier, "Religious Freedom and Democratic Change in Spain," *Brigham Young University Law Review* 3 (2006): 777-809.

Martínez-Torrón, Javier, *Religion and Law in Spain*, Alphen aan den Rijn: Kluwer, 2013.

Meer, Fernando de, *La cuestión religiosa en las Cortes constituyentes de la Segunda República Española*, Pamplona: Eunsa, 1975.

Meseguer, Silvia, "Hacia una nueva comprensión de la regulación estatal del patrimonio cultural eclesiástico," *Revista General de Derecho Canónico y Derecho Eclesiástico del Estado* 29 (2012): 8-10.

Navarro-Valls, Rafael, "Cómo actuó la Iglesia frente a la Guerra?," in VV.AA., *La Iglesia frente a la Guerra (noviembre 1937)*, Madrid: Unidad, 2005, pp. 203 ff.

Olmos, M Elena, "Personalidad jurídica civil de las entidades religiosas y Registro de Entidades Religiosas," in *La libertad religiosa y su regulación legal,* ed. Rafael Navarro-Valls, Joaquín Mantecón and Javier Martínez-Torrón, Madrid: Iustel, 2009, pp. 577-620.

Ortiz, Ferrer, "Los principios constitucionales del derecho eclesiástico como sistema," in VV.AA., *Las relaciones entre la Iglesia y el Estado. Estudios en memoria del profesor Pedro Lombardía*, Madrid: Edersa 1989, pp. 309-322.

Otaduy, Jorge, "Las cláusulas de salvaguarda de la identidad de las instituciones religiosas. Doctrina y jurisprudencia", in VV.AA., *Las relaciones entre la Iglesia y el Estado: estudios en memoria del Profesor Pedro Lombardía,* Madrid: Edersa, 1989, pp. 363-390.

Palomino, Rafael, *Religión y derecho comparado*, Madrid: Iustel, 2007.

Palomino, Rafael, "Iglesias, confesiones y comunidades religiosas: el concepto legal de confesión religiosa en la LOLR y la doctrina", in *La libertad religiosa y su regulación legal,* ed. Rafael Navarro-Valls, Joaquín Mantecón and Javier Martínez-Torrón, Madrid: Iustel, 2009, pp. 556-575.

Palomino, Rafael, "Religion and Neutrality: Myth, Principle and Meaning," *Brigham Young University Law Review* 3 (2011): 657-689.

Payne, Stanley G., *Spanish Catholicism: An Historical Overview*, Madison: University of Wisconsin Press, 1984.

Reina, Victor, and M Ángeles Félix (eds.), *Acuerdos del Estado español con confesiones religiosas minoritarias*, Madrid: Marcial Pons, 1996.

Rodríguez Chacón, Rafael, *El factor religioso ante el Tribunal Constitucional*, Madrid: Universidad Complutense, 1992.

Rossell, Jaime, "El derecho de acceso de las minorías religiosas a los medios públicos de comunicación", in VV.AA., *Medios de comunicación y pluralismo religioso*, Barcelona: Consejo del Audiovisual de Cataluña, 2010, pp. 127-150.

Ruano Espina, Lourdes, "Objeción de conciencia a la Educación para la Ciudadanía," *Revista General de Derecho Canónico y Derecho Eclesiástico del Estado* 17 (2008): 1-61.

Spanish Constitutional Court, STC 49/1982, FJ 2, 14 July 1982.

Spanish Constitutional Court, STC 144/1988, FJ 1, 12 July 1988.

Spanish Constitutional Court, STC 45/1989, FJ 4, 20 February 1989.

Suárez, Federico, "Génesis del Concordato de 1851," *Ius Canonicum* 3 (1963): 65-249.

Tirapu, Daniel, "Acuerdos Iglesia-Estado en España," in VV.AA., *Europa: una realidad en camino*, Jaén: Seminario Diocesano de Jaén, 1991, pp. 185-208.

Tusell, Javier, "El impacto del Concilio Vaticano II en la política y en la sociedad española," in VV.AA., *El posconcilio en España*, Madrid: Encuentro, 1988, pp. 377-390.

Tusell, Javier, *Spain: From Dictatorship to Democracy*, Malden: Blackwell, 2007.

Villa Robledo, María J, "Reflexiones en torno al concepto de 'notorio arraigo' en el art. 7 de la Ley Orgánica de libertad religiosa," *Anuario de Derecho Eclesiástico del Estado* 1 (1985): 143-184.

Religious Neutrality and its Enemies: The Polish Experience

Wojciech Brzozowski

A. Why Neutrality?

The title of the present chapter clearly alludes to the brilliant and influential work of Karl Popper, *The Open Society and its Enemies*. It is therefore understandable that the opening remarks should justify this intellectual loan which requires both providing an explanation to the metaphor and exploring its limits. Popper's passionate writing was aimed at examining the philosophical roots of totalitarian ideologies as well as defending the principles of liberal democracy and limited government. Obviously, the objectives of this short chapter have not much to do with the political philosophy nor could it be compared by any measure to Popper's astonishing critique of Plato and his followers. The aim of the chapter is to present a critical analysis of the Polish model of Church-State relations, as designed by the Constitution of 1997 and against the background of the European understanding of religious freedom.

It has to be noted that the Republic of Poland, being a member state of the Council of Europe and of the European Union, is supposed to observe the standards of the European legal space.[1] However, when it comes to the relations between the state and religious groups, these standards, in many cases, admit a variety of models to be implemented at the domestic level, in order to respect national traditions of the member states.

The author of the paper does not intend to provide another overview of the Polish model and to briefly cover every important element of the Church-State relations, given that the existing contributions on that topic

1 However, it may be argued that the Polish road towards democracy was largely driven by the European integration but after achieving membership in the EU in 2004 that benchmark lost its importance. The quality of the Polish democracy decreased during the years 2005-2007 and the EU seemed helpless as far as disregard for human rights was concerned, see Bodnar, "Poland: EU driven democracy?," 2010, p. 41; Sadurski, "The Constitutional Order," 2008, pp. 15-30.

seem to be sufficient.[2] In contrast, the study is focused on one of the essential elements of the above-mentioned relations: the state's neutrality in matters of personal convictions. It may be worthwhile to examine how the Polish state, in which the vast majority of population belongs to the Roman Catholic Church, has managed to overcome the embarrassing legacy of undemocratic ecclesiastical policy. The Polish public authorities used to be excessively supportive of the Church before the Second World War[3] and undoubtedly hostile towards religion during the communist regime,[4] until its late period.[5] Did the pendulum stop swinging after the decline of communism, or did the changes of 1989 simply result in the state making another U-turn in its relations with the religious bodies?

It is for a reason that the principle of religious neutrality is the key concept of this chapter. The Polish democracy retained a separation-based model of relations with the religious denominations and proclaimed neutrality at the dawn of transformation of 1989, but the state can hardly be described as taking both of these principles seriously. Apparently, it is religious neutrality that should be seen as a missing element to the Polish ecclesiastical policy in recent years.

In the Constitution of 1997, the principle of religious neutrality stems from Article 25 para. 2, according to which "Public authorities in the Republic of Poland shall be impartial in matters of personal conviction, whether religious or philosophical, or in relation to outlooks on life, and shall ensure their freedom of expression within public life." The reasons for replacing the term 'neutrality' with the surprising term 'impartiality' will be discussed later in the paper, but it may be assumed at this point that both terms should be considered equivalent. It is notable that the principle of ideological neutrality, under the name of 'neutrality', and not 'impartiality', was first introduced to the Polish law in the last days of the com-

2 See Krukowski, "Polish Law on the State-Church Relations," 2009; Mazurkiewicz, "Autonomy of the Church and Freedom of Religion in Poland," 2001; Pietrzak, "Church and State in Poland," 2003; Rynkowski, "State and Church in Poland," 2005; Stanisz, "The Principles of the Relationship Between Church and State in the Constitution of the Republic of Poland of 2nd April, 1997," 2007, pp. 131-143.

3 See Pease, *Rome's Most Faithful Daughter: The Catholic Church and Independent Poland, 1914-1939*, 2009.

4 See Monticone, *The Catholic Church in Communist Poland 1945-1989: Forty Years of Church-State Relations*, 1986; Diskin, *The Seeds of Triumph: Church and State in Gomulka's Poland*, 2001.

5 See Osuchowski, "The New Legislation in Religious Matters," 1990, pp. 51-67.

munist regime, and it was proclaimed in a statute.[6] In 1989, the concept of neutrality of the state was seen as a first element of democratic changes and it enjoyed the political support of the Catholic Church. This is understandable given that it put an end to the involvement of the state in promoting the Marxist ideas and demonstrating hostility towards religion. Still, it did not take long for the Church to notice that the state's neutrality in matters of personal conviction cuts both ways: it prevents the public authorities from fighting against religion, but also from supporting the active role of religious organizations in the public sphere. As a consequence, the Catholic Church has been, over the last two decades, the most tenacious opponent of the neutrality principle.

Of course, the metaphor used in the title of this chapter has its limits. It would probably be wrong to conclude that all the *dramatis personae* to be presented are sworn enemies of religious neutrality. 'Enemy' is a strong word; it implies hostility and unceasing willingness to cause harm. As a matter of fact, religious neutrality has some enemies in the strict meaning of this word, but there are many to whom it is rather unimportant or simply negligible. It is because of their passivity and proclivity to concessions in fundamental matters that the principle of religious neutrality in Poland remains a challenge for the future.

I will argue that the deficiency of religious neutrality is a result of coexistence of many factors which are: ignoring and violating the principle of neutrality by the political power, reluctance to enforce the constitutional standard by the judicial power (in particular the Constitutional Tribunal), and quiet assistance of some legal scholars who justify departing from that standard. Let us carefully examine each of these elements.

B. Careless Legislator

As far as law-making and enforcement is concerned, the burning issues are so numerous that it would be difficult even to mention all of them. For this reason, I will just concentrate on those which seem either most serious or most spectacular.

6 The Act on Guarantees of Freedom of Conscience and Religion of 17 May 1989; the English version may be found in Osuchowski, "The New Legislation in Religious Matters," 1990, p. 69.

Traditionally, the battlefield where the regulatory ambitions of the state and of the religious communities tend to meet has been religious instruction in public schools. Whether such instruction is admissible or not and how deeply it is integrated with the schools' curriculum does not necessarily have to affect the religious freedom. In the light of the European Convention on Human Rights which sets the standards applying to the European legal space, various solutions are acceptable. Public schools may offer no religious instruction at all, teach about diverse religions and philosophical traditions or provide the students with alternative courses in particular religions. None of these models should be seen as incompatible *per se* with the Convention. However, if religious instruction is compulsory, certain legal mechanisms should be applied in order to ensure that there is no violation of religious freedom. In addition, it has to be noted that regardless of the adopted model, the state should remain neutral in matters of religious convictions and ensure that the religious freedom of all persons is respected. The European Court of Human Rights reiterates that in regard to education and teaching the state authorities must ensure that information or knowledge included in the curriculum is conveyed in an "objective, critical and pluralistic manner."[7] This duty corresponds with the state's role as a "neutral and impartial organiser of the exercise of various religions, faiths and beliefs."[8]

The solution adopted by the Polish Constitution falls into the third of the above-mentioned models. According to Article 53 para. 4, "The religion of a church or other legally recognized religious organization may be taught in schools, but other people's freedom of conscience and religion shall not be infringed thereby." To be exact, such a possibility was recognized by the law some years before the present constitution was passed – in the early 1990s, during the transition period – and the Constitution of 1997 merely confirmed it.

It looks promising as the enforcement of the cited provision should result in teaching many religions and, as a consequence, in satisfying the

7 See, in particular, *Kjeldsen, Busk Madsen and Pedersen v Denmark*, 7 December 1976, Applications No. 5095/71, 5920/72, 5926/72, § 53; *Folgerø and Others v Norway*, 29 June 2007, Application No. 15472/02, § 84; *Lautsi and Others v Italy*, 18 March 2011, Application No. 30814/06, § 62.

8 See, in particular, *Leyla Şahin v Turkey*, 10 November 2005, Application No. 44774/98, § 107; *Dogru v France*, 4 December 2008, Application No. 27058/05, § 62.

needs of people belonging to various religious traditions, thus enabling them to coexist peacefully in the school environment. This, however, did not happen and there are certain reasons for it.

Above all, the obligation to offer courses in religion of a particular confession depends on the number of interested pupils. According to the regulation of the Minister of National Education of 14 April 1992 on the conditions and methods for organizing religious instruction in public kindergartens and schools, there must be a minimum of seven pupils belonging to a particular denomination in a school in order to apply for religious education. If this minimum is not satisfied, it is possible to request a course outside of pupil's home institution. Until recently, a minimum of three pupils for an interscholastic group was required. This changed in 2014, when the regulation was eventually amended, but the minimum for organizing religious instruction within the home institution (seven pupils) remains in force which creates obvious obstacles in a country marked with an overwhelming predominance of the Roman Catholic Church and religious minorities amounting to 10%. It appears that providing the pupils with easily accesible non-catholic religious instruction is possible only in certain areas where the minority population is significant.[9] Thus, the state authorities indirectly support the dominant religious group, which is the only denomination able to spread its teachings effectively within the framework of the public education system. The threshold required to organize religious instruction can also be described as amounting to infringement of the principle of equal rights of religious denominations (Art. 25 para. 1 of the Constitution). In practice, some religious communities asked educational bodies for access to public school classrooms on Saturdays and Sundays.[10] Nonetheless, grades earned in courses held outside the educational system cannot be recorded on the final grade report.[11] It has to be repeated that these limits are not prescribed by a statute, but they were set in an executive regulation, without a proper statutory authorization

9 The Orthodox religious instruction is available mainly in Podlachia region (*Podlasie*), whereas the Lutheran confession prevails in Cieszyn Silesia (*Śląsk Cieszyński*).

10 This is how the Islamic religious education was made available in certain regions of Poland, see Nalborczyk and Borecki, "Relations between Islam and the state in Poland: the legal position of Polish Muslims," 2011, pp. 351-352.

11 As found by the Constitutional Tribunal in 1993 (U 12/92).

which was an infraction of the Polish rules governing the constitutional system of sources of law.

The pupil may choose an alternative course in ethics which is provided by very few schools or decide not to attend any of these courses. However, if he/she decides the latter, such a decision will be reflected on his/her final school report by a straight line instead of a mark against the subject 'religion/ethics'. Thus, the school reports and leaving certificates which are public documents reveal the pupil's convictions to those to whom such documents may be presented: future employees, high schools, etc. It seems that the pupils are indirectly encouraged by the state to choose a course in religion in order to avoid identification as being non-religious or a member of a minority denomination. In addition, this situation is clearly incompatible with the constitutional provision stating that "No one may be compelled by organs of public authority to disclose his philosophy of life, religious convictions or belief" (Art. 53 para. 7 of the Constitution).

In June 2010 that issue was examined by the European Court of Human Rights. The applicants had made several requests to the school authorities asking for their son to be allowed to follow a course in ethics instead of religious instruction. None of the primary schools attended by their son had provided a course in ethics. The refusals had been based on the lack of suitable teachers, financial reasons and insufficient numbers of pupils asking for a course in ethics. As a consequence, in the school report of their child there was a straight line against the subject "religion/ethics" and the word "ethics" was crossed out. The Court noticed that the message conveyed by such a school report was "unambiguous and anything but neutral: the ethics class was not available as an optional subject to the third applicant and he chose not to attend religion class," accordingly, the Court found that there had been a violation of Article 14 taken in conjunction with Article 9 of the European Convention of Human Rights.[12] The judgment sparked off a lively debate in Poland.

The catalogue of legal shortcomings concerning the implementation of the constitutional right to religious instruction could be longer. It is probably worth noticing that, contrary to early declarations, religious teaching is subsidized by the state which in the Polish reality means that the dominant religion relies considerably on public funding. Another burning issue was the Regulation of the Minister of National Education of 2007 which stipu-

12 *Grzelak v Poland*, 15 June 2010, Application No. 7710/02.

lated that the grades for the subject 'religion/ethics' be included in the calculation of a grade point average (GPA), a fact that encouraged many pupils to attend religious classes.

The history of religious instruction in Polish public schools is a good illustration of how the state abandoned the idea of neutrality in religious matters and found itself entangled in supporting religion being in practice the religion of the majority of the population. It is the combination of various defective mechanisms that brought about the state's profound involvement in religious affairs. The public authorities are not mere witnesses of the advancement of the Catholic Church, but also its devoted supporters who actively give assistance to the process of spreading the Christian faith and that includes financial aid since the religion teachers are entirely remunerated by the state. Interestingly, such an attitude was reflected, until 2017, in the preamble to the Educational System Act of 1991 which stated that "Teaching and education, respecting the Christian values, shall be based on the universal principles of ethics." One could ask if the Christian values were the only values recognized and respected by the Polish public schools.

Of course, difficulties with implementing the principle of neutrality arise not only in respect to the education system. The obligation to respect the Christian values was also introduced into the Act on Radio and Television Broadcasting of 29 December 1992. According to the Act, the public radio and television broadcasting programmes should "respect Christian values while adopting universal ethical principles as the basis" (Art. 21 para. 2 subpara. 6) and the broadcasts should "respect the religious convictions of the viewers and listeners, in particular the Christian system of values" (Art. 18 para. 2). The latter obligation was also made a part of a legal definition of a social broadcaster (Art. 4 item 10). The problem could seem trivial since in many cases such provisions have the tendency to become empty declarations. In fact, the National Broadcasting Council is authorized to control broadcasters' activities within the framework of the law and even to withdraw the broadcast license. This is not just a theoretical possibility given that some time ago the Council admonished one of the broadcasters for having mocked the idea of premarital abstinence.[13] Therefore, it could hardly be said that it is just a minor infraction of the

---

13 See Wyrzykowski, "Seks przedmałżeński a konstytucyjny porządek państwa," 2007, pp. 175-188.

neutrality principle. The above-cited provisions directly affect several constitutional rights and freedoms.

In many cases the preference towards the dominant church or Christianity in general, is demonstrated openly in the official acts of the state. The problem becomes particularly difficult if these acts are of non-normative nature which is the case of many appeals and resolutions that reveal the official standpoint of the public powers without creating any legal obligations.

After the European Court of Human Rights delivered the first judgment in the case *Lautsi v Italy* (Application No. 30814/06), finding that the display of crucifixes in Italian public schools had been a violation of the Convention, a heated debate started in many European countries and Poland was no exception. The judgment provoked an unprecedented reaction of the Polish parliament with both chambers opposing fiercely to the Court's findings.[14] The lower house (Sejm) passed a resolution which recalled the acts of hostility towards religion in times of fascist and communist rules, the argumentation was far from subtlety and expressed deep concern about the religious freedom, rights and feelings of the believers and the social peace allegedly threatened by the judgment. It also emphasized "the fundamental and positive contribution of Christianity to the development of human rights." The upper house (Senate) declared that the crucifix had accompanied Poland in all breakthrough moments of its history and therefore every attempt to ban the cross from schools, hospitals, institutions and public places in Poland had to be seen as a violation of the Polish tradition, remembrance and national dignity. Also, the resolution of the Senate contained a bizarre appeal calling to "treat the judgment of the European Court of Human Rights with reserve" although the exact nature of the attitude desired by the Senate remained unclear. However, it should be remembered that controversy over that judgment was not limited to Poland, and eventually the Grand Chamber of the Court, being subjected

14 Resolution of the Sejm of 3 December 2009 on the protection of freedom of religion and values constituting the common heritage of Europe; Resolution of the Senate of 4 February 2010 on respecting the Crucifix (both acts are available in English: http://humanrightshouse.org/Articles/14397.html).

to international political pressure,[15] decided the matter again, this time in a diametrically opposed way.[16]

The above examples demonstrate that the implementation of the principle of religious neutrality is an uneasy task and apparently not a matter of great concern to the political power. Of course, not every act of this power is subject to judicial review and that is the case of appeals, resolutions, and also spontaneous declarations, oral or written, made by the persons exercising high offices. It appears that to some extent the neutrality principle cannot but remain *lex imperfecta*. Nevertheless, as far as the legislation is concerned partiality should be eliminated by means of constitutional review. It may therefore be instructive to examine the role of the Polish Constitutional Tribunal in reference to religious neutrality of the state.

C. Reluctant Judiciary

The Constitutional Tribunal has adjudicated several times upon the acts regarding matters of religion or personal convictions.[17] There is no doubt that a consistent support to the principle of neutrality would have helped to restore the conformity of the law with the Constitution.

Regrettably, the Polish *acquis constitutionnel* proves that safeguarding religious neutrality of the state is one of the Tribunal's weak points. Moreover, the analysis of judgments delivered in cases concerning this issue brings the reader to some rather disturbing conclusions about the strategies applied by the Tribunal in this respect.

Firstly, whenever it is possible the Tribunal tries to avoid any decision-making. That is exactly what happened in the case concerning the state budget funding of construction works of the Temple of Divine Providence (*Świątynia Opatrzności Bożej*) in Warsaw. The Tribunal waited with the delivery of the judgment until January of the subsequent year, thus finding itself obliged to discontinue the proceedings because the challenged act – the Budget Act which is, by its nature, adopted for a period of one year –

15 Zoethout, "Rethinking Adjudication under the European Convention," 2012, p. 420.

16 *Lautsi and Others v Italy*, 18 March 2011, Application No. 30814/06.

17 The judgments delivered until 2000 are discussed by Mączyński, "Freedom of Conscience and Religious Liberty in the Jurisdiction of the Polish Constitutional Tribunal," 2000.

had ceased to have effect prior to the delivery of a judicial decision (Art. 39 para. 1 subpara. 3 of the Constitutional Tribunal Act of 1 August 1997).[18]

The reluctance to decide came into play again when the Tribunal adjudicated upon the regulation according to which the grades for 'religion/ethics' were to be included in the calculation of a grade point average (GPA).[19] That case seemed simple as the core of the problem was the unconstitutionality of the statutory authorization to issue the regulation in question. It was therefore a technical problem rather than an axiological one. What is more important, the Tribunal itself had expressed the view that the authorization was invalid.[20] This made the applicants reduce their argumentation to a brief reference to the Tribunal's own opinion. Despite their confidence that this would be enough, the Tribunal found that the application lacked reasons for the claim because the applicants failed to present their own arguments. Presenting excerpts from the Tribunal's jurisprudence in which the challenged authorization had been explicitly questioned by the Tribunal was considered insufficient. As a result, the Tribunal refused to carry out the review in this respect. Such a decision is hard to defend and it could be said that the Tribunal played hide-and-seek with the applicant. It is noteworthy that one of the justices (Ewa Łętowska) concluded in her separate opinion that the judgment actually amounted to a denial of justice.

Another example could be the adjudication upon the provisions on the restitution of the confiscated property to the Catholic Church. The issue was a burning one since the exact damage suffered by the Church in times of communist regime cannot be determined and the rough estimation provided by the Church is questioned by many. Still, it took the Tribunal more than two years to decide on the conformity of the challenged provisions with the Constitution and by the time when the long awaited judgment was finally delivered[21] most of the property had already been restored to the Church.

Secondly, the Constitutional Tribunal avoids setting stable standards as to the meaning of religious neutrality. As a result, the notion remains vague and unclear. It seems that the best way to achieve coherence and

18 The judgment was thus delivered in 2007 (K 16/06).
19 The judgment in question was delivered in 2009 (U 10/07).
20 That view was expressed in a signal decision (S 1/07).
21 In 2011 (K 3/09).

stability in this respect would be to design 'a test of neutrality' that is a set of criteria which must be met in order to declare that a challenged provision is compatible with the neutrality principle. Unfortunately, the Tribunal has failed to provide such a test so far.

In general, the stability of jurisprudence is one of the missing elements in the Tribunal's approach towards the state's neutrality. Some judicial bodies, like the European Court of Human Rights, have developed certain statements or phrases related to religious freedom, which are commonly cited and automatically recognized as the court's legal opinion on that matter.[22] The Polish Constitutional Tribunal makes use of these phrases from time to time usually with the intention of decorating the assessment with a handy quotation. It did not come up with a coherent concept of neutrality, nor is there any such thing as neutrality *à la polonaise* which could serve as an inspiration to the foreign legal systems.

However, probably the most irritating discrepancy in the constitutional jurisprudence regarding the issue of neutrality is the admissibility of interpreting 'impartiality' as 'neutrality'.

As indicated above, the term 'impartiality' was introduced to the Polish Constitution of 1997 in order to avoid the term 'neutrality' which was unpleasant to the Catholic Church and its political supporters. Theoretically, one could look for differences between these two terms. The concept of neutrality assumes not being a party and not acting as a judge in a conflict, whereas the idea of impartiality is precisely a quality expected of a judge: someone who shows no prejudice towards the parties of a conflict, but eventually is supposed to deliver a final ruling. If this distinction was to be taken seriously, one would have to accept the conclusion that the Polish public powers are authorized to settle a theological debate as long as they remain impartial. Such a conclusion would obviously be absurd and incompatible with the idea of religious freedom. Nonetheless, ever since the Constitution was adopted, some legal scholars have expressed the view that maybe the introduction of the term 'impartiality' to the Constitution meant that its authors had expected Poland to implement a mild version of neutrality or 'neutrality light' or even something far from neutrality.[23] In

---

22 E.g. the phrase about religious freedom being "a precious asset for atheists, agnostics, sceptics and the unconcerned," was often repeated by the European Court of Human Rights.

23 See, in particular, Krukowski, *Polskie prawo wyznaniowe*, 2005, pp. 55-57; Królikowski and Szczucki, "Państwo świeckie, neutralne, czy bezstronne?," 2010.

other terms, accepting the assumption that the constitutional notion of impartiality should not be interpreted as neutrality usually serves as a justification of non-implementing that principle or implementing it only to a very limited extent.

The Constitutional Tribunal had the opportunity to address this issue explicitly in two cases and the judgments in both cases were delivered in December 2009 over the course of less than two weeks. Surprisingly, opposing views were expressed in those judgments. In the first one, the Tribunal used the term 'impartiality and neutrality' and stated openly: "it follows from the Constitution, in particular from Articles 25 and 53, that the character of the state is neutral, in matters of worldview, and secular." Also, the Tribunal sustained its earlier view, asserting that:

> The interpretation adopted by the Constitutional Tribunal is in line with the understanding of secularism, neutrality and the separation of Church and state in those European democratic states where religion is taught in state schools, sometimes even on a compulsory basis. Moreover, this is compliant with international conventions of human rights.[24]

The above cited judgment was given in full bench. Nevertheless, it was not later than after twelve days that the Tribunal, sitting in a bench of five judges, delivered a judgment in which the following words appeared:

> It is of vital importance that the Polish constitution-makers did not apply the term «neutrality» but they mentioned «impartiality». According to many Polish legal scholars, the notion of impartiality is not identical with the notion of ideological neutrality which is accepted in the legal science. In the legal scholarly writing it is frequently remarked that the notion of impartiality, contrary to neutrality, admits active involvement of the state aimed at enabling individuals to enjoy their freedom of conscience and religion. [...] In general terms, the notion of impartiality is commonly considered in the legal science as more friendly towards religion and admitting wider scale of public powers' activity.[25]

As evidenced above, the Tribunal's standpoint regarding the issues of Church-State relations can hardly be considered clear since even the basic terms are defined in various ways. It has to be emphasized that by failing to define religious neutrality the Tribunal contributes to the process of depriving the constitutional provisions of any real meaning. In addition, the Tribunal has never repealed any provision challenged on the grounds of

---

24 Excerpt from judgment U 10/07.
25 Excerpt from judgment K 55/07.

being excessively supportive of the Church, thus violating the neutrality principle, even though in certain cases this should have happened.

D. Over-indulgent Legal Scholars

It is now time to examine the role of the last 'enemy' of the neutrality principle. There is no doubt that the legal scholars have an important role to play as far as the interpretation of the above-mentioned principle is concerned. On the one hand, they may solve the problems which appear in the constitutional practice, provide valuable comments to latest developments and challenges or even inspire the law-makers to develop and reform the legal system. On the other hand, they may just as well ignore the legislative mistakes, offer partial interpretations and justify the infringements of the Constitution.

The suggestion that the Polish legal scholars oppose the idea of neutrality would be obviously oversimplified. In Poland, as in any other country, legal experts subscribe to various views and promote diverse interpretations. Therefore, it cannot be said that the Polish academics unconditionally support the standpoint of the Catholic Church in every conflict over the legal status of religious denominations.

Nonetheless, since the beginning of the democratic transformation of 1989 some legal scholars have acted as advocates of interpretations of religious freedom which could never be reconciled with the idea of religious neutrality. Alternatively, they have supported such understanding of this concept as to make it impossible to implement. It may be interesting to identify and to briefly examine some of the strategies serving these purposes.

Firstly, it is not uncommon to encounter opinions that the concept of religious neutrality is 'not workable' or even self-contradictory and therefore logically impossible. In that view, the state always accepts some set of values, so introducing such a declaration of axiological indifference to the Constitution is a promise never to be fulfilled.[26] Following that opinion, every action undertaken by the state is motivated by some axiological system and because of that, the constitutional provision imposing an obli-

---

26 See e.g. Olszówka, "Interferencja zasad prawa wyznaniowego instytucjonalnego," 2010, p. 80.

gation of neutrality should be treated as non-existent (*interpretatio per non est*). Some legal scholars even claim that it would probably be more honest if the state openly declared which religious convictions it supports.[27]

The above-mentioned opinion is based on an obvious misunderstanding. There is no doubt that the idea of 'total neutrality' would be unreasonable. Yet, nobody calls for this concept to be implemented. The reason for the state to remain neutral is to defend certain values determining the nature of the political community: tolerance, mutual understanding, respect for human liberty and dignity, openness to dialogue. The state may not (and should not) remain neutral with respect to these values; on the contrary, it should affirm and implement them. These values which constitute the idea of public morality have to be distinguished from private morality being related to individual choices and to various concepts of a good life. As far as the private morality values are concerned the state is obliged to stay neutral given that it is the only way of safeguarding the democratic order. Blurring the distinction between the private and the public morality, in order to question the very possibility of the state remaining neutral, is a common strategy of delegitimization of the neutrality principle.

Secondly, one may come across an opinion that the Polish mutation of neutrality is somehow different from the traditional concept as it has been known in the Western legal tradition. To this aim, some legal scholars put forward an unsettling idea of making a distinction between 'open' and 'closed' neutrality, sometimes depicted as an opposition between the 'friendly' and 'unfriendly' neutrality which is another wording for the same concept.[28] Such an interpretation is disputable since it can be argued that a neutral attitude is neither friendly nor unfriendly: it is neutral, as the name itself suggests. Still, similar interpretations are sometimes offered in international legal science. What is far less understandable, however, is that the state which is cast as an example of the 'closed' (or 'unfriendly') model, that is France, could be described as demonstrating open hostility towards religion and placed on the same level as the Soviet Union.[29] Many readers would find the idea of comparing France and the Soviet Union somewhat disturbing. Still, such a comparison is made for a reason: it helps some legal scholars deny any advisability of implementing the state's neutrality and dilute the meaning of that constitutional principle by

27 See Łączkowski, "«Bezstronność» władz publicznych," 2006, p. 214.

28 See Krukowski, *Polskie prawo*, pp. 55-56.

29 See ibid., pp. 27-29.

means of unfavourable interpretations. In that view, the Polish model appears to be closer to the American one, despite different historical experiences and incomparable religious structures of both societies. The aim of inventing such theories is based on the assumption that if the Polish model of Church-State relations must contain the element of neutrality then the only way out of this situation is to reshape and reinvent the very idea of neutrality. Accordingly, there is a separate 'Polish path to neutrality', to put it this way, while the French model has nothing to do with neutrality: it is about hostility and close to Soviet standards. In fact, this 'Polish path' seems to be a pleasant label for a model implementing an incomplete standard of religious neutrality.

Thirdly, surprising conclusions are drawn from the presence of the Catholic Church's name in the body of the Constitution. The Catholic Church is mentioned once in the text, in a provision that states that "The relations between the Republic of Poland and the Roman Catholic Church shall be determined by international treaty concluded with the Holy See, and by statute" (Art. 25 para. 4 of the Constitution). As far as the relations between the state and the non-catholic denominations are concerned, they are supposed to be determined by statutes adopted pursuant to agreements concluded between their appropriate representatives and the Polish government (Art. 25 para. 5 of the Constitution).

The reason for that difference in treatment is sometimes explained by assuming that the Catholic Church was somehow privileged by the Constitution. Thus, the reference to the dominant church is interpreted by some legal scholars as an exception to the general principle of equal rights of religious communities.[30] It is an old tune in the Polish constitutional law since it brings back the echoes of the Constitution of 1921, which stated: "The Roman Catholic religion, being the religion of the preponderant majority of the nation, occupies in the state the leading position among equal confessions" (Art. 114). The 'leading among the equal' concept, or the *primus inter pares* principle, was an obvious contradiction and it deprived the equality concept of any real meaning. It should therefore be regretted that the idea of restoring the pre-war model of Church-State relations was vigorously accepted by the Constitutional Tribunal which in 2009 asserted that:

30 See Olszówka, "Kilka uwag o (nie)równouprawnieniu związków religijnych (na tle orzecznictwa Trybunału Konstytucyjnego)," 2012.

> There is no doubt that Article 25(4) of the Constitution and the concordat specify the special institutional position of the Roman Catholic Church in the legal system of the Republic of Poland, reflecting its dominant position within the religious structure of Poland.[31]

The fact is that the reason for designing the legal status of the Catholic Church on a separate basis has nothing to do with the idea of granting special privileges to the dominant confession. The provisions referring to the Catholic Church and those applying to the non-catholic denominations derive from the same assumption: the basis for the relations between the state and the religious entities should be the bilateral agreements. The separate provision referring to the Catholic Church is a natural consequence of its unique features: "Since the Holy See is a separate legal entity in international law (which has no equivalent in the case of non-catholic denominations), the special procedure for regulating the legal situation of the Catholic Church seems to be fully justified."[32] It is therefore unconvincing to assume that the reason for putting the name of the dominant church was to acknowledge its special position in the religious composition of the society.

E. Conclusion

The aim of this paper was to provide an explanation to the deficiency of neutrality in the Polish constitutional practice. It can be reasoned that the Constitution itself is not enough to determine the actual model of relations between the state and the religious entities if that model may not count on support of the main actors of the public life.

The conclusions reached so far may give little hope for the situation to change as apparently neutrality is of nobody's concern. Still, in spite of much criticism deserved, the Polish political elites have proven many times their maturity and ability to converge on the European standards in the long run. Hopefully, this should be the case of religious neutrality.

---

31 Excerpt from judgment U 10/07.

32 Stanisz, "The Principles of the Relationship Between Church and State in the Constitution of the Republic of Poland of 2nd April," 1997, pp. 138-139.

Bibliography

Bodnar, Adam, "Poland: EU driven democracy?," in *Democratization and the European Union: Comparing Central and Eastern European post-communist countries*, ed. Leonardo Morlino and Wojciech Sadurski, London & New York: Routledge, 2010, pp. 19-44.

Constitutional Tribunal of Poland, 20 April 1993, *U 12/92.*

Constitutional Tribunal of Poland, 6 February 2007, *K 16/06.*

Constitutional Tribunal of Poland, 2 December 2009, *U 10/07.*

Constitutional Tribunal of Poland, 14 December 2009, *K 55/07.*

Constitutional Tribunal of Poland, 8 June 2011, *K 3/09.*

Diskin, Hanna, *The Seeds of Triumph: Church and State in Gomułka's Poland*, Budapest: Central European University Press, 2001.

European Court of Human Rights, *Kjeldsen, Busk Madsen and Pedersen v Denmark*, 7 December 1976, Application No. 5095/71, 5920/72, 5926/72.

European Court of Human Rights, *Leyla Şahin v Turkey*, 10 November 2005, Application No. 44774/98.

European Court of Human Rights, *Folgerø and Others v Norway*, 29 June 2007, Application No. 15472/02.

European Court of Human Rights, *Dogru v France*, 4 December 2008, Application No. 27058/05, § 62.

European Court of Human Rights, *Grzelak v Poland*, 15 June 2010, Application No. 7710/02.

European Court of Human Rights, *Lautsi and Others v Italy*, 18 March 2011, Application No. 30814/06.

Królikowski, Michał, and Krzysztof Szczucki, "Państwo świeckie, neutralne, czy bezstronne?," *Więź* 625 (2010): 21-33.

Krukowski, Józef, "Polish Law on the State-Church Relations," in *A Synthesis of Polish Law: Part 1*, ed. Tadeusz Guz, Jan Głuchowski, and Maria R. Pałubska, Frankfurt am Main: Peter Lang, 2009.

Krukowski, Józef, *Polskie prawo wyznaniowe*, Warszawa: LexisNexis, 2005.

Łączkowski, Wojciech, "«Bezstronność» władz publicznych," *Ruch Prawniczy, Ekonomiczny i Socjologiczny* 68, 2 (2006): 209-219.

Mazurkiewicz, Piotr, "Autonomy of the Church and Freedom of Religion in Poland," in *Church Autonomy: A Comparative Survey*, ed. Gerhard Robbers, Frankfurt am Main: Peter Lang, 2001, pp. 359-380.

Mączyński, Andrzej, "Freedom of Conscience and Religious Liberty in the Jurisdiction of the Polish Constitutional Tribunal," in *Constitutional Jurisprudence in the Area of Freedom of Religion and Beliefs*, Warsaw: Office of the [Polish] Constitutional Tribunal, 2000.

Monticone, Ronald C., *The Catholic Church in Communist Poland 1945-1989: Forty Years of Church-State Relations*, New York: Columbia University Press, 1986.

Nalborczyk, Agata S., and Paweł Borecki, "Relations between Islam and the state in Poland: the legal position of Polish Muslims," *Islam and Christian-Muslim Relations* 22 (2011): 343-359.

Olszówka, Marcin, "Interferencja zasad prawa wyznaniowego instytucjonalnego," *Przegląd Prawa Wyznaniowego* 2 (2010): 63-86.

Olszówka, Marcin, "Kilka uwag o (nie)równouprawnieniu związków religijnych (na tle orzecznictwa Trybunału Konstytucyjnego)," *Studia Politologiczne* 23 (2012): 247-265.

Osuchowski, Janusz, "The New Legislation in Religious Matters," *Droit Polonais Contemporain/Polish Contemporary Law* 1 (1990): 51-67.

Pease, Neil, *Rome's Most Faithful Daughter: The Catholic Church and Independent Poland, 1914-1939*, Athens: Ohio University Press, 2009.

Pietrzak, Michał, "Church and State in Poland," in *Law and Religion in Post-Communist Europe*, ed. Silvio Ferrari, W. Cole Durham, Jr., and Elizabeth Sewell, Leuven, Paris, Dudley: Peeters, 2003, pp. 215-238.

Rynkowski, Michał, "State and Church in Poland," in *State and Church in the European Union*, ed. Gerhard Robbers, Baden-Baden: Nomos, 2005, pp. 419-438.

Sadurski, Wojciech, "The Constitutional Order," in *Democracy in Poland 2005-2007*, ed. Lena Kolarska-Bobińska, Jacek Kucharczyk, and Jarosław Zbieranek, Warsaw: The Institute of Public Affairs, 2008, pp. 15-30.

Stanisz, Piotr, "The Principles of the Relationship Between Church and State in the Constitution of the Republic of Poland of 2nd April, 1997," *Soter: Journal of Religious Science* 22, 50 (2007): 131-143.

Wyrzykowski, Mirosław, "Seks przedmałżeński a konstytucyjny porządek państwa," in *Państwo – prawo – polityka w przestrzeni konstytucyjnej*, ed. Jan Majchrowski, Warsaw: Liber, 2007, pp. 175-188.

Zoethout, Carla M., "Rethinking Adjudication under the European Convention," in *The Lautsi Papers: Multidisciplinary Reflections on Religious Symbols in the Public School Classroom*, ed. Jeroen Temperman, Leiden, Boston: Martinus Nijhoff Publishers, 2012, pp. 413-426.

Situating Indian Secularism and Hindu Nationalism

Ronojoy Sen

A. Introduction

India is often described as one of the most diverse countries when it comes to religion. This is borne out by statistics alone. According to the 2011 Census, Hindus are an overwhelming majority in India accounting for nearly 80 per cent of India's 1.3 billion-plus population. They are followed by Muslims (13.4%), Christians (2.3%), Sikhs (1.9%) and Buddhists (0.8%). While the individual percentages for non-Hindu religions are small, their actual numbers are not. For example, Muslims, as the largest minority in India, have 138 million followers in India, which makes them the fourth largest group of Muslims worldwide. Even its Christian population of 24 million exceeds the followers of this religion in several European countries combined.

That India has managed to survive relatively peacefully – despite periodic conflicts – over the course of its independent existence is a tribute to the tolerance that exists among its religious communities and the strength of the secularism crafted by the founders of the Indian constitution. This achievement is particularly remarkable since global surveys demonstrate that India is one of the most religious countries with over 90 per cent of its citizens professing to be believers. Even so, several recent episodes of religious conflict have rocked the tranquility of the Indian nation and caught international attention as well. While it may be argued that religion *per se* was not the sole cause of these conflicts, it was one of the principal elements that mobilized them. Some of the most prominent among these religious conflicts would be the destruction of the Babri Masjid in 1992 followed by the Gujarat riots in 2002 that resulted in widespread violence against Muslims.

In this essay, I explore secularism in theory and practice. First, I discuss the constitutional basis of Indian secularism followed by a brief comparison of it with other variants of secularism. Second, I look at the practice of secularism in India by analysing an important Supreme Court ruling, which legitimized the use of Hindutva or "Hinduness" as a core ideology of the Hindu nationalists, and then examining the politics of Hindu nationalism. I conclude with a brief assessment of the rise and impact of Hindu nationalist forces in India.[1]

B. Types of Secularism

In his classic, *India As A Secular State*, Donald Eugene Smith observed that the Constitution of India provided "a relatively sound basis for the building of a secular state." Smith believed that there was a good chance that twenty years following the 1963 publication of his work that "many of India's constitutional anomalies regarding the secular state will have disappeared."[2] Meanwhile, another scholar, Ved Prakash Luthera, argued that India was neither a secular state nor was it desirable for it to be one in the absence of an organized structure for the Hindu religion. He preferred to call India a "jurisdictionalist state" where the state balanced the power of religious authorities.[3] More than four decades after Smith made his predictions, and over sixty years after Indian independence, the anomalies that troubled Smith – the existence of separate personal laws for religious groups, the intervention of the state in religious institutions, and the practices and reservations for groups defined by caste – continue to loom large. In hindsight, one could reasonably challenge Smith's prediction, because he was writing at a time when theories about the decline of religion were dominant and the growth of secularism was "often interpreted as a natural concomitant to the spread of science, education, and technology."[4] The following statement by Smith is fairly typical of the time: "The forces of Westernization and modernization at work in India are all on the side of the secular state. Industrialization, urbanization, the break-up of the joint family system, greatly increased literacy, and opportunities for higher education – all tend to promote the general secularization of both private and public life."[5]

---

1 Sections of this essay are drawn from Ronojoy Sen, *Articles of Faith: Religion, Secularism, and the Indian Supreme Court*, 2012.
2 Smith, *India as a Secular State*, 1963, p. 14.
3 Luthera, *The Concept of the Secular State and India*, 1964.
4 Keddie, "Secularism & its Discontents," 2003, p. 16.
5 Smith, "India as a Secular State," 1999, p. 224.

The current understanding is the impact of Westernization and modernization on religion and religious beliefs is far more complicated, and the thesis of progressive secularization of society is not borne out. Peter Berger, one of the leading proponents of secularization in the 1960s, changed his views to: "The world today, with some exceptions [...] is as furiously religious as it ever was, and in some places more so than ever."[6] Even Pippa Norris and Ronald Inglehart, who have authored a study supporting the thesis of a decline of religion in industrialized societies, argue against a simple correlation between modernization and secularization.[7] As Jean Bethke Elshtain puts it, "The secularization thesis has failed, and failed spectacularly."[8] In the aftermath of 9/11 and the global surge in Islamist terrorism, there are a slew of books on the role of religion in general[9] and Islamic fundamentalism in particular, in fuelling violence and intolerance.

These debates have greater resonance in India, which ranks as one of the most religious countries in the world, and in recent years, India has become one of the principal targets of Islamist terrorism. A Pew Global Attitudes Project survey in 2002 reported that 92 per cent of respondents in India said that religion was very important to them. As a special report on religion and public life in a popular magazine says:

> Today, India is a test tube for religious politics. The birthplace of four big religions (Buddhism, Jainism, Sikhism and Hinduism), it has remained religious even as it has modernized.[10]

In the aftermath of the Gujarat riots in 2002, one scholar went so far as to say that "tensions between religious communities were increasingly defining lives in many regions of India."[11] There are, of course, others who believe that the potential for religious violence is vastly overstated. Author

6 Berger, *The Desecularization of the World*, 1999, p. 224.

7 See Norris and Inglehart, *Sacred and Secular: Religion and Politics Worldwide*, 2004.

8 Elshtain, "Religion and Democracy," 2009, p. 16.

9 On religion, see, for instance, Harris, *The End of Faith: Religion, Terror, and the Future of Reason*, 2004; Dawkins, *The God Delusion*, 2006, and Hitchens, *God is Not Great: How Religion Poisons Everything*, 2007. On Islam, see Roy, *Globalized Islam: The Search for a New Ummah*, 2004, and Lewis, *The Crisis of Islam: Holy War and Unholy Terror*, 2004.

10 "Bridging the Divide," *The Economist* (Singapore), November 3, 2007.

11 Nussbaum, *The Clash Within: Democracy, Religious Violence, and India's Future*, 2007, p. 9.

and former bureaucrat, Pavan Varma, for instance, writes that the very nature of Hinduism makes it inimical to religious violence:

> The paranoia that Hinduism is under siege, and needs to assert itself aggressively, has been whipped up only recently by fringe fundamentalist groups whose credentials to speak for all Hindus is very doubtful. Moreover, Hindus are temperamentally opposed to any prolonged instability or disorder that could be a consequence of religious violence, especially since it is amply clear that there is no practical alternative to coexistence.[12]

He adds that the large Muslim population, which no "political party with the ambition to come to power can ignore,"[13] acts as a bulwark against religious violence. His views mirror Smith's analysis of secular state.

In his conception of the secular state, which forms the other lynchpin in his analysis, Smith saw it as one derived from the "liberal-democratic tradition of the West." More importantly, the secular state involves three sets of relations: religion and the individual (freedom of religion); the state and the individual (citizenship); the state and religion (separation of church and state). In liberal-democratic theory, these relations can be classified under the three broad principles of liberty, equality, and neutrality. For Smith, a secular state is one where freedom of religion is guaranteed, all citizens are equal irrespective of their religion, and the state is not connected in any way to religion. In this scheme, the Indian state falls short a secular state status on several counts.

There are indeed several departures in the Indian Constitution from the model that Smith utilized for his analysis. For example, Article 25 enshrines the right to individual freedom of religion while also empowering the state to intervene in Hindu religious institutions. Similarly, Article 17 requires the state to abolish untouchability, one of the most abhorrent practices of Hindu society. Although equality of citizenship is guaranteed by its Constitution, there are provisions for reservations or affirmative action in elections, educational institutions, and government jobs for lower castes and tribals. Similarly, although no one is required to take part in religious instruction or prayer in educational institutions, the state is committed to giving aid to institutions run by religious communities. Finally, there are personal laws in place for different religious communities, with a non-justiciable "directive principle" in the Constitution calling for a uni-

12 Varma, "Citizen India: The Many are One," 2009, p. 50.
13 Ibid.

form civil code in the future. As Gary Jacobsohn points out, "religious and secular life are so pervasively entangled [in India] that a posture of official indifference cannot be justified either politically or constitutionally."[14] Evidence suggests India balances its support for religion and secularism, but the idea of secularism itself is challenged at times.

Although the Christian roots of the term "secular" are acknowledged by most scholars, there is at the same time recognition that secularism has relevance for non-Christian societies. It is now recognized that separation of church and state is not the only viable model for secularism. As Charles Taylor writes, "Some kind of distancing is obviously required by the very principle of equidistance and inclusion which is the essence of secularism. But there is more than one formula that can satisfy this. Complete disentanglement of government from any religious institutions is one such, but far from the only one."[15] Moreover, Gurpreet Mahajan points out that there are variations in the way Western democracies deal with religion, with only some nations conforming to the "wall of separation" doctrine.[16] Marc Galanter, too, argues that instead of seeing the Indian secular state as playing catch up with the West, one must accept that India has "as long or a longer tradition of secular government in many respects than most of Western Europe or North America." This in effect means working with a conception of secularism that does not mark a clear break between church and state, since the former in the Christian sense did not exist in the Indian context.

One can broadly distinguish among three types of secularism. The first is the American model. Unlike the many articles in the Indian Constitution, which define the relationship of the state to religion, the American Constitution is fairly brief on the issue. Also, the use of the word "secular" is absent in the American Constitution. The First Amendment of the US Constitution merely says: "Congress shall make no law respecting an establishment of religion, or prohibiting the free exercise thereof." This has been usually separated to denote two aspects of the relationship of the state to religion: the establishment clause, which prohibits the government from advancing the interests of any one faith, and the free exercise clause, which guarantees religious freedom. It is common to describe this arrange-

14 Jacobsohn, *The Wheel of Law: India's Secularism in Comparative Constitutional Context*, 2003, p. 10.

15 Taylor, "Modes of Secularism," 1998, p. 52.

16 Mahajan, *Identities and Rights: Aspects of Liberal Democracy in India*, 1998.

ment as a "wall of separation" following Jefferson's immortal words written in a letter to the Danbury Baptists in 1802.[17] Justice Hugo Black famously used this phrase in *Everson v Board of Education Ewing*,[18] which made the "wall of separation" the foundation of subsequent jurisprudence.

However, in practice Jefferson's separation has been far more difficult to implement. Like in India, in the US, too questions of how much the government should accommodate the religious practices and conscientious objections of individuals or groups as well as the distance it should maintain from religion have frequently come up before the courts. Five years after *Everson*, Justice William Douglas in *Zorach v Clauson*, while upholding the idea of separation, said that the First Amendment did "not say that in every and all respects there shall be a separation of Church and State."[19] Again in *Lemon v Kurtzman*, Justice Warren Burger said, "The line of separation, far from being a 'wall', is a blurred, indistinct and variable barrier depending on all the circumstances of a particular relationship."[20]

The second model is the European one where there is a good deal of variation across countries and the boundary between state and religion is more porous than in the U.S. A common feature in many European nations is that the state privileges one religion although there is no discrimination against other religions. Example of this model may be found across Europe. In Spain, Article 16 in the Constitution of 1978 states that "no religion shall have a state character," while it also provides that: "The public authorities shall take into account the religious beliefs of Spanish society and shall consequently maintain cooperative relationships with the Catholic Church and other religions." Italy, for example, is one of several states that monetarily support religious groups. Its government paid the salaries of Catholic priests, but this practice changed in 1984 when the government began allowing taxpayers to choose which religious groups received their financial support. Sweden is another example of a state monetary support of religion, where the proceeds of a new religious tax

17 Jefferson had written: "I contemplate with sovereign reverence that act of the whole American people which declared that their legislature should 'make no law respecting an establishment of religion, or prohibiting the free exercise thereof,' thus establishing a wall of separation between Church and State.".

18 US Supreme Court, *Everson v Board of Education Ewing*, 330 U.S. 1 (1947).

19 US Supreme Court, Zorach v Clauson, 343 U.S. 306 (1952).

20 US Supreme Court, *Lemon v Kurtzman*, 403 U.S. 602 (1971).

are divided according to taxpayer preference to different religious groups. Its government ultimately relinquished its formal control over the Church of Sweden by replacing its church tax with an annual fee that its tax authorities collect from Church of Sweden members. A government-run commission provides money to registered religious groups outside the Church of Sweden. Thus, the state-sponsored funding of religion is declining, but states may continue their support religion through education. It is not uncommon for countries, such as Germany and Spain, to allow their academic and religious authorities to hold religion classes in public schools. Finally, it is not unusual for European constitutions to also contain references to God, but there are exceptions within the European community.

France and its policy of *laicite*, which originally assured the equality of all citizens before the law irrespective of race or religion, is a contrast to the rest of Europe, because it establishes a strict separation between church and state. French secularism has also probably been the most hotly debated in recent times, because its policies towards minorities may restrict the open expression of religion, particularly Muslims. Some French scholars have argued that *laicite* has no adequate English translation, though the adjective *laique* is usually translated as "secular". These scholars have stressed on the historical background of *laicite*, including the confrontational nature of church-state relations, which has contributed to its singular nature. The origins of *laicite* can be traced back to the French revolution and the idea of a state-sponsored republicanism which envisioned a uniform, secularized French identity. However, it was only in 1905 that a law codified the formal separation of church and state. The traditions of *laicite* have been especially critical in French educational policy, and they were the subject of controversy when France's National Assembly passed a law banning prominent religious symbols in schools. This sparked serious concerns among France's Muslims – who make up 8 per cent of the country's population – since it prevented Muslim girls from wearing the *hijab* (veil) in schools. More recently, when an immigrant Muslim woman applied for French citizenship, France's highest administrative court denied citizenship on the grounds that her practice of Islam was incompatible with French values.

The only European country that practices a version comparable to France's version of "hard" secularism is Turkey, where the relationship between religion and state is unique for a Muslim-majority nation. Turkey embarked on this unique journey in the 1920s when the founder of modern

Turkey, Kemal Ataturk, imposed Western-style secularism on the country. Ataturk abolished the caliphate in 1924, changed the alphabet into Latin letters, placed mosques under state control and crushed the religious hierarchy. This version of secularism was enforced by a small, but powerful, elite comprising the military and judiciary. This consensus has cracked over the past few years with the rise of Islamist forces to power, especially the Justice and Development Party (AKP). Ever since AKP became Turkey's governing party, the tensions between the secularist and Islamist forces have become more apparent. In 2008, the AKP pushed through a controversial constitutional amendment lifting the ban on women wearing headscarves in universities. A constitutional court later struck it down, and this judicial action led to an attempt by state prosecutors to ban the AKP, which was eventually turned down by the constitutional court by the slimmest of margins.

Commenting on the forms of secularism in modern states, Talal Asad says that that picture is far from uniform: "Even in modern secular countries the place of religion varies. Thus, although in France both the highly centralized state and its citizens are secular, in Britain the state is linked to the Established Church and its inhabitants are largely nonreligious, and in America the population is largely religious but the federal state is secular. Consequently, although the secularism of these three countries have much in common, the mediating character of the modern imaginary in each of them differs significantly."[21] Sunil Khilnani makes a similar point when he says that "there is no one paradigmatic form of secularism or of the secular state."[22]

C. *Theories of Indian Secularism*

Obviously India is not alone among secular democracies where the relationship between state and religion is contested. It is also equally true that Indian secularism is radically different from countries such as France where there is a hard division between state and religion, or other European countries where one religion is a state religion or receives privileged status. Perhaps the closest to the Indian model is the American one where

---

21 Asad, *Formations of the Secular: Christianity, Islam, Modernity*, 2003, pp. 5-6.
22 Khilnani, "Secularism: Western and Indian," 2007, p. 43.

the separation between state and religion exists but in effect has been most difficult to define. Though the contexts of the cases in India and America have usually been very different the underlying issues have some similarities. Indeed, it is acknowledged that the framers of the Indian Constitution were greatly influenced by the American Constitution. However, on the issue of religion, the Indian Constitution is significantly different from the American and European models. As Mahajan points out, "Independent India followed neither the English nor the American model. It chartered a different route wherein non-establishment of religion was combined with the absence of separation."[23] She says that by placing religion "squarely in the public domain," the Indian Constitution "endorsed a position that was significantly different from the perspective that was expressed by the dominant liberal framework of that time."[24] This was a policy that brought "religion frontally to the public arena, but at the same time also allowed the state to engage with matters of religion as also with the affairs of religious communities."[25]

In the Indian context, plenty has been written on secularism since Smith published *India as a Secular State* was published. Shortly after his publication, Galanter critiqued Smith's conception of secularism and challenged it by noting the difficulty of separating the religious and secular. Moreover, he pointed out that underlying Smith's model of the secular state in India was the belief that the "notion of the religious may be readily distinguished from the 'secular' or non-religious."[26] Galanter, in fact, argued that the Indian state was not in the business of promoting freedom of religion but concerned with religious reform: "The freedom that is a principle of the secular state is not freedom of religion as it is (in India) but freedom of religion as it ought to be. The ultimate argument for the secular state then is not to maximize the presently desired freedoms but to substitute a new and more appropriate or valuable kind of freedom."[27] This is what Jacobsohn also alludes to when he labels Indian secularism as an ameliorative model that "embraces the social reform impulse of Indian na-

23 Ibid., p. 303.
24 Mahajan, "Religion and the Indian Constitution: Questions of Separation and Equality," 2008, p. 298.
25 Ibid., p. 305.
26 Galanter, *Law and Society in Modern India*, 1997, p. 253.
27 Ibid., p. 258.

tionalism in the context of the nation's deeply rooted religious diversity and stratification."[28]

The destruction of the Babri Masjid, a sixteenth century mosque located in Ayodhya, by Hindu fanatics in 1992 and the electoral success of the Hindu nationalist Bharatiya Janata Party (BJP), over the last two decades inspired several articles questioning the premises and viability of the Indian secular state. Scholars such as Ashis Nandy and T.N. Madan believe that the secular state was doomed to failure in India. Moreover, Madan observes that "secularism in South Asia as a generally shared credo of life is impossible, as a basis for state action impractible, and as a blueprint for the foreseeable future impotent."[29] To Madan, the ideology of secularism, with its origins in the West, is incapable of dealing with the all-embracing character of religion in India. Nandy goes even further by identifying secularism as part of a larger package consisting of development, mega-science, and national security, which is used by the state to silence its "nonconforming citizens."[30] He also makes a distinction between religion as faith and religion as ideology, going on to posit that the "modern state always prefers to deal with religious ideologies rather than with faiths."[31] According to Nandy, "Secularism may once have been an emancipatory idea but for too long it has had a built-in principle of exclusion."[32] In Nandy's view, the ideology of secularism in India is thoroughly discredited by frequently having to fall back on examples of tolerance such as Ashoka, Kabir or Mahatma Gandhi, none of whom "drew their principles or values from the ideology of secularism."[33] He, thus, calls instead for a religious tolerance outside the bounds of secularism.

28 Jacobsohn, *The Wheel of Law*, p. 50.

29 Madan, "Secularism in its Place," 1998, p. 298.

30 Nandy, "The Politics of Secularism and the Recovery of Religious Toleration," 1998, p. 333.

31 Ibid., pp. 322-323.

32 Nandy, "Closing the Debate on Secularism: A Personal Statement," in 2007, p. 114. Nandy adds that unlike him Madan has not "jettisoned the idea of secularism." Ibid., p. 112.

33 Ibid.

D. *What the Founders Thought*

It is apparent that the Indian version of secularism differs from the American or the European model. If one does not discard the relevance of secularism in the Indian context, as Madan and Nandy do, what model does one employ? The Constituent Assembly, which drafted the Indian Constitution between 1946 and 1949, is a good place to locate the thinking behind the Indian secular state.[34] The Assembly debates represent an incredibly rich source for the thinking behind the Indian secular state. And one does not have to be an originalist to go back to the debates. As Rajeev Bhargava points out:

> The underlying point of secularism must have been articulated with a greater deal of perspicacity at that time than is possible even in this current phase of communalization. In short, to get a handle on current constitutional practices, to grasp their value and meaning, we may have no option but to go back in time to the Constituent Assembly debates and perhaps even further back to the colonial era.[35]

One has tried to do this wherever possible.

The Assembly debates reveal that there were real differences on the direction that Indian secularism should take. Though there were attempts to insert the term "secular state" in the draft Constitution on the one hand and to begin the preamble by invoking God on the other, these did not succeed. Members, such as H.V. Kamath, Govind Malaviya, and S.L. Saxena, wanted to begin the preamble to Indian Constitution with the phrase, "In the name of God."[36] After a heated discussion on the merits of this proposal, Kamath's amendment was put to vote and defeated. The same fate befell Brajeshwar Prasad's proposal to begin the preamble with the following words: "We the people of India, having resolved to constitute India into a secular cooperative commonwealth to establish socialist order..." It was only in 1976, during the Emergency, that "secular" (as well as "socialist") was inserted into the Preamble of the Constitution through its Forty-second Amendment.

There were, however, several voices in the Assembly, including B.R. Ambedkar, who wanted to severely restrict the role of religion in the pub-

---

34 For details of the composition and functioning of the Constituent Assembly see Austin, *The Indian Constitution: Cornerstone of a Nation*, 2000, ch. 1.

35 Bhargava, "Introduction," 2008, p. 12.

36 *Constituent Assembly Debates*, Vol. 10, p. 439.

lic sphere. Economist K.T. Shah raised the demand that there be an article expressly stating that the Indian state has "no concern with any religion, creed or profession of faith." He said,

> The State of India, if it claims to be secular, if it claims to have an open mind, should have, in my opinion, a right not merely to regulate and regulate such [religious] practices but also absolutely to prohibit them.[37]

He also proposed a strict separation where the Indian state "shall have no concern with any religion, creed or profession of faith," which was rejected. Similarly India's future president Sarvepalli Radhakrishnan said during the debates, "Nationalism, not religion, is the basis of modern life."[38]

On the other side, there were members such as the Hindu traditionalist, K.M. Munshi, who believed the state must take into account that the religiosity of Indians and articulated religious tolerance in Hindu terms: "We are a people with deeply religious moorings. At the same time, we have a living tradition of religious tolerance – the result of the broad outlook of Hinduism that all religions lead to the same god." [39] He felt that the non-establishment clause of the American Constitution was "inappropriate to Indian conditions and we had to evolve a characteristically Indian secularism," and the Indian state could not "possibly have a state religion, nor could a rigid line be drawn between the state and church as in the US."[40] He added, "A secular state is not a Godless State. It is not a state which is pledged to eradicate or ignore religion. It is not a state which refuses to take notice of religious belief in this country." Members such as H.V. Kamath expressed similar views.

Ultimately, it was the "equal respect"[41] theory – where the state respects and tolerates all religions – that won the day. This was also the Nehruvian formulation of secularism. This is a position that oscillates between *sarvadharma samabhava* (goodwill towards all religions) and *dharma nirpekshata* (religious neutrality). It is no secret that Jawaharlal Nehru saw religion as a force that checked the "tendency to change and progress." But he did not let his personal convictions colour his concep-

---

37 *Constituent Assembly Debates,* Vol. 7, p. 827.

38 Shiva Rao, *The Framing of India's Constitution: Select Documents, Vol. 2*, 1968, p. 16.

39 Munshi, *Indian Constitutional Documents, Vol. 1*, 1967, p. 309.

40 Ibid.

41 I borrow this term from Jha, "Secularism in the Constituent Assembly Debates: 1946-50," 2002.

tion of the secular state. He wrote, "A secular state does not mean an irreligious state: it only means that we respect and honour all religions giving them freedom to function."[42] On another occasion, Nehru defined a secular state as one where there is "free play for all religions, subject only to their not interfering with each other or with the basic conceptions of our state."[43] This conception of a secular state is what Rajeev Bhargava describes as "principled distance," which he believes is the primary characteristic of Indian constitutional secularism. In this interpretation, a secular state "neither mindlessly excludes all religions nor is merely neutral towards them."[44] Neera Chandoke, too, subscribes to this view of "principled distance" as the defining characteristic of secularism in India. She writes, "Secularism, we can say, outstripping provisions for freedom and equality, stipulates that the state will maintain an attitude of principled distance from all religious groups."[45] She further explains that Indian secularism was "designed to allow people to live together in civility. This is what contemporary critiques of secularism seem to forget."[46]

These contestations over the secular state raise important questions on the nature of Indian secularism, the constitutional provisions governing the relationship between the state and religion and their actual implementation by the Indian state. The reformist element with regard to religion in the Indian Constitution makes the "principled distance" argument somewhat problematic. One could question what exactly "principled" amounts to and who decides its content. Another description of constitutional secularism is offered by Rajeev Dhavan who disaggregates Indian secularism into three components: religious freedom, celebratory neutrality, and reformatory justice.[47] Religious freedom covers not only religious beliefs, but also it encompasses rituals and practices. Celebratory neutrality entails a state that assists, both financially and otherwise, in the celebration of all faiths. Reformatory justice involves regulating and reforming religious institutions and practices, setting aside some core elements that are beyond regulation.

42 *Jawaharlal Nehru's Speeches V*, 1996, p. 59.
43 Sarvepalli Gopal, *Jawaharlal Nehru: An Anthology,* 1980, p. 327.
44 Bhargava, "India's Secular Constitution," 2002, p. 117.
45 Chandoke, *Beyond Secularism: The Rights of Religious Minorities*, 2002, p. 48.
46 Ibid., p. 50.
47 Dhavan, "The Road to Xanadu: India's Quest for Secularism," 2001.

In an introduction to a collection of essays on Indian secularism, the editors flag its unusual nature by observing that:

> In the West secularism historically sought the separation of the spheres of state and religious authority, broadly to correspond to the domains of public and private life. The Indian state has chosen to interpret secularism differently: it has undertaken the charge to ensure the protection of all religions. It therefore makes a huge investment in matters of religion, unlike any nation in the West – for example, by administering religious trusts, declaring holidays for religious festivals, preserving the system of different personal laws for different communities, undertaking the reform of religious law, having secular courts interpret religious laws, and so on. The raises the problem of where the boundaries of state secularism are to be drawn.[48]

E. The Hindutva Ruling

The "Hindutva judgments" is the collective name given to seven decisions handed down by the Supreme Court in 1996. The cases involved 12 members of Hindu nationalist parties, such as the BJP and Shiv Sena. The 12 members, who included Shiv Sena chief Bal Thackeray and then Maharashtra Chief Minister Manohar Joshi, were charged with violating Section 123 of the Representation of People Act, 1951 (RPA) by appealing to Hindutva. Section 123(3) prohibits election candidates from appealing for votes on the grounds of religion or religious symbols among other things. Section 123(3A) prohibits attempts to promote enmity on grounds of religion, race, community or language. On the specific question of whether an appeal to Hindutva constitutes a violation of the RPA, the main opinion of the Court was delivered in *Prabhoo v. Kunte*[49] where Ramesh Yeshwant Prabhoo, then mayor of Bombay, and his election agent, Thackeray, faced charges of a corrupt practice i.e. appealing for votes on religious grounds or promoting enmity on religious grounds.

The Court first dealt with the question of the constitutionality of section 123 of the RPA, which was challenged by the appellants. The Court upheld the constitutionality of the relevant sections of the RPA on the grounds that they were "enacted to so as to eliminate from the electoral process, appeals to those divisive factors which arouse irrational passions

48 Needham and Rajan, "Introduction," 2007, p. 20.

49 See Cossman and Kapur, *Secularism's Last Sigh? Hindutva and the (Mis)Rule of Law*, 1999, chapter 2, for details on the Hindutva cases.

that run counter to the basic tenets of our Constitution, and, indeed of any civilized political and social order."[50] Writing for the Court, Justice J.S. Verma said: "Under the guise of protecting your own religions, culture or creed you cannot embark on personal attacks on those of others or whip up low hard instincts and animosities or irrational fears between groups to secure electoral victories."[51]

On the basis of speeches by Thackeray,[52] the Court held that there was an appeal to voters to elect Prabhoo because he was a Hindu. The Court also held that one of Thackeray's speeches included derogatory references to Muslims. On these counts, the Court concluded that Prabhoo and Thackeray were guilty of corrupt practices.[53] However, in another of the Hindutva cases the court acquitted Manohar Joshi, possibly the most high profile candidate accused of corrupt practice. The chief minister was found not guilty for declaring in a public speech that the "first Hindu state will be established in Maharashtra." The Court in this instance ruled: "A mere statement that the first Hindu state will be established in Maharashtra is by itself not an appeal for votes on the grounds of his religion but the expression, at best, of such a hope."

The most important aspect of the ruling was the discussion on the legitimacy of appealing to 'Hindutva' during the election campaign. In discussing Hindutva, Justice Verma first went over the definition of Hinduism presented in an earlier case *Yagnapurushdasji*. Basing his opinion on his reading of the inclusivist Hinduism of *Yagnapurushdasji* and on another later decision,[54] Verma proceeded to conflate Hindutva with Hin-

50 Supreme Court of India, AIR 1996 SC 1124.

51 Ibid.

52 Some of Thackeray's speeches, which were quoted by the Court, included passages like: "We are fighting this election for the protection of Hinduism. Therefore, we do not care for the votes of Muslims. The country belongs to Hindus and will remain so."

53 In contrast, in another of the Hindutva cases, then Maharashtra chief minister Manohar Joshi was found not guilty for declaring in a public speech that the "first Hindu state will be established in Maharashtra." The Court ruled: "In our opinion, a mere statement that the first Hindu state will be established in Maharashtra is by itself not an appeal for votes on the grounds of his religion but the expression, at best, of such a hope."

54 Supreme Court of India, *Commissioner of Wealth Tax, Madras v. Late R. Stridharan by L.R.s*, (1976) Supp SCR 478. Here the Court said: "It is a matter of common knowledge that Hinduism embraces within self [sic] so many diverse forms

duism by arguing that Hindutva was a "way of life" and could not be equated with "narrow fundamentalist Hindu religious bigotry."[55]

Thus, it cannot be doubted, particularly in view of the Constitution Bench decisions of this Court that the words 'Hinduism' and 'Hindutva' are not necessarily to be understood and construed narrowly, confined only to the strict Hindu religious practices unrelated to the culture and ethos of the people of India, depicting the *way of life* of the Indian people. Unless the context of a speech indicates a contrary meaning or use, in the abstract these terms are indicative more of a *way of life* of the Indian people and are not confined merely to describe persons practicing the Hindu religion as a faith (italics added).[56]

In conflating Hindutva with Hinduism, the Court ignored the sacred soil and birth/race aspects of Hindutva as defined by Savarkar and Golwalkar.

The Court, however, did not stop at equating Hinduism with Hindutva. Quoting from a book on Indian Muslims,[57] Verma then went on to opine that "the word 'Hindutva' is used and understood as a synonym for 'Indianisation', i.e. development of uniform culture by obliterating the differences between all the cultures co-existing in the country."[58] According to the Court, the terms Hinduism and Hindutva by themselves did not violate the provisions of the RPA.

> Considering the terms 'Hinduism' or 'Hindutva' per se as depicting hostility, enmity or intolerance towards other religious faiths or professions, proceeds from an improper appreciation and perception of the true meaning of these expression emerging from the discussions in earlier authorities of this Court… It is indeed very unfortunate, if in spite of the liberal and tolerant fea-

---

of beliefs, faiths, practices and worship it is difficult to define the term 'Hindu' with precision."

55 Supreme Court of India, AIR 1996 SC 1130.

56 See ibid., 1129.

57 See Khan, *Indian Muslims: The Need for a Positive Outlook*, 1994. The exact quote was: "The strategy worked out to solve the minorities problem was, although differently worded, that of Hindutva or Indianisation. This strategy, briefly stated, aims at developing a uniform culture by obliterating the differences between all the cultures co-existing in the country." However Cossman and Kapur point out that it is a cause of concern that the quoted passage is a description of the strategy of the Jana Sangh, which is something that the Court does not mention or seems to be bothered about. See also Noorani, *Savarkar and Hindutva: The Godse Connection*, 2002, p. 74. Noorani writes that the Maulana was not writing in praise of Hindutva but censuring it.

58 Supreme Court of India, AIR 1996 SC 1130.

tures of Hinduism recognized in judicial decisions, these terms are misused by anyone during the elections to gain any unfair political advantage.[59]

But unfortunately, these terms could be and arguably were misused in the way specified.

Though Verma assimilated Hinduism and Hindutva, he was silent on the antecedents of Hindutva. For example, he did not consider Savarkar and Golwalkar's use of sacred soil and race to include some and exclude others as foreigners. However, the intense debate generated by the Hindutva judgment brought out some of the important ramifications of the ruling. Commentators were troubled by the fact that the Court by inferring the meaning of Hindutva from Hinduism had "obscured the historical background as well as the contemporary political context"[60] of Hindutva. It was argued that the Court failed to "recognize that Hindutva as an expression has a special meaning and is associated with the social and political philosophy of V.D. Savarkar and M.S. Golwalkar."[61] It was further pointed out that the judgment implied that "Hinduism, the religion of the majority of Indians, comes to reflect the way of life of *all* Indians."[62]

At the other end of the spectrum, the Hindu nationalists were jubilant about the judgment. Soon after *Prabhoo*, an editorial in the *Organiser*, the journal of the RSS, stated, "The apex court has fully and unambiguously endorsed the concept of Hindutva which the [BJP] has been propounding since its inception."[63] A contemporary Hindu nationalist ideologue and a minister of the BJP-led NDA government, Arun Shourie, argued, "The Court accepted, indeed adopted in toto the definition of Hindu, of Hindutva which the RSS and BJP have been maintaining is what they have meant whenever they have used these expressions."[64] The BJP referred to the judgment in the party's 1999 election manifesto:

> Every effort to characterize Hindutva as a sectarian or exclusive idea has failed as the people of India have repeatedly rejected such a view and the Supreme Court, too, finally, endorsed the true meaning and content of Hinduism as being consistent with the true meaning and definition of secularism.

---

59 Ibid., 1131.

60 Cossman and Kapur, *Secularism's Last Sigh?*, p. 34.

61 Nauriya, "The Hindutva Judgements: A Warning Signal," 1996, p. 11.

62 Cossman and Kapur, *Secularism's Last Sigh?*, p. 33.

63 *Organiser*, "Editorial," December 24, 1996.

64 Shourie, "The Hindutva Judgments: The Distance That Remains," 1996, at http://www.bjp.org/index.php?option=com_content&task=view&id=2653&Itemid=376.

F. The Politics of Hinduism

There are many who have argued powerfully that the division of the Indian population into religious communities was the result of British rule. Colonial policies – the census and the legal system in particular – classified the population along religious lines and helped solidify religious identities. This is not to say that there was no sense of religious identity before the British came to India. But this sense of identity did not translate into pan-Indian political movements. Indeed, there is sufficient reason to believe that Hinduism itself might have been a construct of Orientalist scholarship.

It is now commonly accepted that use of the term 'Hinduism' or 'Hindu' to denote a single religious community is of recent origin. It was only from the nineteenth century that the term Hinduism came to be in vogue. In large measure British scholars, missionaries, and administrators introduced it. Needless to say the fixation with defining Hinduism was not confined to the Western scholar. The definition or redefinition of Hinduism by Hindu intellectuals was most often a response to the relentless critiques of European missionaries and Orientalists. The search by Hindu intellectuals for a more pure form of Hinduism was initiated by Rammohun Roy, who is recognized as a seminal figure in the reform of Hinduism and hailed as the 'father' of modern India.

This 'cleansing' of Hinduism and an adoption of, what historian Romila Thapar has referred to as, the Semitic model would be a recurrent theme among Hindu reformers in the nineteenth century and later. There were broadly two strands of reformist Hinduism: an 'inclusivist' and an 'exclusivist' model. The most prominent proponents of an inclusivist Hinduism were Swami Vivekananda (1863-1902) and Sarvepalli Radhakrishnan (1888-1975). The exclusivist strand was associated with the founder of contemporary Hindu nationalism, Vinayak Damodar Savarkar (1883-1966), and his notion of 'Hindutva' (Hinduness). Like many Hindu intellectuals before him, Savarkar, too, engaged with the problem of how to define 'Hinduism' and 'Hindu'. In tracing the origin of the term 'Hindu', Savarkar refused to accept standard interpretations that held that the term was coined by outsiders to describe the people living across the Indus River. In his seminal text, *Hindutva*, he wrote, "Thus Hindu would be the name that this land and the people that inhabited it bore from time immemorial that even the Vedic name Sindhu is but a later and secondary form of it."[65]

The key innovation by Savarkar was giving the concept of Hindu a territorial component. "We have found," Savarkar writes, "the first important essential qualification of a Hindu is that to him the land that extends from Sindhu to Sindhu is the Fatherland (Pitribhu), the Motherland (Matribhu) the land of his patriarchs and forefathers."[66] More importantly, Savarkar specified that the "Dharma of a Hindu being so completely identified with the land of the Hindus, this land to him is not only a Pitribhu but a Punyabhu, not only a fatherland but a holyland."[67] This meant that Muslims and Christians, who might have been born in the "common Fatherland", could not be regarded as Hindus. Savarkar coined the word 'Hindutva' to substitute for Hinduism which, in his book, "meant a theory or code more or less based on spiritual or religious dogma or system." According to Savarkar it was of paramount importance to distinguish between Hinduism and Hindutva: "Hinduism is only a derivative, a fraction, a part of Hindutva [...]. Hindutva embraces all the departments of thought and activity of the whole Being of our Hindu race."[68]

The exclusivist logic of Savarkar was extended by M.S. Golwalkar. He was the most prominent ideologue of the Rashtriya Swayamsevak Sangh (RSS). Founded in 1925, the RSS aimed to revitalize India's cultural life by organizing branches (*sakhas*) where the country's youth could learn discipline and devotion to the nation. In 1938, two years after he became *sarsanghchalak* (supreme director) of the RSS, Golwalkar published *We or Our Nationhood Defined.* Regarding the origins of the Hindus, Golwalkar declared in his book that Hindus came "into this land [Hindusthan] from nowhere, but are indigenous children of the soil always, from times immemorial and are natural masters of the country."[69] Borrowing from extant notions of nationalism, Golwalkar stressed that the 'Hindu' nation was founded on a defined territory, race, religion, culture and language. This concept of the Hindu nation was marked by exclusivity: "All those not belonging to the national, i.e. Hindu Race, Religion, Culture and Lan-

65 Savarkar, *Hindutva: Who is a Hindu?*, 1969, p. 10.
66 Ibid., p. 110.
67 Ibid., p. 111.
68 Ibid., p. 3-4.
69 Golwalkar, *We or Our Nationhood Defined,* 1947, p. 13.

guage naturally fall out of the pale of 'National' Life." Golwalkar's message to the non-Hindus was unambiguous and draconian:

> The non-Hindu peoples in Hindusthan must either adopt the Hindu culture and language, must learn to respect and hold in reverence Hindu religion, must entertain no idea but those of glorification of the Hindu race and culture [...].[70]

In post-1947 India, the BJP and its predecessor, the Jana Sangh, became the political face of Hindu nationalism. After a Hindu fundamentalist, Nathuram Godse, shot dead Mahatma Gandhi in 1948, the RSS was banned. When the ban was lifted in 1949, the RSS kept away from explicitly political work. Another important member of the Sangh Parivar (saffron brotherhood) is the Vishwa Hindu Parishad, which was founded in 1964. For a large part of India's independent history, the Hindu nationalist groups remained on the margins of India's politics. In the 1984 elections following Indira Gandhi's assassination, the BJP won a mere two seats in the national elections. However, from the late-1980s onwards, the BJP's fortunes improved. There were certain critical events that pushed the Hindu nationalist groups to the forefront and led to a sharp rise in their popularity.

More than any single factor, it was the Ayodhya issue that propelled the Sangh Parivar from the periphery to the mainstream. In 1984, the VHP passed a resolution intending to liberate the disputed Ram Janambhoomi site in Ayodhya, a town in north India where Rama, a popular Hindu god, is believed to have been born. This was a divisive issue since a mosque – the Babri Masjid (so named since a commander in Mughal emperor Babur's army is said to have destroyed a temple and built a mosque over it) – stood on the site of the Ram Janambhoomi. The site had been kept under local and key ever since an idol of Rama mysteriously appeared inside the mosque in 1949. The VHP mobilized support around this issue by asking Hindus all over India to make special bricks, which would be consecrated in a ceremony called Ram *shilan puja* and then sent to Ayodhya in special chariots. This campaign was marked by considerable tension between Hindus and Muslims and acts of violence across India.

The VHP mobilization and religious polarization around the Ayodhya issue was not the only factor behind the success of the BJP. In 1985, when the Congress under Rajiv Gandhi was heading the central government, the

70 Ibid., p. 55-56.

locks of the temple inside the Babri Masjid was opened after a writ petition was filed by the VHP in a local court. The same year the Indian Supreme Court passed the famous Shah Bano judgment where a divorced Muslim woman was granted maintenance. This was seen by many Muslim leaders as infringing Islamic personal law. Faced with massive protests from conservative Muslims, the Rajiv Gandhi government capitulated and passed a legislation, which annulled the court ruling. The BJP would exploit this in its election campaign accusing the Congress of "pseudo-secularism" and "minority appeasement." Shah Bano also provided ammunition to the BJP's demand for a uniform civil code for all Indians, irrespective of religion, instead of different sets of civil laws for Hindus, Muslims, Christians, and Parsis. The 1980s also saw the telecast of the enormously popular serials based on the epics *Ramayana* and *Mahabharata* on the state-run television channel, Doordarshan. These, too, played their role in the mobilization by the Sangh Parivar. The immediate effect of this mobilization programme was felt in the 1989 elections. The BJP's tally of parliamentary seats jumped to 89. The next year, the BJP formed government in the states of Madhya Pradesh, Rajasthan, and Himachal Pradesh.

In 1990, the BJP undertook its most important campaign ever to reach out to and consolidate its support base. BJP leader Lal Krishna Advani launched a *rath yatra* (a procession in a chariot) in September from the Somnath temple in Gujarat with the intention of traveling some 10,000 kilometres across northern and western India before finishing up at Ayodhya. The *yatra* was highly successful, but it also left a trail of religious tension and violence. In October 1990, Advani was arrested in Bihar leading to the BJP withdrawing support to the coalition government in New Delhi and fresh elections in 1991. The assassination of Rajiv Gandhi during the campaigning for the elections generated a sympathy wave in favour of the Congress. In spite of this, the BJP emerged as the second largest party with 119 seats in Parliament and a vote share of nearly 20 which was nearly double its share in 1989. The main support for the BJP came from the urban, Hindu middle class.

It was during the Narasimha Rao-led Congress government's tenure that Indian secularism suffered one of its most dramatic setbacks. Though the BJP had by now come to power in Uttar Pradesh – the state where Ayodhya is located – in 1991, the party did not take any steps to 'liberate' the Ram Janambhoomi. However, from October 1992 onwards, the VHP began a campaign of *kar seva* (voluntary service) for temple construction at Ayodhya. It announced that on December 6, 1992 it would start *kar seva* in Ayodhya and not stop until the temple was built. On the appointed day, some 200,000 *kar sevaks* (volunteers) congregated in Ayodhya. For five hours, an army of *sevaks* assaulted the Babri Masjid, which finally caved in by evening.

The demolition of the Babri Masjid was a low point in the history of Indian secularism. Its repercussions were felt far beyond Ayodhya. The Uttar Pradesh government was dismissed by the Centre. Within a week, the BJP governments in Madhya Pradesh, Himachal Pradesh, and Rajasthan were dismissed and several prominent BJP leaders, including Advani, were arrested. There were several clashes between Hindus and Muslims following the demolition, the worst being the two-week long Mumbai riots in January 1993. Though the Ram Janambhoomi movement petered out, the Babri Masjid demolition had the effect of breeding animosity between Hindus and Muslims across northern India. The political fallout of Ayodhya and Babri Masjid was mixed. The BJP lost heavily in elections in Himachal Pradesh and Madhya Pradesh though it was re-elected in Rajasthan. However, in Uttar Pradesh it lost out to a coalition of two parties – the Samajwadi Party and the Bahujan Samaj Party – which drew heavily on votes from Muslims and lower castes. But in spite of the reversal of fortunes, the BJP remained the single largest party in Uttar Pradesh.

The rise of the BJP from the late 1980s was accompanied by a steady loss of support for the Congress, which had been India's pre-eminent party since independence. The 1990s also saw the emergence of a host of caste-based as well as regional parties that challenged the hegemony of the Congress. Though the BJP emerged as the largest party in the 1996 general elections and was invited to form the government, it could not survive for more than 13 days. Between 1998 and 1999 the BJP formed a government that lasted only a year. Finally, the BJP stitched together a coalition – the National Democratic Alliance – which lasted a full term from 1999-2004 with Atal Bihari Vajpayee as prime minister. The NDA government would also mark a phase of moderation in BJP policy since it had to carry along several coalition partners. Most of its pet projects such as Ayodhya and the uniform civil code were put on the backburner.

However, the BJP coalition's term was marked by one of the worst incidents of religious violence in independent India. If the destruction of the Babri Masjid was a low point of Indian secularism, the 2002 Gujarat riots marked a nadir in Hindu-Muslim relations. The immediate provocation of the riots was the setting on fire of a train bogey carrying *kar sevaks* returning from Ayodhya in a station called Godhra in Gujarat. Fifty-seven people died in that fire. On the suspicion that Muslims might have been behind the act, bloody violence broke out across the state. Nearly 1,100 people, most of them Muslims, were killed over a month-long orgy of violence. Riots have not been uncommon in India, however, the Gujarat riots were unprecedented – with the exception of the post-partition riots in 1947 and the anti-Sikh riots in 1984 after Indira Gandhi's assassination – in scale. It was also characterized by what was seen a tacit compliance with and abetment of the violence by the Gujarat administration led by then Chief Minister Narendra Modi. There are many who believe that the Gujarat violence was a progrom by the Modi government where Muslims were deliberately targeted.

Even the BJP government in New Delhi sought to distance itself from the Gujarat violence with then Prime Minister Vajpayee saying on April 4, 2002, in Ahmedabad (the capital of Gujarat), "A ruler should not make any discrimination between his subjects on the basis of caste, creed and religion."[71] In a direct indictment of the state administration, the National Human Rights Commission in its annual report said:

> The tragic events in Gujarat, starting with the Godhra incident and continuing with the violence that rocked the state over two months, have greatly saddened the nation. There is no doubt, in the opinion of the Commission, that there was a comprehensive failure on the part of the state government to control the persistent violation of the rights to life, liberty, equality, and dignity [...].[72]

In the next national elections in 2004, the BJP-led coalition lost in spite of presiding over a period of high economic growth. Indeed, one of the planks of its election campaign was the 'Shining India' slogan. To the surprise of most political pundits, the Congress-led United Progressive Alliance (UPA) ousted the BJP at the Centre. In the subsequent years, the BJP presented a picture of confusion, uncertain about how to regroup and go forward. There were also few national-level leaders to replace an ailing Vajpayee and Advani. More importantly, there was confusion within the

71 "Prime Minister, Atal Behari Vajpayee on Gujarat," *Outlook* Novemer 2002, at https://www.outlookindia.com/website/story/prime-minister-atal-behari-vajpayee-on-gujarat/218032.

72 National Human Rights Commission, "Report on the visit of NHRC Team headed by Chairperson, NHRC to Ahmedabad, Vadodra and Godhra," 2002, at http://nhrc.nic.in/guj_annex_1.htm.

party on whether to pursue hardline Hindutva or to follow a moderate policy.

Amid this uncertainty, one man's fortune shone brighter than ever: Narendra Modi. The known details of Modi's life have been widely publicized. From a lower caste (Ghanchi) though by no means the lowest, he had a formal marriage at an early age but seems never to have lived with his wife. He joined the RSS as a young man. In 1988, he was appointed organising secretary of the BJP's Gujarat unit. He played a crucial role in the 1995 and 1998 Gujarat state elections before becoming chief minister in 2001 after the huge earthquake in the state. Soon after the 2002 Gujarat riots, Modi was re-elected, silencing his many critics within India and outside. Since then he was returned to power in Gujarat in two successive elections. Such was the dominance of the BJP across Gujarat that a new term was coined to describe Modi's politics – Moditva – to replace the earlier Hindutva of the BJP. The success of Modi was all the more remarkable since there was considerable dissent within the BJP against Modi and his autocratic style of functioning.

Though the UPA returned to power in 2009 the second tenure of the government, especially its last two years, was marked corruption scandals and policy paralysis. This meant that the BJP was able to bounce bank in the 2014 national elections. Much of the credit for the decisive nature of the BJP's victory has to go to India's newly-appointed Prime Minister, Narendra Modi. When the BJP announced Modi as its prime ministerial candidate in 2013, there were many who were sceptical of his ability to reach out to voters beyond the party's traditional catchment area of northern and western India. The 2002 riots in Gujarat were a serious concern for many, particularly minorities. But not only did he enthuse voters across India, including eastern and southern India where the BJP is not traditionally strong, but also he helped the party win an unprecedented number of seats from the north and west.

Among the factors crucial to the BJP's success was the presidential-style campaign run by Modi. Perhaps the only other prime ministerial aspirant in India who ran a similar campaign was Indira Gandhi in the 1971 election. Given the fragmentation of the polity there were doubts about the efficacy of such a campaign. But Modi was helped by the fact that the electorate, particularly younger voters, was receptive to his message. There were several reasons why Modi's campaign was so successful. First, Modi spoke the language of development and governance, rather than the divisive agenda of Hindutva, which appealed to voters. The BJP's campaign was extremely well packaged and funded, using both the traditional and social media to tremendous effect. Modi, who addressed some 450 rallies across India during the campaign period, also used innovative methods such as hologram technology to address multiple rallies without actually being physically present. This allowed Modi to transcend the BJP's traditional vote base of upper caste Hindus and its regional limitations.

On the ground, however, the BJP worked actively to consolidate the Hindu vote. This paid dividend in states like Uttar Pradesh, which sends 80 MPs to the Lok Sabha, and Bihar which elects 40 MPs. Both states saw communal violence in the run-up to the polls which possibly helped the Hindu vote consolidate in favour of the BJP and enabled it to win an astounding 93 out of 120 seats compared to only 22 seats in the 2009 election. The BJP was also able to woo lower castes, who traditionally do not vote for the BJP, by consistently emphasizing Modi's lower-caste background; it also made crucial alliances with parties such as the Lok Janshakti Party (LJP), which has considerable support among the lower castes, in Bihar.

Second, the Congress-led United Progressive Alliance (UPA) was facing severe anti-incumbency on various counts, including high inflation, a raft of corruption scandals and policy paralysis, and the BJP seemed to many voters the only credible, national alternative. A demoralised Congress ran a lackadaisical campaign which was a pale shadow of the BJP's. It helped the BJP that India's corporates as well as some media houses were heavily backing Modi.

Third, the RSS pulled out all stops to get Modi elected. Though Modi, a former RSS volunteer, has had his run-ins with his parent organization. It was the RSS which was instrumental in getting Modi selected as prime ministerial candidate and then backing him to the hilt. Fourth, many had felt that the minority Muslim community's mistrust of Modi would prove to be an obstacle for the BJP. However, the Muslim vote, which is rarely a majority in any constituency, got divided among the parties contesting against the BJP. This was especially true in UP and Bihar, where the BJP won most of the seats where there is a heavy concentration of Muslim voters.

During electioneering Modi largely eschewed the Hindu nationalist rhetoric and focused on governance, which was the theme of his campaign. The record of the Vajpayee government, which had allies to contend with, shows that the BJP has tended to become centrist in power. It might not be so easy for Modi to ignore the RSS, which is an organization that schooled him and also one with a considerable cadre he mobilized to ensure the BJP's win. Though the RSS is not involved in day-to-day administration it plays a significant role in major decisions within the BJP.

It is too early to predict how the Modi government will impact Indian secularism. At the time of writing, over the two years that the BJP has been in government, as was expected an overt assault on secularism has not occurred. There have, however, been several incidents of religious intolerance involving Hindu nationalist organisations, including forced reconversion of Muslims and Christians, the lynching of a Muslim man for consuming beef and incendiary statements by some BJP and RSS leaders. Prime Minister Modi himself has sought to distance himself from these controversies, often condemning them when it became absolutely necessary. This has given rise to the suspicion that he has turned a blind eye to religious polarisation and intolerance. Noted political analyst Pratap Bhanu Mehta has commented, "The blame […] has to entirely lie on Modi. Those who spread this poison enjoy his patronage."[73] At the same time, the BJP government has appointed several persons affiliated to the RSS to head educational and cultural institutions, paving the way for a more long term impact on Indian secularism.

Bibliography

Asad, Talal, *Formations of the Secular: Christianity, Islam, Modernity*, Stanford: Stanford University Press, 2003.

Austin, Granville, *The Indian Constitution: Cornerstone of a Nation*, Oxford: Oxford University Press, 2000.

Berger, Peter L., *The Desecularization of the World: Resurgent Religion and World Politics*, Washington D.C.: Ethics and Public Policy Center; W.B. Eerdmans Pub. Co, 1999.

Bhargava, Rajeev, "Introduction," in *Politics and Ethics of the Indian Constitution*, ed. Rajeev Bhargava, New Delhi: Oxford University Press, 2008, pp. 1-40.

Bhargava, Rajeev, "India's Secular Constitution," in *India's Living Constitution: Idea, Practices, Controversies*, ed. Zoya Hasan, E. Sridharan and R. Sudarshan, Delhi: Permanent Black, 2002, pp. 105-133.

73 Mehta, "Dadri reminds us how PM Modi bears responsibility for the poison that is being spread," 2015. Also see Mehta, "The Drummer's Silence," 2015.

Chandoke, Neera, *Beyond Secularism: The Rights of Religious Minorities*, New Delhi: Oxford University Press, 2002.

Cossman, Barbara, and Ratna Kapur, *Secularism's Last Sigh? Hindutva and the (Mis)Rule of Law*, New Delhi: Oxford University Press, 1999.

Dawkins, Richard, *The God Delusion*, Boston: Houghton Mifflin Co, 2006.

Dhavan, Rajeev, "The Road to Xanadu: India's Quest for Secularism," in *Religion and Personal Law in Secular India*, ed. Gerald Larson, Bloomington: Indiana University Press, 2001, pp. 301-329.

Elshtain, Jean Bethke, "Religion and Democracy," *Journal of Democracy* 20, 2 (2009): 7-17.

Galanter, Marc, *Law and Society in Modern India*, New Delhi: Oxford University Press, 1997.

Golwalkar, M.S., *We or Our Nationhood Defined,* Nagpur: Bharat Prakashan, 1947.

Harris, Sam, *The End of Faith: Religion, Terror, and the Future of Reason*, New York: W.W. Norton & Co, 2004.

Hitchens, Christopher, God is not Great: How Religion Poisons Everything, 1st ed., New York: Twelve, 2007.

India, Parliament, *Constituent Assembly debates: Official report, Vol. 1-12,* New Delhi: Lok Sabha Secretariat, 1999.

Jacobsohn, Gary Jeffrey, *The Wheel of Law: India's Secularism in Comparative Constitutional Context*, New Delhi: Oxford University Press, 2003.

Jha, Shefali, "Secularism in the Constituent Assembly Debates: 1946-50," *Economic and Political Weekly* 37, 30 (2002): 3175-3180.

Keddie, Nikki R., "Secularism & its Discontents," *Daedalus* 132, 3 (2003): 14-30.

Khan, Maulana Wahiuddin, *Indian Muslims: The Need for a Positive Outlook*, New Delhi: Al-Risala Books, 1994.

Khilnani, Sunil, "Secularism: Western and Indian," in *The Secular State and Islam in Europe*, ed. Kurt Almqvist, Stockholm: Axel and Margaret Ax:son Johnson Foundation, 2007.

Lewis, Bernard, *The Crisis of Islam: Holy War and Unholy Terror*, London: Phoenix, 2004.

Luthera, Ved Prakash, *The Concept of the Secular State and India*, London, New York: Oxford University Press, 1964.

Madan, T. N., "Secularism in its Place," in *Secularism and Its Critics*, ed. Rajeev Bhargava, New Delhi: Oxford University Press, 1998, pp. 297-320.

Mahajan, Gurpreet, *Identities and Rights: Aspects of Liberal Democracy in India, Delhi*, Oxford: Oxford University Press, 1998.

Mahajan, Gurpreet, "Religion and the Indian Constitution: Questions of Separation and Equality," in *Politics and Ethics of the Indian Constitution*, ed. Rajeev Bhargava, New Delhi: Oxford University Press, 2008, pp. 297-310.

Mehta, Pratap Bhanu, "Dadri reminds us how PM Modi bears responsibility for the poison that is being spread," *The Indian Express*, October 3, 2015.

Mehta, Pratap Bhanu, "The Drummer's Silence," *The Indian Express*, July 3, 2015.

Ministry of Information and Broadcasting, Government of India, *Jawaharlal Nehru's Speeches V*, New Delhi: Publications Division, Ministry of Information and Broadcasting, Government of India, 1996.

Munshi, K. M., *Indian Constitutional Documents, Vol. 2*, Bombay: Bharatiya Vidya Bhavan, 1967.

Nandy, Ashis, "The Politics of Secularism and the Recovery of Religious Toleration," in *Secularism and Its Critics*, ed. Rajeev Bhargava, New Delhi: Oxford University Press, 1999, pp. 321-344.

Nandy, Ashis, "Closing the Debate on Secularism: A Personal Statement," in *The Crisis of Secularism in India*, ed. Anuradha Dingwaney Needham and Rajeswari Sunder Rajan, Ranikhet: Permanent Black, 2007, pp. 107-117.

National Human Rights Commission, "Report on the visit of NHRC Team headed by Chairperson, NHRC to Ahmedabad, Vadodra and Godhra," 2002, at http://nhrc.nic.in/guj_annex_1.htm.

Nauriya, Anil, "The Hindutva Judgements: A Warning Signal," *Economic and Political Weekly* 31, 1 (1996): 10-13.

Needham, Anuradha Dingwaney, and Rajeswari Sunder Rajan, "Introduction," in *The Crisis of Secularism in India*, ed. Needham and Rajan, Ranikhet: Permanent Black, 2007, pp. 1-42.

Nehru, Jawaharlal, and Sarvepalli Gopal (eds.), *Jawaharlal Nehru: An Anthology*, Delhi, Oxford: Oxford University Press, 1980.

Noorani, Abdul Gafoor, *Savarkar and Hindutva: The Godse Connection*, New Delhi: LeftWord Books, 2002.

Norris, Pippa, and Ronald Inglehart, *Sacred and Secular: Religion and Politics Worldwide*, Cambridge: Cambridge University Press, 2004.

Nussbaum, Martha C., *The Clash Within: Democracy, Religious Violence, and India's Future*, New Delhi: Permanent Black, 2007.

Roy, Olivier, *Globalized Islam: The Search for a new Ummah*, New York: Columbia University Press, 2004.

Savarkar, V.D., *Hindutva: Who is a Hindu?*, Bombay: Veer Savarkar Prakashan, 1969.

Sen, Ronojoy, *Articles of Faith: Religion, Secularism, and the Indian Supreme Court*, New Delhi: Oxford University Press, 2012.

Shiva Rao, Benegal, *The Framing of India's Constitution: Select Documents, Vol. 2*, Nasik: Government of India Press, 1968.

Shourie, Arun, "The Hindutva Judgments: The Distance That Remains," 1996, at http://www.bjp.org/index.php?option=com_content&task=view&id=2653&Itemid=376.

Smith, Donald Eugene, *India as a Secular State*, Princeton N.J.: Princeton University Press, 1963.

Smith, Donald Eugene, "India as a Secular State," in *Secularism and Its Critics*, ed. Rajeev Bhargava, New Delhi: Oxford University Press, 1999, pp. 177-233.

Supreme Court of India, AIR 1996 SC 1124.

Supreme Court of India, AIR 1996 SC 1130.

Supreme Court of India, *Commissioner of Wealth Tax, Madras v. Late R. Stridharan by L.R.s*, (1976) Supp SCR 478.

Taylor, Charles, "Modes of Secularism," in *Secularism and Its Critics*, ed. Rajeev Bhargava, New Delhi: Oxford University Press, 1998, pp. 31-53.

US Supreme Court, *Lemon v Kurtzman*, 403 U.S. 602 (1971).

US Supreme Court, *Zorach v Clauson,* 343 U.S. 306 (1952).

US Supreme Court, *Everson v Board of Education Ewing*, 330 U.S. 1 (1947).

Varma, Pavan K., "Citizen India: The Many are One," *World Policy Journal* (Spring 2009): 45-52.

Cultivating Co-existence Through Control and Cooperation: 'Secularism with a Soul' and the Singapore Model of Regulating Religious Freedom and Maintaining Religious Harmony

Li-ann Thio

A. Introduction

There are a plurality of approaches adopted in constitutional arrangements structuring state-religion relations within secular constitutional orders which do not identify with any specific religion.[1] The model of secularism employed, whether anti-theocratic or anti-religious, whether the state is hostile, supportive, cooperative or accommodative towards religion, will impact the scope of religious freedom. Where a constitutional order recognises a degree of legal pluralism as a facet of respecting the right of religious minorities, and where religious tenets or religious law conflict with general law, this presents a perennial problem of managing or resolving conflicts regarding competing claims of authority between state and religion.

This chapter examines the Singapore model of state-religion relations where the state has displayed some degree of ambivalence towards religion. Religion is recognised as a positive and constructive social force (particularly in relation to welfare provision and sustaining social mores), as being "for many Singaporeans the source of their sense of morality, social duty and concern for their fellow men."[2] However, the 'dark side' of religion also presents a concern, insofar as it is viewed as a source of conflict where religion poses a challenge to political authority, or where intergroup religious tensions threaten to undermine the prioritised objective of

---

1 When Singapore seceded from the Malaysian Federation in 1965, it adapted its existing state constitution to become the Republic's new independence constitution. Notably, the Malaysian article 3 reference to Islam as the Federation's religion was omitted, in Singapore's early commitment to a form of democratic secularism. For an 8 model typology, see Hirschl, "Comparative Constitutional Law and Religion," 2011, pp. 422-440.

2 Para 45. Maintenance of Religious Harmony white paper (Cmd 21 of 1989).

'racial and religious harmony'. Historically, the race riots of the 1950s-1960s which has had a deep psychological impact on Singapore's founding fathers has been exacerbated by the close sociological relation between ethnicity and religion, specifically, Malays and Islam. Within Singapore, most Malays are overwhelming Muslim as a sociological fact (98.7%).[3] Geo-politically, the Chinese majority island city-state has been described as being a "red dot in a sea of green,"[4] given its location within a Malay region dominated by Muslim-majority Malaysia and Indonesia. The prospect of race-religion tensions in this context is self-evident.

Whether the government adopts a 'cooperation' or 'control' model towards religion depends on the nature of the religious activity and expression. Specific instances of 'cooperation' and 'control' are examined in this chapter, which should illuminate both the local understandings of secularism and the health of religious liberties extant in Singapore. In addition, it must be underscored that maintaining religious harmony is not merely a matter of public order or the absence of disorder, but it goes to the quality of relationship,[5] the sustainability of good relations between disparate religious groups in what may be described as a secular state, but a religious society. As Prakash J noted in *Chen Cheng v Central Christian Church*,[6] "Singapore is a secular state with divers religions and there is a very high degree of religious tolerance."

Nonetheless, there are increasing signs of intolerance towards religion by militant secularists, and the perennial fear of inter-religious conflict.[7]

Indeed, 'racial and religious harmony' may be considered a quasi-constitutional value and an integral aspect of the brand of Singapore communitarian constitutionalism and national identity. Securing the pacific co-existence of disparate ethnic and religious groups is considered key to social stability, a necessary but insufficient precondition to nurturing community, if not solidarity. Both legal and non-legal approaches towards managing

---

3 See 2010 Population Census (Demographic Characteristics, Education, Language and Religion) at www.singstat.gov.sg.

4 Former Indonesian President BJ Habibie made this derogatory reference: "President unhappy with Singapore, says AWSJ," *Straits Times* (Singapore), 5 August 1998, p. 16.

5 See Thio, "Relational Constitutionalism and the Management of Inter-Religious Disputes: The Singapore 'Secularism with a Soul' Model," 2012, pp. 1-24.

6 [1997] 1 SLR 94 at 103.

7 See Thio, "Between Eden and Armageddon: Navigating 'Religion' and 'Politics' in Singapore," 2009, pp. 365-405.

religious harmony are deployed, influenced by whether sanction and deterrence, or reconciliation, is the desired goal.

B. Setting the Context: Religion and the Singapore Constitutional Order

Constitutionalism as a commitment to limited government and effectuating fundamental principles of a polity does not in itself require metaphysical skepticism.[8] In negotiating the management of power, justice and culture, constitutionalism sits where "national history, custom, religion, social values and assumptions about government meet positive law."[9]

C. Secularism with a Soul – The Singapore Model

The indigenised model of state-religion relations in Singapore has been described as a form of 'secularism with a soul', which suggests the co-existence of the material and the metaphysical, where the state is not hostile to religion but allows religious groups a role to play in forging a harmonious, cohesive society. As Senior Minister of State ZA Rasheed noted:

> Secularism here is unique. It is not like the secularism in Turkey or France where the relationship between the state and the religion has brought about many problems, and even threatening their stability. We thank God that the situation here is different. There is mutual respect between the two. In fact, there is cooperation.[10]

Another minister noted that secularity does not connote anti-theism as Singapore's government is secular, but it is certainly not atheistic. It is neutral. This is an important principle because all the major religions of the world are represented here."[11] The Prime Minister in 2009 noted that: "We are not against religion. We uphold sound moral values."[12] The state is impartial insofar as it neither favours nor disfavours any religion. In contrast

8 See Walker, "The Idea of Nonliberal Constitutionalism," 1997, p. 154; Thio, "Constitutionalism in Illiberal Polities," 2012, pp. 133-152.

9 Beer, *Constitutional Systems in Late Twentieth Century Asia*, 1992, p. 4.

10 Zainul Abidin Rasheed, in *Singapore Parliamentary Debates*, vol. 74 (23 May 2002).

11 "Government is secular: not atheistic: BG Yeosd," *Straits Times* (Singapore), 8 October 1992, p. 2.

12 Prime Minister Lee Hsien Loong, "National Day Rally Speech," 2009.

to Malaysian practice, the Constitution of Singapore does not conflate ethnicity with religion; the government does not meddle with theology and refuses to recognise deviant sects or cults, which presupposes an espousal of religious orthodoxy.[13] During times of national disasters, religious and political leaders have shared the stage in national mourning rituals.[14] Political leaders also attend religious festivals.[15]

Secularism in this context is anti-theocratic, not anti-religious and has certain key features. First, secularism relates to the source of *political authority*, the "supreme source" being the Constitution of Singapore.[16] Political rights and democracy are to be secured not by religious institutions but through secular safeguards, including the press, judicial review, parliament and the ballot box.[17] Thus, beyond the *Syariah* court system, divine law is not an accepted source of *legal authority.*[18] Second, the Singapore model is distinct from the French *laïcité* or the Turkish model of strict *separation*, and it does not preclude the *co-operation* of religion and state,[19] for example, in delivering social welfare services. The government is "secular

---

13 The government stated that as a secular body it is not concerned "with issues of religious doctrinal purity or deviance," 71 *Singapore Parliament Reports*, 6 March 2000, col 1141 (Oral Question on Cults).

14 Tracy Sua and Sharlene Tan, "Thousands gather to pray for tsunami victims," *Straits Times* (Singapore), 31 January 2005; Zuraidah Ibrahim, "The nation mourns," *Straits Times* (Singapore), 31 December 1997, p. 1. See PM Lee Hsien Loong, "Tsunami Disaster Memorial Service," 9 January 2005, at http://www.mfa.com.sg/content/mfa/overseasmission/tokyo/press_statements_speeches/2005/200501/press_200501_2.html.

15 Prime Minister Lee delivered a speech at a Buddhist meeting at the Singapore Indoor Stadium where prayers for peace were made for the nation. He said: "Here we have created an environment where people of all faiths live in harmony and peace with one another." "Buddhist devotees light candles for Singapore's peace," *Straits Times* (Singapore), 18 November 2013, A9. The Singapore President has also attended an inter-religious prayer meeting organised by the Franciscan Friars: "Inter-religious prayer for peace," *Straits Times* (Singapore), 28 October 2013, B2.

16 President Wee Kim Wee, "President's Address" in *Singapore Parliamentary Debates*, vol. 52, col. 11 (9 January 1989).

17 *MRH White Paper*, para. 21.

18 The court in *Pte Chai Tshun Chieh v Chief Military Prosecutor* [1998] M.C.A. 1 rejected the argument by a pacifist Jehovah's Witnesses that he was not bound to obey secular military orders as his religion's sacred texts was a higher law than man-made law.

19 Kuah-Pearce, "The Poetics of Religious Philantrophy: Buddhist Welfarism in Singapore," 2008, pp. 167-187.

but not atheistic"[20] and it represents Singaporeans of "all beliefs, including those without a religion."[21] The government does not promote religious orthodoxy or punish heresy[22] and it seeks to treat religions even-handedly to keep the peace.[23] Religious groups are subject to public order laws such as those which regulate unlawful assembly.

The brand of secularism practised in Singapore is pragmatic rather than dogmatic. It is inclusionist rather than exclusionist, in seeking both to accommodate the expression of religiously influenced convictions in the public square as an aspect of preserving a democratic society[24] as well as religious participation in public life. An example of this is the celebration of the Jewish festival of Hannukah with a public menorah, first held in 2011.[25] However, while recognising the right of all citizens of whatever religious or non-religious profession, to participate in public debate,[26] the government is wary of religious groups forming political parties (though there are no laws banning this) or of religious leaders seeking to mobilise their flocks against the government and thereby intruding into the political realm and regularly cautions against this.[27] This reticence is tempered by the appreciation of the dangers of secular fundamentalism manifested

20 "Government is secular: not atheistic: BG Yeo," *Straits Times* (Singapore), 8 October 1992, p. 2.

21 "SM: Guard against religious enclaves," *Straits Times* (Singapore), 3 August 2009.

22 Part IX of the Administration of Muslim Law Act (1999) lists Muslim-specific offences such as cohabitation outside marriage which the *Syariah* courts implement.

23 PM Lee Hsien Loong, "National Day Rally Speech," 16 August 2009.

24 Thio, "Religion in the Public Sphere of Singapore: Wall of Division or Public Square," 2008, pp. 73-104.

25 "First Public Menorah in Singapore," *Straits Times* (Singapore), 25 December 2011, Community News Service at http://www.collive.com/ show_news.rtx?id=17 782.

26 Thio, "Religion in the Public Sphere of Singapore: Wall of Division or Public Square," 2008, pp. 73-104.

27 See Maintenance of Religious Harmony Act. Under this Act, the Minister can issue non-justiciable restraining order against a religious leader, or someone who incites a religious leader, prohibiting him from addressing a certain congregation on specified topics or from publishing material on certain topics, for a maximum of a two year period. This relates to instances where religion and politics is 'mixed', so as to incite disaffection against the government or inter-religious hostility. If the Presidential Council of Religious Harmony set up under the Act and composed primarily of religious leaders disagrees with the Minister's decision, the president has the power to override the ministerial order. This involves non-government actors in the moderation of government power.

where the state is hostile to religion, as opposed to taking "a neutral position with regard to religion."[28] Thus, negotiating the fluid boundary lines between 'religion' and 'politics' is a perennial problem of governance in Singapore. As a corrective, the government withdrew its ill-fated religious knowledge programme implemented in public schools in the 1980s, as this programme gave rise to the unexpected consequence of religious fervour, which was contrary to the espoused goal of co-opting religions to promote civic virtues rooted in self-discipline and the work ethic.[29] The Education Minister explained that the withdrawal was motivated by the feeling the government "had not been entirely neutral in the matter of religions" as only certain religions whose values were thought to be in alignment with government values were chosen for the scheme. The principle of subsidiarity is evident in the statement that imparting religious beliefs to children was "the province of the home and not that of the school," with the programme replaced by one on civics education based on "our shared values."[30]

While the constitution itself does not contain an express commitment to the principle of secularity, this is evident through constitutional history and contemporaneous understandings of the Singaporean polity, expressed in parliamentary debates, white papers, and ministerial statements.[31] Executive statements are given great weight in the Singapore context.[32] Here, a modified version of the English parliamentary system is practiced where the ruling People's Action Party currently controls 80 of 87 elective states and has ruled continuously within a dominant party state since Indepen-

---

28 Foreign Affairs Minister of State ZA Rasheed, *Forum on Religion and Multiculturalism*, National University of Singapore University Scholars Programme, 8 January 2010.

29 Tamney, *The Struggle over Singapore's Soul: Western Modernisation and Asian Culture*, 1996, pp. 25-49.

30 Tan, "Crucial for Government to be Neutral in Religious Matters," Statement on the phasing out of Religious Knowledge in schools, reported in *Straits Times* (Singapore), 27 October 1989, pp. 23-25. In 1990, a white paper on five 'shared values' was adopted, being: (a) Nation before community and society above self; (b) Family as the basic unit of society; (c) Regard and community support for the individual; (d) consensus instead of contention and (e) racial and religious harmony.

31 Para. 46 of the Shared Values white paper (Cmd 1 of 1991) states that "Singapore is a secular state." See also Thio, *A Treatise on Singapore Constitutional Law*, 2012, pp. 205-218.

32 See Thio, "Soft Constitutional Law in non-liberal Asian Constitutional Democracies," 2010, pp. 766-799.

dence was gained in 1965.[33] The apex Court of Appeal has described the Singaporean model of "accommodative secularism" as one predicated on "removing restrictions to one's choice of religious belief."[34] Freedom of conscience is a cardinal value underlying religious liberty in Singapore,[35] disallowing state protection of religious orthodoxy or apostasy laws, such as those extant in Malaysia where the state has adopted a protectionist attitude towards Sunni Islam, despite the historical Malaysian commitment to a secular state.[36]

Currently, more than 80% of Singaporeans profess a commitment to a religious faith (as opposed to belief in a secular faith). Buddhists and Taoists form the majority religious group (44.21%), followed by Christians (18.3%), Muslims (14.7%), Hindus (5.1%) other religions (0.7%) and atheists or agnostics (17%).[37] Singapore thus bucks the 'secularisation' thesis as modernity has not diminished religiosity. Unlike many parts of the humanistic West,[38] religion is taken seriously and not marginalised or trivialised, in many Asian countries, including Singapore. Whether or not all aspects of religious expression enjoy reasonable accommodation within the constitutionally permitted limitations on the basis of public order, health and morality, is a continuing subject of enquiry. This sheds light on the extent to which a genuine communitarianism is practised, where the

---

33 Thio, "The Right to Political Participation in Singapore: Tailor-Making a Westminster-Modelled Constitution to fit the Imperatives of 'Asian' Democracy," 2002, pp. 181-243.

34 *Nappalli Peter Williams v Institute of Technical Education* [1999] 2 SLR 569 at 576G (Court of Appeal).

35 Para 18(c) of the white paper on Maintenance of Religious harmony states as crucial the duty to "to respect the right of each individual to hold his own beliefs and to accept or not to accept any religion." The official view of Islam espoused by the Islamic Religious Council of Singapore is that "Islam does not believe in compulsion in religion" drawing from Surah 256: http://www. muis.gov.sg/websites/khut bah/ser-220621.asp.

36 See Fernando, *The Making of the Malayan Constitution*, 2002.

37 2010 Population Census (Demographic Characteristics, Education, Language and Religion), at www.singstat.gov.sg.

38 E.g. on 'secular fundamentalism', see Ekins, "Secular Fundamentalism and Democracy," 2005, pp. 81-93; Ocvirk, "Secularist Christophobic Fundamentalism and Islamic Monoreligionism: Obstacles for Dialogue and Peaceful Co-existence," 2009, pp. 423-433, available at http://www.teof.uni-lj.si/uploads/File/BV/BV-09-Ocvirkp2.pdf; Ogilvie, "After the Charter: Religious Free Expression and Other Legal Fictions in Canada," 2002, pp. 219-235; Campos, "Secular Fundamentalism," 1994, pp. 1814-1827.

existence of religious groups as intermediating institutions is valued in its role in promoting democracy and acting as a check against the organic, 'totalising' state which insists of being the final arbiter of all values, or whether statism prevails, to the determine of liberty in general, and religious freedom in particular.

D. Constitutional and Legal Framework

Religious liberties are guaranteed under article 15 of the Singapore Constitution which reads:

> 15.—
>
> (1) Every person has the right to profess and practise his religion and to propagate it.
> (2) No person shall be compelled to pay any tax the proceeds of which are specially allocated in whole or in part for the purposes of a religion other than his own.
> (3) Every religious group has the right —
> - to manage its own religious affairs;
> - to establish and maintain institutions for religious or charitable purposes; and
> - to acquire and own property and hold and administer it in accordance with law.
>
> (4) This Article does not authorise any act contrary to any general law relating to public order, public health or morality.

Notably, unlike the Malaysian constitution, there is no constitutional authorisation to enact anti-propagation legislation,[39] which would curtail the external expression of religious freedom in Singapore, nor state underwriting of Islamic institutions.[40] While freedom of conscience and profession of faith (the *forum internum*) is absolute, religious practice, and propagation (*forum externum*) may be subject to legislative regulation on the grounds list in article 15(4). Notably, religious freedom has the status of a non-derogable right as it cannot be curtailed by anti-subversion or Emer-

39 The 1966 Constitutional Commission Report stated at paragraph 38 that an anti-propagation clause which singled out a particular religion for special treatment" would be "inappropriate" and "inconsistent" in a "democratic secular state such as Singapore." (Singapore Government Printers, 1966).

40 Articles 3, 12(2) and 11(4), Federal Constitution of Malaysia (1957).

gency laws exceptionally permitted under articles 149 and 150 of the Constitution.

Religious groups have the right under article 15(3) to manage their own religious affairs, maintain religious charities, and administer property. Under article 16(2), religious groups have the right to establish and maintain religious institutions to instruct children in their own religion; except where the Constitution expressly permits, non-discrimination on grounds of religion is prohibited under article 12. In deference to religious minorities and the demands of religious pluralism, article 12(3) provides that the equality clause does not invalidate laws regulating religious personal laws or religiously mandated restrictions in relation to religious office or employment. Reservations were attached to articles 2 and 6 (modification or abolition of laws and customs that discriminate against women) when Singapore acceded to the UN Convention on the Elimination of All Forms of Discrimination against Women (CEDAW) "where compliance with these provisions would be contrary to their religious or personal laws."[41]

Singapore does not have a confessional constitution nor is there a clause prohibiting the establishment of religion after the American model.[42] 'Establishment' entails the state giving official recognition, financial or non-pecuniary or support to a particular faith. Indeed, the state indirectly protects Islam insofar as Article 152 of the Constitution recognises that the Malays are indigenous peoples to whom the government owes a duty "to protect, safeguard, support, foster and promote their political, educational, religious, economic, social and cultural interests and the Malay language." While article 152 does not embody a justiciable entitlement nor mandate a system of affirmative action or other forms of positive entitlement, it does oblige the government to devise and implement a programme to meet the needs of the Malays.

General laws seek to safeguard religious harmony. Under the Singapore Penal Code (Cap 224), it is an offence under section 298 to utter words with a deliberate intent to wound the religious or racial feelings of anoth-

41 The text of Singapore's reservations to CEDAW and objections to these may be found at the website of the UN Department for the Advancement of Women, at http://www.un.org.libproxy1.nus.edu.sg/womenwatch/daw/cedaw/reservations-country.htm.

42 *Colin Chan v. Public Prosecutor* [1994] 3 S.L.R. 662 at 681F. Contrast this with the anti-establishment U.S. First Amendment: "Congress shall make no law respecting an establishment of religion, or prohibiting the free exercise thereof.".

er; under section 298A words or acts which promote on grounds of religion or race, disharmony prejudicial to maintaining harmony between different religious or racial groups is a crime punishable with imprisonment. Section 3 of the Sedition Act (Cap 290) also adopts a capacious understanding of 'sedition' to encompass 'horizontal' relations between private actors insofar as speech promotes "feelings of ill-will and hostility between different races or classes of the population in Singapore." 'Race' has been broadly applied to encompass 'religion', at least where Islam is concerned, given the close nexus between Malays and Islam in the Singaporean context.[43] These laws reflect the importance accorded to the maintenance of racial and religious harmony, as does the specific legislation such as the Maintenance of Religious Harmony Act (Cap 167A), discussed below. Both manifest a desire to cater to the needs and 'feelings' of the Emotional Man, rather than the Rational Man.[44]

E. *The Accommodation of Muslim Minorities and Promoting Pacific Coexistence Through Autonomy Schemes*

The constitutional regime for negotiating religion and law and separating potential conflicts of jurisdiction is grounded in article 153 which essentially mandates legal pluralism. This is effectuated by the Administration of Muslim Law Act (Cap 3) (AMLA), which establishes religious courts with limited jurisdiction over matters relating to personal law, testamentary disposition, marriages, and divorces.

AMLA derives its authority not from a divine text but through secular fiat. To protect religious minorities, the law allows for religious-based exemptions.[45] There is some interaction of law and religion, even if secular law facilitates, and thereby, limits some aspects of *Syariah* (religious) law.

---

43 For an analysis of the provisions and relevant case law, Thio, "Contentious Liberty: Regulating Religious Propagation in a Religiously Diverse Secular Democracy," 2010, pp. 484-515; Tan, "Sedition and its new clothes in Singapore," 2011, pp. 212-236; Neo, "Seditious in Singapore! Free Speech and the offence of promoting ill-will and Hostility between different Racial Groups," 2011, pp. 351-372.

44 A Rational Man would be able to see the broader values of free speech and thus tolerate offensive speech which 'hurts' feelings. Laws which minister to hurt feelings deal with emotions rather than rationality and are more realistic than utopian.

45 E.g., madarasahs (religious schools) are exempt from the Compulsory Education Act (2001).

This may be characterised as a scheme of autonomy rather than what has been described as a 'sphere sovereignty' model which envisages two structurally distinct spheres where religion and state are sovereign within their spheres. Within a scheme of autonomy which is monist, a superior power concedes or delegates authority to a subordinate power.[46]

The pragmatic Singapore model of secularism is not contravened by the involvement of statute-based religious bodies like the Majlis Ugama Islam Singapura (MUIS) or Islamic Religious Council which regulates matters such as *halal* certification of food. Contrariwise, the stricter separation of church and state in the Philippines which "shall be inviolable"[47] rendered it unconstitutional for a Philippines government agency to be involved in halal certification.[48] This results from "classifying a food product as *halal* is a religious function because the standards used are drawn from the Qur'an and Islamic beliefs" and involving government in this matter infringed the religious freedom of Muslim organisations to "interpret for Filipino Muslims what food products are fit for Muslim consumption" was encroached upon. In addition, "by arrogating to itself the task of issuing *halal* certifications, the State has in effect forced Muslims to accept its own interpretation of the Qur'an and Sunnah on *halal* food."

Indeed, the Singapore government's friendly, protective approach towards the Muslim minority is evident in enforcement of secular laws protecting Muslim dietary requirements by civil courts. In *Angliss Singapore Pte. Ltd. v. PP*[49], the High Court upheld a conviction under section 88 of AMLA which makes the selling by a Muslim or non-Muslim of halal food without MUIS certification a strict liability offence. In this case, the food, "Dewfresh" chicken nuggets, was *halal* but exhibited the wrong label, lacking MUIS approval. In noting absolute liability and the fact that there was no intent to provoke racial discord, Justice Rajah observed that: "Parliament has deemed it fit that the religious sensitivity or welfare of the general public should warrant a high standard of care by all those engaged in the particular activities governed by statutes imposing strict liability" and that: "Parliament views *halal* certification as an issue of vital impor-

46 See generally van der Vyver, "The Jurisprudential Legacy of Abraham Kuyper and Leo XIII," 2002, pp. 211-249.

47 Article II, Section, 1987 Philippines Constitution.

48 *Islamic Da'Wah Council of the Philippines Inc v. Office of Muslim Affairs* G.R. No. 153888 (July 9, 2003).

49 [2006] 4 Sing. L. R. 653.

tance."[50] In so doing, the government discharges its article 152(2) responsibility to protect the Malays on the basis of indignity. Indeed, Judge Rajah (who is not a Muslim) suggested that AMLA should be amended to allow for the prosecution of corporate offenders. When AMLA was in fact amended in 2008, the Minister of Muslim Affairs referenced the Judge's observations, stating that "every Muslim in Singapore will take comfort in knowing that the authorities take a serious view of a matter that is important to all Muslims."[51] Thus, a dialogical relationship is evident between the courts and Parliament where the former suggests legal reform in the interests of protecting religious minorities, which is treated as an aspect of the common good.

Nonetheless, potential jurisdictional clashes between religious and civil courts have not occurred in Singapore where there is no mainstream effort to politicise Islam; where there is civil court jurisdiction over religious bodies, this is done respectfully to minimise a sense of intrusion into religious affairs. The High Court has held that religious bodies such as the MUIS fatwa committee which was involved in property disposition are subject to rules of natural justice as: "[i]t is an important principle of Western as well as Muslim jurisprudence that a person cannot be a judge in his own cause."[52]

The practice of legal pluralism in demonstrating respect for the Muslim minority which promotes relational well-being for the entire community is evident in two further matters. First, religious concerns qualified public health considerations when Muslims were allowed an exception from the policy of requiring victims of Severe Acute Respiratory Syndrome (SARs) to be immediately cremated, by allowing Muslim victims to be immediately buried in two sealed body bags.[53] Second, the government took a gradual approach before including the Muslim community in the application of the 'presumed consent' regime under Human Organ Transplant Act (Cap 131A);[54] this was first introduced in 1987 when prevailing religious

50 Ibid., at paras. 29, 31.

51 85 *Singapore Parliamentary Debates*, 17 Nov 2008, Administration of Muslim Law (Amendment Bill).

52 *Mohamed Ismail bin Ibrahim v Mohammad Taha bin Ibrahim* [2004] 4 SLR(R) 756 at 780.

53 "No wakes for suspected SARs deaths," *Straits Times* (Singapore), 24 April 2003, H4.

54 A person between the ages of 21 and 60 is presumed to have agreed to donate his kidneys, heart, liver and corneas when he dies, unless he has opted out.

opinion deemed this forbidden; however, the government allowed the Muslim community time to deliberate and come to a consensus that organ donation was beneficial and permissible before HOTA was extended to apply to Muslims in 2008.[55] In seeking consensus rather than imposing a fiat, the government demonstrated it was treating the Muslim community with concern and respect, while trying to promote public health policies in a manner which did not unduly disrupt religious sensitivities.

Nonetheless, the Muslim community is aware that an 'accommodation' model which seeks to maximise freedom without forsaking inter-group or social harmony requires some give and take. The government seeks to negotiate this through a 'common/separate domain' policy. Where a Muslim school principal tried to ban non-halal food from the school canteen, he was rapped by the Ministry of Education which requires canteen to provide a mix of halal and non-halal food suitable for children of all religions. Mosque leaders were quoted by the press as acknowledging the regressive nature of declaring a school canteen a *halal zone* as it would make non-Muslims think Muslims are not accommodating towards others.[56] There has also been some disquiet over the ban on wearing religious dress (tudung) by primary schoolgirls though the government sought to placate parents by urging them to consider the importance of education rather than pulling their daughters out of school. There is no absolute ban on wearing religious dress in public institutions, including secondary schools and universities. Indeed, the Speaker of Parliament, Madam Halimah Yacob, wears the hijab in discharging the duties of her office.[57] The rationale for banning religious dress from public primary schools was the government's desire to maintain such venues as common domains where commonality rather than difference is emphasised, though the government has also stated such policies were not writ in stone and open to continual negotiation.[58] This too reflects the attempt to balance religious liberties with public inter-

---

55 "Muslims to be included in the Act from Aug 1," *Straits Times* (Singapore), 22 January 2008.

56 "All schools must have mix of halal and non-halal food," *Straits Times* (Singapore), 6 February 2008; "'Halal zone' would've been a step backwards," *Straits Times* (Singapore), 6 February 2008.

57 Halimah Yacob: "I must be fair and impartial," *Supper Club, Singapolitics*, 22 May 2014, at http://www.singapolitics.sg/supperclub/halimah-yacob-i-must-be-fair-and-impartial.

58 On the tudung controversy, see Thio, "Recent Constitutional Developments: Of Shadows and Whips, Race, Rifts and Rights, Terror and Tudungs, Women and

ests, without impairing relational harmony which top-down approaches to governance are liable to impair – unhappiness is managed by continual dialogue and an invitation to cooperate and work within the system.

Indeed, when the government was dealing with the terrorist threat emanating from an extremist sector of the Muslim community in relation to the Jemaah Islamiyah arrests of 2002 for a bomb plot, it underscored the need not to "disrupt the legitimate practices and peaceful activities of the local Muslim community." It urged the Muslim community to adopt self-regulatory practices to weed out extremist teachings, and also urged all Singaporeans to be vigilant and not allow fears to disrupt religious harmony and relations. The government also sphere-headed reconciliatory efforts among Singaporeans by promoting dialogue and initiating the adoption of a declaration on religious harmony by religious leaders, as a code of conduct meant to promote self-restraint and good-will among the religious groups and races.[59]

F. Cooperation of Religion and State

Where the values of religious groups are in alignment with state policy, the state adopts a co-operationist or partnership approach towards them. This is evident in the delivery of welfare services[60] within the context of a non-welfare State, where the government administers welfare programme as a matter of discretionary powers rather than justiciable entitlements. The government pro-actively encourages community groups, religious or otherwise, to provide social welfare services through providing land at nominal prices or leasing property at below market rents to religious groups which run services e.g. hospitals, tuition centres, as part of their mission to serve the larger community. For example, a Christian group set up the All Saints Home to provide nursing care for the elderly sick of all

Wrongs," 2002, pp 328-373. For the more recent hijab controversy, see "Allowing hijab problematic for some jobs: Yaacob," *Today*, 1 Nov 2013 at http://www.todayonline.com/singapore/allowing-hijab-problematic-some-jobs-yaacob.

59 White Paper, Jemaah Islamiyah Arrests and the Threat of Terrorism (Cmd 2 of 2003), pp. 22-23. See also Thio, "Constitutional 'Soft' Law and the Management of Religious Liberty and Order: The 2003 Declaration on Religious Harmony," 2004, pp. 414-443.

60 Thio, "The Cooperation of Religion and State in Singapore: A Compassionate Partnership in Service of Welfare," 2009, pp. 33-45.

races and religions, which the government partially funded, such that the Home reserves 90% of its beds for Ministry of Health referrals.

The government also sounds a conciliatory note towards religious groups, even when policies such as building casinos, displease them. In 2005, when announcing the government's plan to reverse the no casino policy, the Prime Minister stated his respect of religious group views but said the government "has to balance the economic pluses against the social fallout and the intangible impact on values, and make an overall judgment whether to proceed." He expressed his hope that religious groups despite their difference perspective would "continue to work for the greater good of Singapore", to "help their fellow citizens, not just gambling addicts, but everyone who is in need of help." He especially hoped "that the religious groups will work together with the government to help to build strong families, which are the basic units of a resilient and stable society."[61]

G. *Limitations on Religious Freedom in the Interests of Public Order/ Security*

While some accommodation is accorded Muslim minorities as a commitment to legal pluralism, the strictest limits to religious freedom apply where national security or public order interests are involved. A series of cases brought by Jehovah's Witnesses in the 1990s attest to this, the leading case being that of *Chan Hiang Leng Colin v Public Prosecutor.*[62]

The Jehovah's Witnesses are a pacifist religious group whose members are forbidden to undertaken military service. This stands in opposition to the Enlistment Act (Cap 93) under which all Singaporean males of a certain age are subject to a compulsory requirement to perform military service. In 1972, the group was deregistered under the Societies Act (Cap 311) such that to attend a Jehovah's Witnesses religious meeting would be to attend an unlawful assembly. Further, under the Undesirable Publications Act (Cap 338), a blanket ban of all publications of the Watch Tower, the Jehovah Witnesses' publishing arm, was imposed.

---

61 Paras 65-66, "Prime Minister's Statement before Parliament, Proposal to Develop Integrated Resorts," 18 April 2005, at http://www.mti.gov.sg/MTIInsights/ Docum ents/Ministerial%20Statement%20-%20PM%2018apr05.pdf.

62 [1995] 1 SLR(R) 388.

The Constitution permits restrictions on religious actions on the basis of public order under article 15(4). Here, the High Court ruled that: "The sovereignty, integrity and unity of Singapore are undoubtedly the paramount mandate of the Constitution and anything, including religious beliefs and practices, which tend to run counter to these objectives must be restrained."[63] *Public order* was effectively deployed as a categorical trump, which is regrettable, as it fails to balance the competing interests such that neither are rendered otiose.[64] The valorisation of public order is evident in the careless equation of "public order" (a permissible derogation under article 15(4)), with "national security" (under article 149, various fundamental liberties, excluding religious freedom, may be 'suspended' by anti-subversion legislation).[65] This approach towards constitutional adjudication effectively decimates constitutional liberty and it is hoped it will be consigned to history, in an age where more calibrated balancing approaches have been evident in judicial methodology.[66] The application of this public order trump was repeated in one further case involving a Jehovah Witness who was a teacher at a technical institute refusing to salute the flag or recite the national pledge during the morning school assembly, as this was considered to be a form of idolatry. His employment was terminated and the issue was whether this was a violation of his religious freedom.

The High Court (upheld by the Court of Appeal) in *Peter William Nappalli v Institute of Technical Education*[67] found not violation of religious freedom, that it was an implied contractual term in the contract of employment where an educational institution was an employer that "its teachers

63 [1995] 1 SLR(R) 388 at [64].

64 *AG v Shadrake Alan* [2011] 2 SLR 445 at [474].

65 "The respective Ministers were clearly of the view that the continued existence of the Jehovah's Witnesses was prejudicial to the national interest. The basis for the de-registration clearly flowed from the danger of allowing absolute freedom of religion which might create a complete denial of a government's authority and ability to govern individuals or groups asserting a religious affiliation. The Jehovah's Witnesses were not mere conscientious objectors to national service but were engaging in conduct which was prejudicial to national security. The activities of the Jehovah's Witnesses were therefore restricted on the basis that they were against the 'public order'," [1995] 1 SLR(R) 388 at 78.

66 See Thio and Chong, "The Chan Court and Constitutional Adjudication: 'A sea change into something rich and strange?'," 2012, pp. 87-119.

67 [1998] SGHC 351.

encourage students to be good and useful citizens... [by] requiring them to lead their students in the taking of the National Pledge and the singing of the National Anthem during school assembly." Tan Lee Meng J, citing the "sovereignty, integrity and unity of Singapore" mantra framed by Yong Pung How CJ in *Chan Hiang Leng Colin v PP*[68] further stated:

> With no natural resources of its own, Singapore's success depends on, among other things, the unity of its multi-racial and multi-cultural population...Surely the Ministry of Education is entitled to take reasonable steps to ensure that future generations of Singaporeans understand the importance of preserving the sovereignty, integrity and unity of Singapore.[69]

In other words, the non-serving of military service was analogised with the unwillingness of a teacher working for a public educational institution to say the national pledge or salute the national flag to be pose a security threat, warranting the curbing of the constitutional liberty of religious freedom. This is regrettably, not a balancing approach and it is hoped that the invocation of this mantra has received its *quietus est.*

Notably, religious propagation has been limited by sedition laws where feelings have been hurt by religious speech. These are instrumental laws directed not at the content of religious propagation but its effects on the Emotional Man.[70] This has lead to the dilution of religious liberty in the interests of placating emotional feelings to serve the declared objective of religious harmony.

H. Pre-Emptive Approaches towards Regulating Religion: The Maintenance of Religious Harmony Act (Cap 167A)

The government holds the fear that if religiously sensitive cases are litigated in open court, it could spark communal disharmony, even riots, as it has done historically. A well known case is the riots surrounding the Maria

68 [1994] 3 SLR 662, 684.

69 Para 46, [1998] SGHC 351.

70 See *Public Prosecutor v Ong Kian Cheong* [2009] SGDC 163. For an analysis, see Thio, "Contentious Liberty: Regulating Religious Propagation in a Religiously Diverse Secular Democracy," 2010, pp. 484-515.

Hertogh case in the 1950s.[71] Indeed, "the especial sensitivity of racial and religious issues in our multi-cultural society" has been judicially noted.[72]

In a white paper explaining the need for legislation on religious harmony, it was observed that:

> Religion is a deeply felt matter, and when religious sensitivities are offended, emotions are quickly aroused. It takes only a few incidents to inflame passions, kindle violence, and destroy the good record of religious harmony built up in recent decades. The Maria Hertogh riots were a classic example.[73]

It went on to explain discomfit with adjudication thus:

> A Court trial may mean considerable delay before judgment is pronounced, and the judicial proceedings may themselves stoke passions further if the defendant turns them into political propaganda.[74]

The white paper also annexed a report entitled "Religious Trends – A Security Perspective" by the Internal Security Department which identified three primary concerns. First, "Aggressive and Insensitive Proselytisation", with the government fear that aggressive evangelism by one religious group would offend other groups; in particular, the work of Protestant churches was felt to threaten religious equilibrium, upsetting Hindus and Muslims, although intra-religious tensions amongst Muslims, Hindus, and Christians were also noted. An example was a sermon delivered by an Evangelical Christian pastor where Islam was identified as the "greatest threat to Christianity."[75] Second, "mixing religion and politics," exemplified by the venturing of various Catholic priests into social action which the government characterised as acting like a "political pressure group." This included criticism of media freedom and labour laws.[76] Third, "Religion and Subversion" captured by the involvement of Catholics in an alleged "Marxist conspiracy" to overthrow the government and establish a Marxist state by first infiltrating various groups like tertiary student societies, the Catholic church and theatre groups.[77] What was not then identified as a threat to social disharmony, which has since emerged, is the tactic

---

71 *In The Matter Of Maria Hertogh*, [1951] MLR 26.

72 *PP v Koh Song Huat Benjamin* [2005] SGDC 272.

73 Para 11, Maintenance of Religious Harmony white paper (Cmd 21 of 1989).

74 Para 31, Maintenance of Religious Harmony white paper (Cmd 21 of 1989).

75 Para 7, Maintenance of Religious Harmony white paper (Cmd 21 of 1989).

76 Para 13, Maintenance of Religious Harmony white paper (Cmd 21 of 1989).

77 Para 30, Maintenance of Religious Harmony white paper (Cmd 21 of 1989).

of militant secularists who as conflict entrepreneurs, may seek to incite inter-religious group tensions to suit their own humanist agenda against a religious group they dislike and so to curb the role of religion in public life.[78]

Thus, there was a perceived need to have some legislation which would allow preventive or pre-emptive action to be taken "to stop a person from repeating harmful provocative acts"; in addition there was a need for a legislative regime which would allow the government to take less severe action than under existing laws such as the Sedition Act (Cap 290) or the Internal Security Act (Cap 143) which allows preventive detention for subversive action, rather than "misuse of religions."[79]

The solution adopted to this perceived problem was the Maintenance of Religious Harmony Act (Cap 167A)[80] under which the relevant Minister could issue non-justiciable restraining orders to effective place an erring religious leader or person "on notice"[81] so that he would cease and desist from repeating the offending action. The government considered the act "not something we are very proud of," a realistic apprehension in the deterioration in inter-religious group relations, a piece of legislation introduced "more in sorrow than with joy" designed to "prevent us from sliding backwards."[82]

The Act identified four grounds upon which such a restraining order could be issued under section 8(1) which warrants reproducing in full:

> 8.—(1) The Minister may make a restraining order against any priest, monk, pastor, imam, elder, office-bearer or any other person who is in a position of authority in any religious group or institution or any member thereof for the purposes specified in subsection (2) where the Minister is satisfied that that person has committed or is attempting to commit any of the following acts:

---

78 E.g. advocates of a pansexualist or sexually libertine agenda who oppose those who morally dissent from their agenda, especially Christian social conservatives. See Thio, "Between Eden and Armageddon: Navigating 'Religion' and 'Politics'," pp. 365-405.

79 Para 32, Maintenance of Religious Harmony white paper (Cmd 21 of 1989).

80 See Sinha, "Theorising 'Talk' about 'Religious Pluralism' and 'Religious Harmony' in Singapore," 2005, pp. 25-40; Winslow, "The Separation of Religion and Politics: The Maintenance of Religious Harmony Act," 1990, p. 327; Thio, "Control, Co-optation and Co-Operation: Managing Religious Harmony in Singapore's Multi-Ethnic, Quasi-Secular State," 2005, pp. 231-244.

81 Para 32, Maintenance of Religious Harmony white paper (Cmd 21 of 1989).

82 Deputy Prime Minister Goh Chok Tong, 51 Singapore Parliament Reports, col. 1148 at 1159 (23 Feb. 1990).

(a) causing feelings of enmity, hatred, ill-will or hostility between different religious groups;
(b) carrying out activities to promote a political cause, or a cause of any political party while, or under the guise of, propagating or practising any religious belief;
(c) carrying out subversive activities under the guise of propagating or practising any religious belief; or
(d) exciting disaffection against the President or the Government while, or under the guise of, propagating or practising any religious belief.

Under the terms of the Act, the restraining order can restrain its subject from addressing any congregation either orally or in writing on identified topics, from publishing any religious publication without prior Ministerial permission and from holding any editorial office with respect to a religious groups, without prior ministerial permission.[83] The subject is afforded some procedural safeguards in the form of a ministerial duty to give notice of intention to issue the order, to receive the supporting grounds and factual allegations and the right to make written representations to the Ministers, in lieu of judicial review. Critics feared that this added another layer of public powers to police what would otherwise be legitimate political dissent and so, undemocratically chill speech.

Restraining orders may also apply to persons instigating a religious group, institution or leader to commit any of the acts specified in section 8(1).[84] Each restraining order applies for a period not exceeding two years and may be renewed. A political safeguard is provided in the form a requirement that the President must confirm a restraining order within 30 days from receiving the recommendation to do so by the Presidential Council for Religious Harmony (PCRH), which is constituted under section 3 of the Act. This provides that the PCRH, which shall be between 6 and 15 members, shall compose of "not less than two-thirds of the members of the Council shall be representatives of the major religions in Singapore and the other members shall be persons who, in the opinion of the Presidential Council for Minority Rights, have distinguished themselves in public service or community relations in Singapore." The PCRH's functions are recommendatory in nature, with respect to matters the Minister or Parliament might refer to it concerning the maintenance of religious harmony in Singapore. Article 22I of the Constitution provides that the

83 Section 8(2), Maintenance of Religious Harmony Act (Cap 167A).
84 Section 9, Maintenance of Religious Harmony Act (Cap 167A).

President acting in his personal discretion may cancel, vary or confirm a restraining order where the advice of the Cabinet is contrary to the recommendations of the PCRH. When the PCRH and Cabinet are in agreement, the presidential 'veto' does not come into operation.

The MRHA has existed on the statute books for 25 years now, and interestingly, not a single restraining order has been issued.[85] In a candid interview in 2001,[86] the then Minister for Home Affairs identified three instances where restraining orders were almost issued: first, where an Islamic leader urged Muslims to vote for Muslim candidates during the 1991 General Election, which was considered to involve mixing religion and politics. Second, in 1992 when a Christian leader was considered to threaten inter-religious relations by criticising other faiths like Buddhism, Taoism, and Catholicism in sermons and publications. Finally, in 1995 Hindus were provoked when a Muslim leader criticised as devilish a Hindu belief that statutes of a Hindu deity, Ganesha, could drink milk offerings.

The authorities have demonstrated a reluctance to invoke MRHA powers where a warning suffices to induce conduct which dissipates tensions. A heavy-handed approach may provoke distrust and disquiet amongst religious citizens, which destroys social trust and harmonious relationships.

I. Conclusion: Managing Religion Through Legal and Non-legal Approaches

Ultimately, the Singapore government outside of the partnership model of managing religion-state relations has a variety of hard and soft, legal and non-legal techniques at its disposal.[87] It can take pre-emptive action to diffuse tensions, through informal warning or through issuing a MRHA restraining order. It may also punish conduct considered inimical to religious harmony, through criminal or sedition law. Last, it may seek to adopt a palliative approach, through encouraging religious leaders to dialogue and

---

85 Minister of Home Affairs Wong Kan Seng, 82 *Singapore Parliament Reports*, 12 February 2007, col 1319.

86 "Govt reins in religious leaders," *Straits Times* (Singapore), 12 May 2001, p. 1.

87 See Thio, "Relational Constitutionalism and the Management of Inter-Religious Disputes: The Singapore 'Secularism with a Soul' Model," pp. 1-24; Tan, "From Clampdown to Limited Empowerment: Hard and Soft Law in the Calibration and Regulation of Religious Conduct in Singapore," 2009, pp. 351-379.

build relations with each other, by setting up bodies like the PCRH, the inter-racial and religious confidence circle (IRCC), and overseeing the drafting of the declaration on religious harmony by religious leaders, as a code of self-restraint and best practices. Deliberative processes build confidence and declarations require interaction which helps to dissipate suspicion, and to give content to "the ground rules of prudence and good conduct."[88] This serves the interest of maintaining sustainable, harmonious long-term relationships between religious groups and between religious groups and the government, which more adversarial or legalistic methods may not engender.

Bibliography

Beer, Lawrence Ward, *Constitutional Systems in Late Twentieth Century Asia*, Washington: University of Washington Press, 1992.

Campos, Paul F., "Secular Fundamentalism," in *Columbia Law Review* 6, 24 (1994): 1814-1827.

Ekins, Richard, "Secular Fundamentalism and Democracy," in *Journal of Markets and Morality* 8, 1 (2005): 81-93.

Fernando, J.M., *The Making of the Malayan Constitution*, Kuala Lumpur: MBRAS Monograph No. 31, 2002.

Hirschl, Ran, "Comparative Constitutional Law and religion," in *Comparative Constitutional Law,* ed. Tom Ginsburg and Rosalind Dixon, Cheltenham: Edward Elgar, 2011, pp. 422-440.

Kuah-Pearce, Khun Eng, "The Poetics of Religious Philantrophy: Buddhist Welfarism in Singapore," in *Religious Diversity and Civil Society: A Comparative Analysis*, ed. Bryan S. Turner, Oxford: Bardwell Press, 2008, pp. 167-187.

Neo, Jaclyn Ling-Chien, "Seditious in Singapore! Free Speech and the offence of promoting ill-will and Hostility between different Racial Groups," in *Singapore Journal of Legal Studies* (2011): 351-372.

Ocvirk, Drago Karl, "Secularist Christophobic Fundamentalism and Islamic Monoreligionism: Obstacles for Dialogue and Peaceful Co-existence," in *Bogoslovni vestnik* 69 (2009): 423-433.

Ogilvie, Mh, "After the Charter: Religious Free Expression and Other Legal Fictions in Canada," *The Oxford University Commonwealth Law Journal,* 2 (2002): 219-235.

Sinha, Vineeta, "Theorising 'Talk' about 'Religious Pluralism' and 'Religious Harmony' in Singapore," *Journal of Contemporary Religion* 20 (2005): 25-40.

88 Para 46, Maintenance of Religious Harmony white paper (Cmd 21 of 1989).

Tamney, Joseph B., *The Struggle over Singapore's Soul: Western Modernisation and Asian Culture*, New York: Walter de Gruyter, 1996.

Tan, Eugene KB, "From Clampdown to Limited Empowerment: Hard and Soft Law in the Calibration and Regulation of Religious Conduct in Singapore," *Law and Policy* 31, 3 (2009): 351-379.

Tan, Yock Lin, "Sedition and its new clothes in Singapore," *Singapore Journal of Legal Studies* (2011): 212-237.

Thio, Li-ann, *A Treatise on Singapore Constitutional Law*, Singapore: Academy Publishing, 2012.

Thio, Li-ann, "Between Eden and Armageddon: Navigating 'Religion' and 'Politics' in Singapore," *Singapore Journal of Legal Studies* (2009): 365-405.

Thio, Li-ann, "Constitutionalism in Illiberal Polities" in *The Oxford Handbook on Comparative Constitutionalism*, ed. Andras Sajo, Michel Rosenfeld, Oxford: Oxford University Press, 2012, pp. 133-152.

Thio, Li-ann, "Constitutional 'Soft' Law and the Management of Religious Liberty and Order: The 2003 Declaration on Religious Harmony," *Singapore Journal of Legal Studies* (2004): 414-443.

Thio, Li-ann, "Contentious Liberty: Regulating Religious Propagation in a Religiously Diverse Secular Democracy," *Singapore Journal of Legal Studies* (2010): 484-515.

Thio, Li-ann, "Control, Co-optation and Co-Operation: Managing Religious Harmony in Singapore's Multi-Ethnic, Quasi-Secular State," *Hastings Constitutional Law Quarterly* 33, 2&3 (2005): 197-254.

Thio, Li-ann, "Recent Constitutional Developments: Of Shadows and Whips, Race, Rifts and Rights, Terror and Tudungs, Women and Wrongs," *Singapore Journal of Legal Studies* (2002): 328-373.

Thio, Li-ann, "Relational Constitutionalism and the Management of Inter-Religious Disputes: The Singapore 'Secularism with a Soul' Model," *Oxford Journal of Law and Religion* 1, 3 (2012): 1-24.

Thio, Li-ann, "Religion in the Public Sphere of Singapore: Wall of Division or Public Square" in *Religious Pluralism and Civil Society: A Comparative Analysis*, ed. Bryan S Turner, Oxford: Bardwell Press, 2008, pp. 73-104.

Thio, Li-ann, "Soft Constitutional Law in non-liberal Asian Constitutional Democracies," *International Journey of Constitutional Law* 8, 4 (2010): 766-799.

Thio, Li-ann, "Between Eden and Armageddon: Navigating 'Religion' and 'Politics'," in *Singapore Journal of International & Comparative Law* 2 (2009): 365-405.

Thio, Li-ann, and David Chong, "The Chan Court and Constitutional Adjudication: 'A sea change into something rich and strange'," in *The Law in His Hands: A Tribute to Chief Justice*, ed. Chao Hick Tin, Andrew Phang Boon Leong, V K Rajah, Yeo Tiong Min, Singapore: Academy Press, 2012, pp. 87-119.

Thio, Li-ann, "Relational Constitutionalism and the Management of Inter-Religious Disputes: The Singapore 'Secularism with a Soul' Model," *Oxford Journal of Law and Religion* 2 (2012): 1-24.

Thio, Li-ann, "The Right to Political Participation in Singapore: Tailor-Making a Westminster-Modelled Constitution to fit the Imperatives of 'Asian' Democracy," *Singapore Journal of International & Comparative Law* 6 (2002): 181-243.

Thio, "The Cooperation of Religion and State in Singapore: A Compassionate Partnership in Service of Welfare," *The Review of Faith & International Affairs* 7, 3 (2009): 33-45.

van der Vyver, Johan D, "The Jurisprudential Legacy of Abraham Kuyper and Leo XIII," *Journal of Markets and Morality* 5, 1, (2002): 211-249.

Walker, Graham, "The Idea of Nonliberal Constitutionalism," in *Ethnicity and Group Rights*, ed. Ian Shapiro, Will Kymlicka, New York City: NYU Press, 1997, pp. 154-184.

Winslow, Valentine S., "The Separation of Religion and Politics: The Maintenance of Religious Harmony Act," *Malaya Law Review* 32 (1990): 327-331.

The Legal-Formal Status of Religions in China

Andre Laliberte[1]

A. Introduction

What is the fate of religion in China under Xi Jinping? How successful has been the Chinese Communist Party (CCP) in ensuring that China keeps religion out of politics? The resilience, and even the growth, of religion in China, suggests that the CCP has accepted a social role for religion in the country. This change coincides with the deepening of China's interaction with the outside world, a phenomenon that brings to mind another question, addressed by others looking into the influence of religion in contemporary societies. What is the poltical leaning of religion in China? The acceptance of religion by the state suggests that the latter believes in its capacity to control a phenomenon that it had hoped to see whither away during the three first decades after 1949. However, it leaves open the question of whether the state is justified to manifest this self-confidence.

To answer these questions, this chapter first looks at the institutional dimension of relations between state and religion. Then, it moves on to present the complex nature of China's religious landscape, marked by an age-old diversity but also by the recent efforts of the state to regulate and to manage this diversity. These defining characteristics of religious life in China, I argue, seriously undermine the ability of any religious actor to challenge significantly and effectively the authority of the state. Then, I will review some of the major themes that these religious actors have articulated when they want to oppose political authority.

1 I would like to thank the Social Sciences and Humanities Research Council of Canada for the research support and the time that were necessary for writing this paper.

B. The Relationship between the Modern State and Religions in China

China does not proclaim a state religion but it does not qualify as a secular state, the way we usually use this concept in Euro-American countries.[2] There, the concept of the secular state defines a state that is neutral on religious matters, and one that upholds the principle of dual toleration, wherein the state does not intervene on religious matters, and religions do not interfere with state affairs.[3] There are many definitions of the secular state, and the historical and culturally specific nature of the secular state invites one to be prudent in applying to other countries a model of relations between religion and politics derived from the particular nature of political power and religious authority in Western Europe.[4] As the work of scholars on the ongoing debates about the nature of the secular state in India demonstrates clearly, we should not underestimate the ability of different societies to adapt to their conditions liberal secular institutions.[5] Closer to China, Taiwan demonstrates that Chinese cultural specificities need not present an obstacle either to develop a secular state.[6] Using the admittedly culturally-specific criteria outlined above, I want to argue in this chapter that China is not a liberal secular state, and its approach to religions is akin to that of a state with a religious establishment, in fact, a state with multiple establishments, which recognizes five religions: Buddhism, Taoism, Islam, Protestant Christianity, and Catholicism. This regime of limited official religious recognition, however, does not cover all dimensions of the relations between religion and state in China.

In many respects socialism with Chinese characteristics functions as a form of state religion. In a short essay, the noted sociologist of religions Ninian Smart noted that the cult of personality that surrounded Mao Zedong in his lifetime, the doctrine promoted by Maoism, the mythology surrounding him, and the attempts at institutionalization surrounding his

2 I use the expression as a shorthand for European countries and their former colonies, all influenced deeply by Eastern and Western Christianity.

3 See Stepan, "The World's Religious Systems and Democracy: Crafting the 'Twin Tolerations," 2001, pp. 213-253.

4 See Asad, "On Re-reading a Modern Classic: W.C. Smith's 'The Meaning and End of Religion'," 2001, pp. 205-222.

5 See Bhargava, "Can Secularism Be Rehabilitated?" 2013; Madan, "Secularism in Its Place," 1998, pp. 297-320; Smith, *India as a Secular State*, 1963.

6 See Laliberte, "The Regulation of Religious Affairs in Taiwan: From State Control to *Laisser-faire*?" 2009, pp. 53-84; Kuo, *Religion and Democracy in Taiwan*, 2008.

'thought' made Mao comparable to a religious leader.[7] In a short essay, Stephan Feuchtwang noted that the mass movements that swept through China during the Cultural Revolution, in their rituals, constituted a form of religious resistance against the bureaucratic state.[8] Finally, the recent declarations by the CCP that the final decision about the legitimation of the succession to the Dalai Lama rests on the organs of the state that it leads, suggesting that the CCP reclaims religious authority.[9] In this chapter, I do not address this issue of the CCP as a form of religion, but I focus on the CCP's relations with religions, understood as visions of the world premised on a belief about the power of the unseen over the affairs of this world. I believe that this definition, used to describe religious realities in Africa,[10] better captures the religious realities of China, than other definitions that are narrower and too closely related to the Euro-American historical realities.[11] In sum, the CCP is an atheist organization that seeks superiority over religions in the name of a teleology that asserts the withering away of the latter, although it has gradually changed its views on the matter and accepts that religion is compatible with socialism. However, this acceptance rests on the principle that religion serves the CCP.[12]

While there is no official religion in China and while the official ideology of the ruling party does not qualify as such – the CCP's materialist philosophy unambiguously rejects any belief that invisible forces could control people's destiny – this does not mean that the legal-formal status of religions in China does not matter. As mentioned above, China is a regime of multiple religious establishments, wherein the state recognizes five national religious associations as legitimate. The nature of the CCP supervision of these religions, however, departs from the idea of a religious establishment in the Euro-American world wherein the state and religious authorities have developed a relation of mutual support and cooperation. The CCP has the ambition to determine the role religious associations can play

7 See Smart, *Mao*, 1974, pp. 83-94.
8 See Feuchtwang, "Religion as Resistance," 2000, p. 165.
9 See Famularo, "Spinning the Wheel: the Policy Implications of the Dalai Lama's Reincarnation," 2012.
10 See Ellis and ter Haar, "Religion and Politics in Sub-Saharan Africa," 1998, pp. 175-201.
11 See Gill, "Religion and Comparative Politics," 2001, pp. 117-138; Smith, "Introduction: Correcting a Curious Neglect, or Bringing Religion Back In," 1996, pp. 1-25.
12 See Ye, "Dui zongjiao lilun he zhengce yaodian de fenxi yu guilei," 2001.

in society, possesses the ability to act as an arbiter if it chooses to do so, and controls the instruments to regulate the internal affairs of religions. The state's own think tanks and directives over decades have determined authoritatively the role of religion in a socialist society, and changed policies accordingly.[13] In declaring the Falungong an 'evil cult', the CCP imposed its verdict on a religious dispute between Buddhists and the leaders of that movement, in what was originally a religious disagreement.[14] Finally, the CCP instructs and provides 'guidance' to the leaders of the religious associations via its United Front Work Department and the State Administration for Religious Affairs. In sum, China is a state where there exists an asymmetric separation between state and religion because state influence permeates religions in almost every aspect, while many mechanisms prevent religions from doing likewise.[15]

Because the state has successfully asserted its institutional hegemony in a corporatist structure of control, there is no tensional competition between secular and religious claims of authority, as far as the five official religions' institutions mentioned above are concerned: they accept the CCP paramount leadership because since 1978 they believe it has supported their associations. However, the religious ecology of China is far more complex than what the regime would like to portray to the outside world.[16] All of the five religions have to contend with dissident forms or movements that claim affiliation with the tradition but do not necessarily recognize the influence of the official association. For example, many Buddhists acknowledge the authority of spiritual leaders such as Chin Kong, whom the official Buddhist Association of China does not accept.[17] Many religious groups that refer to Christian soteriology, such as the Church of

13 See Wang, *Zhongguo de zongjiao wenti he zongjiao zhengce*, 2002.

14 See Tong, *Revenge of the Forbidden City: The Suppression of the Falun Gong in China*, 2009; Ownby, *Falun Gong and the Future of China*, 2008; Palmer, *La fièvre du qigong: guérison, religion et politique en Chine*, 2005.

15 One of the most fundamental of these mechanisms is the obligation for CCP members to be atheist. Although the CCP tolerates exceptions for cadres from the minorities, or local cadres may participate in communal religious activities, it remains an obstacle to promotion to higher ranks and limits participation of religious believers in national politics.

16 On this concept of religious ecology, see Sun, "The Chinese Buddhist ecology in post-Mao China," 2011, pp. 498-510.

17 See Dutournier and Ji, "Expérimentation sociale et 'confucianisme populaire': Le cas du Centre d'éducation culturelle de Lujiang," 2009, pp. 71-86.

the Almighty God, reject the official Three-Selves Committee for the Patriotic Church of China, the official Protestant Christian association.[18] Besides these contestations for authority in the margins of the official organizations, episodic leaks from the domestic security and police bureau reveal the proliferation of an unknown number of small congregations around self-proclaimed spiritual masters that are sanctioned as 'reactionary sects,' or 'feudal superstitions'.[19] Last but not least, but difficult to measure and account for, are the local communal religions in the countryside that structure social life, sometimes even with local officials' assent.[20] Mounting evidence from fieldwork also shows that urban centers with migrant workers reproduce such forms of religiosity.[21]

The corporatist framework of governance for religious affairs is becoming increasingly legalistic.[22] That is, a growing number of laws, regulations, directives, rules, and legal opinions, are shaping the framework under which religions can operate legally.[23] As the broader issue of noncompliance with international treaty on human rights demonstrates, however, the constitutional framework of China remains a work in progress.[24] The Constitution is not a foundational document for national politics but rather a document that endorses already established policies adopted by the ruling party. The expansion of the legal system in all spheres of society

---

18 See Dui, "China's 'Almighty God' Rises with Threat of Apocalypse," 2012.

19 Allen-Ebrahimian, "Chinese State Media Warns Against 14 'Evil Cults'," 2014.

20 See Chau, *Miraculous Response: Doing Popular Religion in Contemporary China*, 2006; Tsai, *Accountability without Democracy: Solidary Groups and Public Goods Provision in Rural China*, 2007.

21 See Remoiville, "*Le renouveau religieux en Chine urbaine contemporaine: le rôle social de la religion dans la vie quotidienne à Hangzhou,*" 2013; Fan, *Dangdai zhongguoren zongjiao xinyang de bianqian: Shenzhen minjian zongjiao xintu detianye yanjiu*, 2005.

22 I am using the classical definition of Schmitter which sees corporatism as a structure in which the state has granted a monopoly of interest representation to institutions that are different from each other in their function. The state licenses or creates these institutions to select their leadership and articulate their interests: Schmitter, "Still the Century of Corporatism?," 1974, pp. 34-35.

23 See Tong, "The New Religious Policy in China: Catching up with Systemic Reforms," 2010, pp. 859-887; Ying, *Religion, State, and Society*, 2006, pp. 347-373; Leung, "China's Religious Freedom Policy: The Art of Managing Religious Activity," 2005, pp. 894-915; Potter, "Belief in Control: Regulation of Religion in China," 2003, pp. 317-337.

24 See Horneman, "China: When will five-fold state-backed religious monopoly end?," 2013. .

represents an immense progress from the Maoist period when the fiction of 'socialist legalism' represented arbitrary rule. However, we should not confuse the existing references by the CCP that it rules and implements policies 'in accordance with the law,' or 'rule *by* law,'[25] with the idea of 'rule *of* law.'[26] In the former, the legal apparatus serves the rulers; in the latter, even the highest-ranking rulers cannot evade sanctions from the justice system. In the context of the former, constitutional guarantees are not solid.[27] As the crackdown on different churches in Zhejiang as recently as 2014 has revealed, its actions demonstrate that the party can ignore constitutional guarantees.[28] This particular case demonstrates that the constitution's effectiveness in protecting religious freedom remains hampered by the unequal enforcement of rights by different local governments.[29]

A look at the formal-legal statements of the constitution about the treatment of religious minorities also reveals some interesting contradictions and inconsistencies. Firstly, if we want to give credence to existing surveys,[30] all religious believers in China qualify as members of a religious minority because only 22% of Chinese are religious believers, that is, they count as believers in one of the five recognized religions.[31] Other estimates quoted officially are much higher, and argue that close to a quarter of the population embraces Buddhism.[32] Yet, this upward revision still makes the religion with the largest number of adherents a minority of the population. Secondly, the numbers are extremely unreliable and do not give a full account of the religious reality of China. They do not count the

25 Fazhi, 法制.

26 Fazhi, 法治.

27 See Cabestan, "The political and practical obstacles to the reform of the judiciary and the establishment of a rule of law in China," 2005, pp. 43-64.

28 See Pedroletti, "China's Christians fear new persecution after latest wave of church demolitions," 2014.

29 See Tong, "The New Religious Policy in China: Catching up with Systemic Reforms," 2010, pp. 859-887.

30 The Horizon Research Consultancy Group did one of the most detailed surveys, the Chinese Spiritual Life Survey, in 2007. The dataset is available at HRCG, 2007.

31 See Yang and Hu, "Mapping Chinese Folk Religion in Mainland China and Taiwan," 2012, p. 513.

32 Liu Zhongyu from the Research Center for Religious Culture, East China Normal University, estimated from his 2005 survey that there are over 300 million Buddhists: Zhang, "Buddhism in China," 2009, at http://www.chinatoday. com.cn/ ctenglish/se/txt/2009-06/19/content_203310.htm.

people who give credence to the world-views of the popular beliefs, communal religions, and practices such as divination, geomancy, that Chinese sociologists are investigating in increasing number, and for whom the constitution and the legal-framework remains vague and unclear.[33] As we have seen above in relation to local authorities, a variety of attitudes suggests that what passes as an 'intangible heritage' that the state must protect in some places can become a 'feudal superstition' to eradicate elsewhere.

In the context of unequal implementation of national norms throughout a country with varying socio-economic conditions, the effectiveness of implementing international norms such as freedom of conscience is bound to be difficult. Moreover, the domestic context of a rising nationalist sentiment promoted by the CCP to offset its deficit of legitimacy makes it increasingly difficult to adopt international standards without appearing to submit to foreign powers. The challenges of the government to be seen as rightful and just, in a context of rampant corruption, has been amply discussed elsewhere to explain the surge of religious fervor in China.[34] The CCP support for nationalism since the patriotic education campaigns in the 1980s, which coincided with the acceleration of the economic policies that departed from the early socialist ambitions, attest to the regime's anxiety about its legitimacy in the eyes of the population.[35] The successive waves of 'religious fervor' China has experienced since 1978 suggest that this phenomenon is independent from the appeals to nationalism, albeit the sponsorship by provincial governments in North China during the 1980s of worship to the Yellow Emperor had revealed a convergence between the state sponsorship of popular belief, if not religion, and ethnic national-

33 The Chinese Spiritual Life Survey (CSLS) estimated adherents of 'folk religions' at over 55.5% of the population. The category 'folk religions adherents' included people believing in gods without formal identity, people practicing 'communal folk religions', 'ancestors worship', 'individual folk religions', 'amuletic practices', worshipping the God of wealth and local deities, consulting fortune-tellers, and observing geomancy (fengshui). (Yang and Hu, "Mapping Chinese Folk Religion in Mainland China and Taiwan," p. 514) However, the CSLS also found that 67% of respondent agreed with the statement "People should not have any religious belief; instead people should only believe in science." (HRCG, "Chinese Spiritual Life Survey," 2007, question 351).

34 See Ostergaard, "Governance and the Political Challenge of Falungong," 2004, pp. 207-225; Aminzade and Perry, "The Sacred, Religious, and Secular in Contentious Politics: Blurring Boundaries," 2001, pp. 155-178.

35 See Gries, "Popular Nationalism and State Legitimation in China," 2005, pp. 25-43.

ism.[36] Ostensibly directed at Taiwanese 'compatriots', the event has receded, but since 2006, the CCP has, through government-organized NGOs, promoted other international religious events, such as the World Buddhist Forum, mixing together religious and nationalist agenda, to promote its own views on Tibet and cross-Strait relations.

C. Religious Ecology and its Impact on Politics

In the institutional and political context exposed above, it is extremely difficult for religions to inform and shape the political order in any fundamental way. None of the five officially sanctioned religions comes close to attract a sufficient number of followers who could theoretically set up a social movement with the capacity to challenge the regime. We can say the same about non-recognized religions such as Falungong, which claim large numbers of adherents, but have never succeeded in generating anything near the support of a majority of the population. We can find exceptions to that rule among the national minorities. For example, although it is impossible to conduct a reliable survey to support this point, it is likely that a significant proportion, if not the majority, of ethnic Tibetans support the Dalai Lama.[37] Nevertheless, even for an aggrieved minority such as the Uyghurs, who are protesting against what they see as attacks against their tradition, there is no rallying around a single leader or a unique organization.[38] Moreover, in the case of both Tibetans and Uyghurs, the grievances that they express are primarily about the protection of their cultural rights, within or without China, but have little to say about the broader political order of China.

We should not conclude from the absence of any religious institution large and powerful enough to generate support from the majority of the population against the political authority that religion has no impact on Chinese politics. Quite the contrary, as John Lagerwey reminds us in his own work as a social historian and anthropologist, the most important reli-

36 See Billeter, *L'empereur jaune: Une tradition politique chinoise*, 2007.

37 See Bentz, "Symbol and power: the Dalai Lama as a charismatic leader," 2012, pp. 287-305.

38 See Chen, *The Uyghur Lobby: Global Networks, Coalitions and Strategies of the World Uyghur Congress*, 2014.

gious institution throughout Chinese history is the state itself.[39] This statement fitted with the notion that kings in ancient and pre-imperial China ruled by divine right, as 'sons of heaven' (tianzi, 天子), or when they invoked the concept of the 'mandate of heaven'(tianming, 天命). Many interpreted the outbreak of natural catastrophes such as flood and earthquakes, and social calamities such as famine and unrest, as a sign that the emperor had lost the mandate. The origins of this theory on legitimacy remain difficult to ascertain, but traces of its impact on popular beliefs linger, to describe the 'right to rule' of the present leaders. In imperial time, the Chinese emperor, like his counterpart in ancient Rome, achieved the fusion of political and religious leadership when he was not only the supreme political leader and the commander of the army, but also the highest priest of the state religion. Because of this fusion between the two spheres of the political and the religious, the rulers interpreted any form of religious dissidence as a direct political challenge, and addressed it as such. The concerns of many emperors were grounded in historical precedents: two movements associated with Taoism, the Yellow Turban and the Five Pecks of Rice, undermined decisively the Han dynasty; the successful rebellion led by the Red Turbans, a secret society that was long associated with Buddhism, led to the fall of the Yuan dynasty.[40]

The Qing dynasty faced a number of uprisings where religion played a role, starting with the White Lotus Rebellion (1794-1804), followed by the Eight Trigrams uprising in 1813,[41] the Taiping rebellion (1850-1864), and the Boxer uprising (1898-1900). Each of these movements increasingly undermined the government and caused considerable damage. The White Lotus Rebellion marked a turning point for the Qing dynasty, which never recovered fully.[42] The Taiping Rebellion, which coincided with Muslim rebellions in the Northwest, killed between twenty to thirty million people, and as such, represented one of the deadliest conflicts in human history.[43] The Boxer uprising, while not as lethal as the Taiping rebellion, neverthe-

39 See Lagerwey, *China: A Religious State*, 2010.

40 See Dubois, *Religion and the Making of Modern East Asia*, 2011.

41 See Naquin, *Millenarian Rebellion in China: The Eight Trigrams Uprising of 1813*, 1976.

42 See Ter Haar, *The White Lotus Teachings in Chinese Religious History*, 1992.

43 See Reilly, *The Taiping Heavenly Kingdom: Rebellion and the Blasphemy of Empire*, 2004; Chun-Li and Frantz, *The Taiping Rebellion: History and Documents. Volume I: History*, 1966.

less terminally weakened the Qing dynasty, and brought an increase of foreign intervention into the country.[44] These religiously inspired upheavals combined different sets of grievances, such as revolts against unfair taxation, protest over local governments' injustice, and desperate responses to the degradation of living conditions caused by natural disasters that state officials seemed unable to address.[45]

Politically, however, many of them were little more than restoration of the status *quo ante*. The Taiping went further than preceding uprisings because it combined elements of Christianity to its millenarian vision, and CCP officials, including Mao, saw in it a revolutionary movement, albeit an 'indiscriminately anti-foreign' one.[46] Recent revisionist historiography even compared some of the leaders of that movement to modernizing reformers.[47] Regardless of the validity of these interpretations, the political significance of the Taiping rests in the demonstration effect that any set of social-economic grievances that is articulated by a movement using the idiom of Chinese traditional religions can easily turn into a powerful political movement. The Chinese state security apparatus since 1949 certainly believes in the explosive consequences incurred by the concatenation of popular beliefs and political unrest, and as a result, has relentlessly persecuted any groups that claimed, or seemed to have, any affiliation to Taoist secret societies, white lotus movements, and relatively more recently, qigong groups.[48]

The existing social and economic conditions of Chinese society, the expansion of the state capacity, and the current religious ecology of China, however, make these fears from the CCP wildly exaggerated. China as a whole is experiencing levels of prosperity that are unprecedented. Despite growing inequities, major problems such as environmental degradation, labor unrest and inter-ethnic tensions, there is no political challenge to the government arising. The state is now able to monitor every facet of society

---

44 See Cohen, *History in Three Keys: The Boxers as Event, Experience, and Myth*, 1997; Esherick, *The Origins of the Boxer Uprising*, 1987.

45 The leader of the Taiping believed that he was the younger brother of Christ and wanted to root out traditional Chinese religions; the Boxers adhered to the belief that the practice of their specific calisthenics protected them from bullets.

46 Mao, "On Practice," 1976, p. 192.

47 See Platt, *Autumn in the Heavenly Kingdom: China, the West, and the Epic Story of the Taiping Civil War*, 2012.

48 See Ostergaard, "Governance and the Political Challenge of Falungong," pp. 207-225; Perry, "Rural Violence in Socialist China," 2002, pp. 275-308.

in ways that were unimaginable even under the totalitarian phase of the Maoist regime. In addition, even though post-totalitarian China grants its citizens more space for personal freedoms such as choices of career, consumption, migration, family matters, leisure, etc., the security bureau and the different branches of the police have the ability to detect any sign of religious dissidence thanks to the extensive monitoring of traffic on the internet.[49] Moreover, the CCP can rely on the official religious associations and their local branches, whose own vested interest is to monitor from within their own organization to nip in the bud any signs of religious dissidence, 'heresy,' or sectarian divisions, that could weaken the leadership and even expose them to state persecution. Finally, the religious ecology of China today is so complex and fluid that no religious institution could possibly muster throughout the whole country the kind of united front rallying a majority of the population that we can observe in other large societies such as India. While the BJP, in the latter, can claim that it 'represents' 75% of the Indian population it identifies as 'Hindus', nothing similar exists in China: the proportion of the population that is counted as Buddhists, the religion with the largest number of adherents, does not come close, as we have seen above.

If our analysis of the political leanings of religions in China focuses only on the existing five religions recognized by the state and their representative association, we can conclude that no religion represents a challenge to the regime. This is the case because they all have a stake in maintaining the existing structure of governance in religious affairs, a fact captures by the felicitous phrase of Ashiwa and Wank, who argued that religions and the modern state mutually constituted themselves.[50] The CCP has successfully implemented a corporatist structure to ensure that each religion it recognizes can manage its own affairs, in accordance with the state's laws and regulations. The representative associations for each religion have established a structure of governance that mirrors that of the state and the party in many respects.[51] For each of the five religions there is a national association conveying to its members instructions and directives from the CCP. These associations manage the affairs of the religious personnel,

49 See Tai, "Casting the Ubiquitous Net of Information Control: Internet Surveillance in China from Golden Shield to Green Dam," 2011, pp. 237-256.

50 See Ashiwa and Wank, *Making Religion, Making the State in China, the Politics of Religion in Modern China*, 2009.

51 See Yang, "Oligopoly dynamics: Official religions in China," 2007, pp. 635-653.

from clerics' training to their welfare, administer places of worship, approve their religious scriptures, and represent them in foreign relations with co-religionists abroad. Each of these religions can also rely on provincial, municipal, and even county-level representative associations, in principle wherever there is a sufficient number of adherents to that religion and/or clerics. At each level, there religious institutions report to their vis-à-vis in the CCP and the government, as well as to the higher-up religious institution. Like the CCP, each of the official religious association relies on a central committee and a secretary-general to manage its affairs, and renews its governance structure periodically in general meetings.

All of the officially recognized religions, as we will see below, must however contend with challenges from within and from without. For example, the Buddhist Association of China, which brings together, within a unique association, adherents of the Mahayana, Theravada, and Tibetan traditions, must confront the reality that many adherents of the Tibetan Buddhist tradition shun the official associations' authority and recognize as their spiritual master the Dalai Lama. Moreover, dissidence from within the Buddhist Association of China existed, as revealed the case of Ven. Shengguang, a monk who had denounced the June 4 massacre and for a time benefitted from the open support of clerics within the association.[52] A similar cleavage exists among Catholics, many of whom do not recognize the legitimacy of the Patriotic Catholic Association of China's leader, and rather defer to the Vatican.[53] To these differences about the legitimacy of the religions' source of authority, we need to add the sectarian diversity within. This diversity refers often to divergences on matter of theology, historical traditions, or both. This issue is salient with respect to Protestant Christianity and Islam, and to a lesser degree to Buddhism and Taoism.

The National Committee of the Three-Self Patriotic Movement of the Protestant Churches in China (for lay people) and the China Christian Council (for clerics) seek to bring under the same two umbrella organizations all Protestant Christians, regardless of denominations, but they could not prevent the occurrence of divisions between the official churches and barely legal 'house churches.' They could not prevent either the emergence of marginal, breakaway organizations such as the Church of the

52 See Jiang, "Chairman of China's Buddhist Association Wrongly Expels Monk, Says HRIC," 2006.

53 See Lynch, "Beijing and the Vatican: Catholics in China and the Politics of Religious Freedom," 2014, pp. 1-10.

Almighty God.[54] In the case of Islam, the cleavage between Sunni and Shia, so pervasive in the Mashrek and in Central Asia, is largely absent from China, the overwhelming majority of Muslims being Sunni. The same remarks hold for the adherence to Islamic law: with the exception of a few Ismaili, the majority follows the Hanbali School of law. The most important cleavage among Muslims relates to ethnicity and language. While Hui, or ethnic Chinese, are generally accepting the existing legal and political framework under which they can practice their faith, ethnic minorities such as the Uyghurs resent the discrimination against their language, customs, and religious practices.[55] Because Christianity and Islam are minority religions, fragmented by cleavages defined by denomination and/or ethnicity, they are unlikely to constitute the basis of any significant political opposition.

We can make similar remarks for Buddhism and Taoism: they are unlikely to challenge the regime because of divisions from within, and they end up representing minorities, albeit large ones. As mentioned above, Buddhism counts three different schools, and there is a disagreement on the supreme authority. Even setting aside the dispute over the Dalai Lama, Buddhists do not agree about the spiritual authority of a single leader. Many spiritual masters, such as Xuecheng[56], may have an important following, but none stands out as an uncontested leader. Moreover, lay Buddhists who have a large following, such as Wu Zeheng, are vulnerable to state repression.[57] Furthermore, and although the denomination of Tibetan Buddhism may suggest that the division between the three schools mirrors ethnic divisions, the reality is more complex: many Han identify with Tibetan Buddhists, along with Manchus, Mongols, and other non-Han people.[58] We can make a similar comment for Taoism, which lacks a leader with a great visibility, and by all accounts from official statistics and independent observations, counts even less followers than Buddhism.[59] If the clerics of these two Chinese religions have political leanings, it is very

54 See Bays, *A New History of Christianity in China*, 2012.

55 See Davis, "Uyghur Muslim Ethnic Separatism in Xinjiang, China," 2008, pp. 15-30.

56 Xuecheng is the President of the Buddhist Associaion of China since 2015.

57 See David, "Buddhist Sect Leader Detained During Raid," 2014.

58 See Jones, "Contemporary Han Chinese Involvement in Tibetan Buddhism: A Case Study from Nanjing," 2011, pp. 540-553.

59 See HRCG, *Chinese Spiritual Life Survey*.

likely that they would be supportive of the regime, which capitalizes on its self-proclaimed mission to promote Chinese cultural heritage. As religions existing on Chinese soil since two millennia, Taoism and Buddhism have a stronger claim than the three other ones to represent the 'essence' of the Chinese nation.

Other organized religions have claims to represent Chinese culture, but the regime considers them as illegal, and has denounced them variously as 'dangerous, heterodox sects,' 'reactionary feudal organizations,' or, more recently, as 'evil cults.'[60] Variously described by scholars as 'redemptive societies',[61] popular religious movements and heterodox sects,[62] or by adherent themselves, as 'self-cultivation societies,' they vary in their beliefs, practices, organizations, and numbers. These various groups share some important characteristics: their members follow a charismatic leader, who preaches a salvationist doctrine distinct from that of the recognized religions; most adherents experience that doctrine through bodily techniques; and these groups promote morality as a condition of salvation.[63] The better known among them are the Way of Unity, or Yiguandao, and Falungong. There are many others, to judge by leaked reports from the security bureaus, who have reported arrests of their leaders.[64] David Palmer noted that in 1949, at the end of the Republican era, there were more adherents to these religions than there were Buddhist monks, Protestant and Christians.[65] In the absence of official recognition, authorities look at their activities as illegal, and any efforts to recruit members and spread their teachings as *ipso facto* subversive. Falungong is an interesting case. It used to be an apolitical movement, albeit with a substantial following and quite an organizational strength. Persecution has transformed it from a purely religious movement into a quasi-political organization.[66] There are other movements but they are small, and none of them able to challenge frontally the regime.

---

60 Ownby, *Falun Gong and the Future of China*, p. 23.
61 Duara, *Sovereignty and Authenticity: Manchukuo and the East Asian Modern*, 2003.
62 See Seiwert and Ma, *Popular Religious Movements and Heterodox Sects in Chinese History*, 2003.
63 See Ownby, *Falun Gong and the Future of China*, pp. 25-26.
64 See Dui, "Identifying Cult Organizations in China."
65 See Palmer, *La fièvre du qigong: guérison, religion et politique en Chine, 1949-1999.*
66 See ibid.

Finally, the basic component of China's religious ecology is the complex reality of 'popular/folk beliefs/religions' and 'communal religions'. This represents the foundation of the Chinese nexus between the political and religious life that has survived the twentieth century revolutions. In imperial times, they were an integral part of the state apparatus and permeated all aspects of society.[67] This enmeshment with the state made these religious practices a target of the reformers since the late Qing dynasty, followed by the most radicals among the KMT modernizers at the beginning of the twentieth century.[68] When the Cultural Revolution broke out, it represented just the last stage of a succession of anti-religious movements. In one of the most remarkable ironies of recent history, however, the CCP seeks to portray itself as a defender of Chinese traditions and therefore proves more lenient than ever to popular religions, which it deems 'intangible heritage'[69], in its quest for legitimacy. What this 'intangible heritage' includes presents some important contradictions. For example, Confucianism represents an ethical system of thought that some scholars would like to see promoted as a state religion.[70] For some other proponents of the Confucian tradition, however, such a promotion of Confucian ethics into a religion would be unacceptable.[71] Other practices, such as divination (ba gua 八卦), geomancy (feng shui □水), and work on the qi (qigong 气功), represent practices that many party members still consider 'superstitions.' Yet, commercial bookstores sell publications that celebrate them, with the approval if not the open support of the authorities.

D. *Political Theologies*

We could infer the political theology of many religions from their position in the Chinese religious ecology. On the one hand, we can expect that the official associations of the five religions recognized by the state have a

67 See Yang, *Religion in Chinese Society: A Study of Contemporary Social Functions of Religion and some of their Historical Factors*, 1994.

68 See Goossaert, "1898: The Beginning of the End for Chinese Religion?," 2006, pp. 307-336.

69 Oakes and Sutton, *Faiths on Display: Religion, Tourism, and the Chinese State*, 2010.

70 See Bell, *China's New Confucianism: Politics and Everyday Life in a Changing Society*, 2008.

71 See de Bary and Tu, *Confucianism and Human Rights*, 1998.

vested interest in approving through their own public utterances and rituals their support for a regime on which they depend to ensure their existence and continued development. Conversely, we can surmise that the religions excluded from this corporatist structure of governance for religious affairs would adopt a political theology more critical of state authorities. But there are some important nuances to keep in mind. As suggested above, albeit the corporatist regulatory regime enforced by the State Administration for Religious Affairs (SARA) tries to 'harmonize' a unified view between and within each of the five religions that is supportive of CCP policies, there are within each of them some important disagreements with important consequences for their political theologies. Conversely, religions unrecognized by the authorities do not necessarily adopt an oppositional attitude: a stance of accommodation and compromise with the state may serve them better, as it shields them from accusation that they are disturbing social stability and from repression. Furthermore, many worshippers, regardless of whether they belong to an approved religious institution, are simply indifferent to politics altogether.

A political theology that emphasizes cooperation with the existing political and social order may obviously serve well religions if it removes a potential source of hostility to them from state officials. However, it is not a guarantee of the latter's benevolence at all times, especially when religious practice, no matter how innocuous it may appear to outsiders, can be interpreted as a veiled critique. The example of Falungong reveals that contradiction very clearly. Falungong was one among many other groups promoting a Chinese form of healing, known as qigong, which some of the official medical authorities supported as an excellent form of preventive care, at a time when the state started to face a growing crisis in public health caused by a rapidly ageing population.[72] The people who practiced the exercises learned in such groups believed that their practice, by promoting activities and a discipline of the body that improved spiritual and physical well-being, helped the state. It did so by diminishing the demand for public health care, under stress since the dismantling of the communes in the 1980s. This belief embodied a convergence of interest between the CCP and qigong groups. This tacit mutual understanding between qigong groups and the state started to unravel, however, when the official reli-

72 See Palmer, *La fièvre du qigong: guérison, religion et politique en Chine, 1949-1999*.

gious institutions interpreted as a challenge to the existing structure of religious supervision the popularity of some of them, which had a religious dimension. It came to a head when the Falungong appeared to criticize, even if obliquely, state social policy.[73] The attempts by Falungong members to respond to what they saw as slander against their practice by established religious associations escalated into a series of polemics that culminated with a fateful demonstration around Zhongnanhai, the headquarters of the CCP in Beijing. By that time, officials saw in Falungong a major potential for subversion.

Detailed survey by David Palmer of the texts written by Li Hongzhi, the founding leader of Falungong, revealed disturbing trends. He found a prevalence of apocalyptic themes, the claim by Li that he is the savior of humanity, the argument that people had to follow his instructions for healing, specifically that they should not follow other traditions and refuse to take medicine.[74] Unsurprisingly, the sudden response of the government in the summer of 1999, which cracked down on all the activities of Falungong and persecuted its followers, reinforced the Manichean perspective of the groups, whose demonizing of the CCP as absolute evil became credible. The popularity of Falungong before its crackdown revealed continuities with themes that existed for centuries, but also innovation that reflected changes in China since the arrival of Western powers. We have seen that the presence of Protestant Christianity in China since the nineteenth century, as mentioned before, indirectly influenced the Taiping rebellion and added the reference to Christian soteriology to the repertoire of religiously inspired rebellions. The emphasis on materialist philosophy and science by the KMT and the CCP has added to that repertoire another element: the discourse of science. The resonance of Falungong in the 1990s was not only the result of borrowings from traditional Buddhist and Taoist themes, but also the successful grafting of a discourse that incorporate references to medical science, but with a twist. The failure of the other qigong movements to reconcile science and their spiritual practices has led Falungong to denounce science as the obstacle to spiritual salvation.[75]

---

73 See Thornton, "Framing Dissent in Contemporary China: Irony, Ambiguity and Metonymy," 2002, pp. 661-681.

74 See Tong, *Revenge of the Forbidden City: The Suppression of the Falun Gong in China, 1999-2005*, 2009, p. 7; Palmer, *Qigong Fever: Body, Science, and Utopia in China*, 2007, pp. 339-370.

75 See ibid., p. 361.

Before discussing themes of Chinese religions' political theologies, it is important to keep in mind the limitations the five official religious associations face as they articulate their respective political theologies, as well as the consequences of these limitations for the expression of a religiously informed political dissidence. We have seen above that the leaders of the Buddhist Association of China and its Taoist counterpart are, unsurprisingly, supportive of the regime for the sake of their own survival. In doing so, they do not depart too far from a long tradition of endorsing the authority of the rulers in imperial time, and that remained in force in Republican China. The performance of state rituals that show the allegiance of the religious community to the political leaders does not exclude that individual monks, nuns, priests, and lay devotees express criticism of the existing social and political order, on the basis of references to religious concepts such as Karmic retribution or the loss of the Mandate of heaven. However, they are the exception within the official associations. Dissidence, when it is expressed in the margins of the official association, can express a wide range of views, from the appeal to compassion expressed by the monk Shengguan in his denunciation of the June 4 Massacre, to the conservative critiques of Ven. Chin Kong that he professed online.

The patriotic associations for Catholic and Protestant Christianity in China face a deeper form of duality, as they try to assert their authority over their very diverse flocks. Protestant leaders have to negotiate with the state more space for worshippers but also seek to maintain authority over 'house churches' and breakaway groups the state considers dangerous sects. The imposition of a unified leadership over Protestantism has to take into account the legacy of a historically diverse faith divided between different denominations, reflective of the diversity existing outside of China. Therefore, it is difficult to assume unity of views among Christians. We cannot infer that the opposition to abortion observed among conservative Christians in North America, for example, will automatically translate to an opposition to the CCP family planning policy, which often implicitly condones abortion: such opposition may come from other sources.[76] Chinese Protestants may experience division in this issue, but we see no visible institutional expression of them because of the unanimity the official associations want to project. Catholics, who share many of the concerns of other Christians, have to contend with the added complication of the unre-

---

76 See Nie, *Behind the Silence: Chinese Voices on Abortion*, 2005.

solved issue of the paramount authority of their Church. While the episcopate has to recognize the authority of the Patriotic Catholic Association, many of the faithful recognize the supremacy of the Vatican. In sum, the same remark made above about Buddhists and Taoists applies to Christians as well: we cannot assume that the leaders of the Christian and Catholic Patriotic associations can always garner obedience from their flocks in all circumstances. We can make a similar remark for Chinese Muslims, with the added complication that their religious concerns intertwine with issues of ethnic identity.

In the next section, I will present two themes that are shared by the popular beliefs found in communal religions, Buddhism and Taoism, and which even the CCP refers to as it present itself as the custodian of Chinese traditions.

I. The Dream of Great Unity

There have been numerous discussions since the end of the nineteenth century about the necessity for a Chinese national religion, but even in its most recent iteration, they were never conclusive. During the last decades of the Qing dynasty, reformers such as Kang Youwei and Liang Qichao promoted the idea of a national religion (guojiao 国教), believing that Western powers had acquired their prominence because of the internal cohesion provided by a national religion.[77] Their projects, which favored at different times Confucianism and Buddhism, met with resistance from conservatives, because the latter resented changing the existing structure of governance. The most important resistance, however, came from radical reformers, who looked at religious tradition itself as part of the problem.[78] These debates under the Qing were inconclusive but the Republican regime reanimated them, this time with the added twist of Christianity's influence among the elites. Sun Yat-sen and Chiang Kai-shek, the prominent leaders of that period, drew a distinction between 'modern' religions such as Christianity, and superstitions. Both leaders and their party gave up on the idea of a national religion. The CCP, for which the idea of religions' resilience was anathema, as we have seen before, was even less in-

77 See Chang, *Chinese Intellectuals in Crisis: Search for Order and Meaning*, 1987.

78 See Goossaert, "1898: The Beginning of the End for Chinese?," 2006, pp. 307-336.

clined to consider seriously this possibility. The party policy between 1921 and 1966 moved between the paradigms of 'religion as the opiate of the masses,' and religion as the expression of 'feudalism' or 'counter-revolution'. In the first version, more lenient, religion was bound to disappear along with society's modernization, and in the second case, the CCP expelled foreign missionaries from the country, returned clerics to lay life, closed places of worship, and thereby sought to hasten the disappearance of religion. However, in another remarkable turnaround at least as important as the changes in economic policies, the CCP under Jiang Zemin and his successors has appeared, at times, to consider the idea of encouraging, if not openly promoting, myths of shared ancestry borrowed from popular beliefs, in the Cult of the Yellow Emperor.[79]

As the CCP recognizes the importance of religion in a modern society and even its compatibility with socialism,[80] and seeks to promote an idea of a unified Chinese culture to rally the population around its authority, academics and officials debated the idea a national religion, although they could not reach any agreement. The central issue is whether 'Chinese religion/popular beliefs', celebrated by the authorities as 'intangible heritage', could ever perform for China the function of a 'national essence/culture/ideology' that Shinto performed before in Japan, as part of the imperial ideology? However, while Japan was almost homogeneous culturally, linguistically speaking, and could engineer a Shinto tradition relevant for all Japanese citizens, China has a much greater cultural diversity: national minorities altogether represent only eight per cent of the Chinese population, but they occupy almost half of its territory.[81] Moreover, the Han population is also very diverse linguistically.[82] As is the case with Shinto, 'Chinese religion/popular beliefs' is/are inherently ethnic, and very likely to remain alien to the national minorities. Even if Chinese authorities wish that the nation's 'intangible heritage' integrates into a single cultural entity the diverse national minorities of the country, this is likely to be very difficult, as many of the minorities have distinct religious traditions that stand at the core of their identity.

---

79 See Billeter, *L'empereur jaune: Une tradition politique chinoise*, 2007.

80 See Ye, "Dui zongjiao lilun he zhengce yaodian de fenxi yu guilei," 2002; Wang, *Zhongguo de zongjiao wenti he zongjiao zhengce*.

81 See Mackerras, *China's Ethnic Minorities and Globalisation*, 2003.

82 See Mullaney, *Critical Han Studies: The History, Representation, and Identity of China's Majority*, 2012.

Even for Han Chinese, at least two kinds of religious realities make it very unlikely that the state could establish a state religion. The first reality is the complicated nature of the 'Chinese religion/beliefs' themselves: even if we accept as a heuristic device the idea of 'Chinese religion' expressed in ideas such as the 'three-in-one[83]', or 'popular beliefs', there is too much regional variety at the local level, seen in the 'communal religions' to make this plausible or even feasible. Linguistic differences making speech mutually unintelligible, specific regional histories that emphasize different heroes and promote different gods, and a variety of local customs, preclude the creation of national myths embraced all over the country. The second reality is that of the growing allegiance of many Chinese to religions that claim an exclusive affiliation, such as Christianity and Islam. In both cases, and in particular in the most institutionalized forms of these religions which, ironically, the state promotes, these religions preclude attempts at syncretism and resist the idea that they could adopt many of the practices of popular beliefs. Adherents to these religions may represent numerical minorities within the Han population, but they would not recognize themselves in any religion that the authorities would like to promote. Finally yet importantly, the important proportion of the Chinese population that remains atheist or indifferent to religion – including the CCP members, who must profess atheism – would oppose such idea.

II. Challenging the Mandate of Heaven

The Mandate of Heaven represented in traditional China the sacralization of political authority. Rulers perceived therefore the emergence of religious leaders who claimed to be saviors preventing the fatality of natural calamities as political as well as religious disputes. Challenges to the Mandate of Heaven have recurred for centuries in China, and despite the numerous regime changes experienced by the country, it represents a constant in the relationship between state and religion. Since the establishment of the PRC, individuals proclaimed challenges to the Mandate of Heaven in China's rural areas, but they were mostly vain resistance of village elites to Land Reform or village feuds at the beginning of the Reform

83 See Dean, *The Lord of the Three-in-One*, 1998.

policy.[84] No major religious movement since the Taiping Rebellion in the mid-Nineteenth century has come close to contest state authority with any credibility. Even if China's government faces several tests on an unprecedented scale, the strength of the state apparatus is such that the kind of religious-political movements comparable to the Red Eyebrows or the Taiping is unlikely to arise. Although the CCP under Jiang Zemin has acted as if Falungong represented such a threat, there are important differences from previous occurrence that prevent us from making such analogies. The Chinese state today is not about to collapse; the economy may slow down as China enters into a new phase of development, but it is not experiencing the kind of widespread calamity that taxed the state before. Theological or religiously inspired responses to crises are more likely to be local, and will be more difficult to detect, as long as local security forces are able to nip in the bud any early signs of unrest by a group of people who claim some form of supernatural support.

The different crises experienced by Chinese are local phenomena and even though reports mention over 130,000 riots per year, most of these incidents are small-scale and local. Most of the actors involved in these conflicts blame low-level party cadres, factory owners, abusive policemen, or other officials, but few criticize the social, economic, and political system that make these abuses possible in the first place. Many of the grievances are expressed in the idiom used by the CCP itself, which has less to do with the Marxist ideology of class struggle, but more to do with the recuperation of themes, such as 'harmonious society', that resonates more with Confucian values. We see very few issues articulated in a language that we can relate to religious world-views, and only a small proportion of the grievances from the public relate to religion.

III. A Variety of Chinese Political Theologies

The challenge to the Mandate of Heaven discussed above has suggested the resilience of some themes in religions' political theologies. However, the institutionalization of the five religions discussed before and the emergence of new religious movements leaves space for new forms of political theology that import themes from abroad such as respect for diversity and

84 See Perry, "Rural Violence in Socialist China," pp. 275-308.

inter-religious dialogues. The institutionalization of religions has also revealed that each of China's religions has the capacity to provide specific values that can guide the lives of its followers, but the possible result is a pillarization of society into different religious communities. China has avoided this fate for most of its history because communal and popular religions integrated in their world-views the diversity inherent in the co-existence of Buddhist, Taoist, and Confucian concepts. The CCP, with its policies encapsulated in the slogan of 'harmonious society' and 'China dream' suggests a continuation of that policy, albeit in a different framework. Nevertheless, as we have seen before, the diversity of religions has revealed that there are specific differences that make it difficult to think of a uniquely Chinese political theology.

We finally need to keep an important caveat in mind as we discuss the impact of religious world-views on Chinese politics. For many religious believers and for the greater number of people who visit temples, practice traditional rituals and do not necessarily identify to a specific religion, 'doing religion' or the simple act of worship, represents an escape from politics. An apolitical posture can be in itself political, as a 'weapon of the weak' or as a covert strategy of resistance to the state.[85] Conversely, we can look at it as an attitude that reinforces the existing social-economic order by 'giving up' on the hope of effecting any change. In that case, we can interpret the retreat from politics as the expression of disenchantment from politics if not outright cynicism. That is, as many people met in the course of my fieldwork over the years have said to me, their interest for having a more religiously-oriented life is strong because they don't think that 'politics can change anything' or even worse, that 'it is inherently corrupt and unlikely to address the reality of decay.'

E. Conclusion

China offers us a fascinating case of a most radical attempt at modernization in the twentieth century with the surprising realization at the beginning of the twenty-first century that salvation may lie with the revival of its religious traditions. The other interesting aspect of China is that its radical modernization, premised on an extreme form of secularization, turned

---

85 See Scott, *Weapons of the Weak: Everyday Forms of Peasant Resistance*, 1985.

out in the twenty-first century to have generated a strong stimulus for the instrumental use of religion by the state. There is more to the persisting role of religion in China than just its resilience or revival. The challenges of aggressive modernization were real and acute and religions became transformed by this occurrence. The functions religion plays in contemporary China are more than those that the state would like to see it play. The challenges of Chinese religions to the existing political order, however, are local, and even if they are offering an alternative set of values and norms for organizing society, they cannot hope to succeed at replacing the existing order. Conflicting sets of values are more likely to oppose religions against each other rather than any of them challenging the political regime.

Bibliography

Allen-Ebrahamian, Bethany, "Chinese State Media Warns against 14 'Evil Cults'," *Foreign Policy* (June 6, 2014), at http://www.foreignpolicy.com/articles/ 2014/06/06/chinese_state_media_warns_against_14_evil_cults.

Aminzade, Ron, and Elizabeth Perry, "The Sacred, Religious, and Secular in Contentious Politics: Blurring Boundaries," in *Silence and Voice in the Study of Contentious Politics*, ed. Ron Aminzade et al., Cambridge: Cambridge University Press, 2001, pp. 155-178.

Asad, Talal, "On Re-reading a Modern Classic: W.C. Smith's 'The Meaning and End of Religion'," *History of Religions* 40, 39 (2001): 205-222.

Ashiwa, Yoshiko and David L. Wank, *Making Religion, Making the State in China, the Politics of Religion in Modern China,* Standford: Stanford University Press, 2009.

Bays, Daniel, *A New History of Christianity in China*, Malden: Wiley-Blackwell, 2012.

Bell, Daniel A., *China's New Confucianism: Politics and Everyday Life in a Changing Society*, Princeton: Princeton University Press, 2008.

Bentz, Anne-Sophie, "Symbol and power: the Dalai Lama as a charismatic leader," *Nations and Nationalism* 18, 2 (2012): 287-305.

Bhargava, Rajeev, "Can Secularism Be Rehabilitated?" in *Secular States and Religious Diversity*, ed. Bruce J. Berman, Rajeev Bhargava, and André Laliberté, Vancouver: University of British Columbia Press, 2013.

Billeter, Térence, *L'empereur jaune: Une tradition politique chinoise*, Paris: Les Indes savantes, 2007.

Cabestan, Jean-Pierre, "The political and practical obstacles to the reform of the judiciary and the establishment of a rule of law in China," *Journal of Chinese Political Science* 10, 1 (2005): 43-64.

Chang, Hao, *Chinese Intellectuals in Crisis: Search for Order and Meaning (1890-1911),* Berkeley: University of California Press, 1987.

Chau, Adam Y., *Miraculous Response: Doing Popular Religion in Contemporary China*, Stanford: Stanford University Press, 2006.

Chen, Yu-wen, *The Uyghur Lobby: Global Networks, Coalitions and Strategies of the World Uyghur Congress,* New York: Routledge, 2014.

Chun-Li, Chang, and Michael Frantz, *The Taiping Rebellion: History and Documents. Volume I: History*, Seattle: University of Washington Press, 1966.

Cohen, Paul A., *History in Three Keys: The Boxers as Event, Experience, and Myth*, New York: Columbia University Press, 1997.

Davis, Elizabeth Van Wie, "Uyghur Muslim Ethnic Separatism in Xinjiang, China," *Asian Affairs: An American Review* 35, 1 (2008): 15-30.

De Bary, William Theodore, and Tu Wei-ming, *Confucianism and Human Rights,* New York: Columbia University Press, 1998.

Dean, Kenneth, *Lord of the three in one: the spread of a cult in Southeast China.* Princeton, N.J.: Princeton University Press, 1998.

Duara, Prasenjit, *Sovereignty and Authenticity: Manchukuo and the East Asian Modern*, Lanham: Rowman and Littlefield, 2003.

Duara, Prasenjit, "Knowledge and Power in the Discourse of Modernity: The Campaigns against Popular Religion in Early Twentieth-Century China," *Journal of Asian Studies* 50, 1 (1991): 67-83.

Dubois, Thomas David, *Religion and the Making of Modern East Asia*, New York: Cambridge University Press, 2011.

Dui Hua, "Identifying Cult Organizations in China," *Reference Materials* (July 10) at http://www.duihuaresearch.org/2014/07/identifying-cult-organizations-in-china.html.

Dui Hua, "China's 'Almighty God' Rises with Threat of Apocalypse," *Human Rights Journal* 2012, at http://www.duihuahrjournal.org/2012/12/chinas-almighty-god-rises-with-threat.html.

Dutournier, Guillaume, and Ji Zhe, "Expérimentation sociale et 'confucianisme populaire': Le cas du Centre d'éducation culturelle de Lujiang," *Perspectives chinoises* 109, 4 (2009): 71-86.

Ellis, Stephen, and Gerrie ter Haar, "Religion and Politics in Sub-Saharan Africa," *Journal of Modern African Studies* 36, 2 (1998): 175-201.

Esherick, Joseph W, *The Origins of the Boxer Uprising,* Berkeley: University of California Press, 1987.

Famularo, Julia, "Spinning the Wheel: the Policy Implications of the Dalai Lama's Reincarnation," Policy paper for the Project 2049 Institute, 2012, at http://project2049.net/documents/spinning_the_wheel_famularo.pdf.

Fan, Lizhu 范麗珠, *Dangdai zhongguoren zongjiao xinyang de bianqian Shenzhen minjian zongjiao xintu detianye yanjiu (當代中國人宗教信仰的變遷: 深圳民間宗教信徒的田野研究*), Taipei: Weibo Wenhua (瑋柏文化), 2005.

Feuchtwang, Stephan, "Religion as Resistance," in *Chinese Society: Change, Conflict and Resistance,* ed. Elizabeth J. Perry and Mark Selden, London: Routledge, 2000, pp. 161-177.

Fisher, Gareth, "In the Footsteps of the Tourists: Buddhist Revival at Museum/Temple Sites in Beijing," *Social Compass* 58, 4 (2011): 511-524.

Gill, Anthony, "Religion and Comparative Politics," *Annual Review of Political Science* 4 (2001): 117-138.

Goossaert, Vincent, "1898: The Beginning of the End for Chinese Religion?," *Journal of Asian Studies* 65, 2 (2006): 307-336.

Gladney, Dru, "Islam in China: Accommodation or Separatism?," *The China Quarterly 174* (2003): 451-467.

Gries, Peter Hays, "Popular Nationalism and State Legitimation in China," in *State and Society in 21st Century China*, ed. Peter Gries and Stanley Rosen, London: Routledge, 2005, pp. 25-43.

Horneman, Magda, "China: When will five-fold state-backed religious monopoly end?" *Forum 18 News Service*, Oslo, 2013, at http://www.forum18.org/ archive.php ?article_id=1876.

Ji, Zhe, "Secularization and Religious Restructuring: Statist Institutionalization of Chinese Buddhism and its Paradoxes," in *Chinese Religiosities: Afflictions of Modernity and State Formation,* ed. Yang Mayfair Mei-hui, Berkeley: University of California Press, 2008, pp. 233-260.

Jiang, He, "Chairman of China's Buddhist Association Wrongly Expels Monk, Says HRIC," *Epoch Times* (August 19, 2006), at http://www.theepochtimes.com/ n3/173 0836-chairman-of-chinas-buddhist-association-wrongly-expels-monk-says-hric/.

Jones, Allison Denton, "Contemporary Han Chinese Involvement in Tibetan Buddhism: A Case Study from Nanjing," *Social Compass* 58, 4 (2011): 540-553.

Kuo, Cheng-tian, *Religion and Democracy in Taiwan,* Albany: State University of New York Press, 2008.

Lagerwey, John, *China: A Religious State*, Hong Kong: Hong Kong University Press, 2010.

Laliberté, André, "The Regulation of Religious Affairs in Taiwan: From State Control to Laisser-faire?," *Journal of Current Chinese Affairs* 2 (2009): 53-84.

Leung, Beatrice, "China's Religious Freedom Policy: The Art of Managing Religious Activity," *The China Quarterly* 184 (2005): 894-915.

Lynch, Andrew P., "Beijing and the Vatican: Catholics in China and the Politics of Religious Freedom," *Sage Open* 4 (2014): 1-10.

Mackerras, Collin, *China's Ethnic Minorities and Globalisation*, New York: Routledge, 2003.

Madan, T. N., "Secularism in Its Place," in *Secularism and Its Critics*, ed. Rajeev Bhargava, Delhi: Oxford University Press, 1998, pp. 297-320.

Madsen, Richard, "Catholic Revival During the Reform Era," *The China Quarterly* 174 (2003): 469-487.

Mao, Zedong, "On Practice," in *The Political Thought of Mao Tse Tung*, ed. Stuart Schram, New York: Praeger, 1976, pp. 281-296.

Mullaney, Thomas S., *Critical Han Studies: The History, Representation, and Identity of China's Majority*, Berkeley: University of California Press, 2012.

Naquin, Susan, *Millenarian Rebellion in China: The Eight Trigrams Uprising of 1813*, New Haven: Yale University Press, 1976.

Nie, Jing-bao, *Behind the Silence: Chinese Voices on Abortion*, New York: Rowman and Littlefield, 2005.

Oakes, Tim, and Donald S. Sutton, *Faiths on Display: Religion, Tourism, and the Chinese State,* New York: Rowman and Littlefield, 2010.

Ostergaard, Clemens, "Governance and the Political Challenge of Falungong," in *Governance in China*, ed. Jude Howell, New York: Rowman and Littlefield (2004): 207-225.

Ownby, David, *Falun Gong and the Future of China*, New York: Oxford University Press, 2008.

Palmer, David, "Chinese redemptive societies and salvationist religion: historical phenomenon or sociological category?," *Journal of Chinese Ritual, Theatre and Folklore* 172 (2011): 21-72.

Palmer, David, *Qigong Fever: Body, Science, and Utopia in China*, Columbia: Columbia University Press, 2007.

Palmer, David, *La fièvre du qigong: guérison, religion et politique en Chine 1949-1999*, Paris: Éditions de l'école des hautes études en sciences sociale, 2005.

Pedroletti, Brice. "China's Christians fear new persecution after latest wave of church demolitions," *The Guardian* (July 5, 2014), at https://www.theguardian.com/world/2014/jul/05/china-christianity-wenzhou-zhejiang-churches.

Perry, Elizabeth J., "Rural Violence in Socialist China," in *Challenging the Mandate of Heaven: Social Protest and State Power in China*, ed. Elizabeth J. Perry, Armonk: M.E.Sharpe, (2002): 275-308.

Platt, Stephen R., *Autumn in the Heavenly Kingdom: China, the West, and the Epic Story of the Taiping Civil War*, New York: Knopf, 2012.

Potter, Pittman B., "Belief in Control: Regulation of Religion in China," *China Quarterly* 174 (2003): 317-337.

Reilly, Thomas, *The Taiping Heavenly Kingdom: Rebellion and the Blasphemy of Empire,* Seattle: University of Washington Press, 2004.

Remoiville, Julie, *Le renouveau religieux en Chine urbaine contemporaine: le rôle social de la religion dans la vie quotidienne à Hangzhou*, PhD thesis, Ecole pratique des hautes études, 2013.

Schmitter, Philip, "Still the Century of Corporatism?," *The Review of Politics* 36, 1 (1974): 85-131.

Scott, James C., *Weapons of the Weak: Everyday Forms of Peasant Resistance*, New Haven: Yale University Press, 1985.

Seiwert, Hubert, and Ma Xisha, *Popular Religious Movements and Heterodox Sects in Chinese History*, Leiden: Brill, 2003.

Smart, Ninian, *Mao*, Glasgow: William Collins and Sons, 1974.

Smith, Christian, "Introduction: Correcting a Curious Neglect, or Bringing Religion Back In," in *Disruptive Religion: The Force of Faith in Social Movement Activism,* ed. Christian Smith, New York: Routledge, 1996, pp. 1-25.

Smith, Donald Eugene, *India as a Secular State*, Princeton: Princeton University Press, 1963.

Stepan, Alfred, "The World's Religious Systems and Democracy: Crafting the Twin Tolerations," in *Arguing Comparative Politics*, ed. Alfred Stepan, Oxford: Oxford University Press, 2011, pp. 213-253.

Sun Yanfei, "The Chinese Buddhist ecology in post-Mao China: Contours, types and dynamics," *Social Compass* 58, 4 (2011): 498-510.

Tai, Zixue, "Casting the Ubiquitous Net of Information Control: Internet Surveillance in China from Golden Shield to Green Dam," in *ICTs for Mobile and Ubiquitous Urban Infrastructures: Surveillance, Locative Media, and Global Networks*, ed. Rodrigo José Firmino, Fábio Duarte, and Clovis Ultramaried, Hershey: Information Science Reference, 2011, pp. 237-256.

Ter Haar, Barend J., *The White Lotus Teachings in Chinese Religious History*, Honolulu: University of Hawaii Press, 1992.

Thornton, Patricia, "Framing Dissent in Contemporary China: Irony, Ambiguity and Metonymy," *The China Quarterly* 171 (2002): 661-681.

Tong, James, *Revenge of the Forbidden City: The Suppression of the Falun Gong in China, 1999-2005*, New York: Oxford University Press, 2009.

Tong, James, "The New Religious Policy in China: Catching up with Systemic Reforms," *Asian Survey* 50, 5 (2010): 859-887.

Tsai, Lily Lee, *Accountability without Democracy: Solidary Groups and Public Goods Provision in Rural China*, New York: Cambridge University Press, 2007.

Tu, Wei-ming, *Confucian Traditions in East Asian Modernity: Moral Education and Economic Culture in Japan and the Four Mini-Dragons*, Cambridge: Harvard University Press, 1996.

Wang, Zuo'an 王作安, *Zhongguo de zongjiao wenti he zongjiao zhengce (中国的宗教□□和宗教政策, China's religious question and religious policy)*, Beijing: Zongjiao wenhua Chubanshe, 2002.

Yang, Ching-Kun, *Religion in Chinese Society: A Study of Contemporary Social Functions of Religion and some of their Historical Factors*, Taipei: SMC Publishing, 1994.

Yang, Fenggang, "Oligopoly dynamics: Official religions in China," in *The Sage Handbook of The Sociology of Religion*, ed. James Beckford and Jay Demerath, London: Sage, 2007, pp. 635-653.

Yang, Fenggang, "The Red, Black, and Gray Markets of Religion in China," *The Sociological Quarterly* 47 (2006): 93-122.

Yang, Fenggang, and Anning Hu, "Mapping Chinese Folk Religion in Mainland China and Taiwan," *Journal for the Scientific Study of Religion* 51, 3 (2012): 505-521.

Yang, Mayfair Mei-hui, *Chinese Religiosities: Afflictions of Modernity and State Formation*, Berkeley and Los Angeles: University of California Press, 2008.

Ye, Xiaowen, "Dui zongjiao lilun he zhengce yaodian de fenxi yu guilei □宗教理□和政策要点的分析与□□," in *Xin Zhongguo zongjiao gongzuo dashi gailan (1949-1999) 新中国宗教工作大事□□*, ed. Luo Changwu □□武, Beijing: Huawen chubanshe □文出版社, 2001, pp. 1-8.

Ying, Fuk-sung, "New Wine in Old Wineskins: an Appraisal of Religious Legislation in China and The Regulations on Religious Affairs of 2005," *Religion, State, and Society* 34, 4 (2006): 347-373.

Zhang, Xueying, "Buddhism in China," *Explaining China to the World*, at http://www.chinatoday.com.cn/ctenglish/se/txt/2009-06/19/content_203310.htm.

Democratic Prophets and Priests During Taiwan's Democratization

Cheng-Tian Kuo

A. Introduction

Before 2008, Taiwan had a number of historical, cultural and political baggages that could have dwarfed, if not decimated the newborn democracy. It inherited from mainland China a Confucian culture which sustained authoritarian rule for three thousand years. From 1949 to 1987, Taiwan maintained the longest martial rule among modern states by a Leninist party, the Kuomintang (KMT, the Nationalist Party), which continued to be the largest political party after the lifting of martial law. Ever since the 228 Massacre of Taiwanese elites in 1947, an ethnic tension existed between the minority mainlanders who migrated from China in 1949 to take over the Japanese colonial government and the majority local Taiwanese.[1] Finally, two hundred kilometers to its west, the Chinese communist regime has persistently claimed sovereignty over Taiwan and vividly demonstrated its resolve via military actions in the past two decades.

Despite these baggages, Taiwan lifted martial law in 1987, conducted the direct election of the president in 1996 in the midst of a missile crisis across the Taiwan Strait, elected the presidential candidate of the opposition party (Democratic Progressive Party, DDP) to replace the KMT in 2000, and passed the "two turnover test" of a consolidated democracy in

---

1 On Feburary 27, 1947, three Monopoly Bureau officers (mainlanders) hurt a Taiwanese vendor woman selling smuggled cigarettes and killed a bystander in Taipei. On the next day, demonstrators clashed with the police and resulted in more casualties. Island-wide riots broke out in the following week. President Jiang Jieshi immediately sent in troops to surpress the riots, killing about 2,000 to 20,000 Taiwanese, most of whom were teachers, journalists, doctors, lawyers, and high-school students. Since then, the massacre has been one of the major contested issues in elections. For more details about the massacre and its impacts on Taiwanese politics, see Roy, *Taiwan: A Political History*, 2003, pp. 67-75.

2008.[2] In less than thirty years, Taiwan has witnessed vast improvement in human rights that took Western democracies hundreds of years to achieve, such as gender equality, aboriginal rights, labor welfare, affordable universal health coverage, religious freedom and tolerance, and environmental protection. What is notable about Taiwan's "democratic miracle" is not only the speed of democratic consolidation but also the absence of bloody and sustained conflicts which often plague other "Third Wave" democracies and, particularly, those Muslim countries after the Arab Spring.[3]

Reasons for the success or failure of democratization are many and complex. But with the revival of religious influence in politics since the 1980s, social scientists began to study the relationships between religion and democracy. This paper argues that the democratic prophetic and priestly roles played by Taiwanese religious groups have contributed to the "democratic miracle." The next section will describe the three stages of state-religion relations in Taiwan from 1949 to the present: statism, separation of state and religion, and checks and balances between the state and religion. Then, representative cases of the Presbyterian Church in Taiwan and the Buddhist Foguangshan are compared via their democratic theology, religious polity, and interaction with the state in order to explain their differences in prophetic role and priestly role, and how they together contributed to Taiwan's "democratic miracle." The last section concludes the analysis.

B. *Three Stages of State-Religion Relations in Taiwan*[4]

From 1945 to the present, state-religion relations in Taiwan can be divided into three stages: statism from 1945 to 1987; separationism from 1987 to

---

2 See Huntington, *The Third Wave: Democratization in the Late Twentieth Century*, 1991, observed that a newborn democracy became consolidated and could not easily break down when it experienced two democratic turnovers of ruling parties.

3 Huntington, ibid., employed the term "Third Wave" democracies for the new democracies established after the late 1970s. The First Wave democracies were Western democracies established before World War II; the Second Wave democracies were former colonies and established after World War II.

4 When Western concept of separation of state and church was introduced to China around 1900, there were two models: the French model promoted a strong state over religion and the American model promoted a separation of state and religion. Most Chinese intellectuals and political leaders preferred the French model. The

2000; and checks and balances from 2000 to the present. In 1945, for the first time in Taiwan's history, the state was able to effectively control religion while religion had little influence over the state.[5] This was largely due to the Leninist state established by Jiang Jingguo, the heir-to-be to President Jiang Jieshi. Although he became a Christian later probably upon his father's request, there was no record showing that he was committed to Christianity or any religion.[6] Once the party-state was established in 1950, it began to penetrate the society by setting up corporatist associations and implanting party cells in all large social organizations.[7]

Under corporatist law, only one national umbrella religious association was allowed to exist for each religion to represent the interests of its clergy and believers. For instance, at the national level, there were the Buddhist Association of the Republic of China, the Daoist Association of the Republic of China, the Chinese Regional Bishops' Conference and the Confucian Association of the Republic of China.[8] No other associations of the same religion were allowed to exist. Although most Christian denominations had their own national associations, such as the Presbyterian Church in Taiwan and the Chinese Baptist Convention, there was no national umbrella association representing all Christian denominations.

Under the KMT regime, the state was able to control religion through both formal and informal means. In addition to general martial law regulations restricting free movement, information and speech, the major formal

---

KMT state brought the French model to Taiwan in 1949, and Jiang Jingguo further strengthened it. For further discussion of statism and separationism in Taiwan, see Kuo, "State-Religion Relations in Taiwan: From Statism and Separatism to Checks and Balances," 2013, pp. 1-38.

5 Comprehensive studies of Taiwan's religion-state relations are few. Notable works include Laliberté, "The Regulation of Religious Affairs in Taiwan: From State Control to Laisser-faire?," 2009, pp. 53-83; and Kuo, *Religion and Democracy in Taiwan*, 2008.

6 See Jiang, *Jiang Jingguo Zhuan (A biography of Jiang Jingguo)*, 1997.

7 Corporatist associations refer to social organizations that are organized according to the criteria of singularity, compulsion, government sponsorship, non-competitiveness and functional differentiation (Schmitter, "The Organizational Development of International Organizations," 1971, pp. 917-937). Wu Naiteh meticulously studied Jiang Jingguo's efforts to establish corporatist controls over Taiwanese society in the 1950s. See Wu, *The Politics of A Regime Patronage System: Mobilization and Control Within An Authoritarian Regime*, 1987.

8 For the relations between the state and Buddhism in Taiwan during the martial law period, see Jones, *Buddhism in Taiwan: Religion and the State,* 1999.

instrument was the Law Regulating Temples and Shrines enacted in 1929 in China but brought to Taiwan by the refugee KMT state in 1949. More effective forms of state control over religion came from various state intelligence-gathering agencies, such as the local police, the Garrison Command, the Investigation Bureau, the military intelligence office and the National Security Bureau.

In addition to the supervision of state bureaucracy over religion, the KMT also implanted party cells in large religious organizations. These party cells assumed at least three functions: to recruit party members within the religion, to monitor religious organizations' political activities and to elect party members to lead national religious organizations. The KMT coordination center was the First Office of the Social Works Department. There was a loose party caucus set up in the Buddhist Association of the Republic of China, but no smaller party cells existed in monasteries or temples. There is no evidence that formal party organizations existed within Christian denominations.

Because of the dual supervision of the state and party machinery, most religious organizations during the martial law period had no choice but to adopt either a submissive position or a one-way separationist attitude toward the state. That is, the state had all the power to interfere with religious affairs while religion was not allow to interfere with political affairs except by the state's request. Even in cases where their religious activities involved social welfare, they refrained from interacting with the state as much as possible.

Taiwan's political and religious environment significantly transformed in the early 1980s when the supreme political leader's health was deteriorating. The opposition movement made great progress in attracting supporters by combining democratic ideals with Taiwanese nationalism. The KMT government finally lifted martial law in 1987. Li Denghui, who succeeded Jiang Jingguo as president in 1988 after Jiang's death, was a devoted Presbyterian. Although he was not involved in the Presbyterian protest movement during the 1970s, he was familiar with and sympathetic to their religious and political causes.[9] Subsequently, most laws and regulations violating human rights were rescinded, and new laws protecting human rights were instituted. Most important among these new laws were the re-

---

9 See Gao, *Shizijia zhi lu: Gao Junming mushi huiyilu (The Road of the Cross: Memoir of Reverent Gao Junming*, 2001, pp. 335-342.

vised Law on the Organization of Civic Groups and the Law on Assembly and Parade, which guaranteed Taiwanese the same freedom of association and movement as citizens in other democratic countries. This meant that the increasing pluralism of religious organizations that began in the early 1980s was finally legally endorsed by the state. The corporatist structure of religious groups soon yielded to mushrooming of all kinds of national religious associations independent of the old ones.[10]

In the post-martial law regime, the state bureaucracy tried to maintain close supervision of religion but its intentions and methods were very different from those of the Leninist state. The increased freedom of association brought about the burgeoning of "new religions", which combined traditional religious practices with personal ideologies of new religious leaders. At the same time, however, sexual and financial scandals in these unregulated new religions were exposed from time to time. Partly due to the concern over their collective image and partly due to strong competition for membership and financial donations from these new religions, most religious groups supported the government's effort to re-regulate all religions.[11] But the content of the proposed law by the Ministry of the Interior, Law of Religious Groups (zongjiao tuantifa), aroused heated debate not only between the state and religious organizations, but also among the principal religions, on issues such as accounting procedures, property management, building construction and internal governing structures. After decades of negotiations, the bill was frequently shuttled between the legislature and the Ministry of the Interior due to the conflicting and ever-changing demands of various religious groups.[12]

The increased political autonomy of religious groups was evident in several ways. With the help of economic prosperity, new religious groups mushroomed outside the state-controlled religious associations, such as the folk religions of Yiguandao (the Unity Sect) and goddess Mazu belief.[13] Religious support of the KMT government and politicians declined.

---

10 See Lu, Johnson, and Stark, "Deregulation and the Religious Market in Taiwan: A Research Note," 2008, pp. 139-153.

11 See Ye, *Relations of State and Religion in Taiwan*, 2000, p. 263.

12 See Laliberté, "The Regulation of Religious Affairs in Taiwan: From State Control to Laisser-faire."

13 See Katz, "Religion and the State in Post-war Taiwan," 2003, p. 395; Laliberté, "Buddhist Organizations and Democracy in Taiwan," 2001, pp. 97-129, and Paper, "Mediums and Modernity: The Institutionalization of Ecstatic Religious Functionaries in Taiwan," 1996, p. 105.

Many religious leaders openly received politicians from various political parties. State and local elites competed for votes by supporting local religious traditions.[14] In turn, religious organizations solicited support from legislators and elected administrators of different political parties in order to maximize government funding for religious affairs. More and more religious organizations supported candidates to run against KMT candidates. Furthermore, some clergy ran for public offices under different party banners. For instance, once a loyal supporter of KMT candidates during the martial rule, the National Association of Yiguandao let local branches to choose their favorite candidates. In the 1992 legislative election, the local branch in Tainan City nominated the son of a branch leader to run against a KMT candidate. In the 1994 Taipei mayoral election, an influential Yiguandao branch helped elect the DPP candidate Chen Shuibian after he was initiated as a believer.[15] However, most religious organizations decided to maintain their separationist position or maintain equal distance from all political forces. Their believers still could not get used to political debate among believers or between the pulpit and the pew.

Other religious leaders found out that politics was detrimental to organizational cohesion. While politicians and political activists freely exercised their freedom of speech and assembly, religious leaders were worried what the same freedoms might do to their organizations. Heated debates among believers over party loyalty and public policies sometimes paralyzed sacred meetings. Some believers left their religious organizations because they disagreed with the religious leader's political preferences. A former colleague of mine, Professor Tsai, who had been a devoted believer of the Buddhist Zongtai Cansi but also a strong supporter of the DPP, decided to leave the Buddhist organization before the 2000 presidential election because its abbot publicly endorsed the KMT candidate while denouncing the DPP candidate. He told me: "I don't know what's in the stupid mind of this bald donkey (*tulu*, a Chinese prerogative term for monk)." This statement was a shock to me because one year before that, he told me that he saw the incarnation of the abbot in a Taipei branch temple while the abbot's true body, at the same time, was leading a scripture study session at the headquarters 200 kilometers away. "The Buddhist leader performed a miracle," he solemly insisted. Others, being "polluted"

---

14 See Katz, "Religion and the State in Post-war Taiwan," p. 412.

15 See Kuo, *Religion and Democracy in Taiwan*, pp. 77-78.

by democratic values, began to challenge the authoritarian rule of religious leaders. By then, there were plenty of choices of religious denominations or religions anyway. Therefore, most religious leaders decided to uphold the separation principle and asked their believers not to bring politics to religious premises.

Meanwhile, the state was very reluctant to intervene in religious affairs unless serious crimes of violence and rape were committed. Most of the controversies involved minor administrative offenses, such as religious properties illegally built on public land, religious cremation facilities violating regulations on cremation, religious buildings violating zoning rules and religious activities violating environmental regulations. In these cases, the government enforced secular regulations without religious discrimination but usually with a lot of discretion. In most cases, the government would have one eye shut or would provide legal advice to correct these misdeameanors before legal punishments were applied.[16]

While the state's negative intervention in religion was reduced, its positive assistance to religion was not. The Bureau of Civic Affairs of the Ministry of Interior routinely provided small grants (up to about US$ 33,000) to religious organizations which planned to hold religious parades, conferences, exhibitions, ceremonies, charity programs or neighborhood activities. These small grants were given to religious organizations without discrimination but proportionality was considered. Larger programs, for instance, the annual Mazu parade which millions of worshipers attended, tended to receive larger funding. Very few, if any, religious organizations complained about the Bureau of Civic Affairs for violating their religious freedom or the separation of state and religion.

I still call this period of state-religion relations as separationist period because it was the dominant voice among intellectuals, including sociologists of religion and legal scholars.[17] Most took the literal meaning of the Chinese translation of separation of state and religion to be strict separation of them. In 1999, the Grand Justice Council (the equivalent of U.S.

---

16 See Hu, *Taiwan zongjiao ziyou quan zhi xin zhidu fenxi (A New Institutional Analysis of Taiwan's Religious Rights)*, 2009, and Zhang, "The Boundaries of Religious Freedom and Religious Sexual Assaults in Taiwan," 2012.

17 See Li, "Lun tsungchiao hsinyang tzuyu chi kuochia paohu iwu: ping sifa yuan da faguan shihtzu ti si chiu ling hao chieh shih (Protection of Religious Freedom and National Obligation: Comment about the Judicial Yuan's Interpretation)," 1999, pp. 39-60.

Supreme Court) delivered the first major decision on religion-state relations in the Council's history. On a controversy involving a Jehovah Witness refusing to serve military duty, the Council briefly stated that the state should not promote or prohibit any religion.[18] This Council decision seemed to agree with the separationist view and confined religious freedom to the "internal" part of people's lives. The short length and low quality of the Council's deliberations on state-religion relations seemed to reflect their lack of knowledge on this subject.

In the mix of a self-withdrawing state and separationist attitudes of many religious leaders and politically assertive believers, there emerged a new mode of state-religion relations around the year 2000, i.e. checks and balances between the state and religion. This new mode of state-religion relations emerged because of changes in the state and the religious market.

In 2000, the Democratic Progressive Party toppled the fifty-five-years rule of the KMT government. DPP President Chen Shuibian who became an initiated believer of the syncretistic religion Yiguandao (unity sect) in the 1990s won the election partly due to large amount of religious swing votes. His Religious White Paper and politically active religious-policy adviser Zhu Wuxian, propagating religious freedom and resolving problems of land acquisition, attracted votes across religions.[19] The first turnover of the Taiwanese government resulted in major restructuring of not only political coalitions but also state-society relations, including state-religion relations.

In 2008, Ma Yingjiu led the KMT to win the 2008 presidential election and passed what Samuel T. Huntington calls the "two turn-over test" for a consolidated democracy. Never having publicly disclosed his religious affiliation, President Ma was nevertheless committed to further promoting religious freedom as part of his commitment to expanding human rights in

---

18 R.O.C, Justices of the Constitutional Court, Grand Justice Council, Judicial Yuan, Interpretation No. 490, 1999.

19 The Religious White Paper laid out the direction of religious policy reforms, such as to legalize the concurrent illegal occupation of public land by temples and shrines in the mountain, to grant license to cremation facilities within the compound of religious organizations, to recognize the validity of diploma issued by religious seminaries, to respect traditional religious rituals of the aboriginals which included hunting endangered species, and to proprogate a new law for religious groups to enhance religious freedom. See Chen Shuibian, "Zongjiao baipishu (Religious White Paper)," 2000, and Kuo, "Religious Participation in Taiwanese Democracy," 2011, p. 266.

general. In May 2009 he signed the International Covenant on Civil and Political Rights as well as the International Covenant on Economic, Social and Cultural Rights, even though Taiwan was not eligible to become a member state of these treaties. Despite the fact that the signing of the two Covenants had a more political than legal effect, the Human Rights Committee of the Ma government has repeatedly cited the two Covenants and diligently monitored different ministries to revise laws and regulations that might have infringed upon human rights, including religious regulations under the jurisdiction of the Ministry of Interior.

Since the year 2000, the state has gradually changed its policies toward religion. In 2001, the Ministry of Education began active promotion of courses related to religion in primary and secondary schools as well as in universities.[20] Primary and secondary schools cooperate with Buddhist, Christian and Yiguandao organizations, among other religious groups, to offer Life Education classes.[21] In universities, Life Education classes are also added to curricula as optional general knowledge classes. These Life Education classes teach students about the meaning of life, their human relationships, and relations with the nature.[22] Most of them are offered by faculty members with different religious backgrounds. Due to the decreasing government subsidy, universities welcome religion-based foundations to sponsor credited classes and lectures in universities. Students and faculty members can choose from a variety of religion-based clubs, freely wear different religious garments or symbols of their faith and live peacefully on campus.

The central and local governments continued to support public religious activities, such as parades and festivals, without discrimination or excessive entanglement. In a landmark decision in 2004, the Grand Justice Council declared many clauses stipulated in the 1929 Law Regulating Temples and Shrines to be violations of constitutional principles of religious equality and state neutrality.[23] The Law should not intervene in the management and autonomy of religious organizations. Different from the

---

20 R.O.C., Ministry of Education (2001).

21 See Lin, *Zongjiao Shengming Jiaoyu Yu Zhengjiao Fenli: Gongli Xuexiao Guomin Jiaoyu Zhong De Zongjiao Shengming Jiaoyu* (*Life education of Religion and the separation of religion and state: Religious education in public schools*), 2012.

22 See the website of the Ministry of Education, at https://life.edu.tw/2014/origin.

23 The No.573 Review of the Grand Justice Council (GTC) involved a complaint by a temple which sold its properties without the approval of the National Buddhist

above No. 490 Interpretation, the Grand Justice Council provided detailed arguments based on extensive reviews of domestic and foreign documents of state-religion relations.[24] Although still using the translation of strict separationism, its substantive explanations of the principle gradually shifted from separation toward checks and balances.

As mandated by this Grand Justice decision, the Ministry of the Interior began to work on a draft of Religious Group Law. Earlier drafts tended to be highly regulative and filled with punishment clauses. The current version has largely tuned down these elements. Most important of all, with regard to the procedure of registration, a report system has replaced the approval system of the LRTS's legacy, which had caused political and religious debates for violating religious freedom. New applicants for the various benefits provided by the Religious Group Law will only need to fill out some simple forms and need not go through complicated approval procedure. This revised bill is sent to the legislature for approval. Most religious groups are optimistic about its outcome this time. At the time of this paper being written (August 2016), the bill still lies in the legislative floor due to the turnover of the government in May 2016.[25]

While the state exercised further self-restraint and withdrew from religion, the Taiwanese religious market significantly increased its political influence. In my two survey studies of the 2000 and 2008 presidential elections, I found that many voters affiliated with certain religious organizations did not vote according to what their religious leaders told them to.[26] In the 2000 election, believers of pro-KMT religious organizations, such as Buddhist Zhongtai Cansi and Foguangshan, exhibited voting preferences not significantly different from those not affiliated with any religious organization. The Christian and Yiguandao communities, which used to support the KMT, were divided in this election. By the end of the twentieth century, the KMT government was so corrupt that most voters decided to overthrow this fifty-years-old government. The core of various

---

Association as required by the LRTS, which regulated Buddhist and Daoist temples but not Christian/Catholic churches. See Xu, *Zongjiao ziyou yu zongjiaofa (Religious Freedom and Religious Law)*, 2005, pp. 249-269.

24 R.O.C, Justices of the Constitutional Court, Grand Justice Council, Judicial Yuan, Interpretation No. 573, 2004.

25 See Laliberté, "The Regulation of Religious Affairs in Taiwan: From State Control to Laisser-faire?," pp. 74-75.

26 Kuo, "Religious Participation in Taiwanese Democracy."

corruption schemes was the KMT's Business Mangement Committee, established in 1993, to promote the expansion of party enterprises. Through various holding companies associated with these party enterprises, the KMT gained control of largest banks and conglomerates in Taiwan. By sending their representatives to the KMT's Business Management Committee, private conglomerates in real estate, stock trading, insurance, and construction acquired privileged information to government policies and reaped lucrative profits.[27] The opposition party, Democratic Progressive Party, won the presidential election in 2000 and was re-elected in 2004. But corruption increased rapidly in the DPP government after 2004, especially in the First Family, for preferential treatments in government procurement projects, bank loans, joint ventures supported by government funds, and appointments of directors in large conglomerates in which the government held significant stocks.[28] In the 2008 presidential election, believers of pro-KMT religious organizations fell in line with their religious leaders. Many Presbyterians, who used to support the DPP, either did not come out to vote, or voted for the KMT candidate. In other legislative or local elections, religious votes became harder to predict, depending on the quality of candidates and local issues.

With steadily narrowing margins of victory in various elections, religious organizations whose memberships range from hundreds of thousands to millions have acquired the ability to influence political issues that are of vital religious values, such as abortion, homosexual education in public schools, legalization of gambling and sex industries and sustainable development. Conservative religious organizations have actively lobbied in the Legislature in order to uphold their religious values. Some liberal bills were postponed or terminated at the preparation stage. Others were passed only after they were watered down drastically, as in the cases of the Regulation on Development in Offshore Islands in 2006 to legalize gambling and the revision of the Social Order Maintenance Ordinance in order to legalize the sex industry in 2010.

As a combined result of the state's self-restraint and the growing political influence of the religious market, religious freedom in Taiwan has greatly expanded since 2000 to a level higher than in traditional dynasties due to the latter's lack of legal protection of basic religious rights (e.g., the

27 Wang, Chen, and Kuo, "Restructuring State-Business Relations," 2016, pp. 248-251.

28 Ibid., pp. 251-257.

suppression of "evil cults" in Ming and Qing dynasties).[29] The U.S. State Department has published annual reports on religious freedom in all parts of the world since 2001. Taiwan has been covered by the "China (includes Taiwan only) Reports" (International Religious Freedom Reports, China, various years). Under the standardized categories of "Legal/Policy Framework," "Restrictions on Religious Freedom," "Forced Religious Conversion" and "Societal Attitudes," Taiwan has received nothing but adulation for full religious freedom.[30]

What explains the quick transition to and consolidation of a healthy relationship between the state and religion in Taiwan? It is probably the result of the combination of a traditional politico-religious culture and the consolidation of democracy. Traditional politico-religious culture in China was probably not one of state control over religion, as many Chinese scholars have argued, but one of tolerance and limited state control over religion.[31] The syncretistic nature of Chinese religions, no matter if it was Buddhism, Daoism, Confucianism or folk religions, might have facilitated religious tolerance and limited state control. The pragmatic and human-oriented nature of Chinese religions further blurred the lines between religion and state.[32] It probably made little sense to talk about "separation of state and religion" or "who controlled whom" in Chinese religious-political culture because rulers were immersed in various (mixed) religions while religions were immersed in the state as well as in the daily lives of common people.

The healthy relationship between the state and religion in Taiwan is also a result of the democratic consolidation. Religious leaders and organizations representing different disadvantaged groups are able to exercise their full political rights to address their concerns and influence public policies. They also learn democratic values and rules when they engage in, sometimes, emotional religious debates. "Holy wars" are fought only in the spiritual world but not in the secular world. After all, democracy is an institution of inclusion. Taiwanese religious leaders and organizations

---

29 Goossaert and Palmer, *The Religious Question in Modern China*, 2011.

30 U.S. State Department, International Religious Freedom Report – Taiwan, various years.

31 Goossaert and Palmer, *The Religious Question in Modern China*; Lagerwey, *China: A Religious State,* 2010.

32 Yao and Badham, *Religious Experience in Contemporary China*, 2007; Tsai, *Religious Experience in Contemporary Taiwan and China*, 2013.

have adapted quickly to this "only game in town" and contributed to the healthy relation of checks and balances between the state and religion.[33]

The following two sections select the Presbyterian Church in Taiwan and Buddhist Foguangshan for comparison to represent two different political roles (democratic prophet and democratic priest) religious organizations can play in order to contribute to democratization.

C. Democratic Prophets: The Presbyterian Church in Taiwan[34]

The Taiwanese Presbyterian churches were established directly by Western Presbyterians and had little connection with Chinese Presbyterians. In 1865, a Scottish Presbyterian doctor came to southern Taiwan and set up a layman's ministry based on medical services. In 1872, Canadian Presbyterians arrived in northern Taiwan and established an evangelical-medical base.[35] During the early period of Japanese rule, the colonial government welcomed the Presbyterian evangelists in order to provide medical and social services to the Taiwanese. But in the later period of colonial rule, especially after the Pacific War broke out, the government harshly cracked down on the Presbyterians for their refusal to worship the Japanese emperor and to follow other ceremonies prescribed by the Japanese national religion Shinto.[36] After 1945, Taiwanese Presbyterians resumed evangelism via indigenous leadership, with foreign missionaries serving as auxiliary arms.[37] From 1954 to 1964, Presbyterians instituted the "Doubling Movement" which contributed to an increase of membership from 59,000 to 103,000. Currently, the Presbyterians claim a membership of about 240,000, with more than 1,200 churches, numerous seminaries, schools, hospitals, publishing companies and social welfare institutions. In 2010,

33 See Przeworski et al., "What Makes Democracies Endure," 1996.

34 The next two sections are adapted and updated from Kuo, "Religion and Democracy in Taiwan," pp. 21-28, 38-45.

35 See Rubinstein, *The Protestant Community on Modern Taiwan: Mission, Seminary, and Church*, 1991.

36 PCT, *Introduction of the Presbyterian Church in Taiwan*, 2000, pp. 3-16.

37 See Heckman and Rubinstein, "The Importance of Noncognitive Skills: Lessons from the GED Testing Program," 2001, p. 66.

they initiated a new "Doubling Movement" which aimed toward a membership of 300,000 by 2015.[38]

The Taiwanese Presbyterians did not develop a democratic theology until the late 1960s. Before then, the Presbyterians closely followed the obedient political teachings of John Calvin who proposed that Christians take a submissive stance toward the government, even if the government is a tyranny.[39] In the late 1960s, a new generation of clergy and theologians emerged and took control of the central leadership of the Presbyterian Church in Taiwan. Motivated by social justice and influenced by liberal theology, they systematically transformed the submissive Calvinist theology into a liberal democratic theology, which treated human rights, political equality, and democratic institutions as being as important as personal salvation. In their writings and sermons, they cited extensively from the prophets in the Bible to severely criticize the political leaders for their unjust policies and practices.[40]

The most creative and practical part of the Taiwanese democratic theology is the mixture of democratic theory, democratic theology, and Taiwanese nationalism, with the last being the guiding principle in this uniquely Taiwanese contextual theology.[41] The Bible does not necessarily support nationalism. Taiwanese Presbyterians claim, however, in a nutshell, that God has mercy on the people living in Taiwan, that all men are created equal and endowed with inalienable human rights, and that the Taiwanese therefore have the right to establish an independent government of, for, and by the Taiwanese people, not of, for, and by the Chinese on the Mainland or the Chinese immigrants in power. The Presbyterians regard themselves as 'God-calling prophets', who hope to inspire the Taiwanese to build a nation of God in Taiwan.[42] This ethno-democratic theology turned out to be political dynamite because it simultaneously satisfied the religious and political needs of those Taiwanese believers who were exploited by the mainlander martial-law government. Hence, Presbyterian

---

38 See Lin, "Life education of Religion and the separation of religion and state: Religious education in public schools".

39 See Calvin, *Institutes of the Christian Religion*, 1989, pp. 670-671.

40 See Chen, *Social and Political Ethics of the Taiwan Presbyterian Church*, 1991.

41 The most representative works include Chen, ibid., and Luo, *Prayers for Taiwan: The Collection of Rev. Rongguang Luo*, 2001. See also a similar conclusion reached by Wachman, *National Identity and Democratization*, 1994, p. 231.

42 Chen, *Social and Political Ethics of the Taiwan Presbyterian Church*, pp. 145-194.

participation in the opposition movement was justified by the sacred trinity of religion, democracy, and nationalism.

After the lifting of martial law, the national association of Presbyterian churches, the Presbyterian Church of Taiwan, expanded the nationalist element in its political theology. After all, many of its democratic appeals materialized because of the lifting of martial law and democratic reforms of the national representative institutions in 1990 and 1991. Taiwan independence was made the new priority. In 1991, the PCT issued the "Declaration of Independence of Taiwan's Sovereignty."[43] After the 2000 presidential turnover, the PCT was satisfied with this democratic achievement. The pursuit of Taiwan independence became even more fervent. The PCT issued the "Declaration of the Movement to Join the United Nations in the Name of the Republic of Taiwan."

But the DPP lost the 2008 presidential election and again in 2012. The PCT issued political statements immediately after these elections, expressing their concerns that President Ma would betray the sacred mission of Taiwan independence and re-iterating PCT's persistent pursuit of a "new and independent Republic of Taiwan."[44] At the same time, the stagnation or even decline in church membership in the early 2000s generated a sense of crisis at the grassroots level.[45] In particular, the aboriginal churches, which had long been staunch supporters of KMT candidates, formed an alliance with the new generation of clergy in the election of PCT leadership in 2004. In 2005, a new generation of PCT leadership was inaugurated and began to shift the church's major focus from political to social and religious issues. In 2010, the PCT established a promotion center to sponsor a new "Doubling Movement" called "One-Leads-One, Doubling Mission Movement" in order to break the stagnation of church growth in the past decades. This shift has been incremental, however. The PCT continues to

---

43 The "Declaration of Independence of Taiwan's Sovereignty" proclaims that "Taiwan has an independent sovereignty" and "Taiwan and China are two different sovereign states." The PCT urges the government to formulate a new constitution, to join the United Nations in the name of Taiwan, and to establish a new relationship with China. See PCT, "Vital Documents," at http://www.pct.org.tw/ab_doc.aspx?DocID=051, accessed October 24, 2016..

44 PCT, "Vital Documents," at http://www.pct.org.tw/ab_doc.aspx, accessed October 24, 2013.

45 PCT, "Church Statistics," at http:/www.pct.org.tw/stat, accessed October 24, 2013.

sponsor large rallies in support of DPP policies to strengthen national defense, to establish Taiwan independence, and to criticize social injustice.[46]

In terms of democratic religious polity, Presbyterian churches had a head start over other Christian denominations in Taiwan. Calvinism provided a detailed description of a democratic religious polity which the Taiwanese Presbyterians adopted immediately after establishing a few churches in the late 19th century. Taiwanese Presbyterians have not had any supreme master and have placed the clergy only slightly above the laity. With democratization expanding in the larger environment, even the last privileges of the clergy are under attack by the laity.

The history of Taiwanese Presbyterians does not record any supreme master as the Buddhists do. The only "supreme master" is probably John Calvin. Most clergy and theologians use Calvin's works as practical guides to theology and religious polity. However, they would not place Calvin's works on par with the Bible, or compare Calvin with Jesus. They are willing to challenge Calvin's works and deeds, as they would any leader in the church hierarchy. One famous leader in the church, Rev. Gao Junming, was put in jail by the KMT government in 1979 for providing shelter to political dissidents. He has earned a lot of respect from believers. But few Presbyterians read his works and he has never been able to dictate the church's major decisions. The polity of the Presbyterian churches prevents the emergence of supreme mastership.

According to the PCT bylaws, the leadership of the PCT General Assembly is composed of the Speaker, Vice Speaker, and General Secretary. As nominal heads of the PCT, the Speaker and Vice Speaker have no real decision-making power except for hosting the biannual assembly. They are elected by assembly representatives and serve only one two-year term. The General Secretary is the most important person in the central leadership, yet this position also has certain constraints. He is recommended by lower-level church organizations and selected by the General Assembly, serving four years per term with a three-term limit.[47] He can plan, coordinate, and execute PCT activities, but only according to the decisions made

46 PCT, "Annual Programs," at http:// www.pct.org.tw/ab_101.aspx, accessed October 24, 2013.

47 In the 1970s, the Speaker served a one-year term, and the General Secretary served a three-year term. See Hu, *The Way to Cross: Memoir of Re. Chunming Kao*, 2001, p. 222.

by the General Assembly.[48] Therefore, unlike their Buddhist counterparts, Presbyterians leaders move up the hierarchical ladder from the bottom through a series of elections. When they finally reach the top, their power and terms are limited.

The superiority of the clergy over the laity that once existed in Presbyterian churches was limited and has gradually been lost. "The Presbyterian polity has put the Protestant motto the priesthood of all believers" into practice. The core of a Presbyterian church is the small committee (*xiaohui*) which is composed of elders and pastors elected by the church members. The pastors are appointed by a medium-level church organization called the medium committee (*zhonghui*). The most senior pastor chairs the small committee and executes the decisions made by the committee. Each pastor has one and only one vote, no more decisive than the elders in the church's collective decision. The pastor can only exercise informal influence in any attempt to have his proposals passed. To avoid offending either side of disputing parties, most pastors abstain from voting. The medium committees and the General Assembly are all composed of relatively equal numbers of pastors and laity, both enjoying the same voting rights.

Finally, with respect to the interaction between church and the state, Presbyterians have been unique among all Taiwanese religions. Before the 1970s, Presbyterian churches were very submissive to and cooperative with both the Japanese colonial government and the KMT government. [49] The nightmares of the 228 Massacre and the White Terror of the 1950s intimidated the postwar first-generation church leaders from thinking otherwise. Instead, they focused their attention and energy on evangelism. However, the success of the "Doubling Movement" from 1954-1964 generated not only self-confidence but also sociopolitical consciousness[50] among the new generation of church leadership. The authoritarian government also became suspicious about this fast-growing denomination. In the 1970s, the PCT issued three public documents challenging the legitimacy of the KMT government. *The Declarations and Suggestions on National Affairs* (Dui guoshi de shengming yü jianyi, 1971) proclaimed that the

48 See Taipei, *Introduction of the Presbyterian Church in Taiwan*, pp. 13-20.

49 See Chen, *Social and Political Ethics of the Taiwan Presbyterian Church*, pp. 80-84.

50 See Rubinstein, "The Presbyterian Church in the Formation of Taiwan's Democratic Society, 1945-2001," 2001.

Taiwanese have the right of self-determination and urged that new elections be held for national representative bodies. *Our Appeals* (Women de huyü, 1975) pleaded with the government to respect religious freedom and autonomy. *The Declaration of Human Rights* (Renquan xuanyan, 1977), addressed directly to American President Jimmy Carter and all the churches in the world, asked for the establishment of a "new and independent nation" for the Taiwanese people. These three documents were severely criticized by the KMT government and by some Mandarin churches as an act of treason and an inappropriate intervention in politics by the church. Attacks also came from within the Presbyterian churches – from those pastors, elders, deacons, and lay believers who were members of the KMT.[51] Nevertheless, the majority of the Presbyterian churches stood firm.

Major confrontation between the Presbyterians and the government broke out in 1979 when the government cracked down harshly on an opposition rally. Leaders of the movement were arrested, along with some Presbyterian pastors who had participated in the demonstration.[52] Finally, the General Secretary of the PCT, Rev. Gao Junming, was arrested and sentenced to four years in prison for providing sanctuary to an opposition leader. The PCT proclaimed Rev. Gao's innocence and kept the position of the General Secretary vacant until he was released from prison. He served in the position for a total of nineteen years until he retired in 1989.[53]

During the martial law period, the PCT supported the opposition movement with concrete actions. Pastors urged their believers to vote for opposition candidates. National and local churches co-sponsored rallies and demonstrations to protest against the KMT government. The anti-government attitude took a sharp turn in 1988 when Li Denghui, a Taiwanese and a Presbyterian, became President of Taiwan. The PCT supported President Li to consolidate his rule over the Chinese-dominated KMT government, while continuing to lend its support to DPP candidates in legislative bodies and in local magistrate elections.[54] During his administration, President

51 See Hu, *The Way to Cross: Memoir of Re. Chunming Kao*, pp. 235-36, 252, 255.

52 See PCT, *Introduction of the Presbyterian Church in Taiwan*, p. 40.

53 See Hu, "A New Institutional Analysis of Taiwan's Religious Rights," pp. 291-297.

54 The phrase "critical support" (*pipingxin de zhichi*) was coined by Rev. Huang Zhanghui, former president of the Presbyterian Seminary in Tainan (Hu, A New Institutional Analysis of Taiwan's Religious Rights, p. 340).

Li spoke of a "Taiwanese exodus": a plan to liberate Taiwanese from of Chinese political and cultural hegemony.

In the 2000 presidential election, President Li stepped down and nominated his Vice President, Lian Zhan, a Taiwanese born in mainland China, to run for the presidency. The PCT leadership actively mobilized its believers to vote for the DPP candidate. After the presidential turnover in 2000, the PCT formulated the "critical support" principle in order to consolidate the new government.[55] Beginning in 2001, the PCT sponsored the annual National Prayer Breakfast for the DPP President and his cabinet members, despite complaints by some Christians of other denominations. The PCT continued to push for reform policies concerning social, economic, and environmental justices, with a particular strong emphasis on Taiwan independence. In fact, the PCT did not hesitate to criticize the DPP government when it made occasional verbal concessions to the opposition parties on independence issues. From 2000 to 2008, the PCT issued sixteen public proclamations; fifteen of them covered political issues. The only theme that consistently ran through all sixteen proclamations was the clear support for Taiwan independence. The DDP lost the presidential elections of 2008 and 2012. In response, the PCT issued twelve public proclamations; all of them covered political issues; and Taiwan independence remained the dominant theme.[56] Indeed, as Rubinstein correctly concludes, "the Presbyterians served as prophets and leaders during each of the four major periods of Taiwan's recent history."[57]

As democratic prophets in other Third Wave democracies, the PCT courageously initiated democratic reforms from the early 1970s to the present. But democratic reforms could be bloody and betrayed by revolutionary elites, as illustrated by most cases of the Third Wave democracies and the recent Arab Spring countries. The PCT were a religious minority and needed help from other major religious groups who played the role of democratic priests in order to smooth the democratic transition and to consolidate the democracy.

---

55 See Rubinstein, "The Presbyterian Church in the Formation of Taiwan's Democratic Society, 1945-2001," p. 63.

56 PCT, "Vital Documents," at http://www.pct.org.tw/ab_doc.aspx, accessed October 24, 2013.

57 Rubinstein, "Christianity and Democratization in Modern Taiwan: The Presbyterian Church and the Struggle for Minnan/Hakka Selfhood in the Republic of China," 2003, p. 248.

Democratic priests do not need to be devoted democrats like democratic prophets who are committed to democratic values and actively support democratic opposition movement. Democratic priests tend to support the pre-existing authoritarian parties but also warmly promote human rights and peaceful transition in general. In his case studies of three Buddhist organizations (Ciji, Foguangshan and Dharma Drum Mountain) and one folk religious organization (Enacting Heaven), Madsen gave credit to these large religious organizations for their contribution to Taiwan's smooth transition to democracy because they "nurtured a spirit of engagement with public affairs and a cooperative attitude toward the government."[58] Although we should not mix up making contribution to "smooth democratization" with making direct contribution to democracy, these large Buddhist organizations did assume a complimentary role of democratic priests. The next section presents the case of Foguangshan as an example.

D. Democratic Priests: Foguangshan (FGS)

Ven. Xingyun (or Hsing Yun) established the FGS in 1967 to promote Humanistic Buddhism which he had studied under the guidance of Ven. Taixü. [59] He was one of the Chinese monks who fled to Taiwan in 1949. After building a religious base in a remote northeastern county, he moved down to southern Taiwan to establish FGS. With the help of local elites, FGS soon developed into an international religious empire consisting of hundreds of temples, museums, libraries, publishers, hospitals, high schools, universities, and welfare organizations, with more than one thousand clergy and about one million registered believers across five major continents.[60]

Ven. Xingyun's writings rarely touched upon political issues. Among the few comments on politics and politicians, democratic jargon is often fused with authoritarian interpretations. In a book published in 1987, before the lifting of martial law, he said, "We are in the democratic era. We

58 Madsen, *Democracy's Dharma: Religious Renaissance and Political Development in Taiwan*, 2007, p. 136.

59 See Laliberté, *The Politics of Buddhist Organizations in Taiwan, 1989-1997*, 1999, p. 83.

60 Foguangshan, *A Special Issue Commemorating the Thirty-First Anniversary of Foguangshan*, 2002, p. 8.

care about democratic politics, but we don't need opposition parties. Liberal democracy has moral standards… How can a few [opposition] politicians serve us as well as the hundreds of thousands of KMT members can?" He equates the politics of Kharma Emperor with a liberal democracy.[61]

In a long essay expounding upon Humanistic Buddhism, Xingyun included a section on the Buddhist political view. He proposed that "politics need assistance and enlightenment from Buddhism, and Buddhism needs protection and assistance from politics." He cites the close relationship between Buddhism and the state in ancient India and China to support his argument. He argues that Buddhists have a responsibility to protect human rights and to promote social welfare. He further urged Buddhists in a democracy to abandon the old isolationist view and adopt a more assertive interpretation of "participating in politics, not governing."[62] In another short pamphlet, he briefly criticized the corrupted public officials of the new democracy.[63] Both statements, however, are derived more from Confucian or Buddhist standards of self-discipline in public officials than from democratic values or institutions.[64] Except for these few works by Xingyun, none of his one thousand clergy teach or write anything about politics. [65]

In contrast to the slow development of a democratic theology, FGS began to develop a nascent democratic religious polity in the early 1990s.[66] The Organic Law of FGS (OLFGS, foguangshansi zuzhi zhang-cheng) was promulgated five years after FGS was established. Although more democratic and institutionalized than its counterparts in other major Buddhist organizations, the OLFGS and other practical norms specify a number of traditional organizational principles. First, the status of Xingyun is unique and supreme. He was the founder and abbot of the religious empire from 1967 to 1985. Even after he voluntarily resigned from the abbot position, he is still the de facto supreme commander in the FGS system. He

61 See Lu and Liu, *Xingyundashi whom we know*, 1987, pp. 282-283.

62 Xingyun, "A Blueprint of Secular Buddhism (II)," 2001.

63 See Xingyun, "The Dignity of the Officials," 2002, pp. 250-252.

64 Laliberté, *The Politics of Buddhist Organizations in Taiwan, 1989-1997*, p. 99, cites another political speech by Xingyun (1984), in which he espoused ethical democracy. Again, this idea is more Confucian than democratic.

65 See Foguangshan, *A Special Issue Commemorating the Thirty-First Anniversary of Foguangshan*, pp. 112-120.

66 See Jones, *Buddhism in Taiwan: Religion and the State,* pp. 191-197.

appoints abbot successors and makes decisions on major organizational affairs, such as the hosting of ceremonies for ordaining clergy and admitting laity.[67] His published works are required reading for all clergy and believers. In the eyes of his followers, Ven. Xingyun can say or do nothing wrong. Therefore, even though the "monastic order strives to function according to a set of fixed rules rather than following a charismatic style of leadership,"[68] the practice has lagged far behind its ideals.

The OLFGS established a nine-member Religious Affairs Committee (Zongwu Weiyuanhui) as the governing body of the FGS. [69] The abbot is elected from the nine members of this committee, who in turn are elected by all clergy with at least ten years of residency. Although this is a more democratic structure than that of other Buddhist organizations in Taiwan, the actual operation of the procedure is not as democratic as one might expect. Xingyun was the abbot for three consecutive terms, facing no competitors in the elections. In 1985, after serving three terms as abbot, Xingyun appointed Ven. Xinping as his successor. Since the nine Committee members were the same until the election of 1990, and Xingyun was still the real decision maker, there was no competitor during Xinping's election. Democratic elements were introduced in the elections of Committee members in 1990 and afterwards. Not only were the elections held more frequently, but younger clergy were also elected. Although the election of the abbot was still influenced by Xingyun, the general clergy possessed more autonomy than before.

In terms of the power relationship between the clergy and the laity, FGS made some progress after the lifting of martial law. According to the OLFGS, the FGS local temples follow the principle of "clergy decide clergy business." The first article of the first chapter of the OLFGS prescribes that FGS "be led by the clergy and assisted by the laity." Although the laity assume auxiliary and subordinate role, increasingly they share decision-making power with the clergy.

In the early 1990s, limited democratic reforms were introduced into the FGS system. First, after the reform in 1992, a female lay believer was elected to the Religious Affairs Committee in 1997. More important was

67 See Foguangshan, *A Special Issue Commemorating the Thirty-First Anniversary of Foguangshan*, pp. 58-74.

68 Laliberté, *The Politics of Buddhist Organizations in Taiwan, 1989-1997*, p. 88.

69 The following information is based on Foguangshan, *A Special Issue Commemorating the Thirty-First Anniversary of Foguangshan*, pp. 12-15.

the establishment of the Buddha's Light International Association (BLIA) in 1991. The BLIA gave the laity a more active role in managing association affairs, including delivering sermons, which traditionally was regarded as an exclusive privilege of the clergy. But the clergy still hold key positions in the BLIA,[70] thus limiting the spread of democratic norms and practices within the organization. In 1993, the BLIA passed a constitutional law to establish the Lay Dharma Teacher/Lecturer system (Tanjiaoshi/Jiangshi). By 2002, the system had generated seven teachers and one hundred and thirty-three lecturers.[71] Lay Dharma Teachers and Lecturers may deliver sermons in BLIA member temples.

In terms of the interaction between state and religion, FGS played a submissive and supportive role in relation to the KMT government prior to 1987. Ven. Xingyun was arrested by the KMT government in China once and was arrested again in 1949 on an espionage charge after the KMT government moved to Taiwan. He took the advice of other prominent clergy to join and support the KMT in order to avoid any future suspicion and harassment from the government.[72] Afterwards, KMT can-didates were able to deliver political speeches and distribute campaign fliers via the FGS system. Ven. Xingyun was elected director or executive director of the state-sponsored BAROC from 1952 to1993.[73] Furthermore, he was a KMT member and elected to an important advisory position in the party in 1988.[74] After the lifting of martial law, FGS began to take a more autonomous role in political affairs. Within the FGS system, free discussion about politics was allowed. Any FGS laity who was a candidate for public office or supporter of other candidates was permitted to conduct limited political advertisements at religious gatherings. In 1995, Ven. Xingyun publicly endorsed independent presidential candidate Chen Lü-an, who was a former Minister of Defense, a devoted Buddhist and a disciple of Ven. Xingyun. Chen did not get the expected support from the rank and file of the FGS system nor from other major Buddhist organizations,

70 See Laliberté, *The Politics of Buddhist Organizations in Taiwan, 1989-1997*, 1999, p. 103.

71 BLIA, *World Headquarters 10th Anniversary Special Edition*, p. 55.

72 See Hou, "A Study on the Relationship between Buddhism and Politics in Taiwan after WWII," 2003, pp. 33-35; Laliberté, *The Politics of Buddhist Organizations in Taiwan, 1989-1997*, p. 101.

73 The Buddhist Association of the Republic of China homepage, at http://www.baroc.org.tw/outwash.htm, accessed October 24, 2013.

74 See Jiang, *A Biographie of Jiang Jingguo*, p. 23.

and performed poorly in the election, receiving only 8% of the total votes.[75] This electoral loss led to a sharp drop in FGS's mem-bership and financial support, which prompted Ven. Xingyun to "seal the mountain" (*fengshan*) in May 1997 to consolidate its financial structure and to reformulate development strategies.[76] Adding insult to injury, the local government began to harass FGS over zoning violations of its buildings.[77] FGS did not reopen until 2001.

However, the "sealing of the mountain" did not spell the end to FGS's contact with politics. After a few months of recuperation, Ven. Xingyun rebuilt his relationship with the KMT by incorporating important KMT politicians into the BLIA. A KMT vice chairman (Wu Boxion) was BLIA's president for two terms, and another vice chairman of the KMT (Wang Jinping) was a member of the board of directors for two terms. Many other important KMT politicians were members of the governing board of the BLIA.[78] With a successful coalition strategy that crossed party lines, FGS pushed a petition through the legislature to make the birthday of Buddha a national holiday.[79] In 1998 and 2002, FGS also hosted two extravagant Buddhist ceremonies to welcome Buddha's relics to Taiwan. Distinguished politicians from all major parties attended these ceremonies. When the FGS reopened its mountain in 2001, FGS warmly welcomed the DPP President in order to reconcile with the new government. In the 2004 election, the FGS continued to favor the KMT/PFP slate, but did not do so publicly. The FGS' persistent support of the KMT finally paid off in the 2008 and 2012 presidential elections, which in turn generated additional benefits to the religious empire. When the US$3 hundred million Buddha Memorial Center, the largest and most expensive Buddhist building in Taiwan, was inaugurated in 2010, all political leaders of major parties in Taiwan came and were greeted by Ven. Xinyun.[80] As a demo-

75 See Laliberté, *The Politics of Buddhist Organizations in Taiwan, 1989-1997*, pp. 94-96.

76 See Jiang, *A biographie of Jiang Jingguo*, pp. 15-17.

77 See Laliberté, *The Politics of Buddhist Organizations in Taiwan, 1989-1997*, p. 97.

78 BLIA, *World Headquarters 10th Anniversary Special Edition*, pp. 98-103. They included Legislators Pan Weigang and Huang Zhaoshun, KMT central committee members Zhao Liyun and Li Zhonggui. Wang Jingping has been the Speaker of the Legislature since 1999.

79 See Ye, *Relations of State and Religion in Taiwan*, p. 268.

80 Foguangshan, "Reports on the Buddha Memorial Center," at http://www.fgs.org.t w /subject/subject_stupa_03.aspx, accessed October 24, 2013.

cratic priest, the FGS has certainly made "equality of all 'political' kindred" and contributed to the smooth transition to and quick consolidation of Taiwanese democracy.

E. Conclusion

Despite several cultural and political baggages, Taiwan distinguishes itself among the Third Wave democracies with the "democratic miracle" which consists of a smooth transition to and quick consolidation of democracy. Religious organizations have made important contribution to this democratic miracle. Among them are those democratic prophets and democratic priests. The democratic prophetic role played by the Presbyterian Church in Taiwan helped initiate major democratic reforms, while the democratic priestly role assumed by Foguangshan made possible the smooth transition and democratic consolidation.

The Taiwanese example provides a new insight in the study on religion-state relations. Before the turn of the century, the "secularization thesis" dominated the researches on democracy, which tended to ignore or devalue religions for their irrationality and undemocratic ethics. The rise of religious fundamentalism in all major religions in the world in the 1980s did not help to alleviate these concerns of democratic theorists and activists. Even in the few cases, such as Poland, the Philippines and the Arab Spring countries, where religions contributed to the establishment of democracy, the anti-democratic behavior of these religions only confirmed these democrats' deepest worry. However, the Taiwanese case suggests that the relationship between religion and democracy is not necessarily negative. Only when religious organizations start to build democratic theology, democratic religious polity and participate in politics by democratic rules can they significantly contribute to democracy. Democratic religion can make better democracy.

Bibliography

Buddha's Light International Association (BLIA), *World Headquarters 10th Anniversary Special Edition*, Hacienda Heights, CA.: BLIA, 2001.

Calvin, John, *Institutes of the Christian Religion*, trans. Henry Beveridge, Grand Rapids, MI: Wm. B. Eerdmans Publishing Co., 1989.

Chen, Nanzhou, *Taiwan jidu zhanglao jiaohui de shehui zhengzhi lunli (Social and Political Ethics of the Taiwan Presbyterian Church)*. Taipei: Yongwang Press, 1991.

Chen, Shuibian, "Zongjia baipishu," (Religious White Paper), Taipei: Chen Shuibian zongtong jingxuan zhihui zhongxin guojia lantu weiyuanhui, 2000.

Foguangshan, *Foguangshan kaishan jinian sanshiyi zhounian nianjian (A Special Issue Commemorating the Thirty-First Anniversary of Foguangshan)*, Kaohsiung: Foguang Press, 2002.

Foguangshan, "Reports on the Buddha Memorial Center," accessed 10/24/13.

Gao, Junming, *Shizijia zhi lu: Gao Junming mushi huiyilu (The Road of the Cross: Memoir of Reverent Gao Junming)*, Taipei: Wangchunfeng, 2001.

Goossaert, Vincent, and David A. Palmer, *The Religious Question in Modern China,* Chicago, IL: University of Chicago Press, 2011.

Heckman, James J., and Yona Rubinstein, "The Importance of Noncognitive Skills: Lessons from the GED Testing Program," *The American Economic Review* 91, 2 (2001): 145-149.

Hou, Kunhong, "Zhanhou Taiwan fojiao yü zhengzhi guanxi zhi yanjiu," (A Study on the Relationship between Buddhism and Politics in Taiwan after WWII), Paper delivered at *Ershi shiji Taiwan minzhu fazhan xueshu taolunhui (Symposium on the Development of Democracy in Taiwan in the Twentieth Century)*, Guoshiguan, Taipei, 24-26 September 2003.

Hu, Huilin, *Shizijia zhilu: Kao junming mushi huiyilu (The Way to Cross: Memoir of Re. Chunming Kao)*, Taipei: Wangchunfong Press, 2001.

Hu, Lizu, *Taiwan zongjiao ziyou quan zhi xin zhidu fenxi (A New Institutional Analysis of Taiwan's Religious Rights)*, Master thesis, Taipei: National Chenchi University, 2009.

Huntington, Samuel, *The Third Wave: Democratization in the Late Twentieth Century,* OK: University of Oklahoma Press, 1991.

Jiang, Nan, *Jiang Jingguo Zhuan (A Biography of Jiang Jingguo)*, Tapei: Qianwei Press, 1997.

Jones, Charles Brewer, *Buddhism in Taiwan: Religion and the State, 1660-1990*, Hawaii: University of Hawaii Press, 1999.

Katz, Paul. "Religion and the State in Post-war Taiwan," in *China Quarterly* 174 (2003): 395-412.

Kuo, Cheng-Tian, *Religion and Democracy in Taiwan*, Albany: SUNY Press, 2008.

Kuo, Cheng-Tian, "Religious Participation in Taiwanese Democracy," in *A Spectacular Century: The Republic of China Centennial Democracy Forums,* ed. Hung-mao Tien and Wen-cheng Lin, Taipei: Institute for National Policy Research Press, 2011, pp. 259-289.

Kuo, Cheng-Tian, "State-Religion Relations in Taiwan: From Statism and Separatism to Checks and Balances," *Issues & Studies* 49(1) (2013): 1-38.

Laliberté, André, *The Politics of Buddhist Organizations in Taiwan, 1989-1997*, Ph.D. dissertation, University of British Columbia, 1999.

Laliberté, André, "Buddhist Organizations and Democracy in Taiwan," *American Asian Review* 19 (2001): 97-129.

Laliberté, André, "The Regulation of Religious Affairs in Taiwan: From State Control to Laisser-faire?", *Journal of Current Chinese Affairs* 38 (2009): 53-83.

Li, Huizong, "Lun tsungchiao hsinyang tzuyu chi kuochia paohu iwu: ping sifa yuan da faguan shihtzu ti si chiu ling hao chieh shih," (Protection of Religious Freedom and National Obligation: Comment about the Judicial Yuan's Interpretation) *Taiwan Law Journal* 5 (1999): 39-60.

Lin, Qiyun, *Zongjiao Shengming Jiaoyu Yu Zhengjiao Fenli: Gongli Xuexiao Guomin Jiaoyu Zhong De Zongjiao Shengming Jiaoyu* (*Life education of Religion and the separation of religion and state: Religious education in public schools*), Master thesis, Taipei: National Chengchi University, 2012.

Lu, Zhenting, and Fang Liu (eds), *Women Renshide Xingyundashi (Xingyundashi whom we know)*, Taipei: Caifeng Publication, 1987.

Lu, Yunfeng, Byron Johnson, and Rodney Stark, "Deregulation and the Religious Market in Taiwan: A Research Note," *The Sociological Quarterly* 49 (2008): 139-153.

Luo, Rongguang, *Wei Taiwan qidao: Luo rongguang mushi wenji (Prayers for Taiwan: The Collection of Rev. Rongguang Luo)*, Taipei: Wangchunfeng Press, 2001.

Lagerwey, John, *China: A Religious State*, Hong Kong: Hong Kong University Press, 2010.

Madsen, Richard, *Democracy's Dharma: Religious Renaissance and Political Development in Taiwan,* CA: University of California Press, 2007.

Paper, Jordan, "Mediums and Modernity: The Institutionalization of Ecstatic Religious Functionaries in Taiwan," *Journal of Chinese Religions* 24 (1996): 105-129.

Przeworski, Adam, Michael Alvarez, Jose Antonio Cheibub, and Fernando Limongi, "What Makes Democracies Endure?," *Journal of Democracy* 7 (1996): 39-55.

Roy, Denny, *Taiwan: A Political History,* Ithaca, NY: Cornell University Press, 2003.

Rubinstein, Murray, *The Protestant Community on Modern Taiwan: Mission, Seminary, and Church,* Armonk: M.E. Sharpe, 1991.

Rubinstein, Murray, "The Presbyterian Church in the Formation of Taiwan's Democratic Society, 1945-2001," *American Asian Review* 19 (2001): 63-96.

Rubinstein, Murray A., "Christianity and Democratization in Modern Taiwan: The Presbyterian Church and the Struggle for Minnan/Hakka Selfhood in the Republic of China," in *Religion in Modern Taiwan: Tradition and Innovation in a Changing Society*, ed. Philip Clart and Clarles B. Jones, Honolulu: University of Hawaii Press, 2003.

Schmitter, Philippe, "The Organizational Development of International Organizations," *International Organization* 25, 4 (1971): 917-937.

Taiwan Jiduzhanglaojiaohui (PCT), *Introduction of the Presbyterian Church in Taiwan*, Taipei: The General Assembly of the Presbyterian Church in Taiwan, 2000.

Taiwan Jiduzhanglaojiaohui (PCT), "Taiwan Zhuquanduli Xuanyan" (Declaration of Taiwan's Sovereignty Independence), 1911.

Tsai, Yen-zen, *Religious Experience in Contemporary Taiwan and China,* Taipei: National Chengchi University, 2013.

U.S. State Department, International Religious Freedom Report – Taiwan, various years, at http://www.state.gov/j/drl/rls/irf/religiousfreedom.

Wachman, Alan M, *National Identity and Democratization,* Armonk, NY: M.E. Sharpe, 1994.

Wang, James W.Y., Shang-mao Chen, and Cheng-tian Kuo, "Restructuring State-Business Relations," in *Taiwan's Democracy Challenged: The Chen Shui-bian Years*, ed. Yun-han Chu, Larry Diamond, and Kharis Templeman, Boulder, CO: Lynne Rienner Publisher, 2016, pp. 241-266.

Wu, Naiteh, *The Politics of A Regime Patronage System: Mobilization and Control Within An Authoritarian Regime*, Ph.D. Dissertation, University of Chicago, 1987.

Xingyun, "Renjian fojiao de lantu (II) (A Blueprint of Secular Buddhism (II))," *Pumen xuebao (Universal Gate Buddhist Journal)* 6 (2001): 28-32.

Xingyun, "Guanyuan de zunyan," (The Dignity of the Officials) *Miwu zhijian (III) (Between Ignorance and Enlightment (III))*, Taipei: Xianghai wenhua, 2002.

Xu, Yudian, *Zongjiao ziyou yu zongjiaofa (Religious Freedom and Religious Law)*, Taipei: Yuanzhao Publisher, 2005.

Yao, Xinzhong, and Paul Badham, *Religious Experience in Contemporary China,* UK: University of Wales Press, 2007.

Ye, Yongwen, *Taiwan zhengjiao guanxi (Relations of State and Religion in Taiwan)*, Taipei: Fengyun Forum Publisher, 2000.

Zhang, Xingwen, *Taiwan zongjiao xingqin yu zongjiao ziyou zhi fenji (The Boundaries of Religious Freedom and Religious Sexual Assaults in Taiwan)*, 2012.

Yasukuni Shrine and the Politics of Religious Freedom in Contemporary Japan

Yijiang Zhong

A. Introduction

On November 1, 2001, a group of 638 citizens filed a lawsuit at the Osaka District Court against the then Prime Minister Koizumi Jun'ichiro's much publicized visit to the Yasukuni Shrine, a registered religious corporation enshrining over two million spirits of soldiers who died in Japan's modern wars, on August 13, 2001. Following this lawsuit, seven more were filed at local courts in Japan against Koizumi as he continued his annual Yasukuni visits during his office from 2001-2006.[1] The plaintiffs of these lawsuits all made the claims that the Prime Minister's visits should be judged unconstitutional and stopped because the visits violated the constitutional principle of state-religion separation and infringed upon the constitutionally guaranteed right to religious freedom of the plaintiffs, most of whom were family members of the dead soldiers. Plaintiffs, however, won none of the lawsuits. Although in two cases Koizumi's visits were judged unconstitutional, respectively at the Fukuoka District Court in May 2004 and the Osaka High Court in September 2005,[2] the local courts' ruling was in both cases overruled by the Supreme Court of Japan. Koizumi was able to continue his visit throughout his incumbency. Whether judging the visits as unconstitutional or not, no court judged that the right of religious freedom of the plaintiffs was violated. As a result, the plaintiffs' requests for compensation for the violation of their religious freedom were in every case rejected. The plaintiffs lost all cases.

At first sight, these court rulings look rather difficult to understand. Doesn't Koizumi Jun'ichiro's visit, conducted in the official capacity of the Prime Minister of Japan, to an explicit religious facility in endorsing

---

1 See Tanaka, *Dokyumento Yasukuni soshō*, 2007, p. 108.

2 See "Yasukuni sanpai iken soshō," at www.geocities.jp/social792/yasukuni/ ikensos you.html, last accessed 27 December 2014.

the doctrine of that facility clearly breach the constitutional prohibition of the state from engaging in religious activity, a prohibition specified by Article 20 of the Constitution: "Freedom of religion is guaranteed to all [...] The state and its organs shall refrain from religious education or any other religious activity?" Don't his visit and worshiping at the Yasukuni Shrine constitute the state's support to this particular religion and therefore encroach upon the freedom of religious belief of citizens who do not follow this religion? If so, why did the Supreme Court never judge it unconstitutional? How should we understand this apparent 'misjudgment'?

This paper looks into two of the cases to examine why and how the courts were able to dismiss all the claims of violation of religious freedom and withhold a ruling of unconstitutionality. Upon close reading, it becomes apparent that these cases are not just about violation and protection of citizens' religious freedom. They are struggles between minority groups and the constitutional state for the very definitions of religion and religious freedom. These struggles for definitions concern whether these minority groups can choose their way of life through defining their relationship with family members enshrined at the Yasukuni Shrine, without sharing the definition of the death of these family members and the dominant national history and national identity represented by the Yasukuni Shrine and reinforced by the Prime Minister's visit. Ultimately, these cases raise the question to what extent the legal status of liberty-bearing citizenship can enable minority groups to define their individual ways of life, by way of defending their religious freedom, when that definition calls into question the bounded nature of the nation-state which, while obligated to protect the freedom and rights of citizens, also requires them to share the dominant conception and image of the nation. I argue that the failure of these legal cases results from, and exposes, the insufficiency of the conventional, belief-centered, privatized definition of religion and religious freedom, a definition that is based on its historical origin in the particular experience of European societies. It is necessary to expand and reconfigure the legal categories of religion and religious freedom to be relational and contextual ones so as to create the conditions for possible legal accommodation in Japan of minority ways of life which choose not to share the dominant, exclusive form of national identity.

Before looking into the Yasukuni cases, I will first provide a short history of the Yasukuni Shrine to show how the question of religious freedom is intertwined with competing ways of remembering the history of imperialism and war of pre-1945 Japan. This will make clear that the Yasukuni lawsuits are as much about religious freedom as about defining national history and the nation. This is followed by a close examination of the aforementioned Osaka case to see how the plaintiffs proposed a widened definition of religious freedom to relate the constitutional principle of religion-state separation to their argument against the PM's visit which, in endorsing the war-affirming historical narrative of the religious corporation Yasukuni Shrine, violated their religious freedom. I will then discuss how the court used a standard, individual-based, privatized definition of freedom of religious belief to reject the plaintiffs' argument, thereby avoiding touching on the contentious historical issues of imperialism and war. I then look at the second case by focusing on a law scholar's defense of the plaintiffs' argument to show how his argument, based on the normative definitions of religion and religious freedom, could not engage the specific issues symbolized by the Prime Minister's visit to the Yasukuni Shrine, issues of religious freedom as well as historical memory. I conclude this paper by calling for a widened definition of religion and religious freedom so that the right to religious freedom can respond to the specific problems of national identity and history in relation to the right to ways of life articulated through religious freedom. As such, these new definitions can point to new ways in which to engage the Yasukuni problem.

B. The Yasukuni Shrine, Past and Present

The Yasukuni Shrine is an ideologically loaded ritual institution attendant to the intertwined processes in the modern period of the construction and operation of the Japanese constitutional state on the one hand and of overseas expansion and imperialism conducted by the Japanese state on the other. The origin of the Yasukuni Shrine goes back to the Meiji Restoration of 1868. The Meiji leaders, while declaring the return of political authority to the emperor and thereby the establishment of a new government, had to fight the military forces of the Tokugawa Bakufu they had reputedly overthrown if the new government had any chance of survival. The leaders soon found that enshrining in a Shinto rather than Buddhist style the spirits of those who died in fighting was an effective strategy in boosting the morale of soldiers because the Shinto enshrinement distinguished the new government from the Tokugawa Bafuku which used Buddhist temples, clergy, and funerals for centuries to realize its rule. These Shinto-style enshrinement facilities came to be known as *shōkonsha* or "spirit-pacifying shrines." In 1879, the ad hoc battlefield strategy of enshrining spirits and defining death was institutionalized by the Meiji government when the *shōkonsha* in the capital Tokyo was renamed the Yasukuni Shrine and elevated to the pinnacle of the nationwide spirit-pacifying shrine network commemorating lives lost in military fighting.[3]

The status of the Yasukuni Shrine as a state-sponsored shrine, however, soon became a problem when the Meiji leadership embarked on the project of modern state building, key to which being the creation of a constitution. The problem arose from the fact that the modern, constitutional state needs to be established as a secular, public political authority by distinguishing itself from religion. Was the Yasukuni Shrine a religious facility? If so, the state then would not be able to support and operate it. The answer of the Meiji government was that the Yasukuni Shrine was not a religion. Through instituting a definition of religion as private individual belief and distinguish this private religion from the national Shinto ritual system, including the Yasukuni Shrine, the Meiji government claimed that rituals performed at Shinto shrines were non-religious public ceremonies for cultivating patriotic feelings rather than for preaching religious doctrines. The religion-state separation as manifested through the distinction between public Shinto ritual and private religion underscored the 1889 imperial constitution which promised to guarantee individuals' freedom of religious belief but at the same time demanding citizens' loyalty to the imperial state, with that loyalty expressed first and foremost by citizens' participation in Shinto shrine rituals including visits to the Yasukuni Shrine.[4]

The Yasukuni Shrine in the pre-1945 period was then a public, non-religious, ritual institution that utilized the death of soldiers for cultivating the public morality of patriotism and loyalty to the emperor. The pre-1945 Yasukuni Shrine was co-administered by the Ministry of Army, the Ministry of Navy, and the Interior Ministry, with funding coming mainly from the Ministry of Army. Soldiers' and school students' visits were regularly arranged. The emperor and imperial family members frequently paid visits as well in order to demonstrate that those dead souls were indeed being honored and taken care of by the emperor for whom those soldiers gave their lives. The claim to be non-religious, however, was contentious due to the fact that the death of soldiers was sanctified and worshiped as gods or

3 See Shigeyoshi, *Irei to shōkon – Yasukuni no shisō*, 1974, pp. 8-14.

4 See Zhong, *The Origin of Modern Shinto in Japan: The Vanquished Gods of Izumo*, 2016, pp. 192-195.

kami in Japanese. There were a few cases where people including Christian converts opposed the visit to the Shrine claiming the worshiping ritual at the Shrine conflicted with their religious belief. But these cases proved useful occasions for the imperial state to reaffirm the distinction of ritual and religion and the appropriateness of its demand for all citizens' participation in Shinto rituals such as those at the Yasukuni Shrine.

In the early Meiji period, the Yasukuni Shrine enshrined over fourteen thousand souls who died during the Meiji Restoration and the subsequent civil war of 1877. That number increased dramatically as Japan embarked on a series of oversea expansionist and imperialist wars. The Russo-Japanese War of 1904-5 added more than thirteen thousand spirits of dead soldiers but the largest amount came as the result of World War II when more than two million soldiers gave their lives and came to be enshrined at the Yasukuni Shrine. The Shrine currently enshrines over 2,466,000 souls in total, including a small number of dead civilians. These spirits are called "glorious spirits" (*eirei*) by the Shrine and conservative politicians, indicating their affirmation of the imperialist wars waged by Japan through 1945. This affirmation is in many cases forced upon the dead soldiers. A huge number of soldiers died not in fighting, supposedly for the emperor, but in extreme battlefield conditions of hunger, exhaustion and despair. Furthermore, enshrinement of the soldiers as "glorious spirits" took place, mainly in the 1950s, without the family members' consent or awareness, or simply against their will. This collective of "glorious spirits" include the spirits of over twenty thousand Korean soldiers and twenty thousand Taiwanese aboriginal soldiers conscripted, involuntarily and voluntarily, into the Japanese imperial military in the 1940s.[5]

Japan's defeat in World War II in 1945 and the subsequent U.S.-led occupation till 1952 brought about a process of reconstitution of the Japanese nation-state. While the International Military Tribunal for the Far East (IMTFE) of 1945-1948 brought the war to an official end by convicting 25 Class-A war criminals, an early step in reconstituting the state was the Shinto Directive (*Shinto shirei*), announced by the Supreme Command of Allied Powers (SCAP) in December 1945, to abolish official support of Shinto shrines which set up the discursive condition for religion-state separation. Then in November 1946, a new constitution that was modeled after that of the U.S. was promulgated. It confirmed the principles of reli-

---

5 See Tanaka, *Dokyumento Yasukuni soshō*, p. 187.

gion-state separation and religious freedom in Article 20, "Freedom of religion is guaranteed to all. No religious organization shall receive any privileges from the State nor exercise any political authority. (2) No person shall be compelled to take part in any religious acts, celebration, rite or practice. (3) The state and its organs shall refrain from religious education or any other religious activity."[6] The new legal structure put in place by the constitution of 1946 necessitated all major Shinto shrines to self-identify as religious and private entities. The Yasukuni Shrine registered with the government as a Religious Juridical Person (*shūkyō hōjin*) in 1946.

The definition of Shinto as religion, however, was protested by many who saw the new constitution as an American imposition and who continued to advocate that Shinto shrines in particular the Yasukuni Shrine are sites of ceremony for the nation as well as customary cultural practices rather than a religious site. As a result, whenever the prime minister of Japan visited the shrine, many support and many protest against it. Supporters argue it is the government's duty to pay respect to and memorialize those who died for the nation whereas protesters argue government officials' visits represent a lack of reflection on history and a mistaken endorsement of Japan's imperialism and wars of pre-1945 period. Protesters also argue that in legal terms the visits constitute a clear case of violation of the principle of religion-state separation of the 1946 Constitution whereas the prewar Meiji Constitution just blatantly negated the religious nature of the Yasukuni Shrine in order to justify citizens' visit to it. The shrine continues to be a hotspot of controversy.

As a religious corporation, the Yasukuni Shrine by legal definition should have no relationship with the state. But the Shrine's connection with the postwar state, which has for most of the past seven decades been under the control of the conservative Liberal Democratic Party, was never completely severed. This connection took three forms. First, the enshrinement of Class-A war criminals. In as early as 1958, the Health Ministry bureaucrats suggested to the Yasukuni Shrine that the Class-A war criminals be enshrined at the shrine, but the suggestion was rejected by the then

---

6 As a comparison, the First Amendment of the U.S. Constitution goes as follows: "Congress shall make no law respecting an establishment of religion, or prohibiting the free exercise thereof; or abridging the freedom of speech, or of the press; or the right of the people peaceably to assemble, and to petition the Government for a redress of grievances."

head priest of the shrine. In 1966, the Health Ministry again pressed for the enshrinement but still the shrine resisted the state's attempt. It was not until 1978 that the fourteen Class-A war criminals were finally apotheosized when a conservative head priest took control of the Yasukuni Shrine.[7] Second, the government's efforts to renationalize the Shrine. From 1969 to 1974, working with the conservative Association of Bereaved Families (*izoku kai*), the ruling Liberal Democratic Party led the effort in proposing every year a nationalization bill for deliberation in the Diet but the bill was rejected every year until it was finally dropped by the LDP. Strong social opposition out of fear of Japan's remilitarization was a key factor contributing to the defeat of the nationalization attempt. After that, the advocates of state support for Yasukuni shifted to promoting the emperor and the Prime Minister's visits to the Shrine, in particular on August 15, the anniversary of Japan's surrender which in Japanese is ambiguously called *shūsen kinenbi*, or "the End-of-War Anniversary." A visit on this specific date would signal Japan government's official confirmation of pre-1945 imperialist wars as justifiable and correct.

The third form in which the Yasukuni Shrine was connected to the state was visits to the shrine to pay tribute to the war dead by high-level officials including the prime minister. These visits, as suggested, make highly significant political statements. Of 35 prime ministers of the postwar period, 15 visited the Yasukuni Shrine, including the current Prime Minister Abe Shinzo who did so on December 26, 2013. Visits by high level officials were always opposed but it is when the Prime Minister Miki Takeo visited the Shrine on August 15, 1973 that the Yasukuni Shrine came to mark a widely known political controversy and became a rallying symbol for political struggles. Prime Ministers who visited on August 15 include Fukuda Takeo (1978), Suzuki Zenkō (1980, 1981, 1982), Nakasone Yasuhiro (1983, 1984, 1985), and Koizumi Jun'ichirō (2006). More PM visits were made on other dates. Whether on August 15 or not, the visits mark the government's positive understanding of Japan's modern history of war and imperialism, an understanding at great odds with that of other Asian countries and opposed by many people in Japan and other East Asian countries. Opposition takes many forms but the legal form of opposition has been to charge government officials with violating the constitu-

7 See Breen, *Yasukuni, the War Dead, and the Struggle for Japan's Past,* 2008, pp. 6-8.

tional principle of religion-state separation and violating citizens' religious freedom. To fend off these legal charges and political opposition, Miki Takeo expediently clarified his visit to be a private one that was based on four NOs: not using official vehicle, not using public fund to purchase offerings, not using the Prime Minister title, and not accompanied by public servants.[8]

But these markers for the non-official nature of Prime Ministers' Yasukuni visit were soon deliberately given up as political opposition decreased. After the civil and student movements receded in the 1970s, the politically progressive social atmosphere that restrained conservative politicians gave way to a general public less and less interested in these political issues. Decreased popular opposition emboldened politicians. During Koizumi Jun'ichiro's election campaign in 2000, he made a well-advertised "promise" to visit the Yasukuni Shrine in the event that he became the Prime Minister and used this "promise" as the rallying slogan to attract voters, full aware that the slogan would not do harm to his campaign because voters are either supporters or without interest in the issue. When Koizumi visited the shrine on August 13, 2001, he wrote down his name as "The Prime Minister Koizumi Jun'ichiro" on the Shrine's register book, marking the official nature of his visit. His visit incurred a lot of criticism but never threatened the safety and stability of his government (he stayed in his post for six years and became the fifth longest serving Prime Minister to date).

Those who oppose the Prime Minister's visits and choose to protest them through legal suits as well as other public means ally with each other in solidarity and take up the form of distinctive minority groups. Consisted of family members of the dead soldiers, Buddhists priests, Christians, ordinary citizens as well as supporting lawyers, these groups usually organize themselves in *kai* or informal associations for waging legal suits, both as plaintiffs and as supporters, as well as conducting rallying campaigns involving street demonstration, publication, lectures and symposiums. These groups are loose in institutional sense but the key elements that bring them together are clear and strong: their publicly expressed opposition to the Prime Minister's visits to the Yasukuni Shrine and to the positive historical understanding of Japan's imperialism and wars represented by these visits. They also share the strategy of using religious freedom as a

8 See Akitetsu, "Yasukuni Jinja to ha nanika," 2006, pp. 69-71.

means to expose the unlawfulness and incorrectness of these visits and to fight for their right to define the death of the Yasukuni spirits, including their family members. These key elements render them increasingly a minority. Not only does the media not have interest in reporting their activities thus reducing their socio-political existence and influence, the general public tends to share less and less their problem, concern, and their outspoken means of opposition. While there are a lot of people who do not agree with the Prime Minister's visit, they tend to keep their disagreement to themselves and not to stand out to support these groups.

C. Religious Freedom, Historical Memory, and Ultimate Values

The complete record of the Osaka case, concluded on February 27, 2004, is downloadable from the official website "Courts in Japan" copyrighted under the Supreme Court of Japan. The following analysis of the case is based on the downloaded record "Case of Request for Confirmation of Unconstitutionality of the Visit to the Yasukuni Shrine [by the Prime Minister Koizumi Jun'ichiro]" (*Yasukuni sanpai iken kakunin seikyū jiken*).[9] The plaintiffs problematized the Prime Minister Koizumi's visit in terms of its violation of the constitutional principle of religion-state separation and violation of their freedom of religious belief. It is notable, however, that most of the plaintiffs do not profess any religious affiliation or belief in a particular religious doctrine. Unable to resort to the conventional notions of religion and religious freedom, they argued that their right to religious freedom includes the right to define without state interference their relationship with departed family members enshrined at the Yasukuni Shrine because that relationship concerns ultimate life principles and values fundamentally important for them; but the Prime Minister's visit interfered into that relationship because the visit prescribed a definition of the death of their family members that is different from theirs and not acceptable to them. In other words, the plaintiffs tried to creatively define religion and religious freedom so as to connect religious freedom with fundamental values and principles that ground a specific individual way of life, and ultimately connect the protection of that freedom with a critique of the

9 See www.courts.go.jp/hanrei/pdf/C12DD1AB8B417CEB49256E4D0008B1EE. pdf, last accessed 10 June 2014.

dominant form of national history and national imagining. But their effort was not recognized by the court which followed a standard definition of religion.

The plaintiffs made two major claims: first, the Prime Minister's visit to the Yasukuni Shrine was unconstitutional because it violated the constitutional principle of religion-state separation; second, the right to religious freedom of the plaintiffs were violated by the PM's visit, and because of that they demanded compensation of 10,000 yen (about 100 US dollars) for each plaintiff. The nominal amount of compensation sought by the plaintiffs is apparently meant to underscore the fact that what they want is not monetary compensation but an official judgment of the unconstitutionality of the Prime Minister's visit so that it can be stopped. Given that the majority of the plaintiffs are not affiliated with any religion and do not claim adherence to any religious creed, in what sense do they claim religious freedom to have been violated? What is the right that is violated by the Prime Minister's visit? The right plaintiffs formulated was

> the right (*kenri* 権利) or interest (*rieki* 利益) to decide on whether and how to remember and to commemorate those who died in war and above all whether to accept the idea that the war dead are enshrined at the Yasukuni Shrine, and do so without interference or pressure from public authority.[10]

They claimed this right/interest was an extension from their right to religious freedom. How, then, did the plaintiffs (and their lawyers and academic supporters) relate the principles of religious freedom and religion-state separation to the right of commemorating dead soldiers without public authority's interference?

The making of their claims in terms of religious freedom consists of three major steps. First, they establish the fact that Prime Minister Koizumi's visit is a religious one and thereby violates Article 20 of the Constitution which forbids state endorsement of religion; second, they put forward a broadened definition of the individual freedom of religious belief, a freedom which they argue includes personal commitment to ultimate values and principles that are essential for an individual. By doing so, they relate religious freedom to people without pronounced institutional religious affiliation and membership. In this regard, it is intriguing to note that they

10 Case of Request for Confirmation of Unconstitutionality of the Visit to the Yasukuni Shrine [by the Prime Minister] (*Yasukuni sanpai iken kakunin seikyu jiken*), hereafter abbreviated as Case of Request at Osaka, p. 1.

did not invoke the negative freedom of religion, i.e., the right not to have a religion or religious affiliation, which might then be violated by the Prime Minister's visit to the shrine. This may have to do with the lack of reference to the right to not have religious affiliation in Article 20 of the constitution. Third, this broadened constitutional right to freedom is then connected to the right to commemorate the dead soldiers which they argue concerns ultimate values essential for their individual life. Through these steps, they claim that their constitution-derived right of commemoration, as the extended right to religious freedom, was violated by Koizumi's anti-constitutional visit to the Shrine. Let us take a closer look at how these connections are made.

The argument for the unconstitutionality of Koizumi's visit consists of three steps. First, the plaintiffs established religious and nationalist nature of the Yasukuni Shrine. The plaintiffs state that before 1945 the Yasukuni Shrine was a religious institution used by the state to produce endless "imperial subjects" with strong fighting valor. As an ideological apparatus of the prewar imperial state, the shrine was a horrible case of fusion of religion and state. In postwar years, the shrine has become an explicitly legally defined religious institution but, the plaintiffs pointed out, the Yasukuni Shrine's ideological nature remained unchanged in the postwar period because it defends the correctness of imperialism and war and its religious practice was made possible by state support such as the Health Ministry's provision of name list of dead soldiers.[11] Therefore, the Yasukuni Shrine is, first, a religious institution, and second, a religious institution that embodies Japanese militarism and imperialist nationalism. Second, Koizumi's visit was a religious action in public capacity. This is because he worshipped the spirits enshrined there and signed his name with the title "Japanese Prime Minister" on the Shrine registration book. Furthermore, the Prime Minister deliberately utilized mass media to arouse national attention to publicize his religious action. Third, the visit accordingly constitutes state support, promotion, and encouragement of religion. This action violated Article 20 of the Constitution, specifically the third clause, "The state and its organs shall refrain from religious education or any other religious activity."[12]

11 See ibid., p. 4.

12 Ibid., p. 8.

The plaintiffs' argument of the violation of their right and interest in terms of the right to religious freedom, is the key part of their petition. It also consists of three steps. First, they argue the principle of religion-state separation in the constitution should be interpreted as a component of the right to freedom of religious belief rather than as a principle that functions as an institutional guarantee of that right. This interpretation of the relationship between religious freedom and religion-state separation apparently reflects their attempt to directly connect the Prime Minister's visit to articulations of their constitutional rights. That means that the visit, if ruled unconstitutional, would constitute in itself a violation of the rights of the plaintiffs. Second, religion ultimately concerns the way of life (*ikikata* 生き方) of an individual. Religion is about private affairs of individuals, they further argue. It is based on the respect for the esteem of each individual that the constitution guarantees protection of religious freedom. The private nature of religion includes two dimensions: privacy and affinity (*shinwasei* 親和性), both of which are to be protected. The prioritization of religious freedom as a private issue, they continue, has led to widened definitions of religion and religious freedom. That is, principles (*shinnen* 信念) that are strongly held by individuals, comparable to religious beliefs and foundational for the ways of life of those who uphold these principles, can be expected to be protected from interference by public authority. Furthermore, emotions resulted from adhering to those principles, just like those arising from religious beliefs, should receive legal protection in that they concern issues of spirituality (*tamashii*) and absolute, ultimate values (*zettai tekina kyūkyoku tekina kachi*). Thus, by emphasizing religious freedom as an issue of the private and interior dimension of an individual (without God or gods), the plaintiffs put forward significantly widened definitions of religion and religious freedom that do not predicate on formal institutional affiliation with established religious organization but are in need of protection.

Third, to argue that the Prime Minister Koizumi's visit violates their principles and way of life, the plaintiffs go on to establish that the visit infringed upon their freedom of religious belief and the principle of religion-state separation, and based on this violation, seek compensation from the state. They argue that the death of their family members constitutes the basis for their life as individuals and they draw meaning of their own lives from contemplating the unreasonable fact of the death of their family members. However, Prime Minister Koizumi's Yasukuni visit affirms the status of the dead soldiers as "glorious spirits"; this affirmation challenges the principles and emotions of the plaintiffs who do not consider the soldiers as "glorious spirits" but as participants in state-led imperialist wars, and as such constitutes a compulsion for the plaintiffs to renounce these principles and emotions. As a result, "the right or interest to decide on whether and how to remember and to commemorate those who died in war and above all whether to accept the idea that the war dead are enshrined at the Yasukuni Shrine, and do so without interference or pressure from public authority" of the plaintiffs is violated by the Prime Minister's Yasukuni visit.

The three judges of the Osaka District Court recognized that Koizumi Jun'ichiro visited the Yasukuni Shrine in official capacity i.e., as the Prime Minister of Japan.[13] Their ruling included a sketch of the postwar history of government officials' Yasukuni visits and recurring controversies but stopped short of determining whether Koizumi's visit was constitutional or not. In order to explain this restraint, scholars have referred to a legal practice in Japan called "judicial passivism" (*shihō shōkyoku shugi*) which means that courts try to avoid making judgment of constitutionality out of respect for the executive branch of the government. Japan's Supreme Court is known for following this "judicial passivism" in constitutional lawsuits.[14] But whether the Osaka District Court applied this legal principle is not clear.[15] One can only imagine some potential but never pronounced reason: the judges tried to avoid making a decision on such a politically controversial and sensitive issue in order to avoid personal safety

---

13 See ibid., p. 28.

14 See Ichikawa, "Nihon ni okeru iken shinsa sei no kiseki to tokucho," 2004, p. 110; Momochi, "Yasukuni sanpai soshō no mondaiten to kongo no kadai," 2008, p. 136.

15 At a more technical level, legal deliberations often refer to the distinction between "purpose and/or effect as criteria" (*mokuteki kōka kijun*) used by courts to decide whether government act including the Prime Minister's visit to the Yasukuni Shrine is a religious act. The Supreme Court in 1989 and 1997 put forward its guideline for deciding as such, "the purpose of the Prime Minister (whether out of religious belief or not) being a factor to be considered, it is necessary to take into account the place the act takes place, the effect it generates for the general populace, and its relation to social customs." See Momochi, "Yasukuni sanpai soshō no mondaiten to kongo no kadai," pp. 138-139. The technical distinction between purpose and effect, however, is not very helpful in understanding why courts withhold judgment of constitutionality in the Yasukuni legal suits because it is based on a normative definition of religion which is to be problematized rather than used without second thought.

being endangered by attacks from right-wing activists. In any case, judicial passivism is not much more than a technical explanation which risks reducing the complex nature of the Yasuku lawsuits to a technical issue. It is beyond doubt that the Prime Minister's visit is most certainly unconstitutional given the above-mentioned constitutional stipulations about religion-state separation and the official definition of the Yasukuni Shrine as religious corporation.

The judges disagree with the plaintiffs' argument for subsuming the religion-state separation principle under the freedom of religious belief. Rather, the decision asserts, the principle is meant to be an institution that indirectly ensure religious freedom, and should not be interpreted as a specific right possessed by citizens.[16] In other words, the judgment rejected the plaintiffs' use of the religion-state separation principle to articulate their right and then to argue for its violation.

The ruling next provides its explanation for the "Freedom of religion is guaranteed to all" clause in Article 20 of the Constitution before it uses that explanation to decide whether the right of religious freedom was violated.

> This freedom of religion means it should not be restricted by public authority, or any disadvantage be imposed on it. For the violation of this freedom to take place, there must be a disadvantageous treatment by a public authority that is connected to the religious belief, or there must exist a compulsion or forced stop [of religious activity]. If these do not exist but there are merely context-based cases of felt pressure or an unpleasant feeling resulting from indirect or reflexive influence, the claim that a violation of religious freedom took place will not be successful.[17]

Here, the judge assumes a substantive definition of religious belief that is based on individual's pronounced commitment to an articulate doctrine that is distinguished from other socially formed values and commitments. This is the standard and widely accepted definition but is based on the Christianity model and is different from the relational and contextual one proposed by the plaintiffs. Mobilizing the articulate and privatized notion of religious belief, the court's definition draws a distinction between intangible hurt feelings and visible, external, disadvantageous treatment, with which the judges can then sever the link made by the plaintiffs between individuals and their family members, and furthermore between constitu-

---

16 See Case of Request at Osaka, p. 29.

17 Case of Request at Osaka, p. 29-30.

tionally protected religious belief on the one hand and feelings, ultimate values, and ways of life on the other. This severing helps the judge avoid engaging with the questions of history and memory, which however lie at the heart of the legal case because the plaintiffs' feelings and way of life are directly connected to the nation-state's history and the ways in which this history is being remembered. This severance thereby enables the judges to cut the link between the question of unconstitutionality of the Prime Minister's visit and the question of violation of religious freedom of the plaintiffs by that visit.

Based on this privatized and substantive definition of freedom of religion, the judges disqualified the plaintiffs' definition of their right to decide on how to commemorate their departed family members as commensurate to the right to religious freedom. This in effect negates the plaintiffs' claim that their specific right to commemorate has been violated by the Prime Minister's Yasukuni visit.

> What the plaintiffs call 'the right or interest to decide on whether and how to remember and to commemorate those who died in war and above all whether to accept the idea that the war dead are enshrined at the Yasukuni Shrine, and do so without interference or pressure from public authority' is a right or interest that can be completely determined by the plaintiffs and cannot be even indirectly affected by the state's pressure or interference. It is in other words difficult to understand it in terms of the right to freedom of religious belief that is protected from actions of direct and indirect influence. Therefore, it is difficult to recognize that this interest is ensured by Article 20 of the constitution which ensures freedom of religious belief.[18]

Overall, because it is difficult to find that the plaintiffs' legal right or interest has been violated, the plaintiffs do not have the right to claim compensation, "consequently, the plaintiffs' request for compensation is dismissed."[19]

At the technical level, the judges' ruling is consistent and logical. The judges adhere to definitions of religion and freedom that are standard, commonsensical, and acceptable for most people. Insofar as religion is understood in terms of belief and the freedom to have religious belief is regarded as a private issue of each individual citizen, the court's reasoning for the lack of violation of the plaintiffs' freedom follows the standard logic of liberal political thought that presupposes an autonomous,

18 Ibid., pp. 30-31.
19 Ibid., p. 31.

sovereign individual whose relationship with the outside world cannot be existential. Such a definition of religious freedom does not recognize the fact that a human being attains a self-identity and a meaningful life by way of their relationships with the world rather than being truly "in-divide-able" and self-sufficient. As such, the plaintiffs' needs to take into their own hands the right to define their personal life and identity by way of defining the relationship with their departed family members was not responded to, let alone their request for the state to address the fundamental relationships of personal life and identity with national memory and history.

Here, the right to religious freedom as possessed by individual citizens proved insufficient in responding to fundamental questions of how they choose to live their life. As a citizen, they are supposed to be able to demand the protection of those rights by the state; but as a national, they are ultimately urged to interiorize a particular version of the history of the nation of which they are a part, and to follow a particular mode of remembering that history, which however conflict with the ways they choose to define their individual being, life, and happiness. The problem is that the right to religious freedom these individuals possess as citizens becomes an obstacle for them to relate to the world and the national community so as to formulate an identity they desired. In this sense, the Yasukuni lawsuits reflect a political situation that keeps producing minority groups as freedom does not serve as the means for them to move out of that social status but rather subjecting them to that minority status.

D. Religious Freedom, Religion, and Political Community

In this section, I will look at the argument made by a "scholar witness" (*gakusha shōnin*) during court debates in another of the eight Yasukuni cases. This case was filed on November 1, 2001, on the same day as the Osaka one, at the Matsuyama District Court of Ehime Prefecture in Shikoku and the ruling came out in March 2006.[20] The court's judgment was the same as that of the Osaka District Court, denying that the plain-

20 See Shikoku Litigation Group of the Unconstitutionality of the Yasukuni Visit by the Prime Minister Koizumi Jun'ichiro (*Koizumi shushō Yasukuni sanpai iken Shikoku soshōdan*), at page.freett.com/shikoku/mokuji.htm and page.freett.com/shikoku/0206.htm, last accessed 10 November 2014.

tiffs' religious freedom was violated by the Prime Minister's visit while also withholding determining the unconstitutionality of the visit. In these Yasukuni cases, scholars provided expert opinions and advice to support the plaintiffs. They also appeared at court to testify as scholar witnesses. The scholar witness in the Matsuyama case was Morone Sadao, the then professor of law of Ehime University. I will look at how Prof. Morone's argument for the unconstitutionality of the Prime Minister's visit and the violation of the plaintiffs' religious freedom is weakened by the difficulty in defining religion and religious freedom, resulting in an inconsistency that undermined the persuasiveness of his argument. This difficulty of definition, as I will show, comes from treating religion and religious freedom as universal categories although these categories arose from the particular historical experience of European and North American societies. This inconsistency makes it difficult to respond to the specific Yasukuni problem that developed out of Japanese and East Asian history. (My purpose here is to look at the difficulty in defining religion and religious freedom rather than to criticize the commendable efforts of Prof. Morone, who was himself a plaintiff in yet another case, in helping plaintiffs fight for legal rights and interests.)

In support of the plaintiffs, Prof. Morone in October 2003 presented to the court a Statement of Position (*ikensho*) titled "On State-Religion Separation and the Prime Minister's Visit to the Yasukuni Shrine."[21] His main goal is to argue that the Prime Minister's visit is unconstitutional because it violated the constitutional principle of state-religion separation and invaded the plaintiffs' right to religious freedom. The 19000-word statement is divided into five sections plus a one-sentence introduction and a short conclusion.

The first section, "significance of the state-religion separation principle," clarifies the significance being 1, to protect the freedom of religious belief which is private affair concerning individual internal conviction in salvation of the soul; and 2, to secure smooth operation of political democracy. The author places religious freedom within an evolutionary, universal (but largely European) history of humanity's struggles for freedom, and states that the right to religious freedom is "a result of many years of

21 Morone, "On State-Religion Separation and the Prime Minister's Visit to the Yasukuni Shrine," (*Seikyō bunri to shushō no Yasukuni sanpai ni tsuite*), at page.freett.com/shikoku/morone01.htm. For the court's ruling, see www.courts. go.j p/hanrei/pdf/20060616145258.pdf, both last accessed Nov. 9, 2014.

human efforts to obtain freedom." Because religion by definition has absolute, uncompromising, exclusive features, Prof. Morone continues, to separate religion from the state is necessary for democracy where citizens conduct open debates. The definition of religion here is clearly based on the model of church-state relation in historical Europe.

The second section, "legal protective benefit of the state-religion separation clause and invasion of the plaintiffs' right," refers to a series of legal cases in the U.S. as precedent rulings, based on which the author argues that Clause 20 of the Constitution, i.e., the state-religion separation clause, is both a legal principle and a specific right-protecting (i.e. right to religious freedom) clause. Here the statement is making a similar argument with the one presented by plaintiffs in the Osaka case by relating the state-religion separation principle directly to articulations of rights. However, there is a big difference.

Whereas the Osaka plaintiffs concretized the state-religion separation principle through a broadened definition of religious belief and connecting war history to this definition, the statement instead approaches state-religion separation from the perspective of minority groups and does so by relating religious freedom of minority groups to the idea of exclusion from political community (*seiji kyōdōtai*). That is, Prof. Morone's argument strategically avoids relating religious freedom violation to the history of imperialism embodied in the Yasukuni Shrine. He wants to develop a strictly legal argument. In connecting minority's religious freedom to exclusion from political community, the statement first quotes the dissenting opinion of Justice Brennan in the case of Lynch v. Donnelly, 465 U.S. 668 (1984) where Justice Brennan makes reference to minority religious groups. In the Lynch v. Donnelly case, the court ruled the action of the town government of Pawtucket in Rhode Island, of putting up a creche of the birth of Jesus Christ in a shopping area, to be constitutional. Justice Brennan, however, argued that the display constituted government's support of religion given the fact that Christianity is the dominant religion among many minority religions.

> For many, the city's decision to include the creche as part of its extensive and costly efforts to celebrate Christmas can only mean that the prestige of the government has been conferred on the beliefs associated with the creche, thereby providing 'a significant symbolic benefit to religion […]' […] The effect on minority religious groups, as well as on those who may reject all reli-

> gion, is to convey the message that their views are not similarly worthy of public recognition nor entitled to public support [...].[22]

The statement then reinterprets Justice Brennan's reference to minority religious groups to mean that the religion-state separation principle forbids the government from sending out messages that those who do not follow the state-endorsed religion do not belong to the political community, i.e., the nation-state. In other words, state endorsement of a particular religion creates the impression of political exclusion of individual citizens from the nation-state. This potential exclusion, the statement argues, brings about hindrance to supposedly freely conducted private religious life and consequently causes spiritual anxieties, burden and pain. As such, the religion-state separation principle functions as both an abstract institutional principle and articulates a concrete, specific right, the right to be free from above anxieties, burden and pain. "Thus reconstituted, the state-religion separation clause of Article 20...instead of being positioned as a clause of institutional nature, can also be understood as a clause of right-articulating nature (*kenri tekina seikaku*) which grants individuals certain interest (*rieki*)."[23]

Section three, "The Public Nature of the Prime Minister' Visit," distinguishes visits to the Yasukuni Shrine, a religious corporation (*shūkyō hōjin*) enshrining deities (*shinrei* 神霊), from visits to tombs and funerals which venerate human spirits (*jinrei* 人霊). Visits to tombs, which are religious in nature, are nevertheless perceived secular and ceremonial thus socially permissible, but visits to the Yasukuni Shrine are unambiguously religious. Based on this distinction, the statement claims that visits to the Yasukuni Shrine are a proper, unambiguous religious activity. The statement then recaps the features of the Prime Minister Koizumi's visit and concludes that he visited a religious facility in the undoubtedly public capacity of the Prime Minister of Japan.

In Section four, the author builds upon previous court rulings to identify a specific criterion with which to judge that the Prime Minister's visits violated the plaintiffs' right to religious freedom. He traces in previous court rulings in similar cases in Japan the development of what he calls the criterion for judging the constitutionality of the relationship between state

22 Lynch v. Donnelly, 465 U.S. 668 (1984), 701, at supreme.justia.com/ cases/federal/ us/465/668/case.html, last accessed 10 November 2014.

23 Morone, "On State-Religion Separation."

and religion. In reference to these previous cases, he argues that the court should judge the constitutionality of the visit in terms that 1, the state's religious activity gives the impression of state support of a particular religion; 2, the court should consider whether the Prime Minister's act of visiting has a religious meaning besides taking into account his stated intention; and 3, whether the state's religious activity may cause democracy-endangering political confusion and division.

Section five summarizes the argument and concludes that the Prime Minister's visit constitutes support for a specific religion which will cause disunity endangering "democratic process of governance" (*minshushugi tekina tōchi katei*). At the same time, the visit carries a message of excluding certain groups from the political community due to religious matters; because of the spiritual anxiety, burden and pain so caused the Prime Minister's visit must be understood as violating the right of the plaintiffs.

As previously pointed out, the Matsuyama District Court ruled that the plaintiffs lost the case. My taking up the statement here does not mean the statement itself was to blame for the loss. It is, however, important to examine how the difficulty in definitions of religion and religious freedom may have undermined the statement from within.

The difficulty of the statement in maintaining consistency in defining religion and religious freedom is enormous. This difficulty manifests in the use of several different definitions that can hardly be related to each other. First, in Section One religious freedom means for the author the freedom to hold convictions in salvation of souls without being interfered by the state; here the author obviously assumes this is the basic element of the definition of religion. Then, in Section Three, according to the author, both visits to tombs and to the Yasukuni Shrine are religious activities but the former can be seen as secular ceremonies and is socially acceptable whereas the Yasukuni visit is not. The differences here, which are fundamental for the author, are between human spirits and gods on the one hand and between social ceremony and religious ritual on the other.[24] This is the most artificial and forced definition of religion in the statement. It is not clear at all on what basis the distinctions between secular ceremony and religious ritual and the distinction between human spirits and gods are made. It is understandable that Prof Morone needed to define the Yasukuni Shrine as a religion. However, how the Yasukuni Shrine's rituals and the

24 See ibid.

visits are related to convictions in salvation of souls, central to the definition of religion in Section one, is left unanswered. It is not clear whether the Yasukuni Shrine is a religion that is exclusive and absolute, which are features of religion identified in Section one. Toward the end, religious freedom changes to freedom from anxiety, burden or pain resulting from feeling possible exclusion from the political community, exclusion resulting from holding a certain religious belief. Neither spirits/gods nor conviction in salvation of souls appear relevant to religious freedom thus defined.

This inconsistency in definition betrays the difficulty in applying a universalized, indeed rigidified, privatized definition of religion and religious freedom to the specific socio-political conditions in Japan. This inconsistency apparently undermined the persuasiveness of the statement from within. Resulting from this inconsistency is the larger problem in the statement: a mismatch of means and goal. That is, this argument risks depoliticizing the Yasukuni issue which, however, stands at the center of these legal cases. In objectifying the Yasukuni gods as qualitatively different from human spirits, the argument essentially homogenized the complex, varied, contested meanings of death of the enshrined soldiers, a heterogeneity of meaning suppressed by the glorious narrative of the Yasukuni Shrine and by the Prime Minister's visit. It is precisely the definition of the meaning of death that the minority groups wanted to gain control from the state. The need to define the Yasukuni Shrine as a religion along the lines of the rigid and de-historicized definition of religion led to ignoring the history and simplifying the Yasukuni Shrine to a gods-enshrining facility with the complex and controversial historical processes of producing and sustaining these gods of war dead all effaced. It is however precisely those historical processes and those non-institutional links between the Shrine and the nation-state that the plaintiffs intended to problematize in order to define a personal life they decided to live.

The author's resort to the idea of a political community in arguing for the unconstitutionality of the Prime Minister's visit is equally revealing. It is completely understandable that the author adopts American legal precedents in particular the freedom of minority religious groups to build up the argument that the PM's visit was unconstitutional. However, from state endorsement of religion to the impression of political exclusion and then to the consequential result of anxiety, burden and pain, the argument assumes the necessary existence of the state as the protector (and simultaneously violator) of the freedom of citizens, that is, both discussion and practice of religious freedom is possible only within the boundary of the liberal democratic nation-state. The author's argument then relies on a presupposition of the nation-state for the existence of rights, which is the essential legal category constituting the individual citizen. This reliance exposes the mutual dependence of rights of individual citizens and the state which is a politicized society consisting of citizens. Recognition of the membership of citizens by the state is the condition for their possession of rights and thereby for becoming a legal modern individual. That is why an exclusion from the political community will bring about anxiety, burden and pain in the first place.

By developing an argument that assumes the bounded political community, Prof. Morone's argument then affirms the exclusiveness and bounded nature of the nation-state even while it pursues the goal of protecting religious freedom of the plaintiffs as minority groups. The argument exposes the dilemma in discussions of protection of minority groups in that the state is invariably affirmed as the entity that protects. But this legal argument is blind to the fact that the political community is a nation-state that requires the adoption of a uniform imagining of the nation by its citizens in so far as this uniformity is necessary for consolidating social integration and solidarity upon which democratic politics are dependent. As such, the argument such as Prof. Morone's cannot respond to the questions of ultimate values and determination of ways of life that are central to the Yasukuni plaintiffs' arguments because the values and the ways of life upheld by the plaintiffs are based on a reflective and critical understanding of the history of imperialism and war that differs from the dominant national history promoted by the Yasukuni Shrine and the Prime Minister's visit there.

Furthermore, it is easy to see how the statement will not make sense to plaintiffs from outside of Japan such as family members of former Korean soldiers enshrined at Yasukuni, who challenged the right of the Yasukuni Shrine in enshrining the spirits of their family members as "glorious spirits" without their consent, because they are outside (or excluded from) the political community from the very beginning. The statement then essentially excluded non-Japanese plaintiffs from his argument and more significantly reduced the transnational nature of the Yasukuni problem to a domestic one limited to Japan. In the end, in presupposing the trans-historical and universal definitions of religion and religious freedom, the argument of the statement became incapable of responding to the specific issues the Yasukuni lawsuit minority groups wanted to deal with: history of imperialism and war, personal memory of it, and how to live a life that can reconcile these painful but inescapable life components and incorporate them into their life.

E. Conclusion

The legal cases against the Prime Minister Koizumi Jun'ichiro's visits to the Yasukuni Shrine during his office in 2001-2006 provide a good chance to explore how religion and religious freedom are tied to the formation of minority groups and their relationship with the state and the society. The appearance of these cases as intriguing legal "misjudgment" raises the question as to why and how the courts could ignore the obvious unconstitutionality of the Prime Minister's visit to the Yasukuni Shrine, a religious facility, and ignore the plaintiffs' claims for violation of religious freedom. I have shown that this "misjudgment" represents a conflict between competing definitions of religion and religious freedom and this conflict exposes the key tension in these cases between the dominant form of national history manifested by the Prime Minister's Yasukuni visits and a contesting form of historical memory sought by minority groups.

The paper first provided a short history of the Yasukuni Shrine from its establishment after the Meiji Restoration of 1868 until today to show that this religious facility has been closely related to imperialism and war of pre-1945 Japan and the question of religious freedom in these legal cases was intertwined with the struggle for alternative ways of remembering the history of imperialism and war in postwar Japan. The plaintiffs fought for both their religious freedom and their freedom to define national history and their relationship with that history. This fight took the shape, in the Osaka case, of the plaintiffs' proposal of a broadened definition of religious freedom with which they could relate the constitutional principle of religion-state separation to their argument that the Prime Minister's visit, in endorsing the war-affirming historical narrative of the religious corporation Yasukuni Shrine, violated their religious freedom. According to this broadened definition, religious freedom included the right to define the relationship of the plaintiffs with their family members enshrined at the Yasukuni Shrine without interference of the state. This paper then examined how the court applied an individual-based, i.e., privatized form of religious freedom to reject the plaintiffs' broadened definition as well as avoiding touching on the historical issues of imperialism and war. Following on that, this paper looked at a law scholar's defense of the plaintiffs' argument in another case and demonstrated how his argument, based on the normative definitions of religion and religious freedom, failed to engage the specific issues of the Japanese Prime Minister's visit to the Yasukuni Shrine, issues of religious freedom as well as historical memory of war and imperialism.

As it is clear that the failure of these legal cases results from, among other reasons, the insufficiency of the conventional, privatized, individual-based definition, I argue that we need to expand the legal categories of religion and religious freedom to be relational and contextual ones in order to accommodate minority ways of life which opt not to share the dominant, exclusive imagining of the nation. We need a widened definition of religion and religious freedom so that the right to religious freedom can respond to the specific problems of national identity and history in relation to the right to ways of life articulated through religious freedom.

Scholars of religion have since the 1990s called into question the normative, belief-based, privatized definition of religion by showing how this definition arose from particular European historical experience but subsequently spread globally in shaping modern transformations of non-Western societies where that definition was prioritized as the normative standard.[25] In transforming itself to resemble the norm and to be modern, Japan in many ways created religion.[26] But the creations were accompanied by problems that remain to be solved even today. The Yasukuni Shrine is a case in point in this regard. How to think about the Yasukuni problem in terms of religious freedom? The anthropologist Talal Asad emphasized the embodied nature of religion and, I would argue, of religious freedom as well.[27] Being embodied means that what the believer holds as ultimate truth informs the whole life of the believer and is expressed through their speech, way of speaking, gesture, clothing, and all other kinds of behavior, and through their various relationships with the world.

---

25 See Asad, *Genealogies of Religion: Discipline and Reasons of Power in Christianity and Islam*, 1993; van de Veer, *Imperial Encounters: Religion and Modernity in India and Britain*, 2001; Masuzawa, *The Invention of World Religions*, 2005.

26 See Zhong, *The Origin of Modern Shinto in Japan: The Vanquished Gods of Izumo*; Maxey, *The Greatest Problem: Religion and State Formation in Japan*, 2014; Yamaguchi, *Meiji kokka to Shukyo*, 1999; Josephson, *The Invention of Religion in Japan*, 2012.

27 See Asad, *Formation of the Secular*, 2003, pp. 67-99.

As such, practice of religion and religious freedom cannot be neatly segmented by the distinction of the public and the private. But this is the distinction that underscores the dominant definitions of religion as a part of private life and religious freedom as a right to be practiced in the private sphere. Indeed, liberal democratic politics of modern nation-states are believed to be premised on this distinction of the private and the public, and religion as private belief is to be excluded from the public sphere.[28] In this argument religion meant first and foremost Christianity and the discussion has religion's long contentious history in Europe in the background. It is necessary to historicize and reshape this argument of exclusion of religion from the public sphere when we think about the question of religion and religious freedom in Japan and East Asia (arguably in other regions including the increasingly culturally diverse Western societies as well). Just like an individual who is in both the public and private spheres, religion is better thought about as traversing both the public and the private as embodied by individuals.

In the case of the Yasukuni plaintiffs, the embodiedness of religion manifests in their relationship with their family members who died in war and are enshrined at the Yasukuni Shrine. The normative definition of religion will not recognize the religiosity contained in the relationship with human kin or ancestors which in the East Asian context however has been the hallmark of religious life of the past and the present. As plaintiffs of the Osaka case argued, their relationship with the family members enshrined at the Yasukuni Shrine is of paramount importance for their life but they could not define that relationship because of the interference caused by the Prime Minister's visit to the Shrine. In replacement of a definition that prioritizes the private nature of individual belief, we need to foreground the individual's relationship with other beings, both human and supra-natural, when these relationships are existential for these individuals. It is only when scholars, lawyers, and plaintiffs themselves reconfigure their definitions of religion and religious freedom and defend the right of plaintiffs along such a reconfigured and broadened definition that a new way of discussing religion and religious freedom can become possible. When such changes evolve to the extent that it generates enough so-

---

28 The renowned philosopher Jürgen Habermas has been most forcibly arguing for the exclusion of religion from the public sphere and if religion is to be allowed entry into the public deliberations it needs to translate its message into secular languages; Habermas, "Religion in the Public Sphere," 2006, pp. 1-25.

cial and legal impacts, the courts will begin to change to adopt these new definitions. Only then can the legal status of citizenship start to enable minority groups to define their individual ways of life through defending their religious freedom without at the same time sharing the positively affirmed national history of imperialism and war.

Bibliography

Asad, Talal, *Formation of the Secular*, Stanford: Stanford University Press, 2003.

Asad, Talal, *Genealogies of Religion: Discipline and Reasons of Power in Christianity and Islam*, Baltimore: John Hopkins University Press, 1993.

Breen, John, *Yasukuni, the War Dead, and the Struggle for Japan's Past*, New York: Columbia University Press, 2008.

Habermas, Jurgen, "Religion in the Public Sphere," *European Journal of Philosophy* 14:1 (2006): 1-25.

Haruyama, Akitetsu, "Yasukuni Jinja to ha nanika," *Refarensu*, No. 666 (July 2006): 49-75.

Ichikawa, Masato, "Nihon ni okeru iken shinsa sei no kiseki to tokucho," *Ritsumeikan hogaku* 294 (2004): 104-119.

Josephson, Jason, *The Invention of Religion in Japan*, Chicago: The University of Chicago Press, 2012.

Masuzawa, Tomoko, *The Invention of World Religions*, Chicago and London: The University of Chicago Press, 2005.

Maxey, Trent, *The Greatest Problem: Religion and State Formation in Japan*, Boston: Harvard Asian Center, 2014.

Momochi, Akira, "Yasukuni sanpai soshō no mondaiten to kongo no kadai," in *Shūkyōhō*, Vol. 27 (2008): 129-148.

Morone, Sadao, "On State-Religion Separation and the Prime Minister's Visit to the Yasukuni Shrine," (Seikyō bunri to shushō no Yasukuni sanpai ni tsuite), at page.freett.com/shikoku/morone01.htm.

Osaka District Court, "Case of Request for Confirmation of Unconstitutionality of the Visit to the Yasukuni Shrine [by the Prime Minister]" (*Yasukuni sanpai iken kakunin seikyu jiken*).

Shigeyoshi, Murakami, *Irei to shōkon – Yasukuni no shisō*, Tokyo: Iwanami Shoten, 1974.

Tanaka, Nobumasa, *Dokyumento Yasukuni soshō*, Tokyo: Iwanami Shoten, 2007.

Van de Veer, Peter, *Imperial Encounters: Religion and Modernity in India and Britain*, Princeton: Princeton University Press, 2001.

Yamaguchi, Teruomi, *Meiji kokka to Shukyo*, Tokyo: Tokyo daigaku shuppankai, 1999.

"Yasukuni sanpai iken soshō," at www.geocities.jp/social792/yasukuni/ ikensosyou.html.

Zhong, Yijiang, *The Origin of Modern Shinto in Japan: The Vanquished Gods of Izumo*, London: Bloomsbury Publishing, 2016.

The Protection of the Existence and Identity of Religious Minorities Under the United Nations Legal Framework: Between the Group-Centered and Person-Centered Approaches

Rodrigo Vitorino Souza Alves[1]

A. Introduction

There is an almost universal consensus that all human beings are entitled to a set of fundamental human rights.[2] However, there is no doubt that the rights of minority groups, especially religious minorities, are being violated in almost every part of the world, a serious problem that jeopardizes the stability of the States and undermines human dignity. Reports from different organizations emphasize the fact that religious minorities need special attention.[3]

In this context, international organizations have an increasingly important role to play regarding the protection of members of religious minorities against human rights abuses. This chapter aims to discuss the protection of the identity and existence of religious minorities under the United Nations minority rights regime, with focus on the problem of the recognition of group rights.

1 Earlier drafts of this chapter were presented at the VI Session of the United Nations Forum on Minority Issues – OHCHR (Geneva, November 2013) and at the Law and Religion Scholars Network Conference (Cardiff, May 2014).

2 For example, 169 States are Parties to the International Convenant on Civil and Political Rights (1966) and 196 States are Parties to the Convention on the Rights of Child (1989).

3 See Pew Research Center, "Rising Restrictions on Religion: One-third of the world's population experiences an increase," August 2011, at http://www.pewforum.org/files/2011/08/RisingRestrictions-web.pdf. See also Grim and Finke, *The Price of Freedom Denied: Religious Persecution and Conflict in the Twenty-First Century*, 2010.

B. Religion and Minority Rights in the United Nations Instruments

The freedom to have, adopt, change, renounce and, either individually or in community with others, to manifest a religion or belief is widely recognized as a basic human right by the international community.[4] However, the legal protection of freedom of religion and belief alone was assumed as incapable of solving the problems faced by religious minorities, which are frequently subjects of hostility on the part of predominant religious or secularist segments of society.

In order to provide a higher level of security for religious minorities, they were included in the United Nations minority rights regime. The two pillars of this regime are the International Covenant on Civil and Political Rights – ICCPR of 1966, and the Declaration on the Rights of Persons Belonging to National or Ethnic, Religious and Linguistic Minorities of 1992.[5]

I. The International Covenant on Civil and Political Rights

The most important legally binding provision that deals with minority rights is Article 27 of the ICCPR, which states that,

> [i]n those States in which ethnic, religious or linguistic minorities exist, persons belonging to such minorities shall not be denied the right, in community with the other members of their group, to enjoy their own culture, to profess and practice their own religion, or to use their own language.

---

4 Within the United Nations, the most important international standards are Article 18 of the Universal Declaration of Human Rights (1948), Article 18 of the International Covenant on Civil and Political Rights (1966) and Article 1 of the Declaration on the Elimination of All Forms of Intolerance and of Discrimination Based on Religion or Belief (1981). The Human Rights Committee has also adopted a general comment on freedom of religion or belief (UN Human Rights Committee, CCPR General Comment No. 22: Article 18, 30 July 1993, CCPR/C/21/Rev. 1/Add.4).

5 Several human rights instruments grant protection to minorities against different kinds of violence and discrimination, such as Article 2 of the Convention on the Prevention and Punishment of the Crime of Genocide (1948), Articles 2 and 4 of the Convention on the Elimination of All Forms of Racial Discrimination (1966), Article 13 of the International Covenant on Economic, Social and Cultural Rights (1966), Article 5 of the UNESCO Convention against Discrimination in Education (1960), Article 5 of the UNESCO Declaration on Race and Racial Prejudice (1978), and Article 30 of the Convention on the Rights of the Child (1989).

Expressed in negative terms, Article 27 does not call for special measures to be adopted and does not explicitly recognize the existence of a right. Notwithstanding, as already affirmed by the Human Rights Committee,[6] since the article prohibits the denial of those rights ('to enjoy their own culture, to profess and practice their own religion, or to use their own language'), it does establish and recognize a right, which is conferred on members of minorities, in addition to all the other human rights enshrined in the ICCPR.[7]

This right has already been formulated as a 'right to identity',[8] as it represents the claim to distinctiveness in terms of ethnicity, religion and/or language. Article 27 protects all individuals not only against forced assimilation, but also from social exclusion, compelling the States to ensure that all members of minorities are free to partake of their group's identity. Therefore, the article reinforces the individual freedom to belong to a minority group and demands the protection of its exercise. For this reason, positive measures of protection are obliquely required against violations carried out by the State, its agents or other persons.[9]

These measures, however, should not promote the 'museumification' of cultures,[10] the creation of 'living museums of peoples'[11] nor the preservation of the cultural 'purity'[12] of a group. As the beneficiaries of the rights under Article 27 are individuals, and not groups or identities themselves, any protective measure must not be misunderstood as the imposition of a cultural duty over the group or its members, such as the duty to maintain a specific individual or collective religious identity.

6 UN Human Rights Committee, General Comment No. 23: The rights of minorities (Art. 27), 8 April 1994, CCPR/C/21/Rev. 1/Add.5, para. 6.1.

7 For a comparison between religious freedom and religious minority rights frameworks, see Ghanea, "Religious or Minority? Examining the Realisation of International Standards in Relation to Religious Minorities in the Middle East," 2008, pp. 304-313.

8 See Thornberry, "Minority Rights," 1995, pp. 332-333.

9 See UN Human Rights Committee, General Comment No. 23: The rights of minorities (Art. 27), 8 April 1994, CCPR/C/21/Rev. 1/Add.5, para. 6.1.

10 Thornberry, "Minority Rights," 1995, p. 332.

11 Wiessner, "The Cultural Rights of Indigenous Peoples: achievements and continuing challenges," 2011, p. 140.

12 Kymlicka, *Multicultural Odysseys: Navigating the New International Politics of Diversity*, 2011, pp. 100-103.

In the context of the conflict of rights, as observed by the Committee[13], none of the minority rights of Article 27 "may be legitimately exercised in a manner or to an extent inconsistent with the other provisions of the Covenant.". Minority rights do not exclude, but complement the other human rights.

Finally, regarding the protection of religious minorities in the jurisprudence of the Committee, the most relevant case is Waldman v Canada, in which a claim under Article 27 was brought by a member of a religious group.[14] The author of the communication was a Canadian citizen and a member of the Jewish faith, who claimed to be a victim of a violation of Articles 26, 18.1, 18.4 and 27 taken in conjunction with Article 2.1 of the ICCPR. He complained that, in the province of Ontario, the Roman Catholic schools were the only non-secular schools receiving full and direct public funding, while other religious schools had to be funded through private sources, including charging of tuition fees. In the view of the Committee, if a State party chooses to provide funding to religious schools, it should make this funding available without discrimination. Since the differential treatment was not justified, there was a breach of Article 26. However, the Committee was of the opinion that no additional issue arose for its consideration under Articles 18, 27 and 2.1 of the ICCPR.[15]

II. Minority Rights Declaration

'Inspired'[16] by Article 27 of the ICCPR, the Declaration on the Rights of Persons Belonging to National or Ethnic, Religious and Linguistic Minorities was adopted by the United Nations General Assembly in 1992. Aiming to supplement the ICCPR, the Declaration acknowledges special rights of persons belonging to minorities, entrusts States with duties, and explicitly adds national minorities as one of the categories protected.[17]

---

13 UN Human Rights Committee, General Comment No. 23: The rights of minorities (Art. 27), 8 April 1994, CCPR/C/21/Rev. 1/Add.5, para. 8.

14 Waldman v Canada (Communication No. 694/96 – d. 1999). For a comment of this case, see Meyler, "The Limits of Group Rights: Religious Institutions and Religious Minorities in International Law," 2007, pp. 549-551.

15 See Waldman v Canada (Communication No. 694/96 – d. 1999, para. 10.4-10.7).

16 See Preamble of the 1992 Declaration.

17 Concerning the minority rights in international law, see, among others, Thornberry, *International Law and the Rights of Minorities*, 1991; Thornberry and Este-

Under the Declaration, on the one hand, States shall protect the existence and identity of religious minorities, ensure that members of religious minorities may exercise their rights, protect them against discrimination, create favorable conditions for the expression and development of the group characteristics, and create measures so that they may participate in the progress of the country. In summary, States shall observe and enforce the cornerstone principles of equality, non-discrimination, non-exclusion, and non-assimilation of religious minorities[18]. On the other hand, persons have the right to enjoy their own culture, to profess and practice their own religion and to use their own language, to participate effectively in every area of social life as well as in political decisions, to associate and establish or keep contact with others, including members of other minority groups and of the mainstream society. In short, those belonging to minorities must be able to exercise all their human rights individually or with others.[19]

Concerning the existence and identity of religious minorities, it is proclaimed in Article 1 of the Declaration that,

> 1. States shall protect the existence and the national or ethnic, cultural, religious and linguistic identity of minorities within their respective territories and shall encourage conditions for the promotion of that identity.
> 2. States shall adopt appropriate legislative and other measures to achieve those ends.

These clauses imply that States have to take into account the minorities within their territory when promoting any policies or measures, and must not cause the elimination or forced assimilation of religious groups nor undermine the religious identity of persons. Religious identity and existence require that States should abstain from violations of minority rights, and that States should adopt positive measures as well, in order to protect members of minorities against human rights violations.

---

banez, *Minority Rights in Europe*, 2004; Ghanea and Xanthaki (eds.), *Minorities, Peoples and Self-Determination: Essays in Honour of Patrick Thornberry*, 2005; Pentassuglia, *Minority Groups and Judicial Discourse in International Law: A Comparative Perspective*," 2009. See also the UN Working Group on Minorities, Commentary of the Working Group on Minorities to the United Nations Declaration on the Rights of Persons Belonging to National or Ethnic, Religious and Linguistic Minorities (E/CN.4/Sub.2/AC.5/2005/2), 2005.

18 Articles 1 and 4 of the 1992 Declaration.

19 Articles 2 and 3 of the 1992 Declaration.

The purpose of the Declaration is to affirm the rights of members of minority groups, including religious minorities. This means that members of religious minorities are protected from violations from the mainstream society, from the other members of their own group and from the group as a whole. The 1992 Declaration clearly acknowledges the rights of persons belonging to religious minorities while it does not recognize any rights of groups qua groups over them. Accordingly, while individuals may claim their rights even against their own group, religious minority or majority groups may not claim any intrinsic rights over their adherents. The protection of the existence and identity of a minority reflects the rights provided mostly under Article 2 of the Declaration.

III. Recommendations of the United Nations Forum on Minority Issues

In order to propose some practical and concrete measures for the implementation of the 1992 Declaration, the United Nations Independent Expert on Minority Issues presented before the Human Rights Council a set of Recommendations on ‘Guaranteeing the rights of religious minorities’.

The document, which is an outcome of the VI Session of the Forum on Minority Issues, is based on the Declaration, as well as other international and regional human rights standards and principles developed by different stakeholders and national legislation. The jurisprudence and general comments of treaty bodies, as well as relevant reports and recommendations from different special procedures, including the work of the Special Rapporteur on freedom of religion or belief, have informed the recommendations. The document also reflects the inputs received from the more than 500 participants in the Forum.[20]

Concerning the existence and identity of religious minorities, the document offers concrete and valuable measures related to: non-discrimination

20 UN Human Rights Council, Recommendations of the Forum on Minority Issues at its sixth session: Guaranteeing the rights of religious minorities (A/HRC/25/66), 2014, para. 4.

standards;[21] separation and non-interference;[22] the protection against incitement to religious hatred, discrimination, hostility and violence balanced with the protection of the freedoms of religion and expression, and the prohibition of blasphemy laws;[23] the protection of religious identity limited by the prohibition of religious or traditional practices that violate the

---

21 "17. States should ensure that there is no discriminatory treatment in regard to the legal and administrative recognition of all religious and belief groups. Any registration and administrative procedures, including those relating to the property and the functioning of places of worship and other religious-based institutions, should be conducted according to non-discrimination standards. International standards do not allow non-recognition of religious or belief groups to result in denial of their rights. Such standards require an inclusive approach to be taken.
18. Existing legislation should be reviewed to ensure that no provisions exist in law that are discriminatory or have a directly or indirectly discriminatory impact on persons belonging to religious minorities. Furthermore, requirements and official procedures resulting from the application of laws – and their possible discriminatory impact on some individuals and groups – should be reviewed and amended.
19. States should adopt domestic anti-discrimination legislation that includes provisions that prohibit direct and indirect discrimination against persons belonging to religious minorities. Governments should ensure the implementation of such legislation, including at local levels. They should further ensure that remedies are available and easily accessible for religious minorities, and that adequate penalties are applied in the event of violation."

22 "20. States should exercise no undue influence over religious minority affairs, including with respect to the appointment of religious leaders, the functioning of places of worship, and any legitimate religion- or belief-based activities."

23 "21. States that have not already adopted laws protecting against incitement to religious hatred, religious discrimination, and hostility or violence against religious minorities, should do so in line with applicable international standards and good practices, and should ensure that penalties are appropriate and are enforced in practice.
22. States should protect the interdependent freedoms of religion and expression that together encompass the rights to teach, proselytize and criticize any religion, while encouraging a respectful and peaceful coexistence.
23. States should ensure that anti-terrorism legislation and policies and their application do not lead to negative consequences for members of religious groups, in particular as a result of religious profiling. Religious profiling in the context of anti-terrorism measures should be prohibited by law.
24. Blasphemy laws as well as provisions on offences related to religions should be repealed and replaced with provisions that are in conformity with applicable international human rights standards, including in relation to the right to freedom of religion or belief, and the right of persons to freely change their religion or belief if they so choose."

human rights of any individual;[24] the prohibition of forced isolation of religious groups aiming to protect the group identity[25]; requirements of reasonable accommodation in workplace[26] and school;[27] and group autonomy for religious minorities concentrated in a particular area.[28]

Even though the Recommendations are not legally binding, they contribute to legitimize the claims of religious minorities as well as to influence States and regional organizations regarding the promotion of religious minorities' human rights.

---

24 "25. Harmful traditional religion- or belief-based practices that violate the human rights of any individual should be prohibited by law and addressed in conformity with international standards. Where appropriate, consultations should be undertaken with leaders and members of religious communities to address such issues and their causes."

25 "29. As provided for in the Declaration, States should engage with neighboring and kin States that religious minorities emanate from and/or maintain peaceful contacts with. They should foster positive exchanges and provide appropriate religious and/or cultural support to religious communities, and support for them to establish and maintain peaceful contacts with other members of their group both within their own country and across State borders."

26 "30. Economic actors, including private businesses, as well as bodies representing employees, such as trade unions, should ensure that religious minorities and their specific religious requirements are reasonably accommodated in the workplace. Trade unions should, for example, develop expertise on the challenges facing religious minorities in the labour market in their country, and seek to engage policymakers and employers in finding solutions."

27 "42. Where public education includes instruction in a particular religion or belief, provision should be made for non-discriminatory exemptions or alternatives to accommodate the wishes and religious education requirements/needs of religious minorities. Instruction in subjects such as the general history of religions, where it is delivered, should be conducted with a view to promoting interfaith and interreligious understanding and dialogue. Measures should be taken to ensure that children (along with their parents/legal guardians) may choose whether to participate in classes of religious education or not."

28 "33. Where religious minorities form the majority in a particular region or locality, cultural and/or political autonomy arrangements may be considered appropriate, with due consideration given to ensuring the rights of those who may form a minority in those localities. Such arrangements should be established with the meaningful participation of minorities."

C. The Concept of Religious Minority

The previous section described some of the international instruments regarding the protection of minorities under the United Nations legal framework and underlined that religious minorities are explicitly recognized as a category of minorities, which grants them special or additional rights. However, there is no legal definition of what should be understood as a 'religious minority', and for this reason, a few remarks will be made about the conceptual discussion.

Concerning the term 'minority', although there is no generally accepted concept, United Nations bodies have already made some approaches towards its definition.[29] According to Francesco Capotorti, the Special Rapporteur of the Sub-Commission on Prevention of Discrimination and Protection of Minorities, a minority is "a group numerically inferior to the rest of the population of a State, in a non-dominant position, whose members – being nationals of the State – possess ethnic, religious or linguistic characteristics differing from those of the rest of the population and show, if only implicitly, a sense of solidarity, directed towards preserving their culture, traditions, religion or language."[30]

Jules Deschênes, as the Canadian member of the United Nations Sub-Commission, follows the efforts of Capotorti and includes the aim 'to achieve equality with the majority in fact and law'. For Deschênes, a minority could be defined as a 'group of citizens of a State, constituting a numerical minority and in a non-dominant position in that State, endowed with ethnic, religious or linguistic characteristics which differ from those of the majority of the population, having a sense of solidarity with one another, motivated, if only implicitly, by a collective will to survive and whose aim is to achieve equality with the majority in fact and law.'[31]

The United Nations Rapporteur Asbjørn Eide also addresses the conceptual problem and suggests that "a minority is any group of persons resident within a sovereign State which constitutes less than half of the popu-

29 For a discussion of these approaches, see: Thornberry, *Indigenous Peoples and Human Rights*, 2002; Hannum, *Autonomy, Sovereignty, and Self Determination: The Accommodation of Conflicting Rights*, 1990.

30 Capotorti, "Study on the rights of persons belonging to ethnic, religious and linguistic minorities," 1979, para. 568.

31 Deschênes, "Proposals concerning a definition of the term minority," 1979, para. 181.

lation of the national society and whose members share common characteristics of an ethnic, religious or linguistic nature that distinguish them from the rest of the population."[32] This definition departs from the previous approaches since it does not distinguish between citizens and non-citizens, or nationals and non-nationals, replacing the criteria of nationality and citizenship for residency. It also defines the size of a minority group and removes the reference to 'sense of solidarity' and to the collective aim, turning the definition of minority into an objective concept.

As noted above, there is no universally accepted definition of minority, and consequently there is no universal definition of 'religious minority'. In spite of this, a working definition for this study would incorporate elements from those three remarkable proposals (Capotorti-Deschênes-Eide).

Although nationality, ethnicity, language, and religion tend to overlap, it is possible to identify religious minorities as a separate category within the minority rights regime. A religious minority can be defined as a group of persons resident within a sovereign State, numerically inferior to the rest of the population, in a non-dominant position, whose members possess a common religion or belief differing from those of the rest of the population and show a sense of solidarity, directed towards preserving their religion or belief, motivated, if only implicitly, by a collective will to survive and whose aim is to achieve equality with the majority in fact and law. In other words, a religious minority is a minority whose members are united by a common religion or belief. They are distinguished from the rest of the population not in terms of ethnicity or language, but because of the possession of a different or specific religious bond.

Concerning the meaning of religion and belief, according to the Human Rights Committee,[33] the ICCPR protects theistic, non-theistic and atheistic beliefs, as well as the right not to profess any religion or belief. Therefore, the Committee interprets the terms 'belief' and 'religion' broadly, and for this reason, the protection should not be limited to traditional religions nor to religions and beliefs with institutional characteristics or practices analogous to those of traditional religions.

32 See Eide, "Working Definition of Minorities, Possible Ways and Means of Facilitating the Peaceful and Constructive Solution of Problems Involving Minorities," 1979, para. 29.

33 See UN Human Rights Committee, CCPR General Comment No. 22: Article 18, 30 July 1993, CCPR/C/21/Rev. 1/Add.4, para. 2.

D. *Religious Groups and the Minority Rights Regime*

Minority rights protections certainly complement and enhance the protection granted to religious minorities, in addition to the protections offered by religious freedom rights. In spite of this, the enjoyment of minority rights by members of religious groups is challenging and should be realistic and informed.[34]

Unlike what happens with national, ethnic and linguistic minorities, ascribing special rights based on religion manifestly raises issues related to Religion-State relations, as international human rights instruments (including the ICCPR) require that legislation, public policies and administrative measures should respect the freedom of religion as well as the right to equality of the whole population. Greater problems, however, are faced when seeking to empower religious minorities with *group* rights.

Each kind of minority group has particularities that should be considered when interpreting the human rights provisions. Accordingly, the United Nations Working Group on Minorities stated that, although the 1992 Declaration does not make any distinctions between the categories,

> [t]his does not exclude the possibility that the needs of the different categories of minorities could be taken into account in the interpretation and application of the various provisions.[35]

In this chapter, it is argued that, under the minority rights regime, the protection of the interests of groups whose members are connected by a religious bond only (*i.e.* religious minorities) should be person-centered, and not group-centered, as they fall into the non-organic group category.

To begin with, non-organic groups and organic groups need to be differentiated.[36] The latter category comprises collectivities of human beings, commonly designated as nations or peoples, which share virtually all aspects of life and demand to be treated differentially *ab initio*. These groups demand the recognition of autonomy in order to protect their identity, de-

---

34 See Ghanea, "Are Religious Minorities Really Minorities?," 2012, pp. 62, 74.

35 UN Working Group on Minorities, Commentary of the Working Group on Minorities to the United Nations Declaration on the Rights of Persons Belonging to National or Ethnic, Religious and Linguistic Minorities (E/CN.4/Sub.2/AC.5/2005/2), 2005, para. 7.

36 See Wiessner, "Faces of Vulnerability: Protecting Individuals in Organic and Non-organic Groups," 1996, p. 218; idem, "The Cultural Rights of Indigenous Peoples: achievements and continuing challenges," 2011, p. 125.

fined by their distinctive cultural, linguistic, ethnic, religious, and other characteristics. Groups that belong to the former category (non-organic), conversely, do not have the same interest in sharing all aspects of life. Their members are primarily concerned about not being discriminated against the mainstream society.

While the organic category includes ethnic and national collectivities, which are encompassing groups[37] that claim to be treated as separate peoples (within the State or not),[38] the non-organic category comprises other groups such as women, children and religious communities, whose members should be recognized as full members of the State's majority people. Regarding organic and non-organic *minority* groups, both categories are protected under the provisions of Articles 6 to 26 of the ICCPR, and especially by its Article 27. However, these provisions do not expressly protect minorities as right-holder groups. Although many of the civil and political rights of the ICCPR have a collective dimension – thus jointly held or shared by a set of individuals (*e.g.* the right to freedom of thought, conscience and religion in Article 18, which can be exercised 'either individually or in community with others') –, those rights are held by the person, *i.e.* by the member of a group.

The idea of the protection of a group as a 'corporate entity'[39] cannot derive from Article 27 itself. This provision requires a person-centered ap-

---

37 According to Margalit and Raz, "National Self-Determination," 1995, pp. 81-85, encompassing groups are groups that combine at least six features that make their culture pervasive: 1) The group has a common character and culture that comprises varied and important aspects of life; 2) People growing up among members of the group will acquire the group culture; 3) Membership in the group is, in part, a subject of mutual recognition; 4) The membership is important for one's self-identification; 5) Membership is a matter of belonging, not of achievement; 6) The groups concerned are not small groups, but anonymous groups where mutual recognition is secured by the possession of group characteristics.

38 Concerning the discussion about secession, independence and autonomy related to ethnic conflicts, Lapidoth, *Autonomy: Flexible Solutions to Ethnic Conflicts*, 1997, p. 23, states that "the rise in ethnic and national consciousness increases the need to search for solutions for the demands of minorities, of indigenous populations, and of peoples. One way to satisfy these demands while preserving the existence of the state and its territorial integrity is by establishing regimes of autonomy."

39 Jones, "Human Rights, Group Rights, and People's Rights," 1999, pp. 83-88, proposes the existence of two different conceptions of group rights, collective rights and corporate rights. While collective rights derive from a commonality that situates a number of individuals together, corporate rights derive from the corporate

proach, as it protects 'persons' (belonging to a minority) or 'members' (of a group), but not the group as such. It can be said, however, that the protection of a minority as a right-holder group within a State's territory is possible only when inferred from the self-determination of peoples,[40] which is provided as a right in the ICCPR[41] and as a principle in the United Nations Charter of 1945,[42] with the condition that the minority group falls into the organic category, *i.e.* if a given minority group can also be regarded as a nation or people.[43]

---

entity, such as a nation or a people. In this study, 'group rights' are restricted to corporate rights.

40 Self-determination is a right and a principle in the international law. Concerning this dual nature, see Xanthaki, "The right to self-determination: meaning and scope," 2005, pp. 21-22.

41 ICCPR, "Article 1. (1). All peoples have the right of self-determination. By virtue of that right they freely determine their political status and freely pursue their economic, social and cultural development. (2). All peoples may, for their own ends, freely dispose of their natural wealth and resources without prejudice to any obligations arising out of international economic co-operation, based upon the principle of mutual benefit, and international law. In no case may a people be deprived of its own means of subsistence. (3). The States Parties to the present Covenant, including those having responsibility for the administration of Non-Self-Governing and Trust Territories, shall promote the realization of the right of self-determination, and shall respect that right, in conformity with the provisions of the Charter of the United Nations."

42 UN Charter, "Article 2. The purposes of the United Nations are: (…); (2). To develop friendly relations among nations based on respect for the principle of equal rights and self-determination of peoples, and to take other appropriate measures to strengthen universal peace."

43 The minority rights of Article 27 of the ICCPR comprehend the rights of members of internal minorities, as an attempt to protect them against discrimination. For that reason, Francesco Capotorti (Study on the rights of persons belonging to ethnic, religious and linguistic minorities, 1979, para. 568) states they should be 'nationals of the State', and Jules Deschênes (Proposals concerning a definition of the term minority, 1985, para. 181) affirms that a minority aims 'to achieve equality with the majority in fact and law'. Although the idea of the requirement of nationality or citizenship is highly controversial and rejected by the Human Rights Committee (Cf. General Comment No. 23: The rights of minorities (Art. 27), 8 April 1994, CCPR/C/21/Rev. 1/Add.5, para. 5.2), it reinforces the notion that Article 27 does not intend to grant a non-organic minority group the right to autonomy. Rather, Article 27 aims to protect their members' full membership of the State against any prejudicial treatment.

Self-determination as a right of the peoples[44] "is of particular importance because its realization is an essential condition for the effective guarantee and observance of individual human rights and for the promotion and strengthening of those rights."[45] It encompasses the freedom to determine a people's political status and the freedom to pursue their economic, social and cultural development. The first dimension implies that all peoples have the right to determine freely their political status in the international community and it is exemplified by the liberation of peoples from colonialism and by the prohibition to subject peoples to alien subjugation, domination and exploitation.[46] The second dimension comprises the the freedom of a people to organize itself, to create its own laws and to determine its aims and objectives, as long as individual human rights are respected and its elected authorities represent the whole population without distinction as to race, color, descent, nationality, or ethnic origin.[47]

Therefore, self-determination is a complex right and grants different levels of emancipation or autonomy, including various forms of political, economic, social, and cultural self-determination. Regarding the current situation of the nations or peoples of the world, it can be said that a people

---

44 Neither the Human Rights Committee nor the Committee on the Elimination of Racial Discrimination (CERD) have postulated a definition of the term 'people'. Although no universally accepted or permanent list of criteria exists, Joseph, Schultz, and Castan, *The International Covenant on Civil and Political Rights: Cases, Materials, and Commentary*, 2005, p. 142, offer the following contribution: "Self-determination is the collective right of the 'peoples'. Various conditions or characteristics of 'peoples' have been put forward, including common historical tradition, racial or ethnic identity, cultural homogeneity, linguistic unity, religious or ideological affinity, territorial connection, common economic life, and consisting of a certain minimum number."

45 UN Human Rights Committee, CCPR General Comment No. 12: Article 1 (Right to Self-determination), The Right to Self-determination of Peoples, 13 March 1984, UN Doc. HRI/GEN/1/Rev. 1 at 12 (1994), para. 1.

46 "The establishment of a sovereign and independent State, the free association or integration with an independent State or the emergence into any other political status freely determined by a people constitute modes of implementing the right of self-determination by that people." (UN General Assembly, Declaration on Principles of International Law concerning Friendly Relations and Cooperation among States in accordance with the Charter of the United Nations, 24 October 1970, A/RES/2625[XXV], n. 1).

47 See UN Committee on the Elimination of Racial Discrimination (CERD), General Recommendation No. 21: Right to self-determination, adopted on 23 August 1996, para. 4.

should be entitled to self-determination against the State in which territory it is based when that people still lives under some kind of colonial domination, or when it is so severely persecuted and its human rights so systematically abused that secession is the only viable option. In those cases, this nation or people would form a new State or be annexed to an existing one. However, regardless of the identification of those conditions that would lead to the recognition of independence, some aspects of self-determination shall protect peoples within a given State, a guarantee that is going to be called internal self-determination.[48]

Internal self-determination allows the community to exercise control over its own future, and thus survive and thrive within the framework of a legally pre-existing order. It is a central component of a group's identity and carries a strong political meaning.[49] Internal self-determination may include cultural autonomy (recognition and protection of cultural diversity, encompassing language, art and traditional practices), political participation (representation of the community in the political bodies of the State) and territorial autonomy (protection of the land and its natural resources). Regarding the latter, the recognition of an autonomous area[50] as the highest level of internal self-determination would allow political autonomy (self-government and self-administration) and the recognition of traditional law (legislation and enforcement).[51]

These forms of protection are group rights[52], since they treat a group as a right-bearing corporate entity, ascribing rights to the group as such. A group right would supervene on the rights of individuals but would not be reducible to an aggregate of individual rights. Some examples are the right

---

48 See Joseph, Schultz, and Castan, *The International Covenant on Civil and Political Rights: Cases, Materials, and Commentary*, pp. 148-149.

49 See Foster, "Articulating Self-determination in the Draft Declaration on the Rights of Indigenous Peoples," 2001, pp. 141-142; Lapidoth, *Autonomy: Flexible Solutions to Ethnic Conflicts*, p. 32.

50 See Crawford, *The Creation of States in International Law*, 1979, p. 211, "Autonomous areas are regions of a State, usually possessing some ethnic or cultural distinctiveness, which have been granted separate powers of internal administration, to whatever degree, without being detached from the State of which they are part."

51 For an account of minorities and self-determination in international law, see Rehman, *The Weakness in the International Protection of Minority Rights*, 2000.

52 In relation to the debate about the existence of a 'group right' and the relation between group rights and human rights, we refer to Casals, *Group Rights as Human Rights: a Liberal Approach to Multiculturalism*, 2006. and Baker, *Group Rights*.

to an autonomous legal system with jurisdiction over internal disputes (a legal system must override the freedoms of its litigants in that they must accept its verdict), the right to administrative autonomy (which establishes a public or *quasi*-public internal authority) and the right to special forms of group participation in public decision-making (*i.e.* to exercise coercive power).[53]

As the rights of one presuppose some duties for another,[54] group rights would imply duties. Basically, group rights derived from the internal aspect of self-determination impose on the State the duty of non-intervention in internal matters as well as they impose on the individuals the duty of subjection or subordination to the group.

In spite of the international recognition of the right to internal and/or external self-determination of peoples, since the interpretation and application of Article 1 of the ICCPR is controversial,[55] and only a people qua people can make claims under the right enshrined in that clause, most of the complaints related to internal self-determination of minority groups are brought to the Human Rights Committee under Article 27,[56] largely in re-

---

53 See Scolnicov, *The Right to Religious Freedom in International Law: Between Group Rights and Individual Rights*, 2011, p. 25.

54 See Green, "Internal Minorities and Their Rights," 1995, p. 258, "X has a right (…) only if X has an interest sufficiently important to warrant holding others to be under some duties to respect or promote that interest. Rights are thus not merely correlates of duties on the part of others; they are the ground for such duties."

55 The relevant jurisprudence of the Human Rights Committee on this matter includes Chief Ominayak and Lubicon Lake Band v Canada (Communication No. 167/84 – d. 1990), E.P v Colombia (Communication No. 318/88 – d. 1990), A.B et al v Italy (Communication No. 413/90 – d. 1990), R. L et al v Canada (Communication No. 358/89 – d. 1991), Diergaardt et al v Namibia (Communication No. 760/97 – d. 2000), Äärelä and Näkkäläjärui v. Finland (Communication No. 779/97 – d. 2001), Gillot v France (Communication No. 932/2000 – d. 2002).

56 See, for example, Kitok v Sweden (Communication No. 197/85 – d. 1988), Chief Ominayak and Lubicon Lake Band v Canada (Communication No. 167/84 – d. 1990), Marshal v Canada (Communication No. 205/86 – d. 1991), Mahuika v New Zealand (Communication No. 547/93 – d. 2000). In the case Kitok v Sweden (para. 6.3), for example, the Committee ruled: "6.3 With regard to the State party's submission that the communication should be declared inadmissible as incompatible with article 3 of the Optional Protocol or as 'manifestly ill-founded', the Committee observed that the author, as an individual, could not claim to be the victim of a violation of the right of self-determination enshrined in article 1 of the Covenant. Whereas the Optional Protocol provides a recourse procedure for indi-

lation to the protection of their economic activities[57] and cultural traditional activities associated with the land.[58]

The recognition of internal self-determination to a minority group in these cases, however, is not a model for every group. These cases involve the protection of the rights of indigenous peoples, which have, beyond a common cultural identity, a bond of ancestry with the original people of the territory.[59] This unique characteristic grants indigenous peoples a special status under international law.[60] Thus, the question of which minority groups should be offered any form of protection under the right to self-de-

---

viduals claiming that their rights have been violated, article 1 of the Covenant deals with rights conferred upon peoples, as such. However, with regard to article 27 of the Covenant, the Committee observed that the author had made a reasonable effort to substantiate his allegations that he was the victim of a violation of his right to enjoy the same rights enjoyed by other members of the Sami community. Therefore, it decided that the issues before it, in particular the scope of article 27, should be examined with the merits of the case."

57 The Human Rights Committee has consistently confirmed that economic activities may come within the scope of Article 27, if they are an essential element of a minority community. See, among others, Chief Ominayak and Lubicon Lake Band v Canada (Communication No. 167/84 – d. 1990, para. 32.2); Kitok v Sweden (Communication No. 197/85 – d. 1988, para. 9.2); and Länsman et al v Finland (Communication No. 511/92 – d. 1994, para. 9.2).

58 The UN Human Rights Committee (General Comment No. 23: The rights of minorities (Art. 27), 8 April 1994, CCPR/C/21/Rev. 1/Add.5, para. 7) recognized that the right of minorities to enjoy their own culture includes "a particular way of life associated with the use of land resources, especially in the case of indigenous peoples. That right may include such traditional activities as fishing or hunting and the right to live in reserves protected by law."

59 See Cobo, "Study of the problem of discrimination against Indigenous Populations," 1986, para. 379, "[I]ndigenous communities, peoples and nations, are those which, having a historical continuity with pre-invasion and pre-colonial societies that have developed on their territories, consider themselves distinct from other sectors of the societies now prevailing in those territories or parts of them. They form at present non-dominant sectors of society and are determined to preserve, develop and transmit to future generations their ancestral territories, and their ethnic identity, as the basis of their continued existence as peoples, in accordance with their own cultural patterns, social institutions and legal systems.".

60 The two major recent developments on the protection of indigenous peoples were the adoption of the American Declaration on the Rights of Indigenous Peoples within the Organization of the American States on June 2016 and the adoption of the United Nations Declaration on the Rights of Indigenous Peoples in 2007. Both documents expressly recognize their right to self-determination.

termination becomes more relevant and remains open in international law.[61]

Although the United Nations recognize national or ethnic, religious and linguistic groups as minorities, these groups do not have the same characteristics. This situation requires from the States and human rights bodies to take into account their particularities in the interpretation and application of the rights enshrined in the ICCPR. As previously stated, each one of those minorities is protected under Article 27 of the ICCPR and the 1992 Declaration, a protection that is person-centered, since these documents recognize the rights of the *members* of minorities, and not of the groups as such. Therefore, Article 27 of the ICCPR (and the Declaration as well) should not be interpreted to grant group rights to non-organic minorities, such as religious minorities. There is no ground under Article 27 for group claims aiming to exercise power or authority over its members nor to restrict their rights or impose duties, situations that are different from an informed and voluntary decision to subject oneself to the group's authority.

Relative to the protection of a collectivity against external interference, it must be highlighted that the legal protection under Article 27 is not limited to the individual exercise of those rights, as it includes the collective exercise as well, in addition to the other rights recognized by the international human rights documents. For that reason, the minority rights framework reinforces the protection of the collectivity against foreign illegitimate intervention. In the case of organic minority groups, they are also protected under Article 1, or at least their minority rights should be interpreted in the light of self-determination (as a principle rather than a right), aiming to empower them with some level or forms of internal self-determination.

According to the Commentary of the United Nations Working Group on Minorities,

> [t]he rights of persons belonging to minorities differ from the rights of peoples to self-determination. The rights of persons belonging to minorities are individual rights, even if they in most cases can only be enjoyed in community with others. The rights of peoples, on the other hand, are collective rights. While the right of peoples to self-determination is well established under in-

---

61 A defense of the interpretation and application of the right to self-determination for minorities in general, as to protect their identity, can be found at Henrard, *Devising and Adequate System of Minority Protection: Individual Human Rights, Minority Rights and the Right to Self-Determination*, 2009.

> ternational law, in particular by common Article 1 of the two International Covenants on Human Rights, it does not apply to persons belonging to minorities. This does not exclude the possibility that persons belonging to an ethnic or national group may in some contexts legitimately make claims based on minority rights and, in another context, when acting as a group, can make claims based on the right of a people to self-determination.[62]

An overlap between some kinds of minorities and the concept of people is, therefore, possible.

In relation to religious minorities, the protection of the group's interests is possible through the exercise, *inter alia*, of the freedoms of assembly and association, the collective dimension of religious freedom ("in community with others"), and the rights of political participation and non-discrimination, enhanced by Article 27. Nonetheless, they could be entitled to internal self-determination if, in addition to the common religious identity, there is a strong national, ethnic, or linguistic (and cultural) bond, which would make them organic groups. Depending on the form of internal self-determination that a minority group claims (such as local and autonomous administration), a territorial bond would be necessary as well.

With this in mind, it is proposed in this study that the interpretation and application of minority rights and self-determination should take into account the distinctions between organic groups and non-organic minority groups; the latter category includes religious minorities. The proposed approach could be outlined as following:

Legal Treatment of Organic Minority Groups should:

- be based on the right to self-determination combined with the rights of members of minorities,

62 UN Working Group on Minorities, Commentary of the Working Group on Minorities to the United Nations Declaration on the Rights of Persons Belonging to National or Ethnic, Religious and Linguistic Minorities (E/CN.4/Sub.2/AC.5/2005/2), 2005, para. 15. Similarly, the Human Rights Committee (General Comment No. 23: The rights of minorities [Art. 27], 8 April 1994, CCPR/C/21/Rev. 1/Add.5, para. 3.1) states that: "The Covenant draws a distinction between the right to self-determination and the rights protected under article 27. The former is expressed to be a right belonging to peoples and is dealt with in a separate part (Part I) of the Covenant. Self-determination is not a right cognizable under the Optional Protocol. Article 27, on the other hand, relates to rights conferred on individuals as such and is included, like the articles relating to other personal rights conferred on individuals, in Part III of the Covenant and is cognizable under the Optional Protocol."

- adopt a group-centered approach that respects individual human rights
- aim the protection of the group's independence or relative autonomy and protect individuals with additional cultural and political rights as a consequence of their group membership (for example, the provision of an individual right to a dual nationality in plurinational countries),
- take into account that membership is a matter of belonging, generally based on nonvoluntary criteria (essentially the local of birth or descent).

Legal Treatment of Religious Non-Organic Minority Groups should:

- be based on the rights to religious freedom and equality reinforced by the rights of members of minorities,
- adopt a person-centered approach,
- aim the protection of group members against discrimination within the society, the accommodation of religious differences (*i.e.* the right of a member to follow the group's religious traditions), and the protection of group's interests as the collective manifestation of individual rights,[63]
- take into account that membership is generally based on a mix of voluntary (*e.g.* free decision) and nonvoluntary criteria (*e.g.* family traditions or cultural environment).

The inclusion of religious groups in the minority rights regime certainly furthers the protection of their interests. However, the rights enshrined in Article 27 should not jeopardize the important elements protected under other human rights standards. Lumping together religion, belief, ethnicity, and other elements of a person or group's identity creates a serious risk of losing out of sight some crucial elements of freedom of religion or belief.[64] In this context, the approach presented in this chapter would en-

---

63 Concerning the group or individual characteristics 'religion' and 'belief', there is no right to the protection of a religion or a religious truth as such. Religions and beliefs do not have rights; only human beings have human rights. See Bielefeldt, "Freedom of Religion or Belief – A Human Right under Pressure," 2012, p. 29, "According to the human rights approach, the right holder is the human being, as an individual and together with others (...) the idea of protecting the honour of religions is at variance with the human rights approach, which claims due respect for the dignity and rights of human beings rather than protecting religions as such."

64 See Bielefeldt, "Freedom of Religion or Belief: A Human Right under Pressure," pp. 31-32.

hance the protection of the individual and collective interests against external violations while securing the person's human rights against abuses from or within his/her own group.[65]

E. Existence and Identity of Religious Minorities

The last part of this chapter discusses the protection of the existence and identity of religious minorities in the light of that proposed approach.

I. Protecting the Existence of Religious Minorities

Concerning the existence of religious minorities, this protection should be limited by the rights to religious freedom and equality. Accordingly, while States have to ensure the freedom to form religious groups and protect them from existential threats, that is, from violations that might cause their (unwanted) extinction, States also have to guarantee that every member has the absolute[66] right to change or keep one's religion,[67] which implies

---

65 Scolnicov, *The Right to Religious Freedom in International Law: Between Group Rights and Individual Rights*, summarizes the main justifications against the granting of religious group rights, *i.e.*, for the preference of religious freedom as an individual right over religious freedom as a group right. Her arguments are: the dual character of religious freedom and the right of the individual both to belong to, and dissent from the group, must be upheld for the effective protection of the individual against the collective use of power; the members of a religious group do not waive their rights when entering that community; the public character of religions mandates respect for individual rights; there is no effective voluntary choice and so individual freedom must be respected both within and without groups; equal protection of members of minorities can and should be achieved through a conception of individual rights; and finally, according religious group rights involves the State in evaluation of the social worth of religious groups, thereby breaching neutrality.

66 The right to change or keep one's religion is an absolute right, De Jong, *The Freedom of Thought, Conscience and Religion or Belief in the United Nations: 1946-1992*, 2000, p. 71, which is derived from the freedom of thought, conscience and religion or belief – the core of a democratic State. Therefore, there should be no margin of appreciation, proportionality analysis or balancing that may cause restrictions on the right to change or keep one's religion.

67 See Bielefeldt, "Freedom of Religion or Belief: A Human Right under Pressure," p. 31: "A source of much confusion is the term 'identity' that plays a major role in

the freedom to learn from other religions, to propose internal changes and to leave the group at any time, even if one's change or renounce causes the decrease or extinction of the group.

The protection of the existence of a religious minority does not imply that States should violate or allow the violation of the individual rights of its members or third parties in order to preserve the group, nor that States should move from a separation model to a regime of establishment, recognition or other. A State protects the existence of religious minorities when it ensures that the members of religious minorities have the conditions to freely manifest their beliefs, individually or collectively, without discrimination. In the case of vulnerable religious groups affected by human rights violations, they should receive even more special protection by means of positive measures to ensure their physical security and the exercise of the right to freedom of religion or belief, and other human rights as well.

In terms of recognition of the existence of a religious minority, the Human Rights Committee has already emphasized, "[t]he existence of an ethnic, religious or linguistic minority in a given State party does not depend upon a decision by that State party but requires to be established by objective criteria."[68] In addition, according to numerous United Nations Resolutions,[69] States should not misuse registration procedures as a means to limit religious freedom. Therefore, even if the minority group is not regis-

---

many current debates on human rights, minority issues and anti-discrimination policies. It is one of those keys terms one can in fact hardly avoid using. However, the problem may arise than an unspecified invocation of 'identity' in the context of freedom of religion or belief can obscure the component of 'change' or 'choice' that forms an integral and indispensable part of this human right. Given the right to also change one's religion or to have and adopt a religion or belief of one's own choice, the notion of identity in the area of religion or belief conceptually differs from, say, identity in the area of ethnicity. When using the somewhat fashionable identity language, at least one has to insist that religious or belief-based identity is always an identity 'in the making', ie in the sense that it can change in most different ways and can also legitimately be exposed to missionary activities, including non-violent forms of provocation. Saying this does not imply denying the possibility of serious changes also in other areas, like ethnicity. But still there remains a conceptual difference that in my opinion receives too little attention."

68 UN Human Rights Committee, General Comment No. 23: The rights of minorities (Art. 27), 8 April 1994, CCPR/C/21/Rev. 1/Add.5, para. 5.2.

69 See, for instance, UN Commission on Human Rights, Resolution 2005/40 on Elimination of All Forms of Intolerance and of Discrimination Based on Religion or Belief, 19 April 2005, E/CN.4/RES/2005/40.

tered nor recognized by the State, their freedom of religion and belief remains protected as a qualified right.

II. Protecting the Identity of Religious Minorities

In respect of the identity of religious minorities, the 1992 Declaration proclaims that its protection is a duty of the State. However, the Declaration does not recognize a group right to religious identity, and by no means should group identity superimpose individual human rights. As a result, States have to protect the identity of religious minorities as the collective expression of a right jointly held or shared by individuals, which means that the members of the group are entitled to the right to decide about their collective identity.

The duty of the State to protect the characteristics of a non-organic minority group is grounded on the rights of the members of the group to enjoy their culture, religion and language, and it is motivated by the importance of the group to the development of individual identities. Therefore, the duty of the State shall be person-centered even though directed towards the protection of the collective identity. The State shall protect the right of individuals to develop, enjoy and change their collective identities rather than promote the identity itself.

Measures oriented by the idea of granting religious communities group rights to self-determination or religious identity would jeopardize equality and religious freedom. Although aiming to preserve the identity of the group, that kind of protective measures could restrict excessively the freedom to search, choose, change, reach out, communicate, convert, and peacefully provoke in the field of religion.[70] Religious groups could also use group rights as an alleged ground to justify violations of the individual rights of their members, arguing that they have a right to internal self-determination and, for this reason, the State would have a duty of non-interference and their members would be subjected to the group's authority. In international relations, the freedom from interference in internal matters is the first refuge of a government's intent to violate rights. In a similar way,

70 See Bielefeldt, "Freedom of Religion or Belief – A Human Right under Pressure," pp. 31-32.

granting group rights to religious minorities could empower them to make decisions that persecute and oppress their own internal minorities.[71]

As an example, the right to have State recognition or enforcement of a *binding* intra-group religious legal and judicial system or of a higher level of autonomy (as granted to indigenous peoples) certainly endangers dissenters within the group[72] and vulnerable individuals, such as women and children (the 'minorities within minorities'[73]). The United Nations Recommendations discussed previously address these issues when it states:

> Harmful traditional religion- or belief-based practices that violate the human rights of any individual should be prohibited by law and addressed in conformity with international standards. Where appropriate, consultations should be undertaken with leaders and members of religious communities to address such issues and their causes.[74]

Likewise, the recognition of a group right to have delegates of religious minorities representing their respective groups as such in the Legislative or Judiciary branches[75] (which occurs in some Latin American countries in relation to indigenous groups) would intensify the problem of the use of religious reasons in public decisions, since the use of coercive power should be justified mostly by public reasons, at least from the perspective of Rawls' political liberalism.[76] In addition, empowering a majority or minority religious community with that kind of right would raise issues related to the relationship between religions and State (that is, separation and neutrality[77]) and could endanger equality, for including religious and

71 See Green, "Internal Minorities and Their Rights," p. 257.

72 See Scolnicov, *The Right to Religious Freedom in International Law: Between Group Rights and Individual Rights*, p. 30.

73 Eisenberg and Spinner-Halev, *Minorities Within Minorities: Equality, Rights and Diversity*," 2005.

74 UN Human Rights Council, Recommendations of the Forum on Minority Issues at its sixth session: Guaranteeing the rights of religious minorities (A/HRC/25/66), 2014, para. 25.

75 *I.e.*, to reserve a certain number of seats to the representatives of religious communities or to use religion as a criterion in the distribution or apportionment of seats in the Legislative and Judiciary branches.

76 See Rawls, *Political Liberalism*, 1993, p. 217; Rawls, "The Idea of Public Reason Revisited," 1997, pp. 783-784; Habermas, "Notes on Post-Secular Society," 2008, p. 28.

77 For a discussion about separation and establishment in the light of political liberalism, see Laborde, "Political Liberalism and Religion: On Separation and Establishment," 2011, pp. 64-86.

equivalent ideological groups altogether in contexts of religious diversity would require a herculean effort in practical terms. However, in contexts where a majority religion is represented in the Legislative or Judiciary branches as such, or in situations of severe discrimination and/or persecution, the inclusion of representatives of religious minorities in the political and judicial arenas would allow their interests to be appropriately presented and could minimize discriminatory treatment. Nonetheless, the person-centered approach does not preclude the right to have a relative autonomy concerning the internal organization of religious institutions, under the protection of freedoms of religion and association. The possibility of having representatives of religious groups in consultative bodies, public hearings and other forms or levels of participation is admissible as well, since the claims of religious groups must be taken into account in the decision-making processes. Religious minorities have to be allowed to participate in every decision that affects them and States cannot deny participation on the grounds of one's religious identity. Rather, States should ensure by positive measures that members of minorities have their participation rights[78] protected, without any discrimination.[79]

F. Conclusion

The core of democracy is civil and political rights, which must be further promoted and safeguarded. International organizations and national governments, as well as NGO's and individuals, must engage in protecting religious freedom and all the other human rights of minorities against acts of

---

78 ICCPR, "Article 25. Every citizen shall have the right and the opportunity, without any of the distinctions mentioned in article 2 and without unreasonable restrictions: (a) To take part in the conduct of public affairs, directly or through freely chosen representatives; (b) To vote and to be elected at genuine periodic elections which shall be by universal and equal suffrage and shall be held by secret ballot, guaranteeing the free expression of the will of the electors; (c) To have access, on general terms of equality, to public service in his country."

79 ICCPR, "Article 26. All persons are equal before the law and are entitled without any discrimination to the equal protection of the law. In this respect, the law shall prohibit any discrimination and guarantee to all persons equal and effective protection against discrimination on any ground such as race colour, sex, language, religion, political or other opinion, national or social origin, property, birth or other status."

discrimination and violence practiced in the name of a religious or secularist truth, to defend the national identity, or based on any other illegitimate motives.

Article 27 of the ICCPR combined with the 1992 Declaration constitute firstly, instruments of counter-majoritarian protection that should inspire and contribute to the development of other regional and national instruments. Secondly, they are transformative instruments, not only of majoritarian religious groups, but also of minorities, since every person is entitled to, as well as constrained by universal human rights.

Bibliography

Alves, Rodrigo Vitorino Souza, "Diversidade cultural e o direito à autodeterminação dos povos indígenas," *Revista Jurídica da Presidência* 16, 110 (2015): 725-749.

Alves, Rodrigo Vitorino Souza, "Pueblos indígenas, diversidad cultural y el derecho a la autodeterminación: desde el derecho internacional al constitucionalismo latinoamericano," *Derecho PUCP* 75 (2015): 119-138.

Baker, Judith (ed.), *Group Rights,* Toronto: University of Toronto Press, 1994.

Bielefeldt, Heiner, "Freedom of Religion or Belief: A Human Right under Pressure," *Oxford Journal of Law and Religion* 1, 1 (2012): 15-35.

Capotorti, Francesco, "Study on the rights of persons belonging to ethnic, religious and linguistic minorities," UN Doc. E/CN.4/Sub.2/384/rev. 1., Geneva, United Nations, 1979.

Casals, Neus Torbisco, *Group Rights as Human Rights: a Liberal Approach to Multiculturalism*, Dordrecht: Kluwer, 2006.

Cobo, Jose R. Martinez, "Study of the problem of discrimination against Indigenous Populations," UN Doc.E/CN.4/Sub.2/1986/7/Add. 1-4., Geneva, United Nations, 1986.

Crawford, James, *The Creation of States in International Law*, Oxford: Clarendon Press, 1979.

De Jong, Cornelis D, *The Freedom of Thought, Conscience and Religion or Belief in the United Nations: 1946-1992,* Antwerp, Groningen and Oxford: Hart/Intersentia, 2000.

Deschênes, Jules, "Proposals concerning a definition of the term minority," UN Doc. E/CN.4/Sub.2/1985/31, Geneva, United Nations, 1985.

Eide, Asbjørn, "Working Definition of Minorities, Possible Ways and Means of Facilitating the Peaceful and Constructive Solution of Problems Involving Minorities," UN Doc. E/CN.4/Sub.2/1993/34, Geneva, United Nations, 1993.

Eisenberg, Avigail, and Jeff Spinner-Halev (eds.), *Minorities Within Minorities: Equality, Rights and Diversity*, Cambridge: Cambridge University Press, 2005.

Foster, Caroline E, "Articulating Self-determination in the Draft Declaration on the Rights of Indigenous Peoples," *The European Journal of International Law* 12, 1 (2001): 141-157.

Ghanea, Nazila, "Religious or Minority? Examining the Realization of International Standards in Relations to Religious Minorities in the Middle East," *Religion, State & Society* 36, 3 (2008): 303-325.

Ghanea, Nazila, "Are Religious Minorities Really Minorities?," *Oxford Journal of Law and Religion* 1, 1 (2012): 57-79.

Ghanea, Nazila, and Alexandra Xanthaki (eds.), *Minorities, Peoples and Self-Determination: Essays in Honour of Patrick Thornberry*, Leiden and Boston: Martinus Nijhoff, 2005.

Green, Brian J., and Roger Finke, *The Price of Freedom Denied: Religious Persecution and Conflict in the Twenty-First Century,* Cambridge: Cambridge University Press, 2010.

Green, Leslie, "Internal Minorities and Their Rights," in *The Rights of Minority Cultures*, ed. Will Kymlicka, Oxford: Oxford University Press, 1995, pp. 257-272.

Grim, Brian J., and Roger Finke, *The Price of Freedom Denied: Religious Persecution and Conflict in the Twenty-First Century*, 2010.

Habermas, Jürgen, "Notes on Post-Secular Society," *New Perspectives Quaterly* 25, 4 (2008): 17-29.

Hannum, Hurst, *Autonomy, Sovereignty, and Self Determination: The Accommodation of Conflicting Rights,* Philadelphia: University of Pennsylvania Press: 1990.

Henrard, Kristin, *Devising and Adequate System of Minority Protection: Individual Human Rights, Minority Rights and the Right to Self-Determination,* Leiden and Boston: Martinus Nijhoff, 2009.

Jones, Peter, "Human Rights, Group Rights, and People's Rights," *Human Rights Quarterly* 21, 1 (1999): 80–107.

Joseph, Sarah, Jenny Schultz, and Melissa Castan, *The International Covenant on Civil and Political Rights: Cases, Materials, and Commentary,* Oxford: Oxford University Press: 2005.

Kymlicka, Will, *Multicultural Odysseys: Navigating the New International Politics of Diversity*, Oxford: Oxford University Press, 2011.

Laborde, Cécile, "Political Liberalism and Religion: On Separation and Establishment," *The Journal of Political Philosophy* 21, 1 (2011): 64-86.

Lapidoth, Ruth, *Autonomy: Flexible Solutions to Ethnic Conflicts,* Washington D.C.: United States Institute of Peace Press, 1997.

Margalit, Avishai, and Joseph Raz, "National Self-Determination," in *The Rights of Minority Cultures*, ed. Will Kymlicka, Oxford: Oxford University Press, 1995, pp. 79-92.

Meyler, Bernadette A., "The Limits of Group Rights: Religious Institutions and Religious Minorities in International Law," *St. John's Journal of Legal Commentary* 22, 2 (2007): 535-558.

Pentassuglia, Gaetano, *Minority Groups and Judicial Discourse in International Law: A Comparative Perspective,* Leiden and Boston: Martinus Nijhoff, 2009.

Pew Research Center, "Rising Restrictions on Religion: One-third of the world's population experiences an increase," August 2011, at http://www.pewforum.org/files/2011/08/RisingRestrictions-web.pdf.

Rawls, John, *Political Liberalism*, New York: Columbia University Press, 1993.

Rawls, John, "The Idea of Public Reason Revisited," *The University of Chicago Law Review* 64, 3 (1997): 765-807.

Rehman, Javaid, *The Weakness in the International Protection of Minority Rights,* The Hague, London and Boston: Kluwer Law International, 2000.

Scolnicov, Anat, *The Right to Religious Freedom in International Law: Between Group Rights and Individual Rights,* London and New York: Routledge, 2011.

Thornberry, Patrick, *International Law and the Rights of Minorities*, Oxford: Clarendon Press, 1991.

Thornberry, Patrick, "Minority Rights," *Collected Courses of the Academy of European Law* 6, 2 (1995): 307-390.

Thornberry, Patrick, *Indigenous Peoples and Human Rights,* Manchester: Manchester University Press, 2002.

Thornberry, Patrick, and Maria Amor Martin Estebanez, *Minority Rights in Europe*, Strasbourg: Council of Europe Publishing, 2004.

United Nations, Commission on Human Rights, Resolution 2005/40 on Elimination of All Forms of Intolerance and of Discrimination Based on Religion or Belief, 19 April 2005, E/CN.4/RES/2005/40.

United Nations, Human Rights Committee, Äärelä and Näkkäläjärui v. Finland (Communication No. 779/97 – d. 2001).

United Nations, Human Rights Committee, CCPR General Comment No. 22: Article 18, 30 July 1993, CCPR/C/21/Rev. 1/Add.4, para. 2.

United Nations, Human Rights Committee, Chief Ominayak and Lubicon Lake Band v Canada (Communication No. 167/84 – d. 1990).

United Nations, Human Rights Committee, Chief Ominayak and Lubicon Lake Band v Canada (Communication No. 167/84 – d. 1990).

United Nations, Human Rights Committee, Diergaardt et al v Namibia (Communication No. 760/97 – d. 2000).

United Nations, Human Rights Committee, E.P v Colombia (Communication No. 318/88 – d. 1990), A.B et al v Italy (Communication No. 413/90 – d. 1990).

United Nations, Human Rights Committee, General Comment No. 23: The rights of minorities (Art. 27), 8 April 1994, CCPR/C/21/Rev. 1/Add.5.

United Nations, Human Rights Committee, Gillot v France (Communication No. 932/2000 – d. 2002).

United Nations, Human Rights Committee, Kitok v Sweden (Communication No. 197/85 – d. 1988).

United Nations, Human Rights Committee, Länsman et al v Finland (Communication No. 511/92 – d. 1994, para. 9.2).

United Nations, Human Rights Committee, Mahuika v New Zealand (Communication No. 547/93 – d. 2000).

United Nations, Human Rights Committee, Marshal v Canada (Communication No. 205/86 – d. 1991).

United Nations, Human Rights Committee, R. L et al v Canada (Communication No. 358/89 – d. 1991).

United Nations, Human Rights Committee, CCPR General Comment No. 12: Article 1 (Right to Self-determination), The Right to Self-determination of Peoples, 13 March 1984, UN Doc. HRI/GEN/1/Rev. 1 at 12 (1994), para. 1.

United Nations, Human Rights Council, Recommendations of the Forum on Minority Issues at its sixth session: Guaranteeing the rights of religious minorities (A/HRC/25/66), 2014, para. 4.

United Nations, Human Rights Council, Recommendations of the Forum on Minority Issues at its sixth session: Guaranteeing the rights of religious minorities (A/HRC/25/66), 2014, para. 25.

United Nations, Working Group on Minorities, Commentary of the Working Group on Minorities to the United Nations Declaration on the Rights of Persons Belonging to National or Ethnic, Religious and Linguistic Minorities (E/CN.4/Sub.2/AC.5/2005/2), 2005, para. 7.

Wiessner, Siegfried, "Faces of Vulnerability: Protecting Individuals in Organic and Non-organic Groups," in *Living Law of Nations: Essays on Refugees, Minorities, Indigenous Peoples, and the Human Rights of Other Vulnerable Groups*, ed. Gudmundur Alfredsson and Peter Macalister-Smith, Kehl am Rhein: N. P. Engel, 1996, pp. 217-226.

Wiessner, Siegfried, "The Cultural Rights of Indigenous Peoples: achievements and continuing challenges," *The European Journal of International Law* 22, 1 (2011): 121-140.

Xanthaki, Alexandra, "The right to self-determination: meaning and scope," in *Minorities, Peoples and Self-Determination: Essays in Honour of Patrick Thornberry*, ed. Nazila Ghanea and Alexandra Xanthaki, Leiden and Boston: Martinus Nijhoff, 2005, pp. 15-33.

List of Contributors

(in alphabetical order)

Slavica Banić

Slavica Banić is lawyer with professional experience in the field of human rights protection, rule of law, independence of judiciary and public administration and former judge of the Croatian Constitutional Court. Since 2015 she has been Senior Research Fellow at the German-Southeast Asian Center of Excellence for Public Policy and Good Governance (CPG).

Wojciech Brzozowski

Dr. habil. Wojciech Brzozowski is Assistant Professor at the Faculty of Law and Administration, University of Warsaw, Poland, and Head of the Department of Law and Religion. Main research areas cover constitutional law, law and religion, international human rights law.

Otto Depenheuer

Prof. Dr. Otto Depenheuer is Professor for Constitutional Law, Public Law, and Philosophy of Law at the University of Cologne. His research interests include theory of the state, constitutional law, philosophy of law and state as well as theory of law and constitutional history.

Dirk Ehlers

Prof. Dr. Dr. h. c. Dirk Ehlers is Professor of Public Law at Westfälische Wilhelms University Münster. Research interests cover public economic law, administrative law, administrative procedure law, municipial law. He was member of the Supervisory Board of the German-Southeast Asian Center of Excellence for Public Policy and Good Governance (CPG). From 2010-2012 he was the Chairman of the Association of German Public Law Professors.

Robert Esser

Prof. Dr. Robert Esser is Chair for German, European and International Criminal Law and Criminal Procedure Law including White Collar Crime at the Faculty of Law of Passau University where he also heads the Research Center "Human Rights in Criminal Proceedings". Research interests cover European criminal law, International Criminal Law, and White Collar Crime. He was member of the Supervisory Board of the German-Southeast Asian Center of Excellence for Public Policy and Good Governance (CPG).

Alessandro Ferrari

Prof. Dr. Alessandro Ferrari is Professor of Law and Religion at the Department of Law, Economy and Cultures of the University of Insubria (Varese and Como- Italy), where is the director of the Research Centre "Religion, Law and Economy in the Mediterranean Area" (REDESM). His present research project focuses on the "Mediterranean Religious Freedom", attempting a diachronic comparison between the "European Model" of "religious freedom" and the recent transformations in the MENA countries.

Silvio Ferrari

Prof. Dr. Silvio Ferrari is Professor of Law and Religion, University of Milan and Catholic University of Leuven. Research areas cover law and religion in the European legal systems, legal status of Islam in Europe, religious liberty and human rights.

Karsten Fischer

Prof. Dr. Karsten Fischer is Chair of Political Theory at the Geschwister Scholl Institute of Ludwig Maximilians University Munich. Focal research areas cover political theory, intellectual history, and the relation between politics and religion.

Andreas Follesdal

Prof. Dr. Andreas Follesdal is Professor of Philosophy and Director of the PluriCourts Center of Excellence for the Study of the Legitimate Roles of the Judiciary in the Global Order. He does research and publishes on a variety of issues concerning human rights, globalization, democracy, and Europeanization.

María Concepción Medina González

Dr. María Concepción Medina González is Professor at the Law School of National Autonomous University of Mexico and an independent consultant of Mexican religious law. Her research interests cover law and religion, religion in public education, and religion under the Mexican Law of Religion.

Henning Glaser

Henning Glaser is the founding director of the German-Southeast Asian Center of Excellence for Public Policy and Good Governance and lecturer at the Faculty of Law, Thammasat University. His research focuses on constitutional politics in Asian countries, legal reform and public policy, as well as Eurasian geopolitics and global governance.

Cheng-tian Kuo

Dr. Cheng-tian Kuo is Distinguished Professor in Political Science Department and Professor in Graduate Institute of Religious Studies at the National Chengchi University, Taiwan. His major research area is religious politics.

Bart Labuschagne

Dr. Bart Labuschagne is Assistant Professor of Philosophy of Law at Leiden University. He takes an interest in the philosophical aspects of the relationship between (foundations of) law, religion, politics and ethics and has devoted several publications and books on this topic. He is interested in Plato, Augustine, Kant, Hegel, Nietzsche, Scheler, Voegelin and Habermas.

André Laliberté

Prof. Dr. André Laliberté is Professor of comparative politics at the School of Political Studies at the University of Ottawa. His research focus lies in the intersection of the political and the religious in China and Taiwan, in the context of democratic transition, authoritarian resilience and the implementation of social policy.

René Pahud de Mortanges

Prof. Dr. is René Pahud de Mortanges is Professor at the Faculty of Law, University of Fribourg, Switzerland, where he teaches legal history, state-religion relationships, religious laws and constitutional law. He also serves as Director of the Institute of Law and Religion, and as Co-Director of the Center of Islam and Society, both at the University of Fribourg, and is Research Fellow at Renmin University in Bejing and Guest Professor at ECUPL in Shanghai.

Ronojoy Sen

Dr. Ronojoy Sen is Senior Research Fellow at the Institute of South Asian Studies and the South Asian Studies Programme, National University of Singapore. His research interests cover Indian politics, history and culture, law and society, as well as religion and politics.

Rodrigo Vitorino Souza Alves

Dr. Rodrigo Vitorino Souza Alves is Professor of Law at the Faculty of Law, Federal University of Uberlandia, Brazil. Research areas cover religious freedom, social tension and security.

Thio Li-ann

Prof. Dr. Thio Li-ann is Provost Chair Professor at the National University of Singapore where she teaches and researches international human rights law, constitutional and administrative law and comparative public law, with a focus on law and religion.

Javiar Martínez-Torrón

Prof. Dr. Javier Martínez-Torrón is Professor of Law at Complutense University Madrid. Research areas cover international protection of religious freedom, religious minorities in Spain, and the historical influence of Canon Law on the Anglo-American legal tradition.

Johannes Zachhuber

Prof. Dr. Johannes Zachhuber is Professor of Historical and Systematic Theology at the Faculty of Theology and Religion, Oxford University. He is a Fellow of Trinity College. His areas of specialization include the history of Christian thought in late antiquity and the nineteenth century; secularization theories; and religion and politics.

Yijiang Zhong

Dr. Yijiang Zhong is associate professor of the Institute for Advanced Studies on Asia, the University of Tokyo. He is a historian of modern Japan with major research interests in religion, nation(alism), and space.